# Fodor's 07

# BAHAMAS

**Where to Stay and Eat
for All Budgets**

**Must-See Sights
and Local Secrets**

**Ratings You Can Trust**

Fodor's Travel Publications   New York, Toronto, London, Sydney, Auckland
**www.fodors.com**

## FODOR'S BAHAMAS 2007

**Editor:** Michael Nalepa

**Editorial Production:** Evangelos Vasilakis
**Editorial Contributors:** Cheryl Blackerby, Jackie Mulligan, Jacinta O'Halloran, Patricia Rodriguez Terrell, Stephen F. Vletas, Chelle Koster Walton
**Maps:** David Lindroth, *cartographer*; Rebecca Baer and Bob Blake, *map editors*
**Design:** Fabrizio La Rocca, *creative director*; Guido Caroti, *art director*; Moon Sun Kim, *cover designer*; Melanie Marin, *senior picture editor*
**Production/Manufacturing:** Colleen Ziemba
**Cover Photo:** Stephen Frink Collection/Alamy

## SPECIAL SALES

This book is available at special discounts for bulk purchases for sales promotions or premiums. Special editions, including personalized covers, excerpts of existing books, and corporate imprints, can be created in large quantities for special needs. For more information, write to Special Markets/Premium Sales, 1745 Broadway, MD 6-2, New York, New York 10019, or e-mail specialmarkets@randomhouse.com.

## AN IMPORTANT TIP & AN INVITATION

Although all prices, opening times, and other details in this book are based on information supplied to us at press time, changes occur all the time in the travel world, and Fodor's cannot accept responsibility for facts that become outdated or for inadvertent errors or omissions. So **always confirm information when it matters,** especially if you're making a detour to visit a specific place. Your experiences—positive and negative—matter to us. If we have missed or misstated something, **please write to us.** We follow up on all suggestions. Contact the Bahamas editor at editors@fodors.com or c/o Fodor's at 1745 Broadway, New York, NY 10019.

PRINTED IN THE UNITED STATES OF AMERICA

10 9 8 7 6 5 4 3 2 1

# Be a Fodor's Correspondent

Your opinion matters. It matters to us. It matters to your fellow Fodor's travelers, too. And we'd like to hear it. In fact, we *need* to hear it.

When you share your experiences and opinions, you become an active member of the Fodor's community. That means we'll not only use your feedback to make our books better, but we'll publish your names and comments whenever possible. Throughout our guides, look for "Word of Mouth," excerpts of your unvarnished feedback.

Here's how you can help improve Fodor's for all of us.

Tell us when we're right. We rely on local writers to give you an insider's perspective. But our writers and staff editors—who are the best in the business—depend on you. Your positive feedback is a vote to renew our recommendations for the next edition.

Tell us when we're wrong. We're proud that we update most of our guides every year. But we're not perfect. Things change. Hotels cut services. Museums change hours. Charming cafés lose charm. If our writer didn't quite capture the essence of a place, tell us how you'd do it differently. If any of our descriptions are inaccurate or inadequate, we'll incorporate your changes in the next edition and will correct factual errors at fodors.com *immediately.*

Tell us what to include. You probably have had fantastic travel experiences that aren't yet in Fodor's. Why not share them with a community of like-minded travelers? Maybe you chanced upon a beach or bistro or B&B that you don't want to keep to yourself. Tell us why we should include it. And share your discoveries and experiences with everyone directly at fodors.com. Your input may lead us to add a new listing or highlight a place we cover with a "Highly Recommended" star or with our highest rating, "Fodor's Choice."

Give us your opinion instantly at our feedback center at www.fodors.com/feedback. You may also e-mail editors@fodors.com with the subject line "Bahamas Editor." Or send your nominations, comments, and complaints by mail to Bahamas Editor, Fodor's, 1745 Broadway, New York, NY 10019.

You and travelers like you are the heart of the Fodor's community. Make our community richer by sharing your experiences. Be a Fodor's correspondent.

Happy traveling!

Tim Jarrell, Publisher

# CONTENTS

## CLOSEUPS

## MAPS

# ABOUT THIS BOOK

## Our Ratings

Sometimes you find terrific travel experiences and sometimes they just find you. But usually the burden is on you to select the right combination of experiences. That's where our ratings come in.

As travelers we've all discovered a place so wonderful that its worthiness is obvious. And sometimes that place is so unique that superlatives don't do it justice: you just have to be there to know. These sights, properties, and experiences get our highest rating, **Fodor's Choice,** indicated by orange stars throughout this book.

Black stars highlight sights and properties we deem **Highly Recommended,** places that our writers, editors, and readers praise again and again for consistency and excellence.

By default, there's another category: any place we include in this book is by definition worth your time, unless we say otherwise. And we will.

Disagree with any of our choices? Care to nominate a place or suggest that we rate one more highly? Visit our feedback center at www.fodors.com/feedback.

## Budget Well

Hotel and restaurant price categories from ¢ to **$$$$** are defined in the opening pages of each chapter. For attractions, we always give standard adult admission fees; reductions are usually available for children, students, and senior citizens. Want to pay with plastic? **AE, D, DC, MC, V** following restaurant and hotel listings indicate whether American Express, Discover, Diner's Club, MasterCard, and Visa are accepted.

## Restaurants

Unless we state otherwise, restaurants are open for lunch and dinner daily. We mention dress only when there's a specific requirement and reservations only when they're essential or not accepted—it's always best to book ahead.

## Hotels

Hotels have private bath, phone, TV, and air-conditioning and operate on the European Plan (aka EP, meaning without meals), unless we specify that they use the Continental Plan (CP, with a continental breakfast), Breakfast Plan (BP, with a full breakfast), or Modified American Plan (MAP, with breakfast and dinner), or are all-inclusive (including all meals and most activities). We always

list facilities but not whether you'll be charged an extra fee to use them, so when pricing accommodations, find out what's included.

### Many Listings
★ Fodor's Choice
★ Highly recommended
⊠ Physical address
✛ Directions
🗐 Mailing address
☎ Telephone
📠 Fax
🌐 On the Web
✉ E-mail
🎫 Admission fee
🕐 Open/closed times
▶ Start of walk/itinerary
Ⓜ Metro stations
▭ Credit cards

### Hotels & Restaurants
🏨 Hotel
🛏 Number of rooms
♨ Facilities
🍴 Meal plans
✕ Restaurant
🍽 Reservations
🏛 Dress code
↘ Smoking
🍸 BYOB
✕🏨 Hotel with restaurant that warrants a visit

### Outdoors
🏌 Golf
⛺ Camping

### Other
🐾 Family-friendly
🔢 Contact information
⇨ See also
⊠ Branch address
☞ Take note

| | |
|---|---|
| **NEW PROVIDENCE ISLAND**  | To some, New Providence has come to be associated largely with Paradise Island—the skinny islet connected to its larger neighbor by bridge (Paradise Island is home to some of the Bahamas' priciest vacation homes and splashiest resorts, including the megaresort and water park, Atlantis). But New Providence Island is also the site of Nassau, the nation's capital. As a historical and cultural center, Nassau is packed with tour-worthy mansions, churches, government buildings, gardens, forts, museums, and monuments, many with a distinctly British accent left over from the old colonial days. As the nation's largest city, Nassau also offers sophisticated shopping and dining, flashy casinos, hot nightlife—and some of the less-pleasant aspects of big city living, including crowds, traffic, pollution, and, despite a crackdown and clean-up, some petty crime. Though the beaches and resorts of 3-mi-long Paradise Island may create all the buzz, some visitors still prefer the restaurant, boutique, and nightclub scene of downtown Nassau, where hip locals and savvy travelers mingle, or the old-school vibe of Cable Beach, a pretty white-sand stretch with a busy hotel row. Choose your Cable Beach lodgings carefully, however—they tend to be less expensive than those on Paradise Island, and some are in need of an update. Of course, New Providence Island's hotel landscape will change again when Cable Beach's new Baja Mar megacomplex is complete. |
| **GRAND BAHAMA ISLAND**  | Grand Bahama may have had its heyday in the Rat Pack era, but thanks to extensive investment and a determined marketing campaign, it has been making a comeback recently as the nation's big-city alternative to New Providence Island. Established in the 1950s and 1960s, the twin cities of Freeport and Lucaya can't match Nassau's colonial charm or Paradise Island's upmarket chic. But as the second largest population center in the islands, Grand Bahama does offer a good variety of places to shop, gamble, golf, or just hang at the beach—at a noticeably lower cost than in the capital. A number of resorts and the cruise-ship harbor have completed large-scale renovations in the past decade, bringing much-needed new life to older properties. And despite Grand Bahama's large-scale tourism, there's still a wild side to this island, the fourth-largest in the chain: visitors can escape their fellow tourists by choosing from a growing list of soft-adventure and ecotours, including kayaking, exploring old-island fishing settlements, and bird-watching. |

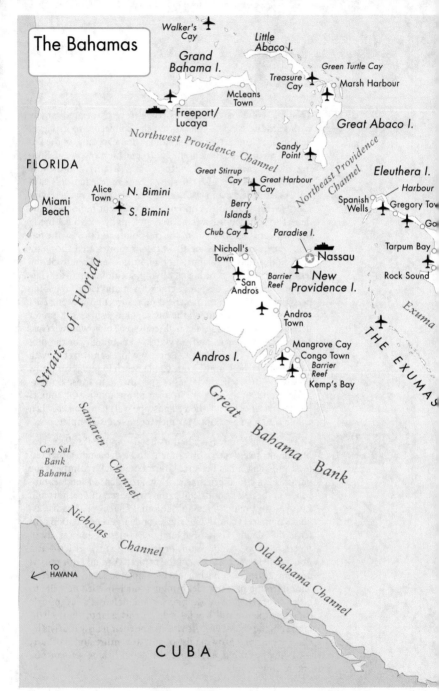

# The Bahamas

Walker's Cay

Little Abaco I.

Grand Bahama I.

Green Turtle Cay

Treasure Cay

Marsh Harbour

McLeans Town

Freeport/ Lucaya

Great Abaco I.

Northwest Providence Channel

Sandy Point

FLORIDA

Great Stirrup Cay

Great Harbour Cay

Northeast Providence Channel

Eleuthera I.

Harbour

Alice Town

N. Bimini

Berry Islands

Spanish Wells

Gregory Tow

Miami Beach

S. Bimini

Go

Chub Cay

Paradise I.

Tarpum Bay

Nicholl's Town

Nassau

Rock Sound

Straits of Florida

San Andros

Barrier Reef

New Providence I.

Andros Town

Exuma

Mangrove Cay

Congo Town

THE EXUMAS

Andros I.

Barrier Reef

Kemp's Bay

Great Bahama Bank

Cay Sal Bank Bahama

Santaren Channel

Nicholas Channel

Old Bahama Channel

TO HAVANA

CUBA

0           50 miles

0           75 km

*ATLANTIC OCEAN*

ernor's Harbour

Arthur's Town

*Mt. Alvernia*   *Cat I.*

New Bight

Port Howe    *San Salvador*

Cockburn
Town

*Rum Cay*

George
Town

Stella Maris

*Great
Exuma I.*   *Long I.*   Deadman's
Cay    *Samana Cay*

*Sound*

*Crooked Island Passage*

*Crooked I.*

Colonel
Hill

Spring Point

*Acklins I.*

*Mayaguana
Passage*

*Mayaguana I.*

*Caicos Passage*

*Providenciales*

*West Caicos*

TO
TURKS AND
CAICOS
ISLANDS

*Little
Inagua I.*

*Great Inagua I.*

Matthew
Town   *Lake
Windsor*

# WHAT'S WHERE

| THE ABACOS | If you're a sailing or yachting aficionado—or if you'd like to be one for a week or two—the Abacos is the place to be. A slim string of small cays, the Abacos were once the nation's boat-building capital. Today, shallow, translucent waters and top-notch marinas make them a hot spot for pleasure-boating and fishing. If you don't bring your own catamaran or powerboat, plenty of places here rent them by the day or week, and idle sails between cays, stopping for picnics on uninhabited islets or for tours of small settlements, are a popular pastime. British Loyalists fleeing the newly independent America first settled here about 225 years ago, and many surviving structures, including candy-color clapboard houses on Green Turtle Cay and Elbow Cay's famous striped lighthouse, make a visit to these isles something of a time-traveling experience. However, that also extends to some of the lodging options. Although there are some spectacular homes and vacation rentals, hotels here in general tend to be not as sophisticated as elsewhere in the nation. Perfect for vacationers who seek isolated beaches by day and unmatched star-gazing by night, these islands might not be for you if you crave nightlife, brand-name shopping, or beaches with a full retinue of Jet Skis, parasailing boats, and hair-braiders. |
|---|---|

| ELEUTHERA & THE EXUMAS | Harbour Island, with its pink-sand beaches; quaint Cape Cod–style architecture in Dunmore Town; upscale restaurants; and intimate, luxurious hotels, makes many "best-of" lists among travelers and travel writers alike. Chic but still friendly, popular but still small enough that a "crowded" stretch of beach might contain a few dozen sunbathers, Harbour Island has grown into something of a celebrity magnet with resorts like Pink Sands and Rock House, and prices have risen accordingly. If you're not a supermodel or an investment banker, you might get sticker shock. On the "mainland" of Eleuthera, visitors will also enjoy friendly hosts, gorgeous beaches, bounteous bougainvillea and other tropical flowers, and fine diving—but at a lower price. Here the hotels tend to be simpler motels, B&Bs, and cottages, without Egyptian-cotton sheets, Aveda bath products, Asian-fusion restaurants, or other trendy trimmings.

The hundreds of little cays that make up the Exumas are prime cruising ground for yachters. Though some fans worried that the 2004 opening of the luxurious Four Seasons Emerald Bay hotel and spa would ruin the region's laid-back charm, these |
|---|---|

fears have so far proved premature. The Exumas remain a quiet destination, albeit with a slowly growing number of options for those who enjoy snorkeling, kayaking, bird-watching, and other active pursuits.

## THE OTHER OUT ISLANDS

The remaining Out Islands are often lumped together as the "Family Islands," since many Bahamians have roots on these smaller and less-populated islands. Each has a casual, small-town atmosphere and abundant natural beauty, but the similarities end there—the different major island groups each fill their own niches. For deep-sea fishing, head to Bimini, once famous for its connections to Ernest Hemingway and illicit rum-runners—and now for its world-class, big-game fishing. For bonefishing, the increasingly trendy sport often done standing on the flats or kayaking in the shallows, try Andros, a lush, green island that's also a lure for bird-watchers and nature-lovers. For a glimpse of the past, visit Cat Island, where remnants of mansions and slave quarters provide a historical backdrop to a quiet community of farmers and fishermen. To really get away from it all, there are the Berry Islands or Crooked and Acklins Islands, among the least-developed in the nation. In general, there are far fewer tourist amenities in the Out Islands, and hotels and restaurants tend to be rustic. (Bimini, with its loads of hotels, restaurants, and bars, and San Salvador, with its large and unusually luxurious Club Med, are among the exceptions.)

## TURKS & CAICOS

The Turks and Caicos, two groups of islands that lie at the bottom edge of the Bahamas, were long considered country cousins to the other Bahamian islands. With far less development and sophistication, the tourism industry here depended largely on divers and budget travelers. But in recent years, T&C has upped the glitz factor, especially in the capital of Providenciales (known to all as simply Provo) and tiny Parrot Cay, which is popular with celebrities. New and newly renovated resorts, spas, and restaurants attract a chic, well-heeled clientele who come for the stunning beaches and terrific diving and snorkeling on the outlying coral reefs (however, the islands' terrain tends toward the dry and scrubby rather than the lush and tropical). Still, many spots in the Turks and Caicos remain charmingly "undiscovered," with few visitors, laid-back locals, simple amenities, and, frankly, not much to do but enjoy the beauty of deserted beaches and sparkling water.

# QUINTESSENTIAL BAHAMAS

## Junkanoo

The Bahamas' answer to Rio de Janeiro's Carnaval and New Orleans' Mardi Gras, Junkanoo is a festival of parades and parties held annually on Boxing Day (the day after Christmas) and New Year's Day. Rooted in West African traditions kept alive by slaves, today's Junkanoo is a raucous, joyful celebration of freedom. Friends and neighbors form groups of as many as 1,000 members to create a theme—complete with elaborate, colorful costumes and choreographed routines that are practiced for weeks. Competition between groups is pitched, as winners receive not just cash prizes but a full year's worth of bragging rights. Much more than just a parade, Junkanoo is a moveable, danceable party, fueled by distinctly Bahamian music created by goatskin drums, clanging cowbells, conch-shell horns, and shrieking whistles. Although Junkanoo festivals occur throughout the islands, the biggest celebrations are in Nassau. And only night owls need apply—the real fun starts long after midnight.

## Conch

Conch, pronounced "konk," is popular for more than just its distinctive, spiral-shape shells; this sea creature, essentially a giant snail, is one of the mainstays of Bahamian cuisine. Firm white conch meat is tenderized, then turned into a variety of dishes. There's cracked conch, fried in seasoned batter and served as a main dish or a sandwich; conch salad, the Bahamian version of ceviche, with raw conch marinated in lime juice with onions and peppers; conch chowder; conch fritters; and conch creole, stewed with tomatoes and spices and served over rice. Islanders often claim that conch has two other magical powers—as a hangover cure (when eaten straight from the shell with hot peppers, salt, and lime) and as an especially tasty aphrodisiac.

Beautiful beaches, crystalline water a dozen shades of blue, luxurious resorts—sure, these images are all trademarks of the Bahamas, but to really get a sense of the islands, you'll want to experience a few of these *highlights* of Bahamian culture and cuisine.

## Rake 'n Scrape

Jamaica has reggae, the Dominican Republic has merengue, and the Bahamas has rake 'n scrape, its own lively brand of traditional, indigenous music. Generations ago, many Bahamians didn't have the money to buy instruments, so at night they would gather and make music, using whatever was at hand. Someone might "play" a saw, someone else made a bass out of string and a tin tub, and another musician kept time by shaking a plastic jug filled with rocks or dried beans, or by beating a goatskin drum. From those humble beginnings came this lilting, highly danceable music, a version of which is often played by bands in nightclubs or at local festivals. Today the best place to hear authentic rake 'n scrape is on Cat Island, where the style is said to have been born, or during Junkanoo celebrations throughout the islands.

## The Straw Markets

Perhaps best known for its "braid ladies" and its sometimes-aggressive vendors, the Nassau straw market is also a bona fide Bahamian tradition. The market was established in the '40s, when Bahamian women, looking for an income source to replace the dying sponge industry, began making and selling baskets, handbags, dolls, and decorations made from dried palm fronds and sisal leaves. Now, many of the products are actually imported or made in the Out Islands. As of this writing, the Nassau market was still in a temporary, tented location, the reconstruction of the permanent market after a 2001 fire not yet complete. Still, for colorful personalities and an array of souvenir choices, this market shouldn't be missed. Just be prepared to haggle, and don't be afraid to say no (nicely) to the many vendors who will approach with a "Hi, sweetie," or a "You all right?"

# WHEN TO GO

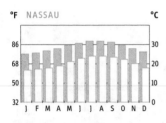

°F  NASSAU                °C

The Bahamas is affected by the refreshing trade-wind flow generated by an area of high atmospheric pressure covering a large part of the subtropical North Atlantic, so the climate varies little during the year. The most pleasant time is from December through May, when the temperature averages 70°F–75°F. It stands to reason that hotel prices during this period are at their highest—around 30% higher than during the less popular times. The rest of the year is hot and humid and prone to tropical storms; the temperature hovers around 80°F–85°F. Hurricane season is from about June 1 through November 30, with greatest risk for a storm from August through October.

Whether you want to join it or avoid it, be advised that Spring Break takes place between the end of February and mid-April. This means a lot of vacationing college students, beach parties, sports events, and entertainment.

## Climate

What follows are average daily maximum and minimum temperatures for Nassau. Freeport's temperatures are nearly the same: a degree or two cooler in the spring and fall, and a degree or two warmer in the summer.

🔲 Forecasts ⊕ www.weather.com.

# IF YOU LIKE

## Beaches

The Bahamas have more than 800 mi of beachfront, more than any other Atlantic or Caribbean nation. Theoretically, it's all yours to explore, since all Bahamian beaches are public up to the high-water mark. In practice, private homes and resorts can make it difficult to reach some stretches of sand, unless you arrive by boat. The best stretches, such as Cabbage Beach on Paradise Island and Cable Beach on New Providence Island, are packed with resorts and resort guests, but there are plenty of more secluded beauties.

- **Harbour Island Beach.** Perhaps the single most famous beach in the Bahamas, thanks to its unusual pink-powder sand, this 3-mi stretch is also among the best spots in the islands to spy Hollywood stars.

- **Old Bight Beach, Cat Island.** Lined with coconut palms and tropical casuarina trees, this rustic (read: no facilities) white-sand beach gives you 5 mi of opportunity for a private picnic, a shell-searching stroll, or a snooze.

- **Guana Cay Beach, Great Guana Cay.** The lightly visited, 7-mi-long western shore of this cay is probably what you envision when you imagine running away to a tropical isle.

- **Treasure Cay beach.** This 3½-mi, sugary white-sand beach borders a shallow, turquoise bay that's perfect for swimming, even for kids. One end brims with vendors hawking watersports equipment, while the other end is often nearly deserted.

## Underwater Sports

Surrounded by some of the most beautiful water in the world—and lots of it—it's no wonder that much of the activity in the Bahamas centers on watersports. And although many think of fishing and sailing first, snorkeling and scuba diving are just as spectacular here, with wrecks and reefs, blue holes and drop-offs, sea gardens and shallow shoals. Thanks to a vast system of coral reefs, diving and snorkeling are good just about everywhere, but the quality of instruction and rental equipment can vary, especially in some of the Out Islands where there are a limited number of operators. Be sure to check out the condition of masks, fins, and dive computers before plopping down your money.

- **Pelican Cays National Park, Great Abaco.** Turtles, spotted eagle rays, and tarpon are among the common sightings in this shallow (25 feet) marine park; you'll need to take a boat to one of the three moorings for the best spots.

- **Thunderball Grotto, Staniel Cay.** Beneath a three-story curved limestone ceiling, this domed cave at the northern end of the Exumas chain has some of the best snorkeling and diving in the Family Islands. James Bond aficionados will recognize it from one of the boat chase scenes in the movie *Thunderball.*

- **UNEXSO (Underwater Explorers Society), Grand Bahama.** The offerings are vast at this famous outfitter: learn to dive, get certified, check out reefs and wrecks, swim with dolphins, and, if you're an experienced diver, witness a shark feeding frenzy.

# IF YOU LIKE

## Golf

Well-designed courses are scattered throughout the islands—and thanks to consistently sunny weather, you can squeeze in a round nearly every day. Greens fees usually remain well under the $200-and-up heights common in Hawai'i and Las Vegas, and most courses offer terrific water views.

- **The Reef Course, Grand Bahamas Island.** This challenging oceanside course, the newest and most acclaimed on Grand Bahama Island, was designed by Robert Trent Jones.

- **Four Seasons Golf Club Great Exuma at Emerald Bay.** Pro golfer Greg Norman designed this 18-hole oceanside course, attached to the exclusive Four Seasons resort.

- **Ocean Club Golf Course, Paradise Island.** Michael Jordan has held his celebrity invitational tournament at this course. Part of the posh One & Only Ocean Club, play here is limited to the club's guests and several others; greens fees are among the highest in the Bahamas.

- **Treasure Cay Golf Course, Great Abaco.** This 18-hole course, designed by Dick Wilson, has a relaxed, friendly atmosphere. No tee times are required, and afternoon golfers often get the course all to themselves.

- **Abaco Club on Winding Bay, Great Abaco.** The only Scottish-style links course in the Bahamas has won rave reviews from golfers for its beauty and drama, with an 18th hole that plays out oceanside, 60 feet above the crashing surf. It's a private club, however, and although you're allowed one visit before joining, memberships start at $75,000.

## One-of-a-Kind Resorts

Spurred partly by competition from other tropical destinations, the luxury market in the Bahamas has grown substantially in the past several years; it's now possible to dine at restaurants opened by internationally famous chefs, relax with a signature treatment at an Eastern-inspired spa, and luxuriate in a $2,000-a-night suite—all without leaving the resort premises.

- **Pink Sands, Harbour Island.** Founded by Chris Blackwell, the Island Records exec who also has luxe properties in Jamaica, this chic, cozy retreat pampers high-rollers with things rarely found in the Out Islands, including imported Indonesian furniture, DVD players, and French coffee presses. Favored by guests in the recording, film, and fashion industries, the resort will roll out the welcome mat for you, too—if you can afford the $500-and-up nightly room rates.

- **One & Only Ocean Club, Paradise Island.** Much smaller and not as frenetically busy as its neighbor, Atlantis, this exclusive resort is for those who want to relax in luxury. Enjoy a complimentary yoga class or shell out for a Balinese massage or an ocean body wrap at the spa, then dine at Dune, the restaurant by famed New York chef Jean-Georges Vongerichten.

- **Atlantis, Paradise Island.** You either love the sprawling Atlantis resort for its thousands of rooms, 20-plus restaurants, loud casino, constant activity, and water park and walk-through aquarium with kitschy Lost City theme—or you hate it, for exactly the same reasons.

# GREAT
# ITINERARY

## WEEKEND IN PARADISE (ISLAND)

### Day 1: Beach It

With lots of direct flights from major U.S. airports, Paradise Island is the perfect long-weekend getaway for those who want their beach with a side of big-city culture. On your first day, get settled into your hotel, then hit the sand. If you'd like a game of pickup volleyball or a parasailing excursion, head to Cabbage Beach, where the music and the crowds are hopping; if you're after more sedate sunbathing, walk a few minutes north to Paradise Beach. For dinner, try Dune at the One & Only Ocean Club or one of the 17 restaurants in the Atlantis complex. Finish the night at Atlantis' casino or at one of the dance clubs on East Bay Street in Nassau, such as the massive Club Waterloo.

### Day 2: City Break

Get oriented to downtown Nassau. In Rawson Square, a popular meeting place between the wharf and the bridge, skip the horse-drawn surreys and go on one of the daily walking tours; official guides dressed in traditional batik vests offer a choice of three itineraries that recall the city's colonial past as a British outpost, touring mansions, cathedrals, forts, and prim-and-proper government buildings. In the afternoon, type A personalities who can handle noise and crowds should do some friendly haggling with the hair-braiders and souvenir sellers at the Straw Market; others might be better off ducking into some of the chic boutiques and duty-free shops along Bay and Parliament streets. For dinner, instead of a five-star extravaganza, try one of the local haunts at Arawak Cay, where cooks pull conch from their shells and make fresh conch salad as you watch.

### Day 3: Sporting & Relaxing

Depending on whether you prefer land- or water-based adventures, book an early tee time at one of Nassau's championship courses, or a morning snorkel or scuba tour. Beginners will enjoy the shallow reefs near Rose Island, though expert divers may prefer a more challenging dive, such as the cliff at Lyford's Cay Dropoff, where your dive partners might include giant grouper, hogfish, and rockfish. After all that strenuous activity, an afternoon at the spa is in order, and you'll still have plenty of time to get back to your room and dress for dinner.

### Optional Add-Ons

Everyone except die-hard cityslickers will have seen enough of Nassau and Paradise Island after three days, so head for one of the remote Out Islands if you have another few days to spend in the Bahamas. Our top picks are Eleuthera and Harbour Island. On the morning of Day 4, catch the fast ferry that delivers you to Harbour Island in about two hours, then catch a taxi to the Harbour Island resort where you'll base yourself for the next few nights. On Day 5, stick around pretty, serene Dunmore Town, which could pass for a New England village if it weren't for all the palms and hibiscus. On Day 6, explore the neighboring island of Eleuthera, making sure not to miss the famous Glass Window Bridge, a narrow strip of the island where the Atlantic meets the Caribbean in a swirl of turquoise, indigo, and aqua waves. On

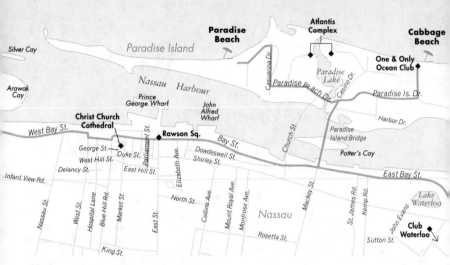

Day 7, you'll have time for a leisurely breakfast—perhaps at local favorite Arthur's Bakery & Cafe—before catching a puddle-jumper for Nassau and connecting to your flight home.

If your Out Island leg is at the end of your vacation, book the earliest possible flight back to Nassau so you'll have time to make your connection back home; Out Island air service has improved in recent years, but delays are still frustratingly frequent.

## TIPS

❶ Water taxis are a fun way to travel between Paradise Island and Nassau, but the departure schedules are definitely on island time—rather than sticking to posted schedules, many operators seem to wait until the boat is full. Also, water taxis only run during daylight hours.

❷ For taxi fares and for shopping at places like the Straw Market, bring lots of small bills; drivers and vendors either won't have change for big bills—or will claim not to in hopes of getting a bigger tip or a higher price for that T-shirt. U.S. money is used interchangeably with Bahamian dollars on a 1-to-1 exchange rate, but spend any Bahamian dollars you get as change first; you'll lose money when you convert Bahamian bills back to U.S. dollars on the way home.

❸ Throughout the Bahamas, the shore snorkeling and diving isn't great. To reach the best spots, you'll usually need to join a tour or rent a boat. A rule to remember about shore snorkeling: the better the sandy beach, the less likely you are to find colorful coral and fish.

# ON THE
# CALENDAR

| | | |
|---|---|---|
| | | The Bahamas is known for its fishing tournaments and sailing regattas, but it's a uniquely Bahamian event—the Carnival-like Junkanoo—that many travelers plan their trips around. |
| **WINTER** | Dec. | The Authentically Bahamian Christmas Trade Show showcases conch shell jewelry, straw handbags, batiks, and other island-made crafts. |
| | | The Bahamas International Film Festival celebrates cinema in paradise, with screenings, receptions, and movie-industry panels in Nassau. |
| | | The National Junkanoo Competition Finals, the "Olympics of Junkanoo," are held on Paradise Island. |
| | | Christmas Day and Boxing Day, December 25 and 26, are both public holidays. Boxing Day coincides with the first of the Junkanoo parades. |
| | | Other annual December doings in Nassau include the Police Band Beat Retreat, Night of Christmas Music, Junior Junkanoo Parade, New Year's Eve Party, and Renaissance Singers Concert. |
| | Jan. | Most churches ring in the New Year with a New Year's Midnight Service. Afterward, the uniquely Bahamian (Mardi Gras–style) Junkanoo festivities continue with the New Year's Day Junkanoo Parade in downtown Nassau. Less extensive celebrations take place in the Out Islands and in the Turks and Caicos—also on January 1, a public holiday. Later in the month, kids get into the act with the Junior Junkanoo Parade on Grand Bahama. |
| | | The New Year's Sailing Regatta at Montagu Bay, Nassau, includes competition among Bahamian-built sloops, whereas the Staniel Cay Annual New Year's Day Cruising Regatta in the Exumas marks the finale of a five-day celebration. |
| | | Pomp and pageantry take over when the Supreme Court opens in Nassau with the Chief Justice inspecting the Royal Bahamas Police Force Guard-of-Honor, accompanied by the acclaimed Bahamas Police Force Band. |
| | | Basketball legend Michael Jordan hosts his annual Michael Jordan Celebrity Invitational Golf Tournament at the One & Only Ocean Club on Paradise Island. The Breitling Golf Tournament is a week of meets on Grand Bahama Island that draws a roster of professional and amateur golfers. |

# ON THE CALENDAR

|  |  |  |
|---|---|---|
|  |  | In Nassau, the Stepping Stones Quilters present an annual Quilt Show, featuring hand-made quilts sewn using traditional Bahamian designs. |
|  |  | The second installment of the Bahamas Wahoo Tournament draws competitive anglers from the Bahamas and Florida. |
|  | Feb. | Miami to Nassau Race Week comprises three days of international sailboat championship racing. |
|  |  | The Bahamas Wahoo Tournament concludes, with the last of its three legs. |
|  |  | Also in the Out Islands, Exuma begins its monthlong Annual Cruising Regatta. |
|  |  | Beginning in February and continuing through April, Whale-watching Trips depart from several islands in the Turks and Caicos. |
|  |  | The Annual Alton Lowe Art Exhibition is at the Nassau Beach hotel beginning at the end of February through the beginning of March; sometimes guest artists also display works. |
|  |  | The E.C. Bethel National Arts Festival, a show by one of the islands' foremost painters, kicks off a nationwide series of events spotlighting music, dance, drama, and Junkanoo; the festivities take place throughout spring. |
| SPRING | Mar. | The tourism ministry sponsors beach parties, music, games, and other celebrations on Grand Bahama and Paradise islands during Spring Break for vacationing college students. |
|  |  | The annual Red Cross Fair at the Queen Elizabeth Sports Centre entertains kids and adults with games, carnival rides, local delicacies, and entertainment. |
|  |  | In Nassau, watch dogs of all classes compete at the International Dog Show & Obedience Trials at the Botanical Gardens. |
|  |  | The weeklong Bacardi Rum Billfish Tournament, which rotates around Grand Bahama and the Out Islands, kicks off the Bahamas billfish season. |
|  |  | Local musicians, Junkanoo groups, and special cultural demonstrations are on tap at the three-day Bahamian Music and Heritage Festival in the Exumas. |
|  | Apr. | Port Lucaya Marina hosts the Dolphin/Tuna Classic Tournament on Grand Bahama. |

| | | The annual Bahamas White Marlin Open at Treasure Cay, Great Abaco, is an all-release tournament, with plenty of parties to complement the fishing. The Bahamas Billfish Championship, consisting of several tournaments throughout the Out Islands, also begins this month. |
| | | The Coconut Festival in Grand Bahama's Pelican Point settlement includes coconut food sampling, coconut tree climbing, and other activities. |
| | | The Royal Nassau Sailing Club presents the Snipe Bacardi Cup & Dudley Gambling Series, an annual race. |
| | | Good Friday, Easter, and the following Easter Monday are public holidays. |
| | | The Bahamas National Youth Choir puts on its annual concert of classical, gospel, and original and traditional Bahamian songs at the Dundas Centre for the Performing Arts in Nassau. |
| | | Develop a strong case of yacht envy at the Annual International Yacht and Jet Show on Providence and Paradise islands, where multimillion-dollar craft are on display. |
| | | One of the biggest annual festivals in the Bahamas, the Exuma Family Island Regatta attracts native sloops from all over the Bahamas for races in Elizabeth Harbour; parties and festivals abound. |
| | May | There are several fishing tournaments in the Out Islands this month, including the continuation of the Bahamas Billfish Championship and the Bimini Festival of Champions. |
| | | The Island Roots Festival celebrates Bahamian traditions with an outdoor party on tiny Green Turtle Cay, while the Cat Island Heritage Festival brings a weekend of performing arts and Bahamian food to Arthur's Town on Cat Island. |
| SUMMER | June | Labour Day, the first Friday of the month, and Whit Monday are public holidays in the Bahamas. Labour Day is marked by parades and picnics throughout the nation. |
| | | Yes, more fishing tournaments: the continuation of the Bahamas Billfish Tournament is a major one this month. |
| | | The Long Island Sailing Regatta in Salt Pond, Long Island, has sloop races, a yacht parade, and lots of activity—both on and off the water. |

# ON THE CALENDAR

| | | |
|---|---|---|
| | | The Cat Island Rake and Scrape Festival celebrates the Bahamas' indigenous rake 'n scrape music. |
| | | Three days of crab races, cook-offs, live rake 'n scrape music, and a performance by the Bahamas Police Band comprise the Crab Fest in Fresh Creek, Andros. |
| | | Nassau's Arawak Cay is transformed into a heritage village every weekend for the cultural festival Junkanoo in June; live performances, crafts, kids' programs, fabulous local dishes, and a costumed Junkanoo Rushout (parading in the streets) occur each night. |
| | | Gregory Town is the scene of the four-day Eleuthera Pineapple Festival, with a Junkanoo parade, crafts displays, tours of pineapple farms, games, contests, and sports events—as well as an opportunity to sample what Eleuthera natives proclaim to be the sweetest pineapple in the world. |
| | | Sailing sloops from throughout the country meet in the Grand Bahama Sailing Regatta, in the exciting "Championship of the Seas." On-shore festivities take place at Taíno Beach and include Junkanoo Rushout parades, dancing, music, and food. |
| | | Grand Turk's Conch Carnival celebrates the Turks and Caicos' favorite culinary icon with four days of music, dancing, kayak races, and conch fritter eating contests. |
| | July | The Bahamas' most important public holiday falls on July 10—Independence Day, which was established in 1973 and marks the end of 300 years of British rule. There's a progression of flag ceremonies on each of the islands, beginning the week before the holiday and culminating in New Providence on July 10. Independence Week is celebrated throughout the Bahamas with regattas, fishing tournaments, and a plethora of parties. |
| | | Eleuthera offers three Homecoming Festivals, in Savannah Sound, Governor's Harbour, and Bluff; all are great ways to mingle with locals over food, drink, games, and general partying. |
| | | Regatta Time in Abaco is an eight-day event with races and tons of on-shore festivities. |
| | | Goombay Festivals—traditional summertime parties with dance troupes and musical groups—take place throughout the summer in Andros and Abaco. |

| | Aug. | **Emancipation Day**, which marks when the English freed Bahamian and Turks and Caicos slaves in 1834, is a public holiday celebrated on the first Monday in August (always August 1 in the Turks and Caicos). |
| | | In the Turks and Caicos, August brings the **Caicos Classic All-Release Fishing Tournament**, which takes place throughout the month. **Provo Summer Festival** spans a week of pageants and cultural shows in Providenciales. Finally, the **Turks and Caicos Music and Cultural Festival** brings together international and Bahamian music stars for several days of outdoor concerts. |
| | | The Nassau **Fox Hill Festival** pays tribute to Emancipation with church services, Junkanoo Rushout parades, music, cookouts, games, and other festivities. |
| | | The annual **Cat Island Regatta** includes parties, fashion shows, and other entertainment. |
| | | Swimming, biking, and running make up the **Great Nassau Triathlon**, which draws more than 200 international competitors. |
| **FALL** | Sept. | More than 200 contestants participate in the grueling **Great Abaco Triathlon**, which includes swimming, running, and biking. The Abaco islands are also the setting for the **All Abaco Sailing Regatta**, a weekend event highlighted by native sloop racing, Junkanoo festivities, dominos competitions, and a food fest. |
| | Oct. | The **Annual Kalik Junkanoo Rushout** gives islanders and visitors on Grand Bahama a reason to party without waiting for the Junkanoo holidays on Taíno Beach. |
| | | The **Annual McLean's Town Conch Cracking Contest**, which includes 20 days of conch-cracking competitions, games, entertainment, and good eating, takes place on Grand Bahama Island as it has for more than 30 years. South Andros holds a smaller version, **Conch Fest**, with a day's worth of music and conching. |
| | | **Discovery Day**, commemorating the landing of Columbus in the islands in 1492, is observed on October 12, a public holiday; you may hear some refer to this holiday as National Heroes Day, intended to honor a wider range of explorers and adventurers. (On Turks and Caicos Islands, it's known simply as Columbus Day.) |
| | | The **North Eleuthera Sailing Regatta** occupies five days of busy sailing. |
| | Nov. | **Christmas Jollification** is an ongoing arts-and-crafts fair with Bahamian Christmas crafts, food, and music held at the Retreat in Nassau. |

# ON THE
# CALENDAR

On Grand Bahama the annual Conchman Triathlon is a swimming-running-bicycling competition for amateurs that raises funds for local charities. Miss it? The EnduraSport Grand Bahama Triathlon is also in November.

The Bahamas Wahoo Tournament, a series of three fishing tournaments in the waters around Grand Bahama and the Abacos, begins its winter run.

# New Providence Island

**WORD OF MOUTH**

"[Potter's Cay is] a mysterious place in Nassau, where you never know quite what you'll see. Fishermen bring in everything from land crabs from the Out Islands, to sharks, spiny lobster, grouper, etc. Piles of conch abound, and they will make a fresh conch salad for you in a makeshift booth. For some reason, not too many tourists visit this haunt, or are aware of it."

–Robert

Updated by
Cheryl
Blackerby

**NEW PROVIDENCE ISLAND, HOME TO TWO-THIRDS OF ALL BAHAMIANS,**
is a palm- and mahogany-shaded flat stretch of white limestone and sand
that is home to an incongruous mix of glitzy casinos and quiet, shady
lanes; trendy, up-to-date resorts and tiny settlements that recall a distant, simpler age; land development unrivaled elsewhere in the Bahamas; and vast stretches of untrod territory. In the course of its history,
the island has weathered the comings and goings of lawless pirates, Spanish invaders, slave-holding British Loyalists who fled the United States
after the Revolutionary War, Civil War–era Confederate blockade runners, and Prohibition rumrunners. Nevertheless, New Providence remains
most influenced by England, which sent its first royal governor to the
island in 1718. Although Bahamians won government control in 1967
and independence six years later, British influence is felt to this day.

Nassau is the nation's capital and transportation hub, as well as the banking and commercial center. Although businesspeople take advantage of
bank secrecy laws that rival Switzerland's and enjoy the absence of in-
heritance, income, and sales taxes, most visitors need look no further
than Nassau's many duty-free shops for proof of the island's commercial vitality.

The fortuitous combination of tourist-friendly enterprise, tropical
weather, and island flavor with a European overlay has not gone unno-
ticed: each year more than a million cruise-ship passengers arrive at Nassau's Prince George Wharf, on short trips from Florida or as a stopover
on cruises to ports farther south in the Caribbean. In keeping with New
Providence's commercial spirit, the welcome center on the wharf offers
much more than maps and directions—it was designed to showcase the
work of Bahamian artisans, and exhibits the handmade wares of more
than 45 vendors. Another joy for hard-bargaining shoppers is Nassau's
Bay Street shops. A 2001 fire destroyed the Straw Market, a premier
Nassau shopping attraction, and it still has not been rebuilt. In the meantime, you can spar with many of the same vendors at a temporary straw
market site, housed under a huge tent on Bay Street while a permanent
market is constructed on the original site a half-block away.

A mile or so east of town, under the bridge from Paradise Island, Potter's Cay Dock is another colorful scene: sloops bring catches of fish
and conch, and open-air stalls carry fresh fruit, vegetables, and local
foods—freshly made conch salad predominates. If the daytime bustle
isn't enough, the nighttime action at the island's nightclubs and casinos
can keep you going into the wee hours of the morning.

Be sure to leave some time for outdoor activities, one of the area's
major draws. From shark diving and snorkeling to bicycle tours, horseback riding, tennis, and golf, active pursuits abound in Nassau. Avid
watersports fans will find a range of possibilities, including waterskiing, sailing, windsurfing, and deep-sea fishing. Or simply cruise the clear
Bahamian waters for a day trip or an evening ride. Although the resorts
have a great deal to offer, it would be a shame not to venture into the
incredible alfresco world that is the Bahamas' calling card.

# GREAT ITINERARIES

*Numbers in the text correspond to numbers in the margins and on the New Providence Island, and Nassau and Paradise Island maps.*

### IF YOU HAVE 3 DAYS

You can take in most of the markets, gardens, and historic sites of ▨ **Nassau** ❶–⓯ in a single day. A good starting point is ▶ **Rawson Square** ❶, in the heart of the commercial area. Do your shopping in the morning, hitting the **Bay Street** strip and the artisans' marketplace at **Prince George Wharf** ❷. To avoid the afternoon heat, visit the cluster of museums near the **Bahamas Historical Society Museum** ⓭, checking out the colonial architecture along the way. Or sit in the shade at one of Nassau's lush public gardens. For a change of pace, spend the next day relaxing at the beach. Decide whether you'd prefer a secluded stretch of sand or a beach right in the middle of the action, such as **Cable Beach**—New Providence has both. Tour ▨ **Paradise Island** ⓰–⓴ on the following day. Try your luck at the casino, and explore the giant aquariums, shops, and restaurants of the **Atlantis** ⓰ megaresort.

### IF YOU HAVE 5 DAYS

Follow the suggested three-day itinerary, and on Day 4, head north for lunch and a bit of local flavor at ▶ **Arawak Cay** ㉘. Visit nearby **Potter's Cay** ⓴, where you can find the freshest seafood and produce on the island. On your final day, drive to ▨ **Western New Providence** ㉓–㉞, stopping in **Adelaide Village** ㉝ and taking a tour of **Commonwealth Brewery** ㉜ or **Bacardi Distillery** ㉞.

### IF YOU HAVE 7 DAYS

A week will give you plenty of time to explore most areas of New Providence and ▨ **Paradise Island** ⓰–⓴. For your first five days, follow the itinerary above. On Day 6, go on a sailing cruise or a guided tour—choose your outfitter and trip based on which area you'd like to see: **Eastern New Providence** ㉑–㉔, or ▨ **Western New Providence** and the **South Coast** ㉕–㉞. Or, keep it mellow and spend more time at the beach and in the water. For your final evening, splurge at one of New Providence's fancier restaurants or hit the ▨ **Nassau** ❶–⓯ nightclub scene. Spend the next day at a spa, finish up that last-minute shopping, or take in your final rays before the trip home.

Most hotels are either on Cable Beach or Paradise Island; just outside downtown Nassau, these tourist areas offer unfettered beach access and proximity to casinos. Cable Beach, so named because the Bahamas' first transatlantic telegraph cable was laid here, is a crescent-shape stretch of sand west of Nassau, rimmed by resorts and the Crystal Palace Casino. Although by no means secluded—a string of high-profile resorts rub up against each other on the shore—Cable Beach is one of New Providence Island's prettiest stretches.

Paradise Island is connected to downtown Nassau's east end by a pair of bridges, one leading to P.I. (as locals call the island), and the original, just east, heading back to Nassau. Its status as an unspoiled alternative to the glitz of Cable Beach is long gone; Paradise Island has been irrevocably changed by the megaresort Atlantis. The tallest building in the Bahamas is home to a beachfront resort complete with a gamut of dining options, the largest casino in the Bahamas or the Caribbean, and some of the region's fanciest shops. Most memorable, however, are the water-based activities, slides, and aquariums. Love it or despise it, it's today's face of Paradise.

## Exploring New Providence

Tourist action is concentrated on New Providence's northeastern side, mostly in the capital city of Nassau and nearby Paradise Island and Cable Beach. You could easily spend your entire trip in those three areas, but if you're staying for more than a few days, you may want to see the rest of this 7- by 21-mi island. This can even be done in a single day, making occasional stops. The terrain is flat, and getting around is easy. Renting a car is your best bet—or pick up a scooter for a more adventurous ride. Wear comfortable shoes, and aim to do most of your walking early in the day, before the Bahamian sun reaches its full midday force.

As competition among Caribbean destinations continues to intensify, the Bahamas government is working toward improving its capital city. A coalition has been established to redesign the downtown area, highlighting the colorful history of the region—including its frequent brushes with pirates and slave traders. Plans also include constructing a harborside boardwalk from the wharf to Potter's Key. In the meantime, Nassau maintains its appeal as a shopping mecca and home to various museums and pink colonial buildings.

### About the Restaurants

New Providence's high-caliber dining ranges from Continental fare to ethnic specialties, including Bahamian, Mediterranean, Asian, Latin, and European eats. Dining out is a major activity, especially now that internationally renowned chefs have started moving to the Bahamas to hone their skills.

Fresh fish is the staple for tourists and locals alike. Most popular are grouper, snapper, and mahimahi (known locally as dolphin), but tuna, wahoo, and conch are also well-liked. Restaurateurs rely on local fishermen and Nassau wholesalers to stock their kitchens.

### About the Hotels

Accommodations in New Providence cater to a myriad of tastes and budgets, from glitzy luxury hotels on Cable Beach to small guesthouses in the western and southern reaches of the island. Consider what type of vacation you want—the ambience, amenities, service, and activities—then study the various options to determine which best suits your style and needs.

## IF YOU LIKE

### BEACHES FOR ALL TYPES

Bahamian beaches make an indelible impression: think warm, blue-green waves lapping up against pink-sand beaches. New Providence beaches, though less secluded and pristine than those on the Out Islands, still tempt travelers with their balmy breezes and aquamarine water. Choose between the more remote beaches of Paradise Island, action-packed strips on Cable Beach, or man-made beaches in downtown Nassau. One of the few peaceful stretches of sand on Cable Beach is the ½-mi strip at the Nassau Beach Hotel. (Many of the big resorts have monopolized the best beaches.) Try Love Beach for snorkeling—here you'll find 40 acres of coral and forests of fern known as the Sea Gardens.

### A CULINARY PLAYGROUND

New Providence is paradise for seafood lovers, adventurous eaters, gourmands, and meat-and-potatoes people alike. The island has a restaurant for every price range—and most every palate. Fresh seafood abounds, in addition to world-class continental fare and ethnic eateries, including Bahamian, Indian, Chinese, French, and Greek. The beauty of dining in New Providence is that you can eat at a grungy local dive for one meal, and feast in an elegant restaurant for the next.

### A FEAST FOR THE EYES

Downtown Nassau intrigues travelers of all types. Shoppers, history buffs, culture mavens, and strollers all seem to find their niche in the blur of colors and aromas. Wander through the straw market, chat with the vendors, then bargain for a hat to shield yourself from the midday sun. Linger in Parliament Square, where pink, colonnaded national government buildings from the early 1800s and palm trees create an old-world ambience. Immerse yourself in the world of booty and high seas adventures at the Pirates of Nassau interactive museum. Visit Festival Place, adjacent to the Prince George Wharf, to buy hand-crafted souvenirs or designer purses. Or sample local culinary specialties such as conch fritters, and take a nap in one of the lush public gardens.

Do you prefer to be in the middle of the action or on a secluded property away from the hubbub? Must the beach be outside your doorstep, or are you willing to drive or take public transportation? Are on-property restaurants and a casino essential to your vacation? If convenience and luxury are your top priorities, an all-inclusive is probably best for you. If you want to mix with the locals and experience a little more of Bahamian culture, choose a hotel in downtown Nassau. Whatever your priorities, you're likely to find what you're looking for in New Providence.

## NEW PROVIDENCE'S TOP 5

**Ardastra Gardens.** Flocks of flamingos, the country's national bird, "march" in three daily shows (you can mingle with the flamboyant pink stars afterward).

**Cracked Conch.** Eat the national dish at the fish shacks next to the water at Arawak Key with a live Bahamian band soundtrack on Friday and Saturday nights.

**Cricket.** Watch cricket games on most Saturday and Sunday afternoons from the balcony of the Bahamas Cricket Club while eating bangers and mash with a Murphy's or Guinness.

**Parliament.** Sit in the public galleries of the Senate and House of Assembly and watch the often-heated and boisterous arguments of members.

**Western Esplanade Beach.** Head to this beach (also known as Long Wharf Beach) and sit in the shade of a coconut palm while admiring a glistening white-sand beach and the mega-cruise ships coming into the harbor (it's only a 10-minute walk from the duty-free shops on Bay Street).

| WHAT IT COSTS In U.S. dollars | | | | | |
|---|---|---|---|---|---|
| | $$$$ | $$$ | $$ | $ | ¢ |
| RESTAURANTS | over $40 | $30–$40 | $20–$30 | $10–$20 | under $10 |
| HOTELS | over $400 | $300–$400 | $200–$300 | $100–$200 | under $100 |

Restaurant prices are for a main course at dinner, excluding gratuity, typically 15%, which is often automatically added to the bill. Hotel prices are for two people in a standard double room in high season, excluding service charges and 6%–12% tax.

### Timing

With the warm Gulf Stream currents swirling and balmy tradewinds blowing, the Bahamas is an appealing year-round destination. The temperature usually hovers in the 70s and 80s, and rarely gets above 90°F on a midsummer's day or below 60°F on a winter's night. June to October tend to be the hottest and wettest months, although rain is often limited to periodic showers.

The best time to visit New Providence, particularly Nassau and Paradise Island, is December through March or April, especially if you're escaping the cold. Be aware that tropical depressions, tropical storms, and hurricanes can plague New Providence during the Atlantic hurricane season from early June to late November.

## AROUND THE ISLAND

Life in the Bahamas is not *all* about glorious laziness. Nassau, the country's capital, is a bustling town on New Providence Island with shops,

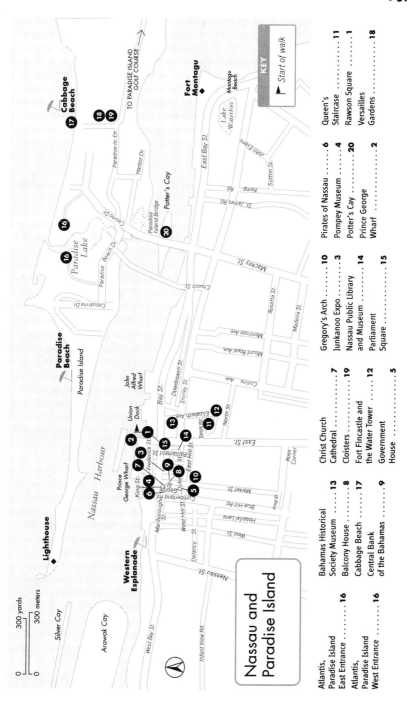

# Nassau and Paradise Island

**KEY**

▲ *Start of walk*

Atlantis,
Paradise Island
East Entrance ....... **16**

Atlantis,
Paradise Island
West Entrance ...... **16**

Bahamas Historical
Society Museum ..... **13**

Balcony House ....... **8**

Cabbage Beach ...... **17**

Central Bank
of the Bahamas ...... **9**

Christ Church
Cathedral ........... **7**

Cloisters ........... **19**

Fort Fincastle and
the Water Tower ..... **12**

Government
House ............. **5**

Gregory's Arch ...... **10**

Junkanoo Expo ...... **3**

Nassau Public Library
and Museum ....... **14**

Parliament
Square ............ **15**

Pirates of Nassau ...... **6**

Pompey Museum ...... **4**

Potter's Cay ......... **20**

Prince George
Wharf ............. **2**

Queen's
Staircase ......... **11**

Rawson Square ...... **1**

Versailles
Gardens ......... **18**

nightclubs, and an enviable array of restaurants, glitzy casinos, and posh hotels. Even in Nassau, though, there are quiet byways and shady lanes where you can escape the main tourist drags' tumult. Shop 'til you drop or wander past buildings that reveal the capital's colonial history. Dine on French cuisine in an elegant restaurant or rub shoulders with Bahamians in a down-home friendly eatery. Drop your dollars in a clangorous casino or escape to Paradise Island's secluded Versailles Gardens. Boogie the night away in a rowdy club or take a nighttime stroll along now-quiet Cable Beach, the daytime crowds just a memory.

Of course, you can flee the hurly-burly altogether and head straight for the water. You'll be hard-pressed to find yourself alone on a stretch of sand, but take heart—relatively secluded beaches do exist, they're just harder to come by.

## Nassau

Nassau's sheltered harbor bustles with cruise-ship activity, while a block away, Bay Street's sidewalks are crowded with shoppers who duck into air-conditioned shops and relax on benches in the shade of mahogany and lignum vitae trees. Shops angle for tourist dollars with fine imported goods at duty-free prices, yet you'll find a handful of shops overflowing with authentic Bahamian crafts, food supplies, and other delights. Most of Nassau's historic sites are centered around downtown.

With its thoroughly revitalized downtown, and the revamped British Colonial Hilton leading the way, Nassau is recapturing some of its past glamour. Nevertheless, modern influences are very apparent: fancy restaurants, suave clubs, and trendy coffeehouses have popped up everywhere. These changes come partly in response to the growing number of upper-crust crowds that now supplement the spring-breakers and cruise passengers who have traditionally flocked to Nassau.

Today the seedy air of the town's not-so-distant past is almost unrecognizable. Petty crime is no greater here than in other towns of this size, and the streets not only look cleaner, they feel safer. Of course, you can still find a wild club or a rowdy bar, but you can also sip cappuccino while viewing contemporary Bahamian art or dine by candlelight beneath prints of old Nassau, serenaded by soft, island-inspired calypso music. Culture and luxury abound: coffeehouses advertise art exhibitions and bistro nights, and along the streets you'll find elegant stores that many bigger towns would be lucky to have.

> **DID YOU KNOW?**
>
> Before 1695, Nassau was known as Charlestown (for Great Britain's Charles I). But it wasn't like the tidy capital you see today—according to ships' logs, sailors could smell the city's stench before they saw land.

### Sights to See

**13** **Bahamas Historical Society Museum.** For those interested in the country's origins and life before European settlement, this small collection contains a wealth of archaeological, historical, and anthropological artifacts.

The museum is staffed by volunteers and is often closed, so call ahead. ✉ *Shirley St. and Elizabeth Ave.* ☎ *242/322–4231* 💲 *$1* 🕐 *Mon. 10–1, Tues.–Fri. 10–4, Sat. 10–noon.*

★ ⑧ **Balcony House.** A charming 18th-century landmark—a pink two-story house named aptly for its overhanging balcony—this is the oldest wooden residential structure in Nassau, and its furnishings and design recapture the elegance of a bygone era. The house was originally built of American cedar. A mahogany staircase, believed to have been salvaged from a ship during the 19th century, is a highlight of the interior. A guided tour through this fascinating building is an hour well spent. (Please note that at this writing Balcony House was closed for renovation.) ✉ *Market St. and Trinity Pl.* ☎ *242/302–2621* 💲 *Donation recommended* 🕐 *Mon.–Wed., Fri. 10–4:30; Thurs., Sat. 10–1.*

⑨ **Central Bank of the Bahamas.** The Central Bank of the Bahamas monitors and regulates the country's financial institutions. The building's cornerstone was laid by Prince Charles on July 9, 1973, during the country's Independence celebrations, and the bank was opened by Queen Elizabeth II in February 1975 (you can find commemorations of these events at the back of the building). Throughout the year, exhibits on two floors of the lobby display emerging Bahamian artists' work. ✉ *Market St. and Trinity Pl.* ☎ *242/322–2193* 🕐 *Weekdays 9:30–4:30.*

★ ⑦ **Christ Church Cathedral.** It's worth the short walk off the main thoroughfare to see the stained-glass windows of this cathedral, which was built in 1837. The white pillars of the church's spacious, airy interior support ceilings beamed with dark wood installed by ship builders. The crucifixion depicted in the east window's center panel is flanked by depictions of the Empty Tomb and the Ascension. Queen Elizabeth II has attended services here. Be sure to spend a few minutes in the small, flower-filled Garden of Remembrance, where stone plaques adorn the walls. Sunday mass is held at 7:30 AM, 9 AM, 11:15 AM, and 6 PM. ✉ *George and King Sts.* ☎ *242/322–4186* 🕐 *Daily 9–5.*

> **DID YOU KNOW?**
>
> Over 35% of Bahamians are Baptist (the islands' number one religion), but many government ceremonies—including the opening of the Supreme Court—are held at the Anglican Christ Church Cathedral (Queen Elizabeth II has attended services here).

⑫ **Fort Fincastle and the Water Tower.** Shaped like the bow of a ship and perched near the top of the **Queen's Staircase,** Fort Fincastle—named for Royal Governor Lord Dunmore (Viscount Fincastle)—was completed in 1793 to serve as a lookout post for marauders trying to sneak into the harbor. It served as a lighthouse in the early 19th century. Climb the stairs or take the elevator to the top of the fort's 126-foot-tall water tower, which is more than 200 feet above sea level. The island's highest point, the tower offers a sweeping view of Nassau and its harbor. ✉ *Top of Elizabeth Ave. hill, south of Shirley St.* 💲 *Water Tower 50¢* 🕐 *Daily 8–5.*

★ ❺ **Government House.** The official residence of the governor-general of the Bahamas since 1801, this imposing pink-and-white building on Duke Street is an excellent example of the mingling of Bahamian-British and American Colonial architecture. Its graceful columns and broad, circular drive recall the styles of Virginia or the Carolinas. But its pink color, distinctive white quoins (cross-laid cornerstones), and louvered wooden shutters (to keep out the tropical sun) are typically Bahamian. Here you can also catch the crisply disciplined but beautifully flamboyant changing of the guard ceremony, which takes place every second and fourth Saturday of the month at 10 AM. The stars of the pomp and pageantry are members of the Royal Bahamas Police Force Band, who are decked out in white tunics, red-stripe navy trousers, and spiked, white pith helmets with red bands. The drummers sport leopard skins. The governor's wife hosts a tea party open to the public from 4–5 PM on the last Friday of the month January–November as part of the People-to-People program. Dress is casual but elegant—no shorts, jeans, or tennis shoes. Entertainment for the free event is provided by musicians, poets, and storytellers. ⊠ *Duke and George Sts.* ☎ *242/322–2020 for changes in ceremony schedule, 242/323–1853 for tea party.*

❿ **Gregory's Arch.** Named for John Gregory (royal governor 1849–54), this arch, at the intersection of Market and Duke streets, separates downtown from the "over-the-hill" neighborhood of **Grant's Town,** where much of Nassau's population lives. Grant's Town was laid out in the 1820s by Governor Lewis Grant as a settlement for freed slaves. Visitors once enjoyed late-night mingling with the locals in the small, dimly lighted bars of Grant's Town. Nowadays you should exhibit the same caution you would if you were visiting the commercial areas of a large city; nevertheless, it's a vibrant section of town. Here you can rub shoulders with Bahamians at a funky take-out food stand or down-home restaurant while catching a glimpse of local life.

❸ **Junkanoo Expo.** Handmade floats and costumes used by revelers during the annual Bahamian Junkanoo celebration are exhibited in an old customs warehouse at the wharf's entrance. Junkanoo, which is celebrated yearly on Boxing Day (the day after Christmas) and New Year's Day, can be likened to Carnaval in Rio de Janeiro and Mardi Gras in New Orleans—although Junkanoo is family-oriented, with children in the parades and families in the stands. Visiting the Expo is the next best thing to seeing the festivities in person. The accommodating staff will tell you everything you want to know about Junkanoo, and the colorful displays speak for themselves. ⊠ *Prince George Wharf* ☑ *$1* ⊙ *Daily 9–5:30.*

⓮ **Nassau Public Library and Museum.** The octagonal building near Parliament Square was the Nassau Gaol (the old British spelling for *jail*), circa 1797. You're welcome to pop in and browse. The small prison cells are now lined with books. The museum has an interesting collection of historic prints and old colonial documents. Check out the exhibit of traditional basket weaving patterns (with names like Bahama Mama, Peas-'n'-grits and Linen Edge) on the second floor, and ask to see the dungeon (usually locked) under the library where you can see wall etchings of clipper ships created by prisoners. ⊠ *Shirley St. between Par-*

*liament St. and Bank La.* ☎242/322–4907 ⬚*Free* ☉*Mon.–Thurs. 10–8, Fri. 10–5, Sat. 10–4.*

**⓯ Parliament Square.** Nassau is the seat of the national government. The Bahamian Parliament comprises two houses—a 16-member Senate (Upper House) and a 40-member House of Assembly (Lower House)—and a ministerial cabinet headed by a prime minister. Parliament Square's pink, colonnaded government buildings were constructed in the late 1700s and early 1800s by Loyalists who came to the Bahamas from North Carolina. The square is dominated by a statue of a slim young Queen Victoria that was erected on her birthday, May 24, in 1905. In the immediate area are a half dozen magistrates' courts (open to the public; obtain a pass at the door to view a session). Behind the House of Assembly is the **Supreme Court.** Its four-times-a-year opening ceremonies (held the first weeks of January, April, July, and October) recall the wigs and mace-bearing pageantry of the Houses of Parliament in London.

> **DID YOU KNOW?**
>
> Judges and barristers still wear wigs in court. Each Supreme Court judge has two wigs—the second one is for formal occasions.

The Royal Bahamas Police Force Band is usually on hand for the event. ✉ *Bay St.* ☎ *242/322–7500 for information on Supreme Court ceremonies* ⬚ *Free* ☉ *Weekdays 10–4.*

**⓺ Pirates of Nassau.** Take a journey through Nassau's pirate days in this interactive museum devoted to such notorious members of the city's past as Blackbeard, Mary Read, and Anne Bonney. Costumed guides greet you at every turn, some of them offering dialogue straight from a period adventure novel. Board a pirate ship, see dioramas of intrigue on the high seas, hear historical narration, and experience sound effects recreating some of the gruesome highlights. Two children under 12 get in free with an adult admission, and after that kids pay half price, making it a fun (if slightly scary) family outing. Be sure to check out the offbeat souvenirs in the Pirate Shop, and the lively Pirate Pub and Courtyard Grill, next door. ✉ *George and King Sts.* ☎ *242/356–3759* ⊕ *www.pirates-of-nassau.com* ⬚ *$12* ☉ *Mon.–Sat. 9–5.*

**⓸ Pompey Museum.** Damaged in the fire of 2001, this museum was closed at this writing. The building, where slave auctions were held in the 1700s, is named for a rebel slave who lived on the Out Island of Exuma in 1830. Exhibits focus on the issues of slavery and emancipation and highlight the works of local artists, such as Amos Ferguson, one of the country's best-loved artists; his folk-art canvases depict a wide variety of subject matter, from religious imagery to nature. ✉ *Bay and George Sts.* ☎ *242/326–2566* ⬚ *$1* ☉ *Weekdays 10–4:30, Sat. 10–1.*

**⓶ Prince George Wharf.** The wharf that leads into Rawson Square is the first view that cruise passengers encounter after they tumble off their ships. Up to a dozen gigantic cruise ships call on Nassau at any one time, and passengers spill out onto downtown, giving Nassau an instant, and constantly replenished, surge of life. A new addition to the wharf is Fes-

# A Playground for Families

**IT MIGHT NOT BE AN EXAGGERATION** to say that the Bahamas is a playground for children—or anyone else who likes building castles in the sand, searching for the perfect seashell, and playing tag with ocean waves.

While water-related activities are the most obvious enticements, these relaxed and friendly islands also offer a variety of indoor options, particularly in Nassau and on adjacent Paradise Island. Nassau is rich in colonial heritage, with historic **Parliament Square** and the **Bahamas Historical Society Museum,** which has a collection of photographs, documents, military uniforms, weapons, and tools, some items dating back to prehistoric days. For tales of the high seas, **Pirates of Nassau** has artifacts and interactive exhibits of the original pirates of the Caribbean.

Both Nassau and Freeport, on Grand Bahama Island, offer the chance to have close encounters of the dolphin kind. **Blue Lagoon Island Dolphin Encounter,** off Cable Beach, lets you stand waist deep in a protected pool of water and interact with trained dolphins, or put on snorkeling gear and swim with them. In Freeport, **UNEXSO** (formerly known as the Underwater Exploration Society, one of whose founders was Jacques Cousteau) has a similar program at Sanctuary Bay, a refuge for dolphins. After a performance of back flips and other tricks, these intelligent creatures literally snuggle up to be petted. Older children and adults also can spend a day learning how these remarkable creatures are trained.

For watersports enthusiasts, snorkeling, parasailing, and boating opportunities abound. In Exuma, rent a power boat and take the kids to Hog Beach, Big Major Island, to see the famous **swimming pigs.** Rumor has it that about 50 years ago, a farmer brought some pigs to the island to forage in the wild and serve as the food supply for his family. The farmer is long gone, but the pigs remain, swimming into the surf to greet arriving boats and beg for day-old bread.

Much of the most incredible scenery of the Bahamas is underwater. Families with children five and older can walk the sea floor to view the kaleidoscope of colors and textures with **Hartley's Undersea Walk.** Participants don diving helmets configured with a special tube and air pump, allowing them to witness life under the sea at a depth of 10–15 feet. But you don't even have to get wet to get a glimpse of some of the 50,000-odd creatures of the sea. At **Atlantis,** a resort on Paradise Island, purchase a day pass and explore the world-class aquarium. For a dose of action and adrenaline, hit the waterslides or float in a tube through a shark-filled lagoon.

Many large hotels, such as Atlantis and **Four Seasons Emerald Bay Exuma,** offer supervised all-day children's programs, and some resorts are free for kids. Even the most remote of the Out Islands can be intriguing to children, and are rich in family-centered activities. Wherever you bring the kids, you're sure to get a warm welcome.

tival Place, designed by Bahamian architect Jackson Burnside in the style of a Bahamian Village. Here you'll find kiosks for 45 Bahamian artisans; vendors selling diving, fishing, and day trips; scooter rentals; and an information desk offering maps. You can also arrange walking tours of Old Nassau here. ⊠ *Waterfront at Rawson Sq.*

**⑪ Queen's Staircase.** These 65 steps are thought to have been carved out of a solid limestone cliff by slaves in the 1790s. The staircase was later named to honor Queen Victoria's 65-year reign. Recent innovations include a waterfall cascading from the top, and an ad hoc straw market along the narrow road that leads to the site. ⊠ *Top of Elizabeth Ave. hill, south of Shirley St.*

**❶ Rawson Square.** Many locals congregate at this square, which connects Bay Street to Prince George Wharf. As you enter off Bay Street, note the statue of Sir Milo Butler, the first post-independence (and first native Bahamian) governor-general. Horse-drawn surreys wait for passengers in Woodes Rogers Walk, which runs down the middle of the square (expect to pay about $10 for a half-hour ride through Nassau's streets). On the Walk's other side, you can look into (or perhaps stop inside) the **hair-braiding pavilion,** where women work their magic at prices ranging from $2 for a single strand to $100 for an elaborate do. An often-overlooked pleasure near the pavilion is Randolph W. Johnston's lovely bronze statue, *Tribute to Bahamian Women.* ⊠ *Bay St.*

## Paradise Island

The graceful, arched Paradise Island bridges ($1 toll for cars and motorbikes from Nassau to P.I.; free for bicyclists and pedestrians), 1 mi east of Nassau's Rawson Square, lead to and from the extravagant world of Paradise Island.

Until 1962, Paradise Island was largely undeveloped and known as Hog Island. A&P heir Huntington Hartford changed the name when he built the island's first resort complex. Although several huge high-rise resorts have been erected since then—as have many million-dollar houses—you can still find several quiet getaway spots. The north shore is lined with white-sand beaches, and the protected south shore, directly across the harbor from Nassau, is a haven for yachts. Aptly renamed, the island *is* a paradise for beach lovers, boaters, and fun lovers. Casinos abound.

### Sights to See

**★ ☺ ⑯ Atlantis, Paradise Island.** The unmistakable sight of this peach fantasia comes into view just as you cross the Paradise Island Bridge. The towering sunstruck visage is actually Royal Towers, the largest and newest wing of the Atlantis resort. With glitzy shopping malls, a cabaret theater, and seemingly unlimited choices for dining and drinks (35 restaurants and bars), Atlantis is as much a tourist attraction as a resort hotel. Many of its facilities, including the restaurants and casino, are open to nonguests. For a peek at the rest—including the world's largest man-made marine habitat, consisting of 11 lagoons—take the guided "Discover Atlantis" tour, which begins near the main lobby at an exhibition called "The Dig." This wonderful series of walk-through aquariums, themed around the lost continent and its re-created ruins, brings you face to face with sharks, manta rays, and innumerable forms of exotic sea life. The rest of the tour tempts you with a walk through the many water slides and pools inaccessible to nonguests. ✉ *Casino Dr.* ☎ *242/ 363–3000* 🖃 *Discover Atlantis tour $25, casino admission free* ⊘ *Tours daily 9–5, casino daily 24 hrs.*

**⑰ Cabbage Beach.** This stretch of white sand along the north side is one of the prettiest on New Providence. Although resorts line much of its length, several minutes' stroll to the east will take you to a nearly uninhabited span of beach overlooking emerald waters and tiny offshore cays.

**★ ⑲ Cloisters.** At the top of the **Versailles Gardens** stand the remains of a 14th-century French stone monastery that were imported to the United States in the 1920s by newspaper baron William Randolph Hearst. (The cloister is one of four to have ever been removed from French soil.) Forty years later, grocery-chain heir Huntington Hartford bought the Cloisters and had them rebuilt on their present commanding site. At the center is a graceful, contemporary white marble statue called *Silence,* by U.S. sculptor Dick Reid. Nearly every day tourists take or renew wedding vows under the delicately wrought gazebo overlooking Nassau Harbour. The Cloisters are owned by the One & Only Ocean Club, but visitors are welcome to look around. ✉ *Paradise Island Dr.*

**★ ⑳ Potter's Cay.** From Nassau, walk the road beneath the Paradise Island Bridge to watch the mailboats heading out to the Bahamas Out Islands loaded down with cars, appliances, passengers, and, yes, mail. You can book a trip on one at the small passenger terminal. You will also see sloops bringing in and selling loads of fish and conch—pronounced *konk.* Along the road to the cay are dozens of stands where you can watch the conch, straight from the sea, being extracted from its glistening pink shell. If you don't have the know-how to handle the tasty conch's preparation—getting the diffident creature out of its shell requires boring a hole at the right spot to sever the muscle that keeps it entrenched—you can enjoy a conch salad on the spot, as fresh as it comes, and take notes for future attempts. Empty shells are sold as souvenirs. Many locals and hotel chefs come here to purchase the fresh catches; you can also find vegetables, herbs, and such condiments as fiery Bahamian peppers preserved in lime juice, and locally grown pineapples, papayas, and bananas.

**⑱ Versailles Gardens.** Fountains and statues of luminaries and legends (such as Napoléon and Josephine, Franklin Delano Roosevelt, David Livingstone, Hercules, and Mephistopheles) adorn Versailles Gardens, the terraced lawn at the One & Only Ocean Club, which was once the private hideaway of Huntington Hartford. The Cloisters grace the top of the gardens. Although the property is owned by the One & Only Ocean Club, visitors are welcome. ✉ *One & Only Ocean Club, Paradise Island Dr.* ☎ *242/363–2501.*

## Eastern New Providence

New Providence Island's eastern end is residential, although there are some interesting historic sites and fortifications here. From East Bay Street, just beyond the Paradise Island bridges, it's a short, scenic drive along Eastern Road, which is lined with gracious homes, to Eastern Point (also known as East End Point)—about 20 minutes, depending on traffic.

## Sights to See

**㉑ Fort Montagu.** The oldest of the island's three forts, Montagu was built of local limestone in 1741 to repel Spanish invaders. The only action it saw was when it was occupied for two weeks by rebel American troops— among them a lieutenant named John Paul Jones—seeking arms and ammunition during the Revolutionary War. The small fortification is in disrepair, and you're not allowed to go inside. The second level has a number of rusted cannons. A narrow public beach stretching for more than a mile beyond the fort looks out upon Montagu Bay, where many international yacht regattas and Bahamian sloop races are held annually. ⊠ *East of Bay St. on Eastern Rd.* 🗹 *Free.*

**㉓ Fox Hill.** Settled by freed slaves who were given land grants, which they paid for either in cash or labor, this residential area was originally four smaller settlements. Today there's not much here of tourist interest—except on the second Tuesday of August, when the community holds its annual Fox Hill Day celebration. It falls a week after the rest of the island celebrates Emancipation Day (some say that's because back in 1834 it took a week for the news of the emancipation to reach the community here). Festivities include music, home-cooked food, and arts-and-crafts booths. Call the Ministry of Tourism for more information. ☎ *242/322–7500.*

**★ ㉒ The Retreat.** Nearly 200 species of exotic palm trees grace the 11 verdant acres appropriately known as the Retreat, which serves as the headquarters of the Bahamas National Trust. Stroll in blessed silence through the lush grounds, past smiling Buddhas, and under stone arbors overhung with vines. It's a perfect break on a steamy Nassau day. Guided tours are available, or walk through this sanctuary on your own. ⊠ *Village Rd.* ☎ *242/393–1317* 🗹 *$2* ⊙ *Weekdays 9–5.*

**㉔ St. Augustine's Monastery.** The Romanesque home of the Bahamas' Benedictine brothers was built in 1946 by a monk named Father Jerome, also famed for his carvings of the Stations of the Cross on Cat Island's Mt. Alvernia. The St. Augustine buildings, home to a college as well as the religious complex, overlook beautiful gardens. This is truly an off-the-beaten-track sight. Call first to see if the monks will give you a tour. ⊠ *Bernard Rd., west of Fox Hill Rd.* ☎ *242/364–1331.*

# Western New Providence & South Coast

Starting from downtown Nassau, West Bay Street follows the coast west past the resorts, posh residential neighborhoods, and ever-increasing new developments of Cable Beach, then past popular Love Beach to Northwest Point. Just beyond is Lyford Cay, the island's most exclusive community, whose residents include actors Sydney Poitier and Sean Connery. Old-money pioneers started settling the cay four decades ago, and along with its 200-odd houses there's a private golf course for residents. Your experience of Lyford Cay is likely to be voyeuristic at best—an entrance gate wards off all but residents and friends.

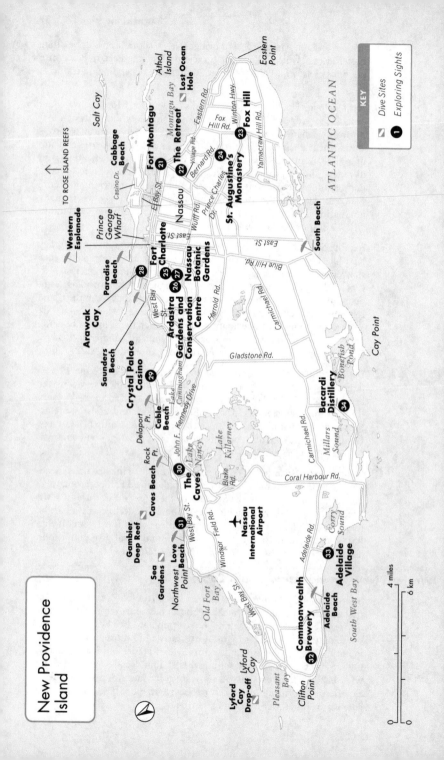

# New Providence Island

TO ROSE ISLAND REEFS

Salt Cay

Athol Island

Lost Ocean Hole

Cabbage Beach

Casino Dr.

Fort Montagu **21**

Montagu Bay

The Retreat **22**

Fox Hill Rd.

Eastern Point

Eastern Rd.

Winton Hwy.

Fox Hill **23**

Village Rd.

Bernard Rd.

St. Augustine's Monastery **24**

Prince Charles Dr.

Yamacraw Hill Rd.

Western Esplanade

Prince George Wharf

E. Bay St.

Nassau

Wulff Rd.

East St.

East St.

Blue Hill Rd.

South Beach

ATLANTIC OCEAN

Paradise Beach

Fort Charlotte

Nassau Botanic Gardens

Harrold Rd.

Carmichael Rd.

Cay Point

Arawak Cay

West Bay St.

Ardastra Gardens and Conservation Centre **26** **27** **25**

**28**

Saunders Beach

Crystal Palace Casino **29**

Cunningham Drive

John F. Kennedy Drive

Lake Cunningham

Gladstone Rd.

Bonefish Pond

Bacardi Distillery **34**

Cable Beach

Delaport Pt.

Rock Pt.

Caves Beach

The Caves **30**

Lake Nancy

Lake Killarney

Blake Rd.

Carmichael Rd.

Millars Sound

Coral Harbour Rd.

Gambier Deep Reef

Sea Gardens

Northwest Point

Love Beach

**31**

West Bay St.

Windsor Field Rd.

Nassau International Airport

Adelaide Rd.

Corry Sound

Adelaide Beach

Adelaide Village **33**

South West Bay

Lyford Cay Drop-off

Lyford Cay

Pleasant Bay

Clifton Point

Old Fort Bay

West Bay St.

Commonwealth Brewery **32**

Adelaide Beach

## KEY

⚓ Dive Sites

**1** Exploring Sights

0    4 miles

0    6 km

Much of the interior and southwestern coast of New Providence is un-developed, with pristine coastal scenery and long, low stretches of pal-metto and pine forest. The loop around the island's west and south coasts can be done in a couple of hours by car or scooter; however, you may wish to take time out for lunch and a swim along the way.

## Sights to See

**33 Adelaide Village.** The small community on New Providence's south-western coast sits placidly, like a remnant of another era, between busy Adelaide Road and the ocean. It was first settled during the early 1830s by Africans who had been captured and loaded aboard slave ships bound for the New World. They were rescued on the high seas by the British Royal Navy, and the first group of liberated slaves reached Nas-sau in 1832. Today, only a few dozen families live in Adelaide. They grow vegetables, raise chickens, and inhabit well-worn, pastel-painted wooden houses, sheltered by bougainvillea and other vegetation. The village has a primary school, some little grocery stores, and locally pop-ular **Avery's Restaurant and Bar** (⊠ Adelaide Rd. ☎ 242/362–1547 ☉ Closed Mon.).

**28 Arawak Cay.** Known to Nassau residents as "The Fish Fry," Arawak Cay is one of the best places to knock back a Kalik beer (brewed right on New Providence Island), chat with the locals, or sample traditional Ba-hamian fare. You can get small dishes such as lobster salad or full meals at one of the pastel-color waterside shacks. Order some steamed, grilled, or fried fish or fresh conch salad, a spicy mixture of chopped conch (just watching the expert chopping is a show as good as any in town) mixed with diced onions, cucumbers, tomatoes, and hot peppers in a lime mari-nade. Twin Brothers and Goldie's Enterprises are two of the most pop-ular stalls. Try their fried "cracked conch" and Goldie's famous Sky Juice (a potent gin and coconut-water concoction).

To reach Arawak Cay, head west along Bay Street, follow the main road around the British Colonial Hilton hotel, and continue west past West-ern Esplanade, which many locals also call Long Wharf Beach. The cay is on the north side of the T-junction of West Bay and Chippingham Road. It's approximately a five-minute drive or 30-minute walk.

**26 Ardastra Gardens and Conservation Centre.** Marching flamingos? These national birds of the Bahamas give a parading performance at Ardas-tra daily at 10:30, 2, and 4. The brilliant pink birds are a delight—es-pecially for children, who can walk among the flamingos after the show. The zoo, with more than 5 acres of tropical greenery and flowering shrubs, also has an aviary of rare tropical birds, native Bahamian creatures such as rock iguanas, and a global collection of small animals. ⊠ *Chipping-ham Rd., south of W. Bay St.* ☎ *242/323–5806* ▣ *$12* ☉ *Daily 9–4:30.*

**34 Bacardi Distillery.** The factory, established in 1962, is open to the public for tours. You can sample a range of its well-known rum products (and, needless to say, purchase some) at the Visitors Pavilion. ⊠ *Bacardi and Carmichael Rds.* ☎ *242/362–1412* ▣ *Free* ☉ *Mon.–Thurs. 10–3.*

**30 The Caves.** These large limestone caverns that the waves have sculpted over the aeons are said to have sheltered the early Arawak Indians. An oddity perched right beside the road, they're worth a glance—although in truth, there's not much to see, as the dark interior doesn't lend itself to exploration. Just a short drive beyond the caves, on an island between traffic lanes, is **Conference Corner,** where U.S. president John F. Kennedy, Canadian prime minister John Diefenbaker, and British prime minister Harold Macmillan planted trees on the occasion of their 1962 summit in Nassau. ⊠ *W. Bay St. and Blake Rd.*

**㉜ Commonwealth Brewery.** Kalik, Nassau's very own beer, pale in color but with a full-bodied taste, is brewed here. The local beverage—by far the most popular among Bahamians—is named for the sound of the cowbells used in the Junkanoo Parade. Free tours are given by appointment only. ⊠ *Clifton Pier and Southwest Rd.* ☎ *242/362–4789.*

**㉙ Crystal Palace Casino.** You can try your luck at baccarat, blackjack, roulette, craps, and Caribbean stud poker—or simply settle for the slots. There's plenty to keep you entertained, including a sports book for betting on your favorite teams, and games from "pai gow poker" to "let it ride" and "war" tables. ⊠ *Nassau Wyndham Resort & Crystal Palace Casino, Cable Beach, Nassau* ☎ *242/327–6200* ☉ *Tables 10 AM–4 AM weekdays, 24 hrs weekends; slots 24 hrs daily.*

★ **㉕ Fort Charlotte.** Built in 1788, this imposing fort comes complete with a waterless moat, drawbridge, ramparts, and a dungeon, where children love to see the torture device where prisoners were "stretched." Young guides bring the fort to life. (Tips are expected.) Lord Dunmore, who built it, named the massive structure in honor of George III's wife. At the time, some called it Dunmore's Folly because of the staggering expense of its construction. It cost eight times more than was originally planned. (Dunmore's superiors in London were less than ecstatic with the high costs, but he managed to survive unscathed.) Ironically, no shots were ever fired in battle from the fort. It's about 1 mi west of central Nassau. Bring a picnic lunch. The fort and its surrounding 100 acres offer a wonderful view of the cricket grounds, the beach, and the ocean beyond. ⊠ *W. Bay St. at Chippingham Rd.* ☜ *$5* ☉ *Local guides conduct tours daily 8–4.*

**㉛ Love Beach.** One of the island's loveliest little beaches is near New Providence's northwestern corner. About 1 mi off Love Beach are 40 acres of coral and sea fan, with forests of fern, known as the Sea Gardens. The clear waters are a favorite with snorkelers.

**㉗ Nassau Botanic Gardens.** Six hundred species of flowering trees and shrubs, a small cactus garden, and two freshwater ponds with lilies, water plants, and tropical fish cover 18 acres. The many trails that wind through the gardens are perfect for leisurely strolls. The Botanic Gardens are across the street from the **Ardastra Gardens and Conservation Centre,** home of Nassau's zoo. ⊠ *Chippingham Rd., south of W. Bay St.* ☎ *242/323–5975* ☜ *$1* ☉ *Weekdays 8–4, weekends 9–4.*

# BEACHES

New Providence is blessed with stretches of white sand studded with palm and seagrape trees. Some of the beaches are small and crescent shaped, whereas others stretch for miles. Right in downtown Nassau is the **Western Esplanade.** Also known as Long Wharf Beach, this stretch of white sand sweeps west from the British Colonial Hilton on Bay Street and offers public restrooms. On Paradise Island, **Paradise Beach,** at the island's far western tip, is a nice stretch of sand. Paradise Island's real showpiece is 3-mi-long **Cabbage Beach,** which rims the north coast from the Atlantis lagoon to Snorkeler's Cove. At the east end you can rent jet skis and nonmotorized pedal boats, and go parasailing.

**Cable Beach** is on New Providence's north shore, about 3 mi west of downtown Nassau. Resorts line much of this beautiful, broad swath of white sand, but there is public access. Jet-skiers and beach vendors abound, so don't expect quiet isolation. Just west of Cable Beach is a rambling pink house on the Rock Point promontory, where much of the 1965 Bond film *Thunderball* was filmed. Tiny, crescent-shape **Caves Beach** is beyond Cable Beach on the north shore, about 7 mi from downtown just before the turnoff on Blake Road that leads to the airport. **Love Beach,** a snorkeler's favorite, is on the north shore beyond Caves Beach, about 9 mi from town (about a 20-minute drive). Access technically lies within the domain of Love Beach residents, but they aren't inclined to shoo anyone away. On the south shore, drive down to **Adelaide Beach,** at the end of Adelaide Village, for sand that stretches down to Coral Harbour. The people who live at New Providence's east end flock to **South Beach,** at the foot of Blue Hill Road on the south shore.

# WHERE TO EAT

With the escalation of Bahamian tourism, meal preparation at the better dining spots has become as sophisticated as that in any leading U.S. city. European chefs brought in by the top restaurants have trained young Bahamians in the skills of haute cuisine. Chinese, Indian, Mexican, Creole, and Japanese fare have also become available.

However, don't neglect the Bahamian food. Several relatively inexpensive spots serve traditional dishes, which now also appear on the ritzier menus: peas 'n' rice, conch (chowder, fritters, and cracked), Bahamian lobster, "stew" or "boil" fish, grouper fingers, fresh local bread, and, for dessert, guava duff, a warm marriage of boiled Guava dough and sweet sauce. Because meats and some seafood often have to be imported, local fish is usually the most economical entrée.

Coffeehouses have sprung up everywhere. Most serve light fare and desserts plus specialty coffees and teas.

Many all-inclusives also offer meal plans for nonguests.

## Nassau

### Bahamian

**$–$$** ✕ **The Poop Deck.** Just east of the bridge from Paradise Island and a quick cab ride from the center of town is this favorite local haunt. You can scan the vista of the Bahamas' largest marina from breezy tables on the large waterfront deck. The restaurant's popularity has resulted in a second Poop Deck on Cable Beach's west end, but for residents, this is still the place. Expect spicy dishes with such names as Mama Mary's steamed fish and Rosie's chicken; there's also an extensive wine list. Save room for guava duff and a calypso coffee spiked with secret ingredients. ⊠ *E. Bay St., at Nassau Yacht Haven Marina, east of bridge from Paradise Island* ☎ *242/393–8175* ⊟ *AE, D, MC, V.*

¢–$$  ✕ **Shoal Restaurant and Lounge.** Saturday morning brings hordes of hungry Bahamians digging into johnnycake and boil fish, the restaurant's specialty. A bowl of this peppery local dish, filled with chunks of boiled potatoes, onions, and grouper, may keep you coming back to this dimly lighted, basic, out-of-the-way "Ma's kitchen," where Bahamian dishes, including peas 'n' rice and cracked conch, are staples. It's just a short cab ride from downtown Nassau. ⊠ *Nassau St., between Meadow St. and Poinciana Dr.* ☎ *242/323–4400* ⊟ *AE, D, MC, V* ⊘ *Closed Wed.*

★ ¢–$  ✕ **Mama Lyddy's Place.** Just off the beaten tourist track, this old house is the place for true Bahamian cooking. Start with a local-style breakfast of souse or "boil fish" and watch Nassau residents stream in for takeout or sit-down meals. For lunch and dinner try fried snapper, cracked conch, minced or broiled crawfish, pork chops, and chicken. All are served with peas 'n' rice or peas 'n' grits and other typical Bahamian side dishes. ⊠ *Market St. at Cockburn St.* ☎ *242/328–6849* ⊟ *No credit cards.*

### Chinese

¢–$$  ✕ **East Villa Restaurant and Lounge.** Nassau residents declare that this restaurant, set back from the busy street, serves the best Chinese food in town. The Chinese-Continental menu includes such entrées as conch with black bean sauce, *hung shew* (walnut chicken), and steak *kew* (cubed prime fillet served with baby corn, snow peas, water chestnuts, and vegetables). The New York strip steak is nirvana. A short taxi ride from Paradise Island or downtown Nassau, this is the perfect spot if you're seeking something a little different from the typical area restaurants. ⊠ *E. Bay St., near Nassau Yacht Club* ☎ *242/393–3377* ⊟ *AE, D, MC, V* ⊘ *No lunch Sat.*

### Contemporary

★ $$  ✕ **The Pink Pearl Café.** The Pink Pearl is set in a 1943 mansion made of limestone and local pine. Its inventive menu and impeccable service draw crowds, as does the live jazz that you can listen to on weekends from the breezy side porch. From the moment you arrive, you know you're in for a treat—aromatic bread arrives in a large calabash shell. Entrées might include roasted grouper with a ragout of onion, tomato, thyme, mushrooms, and potatoes, or grilled conch drizzled with tamarind barbecue sauce. ⊠ *E. Bay St., east of bridge from Paradise Island* ☎ *242/394–6413* ⊟ *AE, D, DC, MC, V* ⊘ *Closed Sun.*

### Continental

★ $$$–$$$$  ✕ **Buena Vista.** High on a hill above Nassau Harbour, this serene restaurant sits secure in its reputation as one of the city's dining institutions; it draws a loyal local clientele. Established in 1946, it occupies what was once a rambling private home built in the early 1800s. Tuxedoed waiters whisk about the dining room, where tables are set with china, crystal, and silver. Although jackets aren't absolutely required, you'll find most gentlemen wearing them. Exemplary entrées include grouper and rack of spring

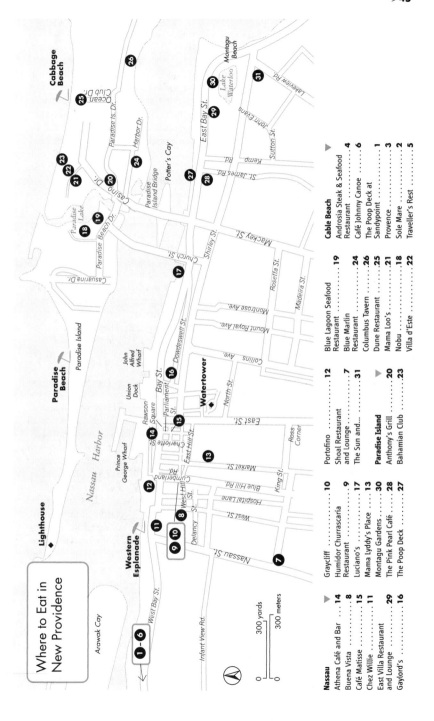

**Where to Eat in New Providence**

0 | 300 yards
0 | 300 meters

**Nassau** ▶
Athena Café and Bar ... **14**
Buena Vista ........... **8**
Café Matisse .......... **15**
Chez Willie ........... **11**
East Villa Restaurant
and Lounge .......... **29**
Gaylord's ............. **16**

Graycliff ............. **10**
Humidor Churrascaria
Restaurant .......... **9**
Luciano's ............ **17**
Mama Lyddy's Place ... **13**
Montagu Gardens ..... **30**
The Pink Pearl Café ... **28**
The Poop Deck ....... **27**

Portofino ............ **12**
Shoal Restaurant
and Lounge .......... **7**
The Sun and... ....... **31**

**Paradise Island**
Anthony's Grill ....... **20** ▶
Bahamian Club ....... **23**

Blue Lagoon Seafood
Restaurant .......... **19**
Blue Marlin
Restaurant .......... **24**
Columbus Tavern ..... **26**
Dune Restaurant ..... **25**
Mama Loo's .......... **21**
Nobu ................ **18**
Villa d'Este .......... **22**

**Cable Beach**
Androsia Steak & Seafood
Restaurant .......... **4**
Café Johnny Canoe ... **6**
The Poop Deck at
Sandypoint .......... **1**
Provence ............ **3**
Sole Mare ........... **2**
Traveller's Rest ...... **5**

lamb. Leave room for Mrs. Hauck's Orange Pancakes, baked in a Grand Marnier sauce—a house specialty for decades. ⊠ *W. Hill and Delancy Sts.* ☎ *242/322–2811* ▤ *AE, D, DC, MC, V* ☉ *Closed Sun. No lunch.*

**$$$–$$$$**  ╳ **Graycliff.** A meal at Graycliff begins in the elegant parlor, where, over live piano music, drinks are served and orders are taken. When your appetizer is ready, you're escorted into one of several dining rooms. Graycliff's signature dishes include roast rack of lamb and the thermidor-style Lobster Graycliff. Prices are no higher than other top-notch Nassau restaurants—except for wine: the cellar contains more than 175,000 bottles that have been handpicked by owner Enrico Garzaroli, some running into the tens of thousands of dollars. You can even buy the world's oldest bottle of wine, a German vintage 1727, for $250,000. ⊠ *W. Hill St. at Cumberland Rd., across from Government House* ☎ *242/322–2796* ⌑ *Reservations essential* ⌂ *Jacket and tie* ▤ *AE, D, DC, MC, V* ☉ *No lunch weekends.*

★ **$$$–$$$$**  ╳ **The Sun and . . .** If you're hoping to catch sight of international superstars, this is a good place to look (assuming that they—or you—make it past the hostess). Dine in a series of rooms surrounding an enclosed garden area with a rock pool and fountain—as magical a dining setting as Nassau offers. Feast on such creations as salmon mousseline and crayfish tails rolled in grouper fillets, topped with Chardonnay-lobster sauce, or veal with porcini mushrooms and white truffle oil. End your meal divinely with one of Belgian owner-chef Ronny Deryckere's six soufflés, which range from almond amaretto to guava. Dress is elegant, but jackets are not required. ⊠ *Lakeview Rd. and E. Shirley St.* ☎ *242/393–1205* ⌑ *Reservations essential* ▤ *AE, D, MC, V* ☉ *Closed Mon., Aug., and Sept. No lunch.*

★ **$$–$$$**  ╳ **Humidor Churrascaria Restaurant.** Carved-wood statues of pipe smokers, imported from Cuba, set the tone at this relaxed restaurant in the Graycliff hotel's Graycliff Cigar Company wing. This spot is a stogie-lover's delight. Here you can get a set meal that includes a selection of cigars. The tasty bistro fare, served by waiters dressed as gauchos, includes tuna tartare, lobster cakes, and risotto with porcini mushrooms and lamb. For postprandial indulgence, retire to the lounge or stroll along the hotel's garden terraces and fountains. ⊠ *W. Hill St., off Cumberland Rd.* ☎ *242/328–7050* ▤ *AE, DC, MC, V* ☉ *Closed Sun.*

**$–$$$**  ╳ **Montagu Gardens.** Angus beef and fresh native seafood—flame grilled and seasoned with home-mixed spices—are the specialties at this romantic restaurant in an old Bahamian mansion on Lake Waterloo. The dining room opens to a walled courtyard niched with Roman-style statues and gardens that lead to a waterside balustrade. Besides seafood and steak (carnivores should try the filet mignon smothered in mushrooms), menu selections include chicken, lamb, pasta, ribs, and several Bahamian-inspired dishes such as conch fritters and minced crawfish with taco chips. A favorite dessert is Fort Montagu Mud Pie. ⊠ *E. Bay St.* ☎ *242/394–6347* ▤ *AE, D, MC, V* ☉ *Closed Sun.*

### Eclectic

**¢–$$$**  ╳ **Portofino.** Nassau's movers and shakers meet here for breakfast, lunch, and dinner. Located at the British Colonial Hilton Nassau, Portofino offers homemade Italian pasta dishes and pizza as well as Bahamian favorites such as pan-seared snapper with mango sauce, conch chowder, and guava duff. The lavish lunch buffet far surpasses the usual hotel fare. For breakfast, don't miss the Bahamian johnnycakes. ⊠ *No. 1 W. Bay St.* ☎ *242/322–3301* ⊟ *AE, D, MC, V.*

★ **$–$$** ✕ **Café Matisse.** Low-slung settees, stucco arches, and reproductions of the eponymous artist's works set a casually refined tone at this restaurant, owned by a husband-and-wife team—he's Bahamian, she's northern Italian. Sit in the ground-floor garden under large white umbrellas or dine inside the century-old house for lunch or dinner. Start with salmon carpaccio, then dive into freshly made pasta such as duck-filled ravioli and lobster cannelloni, or such delights as pizza *frutti di mare* (topped with fresh local seafood). ⊠ *Bank La. and Bay St., behind Parliament Sq.* ☎ *242/356–7012* ⊟ *AE, D, MC, V* ☽ *Closed Sun. and Mon.*

### French

**$$$** ✕ **Chez Willie.** Elegant and romantic, this restaurant specializes in French cuisine with a Bahamian twist. Dine by candlelight in the intimate dining room or alfresco on the patio overlooking the lush gardens. Start with caviar or goose liver pâté, then try the signature grouper served in a puff pastry with crabmeat and coconut cream sauce. Or go with someone you love and share the chateaubriand for two. ⊠ *W. Bay St.* ☎ *242/322–5364 or 242/322–5366* ⊲ *Reservations essential* ⊟ *AE, MC, V* ☽ *Dinner only.*

### Greek

**$–$$** ✕ **Athena Café and Bar.** A mainstay since 1960, this Greek restaurant provides a break from the Nassau culinary routine. Sit on the second floor among Grecian statuary, or on the balcony overlooking the action below. Enjoy souvlaki, moussaka, and spanakopita, among other specialties, along with Greek beer in a relaxed and friendly atmosphere. Gregarious owner Peter Mousis and his family serve tasty fare at moderate prices. ⊠ *Bay St. at Charlotte St.* ☎ *242/322–8833* ⊟ *AE, D, MC, V* ☽ *Closed Sun.*

### Indian

**$–$$** ✕ **Gaylord's.** Plates, plaques, and other Indian works of art decorate the walls of the two dining areas in this historic building, which dates from the 1870s. Draped silk adorns the ceilings. Begin with a *samosa* (a savory vegetable or meat filling enveloped in pastry and then deep fried). Next try one of the tandoori dishes cooked in a special clay oven, including naan bread (plain, or stuffed with chicken, cheese, garlic, or lamb), and mild *korma* (lamb or chicken in a rich cream sauce) or fiery vindaloo. ⊠ *Dowdeswell St. near Victoria Ave.* ☎ *242/356–3004* ⊟ *AE, D, MC, V* ☽ *Closed Sun. No lunch weekends.*

### Italian

**$–$$$** ✕ **Luciano's.** Green Roofs, the sprawling former residence of the late Sir Roland Symonette (the country's first premier) houses this harborside restaurant. The mansion's mahogany woodwork, gardens, and terraces create a romantic setting for dining on Tuscan fare, including Escarole White Bean and Sausage Soup, Bistecca Fiorentina, Snapper *al Cartoccio* baked in parchment with julienne vegetables, and homemade pastas—including risotto with chicken and wild mushrooms. The sweeping view of Paradise Island and the towers of Atlantis is particularly lovely at sunset. Reservations are essential for waterside tables. ⊠ *E. Bay St. 2 blocks west of Paradise Island bridge* ☎ *242/323–7770* ▤ *AE, D, MC, V.*

## Paradise Island

### Caribbean

¢–$$$  ✕ **Anthony's Grill.** Color is the standout feature of Anthony's: bright red, yellow, and blue tablecloths spiked with multihue squiggles; yellow-and-green walls with jaunty cloths hanging from the ceilings; booths printed with bright sea themes; and buoyant striped curtains. The lively spirit is reflected in the cheery service you'll receive at breakfast, lunch, or dinner. Specialties include penne pasta, fresh seafood such as herb-crusted red snapper, steaks, burgers, and salads. ⊠ *Paradise Village Shopping Plaza* ☎ *242/363–3152* ▤ *AE, D, MC, V.*

### Chinese

$$–$$$  ✕ **Mama Loo's.** This dinner-only restaurant in Atlantis serves Chinese fare amidst a tropical-Chinese decor enhanced with huge porcelain urns, carved wood ceilings, lush floral arrangements, and black-lacquer chairs. Pick grouper stir-fry, braised duck, cashew chicken, or beef with oyster sauce. ⊠ *Atlantis, Paradise Island* ☎ *242/363–3000* ⚝ *Reservations essential* ▤ *AE, D, DC, MC, V* ⊗ *Closed Mon. No lunch.*

### Contemporary

★ $–$$$$  ✕ **Dune Restaurant.** At Dune you'll feast on intricately prepared dishes while overlooking Cabbage Beach at the renowned One & Only Ocean Club. Go for breakfast or lunch for the most reasonable prices. For breakfast, try the smoked salmon with potato pancake and chive sour cream or the egg-white omelet with fresh herbs. Dinner entrées include roasted grouper, rack of lamb, and sirloin steak. It's a great place to unwind amid ocean breezes. ⊠ *Ocean Club Dr.* ☎ *242/363–3000 Ext. 64739* ▤ *AE, D, MC, V.*

### Continental

$$$–$$$$  ✕ **Bahamian Club.** Reminiscent of a British country club, this handsome restaurant has walls lined with dark oak, overstuffed chairs, and leather banquettes. Meat is the house specialty—grilled T-bone steak, veal chop, roast prime rib, and chateaubriand for two—but grilled swordfish steak, Bahamian lobster, salmon fillet, and other fresh seafood dishes are all prepared with finesse. Dinner is accompanied by soft piano music; between courses, couples can waltz on the small dance floor. ⊠ *Atlantis, Paradise Island* ☎ *242/363–3000* ⚝ *Reservations essential* ▤ *AE, D, DC, MC, V* ⊗ *No lunch.*

### Eclectic

$$$–$$$$  ✕ **Nobu.** The innovative Japanese restaurant conceived and run by chef Nobu Matsuhisa opened December 2005 in Atlantis's Royal Towers, adjacent to the casino. The central dining room is surrounded by a Japanese pagoda, and guests seated at a long communal sushi bar can watch the chefs work. Reservations are suggested. ⊠ *Atlantis, Paradise Island* ☎ *242/363–3000* 🏛 *Jacket required* ▤ *AE, D, DC, MC, V* ⊗ *No lunch.*

### Italian

$$$–$$$$  ✕ **Villa d'Este.** Upscale Northern Italian cuisine is served in an Italianate room with dark wood, upholstered chairs, statuary, and an impressive fresco on the ceiling. The antipasti display whets the appetite for such dishes as veal in Madeira and asparagus sauce or spaghetti *alla carbonara* (pasta with a rich sauce made of cream, Parmesan cheese, eggs, and bacon). The dessert pastries are delectable. ⊠ *Atlantis, Paradise Island* ☎ *242/ 363–3000* ▤ *AE, D, DC, MC, V* ⊘ *No lunch.*

### Seafood

$$–$$$  ✕ **Blue Lagoon Seafood Restaurant.** The decor tends toward the nautical, with hurricane lamps and brass rails, in this narrow third-floor dining room looking out to Nassau on one side and Atlantis to the other. Choose from simply prepared dishes such as broiled Bahamian lobster tail or grouper, or fancier selections such as almond-fried shrimp and stuffed grouper au gratin. ⊠ *Club Land'Or* ☎ *242/363–2400* ⌔ *Reservations essential* ▤ *AE, DC, MC, V* ⊘ *No lunch.*

$$–$$$  ✕ **Columbus Tavern.** Watch the boats in Nassau Harbour through this restaurant's enormous open windows as you dine on lobster, grouper, and conch. Or set aside your seafaring ways and try the steak Diane flambé— it's served flaming, as the name implies. The tavern serves three meals a day, every day. ⊠ *Paradise Island Dr.* ☎ *242/363–2534* ▤ *D, MC, V.*

$–$$  ✕ **Blue Marlin Restaurant.** A longtime favorite in Hurricane Hole Plaza, Blue Marlin is (no surprise) known for seafood—try seafood linguine, lobster thermidor, or the ever-popular cracked conch—although dishes like Eleuthera Coconut Chicken and Guava Ribs are good as well. Limbo and steel-pan band shows, as well as reasonably priced lunch and dinner specials, keep the place hopping. The restaurant upstairs, Bahama Mama's, uses the same kitchen but adds some Italian dishes. ⊠ *Hurricane Hole Plaza* ☎ *242/363–2660* ▤ *AE, D, MC, V.*

## Cable Beach

### Bahamian

$–$$  ✕ **Café Johnny Canoe.** Johnny Canoe is said to have been a wild-living African chieftain from whose name, most believe, the word *Junkanoo* is derived. If you can't make it to the Junkanoo festivals on Christmas Day and New Year's Day, this is your best opportunity to see a mini-Junkanoo parade. Complete with real costumes and Junkanoo music, the show winds among this crowded restaurant's tables each Friday night at 8. With spacious outdoor seating and a menu of traditional Bahamian fare—cracked conch and grouper fillet—as well as burgers, chicken, ribs, and tropical drinks, this has become a favorite casual hangout for visitors. Desserts include guava duff and Bacardi rum cake. Breakfast is also served. ⊠ *W. Bay St., next to Nassau Beach Hotel* ☎ *242/ 327–3373* ▤ *AE, D, MC, V.*

### Continental

$$$–$$$$  ✕ **Androsia Steak & Seafood Restaurant.** You'll find a wide selection of seafood at this comfortably upscale restaurant, but the specialty is Peppersteak au Paris, a New York sirloin served with Dijon mustard, cracked peppercorns, cream, and brandy. Rich striped curtains add el-

egance, and starfish and lanterns on the wall lend a nautical flavor. ⊠ *W. Bay St., in Shoppers Haven Plaza* 🕿 *242/327–7805 or 242/327–6430* 🖃 *AE, D, MC, V* 🖄 *Closed Sun. No lunch.*

### Italian

★ **$$–$$$** ✕ **Sole Mare.** The elegant ocean-view setting, excellent service, and expertly prepared entrées make this one of the best Italian restaurants on the island. Start off with imported meats and cheeses for your antipasti, and follow it up with lobster fra diavolo or chicken with white wine and artichokes. End the meal with a Marsala-strawberry or chocolate-ricotta soufflé. ⊠ *Nassau Wyndham Resort & Crystal Palace Casino* 🕿 *242/327–6200 Ext. 6861* 🖃 *AE, D, DC, MC, V* 🖄 *Open Fri. and Sat. only.*

### Mediterranean

★ **$$–$$$$** ✕ **Provence.** Provence draws the well-to-do and Hollywood set. The chef bills his fare as "Cuisine Du Soleil"—you can see why with the fiery grilled rib-eye steak in peppercorn sauce, and the oven-roasted Atlantic salmon with citrus butter. At dinner, try the Mediterranean bouillabaisse, braised osso buco, or pan-seared sea bass and black grouper fillets. Or just drop by the Tapas Bar for tasty appetizers, such as escargots fricassee and pan-seared sea scallops. ⊠ *Old Town Sandyport* 🕿 *242/327–0985* 🖃 *AE, D, MC, V* 🖄 *Closed Sun.*

### Seafood

**$$–$$$$** ✕ **The Poop Deck at Sandyport.** A more upscale version of the other Poop Deck, this waterside restaurant has soaring ceilings, a cool pink and aqua color scheme, and a dazzling view of Cable Beach. Start with sweet-potato fish cakes or grilled shrimp and Brie before diving into the fresh seafood, paired with a selection from the extensive wine list. There's a smattering of choices for the seafood-phobic. ⊠ *W. Bay St.* 🕿 *242/327–3325* 🖃 *AE, D, DC, MC, V* 🖄 *Closed Mon.*

## Western New Providence & South Coast

### Bahamian

**$–$$** ✕ **Traveller's Rest.** A scenic 10-mi drive along the coast from downtown Nassau brings you to this relaxed family restaurant, which has a great ocean view. The fresh seafood dinner served just steps from the beach is a real treat—conch, grouper, and crawfish are the heavy hitters. Try the "smudder fish"—a tasty local fish literally smothered in onions, peppers, and other vegetables. Dine outside or in, and toast the sunset with a fresh-fruit banana daiquiri—a house specialty. ⊠ *W. Bay St., Gambier* 🕿 *242/327–7633* 🖃 *AE, D, MC, V.*

# WHERE TO STAY

New Providence Island is fortunate to have an extensive range of hotels, from quaint, family-owned guesthouses to the megaresorts at Cable Beach and on Paradise Island. Downtown Nassau's beaches are not beautiful; if you want to be beachfront on a gorgeous white strand, stay on Cable Beach or Paradise Island's Cabbage Beach. Reasons to stay in Nassau include proximity to shopping and affordability (although the cost

1

of taxis to and from the better beaches can add up). Nassau's British Colonial Hilton, for instance, is a top-rate hotel; but its man-made beach, although pretty, can't compare to Cabbage Beach or Cable Beach.

The homey, friendly little spots will probably not be on the beach—and you'll have to go out to eat unless you have access to a kitchen (although some inns will prepare meals for you on request). On the flip side, your stay is likely to be relaxing, low-key, and less removed from everyday Bahamian life. The plush resorts are big and beautiful, glittering and splashy, but they can be overwhelming. In any case, these big, top-dollar properties generally have more amenities than you could possibly make use of, a selection of dining options, and a full roster of sports and entertainment options. The battle for the tourist dollar rages ceaselessly between Cable Beach and Paradise Island. The competition encourages agents to put forth an endless stream of travel deals, with enticements such as free snorkeling gear, free scuba lessons, and free admission to Las Vegas–style revues.

Paradise Island was once the quieter alternative to more active resorts on Cable Beach. With the spread of the Atlantis Resort, however, all that has changed. There are still a few peaceful retreats on P.I., but the boisterous megaresort has eliminated most of the quiet strolling lanes and brought its own brand of flash to the island. However, Cable Beach probably still tilts younger in its orientation. Some prefer the lineup of resorts along the Cable Beach strip, others like the look of P.I., which has hotels scattered around every corner (and which is, unlike Cable Beach, walkable from downtown).

A tax ranging from 8% to 10%, representing resort and government levies, is added to your hotel bill. Some hotels also add a gratuity charge of between $2.50 and $4 (or higher) per person, per day, for the housekeeping or pool staff.

The prices below are based on high-season (winter) rates, generally in effect from December through March. Expect to pay between 15% and 30% less off-season at most resorts. In general, the best rates are available through packages, which almost every hotel offers. Call the hotel directly or ask your travel agent.

## Nassau

★ $$–$$$   ✕▢▢ **Graycliff.** The old-world flavor of this Georgian Colonial landmark—built in the 1720s by ship captain Howard Graysmith—has made it a perennial favorite with the upscale crowd. Past guests have included the Duke and Duchess of Windsor, Winston Churchill, Aristotle Onassis, and the Beatles. Al Capone stayed here when his sweetie, Polly Leach, owned it during the Roaring '20s, and Lord Mountbatten visited when Lord and Lady Dudley were the proprietors. It's easy to forget that you're steps from downtown Nassau when you stay here. Thick foliage envelops a series of garden villas and cottages, amid limestone courtyards with ponds and fountains. For refined Continental fare, the hotel's original restaurant, Graycliff, is one of the island's premier places to dine. ✉ *W. Hill St., Box N-10246* ☎ *242/322–2796 or 800/*

*688–0076 ≞242/326–6110 or 242/326–6188 ⊕www.graycliff.com ☞7 rooms, 13 suites ⚲ 2 restaurants, in-room hot tubs, 3 pools, health club, hair salon, massage, sauna, 3 bars, business services ▤ AE, D, MC, V.*

★ **$$** ▥ **British Colonial Hilton Nassau.** The first Colonial Hotel, built by Standard Oil co-founder Henry Flagler in 1899, attracted socialites, royals, and industrialists who arrived by yacht at the hotel's pier at the turn of the 20th century and during the boom years of Prohibition. That building was destroyed by fire in 1921, and the present Mediterranean-style British Colonial—an exact replica—opened a year later, featuring a lustrous saffron facade, gleaming marble floors, and soaring arched ceilings. This landmark building is the social heart of Nassau, the setting for political meetings and the city's most important events. Guest rooms have dark mahogany furniture and marble baths; most have ocean views. Bahamian star Jay Mitchell sings Wednesday, Thursday, and Sunday night from 8 PM to midnight, and Friday and Saturday from 9 PM to 1 AM in the Palm Court. The resort sits on 8 lush acres next to a white-sand beach, where guests have front-row seats for watching the cruise ships sail into the harbor. With the Nassau Stock Exchange in an adjacent wing, this hotel is the best business choice in the Bahamas. It's also a popular spot for weddings. Watch for brides descending the grand staircase in the lobby on Saturday and Sunday afternoons. ⊠ *1 Bay St., Box N-7148* ☎ *242/322–3301* ≞ *242/302–9009* ⊕ *www. hiltoncaribbean.com/nassau ☞ 270 rooms, 21 suites ⚲ 2 restaurants, room service, in-room safes, cable TV, in-room broadband, pool, health club, hair salon, massage, spa, beach, dive shop, snorkeling, volleyball, lounge, shops, babysitting, laundry service, concierge floor, Internet room, business services, convention center, meeting rooms, car rental* ▤ *AE, D, DC, MC, V.*

★ **$** ▥ **Dillet's Guest House.** You're in for something special the minute you enter the lounge of this family-run guesthouse—the arched entry, ceiling fans, wicker furniture, caged birds, and massive flower arrangements exude old Nassau charm. Crisp and clean, the place is furnished with true island flair. Rooms are named for island fruits, marked by hand-painted pieces of driftwood on the doors. A few miles from downtown Nassau, this place is ideal for those who prefer Bahamian style to a standard hotel room. It's also popular for weddings. ⊠ *Dunmore Ave. and Strachan St., Box N-204* ☎ *242/325–1133* ≞ *242/325–7183* ⊕ *www.islandeaze.com/dillets/ index.html ☞ 7 rooms ⚲ Dining room, some kitchenettes, minibars, microwaves, Wi-Fi, pool, bicycles, library* ▤ *AE, MC, V* ⟋⟍*CP.*

**$** ▥ **El Greco Hotel.** Pleasant Greek owners and a friendly staff create an ambience more in keeping with a cozy guesthouse than a hotel. Although the decorations are not elaborate, the rooms are large, quiet, and have soothing earth tones. They surround a small pool tucked within a bougainvillea-filled courtyard. The El Greco is a few minutes walk from Bay Street and downtown and is directly across the street from the public Western Esplanade beach. The hotel appeals primarily to a European crowd, and for those on a budget who want to be in Nassau, El Greco is a pleasant find. ⊠ *W. Bay St., Box N-4187* ☎ *242/325–1121* ≞ *242/ 325–1124* ⊕*www.bahamasnet.com/elgrecohotel ☞26 rooms ⚲ Restaurant, cable TV, pool, bar, babysitting* ▤ *AE, D, MC, V.*

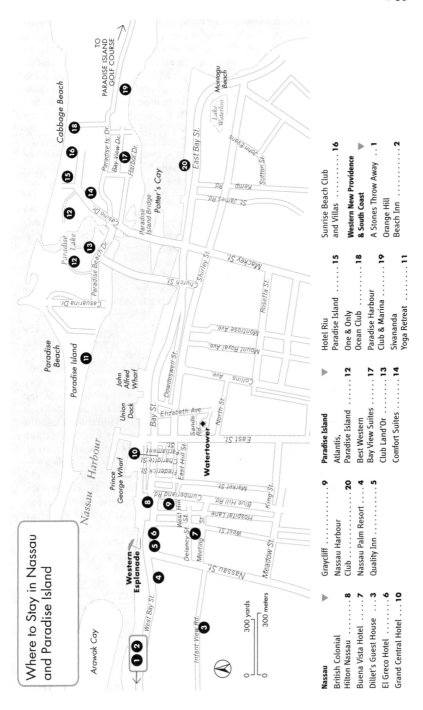

# Where to Stay in Nassau and Paradise Island

**Nassau**

British Colonial Hilton Nassau ...... **8**
Buena Vista Hotel .... **7**
Dillet's Guest House ... **3**
El Greco Hotel ...... **6**
Grand Central Hotel ... **10**
Graycliff ............ **9**
Nassau Harbour Club .... **20**
Nassau Palm Resort .... **4**
Quality Inn ........ **5**

**Paradise Island**

Atlantis, Paradise Island ...... **12**
Best Western Bay View Suites ...... **17**
Club Land'Or ....... **13**
Comfort Suites ...... **14**
Hotel Riu Paradise Island ...... **15**
One & Only Ocean Club ......... **18**
Paradise Harbour Club & Marina ...... **19**
Sivananda Yoga Retreat ....... **11**
Sunrise Beach Club and Villas ......... **16**

**Western New Providence & South Coast**

A Stones Throw Away ... **1**
Orange Hill Beach Inn ......... **2**

$ 🏨 **Nassau Harbour Club.** The Harbour Club is popular with international sailing aficionados and hordes of students on spring break, which, along with its location a mile down the main road into town, does not make it an oasis of peace and quiet. Locals and tourists gather at the downstairs Dockside Bar and Grill to watch televised sports or sit outside on the deck overlooking the harbor. On the hotel's main floor, up a spiral wooden staircase from the bar, is the Santorini restaurant. ⊠ *E. Bay St., Box SS-5755* ☎ *242/393–0771* 🖷 *242/393–5393* 🛏 *50 rooms* ⚹ *Restaurant, pool, dock, bar* ▭ *AE, D, MC, V.*

$ 🏨 **Nassau Palm Resort.** This modern, well-managed five-story hotel is a moderately priced option a few minutes west of downtown, across the street from the pretty Western Esplanade beach. An activities desk in the lobby will help coordinate your island adventures. Some suites come with hot tubs and/or bunk beds. ⊠ *W. Bay St., Box SS-19055* ☎ *242/356–0000 or 800/465–4329* 🖷 *242/323–1408* ⊕ *www.nassau-hotel.com* 🛏 *183 rooms, 12 suites* ⚹ *Restaurant, room service, in-room safes, cable TV, in-room data ports, 2 pools, health club, hot tub, bar, shop, laundry service, business services, meeting rooms* ▭ *AE, D, DC, MC, V.*

¢–$ 🏨 **Quality Inn.** This beachfront hotel is a welcome addition to the Providence Island budget lodging market. It's clean and well-kept, with pleasantly decorated rooms. Ask for a room with an ocean view, as many rooms have only a partial view or none at all. Be aware that each guest must pay a daily service charge of $11.50. ⊠ *West Bay St. and Nassau St., Box N-1836, Suite A081* ☎ *242/322–1515* 🖷 *242/322–1514* ⊕ *www.qualityinn.com* 🛏 *63 rooms* ⚹ *Restaurant, in-room data ports, bar, lounge, business services* ▭ *AE, D, DC, MC, V.*

¢ 🏨 **Buena Vista Hotel.** Surrounded by a beautiful 3-acre garden, this 19th-century plantation house is ½ mi from downtown Nassau. The two-story building is better known for its restaurant, but the spacious, simple, and rather imposingly dark rooms—surprisingly affordable in this elegant setting—are individually decorated with solid-wood furniture. Climb the aqua-hue staircase from the low-key, tasteful lobby, which is filled with tropical greenery, to a long hallway where the rooms are all but invisible to the restaurant guests. The public beach is a 10-minute walk away. ⊠ *Delancy St., Box N-564* ☎ *242/322–2811* 🖷 *242/322–5881* 🛏 *5 rooms* ⚹ *Restaurant, refrigerators, cable TV, bar* ▭ *AE, D, MC, V.*

¢ 🏨 **Grand Central Hotel.** Since the early 1940s when George Constantakis arrived from Greece and opened this hotel, the Grand Central has been an affordable inn with a perfect location, steps away from Bay Street in downtown Nassau. Horse-drawn surreys pass by on the narrow lane of Charlotte Street, making it easy to picture yourself in Colonial Nassau. Ask for a room that opens onto a balcony with views of the cruise ships docked at the end of the street. Guestrooms are clean and tidy, with two double beds or one double bed and a single, new pine furniture, and private baths with tubs and showers. Eleven rooms are in a guesthouse next door. Jimmy's take-out restaurant, next door, offers authentic Bahamian breakfasts and lunches, including fried chicken and pan-seared snapper. This hotel is the best deal in Nassau, and room prices include taxes and service. ⊠ *Charlotte St., Box N-4084* ☎ *242/322–8356* 🖷 *242/325–2018* ⊕ *www.grand-central-hotel.com* 🛏 *35 rooms* ⚹ *Cable TV* ▭ *AE, MC, V.*

## Paradise Island

**$$$$**   🏨 **One & Only Ocean Club.** Once the private hideaway of A&P heir Hunt-
Fodor'sChoice    ington Hartford, this ultra-expensive resort on magnificent Cabbage
★    Beach's quietest stretch provides the ultimate in understated—and de-
cidedly posh—elegance. Its Versailles Gardens includes 35 acres of terraced serenity and an imported French cloister. Set amid private gardens,
the spacious colonial-style rooms have intricately carved furniture and
marble bathrooms. The open-air restaurant, Dune, is perched over the
beach. ⊠ *Ocean Club Dr.* ⌂ *Box N-4777, Nassau* ☎ *242/363–2501
or 800/321–3000* 🖷 *242/363–2424* ⊕ *www.oneandonlyresorts.com*
🛏 *87 rooms, 14 suites, 5 cottages* ⚿ *3 restaurants, room service, cable
TV, golf privileges, 9 tennis courts, pool, health club, spa, beach, snorkeling, windsurfing, boating, waterskiing, bicycles, 2 bars, babysitting,
laundry service* ☰ *AE, D, DC, MC, V.*

**♺ $$$–$$$$**    🏨 **Atlantis, Paradise Island.** A bustling fantasy world—part water park,
Fodor'sChoice    entertainment complex, megaresort, and beach oasis—this is by far the
★    biggest and boldest resort in the country. The overriding theme here is
water—for swimming, snorkeling, and observing marine life, as well as
for mood and effect, in lagoons, caves, waterfalls, and several walk-through
aquariums (touted as the largest artificial marine habitat in the world).
The public areas are lavish, with fountains, glass sculptures, and gleam-
ing shopping arcades. Numerous sporting activities are available, and there
is plenty of nightlife on the premises; the casino, ringed by restaurants,
is the largest in the Bahamas and the Caribbean. The most expensive rooms
are in the glamorous, high-rise Royal Towers. ⊠ *Casino Dr.* ⌂ *Box N-
4777, Nassau* ☎ *242/363–3000 or 800/285–2684* 🖷 *242/363–3524*
⊕ *www.atlantis.com* 🛏 *2,097 rooms, 230 suites* ⚿ *17 restaurants,
room service, in-room safes, cable TV, in-room broadband, golf privi-
leges, 10 tennis courts, 11 pools, health club, hair salon, spa, beach, dock,
snorkeling, windsurfing, boating, basketball, volleyball, 18 bars, casino,
comedy club, nightclub, shops, babysitting, children's programs (ages 4–12),
concierge floor, business services, convention center, meeting rooms, car
rental, travel services* ☰ *AE, D, DC, MC, V* ⫩ *MAP.*

**$$$**    🏨 **Hotel Riu Paradise Island.** The all-inclusive, high-rise Riu is not as grand
as Atlantis next door, but it isn't far from its neighbor's casino and shares
a quieter bit of the same lovely beach. The price of $158 per person in-
cludes meals, snacks, drinks, activities, entertainment, taxes, and gra-
tuities. ⊠ *6307 Casino Dr.* ⌂ *Nassau* ☎ *242/363–3500 or 888/666–
8816* 🖷 *242/363–3900* ⊕ *www.riu.com* 🛏 *379 rooms* ⚿ *Restaurants,
spa, in-room safes, minibars, cable TV, tennis court, pool, health club,
beach, dive shop, snorkeling, windsurfing, boating, hair salon, babysitting* ☰ *AE, D, DC, MC, V.* ⫩ *AI.*

**★ $$$**    🏨 **Sunrise Beach Club and Villas.** Lushly landscaped with crotons, coconut
palms, bougainvillea, and hibiscus, this low-rise, family-run resort on
Cabbage Beach has a tropical wonderland feel. Two pools sustain the
ambience with statuary and tropical plantings, and the beach is acces-
sible via a long flight of wooden stairs built right into the cliff. Paths
wind through the floral arcadia, past trickling fountains, archways,
and terra-cotta tiles with color insets. Choose from one-bedroom town
houses with spiral staircases that lead to an upstairs bedroom, two-bed-

room apartments, or three-bedroom villas. All have fully equipped kitchens, king-size beds, and patios. ⊠ *Casino Dr.* ☎ *Box SS-6519, Nassau* ☎ *242/363–2234* 📠 *242/363–2308* ⊕ *www.sunrisebeachvillas. com* 🛏 *18 1-, 2-, and 3-bedroom units* ⚲ *Kitchens, microwaves, cable TV, 2 pools, beach, bar, babysitting, laundry facilities, Internet room* 🖃 *AE, D, MC, V.*

**$$–$$$**   🏠 **Club Land'Or.** In Atlantis's shadow just over the bridge from Nassau, this friendly time-share property has one-bedroom villas with full kitchens, bathrooms, living rooms, desks, and patios or balconies that overlook the lagoon, the gardens, or the pool. The units are described as accommodating four people, but they seem better suited to couples. The Blue Lagoon Seafood Restaurant is a favorite of locals and guests. Many activities are planned throughout the week. ⊠ *Paradise Beach Dr.* ☎ *Box SS-6429, Nassau* ☎ *242/363–2400* 📠 *242/363–3403* ⊕ *www.clublandor.com* 🛏 *72 villas* ⚲ *Restaurant, kitchens, microwaves, cable TV, pool, bicycles, 2 bars, shops, babysitting, laundry facilities* 🖃 *AE, D, MC, V* 🍽 *EP, MAP.*

**$–$$$**   🏠 **Paradise Harbour Club & Marina.** With a marina and an enviable location, this collection of oversize, comfortable apartments is a great choice for those who want the freedom of a private residence with the facilities of a large resort. Full kitchens (complete with refrigerator, minibar, and dishwasher) lend a homey feeling to these somewhat characterless but very cushy lodgings. Commodious closet and sink space are among the extras. If you prefer a view, opt for the top-floor digs. ⊠ *Paradise Island Dr.* ☎ *Box SS-5804, Nassau* ☎ *242/363–2992* 📠 *242/363–2840* ⊕ *www. phc-bahamas.com* 🛏 *22 units* ⚲ *Restaurant, kitchenettes, tennis court, pool, hot tub, boating, bicycles, bar* 🖃 *AE, MC, V.*

**$$**   🏠 **Comfort Suites.** This all-suites, three-story pink-and-white hotel has an arrangement with Atlantis that allows guests to use that resort's facilities. Kids can also enroll at Atlantis's Discovery Channel Camp. For many, that's reason enough to stay here, in the middle of the Paradise Island action. If you'd rather stay on the grounds, try a poolside lunch and a drink at the swim-up bar. Cozy rooms have sitting areas with sofa beds. Cabbage Beach is just a hop, skip, and a jump away. ⊠ *Paradise Island Dr.* ☎ *Box SS-6202, Nassau* ☎ *242/363–3680 or 800/228–5150* 📠 *242/363–2588* ⊕ *www.choicehotels.com* 🛏 *228 junior suites* ⚲ *Restaurant, in-room safes, minibars, cable TV, pool, bar, babysitting* 🖃 *AE, D, MC, V* 🍽 *CP.*

**$–$$**   🏠 **Best Western Bay View Suites.** This 4-acre condominium resort has a lush, intimate feel. Guests socialize around three pools (two for general use, one reserved for the villas) that are surrounded by tropical plants, including several hibiscus and bougainvillea varieties. Choose between one- and two-bedroom apartments and two- and three-bedroom villas, all of which are spacious, clean, comfortable, and decorated in bright island style. All rooms have private balconies or garden terraces. Cabbage Beach is a 10-minute walk away. ⊠ *Bay View Dr.* ☎ *Box SS-6308, Nassau* ☎ *242/363–2555 or 800/757–1357* 📠 *242/363–2370* ⊕ *www. bayviewvillage.com* 🛏 *22 villas, 12 townhouses, 32 1-bedroom suites, 6 penthouses* ⚲ *Snack bar, fans, kitchens, microwaves, cable TV, tennis court, 3 pools, bar, babysitting, laundry facilities* 🖃 *AE, D, MC, V.*

¢ ⊞ **Sivananda Yoga Retreat.** Accessible only by boat, this resort is the antithesis of high-rollers' Atlantis down the road on Paradise Island. Guestrooms in the main house and tiny one-room bungalows overlook a gorgeous white-sand beach in a 5-acre compound that stretches from Nassau Harbour to the ocean; air conditioning is an additional $10 per day. Tent sites are also available for $55 per person. This retreat is for those who are serious about yoga and good health: two two-hour meditations—the first one starting at 5 AM—and two two-hour yoga classes are mandatory each day. However, there's free time from 10 AM to 4 PM, and the retreat's shuttle boat will take guests to Nassau for shopping and sightseeing. The price, which is per person, includes two vegetarian meals each day. Rooms are austere, and guests are expected to help clean communal bathrooms. Alcohol, coffee, tea, meat, fish, cigarettes, radios, and TVs are not allowed. For more than 30 years, the ashram has been a tranquil oasis for yoga devotees, including the late Beatle George Harrison, CEOs, and families. Yoga class platforms are next to the beach and harbor. There are also meditation rooms, frequent guest lecturers, and special classes for advanced teacher certification. ⊠ *Paradise Island* ✍ *Box N-7550, Nassau* ☎ *242/363–2902 or 800/ 441–2096* 🖶 *242/363–3783* ⊕ *www.sivananda.org/locations/ashrams. html or www.my-yoga.net* ⤳ *35 single private rooms, 7 dormitory-style rooms, 12 rooms facing the beach, and tent sites* ⊟ *AE, MC, V* ❯❮❘ *AI.*

## Cable Beach

$$$$ ⊞ **Guanahani Village.** These substantial, well-furnished time-share and rental accommodations are perfect for young families or groups of friends traveling together. The stucco units are spread across landscaped grounds. Tiled three-bedroom luxury villas, oceanfront or garden side, sleep six comfortably—up to eight using roll-aways (so the price, although in the top category, is really quite reasonable when shared by several people). Each unit has oversize rooms, a delightful secluded patio, a fully equipped kitchen, a washer and dryer, and a dishwasher. The pool overlooks the ocean, although beaches are a bit of a walk. ⊠ *W. Bay St.* ✍ *Box CB-13317, Nassau* ☎ *242/327–7568 or 242/327–4254* 🖶 *242/327–8311* ⊕ *www.guanahanivillage.com* ⤳ *35 units* ⚇ *Snack bar, kitchens, cable TV, tennis court, pool* ⊟ *AE, D, MC, V.*

$$$$ ⊞ **Sandals Royal Bahamian Resort & Spa.** Cable Beach's most expensive spot presents elegantly furnished rooms with views of the ocean, pool, or grounds replete with pillars and faux Roman statuary. There's a state-of-the-art fitness club, and a multilingual concierge service that assists foreign guests. Eight restaurants offer cuisines ranging from Caribbean to Japanese (make reservations well in advance), and nightly entertainment takes place in the resort's amphitheater. ⊠ *W. Bay St.* ✍ *Box CB-13005, Nassau* ☎ *242/327–6400 or 800/726–3257* 🖶 *242/327–6961* ⊕ *www.sandals.com* ⤳ *77 rooms, 327 suites* ⚇ *8 restaurants, room service, cable TV, in-room broadband, 2 tennis courts, 5 pools, gym, health club, spa, beach, dive shop, snorkeling, windsurfing, boating, waterskiing, basketball, croquet, shuffleboard, volleyball, 7 bars, dance club, recreation room, meeting rooms* ⊟ *AE, D, MC, V* ❯❮❘ *AI.*

## Changes at Cable Beach

**CABLE BEACH, A SLEEPY STRING OF RESORTS** on a white-sand beach west of Nassau, is getting a makeover so massive that it's expected to rival Las Vegas when everything is completed in 2010. A mammoth, new $1.6-billion resort called Baha Mar will include six luxury hotels—a Westin, W, St. Regis, Sheraton, Wyndham, and Caesars Resort & Casino. The 3,550-room beachside complex—owned by the Baha Mar Development Company, Harrah's Entertainment, and Starwood Resorts—is the single largest investment in the history of the Bahamas.

Baha Mar will replace Cable Beach's three largest resorts—the Radisson, the Wyndham Nassau Resort & Crystal Palace Casino, and the Nassau Beach Hotel—which are operating as Cable Beach Resorts during renovations. Baha Mar's attractions will include a 100,000-square foot casino, a half-dozen spas, the West Bay Village shopping and restaurant complex, and entertainment venues—all connected by a series of canals and wide pedestrian paths—as well as a Jack Nicklaus Signature golf course.

Michael Hong, known for his work on the $1.6-billion Bellagio Resort and

Wynn Resort in Las Vegas, will lead the design team for Baha Mar, which will sprawl across 1,000 acres. The Radisson Cable Beach Resort will emerge from construction as a Sheraton, the Nassau Beach Hotel will close in 2007, and the Wyndham will remain open throughout the construction—but two of its trademark towers will be taken down and replaced with new buildings.

Across the harbor on Paradise Island, Kerzner International, the owner of Atlantis, is planning an $800-million expansion that will include a new tower with 1,500 guest rooms—bringing the number of rooms at Atlantis to 3,855. The resort currently has a luxury spa, a 10-acre marina capable of holding yachts up to 200 feet, the world's largest outdoor aquarium, 11 swimming pools, and a water slide that goes down the side of a replica Mayan pyramid.

For more information on Baha Mar, visit www.bahamar.com or www. CableBeachResorts.com, or call 800/222-7466. For Atlantis updates, call 888/528-7155 or visit www. atlantis.com.

---

**$$$–$$$$**  **SuperClub Breezes Bahamas.** Right on Cable Beach, this property offers couples and singles (age 16 or older) an all-inclusive rate that covers lodging, entertainment, unlimited food and beverages, land and watersports, airport transfers, taxes, and gratuities. Take advantage of the fitness center, five freshwater pools, swim-up bar, and nightly entertainment, including local bands, toga or pajama parties, and karaoke. A huge fish chandelier and multicolor tile floor decorate the open-air lobby. Large, modern rooms are pleasant, although not striking. ⊠ W. Bay St. ✑ Box CB-13049, Nassau ☎ 242/327–5356 or 800/859–7873 ☒ 242/327–5155 ⊕ www.breezesbahamas.com ➱ 400 rooms ♦ 5 restaurants, snack bar, cable TV, in-room broadband, 3 tennis courts, 5 pools, health club, beach, windsurfing, boating, bicycles, basketball, billiards, volleyball, 4 bars, dance club ☰ AE, MC, V ❢◎❢ AI.

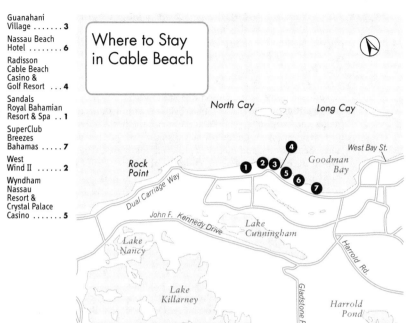

**Where to Stay in Cable Beach**

North Cay    Long Cay

West Bay St.

Rock Point    Goodman Bay

Dual Carriage Way

John F. Kennedy Drive    Lake Cunningham

Lake Nancy

Harrold Rd.

Lake Killarney

Gladstone Rd.

Harrold Pond

0    2 miles
0    3 km

$$ 🏨 **West Wind II.** Privacy is the lure of these cozy villas on Cable Beach's west end, 6 mi from downtown. Two-bedroom, two-bath condominiums have fully stocked kitchens and balconies or patios overlooking the ocean or pools. The reasonable prices and relaxed atmosphere are ideal for families or groups on a budget, and the pleasant, quiet location—off the road amid manicured lawns and pruned gardens—gives children the freedom to play outdoors. The spectacular sea view somewhat compensates for the tiny and very windy beach. A bus stop and taxi stand are right outside. ⊠ *W. Bay St.* ☝ *Box CB-11006, Nassau* ☎ *242/327–7211 or 242/327–7019* 🖷 *242/327–7529* ⇨ *54 villas* ⚓ *Snack bar, kitchenettes, cable TV, 2 tennis courts, 2 pools, beach, snorkeling, boating, babysitting, laundry service, travel services* ▤ *MC, V.*

$$ 🏨 **Wyndham Nassau Resort & Crystal Palace Casino.** If you prefer glitz and glitter, stay at the Wyndham on Cable Beach. The resort's five towers are illuminated with bands of varying colors, making the hotel look like a giant rainbow reflecting off the ocean. High-rollers love the Crystal Club, three concierge floors at the top of the Casino Tower with 30 spectacularly decorated executive suites. The resort has its own palm-fringed beach and lagoon, a health club with top-notch equipment and daily aerobics classes, and the 35,000-square-foot Crystal Palace Casino. ⊠ *W. Bay St.* ☝ *Box N-8306, Nassau* ☎ *242/327–6200 or 800/222–*

7466 ⬛ 242/327–6459 ⊕ *www.wyndhamnassauresort.com* ⬗ *743 rooms, 124 suites* ⚲ *6 restaurants, room service, cable TV, pool, fitness classes, health club, hair salon, beach, snorkeling, windsurfing, boating, 5 bars, casino, recreation room, theater, shops, babysitting, children's programs (ages 4 and up), concierge floors, Internet room, meeting room* ▭ *AE, D, DC, MC, V* ⍩ *FAP, MAP.*

**$–$$** ▦ **Radisson Cable Beach Casino & Golf Resort.** This high-rise property is smack in the middle of the Cable Beach action. Connected by a shopping arcade to the Crystal Palace Casino, the hotel buzzes with activity. Daytime options include dance lessons by the pool, beach volleyball, free scuba lessons, and plenty of children's activities. Guests get special rates at the hotel's challenging 18-hole Cable Beach Golf Club. At night, select from a slew of dining possibilities, beach parties, revues, and—of course—gambling. All rooms have balconies and face either the beach and pool or gardens. ⊠ *W. Bay St.* ⬗ *Box N-4914, Nassau* ☎*242/ 327–6000* ⬛ *242/327–6907* ⊕ *www.radisson-cablebeach.com* ⬗ *669 rooms, 31 suites* ⚲ *6 restaurants, room service, cable TV, in-room broadband, 18-hole golf course, 5 tennis courts, 3 pools, health club, hair salon, beach, snorkeling, boating, bicycles, racquetball, squash, volleyball, 2 bars, casino, shops, babysitting, children's programs (ages 4–11), meeting room* ▭ *AE, D, DC, MC, V* ⍩ *AI, EP.*

**¢–$$** ▦ **Nassau Beach Hotel.** For a low-key atmosphere, try this Cable Beach mainstay, built in the 1940s on a ½-mi sandy beach. Be sure to ask for one of the refurbished rooms, decorated in colonial style. All rooms have balconies, but the views vary. Guests have use of all nonmotorized watersports equipment. Tennis on the six courts (three are lighted) is free before 5 PM, $7 per person hourly during "prime time" (5–9). The hotel has indoor and outdoor restaurants on-site, as well as a shopping arcade. The Crystal Palace Casino is next door, and the Cable Beach Golf Club is across the street. ⊠ *W. Bay St.* ⬗ *Box N-7756, Nassau* ☎ *242/ 327–7711 or 888/627–7282* ⬛*242/327–8829* ⊕*www.nassaubeachhotel. com* ⬗ *400 rooms* ⚲ *5 restaurants, cable TV, 6 tennis courts, 2 pools, gym, beach, snorkeling, windsurfing, boating, 3 bars, shops, babysitting, meeting rooms* ▭ *AE, D, MC, V* ⍩ *BP, EP, FAP, MAP.*

## Western New Providence & South Coast

**★ $$–$$$** ▦ **A Stone's Throw Away.** Featuring seaside comfort in fashionable surroundings, this "gourmet bed and breakfast"—as the French and Belgian owners describe it—is the latest luxury boutique hideaway for celebrities. The three-story Colonial-style inn with wraparound verandahs is perched on a limestone cliff overlooking the beach, 13 mi west of Nassau. The public rooms and guestrooms have the atmosphere of a century-old manor house with pickled wood ceilings, pine plank floors, oriental rugs, leather plantation chairs, mahogany antiques, and a dining room that serves breakfast, lunch, and dinner. Guests can read on the porch, walk to the beach, or relax by a small pool and waterfall. ⊠ *Tropical Garden Rd. and W. Bay St., Gambier* ⬗ *Box SS-5412 Nassau* ☎ *242/327–7030* ⬛ *242/327–7040* ⊕ *www.astonesthrowaway. com* ⬗ *10 rooms* ⚲ *Restaurant, room service, pool, massage, beach, bar* ▭ *AE, MC, V.*

**$**  🏠 **Orange Hill Beach Inn.** If you prefer down-home coziness over slick glamour, then this charming inn—on the site of a former orange plantation perched on a hilltop overlooking the ocean—is the place to stay. Guests are treated like family, and the homey feel extends to the comfortably eclectic living room and daytime honor bar. Danny and Judy Lowe—he's Bahamian, she's Irish—have owned the inn for more than 20 years. Orange Hill has a reputation as an inexpensive alternative for honeymooners and scuba divers. It's a half-hour drive from town, 15 minutes from the casino, and 300 feet from a pleasant roadside beach. Rooms and apartments vary considerably in size. Two cottages, including a hexagon-shape cabin with a pitched pine ceiling and a sweeping view of the ocean, were added in 2005. ⊠ *W. Bay St.* ☍ *Box N-8583, Nassau* ☎ *242/327–5184* 🖷 *242/327–5186* ⊕ *www.orangehill.com* ⤷ *32 rooms* ♿ *Restaurant, some kitchenettes, cable TV, pool, basketball, bar, laundry facilities* ▭ *D, MC, V.*

# NIGHTLIFE & THE ARTS

## Nightlife

Cable Beach and Paradise Island resorts have their own flashy clubs where residents and visitors alike come to enjoy late-night entertainment. The attire for attending these soirees is typically as casual as the atmosphere, although some clubs require dressier duds. The casinos are also casual, so leave your black tie at home. You have to be at least 18 years old to gamble; Bahamians and permanent residents are not permitted to indulge. Most coffeehouses are open late into the evening, but note that a few close around 6.

### Cable Beach

CASINOS  **Crystal Palace Casino.** Slots, craps, baccarat, blackjack, roulette, Big Six, and face-up 21 are among the games in this 35,000-square-foot space. There's a Sports Book facility equipped with big-screen TVs that air live sporting events. Both VIPs and low-limit bettors have their own areas. Casino gaming lessons are available for beginners. Tables and slots are open 24 hours daily. ⊠ *Nassau Wyndham Resort & Crystal Palace Casino, Cable Beach* ☎ *242/327–6200* ⊕ *www. wyndhamnassauresort.com.*

### Nassau

COFFEEHOUSES  **Café Paradiso.** On Bay Street's eastern end, this pleasant coffeehouse serves up sandwiches and salads—try the chicken Caesar or spicy mango shrimp. Tasty desserts include Grandma's homemade brownies and a chocolate-apricot torte. ⊠ *E. Bay St., between Elizabeth St. and Victoria Ave.* ☎ *242/356–5282* ⊗ *Closed Sun.*

**Caffè Caribe.** In the Logos Bookstore, this tiny spot has a simple, modern look with high tables and stools. Salads, quiches, and sandwiches supplement the coffee selection; there's a long list of fruity- and nutty-flavored espressos. It closes at 6 PM. ⊠ *Harbour Bay Shopping Centre, E. Bay St.* ☎ *242/394–7040* ⊗ *Closed Sun.*

**Cappuccino Café and Specialty Shop.** Although a bit out of the way (and only open until 6 PM), this little upscale deli and coffeehouse has a bright, appealing look. There's an extensive gourmet food selection as well as coffeehouse standards. ⊠ *Royal Palm Mall, Mackey St.* ☎ 242/394–6332 ⊙ *Closed Sun.*

**Flamingo Cigars and Gourmet Café.** This simple shop is a refuge from Bay Street's shopping frenzy. The smoker's lounge upstairs is a hidden wood-panel nook in which to savor the Cohibas and Montecristos for sale. ⊠ *1 Bay St., east side of Colonial Hilton Hotel* ☎ 242/325–8510 ⊙ *Closed Sun.*

**Le Bistro.** A two-story European-style bistro in the heart of downtown Nassau, Le Bistro serves coffee, wine, bar drinks, and pastries, as well as Edy's ice cream. Early birds and late-nighters love the long hours, 9 AM–midnight (2 AM on Saturday). ⊠ *Charlotte St., north of Bay St.* ☎ 242/326–0206 ⊙ *Closed Sun.*

NIGHTCLUBS **Club Waterloo.** Claiming to be Nassau's largest indoor-outdoor night-club, this club has five bars and nonstop dancing Monday through Saturday until 4 AM, and there are live bands on the weekend. Try the spring-break-special Waterloo Hurricane, a tropical mixture of rums and punches. ⊠ *E. Bay St.* ☎ 242/393–7324.

**Fluid Lounge.** The hottest nightclub in Nassau is also the hardest to find. Look for the sign on downtown Bay Street in the Kings Court building. You'll walk downstairs to two bars and two dance floors, where a well-dressed crowd moves to Top 40s hits and R&B. Ladies get in free every night before 11 PM. ⊠ *W. Bay St., between Market and Frederick, Downtown* ☎ 242/356–4691 ⊕ *www.clubfluidbahamas.com* 🔒 *$15 admission; $5 with taxi pass, buy one for $5 from any taxi driver* ⊙ *Tues.–Sun. 10 PM–4 AM.*

## Paradise Island

CASINOS **Paradise Island Casino.** At 50,000 square feet (100,000 if you include the dining and drinking areas), this is the Caribbean/Bahamian area's largest facility. Featuring a spectacularly open and airy design, the casino is ringed with restaurants and offers more than 1,100 slot machines, baccarat, blackjack, roulette, craps tables, and such local specialties as Caribbean stud poker. There's also a high-limit table area, and most of the eateries have additional games. Tables are open from 10 AM to 4 AM daily; slots, 24 hours. ⊠ *Atlantis, Paradise Island* ☎ 242/363–3000.

COFFEEHOUSES **News Café.** In Paradise Island's Hurricane Hole Plaza, this is the perfect place to refuel with a light, inexpensive lunch or just a delicious milk shake before heading into town or indulging in some P.I. shopping. Enjoy coffee, muffins, and excellent $5–$6 sandwiches served on your choice of fresh bread. Use the Internet, or choose from their collection of foreign magazines and newspapers. ⊠ *Hurricane Hole Plaza, Paradise Island* ☎ 242/363–4684 ⊙ *7:30 AM–10 PM.*

NIGHTCLUBS **Dragons Lounge and Dance Club.** Part of the Atlantis casino's dining–entertainment complex, Dragons offers music and dancing just steps away from the high-rolling action. ⊠ *Atlantis Resort* ☎ 242/363–3000.

**Oasis Lounge.** There's live piano or vocal music here nightly from 7:30 to midnight. ⊠ *Club Land'Or* ☎ 242/363–2400.

CLOSE UP

# Junkanoo

**IT'S AFTER MIDNIGHT, AND THE STREETS OF NASSAU** are crowded but hushed; the only sound is a steady buzz of anticipation. Everyone is waiting. Suddenly the streets erupt in a kaleidoscope of sights and sounds–the Junkanoo groups are rushing down Bay Street. Their vibrant costumes sparkle in the light of the street lamps, and the crowd shouts with delight. Best of all is the music. The revelers bang on goatskin drums, clang cowbells, and blow on conch-shell horns, hammering out a steady beat of celebration. It's Junkanoo time again!

Junkanoo holds an important place in the history of the Bahamas, but the origin of the word *Junkanoo* remains a mystery. Many believe it comes from John Canoe, an African tribal chief who was brought to the West Indies in the slave trade and then fought for the right to celebrate with his people. Others believe the word stems from the French *gens inconnus*, which means "the unknown people"– significant because Junkanoo revelers wear costumes that make them unrecognizable.

The origin of the festival itself is more certain. Though its roots can be traced back to West Africa, it began in the Bahamas during the 16th or 17th century when Bahamian slaves were given a few days off around Christmas to celebrate with their families. They left the plantations and had elaborate costume parties where they danced and played homemade musical instruments. They wore large, often scary-looking masks, which gave them the freedom of anonymity, so they could let loose without fear of being recognized.

Junkanoo is an important part of the Christmas season in the Bahamas. Parades are held in the wee hours of the morning (1 or 2 AM until dawn) on Boxing Day (December 26) and again on New Year's Day. Surprisingly, what appears to be a random, wild expression of joy is actually a very well-organized and planned event. Family and friends gather in large groups (often as many as 500–1,000) and perform together in the parade.

Competition is heated among the groups, who choose a different theme each year and keep it a closely guarded secret until Junkanoo day, when their efforts are revealed. Most groups spend months preparing for the big day at what they call their "base camp" or "shack." They choreograph dance steps, choose music, and design intricate costumes. Then it's time to practice, practice, practice. Judges watch the event closely and award prizes for best music, best costumes, and best overall group presentation. With thousands of dollars of prize money up for grabs, people go to extremes to please the crowd and put on the best show.

The grandest Junkanoo celebration is in Nassau, where the best views are upstairs on Bay Street or on the benches that line the streets. Plan ahead and arrive early to secure a good spot. You can also experience Junkanoo on Grand Bahama Island, Eleuthera, Bimini, and Abaco. If you miss the festivities, be sure to stop by the **Junkanoo Expo** in downtown Nassau to see some of the most memorable costumes and floats from years past.

## The Arts

### Cable Beach

THEATER   **Rainforest Theatre.** The redesigned theater, which now has an atmosphere true to its name, presents lavish shows. Check with the resort for the latest offerings (and the weather report). ⊠ *Wyndham Nassau Resort & Crystal Palace Casino, Cable Beach* ☎ 242/327–6200 Ext. 6758.

### Nassau

THEATER   **Dundas Centre for the Performing Arts.** Plays, concerts, ballets, and musicals by local and out-of-town artists are staged here throughout the year. The box office is open from 10 AM to 4 PM. ⊠ *Mackey St.* ☎ 242/ 393–3728.

# SPORTS & THE OUTDOORS

For all of its dining, shopping, and nightlife possibilities, Nassau's draw—as with all of the Bahamas—remains its outdoor life; with flawless weather nearly year-round, few visitors to New Providence fail to experience at least some of the natural delights that remain, even among the frenzied construction. Many of these pleasures revolve around the water, and everyone from experienced boaters and divers to novice snorkelers can enjoy seeing (in the words of one local promotion) "how the other two-thirds live." You can participate in sports activities or lie back and enjoy a cruise, often with snorkeling or other water-based fun involved.

> **DID YOU KNOW?**
>
> Bahamians are crazy about two sports: rugby (Sept.–April) and cricket (March–Oct.).

## Boating

From Chub Cay—one of the Berry Islands 35 mi north of New Providence—to Nassau, the sailing route goes across the mile-deep Tongue of the Ocean. The Paradise Island Lighthouse welcomes yachters to Nassau Harbour, which is open at both ends. The harbor can handle the world's largest cruise liners; sometimes as many as eight tie up at one time. Two looming bridges bisect the harbor connecting Paradise Island to Nassau. Sailboats with masts taller than the high-water clearance of 72 feet must enter the harbor from the east end to reach marinas east of the bridges. On the Nassau side of the harbor, **Nassau Yacht Haven** (☎ 242/393–8173 ⊕ www.nassauyachthaven.com) is a 150-berth marina—the largest in the Bahamas—that also arranges fishing charters. **Brown's Boat Basin** (☎ 242/393–3331), on the Nassau side, offers a place to tie up your boat, as well as on-site engine repairs. **Nassau Harbour Club** (☎ 242/393–0771) is a hotel and marina on the Nassau side with 50 slips. Sixty-five-slip **Hurricane Hole Marina** (☎ 242/363–3600) is on the Paradise Island side of the harbor. The marina at **Atlantis, Paradise Island** (☎ 242/363–3000) has 63 "mega-yacht slips." At the western end of New Providence, **Lyford Cay** (☎ 242/362–4131), a posh development for the rich and famous, has an excellent marina, but there is limited availability for the humble masses.

If your children would enjoy sitting in a row on a rubber banana and bouncing along behind a motorboat, ride the big banana at **Premier Watersports** (☎ 242/324–1475, 242/427–0939 cellular), at the beach at the Sheraton Grand and Atlantis.

## Fishing

The waters here are generally smooth and alive with many species of game fish, which is one of the reasons why the Bahamas has more than 20 fishing tournaments open to visitors every year. A favorite spot just west of Nassau is the Tongue of the Ocean, so called because it looks like that part of the body when viewed from the air. The channel stretches for 100 mi. For boat rental, parties of two to six will pay $300 or so for a half day, $600 for a full day.

**Born Free Charters** (☎ 242/393–4144) has three boats and guarantees a catch on full-day charters—if you don't get a fish, you don't pay. **Brown's Charters** (☎ 242/324–2061) specializes in 24-hour shark fishing trips, as well as reef and deep-sea fishing. The **Charter Boat Association** (☎ 242/393–3739) has 15 boats available for fishing charters. **Chubasco Charters** (☎ 242/324–3474 ⊕ www.chubascocharters.com) has two boats for sportfishing and shark fishing charters. **Nassau Yacht Haven** (☎ 242/393–8173 ⊕ www.nassauyachthaven.com) runs fishing charters out of its 150-slip marina.

## Fitness Clubs & Spas

Nassau has a number of health clubs and gyms for those in the mood for an indoor workout or some spa pampering—an energizing alternative to shopping on an overcast day. Most clubs are stocked with the latest high-tech machinery, including stair climbers, treadmills, and exercise bikes, and offer aerobics and other fitness classes. If you plan to stay in the area for a stretch, check to see if package rates are available.

**Azure Spa** (✉ British Colonial Hilton, Bay St. ☎ 242/325–8497) offers quality à la carte services including facials (50-minute steam, massage, and mask is $70), body scrubs and wraps, hydrotherapy ($45 for 25 minutes), and numerous types of massages (hour-long aromatherapy is $80). **Palace Spa** (☎ 242/327–6200), in the Wyndham Crystal Palace complex and adjoining the Radisson Cable Beach, is a full-service gym with all the amenities and aerobics classes. Exercise bikes face the water, and the spa has stair machines and excellent showers. Pamper yourself at the relaxing hot tub and sauna. Fees are $10 daily and $35 weekly (Nassau Wyndham Resort and Nassau Beach Hotel guests receive a discount rate). **Planet Fitness** (✉ Bridge Plaza, just over eastern Paradise Island bridge ☎ 242/394–4653) has aerobics, step, and cardio-funk classes, as well as top-of-the-line fitness equipment, a juice bar, and a nursery. A full-access day pass is $8. **Windermere Day Spa at Harbour Bay** (✉ E. Bay St. ☎ 242/393–8788) offers a variety of ultramodern spa treatments—such as hydrotherapy and salt glows—as well as top-quality facials, massages, manicures, and pedicures. There's also a small, exclusive training center.

## Golf

Guests at affiliated hotels receive discounts at the following courses; prices quoted are for nonguests.

**Cable Beach Golf Club** (7,040 yards, par 72), the oldest golf course in the Bahamas, recently reopened after a renovation. The links are owned by the Radisson Cable Beach Casino & Golf Resort, whose guests get discount rates. ✎ *Box N-4914, Nassau* ☎ *242/327–6000 Ext. 6189* ✉ *18 holes $95, 9 holes $70; carts included. Clubs $25* ⊕ *Daily 7–5:30; last tee-off at 5:15.*

**One & Only Ocean Club Golf Course** (6,805 yards, par 72), formerly the Paradise Island Golf Club, had a major face-lift, care of Tom Weiskopf. The championship course is surrounded by the ocean on three sides, which means that winds can get stiff. Call to check on current availability and up-to-date prices (those not staying at Atlantis or the One & Only Ocean Club may find themselves shut out completely). ✉ *Paradise Island Dr., next to airport* ✎ *Box N-4777, Nassau* ☎ *242/363–3925, 800/321–3000 in U.S.* ✉ *18 holes $225. Clubs $35* ⊕ *Daily 7–6.*

**South Ocean Golf Club** (6,707 yards, par 72), in western New Providence, past Cable Beach, is the newest course to surrender its divots to visiting players. Narrow fairways are a notable feature. The course was designed by Joe Lee and built in 1969. ✎ *Box N-8191, Nassau* ☎ *242/362–4391 Ext. 23* ✉ *18 holes $90, 9 holes $50; carts included. Clubs $20. Reductions for South Ocean Golf and Beach Resort guests* ⊕ *Daily 7–6.*

## Horseback Riding

**Happy Trails Stables** gives guided 90-minute trail rides, including basic riding instruction, through remote wooded areas and beaches on New Providence's southwestern coast. Two morning group rides are offered, but private rides can be arranged at any time. Courtesy round-trip bus transportation from hotels is provided (about an hour each way). Tours are limited to eight persons. There's a 200-pound weight limit, and children must be at least nine years old. Reservations are required. ✉ *Coral Harbour* ☎ *242/362–1820 or 242/323–5613* ✉ *$95 per person* ⊟ *MC, V* ⊕ *Mon.–Sat.*

## Jet Skiing

A number of outfitters rent jet skis in front of Atlantis and the Sheraton Grand on Cabbage Beach. **Premier Watersports** (☎ 242/324–1475, 242/427–0939 cellular) is the most reliable, and charges $55 for 30 minutes.

## Parasailing

**Premier Watersports** (☎ 242/324–1475, 242/427–0939 cellular) gives you the chance to be lifted off a platform and into the skies for five to eight minutes—at $45 a pop. Ask for Captain Tim or his crew on Cabbage Beach in front of the large hotels.

## Sailing

**Nassau Beach Hotel** (☎ 242/327–7711 Ext. 6590) rents Sunfish sailboats for $35 per hour and 16-foot catamarans for $50 per hour.

## Scuba Diving & Snorkeling

Diving operations are plentiful in Nassau. Most hotels have diving instructors who teach short courses, followed the next day by a reef trip. Many small operations have sprung up in which experienced divers with their own boats run custom dives for one to five people; these are often one-person efforts. In many cases, the custom dive will include a picnic lunch with freshly speared lobster or fish cooked over an open fire on a private island beach.

### Dive Sites

New Providence Island has several popular dive sites and a number of dive operators who offer regular trips. The elusive (and thus exclusive) **Lost Ocean Hole** (east of Nassau, 40–195 feet) is aptly named because it's difficult to find. The rim of the 80-foot opening in 40 feet of water is dotted with coral heads and teeming with small fish—grunts, margate, and jacks—as well as larger pompano, amberjack, and sometimes nurse sharks. Divers will find a thermocline at 80 feet, a large cave at 100 feet, and a sand ledge at 185 feet that slopes down to 195 feet. The series of shallow reefs along the 14 mi of Rose Island is known as **Rose Island Reefs** (Nassau, 5–35 feet). The coral is varied, although the reefs are showing the effects of the heavy traffic. Still, plenty of tropical fish live here, and the wreck of the steel-hulled ship *Mahoney* is just outside the harbor.

**Gambier Deep Reef,** off Gambier Village about 15 minutes west of Cable Beach, goes to a depth of 80 feet. **Sea Gardens** is off Love Beach on the northwestern shore beyond Gambier. **Lyford Cay Drop-Off** (west of Nassau, 40–200-plus feet) is a cliff that plummets from a 40-foot plateau almost straight into the inky blue mile-deep Tongue of the Ocean. The wall has endless varieties of sponges, black coral, and wire coral. Along the wall, grunts, grouper, hogfish, snapper, and rockfish abound. Off the wall are pelagic game fish such as tuna, bonito, wahoo, and kingfish. The south-side reefs are great for snorkelers as well as divers because of the reefs' shallowness.

### Operators

All dive shops listed below are PADI facilities. Expect to pay about $65–$70 for a two-tank dive or beginner's course. Shark dives run $100–$125, and certification may cost $400 and up.

**Bahama Divers Ltd.** (☎ 242/393–1466 or 800/398–3483 ⊕ www.bahamadivers.com), the largest and most experienced dive operation in the country, offers twice-a-day dive safaris as well as half-day snorkeling trips. PADI certification courses are available, and there's a full line of scuba equipment. Destinations are drop-off sites, wrecks, coral reefs and gardens, and an ocean blue hole. For Paradise Island guests, Bahama Divers has opened a small dive operation (which also carries snorkel equipment for rent) in the Sheraton Grand.

**Dive Dive Dive, Ltd.** (☎ 242/362–1143, 242/362–1401, or 800/368–3480) specializes in small groups. Dives include trips to walls and reefs, night dives, and shark dives. Transportation is provided.

**Diver's Haven** (☎ 242/394–8960), part of Nassau Island Cruises, offers three daily dives, equipment rental, classes at several area hotels, and a four-day scuba certification course. Two-tank dives are available, or, for the more adventurous, dive trips to the Out Islands can be arranged.

**Stuart Cove's Dive South Ocean** (☎ 242/362–4171 or 800/879–9832), at South Ocean Golf and Beach Resort on the island's south shore, is considered by aficionados to be the island's leading dive shop. Although they're pros at teaching beginners (scuba instruction and guided snorkel tours are available), experienced thrill-seekers flock to Stuart Cove's for the famous shark dives (Cove is one of the world's leading shark handlers). Also popular are his Out Island "Wilderness Safaris," and "Wall Flying Adventures," in which you ride an underwater scooter across the ocean wall. Check out the collection of celebrity photos. The shop runs dive trips to the south-shore reefs twice a day.

## Spectator Sports

Among other imperishable traditions, the British handed down to the Bahamians such sports as soccer, rugby, and cricket. The latter, somewhat confusing sport (bring an expert with you, or you'll never know what's going on), is played at Haynes Oval. Baseball games take place at Queen Elizabeth Sports Center, rugby at Winton Estates, and softball at Clifford Park. For information on spectator sports, call the **Ministry of Tourism** (☎ 242/322–7500 or 800/2242627), or check the local papers for sports updates and calendars.

## Tennis

Most people play at the hotel where they're staying. Fees below are for nonguests.

The **Nassau Beach Hotel** (☎ 242/327–7711) tennis shop charges $5 per person from 9–6 and $7 per person until 9 PM. Three of the six courts are lighted, and rackets can be rented for an hourly rate of $6 per person. Monday evenings are reserved for members.

## Waterskiing

You'd be hard-pressed to find anyone waterskiing these days (most prefer jet skiing), but if the desire strikes, Captain Tim at **Premier Watersports** (☎ 242/324–1475, 242/427–0939 cellular) can make it happen.

## Windsurfing

**Nassau Beach Hotel** (☎ 242/327–7711 Ext. 6590) rents sailboards for $20 per hour; more advanced boards cost $30 per hour.

# SHOPPING

For many, shopping is one of Nassau's greatest delights. Bargains abound between Bay Street and the waterfront. For more upscale items, don't forget to look in the hotel arcades. You can return home with a suitcase full of handmade Bahamian goods or splurge at duty-free shops that offer savings so good that you simply have to load up. You'll find duty-free prices—generally 25%–50% less than U.S. prices—on imported items such as crystal, linens, watches, cameras, sweaters, leather goods, and perfumes. Prices here rival those in other duty-free destinations.

Most of Nassau's shops are on Bay Street between Rawson Square and the British Colonial Hotel, and on the side streets leading off Bay Street. Some stores, however, are beginning to pop up on the main shopping thoroughfare's eastern end. Be aware that prices in shops are fixed, and do observe the local dress customs when you go shopping: shorts are acceptable, but beachwear is not.

Although a few shops will be happy to mail bulky or fragile items home for you, most won't deliver purchases to your hotel, plane, or cruise ship.

## Markets & Arcades

The **International Bazaar,** a collection of shops under a huge, spreading bougainvillea, sells linens, souvenirs, and offbeat items. This funky shopping row is on Bay Street at Charlotte Street. The **Nassau Arcade** (☎ 242/325–0338), on Bay Street between East Street and Elizabeth Avenue, just east of Parliament Square, houses a few small stores, including the Bahamas' Anglo-American bookstore, a tiny storefront with a smattering of interesting reading material. **Prince George Plaza,** which leads from Bay Street to Woodes Rogers Walk near the dock, just east of the International Bazaar, has about two dozen shops with varied wares.

## Specialty Shops

### Antiques, Arts & Crafts

**Bahamacraft Centre** (⊠ Paradise Island Dr., across from Hurricane Hole Plaza ☎ No phone) offers some top-level Bahamian crafts, including a selection of authentic straw work. Dozens of vendors sell everything from baskets to shell collages inside this vibrantly colored building, designed by noted architect Jackson Burnside of Doongalik Studios. You can catch a shuttle bus from Atlantis to the center.

**Balmain Antiques and Gallery** (⊠ Bay St. ☎ 242/323–7421) collects Bahamian artwork as well as antique maps, prints, and bottles.

**Doongalik Studios** (⊠ 18 Village Rd. ☎ 242/394–1886) offers dynamic canvases inspired by Junkanoo celebrations, vibrantly painted furniture, Junkanoo masks, and kaleidoscopic sculpture. Don't miss the sculpture garden or the re-creation of a traditional Bahamian home that serves as a display room for handmade Christmas ornaments, art cards, and other inexpensive and unique gifts. You can watch a Junkanoo video while you shop.

**Marlborough Antiques** (⊠ Marlborough St. ☎ 242/328–0502) specializes in English furniture and bric-a-brac. You can also find Bahamian art, rare books, European glassware, and Victorian jewelry.

**Soft Touch Productions** (⊠ Market St. ☎ 242/323–2128), known for its wire-sculpted dolls depicting local characters and scenes, also sells wicker and straw baskets and other souvenirs.

## Baked Goods

**The Bread Shop** (⊠ Shirley St., east of Mackey St. ☎ 242/393–7973) is, as the sign proclaims, "The home of Rosie's Raisin Bread." Cinnamon rolls, pound and banana cakes, and other sweet delights are also offered in this amiable spot in Nassau's east end.

**Kelly's Bakery** (⊠ Market St. ☎ 242/325–0616) is a convenient place to stop for muffins, cakes, and other goodies.

**Model Bakery** (⊠ Dowdeswell St. ☎ 242/322–2595), in Nassau's east end, is another great local bakery. Be sure to try the cinnamon twists.

## China, Crystal, Linens & Silver

**Linen Shop** (⊠ Bay St. ☎ 242/322–4266) sells fine embroidered Irish linens and lace.

**Solomon's Mines** (⊠ Bay St. locations: between Charlotte and Parliament Sts., at the corner of Charlotte and Bay, and between Frederick and Market; Hurricane Hole Plaza; Atlantis on Paradise Island ☎ 242/356–6920) sells, among other names, Waterford, Hummel, Lladró, Wedgwood, Lenox, Lalique, Baccarat, Bally of Switzerland, Hermes, and Salvatore Ferragamo.

## Cigars

Expansive displays of Cuban cigars, imported by Bahamian merchants, lure aficionados to the Bahamas for cigar sprees. Be aware, however, that some merchants on Bay Street and elsewhere in the islands are selling counterfeits—sometimes unwittingly. If the price seems too good to be true, chances are it is. Check the wrappers and feel to ensure that there's a consistent fill before you make your purchase. A number of stores along the main shopping strip stock only the best authentic Cuban stogies.

**The Cigar Box** (⊠ Bay St. ☎ 242/326–7352), next to Planet Hollywood, offers all the well-known Cuban brands as well as a small selection of humidors.

**Graycliff** (⊠ West Hill St. ☎ 242/322–7050 ⊕ www.graycliff.com) carries one of Nassau's finest selections of hand-rolled cigars, overseen by the prestigious Avelino Lara, who created some of Cuba's best-known cigars. In fact, Graycliff's operation is so popular that it has expanded the hotel to include an entire cigar factory, which is open to the public for tours and purchases. A dozen Cuban men and women roll the cigars; they live on the lovely premises and work here through a special arrangement with the Cuban government. True cigar buffs will seek out the Graycliff's owner, Enrico Garzaroli.

**Havana Humidor** (⊠ Crystal Court at Atlantis, Paradise Island ☎ 242/363–5809) has the largest selection of authentic Cuban cigars in the Bahamas. Watch cigars being made, or browse through the cigar and pipe accessories.

**Pipe of Peace** (⊠ Bay St. and East St. ☎ 242/322–3908) has a wide selection of cigars, pipes, and cigarettes, including all major Cuban cigars. Although the cigar counter occupies just a small portion of the eclectic souvenir shop, it's well known as a good source.

**Tropique International Smoke Shop** (⊠ Nassau Wyndham Resort & Crystal Palace Casino ☎ 242/327–7292) has well-stocked atmosphere-controlled humidors; the well-trained staff provides knowledgeable guidance.

## Eclectic

**Far East Traders** (⊠ Prince George's Plaza, Bay St. ☎ 242/325–7095) has embroidered linens from Asia, silk nighties and kimonos, and handwoven blouses and vests.

**Green Lizard** (⊠ Bay St. ☎ 242/323–8076) is home to a cornucopia of native and imported gifts, including a specialty item you might be tempted to use during your stay: string hammocks.

**House of Music** (⊠ Mackey St. ☎ 242/393–0331) has the best selection of island calypso, soca, reggae, and Junkanoo music.

**The Island Shop and Island Bookstore** (⊠ Bay St. ☎ 242/322–4183) has two floors of travel guides, novels, paperbacks, gift books, and international magazines, as well as clothing, swimwear, and souvenirs. Take a peek at the Bahamian section, which has books on everything from history to cookery.

**Island Tings** (⊠ Bay St. ☎ 242/326–1024) carries a variety of items, some Bahamian, some not (look carefully before assuming you're buying local work). Art includes prints by Eleutheran artist Eddie Minnis, wood carvings, and Androsia fabric—produced on the island of Andros. There's also a sizable food section.

**Royal Palm Trading Co.** (⊠ Bay St. ☎ 242/322–5131) is an upscale store carrying designer clothing lines such as Tommy Bahama and Androsia. It also sells Fashion Fair cosmetics, placemats, and other gift items.

## Fashion

Clothing is no great bargain in Nassau, but many stores sell fine imports. Perhaps the best local buy is brightly batiked Androsia fabric—available by the yard or sewn into sarongs, dresses, and blouses.

**Brass and Leather** (⊠ Charlotte St. off Bay St. ☎ 242/394–5676) sells leather goods for men and women, including bags, shoes, and belts.

**Cole's of Nassau** (⊠ Parliament St. ☎ 242/322–8393 ⊠ Crystal Court at Atlantis, Paradise Island ☎ 242/363–4161 ⊠ Bay Street, next to John Bull ☎ 242/356–2498) is a top choice for designer fashions, sportswear, bathing suits, shoes, and accessories.

**Fendi** (⊠ Bay St. at Charlotte St. ☎ 242/322–6300) occupies a magnificent old building and carries the Italian house's luxury line of handbags, luggage, watches, jewelry, and shoes.

**Tempo Paris** (⊠ Bay St. ☎ 242/323–6112) offers men's clothing by major designers, including Ralph Lauren, Calvin Klein, and Gianni Versace.

### Jewelry, Watches & Clocks

**Coin of the Realm** (✉ Charlotte St. off Bay St. ☎ 242/322–4862 or 242/322–4497) has Bahamian coins, stamps, native conch pearls, tanzanite, and semi-precious stone jewelry.

**Colombian Emeralds International** (✉ Bay St. near Rawson Sq. ☎ 242/326–1661 ✉ Atlantis, Paradise Island ☎ 242/322–3020) is the local branch of this well-known jeweler; the stores carry a variety of fine jewelry in addition to their signature gem.

**The Jewelry Box** (✉ Bay St. ☎ 242/322–4098) specializes in tanzanite jewelry. It's the largest Bahamian supplier of this gem—mined in the foothills of Mt. Kilimanjaro—but it also sells other precious and semi-precious stones and 14-karat gold jewelry.

**The Jewelry Mart** (✉ Bay St. ☎ 242/328–8869) offers Movado, Bulova, and other watches as well as gold jewelry and pieces fashioned from tanzanite, rubies, emeralds, and other gems.

**John Bull** (✉ 284 Bay St. ☎ 242/322–4252 ✉ Crystal Court at Atlantis, Paradise Island ☎ 242/363–3956), established in 1929 and magnificently decorated in its Bay Street incarnation behind a Georgian-style facade, fills its complex with wares from Tiffany & Co., Cartier, Mikimoto, Nina Ricci, and Yves Saint Laurent. The company has 15 locations throughout Nassau.

**Solomon's Mines** (✉ Bay St. locations: between Charlotte and Parliament Sts., at corner of Charlotte and Bay, and between Frederick and Market; Hurricane Hole Plaza; Atlantis on Paradise Island ☎ 242/322–8324 or 877/765–6463) is the place to buy duty-free watches by Tag-Heuer, Omega, Borel, Swiss Army, and other makers. The store also carries African diamonds, as well as Spanish pieces of eight in settings.

### Perfumes

**The Body Shop** (✉ Bay St. ☎ 242/356–2431) sells the company's internationally acclaimed line of all-natural body lotions, shampoos and conditioners, and makeup.

**John Bull** (✉ 284 Bay St. ☎ 242/322–4252 ✉ Crystal Court at Atlantis, Paradise Island ☎ 242/363–3956) has fragrances by Chanel, Yves Saint Laurent, and Estée Lauder. There are 15 locations throughout Nassau.

**Perfume Bar** (✉ Bay St. ☎ 242/325–1258) carries the best-selling French fragrance Boucheron and the Clarins line of skin-care products, as well as scents by Givenchy, Fendi, and other well-known designers.

**The Perfume Shop** (✉ Bay and Frederick Sts. ☎ 242/322–2375) is a landmark perfumery that has the broadest selection of imported perfumes and fragrances in the Bahamas.

**Solomon's Mines** (✉ Bay St. locations: between Charlotte and Parliament Sts., at corner of Charlotte and Bay, and between Frederick and Market; Hurricane Hole Plaza; Atlantis on Paradise Island ☎ 242/356–6920 or 877/765–6463), one of the Caribbean's largest duty-free retailers, stocks French, Italian, and U.S. fragrances, skin-care products, and bath lines.

# NEW PROVIDENCE ISLAND ESSENTIALS

1

*To research prices, get advice from other travelers, and book travel arrangements, visit ⊕ www.fodors.com*

## Transportation

### BY AIR

Nassau International Airport (NAS), 8 mi west of Nassau by Lake Killarney, is served by an increasing number of airlines. With the closure of the Paradise Island Airport, it's the only game in town now.

Air Canada flies from Montréal and Toronto. American Eagle, an American Airlines subsidiary, flies into Nassau daily from Miami and Fort Lauderdale. Bahamasair, the national carrier, has daily flights from Miami and Fort Lauderdale, as well as five flights weekly from Orlando. Continental flies in daily from Newark under service operated by Nassau–Paradise Island Express, and daily from West Palm Beach, Fort Lauderdale, and Miami on Gulf Stream International, another Continental partner. Delta is one of the busier carriers, with daily flights from Atlanta, New York City, Cincinnati, Charleston, and Orlando. US Airways flies in daily from Charlotte, NC, and offers seasonal services from Philadelphia.

 Airlines & Contacts **Air Canada** ☎ 242/377-8411 or 800/776-3000. **American Eagle** ☎ 800/433-7300. **Bahamasair** ☎ 242/377-5505 or 800/222-4262. **Continental** ☎ 242/377-2050 or 800/231-0856. **Delta** ☎ 800/221-1212. **Gulf Stream International** ☎ 242/377-4314 or 800/992-8532. **US Airways** ☎ 242/377-8887 or 800/622-1015.

 Airport Information **Nassau International Airport (NAS)** ☎ 242/377-7281.

### BY BOAT

Nassau is a port of call for a number of cruise lines, including Carnival Cruise Lines, Celebrity Cruises, Costa Cruise Line, Disney Cruise Line, Premier Cruise Lines, Regal Cruises, Royal Caribbean International, and Silversea Cruises. Ships dock at Prince George Wharf, in downtown Nassau.

Ferries operate during daylight hours (usually 9–5:30) at half-hour intervals between Prince George Wharf and Paradise Island. The one-way cost is $3 per person.

### BY BUS

No bus service is available from Nassau International Airport to New Providence hotels, except for guests on package tours. (Breezes, Sandals, and Atlantis have promotional booths at the airport.)

For the adventuresome, consider jitney (bus) service to get around Nassau and its environs. Rides in these buses, which career along with windows open and music blaring, range from smooth sailing to hair-raising. If you want to join locals on a jitney, hail one at a bus stop, hotel, public beach, or in a residential area. Most carry their owner's name in boldly painted letters, so they're easy to spot, and with downtown's main streets being one-way, it's not hard to tell where they're going. If you're not sure of the jitney's direction, ask your concierge on which side of the street to stand, or check with the friendly drivers. The fare is $1; exact change is required. Call out to the driver as your stop approaches.

In downtown Nassau, jitneys wait on Frederick Street between Bay Street and Woodes Rogers Walk. Bus service runs throughout the day until 7.

### BY CAR
For exploring at your leisure, it's best to have a car. Rentals are available at Nassau International Airport, downtown, on Paradise Island, and at some resorts. Plan to pay $80–$120 per day, depending on the type of car. Gasoline costs around $3 a gallon. Remember to drive on the left.

Avis Rent-A-Car has branches at the Nassau International Airport, on Paradise Island in the Paradise Village Shopping Centre, and downtown, just west of the British Colonial Hotel. Budget has branches at the Nassau International Airport and on Paradise Island. Dollar Rent-a-Car, which often has the lowest rates (there are often $39 rentals available), can be found at Nassau International Airport and downtown, at the base of the British Colonial Hotel. Hertz has branches at Nassau International Airport and on East Bay Street, a block east of the bridge from Paradise Island. Thrifty has a branch at the airport.

**Major Agencies Avis Rent-A-Car** ☎ 242/377-7121 or 800/288-0668. **Budget** ☎ 242/377-9000 or 242/363-3095. **Dollar Rent-a-Car** ☎ 242/377-8300. **Hertz** ☎ 242/377-6231, 242/377-6866, or 800/654-3131.

### BY CARRIAGE
Beautifully painted horse-drawn carriages will take as many as four people around Nassau at a rate of $10 per adult and $5 per child for a 30-minute ride; don't hesitate to bargain. Most drivers give a comprehensive tour of the Bay Street area, including an extensive history lesson. Look for the carriages on Woodes Rogers Walk, in the center of Rawson Square.

### BY SCOOTER
Two people can ride around the island on a motor scooter for about $40 for a half day, $50 for a full day. Helmets and insurance for both driver and passenger are mandatory and are included in the rental price. Many hotels have scooters on the premises. You can also try Knowles, on West Bay Street, in the British Colonial Hilton parking lot, or check out the stands in Rawson Square. Remember to drive on the left.

**Knowles** ☎ 242/356-0741.

### BY TAXI
Taxis are generally the best and most convenient way to get around New Providence. Fares are determined by zone. The fare is $6 for trips within downtown Nassau and on Paradise Island (which includes the bridge toll), $9 from Paradise Island to downtown, and $18 from Cable Beach to Paradise Island (including toll). Fares are for two passengers; each additional passenger is $3, regardless of the destination. It's customary to tip taxi drivers 15%. You also can hire a car or small van for about $50 per hour.

A taxi ride from the airport to Cable Beach costs $15; to Nassau, $22; and to Paradise Island, $28 (this includes the $1 causeway toll). These are fixed costs for two passengers; each additional passenger is $3.

Bahamas Transport has radio-dispatched taxis. You can call the Taxi Cab Union directly for a cab. There are also stands at major hotels, or the front desk can call you a cab.

🚖 Taxi Companies **Bahamas Transport** ☎ 242/323-5111, 242/323-5112, 242/323-5113, or 242/323-5114. **Taxi Cab Union** ☎ 242/323-4555 or 242/323-5818.

## Contacts & Resources

### BANKS & EXCHANGING SERVICES

Principal banks on New Providence Island are Bank of the Bahamas, Bank of Nova Scotia, Barclays Bank, Canadian Imperial Bank of Commerce, Citibank, and Royal Bank of Canada. Banks are open on the island Monday through Thursday from 9:30 to 3 and Friday from 9:30 to 5. Banks are closed on the weekend.

### CONSULATES & EMBASSIES

🏛 **U.S. Embassy** ✉ Queen St., across from British Colonial Hilton ☎ 242/322-1181 📠 242/328-7838.

### EMERGENCIES

In an emergency dial 911. Princess Margaret Hospital is government operated, and Doctors Hospital is private.

🚑 **Ambulance** ☎ 911 or 242/322-2881. **Police** ☎ 911 or 242/322-4444.

🏥 Hospitals **Doctors Hospital** ✉ Collins Ave. and Shirley St. ☎ 242/322-8411. **Princess Margaret Hospital** ✉ Shirley St. ☎ 242/322-2861.

### TOUR OPTIONS

More than a dozen local operators provide tours of New Providence Island's natural and commercial attractions. Some of the many possibilities include sightseeing tours of Nassau and the island, glass-bottom boat tours to Sea Gardens, and cruises to offshore cays, all starting at $12. A full day of ocean sailing will cost around $60. In the evening, there are sunset and moonlight cruises with dinner and drinks ($35–$50) and nightlife tours to casino cabaret shows and nightclubs ($28–$45). Tours may be booked at hotel desks in Nassau, Cable Beach, and Paradise Island or directly through tour operators, which have knowledgeable guides and a selection of tours in air-conditioned cars, vans, or buses.

CRUISE TRIPS    One of the best ways to enjoy Nassau's seafaring pleasures is to sign up with one of the many day or evening cruise operators, typically on a catamaran or similar sailboat. These offerings range from three-hour snorkeling trips to romantic sunset cruises or full-day excursions. Prices are fairly standard among the operators: A half-day snorkeling cruise will run about $45, and a full day $60, usually including a drink and snacks; prices for a sunset sail, with drinks and hors d'oeuvres, are around the same. Full-day or dinner cruises, both with meals, cost around $50. Hotel transportation is generally included.

Barefoot Sailing Cruises transports you to a secluded Rose Island beach for snorkeling and sunbathing on a half-day sail or snorkel cruise; other options include an all-day island barbecue and champagne sunset cruise. Feeling luxurious? Arrange a private dinner cruise.

Flying Cloud runs half-day catamaran cruises at 9:30 and 2, as well as sunset "sail-and-a-dinner" cruises on which you can enjoy a candlelight meal in a secluded cove. A five-hour Sunday cruise departs at 10 AM.

Island Tours offers a half-day catamaran excursion to Rose Island beach for beach volleyball and snorkeling. Snacks and an open bar are included, as are bus transfers to and from your hotel.

Sea Island Adventures runs half- and full-day trips to Rose Island for snorkeling and a tropical lunch, as well as sunset cruises. Private charters can also be arranged.

🛥Cruise Lines **Barefoot Sailing Cruises** ☎242/393-0820 ⊕www.barefootsailingcruises. com. **Flying Cloud** ☎ 242/363-4430 ⊕ www.bahamasnet.com/flyingcloud. **Island Tours** ☎242/327-8653. **Sea Island Adventures** ☎242/325-3910 ⊕www.bahamasnet. com/seaislandadventure.

OUT ISLANDS TRIPS
Several options exist for getaways to the less-frequented Out Islands. Expect to pay from $90 for no-frills ferry service to several hundred dollars for full-day excursions with meals, snorkeling, and sightseeing.

Bahamas Fast Ferries provides a wonderful way to escape to Harbour Island—possibly the most charming island in the Bahamas—Spanish Wells, or unspoiled Eleuthera; the high-speed, colorful, and extremely safe *Bo Hengy* catamaran whisks you from Nassau to Out Island getaways in two hours. Book just transport or, better yet, the Bo Hengy Harbour Island package ($159 for adults, $99 for children), which includes a historic walking tour of Harbour Island, a great lunch, and beach time at the famous pink sands—Fast Ferries has its own fully equipped cabana on the beach with complimentary refreshments. Horseback riding is usually available on the beach. You'll be back in Nassau by nightfall.

Exuma Powerboat Adventures offers full-day excursions to the Exuma Cays on their three speedboats. You can feed iguanas at Allan's Cay, participate in a nature walk, and do some snorkeling in the Exumas' Land and Sea Park. There are also shallow-water shark feeds. It's a great way to experience some of the beauty of the less-developed islands outside Nassau. Lunch is included.

Island World Adventures offers full-day excursions to Saddleback Cay in the Exumas on a high-speed powerboat. You can take a guided trek and learn about Bahamian flora and fauna, or just snorkel and sunbathe the day away. Lunch, soft drinks, beer, and rum punch are included.

Seaplane Safaris utilizes low-flying craft for the Exuma Cays trip, allowing you to glide right over the water's surface. You can swim right off the seaplane into Thunderball Grotto, an eerie natural formation (scenes from the James Bond movie bearing its name were filmed here), and enjoy some snorkeling, explore nature trails, or simply loll on the beach on Warderick Wells, the headquarters of the Land and Sea Park. Lunch is included, and the trip takes a full day.

🚢 **Bahamas Fast Ferries** ☎ 242/323-2166 ⊕ www.bahamasferries.com. **Exuma Powerboat Adventures** ☎ 242/393-7116 ⊕ www.powerboatadventures.com. **Island World Adventures** ☎ 242/363-3333 ⊕ www.islandworldadventures.com. **Seaplane Safaris** ☎ 242/393-2522 or 242/393-1179.

SPECIAL-
INTEREST TOURS

During the Close Encounter ($75 per person) arranged by Dolphin Encounters on Blue Lagoon Island (Salt Cay), just east of Paradise Island, you stand in waist-deep water while dolphins play around you. The two-hour program consists of an educational session as well as the encounter. Trainers are available to answer questions. Swim-with-the-Dolphins ($145 per person) actually allows you to swim with these friendly creatures for about 30 minutes. For more complete involvement, try the Assistant Trainer for a Day program ($195 per person, 16 years old minimum), where you learn about dolphin care and training by helping with feeding, cleaning, and food preparation. Programs are available daily 8–5:30, and the cost includes transfers from your hotel and the boat ride to the island. Make reservations as early as possible.

Hartley's Undersea Walk takes you for a stroll on the ocean floor. Special helmets protect hair, eyeglasses, and contacts while allowing you to see the fish and flora. Hartley's yacht, the *Pied Piper,* departs daily at 9:30 and 1:30 from the Nassau Yacht Haven on East Bay Street. Reserve in advance to guarantee a spot.

Pedal & Paddle Ecoventures is a unique, full-day ecotourism adventure that combines all-terrain bicycle rides through forests and along coastlines with kayaking tours through mangrove creeks and sheltered waters. Lunch is included in the full-day tours, which can be booked at most hotel desks. Half-day tours are also available.

Seaworld Explorer is a "semi-submarine" that cruises through the harbor as it makes its way to Sea Gardens Marine Park; you can sit above water on the deck or descend to view the ocean life firsthand through undersea windows.

Stingray City, on Blue Lagoon Island, takes you snorkeling and even allows you to feed a surprisingly friendly stingray or two.

🚢 **Dolphin Encounters** ☎ 242/363-1003 ⊕ www.dolphinencounters.com. **Hartley's Undersea Walk** ☎ 242/393-8234 ⊕ www.underseawalk.com. **Pedal & Paddle Ecoventures** ☎ 242/362-2772. **Seaworld Explorer** ☎ 242/356-2548. **Stingray City** ☎ 242/363-3333 ⊕ www.nassaucruisesbahamas.com.

WALKING TOURS

A walking tour around Historic Nassau, arranged by the Tourist Information Office at Rawson Square, is offered daily. The cost is $10. Call ahead for information and reservations.

🚢 **Historic Nassau** ☎ 242/322-7500.

## VISITOR INFORMATION

The Ministry of Tourism's Help Line is an information source that operates from 8 AM to midnight daily. The ministry also operates tourist information booths at Nassau International Airport, open daily from 8:30 AM to 11:30 PM, and at the Welcome Center (Festival Place) adjacent to Prince George Wharf, open daily from 9 AM to 5 PM. The telephone numbers are 242/323–3182 and 242/323–3183. Ask about Bahamahosts, specially trained tour guides who will tell you about island history and culture and pass on their individual and imaginative knowledge of Bahamian folklore.

The Ministry of Tourism's People-to-People Programme is designed to let a Bahamian personally introduce you to the Bahamas. By prearrangement through the ministry, you can spend a day with a Bahamian family with similar interests to learn local culture firsthand or enjoy a family meal. It's best if you make arrangements—through your travel agent or by calling direct—prior to your trip. (This is not a dating service!) People-to-People also holds teas at Government House (call for details) and sponsors activities for spouses of conference attendees, student exchanges, and pen pal programs.

🚹 Visitor information **Ministry of Tourism** ✑ Box N-3701, Nassau ☎ 242/322–7500 or 242/302–2000 🖷 242/302–2098 🌐 www.bahamas.com ☎ 242/326–4357 Help Line ✉ Nassau International Airport booths ☎ 242/377–6833, 242/377–8606, or 242/377–6782 🖷 242/326–9772 Rawson Square. **People-to-People Programme** ☎ 242/326–5371 or 242/356–0435.

WEDDINGS  Fallen in love? The Ministry of Tourism's Wedding Division arranges weddings for visiting couples. Formerly run by People-to-People, the weddings have proven so popular that the ministry has established a separate department to handle them. Ministry staff will take care of all the paperwork and set up ceremonies ranging from a simple seaside "I do" to more outrageous nuptials. Underwater vows, anyone?

🚹 **Wedding Division** ☎ 242/356–0435.

# Grand Bahama Island

**WORD OF MOUTH**

"Our Lucaya is expensive, so be prepared to pay quite a bit for food and drink. I strongly recommend eating at the Port Lucaya Marketplace across the street, or at Billy Joe's, a local place just off the property line of Reef Village, unless you are on an AI."
—Fasst1

"Rent a scooter and head out to Gold Rock Beach, a really fun day trip, and the beach is superb. There are many beaches along the way that were totally empty of people, really nice."
—soboyle

Updated by
Chelle Koster
Walton

**GRAND BAHAMA, THE FOURTH-LARGEST ISLAND IN THE BAHAMAS** after Andros, Eleuthera, and Great Abaco, lies only 52 mi off Palm Beach, Florida. The Gulf Stream's ever-warm waters lap its western tip, and the Little Bahama Bank protects it from the northeast.

In 1492, when Columbus set foot on the Bahamian island of San Salvador, Grand Bahama was already populated. Skulls found in caves here attest to the existence of the peaceable Lucayans, who were constantly fleeing the more bellicose Caribs. The skulls show that the parents flattened their babies' foreheads with boards to strengthen them, making them less vulnerable to the cudgels of the Caribs, who were reputedly cannibalistic.

Spanish conquistadors visited the island briefly in the early 16th century. They used it as a watering hole but dismissed it as having no commercial value and went on their way. In the 18th century, Loyalists settled on Grand Bahama to escape the wrath of American revolutionaries who had just won the War of Independence. Remnants of that colonial exodus—including 150-year-old St. Peter's Anglican Church and rock walls built by the early colonists—crop up around the settlement of Eight Mile Rock, just west of Freeport Harbour. When Britain abolished the slave trade early in the 19th century, many of the Loyalists' former slaves settled here as farmers and fishermen.

Grand Bahama took on new prominence in the Roaring '20s, when the island's western end and Bimini to the south became convenient jumping-off points for rumrunners ferrying booze to Florida during Prohibition. But it was not until the 1950s, when the harvesting of Caribbean yellow pine trees (now protected by Bahamian environmental law) was the island's major industry, that American financier Wallace Groves envisioned Grand Bahama's grandiose future. Groves dreamed of establishing a tax-free port for the shipment of goods to the United States, a plan that involved building a city.

On August 5, 1955, largely due to Groves's efforts and those of British industrialist Sir Charles Hayward, the government signed an agreement that set in motion the development of a planned city and established the Grand Bahama Port Authority to administer a 200-square-mi area near the island's center. Settlers received tax concessions and other benefits. In return the developers built a port, an airport, a power plant, roads, waterways, and utilities. They also promoted tourism and industrial development.

From that agreement, the city of Freeport and later Lucaya evolved. They are separated by a 4-mi stretch of East Sunrise Highway (aka Churches Row, for all the houses of worship that line it), although few can tell you where one community ends and the other begins. A modern industrial park has developed west of Freeport, close to the harbor. Major companies were drawn here because there are no corporate, property, or income taxes and no customs duties or excise taxes on materials used for export manufacturing. In return the companies hire local workers and participate in community activities and charities.

# GREAT ITINERARIES

*Numbers in the text correspond to numbers in the margins and on the Grand Bahama Island and Freeport-Lucaya maps.*

### IF YOU HAVE 3 DAYS

Begin in the morning with a shopping binge at ▶ **Port Lucaya Marketplace** ❸. Stop at **UNEXSO** ❹ next door to make reservations for tomorrow's swim with dolphins, resort dive course, or excursion. Have lunch at the marketplace before heading to the beach across the street for an afternoon of sunning and watersports. Hit the restaurants and bars at the marketplace for the evening's entertainment. The next day, after your trip, explore the 🏠 **Freeport** area, beginning at **International Bazaar** ❶ for more shopping. Get a quick taste of Bahamian nature at **Bahamas National Trust Rand Nature Centre** ❻. Finish the day with a visit to **Water World** for family entertainment. On Day 3, head west to **Taíno Beach** for great beach action, lunch, watersports, and sunning. Catch an evening dinner cruise and show with **Bahama Mama Cruises.**

### IF YOU HAVE 5 DAYS

With an extra two days, follow the three-day itinerary above and spend Day 4 on an all-day eco- or heritage tour. The next day, catch a tour bus to **West End** for an eyeful of local culture. Have dinner in Freeport and prowl the nightclubs around International Bazaar for after-dark fun.

### IF YOU HAVE 7 DAYS

A week allows you to explore in greater depth the island's environmental treasures. For the first five days use the itinerary above, and on Day 6 visit ▶ **Lucayan National Park** ❼ and its beach—either on your own or with a tour group. In the afternoon, visit **Pirates of the Bahamas** and stay for the bonfire party, which is held Tuesday, Thursday, and Sunday nights. Spend your last morning horseback riding down the beach. In the afternoon, go on a fishing or glass-bottom boat tour. Have dinner at Taíno Beach or Smith's Point.

Most of Grand Bahama's commercial activity is concentrated in Freeport, the Bahamas's second-largest city. On average about 15% of the roughly 4 million people who come to the Bahamas each year visit Freeport and neighboring waterfront Lucaya. Cruise-ship passengers arrive at Lucayan Harbour mostly from the Florida ports of Fort Lauderdale and Cape Canaveral. The harbor has undergone a $10.9 million renovation and expansion with a clever Bahamian-style look, expanded cruise-passenger terminal facilities, and an entertainment-and-shopping village. Still more expansion is under way for cruise and container shipping. The airport has also been improved. In 2005 a new $30 million terminal building opened; the old terminal is still used for domestic inter-island flights.

Lucaya, with the debut of the grand and sprawling Our Lucaya Beach & Golf Resort, stepped up to the role of island tourism capital. With its modern shopping complex, as well as a 19,000-square-foot casino, it raised the bar for the island. In West End, Our Lucaya's challenge was met with the opening and expansion of the deluxe Old Bahama Bay and the groundbreaking for the future Bootle Bay home-and-resort development.

Despite the bustle of business and the influx of tourists, Grand Bahama offers many opportunities to enjoy solitude and nature. For decades, tourism forces have shifted the emphasis away from Freeport to Grand Bahama Island to raise awareness of what lies beyond shopping and gambling. As far as nature-lovers are concerned, two spots in and around Freeport shouldn't be missed: the Bahamas National Trust's (BNT) Lucayan National Park and the BNT Rand Nature Centre.

Ecosensitivity has spawned stimulating ecotourism adventures, including kayak trips through the national park, adventure tours to the island's East End, bird-watching excursions to spot species not found elsewhere in North America, snorkeling tours of coral reefs, and horseback rides through pine forests and along ocean beaches.

Grand Bahama Island also affords a plenitude of opportunities for heritage tourism. The friendly local population is accessible in daily interaction and through the People-to-People Programme (call 242/352–8044 for more information), which can hook you and your family up with hospitable locals with like interests. Most restaurants outside the large resorts serve Bahamian cuisine, and many attractions and tours explore the island's history and culture. For a potent taste of island tradition, plan your visit during Junkanoo celebrations at Christmas and in summer. A throwback to slavery days, Junkanoo colorfully showcases the song, dance, and spirit of Grand Bahama Island with bright and extravagant costumes, horns, bells, drums, and whistles.

## Exploring Grand Bahama

Shopping, golfing, and gambling initially drew many of Grand Bahama's first tourists, but today, beach-going, kayaking, and exploring the island's old fishing settlements are also popular on visitors' to-do lists. Freeport is the hub of the gambling and commercial scenes, but long before it arose as an exotic playground for high-rollers and shoppers, settlements clustered around coastal areas where islanders made their living from the sea. That way of life remains intact in the island's far-reaching areas on the West End and East End, especially in the offshore island of Sweeting's Cay. Driving to these far-flung areas is a cinch, as traffic is practically nonexistent, especially out toward East End. Roads are good, and the billboards are entertaining, if instructive: "Undertakers love overtakers" (i.e., people who pass), and "Littering is stupid; don't do it" (how's that for straightforward?).

The best way to taste local culture is in the restaurants and natural areas. Even in the middle of town, environmental attractions introduce visitors to the curly tailed lizards, Bahamian parrot, pink flamingos, and "flutterbys" (the Bahamian word for butterflies) that make their home

# IF YOU LIKE

### HITTING THE SAND

What Bahamas vacation is complete without a beach? And Grand Bahama Island has more than its share fringing its 96-mi length. All dusted with platinum sands, some are bustling with watersports activity—while others lie so far off the beaten path it takes a four-wheel-drive vehicle and local knowledge to find them. Taíno Beach is the most accessible to the general public. Restaurants and bars provide visitors an anchor and offer watersports rentals and tours. Many resorts off the beach provide free shuttles, and some beach bars have vans that will pick you up at your hotel.

### GOLF

Golf was a big deal on the island long before it became fashionable in the late 1990s. This means that many of the golf courses have a classic design, though most have been renovated in recent years. With plenty of room to build, early designers made the fairways long and scenic, while challenging golfers with lots of water. Today's courses retain those characteristics, but have been renovated and improved upon, one notable addition being the first-class golf academy at Our Lucaya's Lucayan Course.

### SHOPPING CLOSE TO HOME

Savvy shoppers head directly to the duty-free shops for great buys on liquor, jewelry, china, perfume, and other luxury items. If you're an experienced Caribbean duty-free buyer, however, you'll quickly realize that these aren't the best deals to be had in the islands—but they are the closest to the United States. At the other end of the scale, the straw markets are fun, colorful, and sell cheap souvenirs that make good gifts. Do realize that most of the items are made in Taiwan or Japan. Look in the galleries and at the new row of local arts-and-crafts shops at the Port Lucaya Marketplace for more authentic island craftsmanship.

### SNORKELING & SCUBA DIVING

Between the shipwrecks, caves, and coral reefs, Grand Bahama Island offers some of the Bahamas' most varied and vivid underwater scenery. Snorkeling can be anything but tame with blue holes and marine life to discover. Most resorts have snorkeling and scuba facilities. A pioneer in diving, Underwater Explorers Society (UNEXSO) has set a high standard for scuba charters. It's particularly famous for its dolphin dives.

### EXPLORING NATURE

Rare birds and stretches of undisturbed wilderness attract nature-lovers to the island's "bush," as natives call it. Explore by foot, bike, kayak, or jeep safari to discover not only the island's natural wonders but its intriguing past. Geological features range from gorgeous sandy beaches to limestone caves and pine forests. With the right guide, you'll learn how social and natural history intertwine on the island, where bush medicine and fishing are only two of the ways man still depends on nature.

2

# Moving Toward Ecotourism

TO EXPAND TOURISM BEYOND the island's traditional gambling and shopping attractions, Freeport-Lucaya is now marketed as Grand Bahama Island. It makes sense, for beyond the 6-mi strip that comprises the island's metropolis lies another 90 mi of unadulterated wilderness. The balance of the island is given to natural and uncrowded beaches, old-island settlements, and untamed "bush," as locals call the wilds.

The emphasis on the island's natural attributes began below the water line with **UNEXSO** diving and the **Dolphin Experience.** UNEXSO's preoccupation with extreme diving led to the exploration of the island's unique cave system and the opening of **Lucayan National Park,** a portal to the underground labyrinth accessible to the public. One of the caves holds a cemetery of the island's aboriginals, the Lucayans. The park also gives intrepid visitors a taste of the beauty and seclusion of out-of-town beaches. When it opened, the park marked the end of civilization. Rutted dirt roads led to rarely visited time-stilled settlements without electricity and telephones, and long stretches of pine and palmetto forest edged in white sand. In the mid-1990s, as paved roads and telephone wires reached the remote East End, tours began to transport visitors to this other world.

Today, kayaking, biking, snorkeling, boating, jeeping, and cultural safaris provide ways for visitors to take in Grand Bahama Island's most precious treasures. **East End Adventures,** one of the best, bumps along off-road to the island's past, visiting the ruins of Old Freetown, the first settlement, and its pristine beach. Along the way,

safari participants peer into a blue hole, learn about bush medicine, and hear old-island tales. At McLean's Town, they jump into a boat for a conch-cracking demonstration at remote Sweeting's Cay, followed by a home-cooked Bahamian lunch on an uninhabited island beach and blue-hole snorkeling. **Kayak Nature Tours,** another top-notch operation, follows backwater trails to Lucayan National Park and other off-the-beaten-path destinations. Knowledgeable native guides give lessons on island ecology along the way. The company also hosts full-day kayak trips to outer islands.

Right in downtown Freeport, the **Bahamas National Trust Rand Nature Centre** was one of the precursors to ecotourism on Grand Bahama Island. It still provides an oasis for rare birds as well as residents and visitors. On the island's other extreme, close to West End, **Paradise Cove** takes you below the waves. Here you can rent snorkeling equipment or kayak to experience the island's best swim-to reef—Deadman's Reef. Its duck pond teems with opportunities for the binoculars crowd.

Ecotourism promises to be a fixture on Grand Bahama Island, attracting a new brand of island vacationer, one more adventurous and ready to experience the less-touted and richer offerings of Grand Bahama's great outback. For more information, contact the **Ecotourism Association of Grand Bahama** (☎ 242/373-2485).

in the islands. Of course, fine shops, greens, and the casino scene still remain prominent to round out the Grand Bahama experience.

## About the Restaurants

For a true Bahamian dining experience, look for restaurants named after the owner or cook—such as Becky's, Geneva's Place, and Georgie's. Conch, grouper, and Bahamian lobster are the specialties, fresh from local waters. Go to the colorful conch beach shacks at Taíno Beach and at Lucaya, just west of Our Lucaya Beach & Golf Resort. Equally colorful are the owners of such places, such as radio personality Tony Macaroni and the inventor of roasted conch, Joe Billy.

The Grand Bahama dining scene stretches far beyond traditional Bahamian cuisine. The resorts and shopping centers have eateries that rate with Nassau's finest, serving up everything from Italian and English fare to fine continental and creative Pacific Rim specialties. Most restaurants conveniently display their menus outside.

## About the Hotels

Accommodations took a step up when Our Lucaya Beach & Golf Resort opened its doors in 2000. It had a rejuvenating effect on an island whose resorts had grown dated and faded, and other smaller hotels around the island took the cue to spruce up. Old Bahama Bay opened at floundering West End and injected new life into the old capital; it continues to thrive and grow.

Despite all the money that's recently been poured into renovations, Grand Bahama Island accommodations remain some of the Bahamas' most affordable, especially those away from the beach. The majority are located near the two major shopping centers and provide free shuttle service to the nearest stretch of sand.

| WHAT IT COSTS | | | | | |
|---|---|---|---|---|---|
| | $$$$ | $$$ | $$ | $ | ¢ |
| RESTAURANTS | over $40 | $30–$40 | $20–$30 | $10–$20 | under $10 |
| HOTELS | over $400 | $300–$400 | $200–$300 | $100–$200 | under $100 |

Restaurant prices are for a main course at dinner, excluding gratuity, typically 15%, which is often automatically added to the bill. Hotel prices are for two people in a standard double room in high season, excluding service charges and 6%–12% tax.

## Timing

Anytime is a good time to take advantage of Grand Bahama Island's sunny skies and Gulf Stream–warmed waters. Summers can get oppressively hot (into the mid- and high 90s) and muggy, however, so unless you're planning on doing a lot of snorkeling, diving, and other watersports, you may want to schedule your trip for cooler months. Afternoon thunderstorms and occasional tropical storms and hurricanes also make summer less attractive weather-wise. The island averages around 20 days of rain per month from June to September, but the good news is that hotel rates plummet and diving and fishing conditions are great.

## GRAND BAHAMA'S TOP 5

**The Dolphin Experience.** Choose your level of involvement, from merely petting dolphins to diving with them.

**East End Eco-adventure.** Venture beyond the city and head out to the national park and quiet fishing settlements east of Freeport. Go it alone, or hook up with one of several tours that concentrate on heritage and the environment.

**Fish Fry.** Head to Smith's Point every Wednesday night to feast and party with the locals on the beach.

**Lucayan National Park.** You can witness a variety of habitats at this natural beauty—from secluded beaches to bat caves.

**Snorkel or Dive.** There's only one way to truly see the beautiful fish and dolphins that populate the incredible reefs and caves around Grand Bahama Island—so grab a snorkel or regulator and hop on in.

As one of the northernmost Bahamas islands, Grand Bahama experiences temperatures dipping into the high 60s and low 70s in January and February, so you may need a jacket and wet suit. On the upside, the migrant bird population swells and diversifies during that time of year. The other timing considerations are seasonal crowds and the subsequent increase in room rates. High tourist season runs from Christmas to Easter, peaking during spring break (late February to mid-April), when the weather is the most agreeable. To avoid the crowds, high prices, heat, and cold, visit from October through mid-December.

# AROUND THE ISLAND

Grand Bahama's appeal lies in its combination of commercial vitality and natural beauty. In the two main towns, Freeport and Lucaya, visitors can find just about everything that bustling Nassau has to offer: resort hotels, fine restaurants, golfing, duty-free shopping complexes, and gambling. But on Grand Bahama, unlike New Providence, the touristy spots take up only a small portion of an island that, on the whole, consists of uninhabited stretches of sand and patches of forest.

Just steps from the action, outdoor opportunities abound, particularly water-related ones. The island is a mecca for scuba divers and is home of the world-famous Underwater Explorers Society (UNEXSO). Surrounding waters lure anglers from around the world to compete in big game and bonefishing tournaments, such as the Bahamas Wahoo Championship, part of which is held in Grand Bahama each November. For many landlubbers, the island's golf courses—known for their long fairways and water challenges—guarantee year-round entertainment. A surge in ecosensitivity has generated an increase in ecotourism opportunities, both land- and water-based. And then there's swimming and snorkeling, perhaps two of the most popular vacation activities in the Bahamas.

## Freeport

Freeport is an attractive, planned city of modern shopping centers, resorts, and other convenient tourist facilities. The airport is just a few minutes from downtown, and the harbor is about the same distance.

### Sights to See

★ ➏ **Bahamas National Trust Rand Nature Centre.** On 100 acres just minutes from downtown Freeport, ½ mi of self-guided botanical trails show off 130 types of native plants, including many orchid species. The center is the island's birding hot spot, where you might spy a red-tailed hawk or a Cuban emerald hummingbird sipping hibiscus nectar. The flamingo flock was killed off by raccoons, but the center is in the process of replacing the birds. The new visitors center hosts changing local art exhibits and some resident animals, including a Bahama boa. Outside you can visit the caged one-eyed Bahama parrot the center has adopted. The reserve is named for philanthropist James H. Rand, the former president of Remington Rand, who donated a hospital and library to the island. ⊠ *E. Settlers Way, Freeport* ☎ *242/352–5438* 🖃 *$5* ☉ *Weekdays 9–4; guided nature walk by advance reservation.*

➊ **International Bazaar.** Though the 2004 post-hurricane closure of the Royal Oasis Resort and Casino has given this once-vibrant shopping area a down-at-the-heels look, some restaurants and shops remain open, along with the straw market. At the entrance stands a 35-foot *torii* arch, a red-lacquered gate that is a traditional symbol of welcome in Japan. ⊠ *W. Sunrise Hwy. and Mall Dr.* ☎ *No phone* 🖃 *Free* ☉ *Mon.–Sat. 10–6.*

★ ➋ **Perfume Factory.** The quiet and elegant Perfume Factory is in a replica 19th-century Bahamian mansion—the kind built by Loyalists who settled in the Bahamas after the American Revolution. The interior resembles a tasteful drawing room. This is the home of Fragrance of the Bahamas, a company that produces perfumes, colognes, and lotions using the scents of jasmine, cinnamon, gardenia, spice, and ginger. Take a free five-minute tour of the mixology laboratory. For $30 an ounce, you can blend your own perfume using any of the 35 scents ($15 for 1.5 ounces of blend-it-yourself body lotion). Sniff mixtures until they hit the right combination, then bottle, name, and take home the personalized potion. ⊠ *Behind International Bazaar, on access Rd.* ☎ *242/352–9391* ⊕ *www.perfumefactory.com* 🖃 *Free* ☉ *Weekdays 9–5, Sat. 11–3.*

## Lucaya

Lucaya, on Grand Bahama's southern coast and just east of Freeport, was developed as the island's resort center. These days, it's booming with a megaresort complex, a fine sandy beach, championship golf courses, a first-class dive operation, Port Lucaya's marina facilities, and a new casino.

### Sights to See

☾ ➎ **The Dolphin Experience.** Encounter Atlantic bottle-nose dolphins in Sanctuary Bay at one of the world's first and largest dolphin facilities, about 2 mi east of Port Lucaya. A ferry takes you from Port Lucaya to the bay to observe and photograph the animals. If you don't mind getting wet,

Fodor'sChoice
★

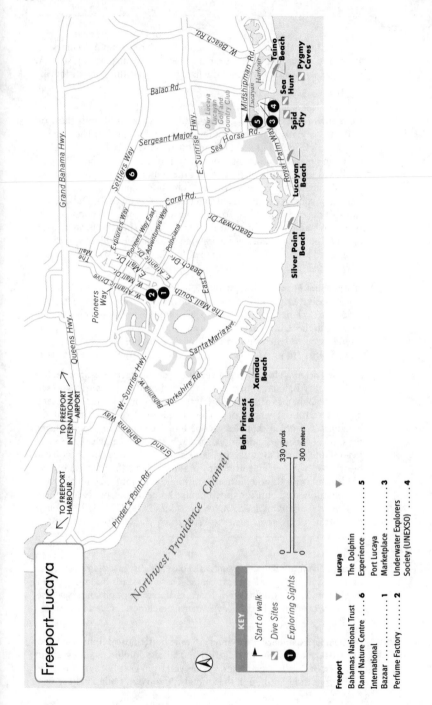

Freeport–Lucaya

**KEY**

▲ Start of walk
🗹 Dive Sites
❶ Exploring Sights

330 yards
300 meters

**Freeport** ▶
Bahamas National Trust
Rand Nature Centre ....**6**
International
Bazaar .............**1**
Perfume Factory ......**2**

**Lucaya** ▶
The Dolphin
Experience ..........**5**
Port Lucaya
Marketplace ..........**3**
Underwater Explorers
Society (UNEXSO) .....**4**

you can sit on a partially submerged dock or stand waist deep in the water, and one of these friendly creatures will swim up and touch you. You can also engage in one of two swim-with-the-dolphins programs, but you must be 55 inches or taller. The Dolphin Experience began in 1987, when it trained five dolphins to interact with people. Later, the animals learned to head out to sea and swim with scuba divers on the open reef. A two-hour dive program is available. You can buy tickets for the Dolphin Experience at the Underwater Explorers Society (UN-EXSO) in Port Lucaya, but be sure to make reservations as early as possible. ⊠ *Dolphin Experience, Port Lucaya* ☎ *242/373–1244 or 800/ 992–3483* 🖷 *242/373–8956* ⊕ *www.unexso.com* 🖃 *2-hr interaction program $75, 2-hr swim program $169, dolphin dive $159, open-ocean experience $199* ⊙ *Daily 9–5.*

★ ❸ **Port Lucaya Marketplace.** Lucaya's capacious and lively shopping complex— a dozen low-rise, pastel-painted colonial buildings whose style was influenced by traditional island homes—is on the waterfront 4 mi east of Freeport and across the street from a massive resort complex. The shopping center, whose walkways are lined with hibiscus, bougainvillea, and croton, has about 100 well-kept establishments, among them waterfront restaurants and bars, and shops that sell clothes, crystal and china, watches, jewelry, perfumes, and local arts and crafts. The marketplace's centerpiece is **Count Basie Square,** where live bands often perform Bahamian music, jazz, and gospel in the gazebo bandstand. Lively outdoor watering holes line the square, which is also *the* place to celebrate the holidays: a tree-lighting ceremony takes place in the festively decorated spot and fireworks highlight the New Year's Eve party there. ⊠ *Sea Horse Rd.* ☎ *242/373–8446* ⊕ *www.portlucaya.com* ⊙ *Mon.–Sat. 10–6.*

❹ **Underwater Explorers Society (UNEXSO).** One of the world's most respected diving facilities, UNEXSO welcomes more than 50,000 individuals each year and trains hundreds of them in scuba diving. Their newest offering, Mini-B Shallow Water Scuba Diving, is a three-tier program for beginners. Mini-B participants use a lightweight and compact scuba kit for short pool and reef dives (up to 20–30 feet). UNEXSO's facilities include a 17-foot-deep training pool with windows that look out on the harbor, changing rooms and showers, docks, equipment rental, and an air-tank filling station. ⊠ *On wharf at Port Lucaya MarketPl.* ☎ *242/373–1244 or 800/992–3483* ⊕ *www.unexso.com* 🖃 *Mini-B adventures $25–$79; dives from $35, night dives $49, dolphin dives $159, shark dives $89* ⊙ *Daily 8–5.*

Fodor'sChoice
★

## Beyond Freeport-Lucaya

Grand Bahama Island narrows at picturesque West End, once Grand Bahama's capital and still home to descendants of the island's early settlers.

Little seaside villages, with concrete block houses painted in bright blue and pastel yellow, fill in the landscape between Freeport and West End. Many of these settlements are more than 100 years old. Their names derive from geographical features or the original homesteaders' surnames, and most residents are descendants of these founders. On your way back east, veer left at the Eight Mile Rock settlement intersection to drive past the town's colonial structures. The seaside backroad eventually returns you to the main road.

The East End is Grand Bahama's "back-to-nature" side. The road east from Lucaya is long, flat, and mostly straight. It cuts through vast pine forest to reach McLean's Town, the end of the road. Curly tailed lizards, raccoons, pelicans, and other native creatures populate this part of the island.

### Sights to See

**⑦** **Lucayan National Park.** In this 40-acre seaside land preserve, trails and

Fodor'sChoice  elevated walkways wind through a natural forest of wild tamarind and

★  gumbo-limbo trees, past an observation platform, a mangrove swamp, sheltered pools containing rare marine species, and what is believed to be the largest explored underwater cave system in the world (7 mi long). You can enter the caves at two access points; one is closed during bat nursing season (June and July). Twenty miles east of Lucaya, the park contains examples of the island's five ecosystems: beach, sandy or white-land coppice (hardwood forest), mangroves, rocky coppice, and pine forest. Across the road, trails and boardwalks lead through pine forest and mangrove swamp to Gold Rock Beach, a beautiful, lightly populated strand of white sand, aquamarine sea, and coral reef. Signs along the trail detail the park's distinctive features. ⊠ *Grand Bahama Hwy.* ☎ *242/352–5438* ✉ *$3; tickets must be purchased in advance at Rand Nature Centre* ⊙ *Daily 8:30–4:30.*

# BEACHES

Some 60 mi of magnificent, pristine stretches of sand extend between Freeport-Lucaya and McLean's Town, the island's isolated eastern end. Most are used only by people who live in adjacent settlements along the way. The outlying beaches have no public facilities, so beachgoers often headquarter at one of the local beach bars. Lucaya hotels have their own beaches and watersports activities, and guests at Freeport hotels are shuttled free to nearby beaches. **Xanadu** is a mile-long strip of white sand with

Fodor'sChoice  an outdoor bar and watersports concessions. **Taíno** appeals to families, wa-

★  tersports enthusiasts, and partyers alike. Its powdery, white sands stretch long and wide, and its beach bars, conch shacks, and watersports concessions provide the makings for a perfect activity-oriented day at the beach.

Local residents prefer the beach at **William's Town,** south of Freeport (off East Sunrise Highway and down Beachway Drive) and east of Xanadu Beach, where sandy solitude is broken only by the occasional passing of horseback riders from Pinetree Stables at the water's edge.

East of Port Lucaya, several delightful beaches run along the **South Shore—Churchill Beach, Smith's Point, Fortune Beach,** and lesser-known **Barbary Beach.** Farther east, at the end of the trail from the Lucayan Na-

★  tional Park, you'll find **Gold Rock Beach,** which is a 20-mi drive from the Lucaya hotels. On the West End, snorkeling beachgoers escape by tour to **Paradise Cove.**

# Grand Bahama Island

LITTLE BAHAMA BANK

Northwest Providence Channel

West End
Boole Bay Village
Queen's Hwy.
Holmes Rock
Eight Mile Rock
Hawksbill Creek
Freeport Harbour
Pinder's Point
Freeport International Airport
Freeport
Bahamas National Trust Rand Nature Centre
Sea House Rd.
William's Town
Xanadu Beach
Midshipman Rd.
Lucaya
Parrot Jungle's Garden of the Groves
Smith's Point
Theo's Wreck
Churchill Beach
Taino Beach
Barbary Beach
Sharp Rock's Point
Ben's Blue Hole
Fortune Beach
Lucayan National Park
Grand Bahama Hwy.
Bevan Town
Freetown
Gold Rock Beach
High Rock
Water Cay
Riding Point
Pelican Point
Rocky Creek
McLean's Town
Sweeting's Cay
Dover Sound

0    10 miles
0    15 km

## KEY

Dive Sites

Exploring Sights

# WHERE TO EAT

Grand Bahama Island's restaurants afford rich opportunities for sampling native cuisine. Practically every restaurant has something made with conch on the menu—the mollusk is both a Bahamian icon and a staple. In the culinary hierarchy of the Bahamian islands, Grand Bahama ranks slightly below Nassau in both sophistication and price, but well above many of the Out Islands in variety and creativity.

You'll find many options in Freeport and Lucaya, from elegant hotel dining rooms and charming waterside cafés to local hangouts and familiar fast-food chains. Menus often combine Continental, American, and Bahamian fare. A native fish fry takes place on Wednesday evening at Smith's Point, east of Lucaya (taxi drivers know the way). Here you can sample fresh fish, sweet-potato bread, conch salad, and all the fixings cooked outdoors at the beach. It's a great opportunity to meet local residents and taste real Bahamian cuisine—and there's no better setting than seaside under the pines and palms. On Friday nights, locals hit Churchill Garden Bar next to the International Bazaar for its well-loved "Mini Crab Fest," featuring land crab dishes indigenous to Andros Island and Gully Wash—a local libation consisting of green coconut juice, sweetened condensed milk, and gin. An automatic 15% gratuity is added to most dining tabs. (⇨ Dining *in* Smart Travel Tips A to Z at the back of the book for general information and price categories)

## Freeport

### American

¢–$$ ✕ **Café Michel's.** Stop by this unpretentious bistro for a light meal or snack. The alfresco tables, with red umbrellas and tablecloths, place you in an ideal people-watching location just off the Bazaar's main promenade; the cozy interior is more intimate. The menu has American and Bahamian dishes such as cracked conch, hamburgers, fried chicken, and lobster tail. ⊠ *International Bazaar* ☎ *242/352–2191* ▤ *AE, MC, V.*

### Bahamian

★ ¢–$$ ✕ **Becky's Restaurant & Lounge.** This popular eatery opens at 7 AM and may be the best place in town to fuel up before a full day of gambling or shopping. Its diner-style booths provide a comfortable backdrop for the inexpensive menu of traditional Bahamian and American food, from conch salad and curried mutton to seafood or a BLT. Pancakes, eggs, and special Bahamian breakfasts—"stew" fish, "boil" fish, or chicken souse (the latter two are soups flavored with lime), with johnnycake or grits—are served all day. ⊠ *E. Beach Dr. and E. Sunrise Hwy.* ☎ *242/352–5247* ▤ *D, MC, V.*

★ ¢–$ ✕ **Geneva's Place.** Geneva's sets the standard for home-cooked Bahamian food. The interior is nothing fancy: a former Italian restaurant whose brick walls have been painted light blue, with a canal-scene mural, wrought-iron grating, and grape leaves. Cook and owner Geneva Munroe will prepare your grouper broiled, steamed, or fried; your pork chops fried or steamed; your conch cracked, or, for breakfast, stewed. Every-

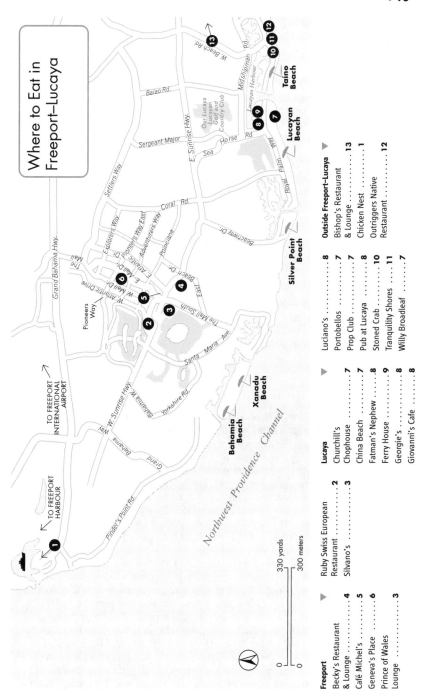

# Where to Eat in Freeport-Lucaya

**Freeport**

Becky's Restaurant & Lounge ......... **4**
Café Michel's ......... **5**
Geneva's Place ......... **6**
Prince of Wales Lounge ......... **3**
Ruby Swiss European Restaurant ......... **2**
Silvano's ......... **3**

**Lucaya**

Churchill's Chophouse ......... **7**
China Beach ......... **7**
Fatman's Nephew ......... **8**
Ferry House ......... **9**
Georgie's ......... **8**
Giovanni's Cafe ......... **8**
Luciano's ......... **8**
Portobellos ......... **7**
Prop Club ......... **7**
Pub at Lucaya ......... **8**
Stoned Crab ......... **10**
Tranquility Shores ......... **11**
Willy Broadleaf ......... **7**

**Outside Freeport-Lucaya**

Bishop's Restaurant & Lounge ......... **13**
Chicken Nest ......... **1**
Outriggers Native Restaurant ......... **12**

thing comes with a big helping of side dishes. The peas 'n' rice are delicious. ⊠ *E. Mall Dr. and Kipling La.* ☎ *242/352–5085* ▭ *D, MC, V.*

### Continental

**$–$$$** ✕ **Silvano's.** In a bright, circular, sunshine-yellow dining room, Silvano's serves a wide selection of Italian-style fish, pasta, and meat. Specialties here include table-flamed filet mignon, veal scallopine, vegetable lasagna, and linguine al pesto. They're located across the street from International Bazaar in a compound of eateries known as Ranfurly Circus, where you'll find some of the best dining options in the downtown area. ⊠ *Ranfurly Circus, opposite International Bazaar* ☎ *242/352–5111* ▭ *AE, D, MC, V* ☉ *Closed Sun. May–Dec.*

**$–$$** ✕ **Ruby Swiss European Restaurant.** The extensive continental menu has seafood, steak, veal, and an all-you-can-eat spaghetti bar for $9.75. Specialties include steak Dianne (flamed with cognac), Wiener schnitzel, lobster thermidor, and desserts flambéed tableside. The wine list's 50-odd varieties represent six countries. Dinnertime guitar music adds a romantic touch to the bustling dining hall scene. Snacks are served into the wee hours. ⊠ *W. Sunrise Hwy., across from Crowne Plaza Tower at Royal Oasis* ☎ *242/352–8507* ▭ *AE, D, DC, MC, V.*

### English

**¢–$** ✕ **Prince of Wales Lounge.** This local favorite is an authentic English-style pub that serves fish-and-chips, sandwiches, steaks, sweet-and-sour baby back ribs, and draft ale in a medieval setting. The adjacent sports bar specializes in pizza. ⊠ *Ranfurly Circus, opposite International Bazaar* ☎ *242/352–2700* ▭ *AE, D, MC, V.*

## Lucaya

### American

**$$$** ✕ **Churchill's Chophouse.** Unwind in the handsome wood piano bar before enjoying a meal in the dining room, surrounded by white wainscoting and French windows. The atrium ceiling over the circular room illuminates Bahamian life with mural scenes and heavy chandeliers, and the atmosphere evokes the plantation era. In this elegant setting, the menu focuses on beef, but escapes single-mindedness with lamb shank bourguignonne, potato-crusted sea bass with cranberry merlot reduction, a lobster surf-and-turf ($68), and other dishes of equal sophistication. ⊠ *Westin Lighthouse Pointe, Our Lucaya Beach & Golf Resort* ☎ *242/373–1333* ▭ *AE, D, DC, MC, V* ☉ *Closed Sun. and Wed. No lunch.*

**☾ $–$$** ✕ **Prop Club.** Spare bits of recovered aircraft wreckage and brightly painted chairs accent this casual resort hangout, which becomes a lively dance floor by night. Giant glass-paned garage doors open to make this an indoor-outdoor place where you can dine and party on the beach. The menu is casual, with offerings like pizza, jerk burger, blackened grouper, and baby back ribs. ⊠ *Westin Breakers Cay, Our Lucaya Beach & Golf Resort* ☎ *242/373–1333* ▭ *AE, D, DC, MC, V.*

**☾ ¢–$$** ✕ **Tranquility Shores.** The primary purpose here is to provide a place for visitors staying off the beach to have their day of fun in the sand. Besides a complete menu of water-sports activities, Tranquility Shores serves a well-rounded selection of American and Bahamian culinary favorites such as Philly cheesesteak sandwiches, conch fritters, grilled grouper, drunken wahoo (local fish fried with Bahamian-brewed Kalik beer batter), and lamb chops. Go for Friday's happy hour (5–9) and enjoy free hors d'oeuvres and drink specials. ⊠ *Taíno Beach, 5 Jolly Roger Dr.* ☎ *242/374–4461* ⊕ *www.tranquilityshores.com* ▤ *AE, D, MC, V* ⊗ *Closed Mon. No dinner Sun.–Thurs.*

> **DID YOU KNOW?**
>
> The local brew, Kalik, gets its name from the sound of the cowbells used at Junkanoo, the islands' holiday-time costumed celebration.

### Bahamian

**$–$$** ✕ **Georgie's.** Sit alfresco at this pleasant, casual spot on the harbor at Port Lucaya Marketplace; it's open for breakfast, happy hour and snacks, lunch, and dinner. Local favorites such as barbecue chicken, conch fritters, lobster, and grouper come with delicious coleslaw and peas 'n' rice. Georgie's cracked conch is the real thing. Inside, the decor is plain, but it's refreshingly air-conditioned. ⊠ *Port Lucaya MarketPl.* ☎ *242/ 373–8513* ▤ *AE, D, MC, V.*

★ **¢–$$** ✕ **Fatman's Nephew.** Owner Stanley Simmons named his restaurant for the two rotund uncles who taught him the trade. One of the better spots to dine in Port Lucaya, this place serves substantial Bahamian fare. The regular menu is somewhat limited, featuring local dishes such as Bahamian turtle, cracked conch, and curried mutton. A blackboard listing a full complement of daily seafood specials widens the offerings. The best seating is on the L-shape outdoor terrace overlooking the waterway and marina. ⊠ *Port Lucaya Market Pl.* ☎ *242/373–8520* ▤ *AE, D, MC, V.*

### Contemporary

**$–$$$$** ✕ **Ferry House.** If you're looking for creative gourmet on Grand Bahama Island, this is the place. Its changing menu—always well executed—leans toward the experimental with dishes like butternut squash soup, octopus salad with kimchi vinaigrette, caribou, three types of lobster, and mixed seafood pan au gratin. A daily tasting menu includes seven courses for $95. Located inside Bell Channel, Ferry House serves as the main restaurant for the Pelican Bay at Lucaya resort, and the windowed dining room hangs over the water just outside the Port Lucaya Marketplace. ⊠ *Port Lucaya Market Pl.* ☎ *242/373–1595* ▤ *AE, MC, V* ⊗ *No dinner Mon.*

Fodor'sChoice ★

### Eclectic

**$** ✕ **Willy Broadleaf.** For an adventure in dining, graze the breakfast buffet line here and sample global dishes such as wild boar sausage, Bahamian specialties, and marvelous pastries. When you've filled your plate, sit down to eat in a Mediterranean marketplace, African village, maharajah's dining hall, Mexican courtyard, or Egyptian market. Breakfast is served from 6:30 to 11. ⊠ *Westin Breaker's Cay, Our Lucaya Beach & Golf Resort* ☎ *242/373–1333* ▤ *AE, DC, MC, V* ⊗ *No lunch or dinner.*

### English

¢–$$  ✕ **Pub at Lucaya.** On the Port Lucaya waterfront, this amiable pub has a reputation for dependable English fare, such as bangers 'n' mash and shepherd's and steak-and-ale pies. You also can't go wrong with the frenched lamb chops, Bahamian lobster tail, or strip sirloin. Lunchtime brings burgers, pasta, and deli sandwiches. The nautical decor incorporates antiques, heavy rustic tables, and ersatz Tiffany lamps suspended from a wood-beam ceiling. Ask for a table on the outside terrace. ⊠ *Port Lucaya Market Pl.* ☎ *242/373–8450* ▭ *AE, DC, MC, V.*

### French

$$–$$$  ✕ **Luciano's.** Linens, soft candlelight, and a twinkling view of the harbor add to the glamour and romance of this sophisticated, second-story
Fodor'sChoice Port Lucaya restaurant. Luciano's has set the standard for fine dining
★ here for many years. Its menu speaks French with English subtitles, including such specialties as *filet au poivre vert* (fillet with green peppercorn sauce), scampi flambé, Dover sole, stuffed quail, and chateaubriand for two, served in the formal, subdued dining room or on the verandah overlooking the marina. For a big finish, order the flamed crêpes suzette for two. ⊠ *Port Lucaya MarketPl.* ☎ *242/373–9100* ▭ *AE, D, MC, V* ⊘ *Closed Sun.*

### Italian

$–$$  ✕ **Giovanni's Cafe.** Tucked away under the bougainvillea at Port Lucaya Marketplace, this corner café evokes a bit of Italy. As you relax on the patio or study the giant mural of an Italian waterway inside the café, treat yourself to local seafood such as lobster in white wine cream sauce and pan-fried grouper in lemon-wine sauce. Full-flavored, classic Italian dishes include spaghetti carbonara and chicken marsala. If you're on a budget, come between 4 and 6 for $10 early-bird pasta dinners. ⊠ *Port Lucaya Market Pl.* ☎ *242/373–9107* ▭ *AE, MC, V* ⊘ *Closed Sun.*

$–$$  ✕ **Portobellos.** The house specialty, seafood spaghetti, unites the best of the Bahamian seas with Mediterranean flair. Other imaginative offerings, all served on colorful dishware, include lobster and asparagus ravioli, grilled marinated veal, and penne with veal and spinach. Sit indoors among classic stone arches or outdoors with a view of the ocean. ⊠ *Westin Breakers Cay, Our Lucaya Beach & Golf Resort* ☎ *242/373–1333* ▭ *AE, D, DC, MC, V.*

### Pan-Asian

★ $–$$  ✕ **China Beach.** Food in this sleek, elegant dining room with its exhibition kitchen extends far beyond Chinese, incorporating elements of Vietnamese, Korean, Thai, Indonesian, Malaysian, and other Pacific Rim styles. From the monthly changing menu, sample sushi, Japanese dumplings, stir-fried conch, Szechuan prawns, and other Asian specialties. ⊠ *Westin Breakers Cay, Our Lucaya Beach & Golf Resort* ☎ *242/373–1333* ▭ *AE, D, DC, MC, V* ⊘ *Closed Mon. and Tues. No lunch.*

### Seafood

$$  ✕ **Stoned Crab.** This long-standing, pyramidal-roof restaurant faces one of the island's loveliest stretches of sand, Taíno Beach. Don't miss the scrumptiously sweet stone crab claws and lobsters, both locally caught. Crabs of

all varieties are the specialty; try stone and snow crab, stuffed crab, and crab cake in the crab sampler. Other specialties include swordfish, grouper, and yellowfin tuna. For meat-lovers, there's also veal loin, strip steak, and more. The sound of the waves will beckon you onto the patio. ⊠ *Taíno Beach* ☎ *242/373–1442* ⊟ *AE, D, MC, V* ⊗ *No lunch Mon.*

## Outside Freeport-Lucaya

Get out of town for a taste of true Bahamian cooking. Many of the island's far-flung restaurants provide courtesy shuttles from hotels.

### Bahamian

★ ¢–$   ✕ **Bishop's Restaurant & Lounge.** A longtime favorite of locals and visitors who venture out into the East End's settlements, Bishop's serves all the Bahamian favorites with homemade goodness and a view of the sea. The cracked conch is light and crunchy; the peas 'n' rice full-flavored. ⌂ *Box F 42029, High Rock* ☎ *242/353–4515* ⊟ *D.*

¢–$   ✕ **Outriggers Native Restaurant.** For Bahamian food fixed by Bahamians, head east to the generational property of an old island family, just beyond Taíno Beach. When you stop at Gretchen Wilson's place for cracked conch, lobster tail, and barbecue chicken down-home style, you'll feel as though you're dining in someone's spotlessly clean home. Wednesday night the quiet little settlement comes to life when Outriggers throws its famous weekly fish fry. In winter the Outriggers Beach Club, across the street, serves light lunch. ⊠ *Smith's Point* ☎ *242/373–4811* ⊟ *No credit cards* ⊗ *Closed Sun. No lunch May–Dec.*

¢   ✕ **Chicken Nest.** Cousins Lovie and Rosie Nixon put together a no-nonsense menu at this simple, home-style West End spot. You can shoot pool while you wait for your order of fish, fritters, conch salad, or homemade sweet-potato bread. If you sit at the bar and order a hard drink, you get the bottle. ⊠ *Bayshore Rd., West End* ☎ *242/346–6440* ⊟ *No credit cards* ⊗ *Closed Mon.*

# WHERE TO STAY

Once a leader in exotic, glamorous resort-casino complexes, Grand Bahama is again setting the standard, with complete makeovers in Freeport, Lucaya, and the West End. You can choose from among Grand Bahama's approximately 4,000 rooms and suites, ranging from attractive one- and two-bedroom units in sprawling resort complexes to practical apartments with kitchenettes to comfortable rooms in economy-oriented establishments. The island's more extravagant hotels include the sprawling, three-prong Our Lucaya; nearby Pelican Bay; Viva Wyndham Fortuna Beach, an all-inclusive east of Lucaya; and the West End's elegant Old Bahama Bay. The latter, like many Grand Bahama resorts, caters to the boating crowd.

Small apartment complexes and time-share rentals are economical alternatives, especially if you're planning to stay for more than a few days. If you value proximity to the beach, stay at Old Bahama Bay, Xanadu, Our Lucaya, Island Seas, or Viva Wyndham Fortuna Beach, which are right on the beach. UNEXSO, Grand Bahama Island's scuba central, and Port Lucaya Marketplace are within easy walking distance of Lucaya's hotels. In 2005, Hurricane Wilma closed down Freeport's largest resort, the Royal Oasis, as well as a few other smaller properties. At press time, there was no news about the future of the Royal Oasis.

The larger hotels offer honeymoon, golfing, gambling, scuba, and other packages. Families will find that many hotels offer babysitting services and children's programs. Some establishments allow children under 12 to stay in your room for free and may not charge you for a crib or roll-away bed.

Resort and government taxes of 6%–12% are added to your hotel bill. Rates from April 15 through December 14 tend to be 25%–30% lower than those charged during the rest of the year. (⇨ Lodging *in* Smart Travel Tips A to Z at the back of the book for general information and price categories)

## Freeport

**$$** ☷ **Island Seas Resort.** This time-share property accommodates nonmembers looking for fun on the beach away from urban bustle. Balconies overlook the flowery courtyard, where thatched-roofed CoCoNuts Grog & Grub and a free-form pool with waterfalls and a swim-up bar are the centerpiece. The beach, used by guests from other non-beachside resorts, is busy with watersports activity. One- and two-bedroom rooms are done in bright modern island style. The property has 117 rooms, but not all are included in the open rental plan. ⌂ *Box F 44735, William's Town, Freeport* ☎ *242/373–1271* 🖷 *242/373–1275* ⊕ *www.islandseas.com* 🖙 *50 rooms* ♴ *Restaurant, pool, beach, boating, parasailing, bicycles, basketball, horseback riding, volleyball, bar* ▭ *D, MC, V.*

★ **$** ☷ **Best Western Castaways.** Near the action in Freeport, this property is one of the nicer budget options in the area. The coral rock–accented lobby introduces four stories of rooms in bamboo and earth and floral tones. Family friendliness is underscored by a playground next to the pool, and a beach shuttle is provided. The restaurant is open only for its famous breakfast, but there's a wide selection of other dining options within easy walking distance. ⌂ *Box F 42629, Freeport* ☎ *242/352–6682 or 800/937–8376* 🖷 *242/352–5087* ⊕ *www.castaways-resort.com* 🖙 *97 rooms, 21 suites* ♴ *Restaurant, pool, 2 bars, nightclub, babysitting, playground, laundry facilities, Internet room* ▭ *AE, D, MC, V.*

**$** ☷ **Royal Islander.** All the amenities without the sticker shock: this two-story, tin-roof, motel-style property near the International Bazaar provides free scheduled shuttle service to Xanadu Beach. The rooms have light-wood and rattan furnishings, lively tropical fabrics, framed pastel prints, and tile floors on the lower level. You'll find carpeted floors upstairs, where no-smoking rooms are available. An inviting white-and-floral lobby faces the spacious pool area. ⌂ *Box F 42549, East Mall Dr., Freeport* ☎ *242/351–6000* 🖷 *242/351–3546* 🖙 *100 rooms* ♴ *Dining room, snack bar, pool, Ping-Pong, bar, shop, travel services, no-smoking rooms* ▭ *AE, D, MC, V.*

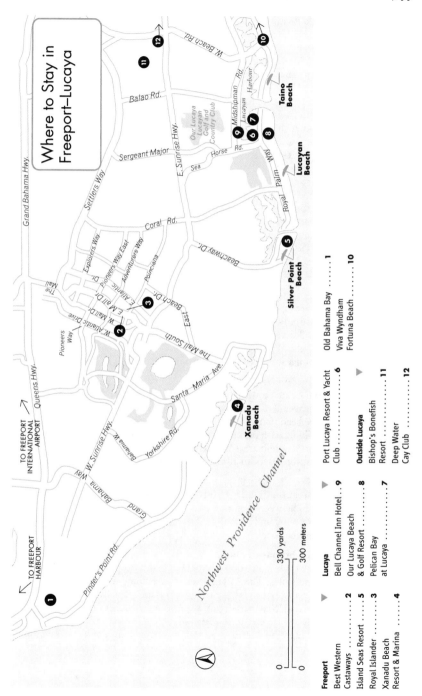

# Where to Stay in Freeport–Lucaya

0 330 yards
0 300 meters

*Northwest Providence Channel*

**Freeport**

Best Western
Castaways . . . . . . . . . . **2**
Island Seas Resort . . . . . **5**
Royal Islander . . . . . . . . **3**
Xanadu Beach
Resort & Marina . . . . . **4**

**Lucaya**

Bell Channel Inn Hotel . . **9**
Our Lucaya Beach
& Golf Resort . . . . . . . . **8**
Pelican Bay
at Lucaya . . . . . . . . . . . **7**

Port Lucaya Resort & Yacht
Club . . . . . . . . . . . . . . **6**

**Outside Lucaya**

Bishop's Bonefish
Resort . . . . . . . . . . . **11**
Deep Water
Cay Club . . . . . . . . . . **12**

Old Bahama Bay . . . . . . **1**
Viva Wyndham
Fortuna Beach . . . . . . **10**

$　🖼 **Xanadu Beach Resort & Marina.** Howard Hughes spent the last few years of his life in the penthouse suite of this landmark hotel, which he owned in the 1970s. Today the resort is making a valiant and dramatic comeback after being devastated by fire and hurricanes. The trademark pink exterior has been repainted yellow, and gold tones with arched brick accents and a fireplace now warm the lobby. Located only a few minutes from town, the property's tower (still known as the Howard Hughes Tower), pool wing, and villas overlook the oval pool and fountain, marina, parking lot, or beach. Rooms show their age but have been spruced up with a new designer look. Coconut palms sway at the wide, gorgeous beach, a three-minute walk from the hotel. Come here for watersports and beach volleyball. An on-site watersports concession has all the wet stuff your vacation needs. ⬚ *Box F 2438, Sunken Treasure Dr., Freeport* ☎ *242/352–6782* 🖷 *242/352–6299* ⊕ *www.xanadubeachhotel.com* ⬚ *137 rooms, 49 suites* ⬚ *Restaurant, snack bar, Wi-Fi, 3 tennis courts, pool, massage, beach, dive shop, dock, snorkeling, boating, jet skiing, parasailing, fishing, billiards, Ping-Pong, volleyball, 2 bars, lobby lounge, shop, babysitting, laundry facilities, Internet room, meeting rooms* ▭ *AE, D, MC, V.*

## Lucaya

$$–$$$　🖼 **Our Lucaya Beach & Golf Resort.** Grand Bahama's grandest resort
**Fodor'sChoice**　　spreads three hotels along 7½ acres of soft-sand beach (the entire resort
★　　covers 372 acres). The focus here is on dramatic play-area water features and golf. The property has a 19,000-square-foot casino, 12 restaurants, lounges, a children's camp, a first-rate spa, and a shopping complex.

🕙　**Sheraton.** Geared toward family vacationers, this resort has a water park with a sugar-mill ruins theme, complete with a zero-entry pool and water slide. The headquarters for children's programs is nearby: a bright, circular building with peekaboo windows for undetected parental spying. The resort's public areas and 511 rooms have a tropical Miami Beach flair. Sheraton offers an all-inclusive plan including alcoholic beverages year-round.

**Westin Breakers Cay.** This 10-floor high-rise resort curves like a wavy cruise ship between the other two, with rooms and suites, restaurants, a long lap pool, and a small half-moon infinity pool encasing a swim-up bar on the beach.

**Westin Lighthouse Pointe.** Two-story structures built to replicate Caribbean-style plantation manors house this property's all-water-view rooms and suites. The 21 lanai suites each come with a butler. A half-moon infinity pool clasps the property and visually blends into the ocean beyond. Stay here if you want to be farther from the hustle and bustle. ⬚ *Sea Horse La., Lucaya* ☎ *242/373–1333, 877/687–5822 in U.S.* 🖷 *242/373–8804* ⊕ *www.westin.com/ourlucaya or www.sheraton. com/ourlucaya* ⬚ *1,151 rooms, 68 suites* ⬚ *14 restaurants, 2 coffee shops, room service, in-room data ports, in-room safes, some kitchenettes,*

2

refrigerators, 2 18-hole golf courses, 4 tennis courts, pro shop, 9 pools, gym, spa, beach, snorkeling, boating, waterskiing, basketball, horseshoes, volleyball, 8 bars, casino, shops, children's programs (ages 2½–12), concierge floor, business services, meeting rooms, travel services ⊟ AE, D, DC, MC, V.

**$–$$**  ⊞ **Pelican Bay at Lucaya.** This is a truly original hotel, Caribbean with
Fodor'sChoice  a European design. A step above typical small-inn Bahamian accommo-
★  dations, Pelican Bay has a tidy, modern appeal and accommodations that overflow with character and decorative elements collected from around the world. Building exteriors are fancifully trimmed in West Indian gingerbread and latticework. Smartly furnished rooms and suites overlook the pool and whirlpool, the channel, and the marina. The newest suites have extras like rain showers, espresso machines, and boxes built into the doors to which fresh pastries are delivered each morning (a full continental breakfast is also available). Pelican Bay is next door to UNEXSO, which makes it popular with divers. It's also only steps away from Port Lucaya Marketplace. The resort has its own marina nearby, and there is a ferry shuttle to Taíno Beach. Lucaya Beach is across the street. ⌂ Box F 42654, Royal Palm Way, Freeport ☎ 242/373–9550 ⎙ 242/373–9551 ⊕ www.pelicanbayhotel.com ⇔ 89 rooms, 94 suites ⌕ 2 restaurants, in-room safes, some microwaves, refrigerators, Wi-Fi, 3 pools, outdoor hot tub, marina, bar, library, laundry facilities, business services, meeting room, no-smoking rooms ⊟ AE, D, MC, V ⦿| CP.

**$**  ⊞ **Port Lucaya Resort & Yacht Club.** Members can dock at the 50-slip marina; others pull in next door at Port Lucaya Marina. Golf carts transport guests to 10 brightly painted buildings around the Olympic-size swimming pool, hot tub, and restaurant. The rooms have garden, pool, or marina views, punctuated sparingly with rattan furniture, tile floors, large wall mirrors, and tropical floral patterns. The walk to the beach takes less than 10 minutes. At night, Port Lucaya Marketplace's celebratory sounds spill into buildings 7, 8, 9, and 10, and guests can enjoy the festivities from their balconies. ⌂ Box F 42452, Bell Channel Bay Rd., Freeport ☎ 242/373–6618 or 800/582–2921 ⎙ 242/373–6652 ⊕ www.portlucayaresort.com ⇔ 157 rooms, 3 suites ⌕ Restaurant, pool, outdoor hot tub, dock, marina, shuffleboard, volleyball, 2 bars, playground, laundry service, no-smoking floors ⊟ AE, D, MC, V.

**¢**  ⊞ **Bell Channel Inn Hotel.** Right on the water near Port Lucaya with easy access to the island's best down-under sites, this hotel is perfect for scuba-oriented travelers. The inn has its own dive shop and lodging-dive packages. The dive boat conveniently leaves from behind the hotel, and the shop is full-service with equipment rentals and certification courses. All but two of the simply furnished rooms are equipped with a small refrigerator; all have a view of the channel and Port Lucaya. The convivial restaurant-bar on property serves seafood and good spirit come happy hour each day. A small pool sits on a wood deck along the water, and the hotel provides free shuttle service to the beach at Island Seas. ⊠ Kings Rd. ⌂ Box F 43817, Freeport ☎ 242/373–1053 ⎙ 242/ 373–2886 ⊕ www.bellchannelinn.com ⇔ 32 rooms ⌕ Restaurant, some refrigerators, Wi-Fi, pool, dive shop, dock, bar ⊟ AE, D, MC, V.

## Outside Freeport-Lucaya

★ $$$$   ▦ **Deep Water Cay Club.** Ideal if you want to get away from it all and angle for bonefish, this private island has Bahamian-style one- and two-bedroom cottages. Activities center around a main lodge with a dining room, self-service bar, and tackle shop. Diversions include beaching, boating, and some of the best bonefishing in the Bahamas. Accommodations are available in three-, four-, or seven-night packages only, including meals and daily guided fishing excursions. The resort can arrange a charter flight from Florida, which lands at the property's own airstrip. ⊠ *Deep Water Cay ℗ Box 280, Richmond Hill, GA 31324 ☎ 912/756–7071 🖷 912/756–3559 ⊕ www.deepwatercay.com ⚓ 10 units ⚐ Dining room, fans, refrigerators, pool, snorkeling, boating, fishing, bar ⊟ No credit cards ⦿ AI.*

$$–$$$$   ▦ **Old Bahama Bay.** Relax and luxuriate in relative seclusion at this hotel
Fodor'sChoice   designed principally for boating vacationers. Waterfront suites, one- and
★   two-bedroom, have heavy wood furnishings and views of the beach through French doors. The suites contain wet bars, bathrobes, cooking utensils, and DVD-CD players (with a complimentary library). Although endearingly intimate and individual, Old Bahama Bay has all the amenities of a full-grown, self-contained resort, making it one of the Bahamas' top small marina properties. ✉ *Box F 42546, West End ☎ 242/350–6500 or 800/444–9469 🖷 242/346–6546 ⊕ www. oldbahamabay.com ⚓ 67 rooms, 6 2-bedroom suites ⚐ 3 restaurants, in-room safes, microwaves, refrigerators, tennis court, pool, gym, spa, snorkeling, boating, marina, fishing, bicycles, 2 bars, shop ⊟ AE, D, MC, V.*

★ ☺ $$$   ▦ **Viva Wyndham Fortuna Beach.** Popular with couples and families, this secluded resort provides a casual, low-stress, all-inclusive getaway. One price covers meals, drinks, tips, nonmotorized watersports, and nightly entertainment. A 1,200-foot private beach bustles with activity. Meals are served buffet style in the huge, gazebo-like dining pavilion or tableside at La Trattoria. Simple rooms in two-story buildings have light-wood furniture, tile floors, and balconies or porches. Kids under age 12 stay free with adults. A $1 million renovation in 2005 added a new restaurant, kid's club, and children's pool. ⊠ *Churchill Dr. and Doubloon Rd., Box F 42398, Freeport ☎ 242/373–4000, 800/996–3426 in U.S. 🖷 242/373–5555 ⊕ www.vivaresorts.com ⚓ 276 rooms ⚐ 3 restaurants, snack bar, in-room safes, 2 tennis courts, pool, outdoor hot tub, fitness classes, gym, beach, dive shop, snorkeling, windsurfing, boating, bicycles, archery, boccie, Ping-Pong, bar, dance club, theater, shops, children's programs (ages 4 and up), playground, laundry service, Internet room, meeting rooms, travel services ⊟ AE, D, MC, V ⦿ AI.*

★ $   ▦ **Bishop's Bonefish Resort.** Stay on the beach in a small community east of Lucaya, without the hefty price tags and bustle of Lucaya. Owned by Bahamian Ruben "Bishop" Roberts, the property comprises eight white-tile, spacious rooms. Bishop will arrange bonefishing excursions to the East End, feed you at his landmark restaurant, and talk politics with you at the bar. Meal packages are available. ℗ *Box F 42029, High Rock ☎ 242/353–4515 🖷 242/353–4417 ⊕ www.gbweekly.com/*

*bishopsbonefish* 🛏 *7 rooms* ♿ *Restaurant, refrigerators, beach, fishing, bar* ▭ *AE, MC.*

## Time-Sharing

2

Contact any of the following for information about rentals. For information about other time-share houses, apartments, and condominiums, check with the Grand Bahama Island Tourism Board.

**Freeport Beach Resort & Club** (✉ Box F 2514, Freeport ☎ 242/352–5371). The 50 suites are in a garden setting close to the International Bazaar and the Royal Oasis Casino. Owners have golf privileges at Royal Oasis courses.

**Mayfield Beach and Tennis Club** (✉ Box F 458, Freeport ☎ 242/352–9776). The rentals here consist of 10 apartments that share a pool, small beach, and tennis court on Port-of-Call Drive at Xanadu Beach.

**Ocean Reef Yacht Club & Resort** (✉ Box F 42639, Freeport ☎ 242/373–4661 ⊕ www.oryc.com). These 63 one- to three-bedroom apartments are midway between the International Bazaar and the Lucayan Beach hotels. The resort has a marina, tennis courts, and pools.

# NIGHTLIFE & THE ARTS

## Nightlife

The casino at Our Lucaya and the shopping-dining complex across the street at Port Lucaya are among the island's top attractions. At Isle of Capri Casino, you can try your luck with state-of-the-art slot machines, craps and blackjack tables, roulette, and baccarat. Tables open at 10 AM. There's no specific dress code, although bathing suits and bare feet are not permitted. You must be at least 18 years old to go into the casino, and residents of the Bahamas are not permitted to gamble. Photography is prohibited.

For noncasino evening and late-night entertainment, Port Lucaya is filled with restaurants and bars, and there's often live entertainment in the middle square. Another option is finding a bonfire beach party or taking a cruise on a sunset party boat. You can also find nightclubs near International Bazaar; they're generally open from 8 or 9 until 3. You may even be able to find some excitement without leaving your resort— many hotels organize their own nighttime entertainment.

### Casino

★ **Isle of Capri Casino** (✉ Our Lucaya Beach & Golf Resort, Sea Horse La. ☎ 888/687–4753 in U.S. ⊕ www.isleofcapricasino.com/Lucaya/), a 35,000-square-foot, bright, tropically decorated casino, has nearly 400 slot machines and 21 game tables consisting of mini-baccarat, Caribbean stud and three-card poker, craps, blackjack, and roulette. There's also a special "Jewel of The Isle" room, featuring high-limit table games and track and sports book betting. The Cove restaurant serves bistro-style fare. The casino is open from 10 AM until 2 AM daily; slot machines are open 24 hours on weekends.

CLOSE UP

# Shaking & Scraping to the Sounds of Bahamian Music

THE RADIO CRACKLES, THE DJ PUTS THE NEEDLE TO THE VINYL, or the band begins to play. The upbeat pulse of Bahamian music circulates through the room. Suddenly you find yourself moving in place, and then across the floor.

Caribbean music seems to create an undeniably contagious urge to dance. Perhaps it's the strong underlying rhythm common to most island music of this region, including the immensely popular **calypso,** originally from Trinidad, and **reggae,** which spread to nearby islands from Jamaica. Both have roots in the drum beats of Africa, which were brought by slaves and spiked with French, British, Spanish, and Portuguese flavors from shipmasters and plantation owners. In the Bahamas, though, the dominant sound is home-grown **soca.**

The fundamental component of soca, calypso, and reggae is the ¼ beat, the base upon which the melody is built. Whereas calypso and reggae emphasize the downbeat, soca music accentuates all four beats evenly—creating tunes that are catchy and easy to dance to. A good Bahamian band can play all three rhythms, often combining them to create a hybrid effect. It's not uncommon to hear a cover of a Bob Marley reggae song in soca style, or a soca-inspired rendition of Harry Belafonte's well-known calypso tune "Maryann."

Soca music has many faces. In some cases its closest relative is calypso, other times it's reggae, dub, ragga, or even hip hop. A single keyboard—or a full symphony orchestra—can create soca. The formula for most contemporary soca songs is a simple melodic line played on a keyboard or an electric guitar, aggressively rapped lyrics, and that characteristic driving rhythm, played on either a beat machine or a drum.

The drums that are so crucial to Bahamian and Caribbean music come in a myriad of forms. Popular with Caribbean bands are the steel pan, originally constructed out of 55-gallon oil drums, and the conga, often associated with Latin music but played throughout the world. The traditional Bahamian drum is a handmade goatskin-covered instrument. It's the mainstay of another well-known Bahamian sound, **rake and scrape** music.

Rake and scrape is typically made using recycled objects. An ordinary saw held in a musician's lap, then bent and scraped, becomes an instrument. Plastic juice bottles are filled with pigeon peas, painted in bright colors, and turned into maracas. Add a goatskin drum, and you have all you need for a rake and scrape ensemble, although many bands now add a guitar, saxophone, or both.

There's a **Rake and Scrape Festival** each June on Cat Island, in which dozens of bands from all over the Caribbean perform. Some people view the festival as an extremely important event, given that rake and scrape is often seen as a dying art. To counter this trend, many of the old-time players teach at local schools to keep the tradition alive for the next generation of Bahamians.

### Nightclubs

★ **Bahama Mama Cruises** (✉ Superior Watersports ☎ 242/373–7863) has some of the best nightlife in Grand Bahama. In addition to sunset "booze cruises," Bahama Mama offers a surf-and-turf dinner with a colorful "native" show (a local term used to indicate entertainment with a traditional cultural flair); $69 for adults, $45 for children (ages 2–12). The Sunset Cruise and Show is $39. Reservations are essential. The dinner cruise is offered Monday, Wednesday, and Friday 6–9 (October–March) or 6:30–9:30 (April–September); the Sunset Cruise and Show runs Monday, Wednesday, and Friday on the same time schedule.

**Club Amnesia** (✉ Across from International Bazaar on East Mall Dr. ☎ 242/351–2582) is one of the hot spots around International Bazaar; it rocks weekend nights with live entertainment and a youthful crowd.

**Harbour Room Night Club** (✉ Port Lucaya MarketPl. ☎ 242/374–4466) overlooks the marina. Hit the floor Tuesday through Saturday and groove to a menu of calypso, salsa, rock, and oldies.

**Prop Club Sports Bar & Dance Club** (✉ Our Lucaya Beach & Golf Resort ☎ 242/373–1333) hosts live music that propels guests out to the giant dance floor, plus karaoke on Tuesday and Thursday at 9 PM. Seating is indoors as well as outdoors on the beach. Open daily for lunch and dinner and nightly entertainment.

## The Arts

### Theater

**Freeport Players' Guild** (☎ 242/352–5533), a nonprofit repertory company, produces Bahamian and American comedies, musicals, and dramas in the 450-seat Regency Theatre during its September–June season.

**Grand Bahama Players** (☎ 242/373–2299) perform at Regency Theatre, staging cultural productions by Bahamian, West Indian, and North American playwrights.

**Port Lucaya Marketplace** (✉ Sea Horse Rd. ☎ 242/373–8446), which opens daily at 10, has a stage that becomes lively after dark, with calypso music and other performances at Count Basie Square (ringed by three popular hangouts: the Corner Bar, the Daiquiri Bar, and the Pub at Port Lucaya).

HERE'S WHERE
The last time locals spotted pirates on Grand Bahama Island was in 2005 when Johnny Depp and his crew were filming two sequels to *Pirates of the Caribbean*. They used a special device in Golf Rock Creek at one of the world's largest open-water filming tanks to give the illusion that the pirate ship was pitching and yawing.

# SPORTS & THE OUTDOORS

## Amusement Parks

**Water World** has two scenic, well-maintained 18-hole courses of miniature golf set among waterfalls and water holes, plus a restaurant, 24-lane bowling alley, video arcade, pool tables, and ice-cream parlor. An

18-hole round of minigolf will set you back $8; bowling is $5 per game. ⊠ *E. Sunrise Hwy. and Britannia Blvd.* ☎ 242/373–2197 ☉ *Miniature golf: daily 10 AM–11 PM; bowling alley: Mon.–Sat. 9 AM–2 AM, Sun. noon–2 AM.*

## Bicycling

By virtue of its flat terrain, broad avenues, and long, straight stretches of highway, Grand Bahama is perfect for bicycling. In November, the island hosts the annual Conchman Triathlon, comprising a 1K swim, 25K bike ride, and a 5K run. When biking, wear sunblock, carry a bottle of water, and look left. Inexpensive bicycle rentals (about $20 a day plus deposit) are available from some resorts, and the Viva Wyndham Fortuna Beach allows guests free use of bicycles.

For a biking tour along quiet beaches and settlements, contact **Grand Bahama Nature Tours** (☎ 866/440–4542 or 242/373–2485 ⊕ www.gbntours.com). The five-hour tour rides along 20 mi of beach and road for $79 per person, including a restaurant lunch.

You can rent a bicycle from **Kayak Nature Tours** (⊠ Queen's Cove ☎ 242/373–2485 or 866/440–4542 ⊕ www.grandbahamanaturetours.com).

## Boating & Fishing

### Charters

Private boat charters for up to four people cost $250–$500 for a half day and $350 and up for a full day. Bahamian law limits the catching of game fish to six dolphinfish, kingfish, or wahoo per person per day.

★ **Capt. Phil & Mel's Bonefishing Guide Services** (⊠ McLean's Town ☎ 242/353–3960 or 877/613–2454 ⊕ www.bahamasbonefishing.net) provides a colorful and expert foray into the specialized world of bonefishing. A whole day (eight hours) for up to two people will run you $400, transportation included; a half day costs $300.

**Reef Tours Ltd.** (⊠ Port Lucaya MarketPl. ☎ 242/373–5880) offers sportfishing for four to six people on custom boats. Equipment and bait are provided free. All vessels are licensed, inspected, and insured. Trips run from 8:30 to 12:30 and from 1 to 5, weather permitting ($100 per angler, $50 per spectator). Full-day trips are also available, as are bottom fishing excursions, glass-bottom boat tours, snorkeling trips, and sailing-snorkeling cruises. Reservations are essential.

### Marinas

**Lucayan Marina Village** (⊠ Midshipman Rd., Port Lucaya ☎ 242/373–8888 ⊕ www.lucayanmarinavillage.com) offers complimentary ferry service to Port Lucaya; the marina has 150 slips accommodating boats up to 200 feet long, a fuel dock, customs and immigrations offices, swimming pools, and a bar and grill.

**Old Bahama Bay** (⊠ West End ☎ 242/350–6500) has 72 slips to accommodate yachts up to 120 feet long. Facilities include a customs and immigration office, fuel, showers, laundry, and electric, cable, and water hookups.

**Port Lucaya Marina** (✉ Port Lucaya MarketPl. ☎ 242/373–9090) offers a broad range of watersports and has 80 slips for vessels no longer than 190 feet.

**Xanadu Marina and Beach Resort** (✉ Sunken Treasure Dr., Freeport ☎ 242/352–6783 Ext. 1333) has 400 feet of dockage and 77 slips; it's an official port of entry.

## Cricket

For a taste of true Bahamian sports, visit the **Lucaya Cricket Club** (✉ Baloa Rd., Lucaya ☎ 242/373–1460). If you feel like joining in, go to training sessions on Tuesday, Thursday, or Sunday. The clubhouse has a bar, gym, and changing rooms. Tournaments take place in April and November.

## Fitness Centers

**Grand Bahama Fitness Centre** (✉ E. Atlantic Dr. off E. Sunrise Hwy., Freeport ☎ 242/352–7867) offers weight and cardio machines, aerobic and yoga classes, and a free nursery. Fees are $8 per day, $20 per week.

**Olympic Fitness Center** (✉ Coral Beach Hotel, Lucaya ☎ 242/373–8181) has Universal machines, weights, and aerobics classes overlooking the hotel's pool. Costs are $7 per day, $20 per week.

★ **Senses Spa** (✉ Our Lucaya Beach & Golf Resort, Lucaya ☎ 242/350–5281) has state-of-the-art cardio and exercise equipment, including free weights, a spinning studio, and fitness classes. The fee is $15 for nonguests per day, which includes use of the sauna facilities.

## Golf

Because Grand Bahama is such a large island, it can afford long fairways puddled with lots of water and fraught with challenge. Two championship golf courses at Our Lucaya and one 9-hole course constitute a major attraction on the island. The Jim McLean School of Golf has replaced the Butch Harmon facility at Our Lucaya. The Our Lucaya Lucayan Course hosts the Breitling Crystal Pro-Am in January. Note that prices tend to be lower in the off-season (mid-May–mid-December).

**Fortune Hills Golf & Country Club** is a 3,453-yard, 9-hole, par-36 course—a Dick Wilson and Joe Lee design—with a restaurant, bar, and pro shop. ✉ *E. Sunrise Hwy., Lucaya* ☎ *242/373–2222* 🏌 *$53 for 9 holes, $70 for 18 holes, cart included. Club rental $14 for 9 holes, $18 for 18 holes.*

Fodor'sChoice **Our Lucaya Lucayan Course,** designed by Dick Wilson, is a dramatic 6,824-
★ yard, par-72, 18-hole course featuring tree-lined holes and fast, well-bunkered greens. The 18th hole has a double lake, and a new clubhouse is being built nearby. The property is the Jim McLean School of Golf's first international location. These state-of-the-art instruction facilities include a practice putting green with bunker and chipping areas, covered teaching bays, and a teaching seminar area. A shared electric cart is included in greens fees. ✉ *Our Lucaya Beach & Golf Resort, Lucaya* ☎ *242/373–1066 or 242/373–1333* 🏌 *$120 for guests, $140 for nonguests.*

**Our Lucaya Reef Course** is a par-72, 6,930-yard course designed by Robert Trent Jones Jr., with lots of water, wide fairways flanked by strategically placed bunkers, and a tricky dogleg left on the 18th hole. ⊠ *Our Lucaya Beach & Golf Resort, Lucaya* ☎ *242/373–2002* ⊠ *$120 for guests, $140 for nonguests.*

## Horseback Riding

★ **Pinetree Stables** runs trail and beach rides Tuesday–Sunday twice a day. All two-hour trail rides are accompanied by a guide—no previous riding experience is necessary. Reservations are essential. ⊠ *Beachway Dr., Freeport* ☎ *242/373–3600* ⊕ *www.bahamasvg.com/pinetree.html* ⊠ *$75 for a 2-hr beach ride* ☉ *Closed Mon.*

## Kayaking

Many resorts rent kayaks for playing in the waves; for more serious adventures, your hotel can hook you up with an outfitter.

★ **Kayak Nature Tours** (⊠ Queen's Cove, Freeport ☎ 242/373–2485 or 866/440–4542 ⊕ www.grandbahamanaturetours.com) leads group kayaking tours of Lucayan National Park and other custom tours. (⇨ Ecotours section in Grand Bahama Island Essentials for more information) **Ocean Motion Watersports** (⊠ Our Lucaya Resorts, Freeport ☎ 242/374–2425 or 242/373–2139 ⊕ www.oceanmotionbahamas.com) rents one- and two-person sea kayaks for $20–$25 per hour.

## Parasailing

**Ocean Motion Watersports** (⊠ Our Lucaya, Freeport ☎ 242/374–2425 or 242/373–2139) charges $60 for its flights from Lucaya Beach. It also has Hobie Cat and wave runner rentals, banana boat rides, and a water trampoline.
**Paradise Watersports** (⊠ Island Seas Resort, Freeport ☎ 242/373–4001) has parasailing tow boats and offers five-minute flights for $50.

## Personal Watercraft

**Ocean Motion Watersports** (⊠ Our Lucaya, Freeport ☎ 242/374–2425 or 242/373–2139 ⊕ www.oceanmotionbahamas.com) rents waverunners for $60 per half hour and conducts one-hour guided tours for $120 per one- to two-person craft.
★ **Tranquility Shores** (⊠ Taíno Beach ☎ 242/374–4460 ⊕ tranquilityshores. com) offers paddleboats, water bikes, kayaks, and snorkel equipment. They also have lunch and happy hour specials.

## Scuba Diving

An extensive reef system runs along Little Bahama Bank's edge; sea gardens, caves, and colorful reefs rim the bank all the way from the West End to Freeport-Lucaya and beyond. The variety of dive sites suits everyone from the novice to the advanced diver. The island is home to UNEXSO, considered one of the finest diving schools and marine research facilities in the world. It also made shark diving synonymous with Grand Bahama Island.

Grand Bahama Island offers dive sites from 10 to 100-plus feet deep. **Ben's Blue Hole** is a horseshoe-shape ledge overlooking a blue hole in 40 to 60 feet of water. **Pygmy Caves,** for moderately experienced divers, provides a formation of overgrown ledges that cut into the reef. **Sea Hunt** site is a shallow dive and is named for the *Sea Hunt* television show, portions of which were filmed here. One of Grand Bahama Island's signature dive sites, made famous by the UNEXSO dive operation, **Shark Junction** is a 45-foot dive where 4- to 6-foot reef sharks hang out, along with moray eels, stingrays, nurse sharks, and grouper. UNEXSO provides orientation and a shark feeding with its dives here. **Spid City** has an aircraft wreck, dramatic coral formations, blue parrotfish, and an occasional shark. You'll dive about 40 to 60 feet down. For divers with some experience, **Theo's Wreck,** a 228-foot cement hauler, was sunk in 1982 in 100 feet of water.

**Caribbean Divers** (✉ Bell Channel Inn, opposite Port Lucaya ☎ 242/373–9111 ⊕ www.bellchannelinn.com) offers guided tours; NAUI, PADI, and SSI instruction; and equipment rental. A resort course allows you to use equipment in a pool and then in a closely supervised open dive for $89. A one-tank dive costs $35. Shark-feeding (two-tank) dives are $90.

Fodor'sChoice **UNEXSO (Underwater Explorers Society)** (✆ Box F 2433, Port Lucaya Marketplace ☎ 242/373–1244 or 800/992–3483 ⊕ www.unexso.com), a world-renowned scuba-diving facility with its own 17-foot dive pool, provides rental equipment, guides, and boats. A wide variety of dives are available for beginners and experienced divers, starting at $25 for a Mini-B Pool Adventure, where beginners use special lightweight equipment. UNEXSO and its sister company, the Dolphin Experience, are known for their work with Atlantic bottle nose dolphins.

**Xanadu Undersea Adventures** (✉ Xanadu Beach Resort ☎ 242/352–3811 or 800/327–8150) offers a resort course for $89, single dives for $37, shark dives for $72, and night dives for $52.

## Snorkeling

★ **East End Adventures** (✉ Freeport ☎ 242/373–6662 ⊕ www.bahamasecotours.com) takes you on a Blue Hole Snorkeling Safari that includes a 55-mi jeep ride and a powerboat jaunt. The five-hour (10–3) excursion is $79 for adults and $49 for children. Snacks and drinks are included.

**Old Bahama Bay** (✉ West End ☎ 242/350–6500) rents snorkel equipment and has mapped out a series of seven snorkeling trails to reefs and wrecks in waters 5–15 feet deep.

★ ♻ **Paradise Cove** (✉ Deadman's Reef ⊕ www.deadmansreef.com ☎ 242/349–2677) allows you to snorkel right offshore at Deadman's Reef, a two-system reef with water ranging from very shallow to 35 feet deep. It's considered the island's best spot for snorkeling off the beach—you're likely to see lots of angelfish, barracudas, rays, and the occasional sea turtle. The resort and famous Red Bar here were closed for several months following Hurricane Wilma in 2005. The bar—a gathering place for watersports enthusiasts—has reopened, and the resort is expected to be back in business by the summer of 2006. There is an access fee of $3 per person; snorkel equipment rentals are available for $10 a day, $5 an hour extra for wet suits or floatation belts. For $35, a snorkel tour includes a briefing, narrated transportation, equipment, and lunch. It's a great deal, especially if you go early and stay late.

**Paradise Watersports** (⊠ Island Seas Resort, Freeport ☎ 242/373–4001) offers a 90-minute Reef 'N' Wreck snorkeling cruise ($35), during which you'll explore coral reefs and a 40-foot wreck.

★ ☾ **Pat & Diane Fantasia Tours** (⊠ Port Lucaya Resort ☎ 242/373–8681 or 888/275–3603 ⊕ www.snorkelingbahamas.com) takes snorkelers to a shallow reef two times a day on cruises aboard a fun-boat catamaran with a 30-foot rock climbing wall and slides into the water. The fee is $40 for the two-hour trip.

## Tennis

★ **Ace Tennis Center** has four lighted courts: grass, rebound, French red clay, and hard. Wimbledon white tennis attire is required on the grass court. Racquet rental and stringing, a ball machine, lessons, and clinics are available. ⊠ *Our Lucaya Beach & Golf Resort* ☎ 242/373–1333 ⌨ *$25–$110 per hr.*

**Xanadu Beach Resort** has two hard courts. ⊠ *Sunken Treasure Dr., Freeport* ☎ *242/352–6782* ⌨ *Guests free, nonguests $5 per hr.*

## Waterskiing

**Paradise Watersports** (⊠ Island Seas Resort, Freeport ☎ 242/373–4001) lets you ski roughly 1½ mi of waves for $30; a half-hour lesson is $40.

# SHOPPING

In the stores, shops, and boutiques in Freeport's International Bazaar and at the Port Lucaya Marketplace, you can find duty-free goods costing up to 40% less than what you might pay back home. At the numerous perfume shops, fragrances are often sold at a sweet-smelling 25% below U.S. prices. Be sure to limit your haggling to the straw markets.

Shops in Freeport and Lucaya are open Monday–Saturday from 9 or 10 to 6. Stores may stay open later in Port Lucaya. Straw markets, grocery stores, and drugstores are open on Sunday.

## Markets & Arcades

**International Arcade** (⊠ Between International Bazaar and Royal Oasis Casino ☎ No phone) has a varied collection of shops, primarily branches of stores found at the adjacent International Bazaar.

★ **International Bazaar** (⊠ W. Sunrise Hwy. and E. Mall Dr. ☎ 242/352–2828) carries imported goods, exotic items, and duty-free merchandise. Heavily impacted by regional hurricane damage in 2004, this once-attractive landmark is in a slump. At press time, 34 shops, restaurants, and bars remained open. A sprightly straw market gathers on one side.

★ **Port Lucaya Marketplace** (✉ Sea Horse Dr. ☎ 242/373–8446) has about 80 boutiques and restaurants in 12 pastel-color buildings—plus a new Arts & Crafts Market building—in a harborside setting. Local musicians often perform at the bandstand in the afternoons and evenings.

★ **Port Lucaya Straw Market** (✉ Sea Horse Dr. ☎ No phone) is a collection of wooden stalls at the Port Lucaya complex's east and west ends. Vendors will expect you to bargain for straw goods, T-shirts, and souvenirs.

## Specialty Shops

### Art

**Art & Nature** (✉ Port Lucaya MarketPl. ☎ 242/373–8326) sells a higher quality of handicrafts than the straw markets and souvenir shops. Look for painted canvases and handbags, and quality wood carvings.

★ **Bahamian Tings** (✉ 15B Poplar Crescent St., Freeport ☎ 242/352–9550) carries well-made Bahamian crafts.

**Flovin Gallery** (✉ International Bazaar and Port Lucaya ☎ 242/352–7564 or 242/373–8388) stocks original paintings in addition to T-shirts and other souvenirs.

**The Glass Blower Shop** (✉ International Arcade ☎ 242/352–8585) features the work of Sidney Pratt, who demonstrates his craft in the shop's front window.

**Leo's Art Gallery** (✉ Port Lucaya ☎ 242/373–1758) showcases the expressive Haitian-style paintings of local artist Leo Brown.

### China & Crystal

**Island Galleria** (✉ International Bazaar and Port Lucaya MarketPl. ☎ 242/352–8194 or 242/373–8404) carries china and crystal by Waterford, Wedgwood, Aynsley, Swarovski, and Coalport, as well as Lladró figurines.

### Cigars

Note: it's illegal to bring Cuban cigars into the United States.

**Havana Trading Company** (✉ Our Lucaya Resort Shops ☎ 242/351–5685) has Cuban cigar rollers at work. The shop also sells liquor.

### Fashion

★ **Androsia** (✉ Port Lucaya MarketPl. ☎ 242/373–8912) specializes in hand-batiked, nature-inspired fashions made on the Bahamian island of Andros—from bikinis to shirts and dresses.

**Animale** (✉ Port Lucaya MarketPl. ☎ 242/374–2066) is known for the wild appeal of its fine ladies clothing and jewelry.

**Bandolera** (✉ Port Lucaya MarketPl. ☎ 242/373–7691 ⊕ www.bandolera. com) sells European-style women's fashions, bags, and jewelry.

**Caribbean Cargo** (✉ International Bazaar ☎ 242/352–2929) has swimwear, beachwear, sarongs, quality souvenir T-shirts, and sea-inspired jewelry.

### Jewelry & Watches

**The Colombian** (✉ Port Lucaya MarketPl. ☎ 242/373–2974) purveys a line of Colombia's famed emeralds plus other jewelry and crystal.

**Colombian Emeralds International** (⊠ International Bazaar, Port Lucaya MarketPl., and Our Lucaya ☎ 242/352–5464, 242/352–7138, 242/373–8400, or 800/666–3889) is *the* place to find emeralds, diamonds, rubies, sapphires, and gold jewelry. The best brands in watches, including Tag Heuer, Breitling, and Omega, are also available here.

### Leather Goods
**Unusual Center** (⊠ International Bazaar and Port Lucaya MarketPl. ☎ 242/352–3994 or 242/373–7333) carries eel-skin leather, peacock-feather goods, and jewelry.

### Perfumes
**Parfum de Paris** (⊠ International Arcade, International Bazaar, Port Lucaya MarketPl., and Our Lucaya ☎ 242/352–8164 or 242/373–8403) offers the most comprehensive range of French fragrances on the island, including Lancome, Fendi, and Tommy.

★ **Perfume Factory** (⊠ International Bazaar ☎ 242/352–9391) sells a large variety of perfumes, lotions, and colognes by Fragrance of the Bahamas. Pink Pearl cologne actually contains conch pearls, and Sand cologne for men has a little island sand in each bottle. You can also create your own scent and brand name and register it.

### Miscellaneous
**Hit Factory** (⊠ International Arcade ☎ 242/352–6004) has the island's best selection of CDs, tapes—and even LPs. Buy reggae, rap, and mainstream American music plus video games.

**Intercity Music** (⊠ International Bazaar and Port Lucaya MarketPl. ☎ 242/352–8820) is the place to buy records, tapes, and CDs of Junkanoo, reggae, and soca music. It also burns its own hit collections.

**Photo Specialist** (⊠ Port Lucaya MarketPl. ☎ 242/373–7858) repairs cameras and carries photo and video equipment.

**Sun & Sea Outfitters** (⊠ UNEXSO, Port Lucaya MarketPl. ☎ 242/373–1244) sells everything water-related, from swimsuits and marine animal T-shirts to dolphin jewelry and sarongs.

# GRAND BAHAMA ISLAND ESSENTIALS

*To research prices, get advice from other travelers, and book travel arrangements, visit* ⊕ *www.fodors.com*

## Transportation

### BY AIR
Grand Bahama International Airport is just off Grand Bahama Highway, about six minutes from downtown Freeport and about 10 minutes from Port Lucaya.

Several United States airlines fly to Grand Bahama International Airport from cities on the east coast, including Atlanta, Chicago, New York City, Miami, and Fort Lauderdale. Interisland flights to and from Nassau and other destinations are also available.

AirTran flies from Atlanta and Baltimore nonstop daily, with connections to major U.S. cities. American Eagle serves Freeport from Miami two to three times daily, with American Airlines connections from many U.S. cities. Bahamasair serves Grand Bahama International Airport with flights from Fort Lauderdale, as well as via Nassau, daily; they have service from Tampa every Monday and Friday. Canada 3000 provides charter flights out of Toronto December through May. Continental/ Continental Connection (Gulfstream) travels daily from Newark, New Jersey, and several cities in Florida (Miami, Fort Lauderdale, Tallahassee, and West Palm Beach). Delta Connection flies twice daily out of Atlanta. Isle Air flies gambling junkets to Isle of Capri Casino from Fort Lauderdale and West Palm Beach Thursday through Sunday. L. B. Ltd. (formerly Laker) flies daily from Fort Lauderdale. US Airways flies directly from Charlotte, North Carolina, daily, and from New York (La-Guardia) and Philadelphia to Freeport on Saturday. TNT Vacations provides nonstop charter service from Boston to Freeport February through May.

Grand Bahama Vacations has airfare packages from Cincinnati and Cleveland, Ohio; Richmond, Virginia; Raleigh-Durham, North Carolina; and Tampa, Florida, with accommodations at seven Grand Bahama Island resorts. Add-on ground and water tours are also available.

🛩 Airlines & Contacts **AirTran** ☎ 800/247-8726. **American Eagle** ☎ 800/433-7300. **Bahamasair** ☎ 242/352-8341 or 800/222-4262. **Canada 3000** ☎ 242/373-7863. **Delta Connection** ☎ 800/221-1212. **Grand Bahama Vacations** ☎ 800/545-1300. **GulfStream Continental Connection** ☎ 242/352-6447 or 800/231-0856. **Isle Air** ☎ 800/843-4753. **L. B. Ltd.** ☎ 242/352-8881 or 800/545-1300. **TNT Vacations** ☎ 242/373-7863 or 800/262-0123. **US Airways** ☎ 800/428-4322.

🛩 Airport Information **Grand Bahama International Airport** ☎ 242/352-6020.

## BY BOAT

Freeport and Lucaya are the ports of call for several cruise lines, including Carnival Cruise Line, Discovery Cruises, and Disney Cruise Lines ( ⇨ Cruise Travel *in* Smart Travel Tips A to Z, at the back of the book). Discovery Cruises provides daily ferry service from Fort Lauderdale, a five-hour trip each way. The Cloud X Fast Ferry departs Palm Beach, Florida at 9:00 AM, Thursday through Monday, for the 3½ hour trip to Freeport; return trips depart Freeport at 3 PM. To pass the time during your passage, you can gamble or hang out in one of the lounges on their luxury catamarans. Round-trip cost, including port tax, is $157.

A free government ferry runs between McLean's Town, at the East End, to Sweeting's Cay. It departs from Sweeting's Cay at 7:10 AM and 4 PM; and from McLean's Town at 8:30 AM and 5 PM. Another ferry travels twice daily from McLean's Town to Crown Haven in the Abacos at 8:30 AM and 4:30 PM; the trip takes an hour.

## BY BUS

Buses are an inexpensive way to travel the 4 mi between downtown Freeport and Port Lucaya Marketplace daily until about 10 PM. The fare is $1. Buses from Freeport to the West End cost $4; to the East End, $8. Exact change is required. Some resorts provide free shuttle service to shopping and beaches. No bus service is available between the airport and hotels.

### BY CAR

If you plan to drive around the island, it's cheaper to rent a car than to hire a taxi. Automobiles, jeeps, and vans can be rented at the Grand Bahama International Airport. Cars start at $60 per day. Some agencies provide free pickup and delivery service to Freeport and Lucaya resorts.

🚗 Major Agencies **Avis Rent-A-Car** ☎ 242/352-7666, 888/897-8448 in U.S. **Dollar Rent-A-Car** ☎ 242/352-9325, 800/800-4000 in U.S. **Hertz** ☎ 242/352-9277, 800/654-3131 in U.S. **Thrifty** ☎ 242/352-9308, 800/367-2277 in U.S.

🚗 Local Agencies **Bahama Buggies** ☎ 242/352-8750. **Cartwright's Rent-A-Car** ☎ 242/351-3002. **KSR Car Rental** ☎ 242/351-5737.

### BY SCOOTER

Grand Bahama's flat, well-paved roads make for good, safe scooter riding. Rentals run about $35 a day with a $200 deposit (about $15 an hour). Helmets are required and provided. Look for rentals at Port Lucaya Marketplace and Pirates of the Bahamas.

### BY TAXI

Taxi fares are fixed by the government (but generally you're charged a flat fee for routine trips, and these rates can vary slightly) at $3 for the first ¼ mi and 40¢ for each additional ¼ mi, regardless of whether the taxi is a regular-size cab, a van, or a stretch limo. If there are more than two people in your party, you will be charged $3 for each additional passenger. Grand Bahama Taxi Union can provide service for visitors arriving by air. There's a taxi waiting area outside the Our Lucaya Beach & Golf Resort.

Taxis meet all cruise ships. Passengers are charged $16 for trips to Freeport and $24 to Lucaya. The price per person drops with larger groups.

Metered taxis also meet all incoming flights. Rides cost about $12 for two to Freeport, $19 to Lucaya.

🚕 Taxi Companies **Grand Bahama Taxi Union** ✉ Grand Bahama International Airport ☎ 242/352-7101.

## Contacts & Resources

### BANKS & EXCHANGE SERVICES

Banks are generally open Monday–Thursday 9:30–3 and Friday 9:30–4:30. Some of the major banks on the island include Bank of the Bahamas, Bank of Nova Scotia, Barclays Bank, and Royal Bank of Canada.

### EMERGENCIES

Dial 911 to reach the police in case of an emergency. Ambulance service and the fire department have separate numbers.

🚑 **Ambulance** ☎ 242/352-2689. **Bahamas Air Sea Rescue** ☎ 242/325-2628. **Fire Department** ☎ 242/352-8888 or 911. **Police** ☎ 911. **Rand Memorial Hospital** ✉ E. Atlantic Dr. ☎ 242/352-6735.

**TOUR OPTIONS**

Tours can be booked through the tour desk in your hotel lobby, at tourist information booths, or by calling one of the tour operators listed below.

A three-hour sightseeing tour of the Freeport/Lucaya area costs $25–$35. A glass-bottom-boat tour to offshore reefs with Reef Tours Ltd. costs $25; sailing tours are $35. A tour of Lucayan National Park runs about $40. Grand Bahama Nature Tours' Bahamas Jeep Safari lets you drive your own open-top vehicle on a convoy through pine forests and along the coast. The cost of the five-hour trip is $99 per person.

For evening entertainment, a dinner cruise will cost around $75, with a show. Sunset "booze cruises" run about $39 each, transportation included ($45 with show).

A host of tour operators on Grand Bahama offer a combination of the tours described above. Executive Tours, H. Forbes Charter & Tours, and Best Island Travel & Tours have sightseeing land tours that can be booked through the major resorts. H. Forbes Charter & Tours also offers trips to Nassau, nightlife bar-hopping excursions, and other adventures. For on-the-water fun, contact Reef Tours Ltd.

**Best Island Travel & Tours** Box F 40869, Freeport 242/352-4811. **Executive Tours** Box F 40837, Freeport 242/373-7863 www.executivetoursbahamas. com. **Grand Bahama Nature Tours** 866/440-4542 or 242/373-2485 www.gbntours. com. **Grand Bahama Vacations** 1170 Lee Wagner Blvd., Suite 200, Fort Lauderdale, FL 33315 800/422-7466 or 800/545-1300. **H. Forbes Charter & Tours** Box F 41315, Freeport 242/352-9311 www.forbescharter.com. **Reef Tours Ltd.** Box F 42609, Freeport 242/373-5880 www.bahamasvg.com/reeftours.

BOAT TOUR  If you don't want to go too far underwater, try an excursion on the Seaworld Explorer semisubmarine, which never fully submerges. Descend into the hull of the boat and observe sea life in air-conditioned comfort from a vantage point 5 feet below the surface. The vessel departs from Port Lucaya and travels to Treasure Reef daily at 9:30, 11:30, and 1:30. The two-hour voyage with transportation and snorkeling costs $39, $25 for children.

**Seaworld Explorer** Port Lucaya Marina, Port Lucaya 242/373-7863.

BREWERY TOUR  A one-hour tour sloshes through the Grand Bahama Brewing Company, the island's only microbrewery, fountainhead of Hammerhead beers, weekdays at 10, 12:30, and 4:40, and Saturday at 10:30 (call ahead on Saturday). Samplings of its four types of beer are available, and the $5 tour price can be credited toward a purchase.

**Grand Bahama Brewing Company** Logwood Rd., Freeport 242/351-5191.

ECOTOURS  Land-and-sea East End Adventures' guided ecotours include a jeep ride along pristine beaches and through dense pine forests to the site of a now-gone early settlement, and a 6-mi boat trip to Sweeting's Cay and Lightbourne Cay, remote islands off Grand Bahama's eastern extreme. Snorkeling a blue hole, nature and bush medicine lessons, a short wilderness hike, and a grilled lunch on the beach are all included in this truly worthwhile experience, which is run by native Bahamians. The eight-hour trips cost $120 per adult. Other tours are shorter and concentrate on off-roading or snorkeling.

Kayak Nature Tours' eco-excursions explore pristine wilderness by kayak, van, snorkel, and foot. The six-hour tour includes 1½ hours of kayaking through Grand Bahama's mangrove environment for a look at bird and marine habitats, a guided nature hike through Lucayan National Park and its caves, swimming on Gold Rock Beach, and lunch. A five-hour excursion combines kayaking and snorkeling at Peterson Cay. The guides are extremely knowledgeable, particularly about flora and fauna. Air-conditioned transport is provided to and from your hotel, all for $79.

🛈 **East End Adventures** ✉ Freeport ☎ 242/373-6662 ⊕ www.bahamasecotours. com. **Kayak Nature Tours** ✉ Queen's Cove, Freeport ☎ 242/373-2485 or 866/440-4542 ⊕ www.grandbahamanaturetours.com.

## VISITOR INFORMATION

The Grand Bahama Island Tourism Board has its main office and a separate tourist information center at International Bazaar in Freeport. Branch offices are at the Grand Bahama International Airport and at the southeast entrance to the Port Lucaya Marketplace. Ask about Bahamahosts, specially trained tour guides who will talk to you about island history and culture and pass on their knowledge of Bahamian folklore. Tourist offices are open weekdays 9–5; information centers, Monday–Saturday 9–5. The airport office is also open on Sunday.

🛈 Tourist Information **Grand Bahama Island Tourism Board** ☎ 242/352-8356, 800/ 448-3386 in U.S. 🖷 242/352-7840 ⊕ www.grand-bahama.com ☎ 242/352-6909 Freeport ☎ 242/352-2052 Grand Bahama International Airport ☎ 242/373-8988 Port Lucaya.

# The Abacos

## WORD OF MOUTH

"There's nothing cooler than finding your own private island you can spend a day on."

—GoTravel

"Other than the rides into town for Island Treats ice cream and the occasional restaurant or grocery run, we stayed at the house enjoying the beautiful sea colors, the peace of the island (the clearest night sky with almost zero artificial light sources . . . magnificent), the incredible empty beaches and the pure sweet island breezes. This is the place to go to really relax, no bars, no casinos, no crowds, no nada . . . perfectly blissful."

—cmcfong, about Man-O-War Cay

Updated by
Stephen Vletas

**THE ATTITUDE OF THE ABACOS** might best be expressed by the sign posted in the window of a Hope Town shop: IF YOU'RE LOOKING FOR WAL-MART—IT'S 200 MILES TO THE RIGHT. In other words, the residents of this chain of more than 100 islands know that there's another world out there, but don't necessarily care to abandon theirs, which is a little more traditional, slow-paced, and out of the way than most alternatives.

The Abacos' calm, naturally protected waters, long admired for their beauty, have helped the area become the Bahamas' sailing capital. The islands' resorts are particularly popular with yachting and fishing enthusiasts because of the fine boating facilities available, among the best in the Bahamas. Man-O-War Cay remains the Bahamas' boatbuilding center; its residents turn out traditionally crafted wood dinghies as well as high-tech fiberglass craft. The Abacos play host annually to internationally famous regattas and to a half dozen game-fish tournaments. Outside the resorts, the oceanside villages of Hope Town and New Plymouth also appeal to tourists for their charming New England ambience.

Many of the 10 or so inhabited cays of the Abacos were first settled more than 200 years ago by New England Loyalists, who in 1783 began fleeing the upstart United States to what they perceived as a safe haven for those loyal to the crown. Joined by plantation owners and their slaves from Virginia and the Carolinas, the newcomers found it hard going on the rocky, infertile land, and soon turned to the sea. Some began fishing and boatbuilding, a way of making a living that some of their descendants still practice today. Others took advantage of the occasional shipwreck.

At the end of the 18th century, Bahamian waters weren't charted, and lighthouses wouldn't be built in the area until 1836. The "wreckers" of the Abacos worked at night, luring unsuspecting ships onto rocks and shoals by shining misleading lights, then plundering the cargo. Of course, not all these wrecks were caused by unscrupulous islanders. Some ships were lost in storms and foundered on hidden reefs as they passed through the Bahamas. Nevertheless, by means fair or foul, wrecking remained a thriving industry in the Abacos until the mid-1800s.

Today the legacy of the British settlers remains intact. Many of the Abacos' 10,000 residents have accents reminiscent of their ancestors—a charming combination of an island cadence with a vaguely Scottish or English lilt. Seafaring is still a major source of income, especially boatbuilding, fishing, and guided fishing trips. Because the Abacos are one of the Out Islands' most visited destinations, an increasing number of residents work in the tourist industry.

## Exploring the Abacos

The Abacos, 200 mi east of Palm Beach, Florida, are a short boat ride from Grand Bahama. Little Abaco Island, Great Abaco Island, and many smaller offshore cays comprise the mini-archipelago, which stretches in a languid crescent for more than 120 mi from Walker's Cay in the north to Hole-in-the-Wall in the south. The dazzling cays lie in the Atlantic, mostly east or north of Great Abaco. Larger populated cays include Walker's, Green Turtle, Great Guana, Man-O-War, and Elbow,

# GREAT ITINERARIES

*Numbers in the text correspond to numbers in the margin and on the Abacos map.*

### IF YOU HAVE 3 DAYS

Make your base in ➤ 🖼 **Marsh Harbour** ①, the biggest city in the Abacos, and spend the first day getting settled in your hotel, exploring the city or a nearby beach, and having a leisurely dinner on Restaurant Row, overlooking the busy marina. On Day 2, get up early and take the ferry to **Hope Town** ⑥, the **Elbow Cay** settlement often considered the most picturesque in the Abacos, with its candy-stripe lighthouse, rows of neat clapboard cottages painted in pastel hues, and plenty of restaurants, shops, and historic sites. Day 3 brings a choice: for another dose of Loyalist history, take the ferry again, this time to **Man-O-War Cay** ⑦, the boatbuilding capital of the region; or stay put and book a diving or fishing trip out of one of the Marsh Harbour marinas.

### IF YOU HAVE 5 DAYS

Follow the suggested three-day itinerary, and on Day 4 go to **Treasure Cay** ⑨ and catch the first ferry to 🖼 **Green Turtle Cay** ⑩, your base for the next two days. Stroll through **New Plymouth** for the remainder of your morning, stopping to wander through the sculpture garden, which memorializes accomplished Bahamians, and the **Albert Lowe Museum,** getting a dose of island history, as well as learning about shipbuilding and hurricane survival. After a lunch of locally caught conch or grouper, spend the afternoon at **Ocean Beach** or on calmer **Gillam Bay,** then dress up for a fancy dinner at one of the two fine resorts on **White Sound.** On your last day, if you're a golfer, you'll want to hit the links at nearby Treasure Cay, where the 18-hole course is considered one of the finest in the Caribbean, yet is so blissfully uncrowded that tee times aren't necessary. And if you're an angler, book a day of bonefishing or offshore fishing with a local guide. Otherwise, rent a small boat and visit some of the uninhabited nearby cays, such as **Nun Jack, No Name,** and **Crab,** where the snorkeling and deserted white-sand beaches are sublime.

### IF YOU HAVE 7 DAYS

Add two days to the 🖼 **Marsh Harbour** portion of the five-day itinerary above. On the first additional day, take a ferry to **Great Guana Cay** ⑧, which has some of the most beautiful beaches in the Abacos and one of the best party-scene restaurants, **Nippers.** On the second day, rent a car and explore the southern reaches of **Great Abaco Island,** perhaps searching for the endangered Bahama parrot at the **Bahamas National Trust Sanctuary** ⑤, or checking out the bronze sculptures at **Pete Johnson's Foundry** in **Little Harbour** ③. Another alternative, if you're a boater, is to rent a boat your first day in Marsh Harbour and spend the week island-hopping. If all that sounds like too much work, consider experiencing life like a local: bring some books, sunblock, and a few swimsuits; rent a cottage, a dinghy, and a golf cart, perhaps on 🖼 **Elbow Cay** or 🖼 **Great Guana Cay** ⑧; and learn to practice the fine art of relaxation.

3

all of which offer full services for boaters and just the right sprinkling of small resorts and enchanting settlements. The majority of the other cays are uninhabited, and together they provide a 100-mi-long sheltered cruising area that beckons to explorers in search of aqua-green bays, coral reefs, hidden coves, and white strands of beach.

The mind-melting serenity of the Abacos is a great tonic for forgetting your problems back home. This sense of well-being often stealthily seeps in a day or two after arrival. All of a sudden, you just feel more relaxed, more at peace. This is a place where you can feel content in an uncrowded environment, yet still have access to whatever levels of accommodation and services you desire. Water-related activities abound, and it's easy to go sailing, boating, diving, snorkeling, beachcombing, or fishing. Ecotourism has become the "in" thing, and hiking and biking are popular through natural areas ripe with bird and plant life. Sea kayaking in pristine protected areas provides a rewarding sense of adventure, and more conventional activities include golf, tennis, and beach volleyball. But if you don't feel like doing anything at all, that's a highly rated activity, too.

On Great Abaco proper you'll find rugged stretches of white limestone bluffs, miles of kelp-strewn beaches devoid of footprints, landlocked lakes, pine forests where wild boar roam, and the Bahamas' third-largest community: the thriving commercial center of Marsh Harbour. The town has a variety of accommodation options, rental cars and boats, groceries, hardware stores, a plethora of restaurants and shops, and the Bahamas' largest marina. The drug stores are decently stocked, and one of the best medical clinics in the islands is here. Up north on Little Abaco, tourism is less prominent, and locals live as they have for the last hundred years—farming, fishing, and spending time with family and friends. This is a good area to explore by car—but be sure to save some time to relax on the stunning beaches around Fox Town.

Convenient commercial air service from Florida or Nassau to the Marsh Harbour and Treasure Cay airports makes reaching the Abacos fairly easy. Air charters from Florida and Nassau are an economical option for families or fishing parties who prefer this extra convenience. If you want to take the casual approach, mailboats from Nassau visit ports up and down the island on a weekly basis. Scheduled ferry service from Marsh Harbour and Treasure Cay to the offshore cays is convenient and reliable, and most ferry boats are covered, so you'll stay dry during rough-weather crossings. You should always be prepared for inclement weather; seasoned travelers always take rain jackets with hoods. Wear either sandals or tennis shoes with good support and traction, since the gunwales of the ferries and the docks are usually slippery.

Many travelers make the case that the Abacos is the best overall destination in the Bahamas. It's really the complete package—immaculate deserted beaches, deluxe full-service marinas, Out Island charm combined with easy travel, and top-quality accommodations. Plus, you can hit the links at world-class golf courses at Treasure Cay and Winding Bay, go bonefishing in the Marls, play tennis, or go diving or snorkeling. Of course, you can also *really* get away from it all in the Abacos.

# IF YOU LIKE

### SNORKELING & DIVING

With clear, shallow waters and a series of colorful coral reefs extending for miles, the Abacos provide both the novice and the experienced underwater explorer plenty of visual stimulation. The reefs, often within swimming distance of shore, are teeming with trigger fish, grouper, parrot fish, green moray eels, angelfish, jacks, damsel fish, sergeant majors, sting rays, sea turtles, dolphins, and even the occasional reef or nurse shark. Dive operators are available in the most heavily touristed areas, but you can also venture out on your own, especially with a rented boat. Good places to start include the reefs near Guana Cay; Fowl Cay National Reserve between Man-O-War and Scotland cays; Pelican Cays National Park, just south of Marsh Harbour; and the reefs around Green Turtle Cay, where a Key West organization called Reef Relief has helped islanders install a series of 18 mooring buoys where you can safely anchor your boat without fear of damaging the fragile reef.

Maps of the buoys, which stretch from uninhabited Nun Jack Cay in the north to No Name Cay in the south, can be picked up at many Green Turtle Cay businesses. Visibility is generally high year-round, but the clear water turns cloudy after heavy storms and high seas. The relatively northern location of the Abacos means you may need a wetsuit from December through March. But no matter what the time of year, the sheer number of good sites and relatively low visitor traffic translate to a fantastic view of life under the sea that you rarely have to share.

### A LIVING HISTORY

Though the Abacos may be most famous for beaches, sailing, and fishing, you'd be missing the boat, so to speak, if you didn't explore the area's rich history. And that doesn't mean spending all those sunny days inside a museum, although there are fine, small museums in Hope Town and New Plymouth, each worth a visit to learn about the boatbuilding and seafaring traditions of the Loyalists who settled these islands.

Because the original settlements have been so well preserved, it's possible to absorb history just by wandering through them. In Hope Town, look for the gingerbread cottages with white picket fences, built 100 or more years ago but still lived in today. In New Plymouth, check out the sculpture garden depicting the accomplishments of famous Bahamians. While you're there, observe the architecture: the neat clapboard homes, shops, and churches, many with carefully tended flower boxes and airy front porches, have survived hurricanes and tropical storms and still look much like they must have when they were built a century ago. On Man-O-War Cay, witness boatbuilding as it's been done for generations, or see women carefully crafting modern bags out of the same cloth their ancestors used for sails. And everywhere in the Abacos, simply try engaging the local residents in conversation. Nearly all of them, but especially those over 60, have some great tales to tell of what it's like to live on an island where many grew up without cars, TVs, telephones, or daily mail service.

## THE ABACOS' TOP 5

**Bonefishing in the Marls.** This is one of the most spectacular wilderness flats regions anywhere, with an endless maze of lush mangrove creeks, hidden bays, and sandy cays. Hire a professional guide to show you the best spots.

**Cay hopping.** Rent your own boat and spend a day or more skipping from Green Turtle to No Name, Great Guana, Elbow, Snake, Tilloo— or whatever your please. Settle onto your own private strip of beach and enjoy.

**Green Turtle Cay nightlife.** When the Gully Roosters play, the island

rocks. Any local will be able to tell you when and where you can catch their next show. (And be sure to stop in at Miss Emily's Blue Bee Bar for a mind-altering Goombay Smash.)

**Little Harbour.** Drop out and kick back; spend a day—or a week—in this serene bayside artists colony pursuing life's simple island pleasures.

**Nippers Beach Bar and Grill on Great Guana Cay.** Their Sunday pig roast is the best beach party of the year—and they have it every week, so there's no excuse for missing it.

Drive into Little Harbour, an artists community, and completely disappear for a week or, if you're an angler, abandon your cell phone and hole up in Sandy Point.

### About the Restaurants

Fish, conch, and lobster—called crawfish by the locals—have long been the bedrock of local cuisine. Although a few menus, mostly in upscale resorts, feature dishes with Italian, Asian, or Continental influences, most restaurants in the Abacos still serve simple Bahamian fare, with a few nods to American tastes. (It's rare to find a place that still serves sheep's-tongue souse, a stew made from the tongue of a sheep and a handful of other ingredients.)

The Abacos are not particularly dieter-friendly. Breakfasts tend toward the hearty, eggs-bacon-and-pancakes variety. At lunch, even in the trendiest spots, you'll likely find variations on a few standards: fresh grouper "burgers," or breaded, fried fish fillets served on slightly sweet Bahamian buns; cracked conch, which is tenderized, deep-fried conch meat; and hamburgers and sandwiches, all usually sided with french fries, coleslaw, or local favorites like peas 'n' rice.

Dinner provides more options. You might eat local favorites like pork chops, fried chicken, or minced lobster cooked with tomatoes, garlic, and onions at a bare-bones diner; or head for a fancier restaurant and choose from an ever-changing array of seafood dishes with international flair, such as lobster risotto, sesame-crusted ahi tuna with wasabi sauce, or monkfish wrapped in pancetta.

Remember that almost nothing is grown locally, so high-quality fruits and vegetables are a rarity, especially right before the weekly boat bearing provisions arrives. (By the same token, don't be surprised if all dishes on the menu aren't available every day.) The remoteness also means meals aren't cheap, even in the humblest spot. Lunch usually costs at least $10 per person, and you can easily spend upward of $30 apiece at dinner, even without drinks.

## About the Hotels

Small, intimate resorts are the rule in the Abacos. There are a few full-scale resorts, with multiple restaurants, bars, pools, and features like tennis courts, but most accommodations are beachside condos or cottages, or hotels with just a handful of rooms and a single small restaurant. What you may give up in modern amenities and bells-and-whistles like spas or 24-hour room service, you'll gain in privacy and beauty. Many hotels have water views, and with a cottage you may even get your own stretch of beach. Although rooms tend to be simple, air-conditioning has become a standard feature, and more places are adding previously un-heard-of luxuries like satellite TV, in-room phones, VCRs, and Internet access. Again, small and remote doesn't equate with inexpensive; it's just about impossible to find lodging for less than $100.

| WHAT IT COSTS | | | | | |
|---|---|---|---|---|---|
| | $$$$ | $$$ | $$ | $ | ¢ |
| RESTAURANTS | over $40 | $30–$40 | $20–$30 | $10–$20 | under $10 |
| HOTELS | over $400 | $300–$400 | $200–$300 | $100–$200 | under $100 |

Restaurant prices are for a main course at dinner, excluding gratuity, typically 15%, which is often automatically added to the bill. Hotel prices are for two people in a standard double room in high season, excluding service charges and 6%–12% tax.

## Timing

Unlike the rest of the Bahamas, which are busiest from December through April, the peak months for the Abacos are in June, July, and early August. That's the best time for sailing, boating, and swimming; the season of the most popular regatta and fishing tournaments; and the time you're likely to pay a premium for hotels, boats, and cars—if you can book them at all. December through May is a pleasant time to visit, though most locals refuse to get in the water during those months. With average high temperatures in the 70s and low 80s, you might disagree, although in January and February, those highs can sometimes dip as low as 50°F when a norther drifts through.

In September and October, typically the peak of hurricane season, the number of visitors drops to a trickle, and many hotels and restaurants shut down for two weeks to two months. If you're willing to take a chance on getting hit by a storm, this can still be a great time to explore, with discounts of as much as 50% at the hotels that remain open.

**DID YOU KNOW?**

Bahamian currency includes a $3 bill. There's also a half-dollar bill and a 15-cent piece, which is square and decorated with a hibiscus.

# THE ABACOS

*Numbers in the margin correspond to points of interest on the Abacos map.*

## Great Abaco Island

❶ Most visitors to the Abacos make their first stop on Great Abaco Island's east coast at **Marsh Harbour,** the Bahamas' third-largest city and the Abacos' commercial center. Besides having the biggest international airport in the Abacos, Marsh Harbour is considered by boaters to be one of the easiest harbors to enter. It has several full-service marinas, including the 190-slip Boat Harbour Marina and the 80-slip Conch Inn Marina.

Stock up on groceries and supplies here on the way to other islands. The downtown area has several supermarkets with a better selection than the sometimes-limited supplies on the smaller islands, as well as a few department and hardware stores. Most of the gift shops are on the main street, which has the island's only traffic light. If you need cash, this is the place to get it as well; the banks here are open every day and have ATMs, neither of which you will find true on the smaller, more remote cays. There are also gas stations, doctors, government offices, and a few good, moderately priced restaurants.

❷ Drive 25 minutes south of Marsh Harbour to get to **The Abaco Club on Winding Bay,** a glamorous private golf and sporting club (for resident and nonresident members) set on 520 acres of stunning oceanfront property. The clubhouse, restaurant, and pool, which sit on 65-foot high white limestone bluffs, offer guests a mesmerizing view of the purple-blue Atlantic Ocean, and the bay has more than 2 mi of sugar sand beaches. Amenities and activities at **The Club** (☎ 242/367–0077 ⊕ www.theabacoclub.com) include an 18-hole tropical links golf course, a luxurious European-style spa and fitness center, scuba diving, snorkeling, horseback riding, tennis, bonefishing, and offshore fishing. Real estate for sale includes 70 exquisite two- and three-bedroom turnkey cottages and 60 estate homesites. The Ritz-Carlton group manages club operations, and they have plans to build a fishing village in Cherokee Sound and a small private marina in Little Harbour.

❸ The small, eclectic artist's colony of **Little Harbour** was settled by the Johnston family more than 50 years ago. **Pete Johnston's Foundry** (☎ 242/477–5487), the only bronze foundry in the Bahamas, is the centerpiece, and sculptor Johnston and his sons and acolytes cast magnificent lifelike bronze figures using the age-old lost-wax method. In **Pete's Pub and Gallery** (☎ 242/366–3503, 242/477–5487, or 954/840–3575 ⊕ www.petespubandgallery.com), you can view the fine bronzes, unique gold jewelry, and other original island art for sale, or chow down on fresh seafood, burgers, and cold drinks. Try the mango-glazed grouper, lemon pepper mahimahi, or coconut cracked conch while you kick back and enjoy a view of the harbor. And don't miss the Saturday wild pig roasts (April through July). By car, Little Harbour is about 30 minutes south of Marsh Harbour.

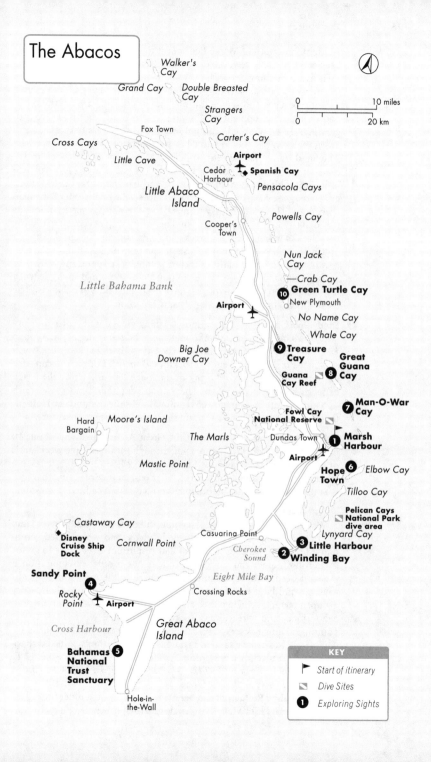

# The Abacos

*Walker's Cay*

*Grand Cay*

*Double Breasted Cay*

*Strangers Cay*

Fox Town

*Cross Cays*

*Carter's Cay*

*Little Cave*

**Airport**

Cedar Harbour

◆ **Spanish Cay**

*Pensacola Cays*

**Little Abaco Island**

Cooper's Town

*Powells Cay*

*Little Bahama Bank*

*Nun Jack Cay*

—*Crab Cay*

⑩ **Green Turtle Cay**

◦ New Plymouth

**Airport**

*No Name Cay*

*Big Joe Downer Cay*

*Whale Cay*

⑨ **Treasure Cay**

⑧ **Great Guana Cay**

*Guana Cay Reef*

⑦ **Man-O-War Cay**

Fowl Cay **National Reserve**

*The Marls*

Dundas Town

**Marsh Harbour** ①

**Airport**

*Hard Bargain*

*Moore's Island*

*Mastic Point*

⑥ **Hope Town**

*Elbow Cay*

*Tilloo Cay*

**Pelican Cays National Park dive area**

*Castaway Cay*

◆ **Disney Cruise Ship Dock**

*Cornwall Point*

Casuarina Point

*Lynyard Cay*

③ **Little Harbour**

*Cherokee Sound*

② **Winding Bay**

**Sandy Point**

*Eight Mile Bay*

*Rocky Point*

④ **Airport**

Crossing Rocks

*Cross Harbour*

*Great Abaco Island*

**Bahamas National Trust Sanctuary** ⑤

Hole-in-the-Wall

| KEY | |
|---|---|
| ▶ | *Start of itinerary* |
| ◪ | *Dive Sites* |
| ① | *Exploring Sights* |

0 — 10 miles
0 — 20 km

About 30 mi south of Marsh Harbour is the seaside settlement of **Cherokee Sound,** home to fewer than 100 families. Most of the residents make their living catching crawfish or working in the growing tourism industry; many lead offshore fishing and bonefishing expeditions. The deserted Atlantic beaches and serene salt marshes in this area are breathtaking, and though development at Winding Bay and Little Harbour are progressing, the slow-paced, tranquil feel of daily life here hasn't changed. Take, for example, the no-name bay just north of the settlement, where **The Sand Bar,** a magnificent wooden pier, juts out into glass-clear waters that are home to schools of bonefish. The pier is over a football field in length, with an open-air restaurant and bar that serves cold Kaliks, grilled burgers, grouper, conch salad, and fries, along with other Bahamian specialties. This place is easy to miss if you're not paying attention, as the road to Cherokee Sound is a winding, curvy strip of cement that skirts the edges of mangrove-lined creeks and bays cut into the coral. About a mile before the settlement, you'll see a sign on your left. Follow the narrow road, park in one of the areas just before locked gate, and walk over to the Sand Bar. It's a nice choice for lunch or afternoon drinks . . . when it's open. Often it's not—you just have to go and take your chances. The more things change, the more they stay the same.

④ **Sandy Point,** a "takin' it easy, mon" fishing village with miles of beckoning beaches and a couple of bonefishing lodges, is slightly more than 50 mi southwest of Marsh Harbour. The Great Abaco Highway leg, which runs into the settlement, ends at **Rickmon Bonefish Lodge.** You can park your car here, have a cold drink in the lodge bar, and enjoy the beach or fish the flats on your own. There are no communities to visit south of Sandy Point, but a major navigational lighthouse stands at **Hole-in-the-Wall,** on Great Abaco's southern tip. It's not open to visitors.

A rugged winding road leads off the Great Abaco Highway, about 40 mi south of Marsh Harbour, passing through the dense pine woodlands

⑤ of the **Bahamas National Trust Sanctuary** (☎ 242/393–1317), a reserve for the endangered Bahama parrot. Your best chance of seeing that bird is at dawn. More than 100 other species have been sighted in this area.

## Where to Stay & Eat

★ $$ ✕ **Wally's.** This two-story pink colonial villa sits across Bay Street from the marina, fronted by green lawns, hibiscus, and white-railed verandahs. This is the Abacos' most popular restaurant—*the* place to go for good food, potent rum cocktails, and serious people watching. Lunch is a scene, especially if you sit outside, where you'll find a mix of locals, tourists, and boat people munching on Greek or Caesar salads, spicy grouper, tarragon chicken, and mahimahi burgers. Inside is a stylish bar, a boutique, and three dining rooms, all adorned with Haitian-style paintings. Dinner is served Friday and Saturday only, and the menu includes wild boar, turtle sautéed in onions and mushrooms, grilled wahoo, and tender lamb chops. Save room for the irresistible Key lime pie. ⊠ *E. Bay St., Marsh Harbour* ☎ *242/367–2074* ▤ *AE, D, MC, V* ☺ *Closed Sun. Closed early Sept. and Oct.*

$–$$ ✕ **Hummingbird Restaurant and Bar.** At this unassuming diner tucked inside Memorial Plaza Mall, locals trade gossip over heaping plates of pancakes and cheese-stuffed omelets at breakfast, then move on to hearty lunches of cracked conch, burgers, and salads. At dinner, the dress code and the vibe remain casual, but the food presentation gets kicked up a notch; try the stuffed pork chops or go Bahamian with a grilled turtle steak. If you want to look like you're in the know, ask for a booth when you make your reservation. ⊠ *Memorial Plaza, Marsh Harbour* ☎ *242/367–2922* ▭ *MC, V.*

**$-$$** ⨯ **Jib Room.** Expect casual lunches of hot wings, conch burgers, fish nuggets, and nachos in this harbor-view restaurant and bar, located inside the Marsh Harbour Marina. The twice-weekly barbecue nights are especially popular; on Wednesday it's baby back ribs and on Saturday it's grilled steak, featuring New York strip. ⊠ *Pelican Shores, Marsh Harbour* ☎ *242/367–2700* ⊕ *www.jibroom.com* ▭ *MC, V* ⊗ *Closed Sun.–Tues.*

★ **$-$$** ⨯ **Mangoes.** An open-air deck, which was rebuilt after the 2005 hurricane season, makes Mangoes a great place for waterside dining. Enjoy cracked conch, grouper tacos, and zesty salads at lunch; at dinner try the house specialties like chicken breast stuffed with crabmeat and sweet peppers, fresh grouper with mango salsa, or the catch of the day grilled, fried, or blackened. If it's wahoo, order it grilled with lots of extra key limes. The bread pudding is an after-dinner highlight, made with bananas, coconut, and sweet, doughy Bahamian bread. The restaurant is part of a complex that contains a boutique selling resort wear and a 29-slip marina—which means you can sail in from the offshore cays, tie up in front, enjoy a meal, and do some shopping. ⊠ *Queen Elizabeth Dr., Marsh Harbour* ☎ *242/367–2366* ⊕ *www.mangoesabaco. com* ▭ *AE, D, MC, V* ⊗ *Closed Oct.*

**$-$$** ⨯ **Sapodilly's.** The colorful bi-level patios will grab your eye—Sapodilly's wooden beams are painted lime green, hot pink, and bright yellow—but the flavorful dishes will hold your attention. Among the best choices are pastas, the grilled grouper kebab, and Marsh Harbour's best burger, topped with blue cheese, bacon, and mushrooms. Or simply go for the drinks and an extensive appetizer menu, including hot wings, conch fritters, escargot, fried shrimp, and onion rings, served with a side of live music on Friday and Saturday nights. To help dance the night away, order their Dilly Willy, a patented run concoction you won't forget. ⊠ *Queen Elizabeth Dr., Marsh Harbour* ☎ *242/367–3498* ▭ *AE, D, MC, V* ⊗ *Closed Sun.*

**¢-$** ⨯ **Jamie's Place.** There's nothing fancy about this clean, bright, diner-style eatery, but the welcome is warm, the Bahamian dishes well-executed, and the prices are right, with most meals clocking in at $10 or under. Choose fried chicken, cracked conch, or fresh-caught dolphin, with a side of mashed or roasted potatoes, peas 'n' rice, macaroni and cheese, or coleslaw. Jamie's is also an ice-cream parlor, with a dozen flavors. ⊠ *Queen Elizabeth Dr., Marsh Harbour* ☎ *242/367–2880* ▭ *No credit cards* ⊗ *Closed Sun.*

**¢** ⨯ **Bahamas Family Market.** At lunchtime, the best bargains in town are at the lunch counter inside this small grocery. Jamaican meat pies stuffed with curried beef or chicken go for $3. A sub sandwich full of Italian salami and cheese, plus chips and a soft drink, is just $5. At breakfast, snag a fresh-baked pastry and coffee for two bucks. There's no eating area, but they'll heat up your order if you'd like. It's also the perfect spot to pack your boat or car cooler for a picnic. ⊠ *Queen Elizabeth Dr., at stoplight, Marsh Harbour* ☎ *242/367–3714* ▭ *No credit cards.*

¢ ✕ **Show-Boo's Conch Salad Stand.** JUST BE NICE implores the hand-lettered sign on this ramshackle stand, across from Sapodilly's restaurant. Follow the instructions and you'll be rewarded with what the proprietor claims to be "the world's best conch salad," often diced and mixed while you watch. Hours are erratic, especially during the September–November off-season. To find out if Show-Boo showed up for business, just swing by around lunchtime and see if there's a line forming in front of his stand. ⊠ *Queen Elizabeth Dr., Marsh Harbour* ☎ *No phone* ▭ *No credit cards.*

☾ **$$–$$$$**
**Fodor'sChoice**
★
✕⊡ **Abaco Beach Resort & Boat Harbour.** One of the liveliest party spots on the island, this place rocks during the half-dozen fishing tournaments it hosts every year. The resort is set on 52 immaculately manicured acres overlooking the Sea of Abaco, just five minutes from the Marsh Harbour airport or a short ferry ride away from Hope Town on Elbow Cay. The spacious ocean-view rooms have natural-stone floors, white wicker furnishings, marble wet bars, built-in hair dryers, and in-room satellite TVs. Dine on roasted rack of lamb with garlic mashed potatoes or a broiled lobster tail at Angler's Restaurant ($–$$), which overlooks gleaming rows of yachts moored in the Marina. The resort's dive shop will arrange fishing charters and boat rentals; use of small sailboats and kayaks is complimentary. Lounge poolside and enjoy fruity rum drinks at the swim-up bar while your kids explore the beach playground. ✍ *Box AB 20511, Marsh Harbour, Abaco* ☎ *242/367–2158 or 800/753–9259* 🖷 *242/367–4154* ⊕ *www.abacoresort.com* ⟳ *72 rooms, 10 suites* ⚘ *Restaurant, refrigerators, 2 tennis courts, 2 pools, gym, dive shop, dock, windsurfing, boating, 190-slip marina, fishing, mountain bikes, 2 bars, lounge, laundry facilities* ▭ *AE, D, MC, V* ⦿ *FAP, MAP.*

**$$$$** ⊡ **Rickmon Bonefish Lodge.** Well-regarded fishing guide Ricardo Burrows operates this comfortable waterside lodge at the end of the road in Sandy Point. The whitewashed, plantation-style building has 11 modern rooms, each with air-conditioning and satellite TV; five overlook the ocean through sliding French doors. Fishing packages, which include top private guides, are the most popular option here, but nonfishing guests can fill their time beachcombing, bird-watching, snorkeling, and boating. The location is great for accessing the flats around Castaway Cay, Moore's Island, and the southern Marls. ⊠ *General delivery, Sandy Point* ☎ *242/366–4477, 242/366–4233, or 800/211–8530* 🖷 *242/366–4478* ⟳ *11 rooms* ⚘ *Restaurant, beach, lounge; no room phones* ▭ *No credit cards* ⦿ *AI.*

**$$–$$$** ⊡ **Pelican Beach Villas.** On a quiet, private peninsula opposite the main settlement of Marsh Harbour sit these waterfront clapboard cottages, cheerily painted in pale pink, yellow, blue, and green. Inside the air-conditioned rooms are rattan furnishings with pastel cushions and porcelain tile floors. A small sand beach is out front, and the cottages are right near Mermaid Reef, a top pick among snorkelers. There's no restaurant on-site, but there's food within walking distance at the Marsh Harbour Marina; for other options, you'll need to rent a car or, better yet, a dinghy, which you can tie up for free at the 100-foot dock. ⌂ *Box AB 20304, Marsh Harbour, Abaco* ☎ *877/326–3180 or 242/367–3600* ⊕ *www.pelicanbeachvillas.com* ⇆ *7 cottages* ⌂ *Kitchenettes, beach, dock, boating, laundry facilities* ⊟ *AE, D, MC, V.*

**$$** 🏨 **Nettie's Different of Abaco.** Owner Nettie Symonette has created an ecowonderland nestled between a freshwater lake and a glorious 8-mi section of powdery beach on Cherokee Sound. This ecoresort embraces the area's natural habitat, which is alive with wild boars, peacocks, herons, and flamingos. Airy, colonial-style rooms have wooden floors, vaulted open-beam ceilings, and handcrafted furniture. Some have air-conditioning, though others depend on fans and gentle sea breezes to keep things cool. Bonefishing packages allow anglers to fish the famous Marls region, one of the most productive fisheries in the islands. Birding, swimming, sea kayaking, and snorkeling are also popular. More than 75 species of birds have been identified on the property, including the rare Bahama parrot. ✉ *Casuarina Point, Box AB 20092, Marsh Harbour* ☎ *242/366–2150 or 877/505–1850* ⊟ *242/327–8152* ⊕ *www.differentofabaco. com* ⇆ *20 rooms* ⌂ *Restaurant, some microwaves, refrigerators, pool, lake, outdoor hot tub, beach, snorkeling, boating, fishing, bicycles, billiards, bar, laundry facilities; no room phones, no room TVs* ⊟ *MC, V.*

**$** 🏨 **Conch Inn Resort & Marina.** This low-key, one-level marina hotel is a good choice for budget travelers, but make reservations well in advance. Each simple room has two double beds, white-tile floors, white-rattan furniture, and color-splashed bedspreads. The Conch Crawl restaurant serves delicious breakfasts, including cheesy omelets and thick, sweet pancakes. The 80-slip marina, one of Marsh Harbour's busiest, is the Bahamas' headquarters for the Moorings sailboat charter service and Nautic Blue Power Yacht Vacations. Top restaurants, shopping, and small beaches are within easy walking distance. ⌂ *Box AB 20469, Marsh Harbour, Abaco* ☎ *242/367–4000* ⊟ *242/367–4004* ⊕ *www.conchinn.com* ⇆ *10 rooms* ⌂ *Restaurant, refrigerators, pool, dive shop, dock, marina, bar, shop, laundry facilities* ⊟ *AE, MC, V.*

**$** 🏨 **Lofty Fig Villas.** Owned by the same family for years, this tidy compound has six spacious villas with pool or harbor views. Kitchens are fully equipped, and the supermarket is about a 10-minute walk away. Restaurants, marinas, bars, and a dive shop are even closer—basically right out the front door. For families or groups on a budget, this is a super option. ✉ *Across from Mangoes Restaurant and Conch Inn Resort, Box AB 20437, Marsh Harbour, Abaco* ☎ *242/367–2681* ⊟ *242/267-3385* ⊕ *loftyfig@mymailstation.com* ⇆ *6 villas* ⌂ *Kitchenettes, pool* ⊟ *D, MC, V.*

## Sports & the Outdoors

BICYCLING **Rental Wheels of Abaco** (☎ 242/367–4643) rents bicycles for $10 a day; they also have Suzuki and Yamaha mopeds.

BOATING You can get around Marsh Harbour, Great Abaco Island, and most of the nearby settled cays by car or ferry, but it's more fun to have your own boat. Marsh Harbour has the biggest selection of rental boats and the largest marinas in the Abacos, so even if you're staying on another cay, you may want to reserve your boat here. You can rent anything from a small dinghy to a 46-foot yacht or catamaran that will sleep six or more. Most rentals are available on a daily, three-day, or weekly basis. Count on spending at least $100 a day for a small boat and $180 for a larger one; the sky's the limit for a deluxe yacht with crew. Reserving your boat in advance is recommended, and remember that rates don't include fuel, which can cost nearly $4 per gallon in the Bahamas. Sailboats can be chartered by the week or longer, with or without crew.

In Marsh Harbour, **Boat Harbour Marina** (☎ 242/367–2158) has 190 fully protected slips and a slew of amenities. **Conch Inn Marina** (☎ 242/367–4000) is one of the busiest in Marsh Harbour and has 80 slips. **Marsh Harbour Marina** (☎ 242/367–2700) has 68 slips and is the only full-service marina on the left side of the harbor, a 10-minute drive from most shops and restaurants. **Mangoes Marina** (☎ 242/367–4255) has 29 slips and a full range of amenities, including on-shore showers, a pool, and a popular restaurant of the same name.

**Florida Yacht Charters** (☎ 242/367–4853 or 800/537–0050 ⊕ www.floridayacht.com), at the Boat Harbour Marina, offers air-conditioning and other amenities on its sailboats, power yachts, and catamarans. **The Moorings** (☎ 242/367–4000 or 888/952–8420 ⊕ www.moorings.com) rents 36- to 47-foot sailboats from its base at the Conch Inn Resort & Marina in Marsh Harbour. **Nautic Blue Power Yacht Vacations** (☎ 242/367–4000 or 800/416–0224 ⊕ www.nauticblue.com) has 34- to 46-foot powerboats.

**Laysue Rentals** (☎ 242/367–4414) is a good option for renting a catamaran in Marsh Harbour. **Rainbow Rentals** (☎ 242/367–4602) has custom-built 22-foot catamarans complete with freshwater showers, as well as powerboats. **Rich's Rentals** (☎ 242/367–2742 ⊕ www.richsrentals.com) is the place for 21- to 26-foot Paramount powerboats, all fully equipped for diving and fishing. **Sea Horse Boat Rentals** (☎ 242/367–2513 ⊕ www.seahorseboatrentals.com) has a variety of boats, from 26-foot Paramounts to 18-foot Boston Whalers. They're on the east side of Marsh Harbour in the Boat Harbour Marina, a more convenient location for people staying on Lubbers Quarters and Elbow Cay. They also have an office in Hope Town.

EVENTS   Several sporting events are held annually in the Abacos. You can catch the **Boat Harbour Billfish Championship** in June. Each July, **Regatta Time in Abaco,** a series of five sailboat races, takes place in five cays, with the party scene attracting even more participants than the races. In September there's a spectator event titled the **All Abaco Regatta,** with native Bahamian sloops competing in races, plus nightly festivals with food stands and live music. For information about Abacos events, call Marsh Harbour's **Abaco Tourist Office** (☎ 242/367–3067). The **Out Island Promotion Board** (☎ 954/475–8315 ⊕ www.myoutislands.com) has information on everything from special events to art galleries.

FISHING   You can find bonefish on the flats, yellowtail and grouper on the reefs, or marlin and tuna in the deeps of the Abacos. **Capt. Creswell Archer** (☎ 242/367–4000) will seek out tuna, wahoo, dorado, marlin and other offshore species during a half day or full day of deep-sea fishing. The

**Heritage Bonefishing Club** (☎ 242/366–2150) lures the fishing crowd to Casuarina Point at Different of Abaco—an angler's paradise. Premier fly-fishing guide **Justin Sands** (☎ 242/367–3526 or 242/359–6890 ⊕ www.thebahamian.com/justfish/) works out of a state-of-the-art Hell's Bay flats skiff that will put you on tailing bones in the skinniest water. Justin was the Abacos bonefish champ two years running, and he will guide you in the Marls or around Snake Cay, Little Harbour, and Cherokee Sound. Advance reservations are a must. Brothers Buddy and Christopher Pinder have a combined 30 years of experience in the local waters, and their **Pinder's Bone Fishing** (☎ 242/366–2163) offers year-round bonefishing on the Marls, a maze of mangroves and flats on the western side of Abaco.

SCUBA DIVING & SNORKELING
There's excellent diving throughout the Abacos. Many sites are clustered around Marsh Harbour, including the reef behind **Guana Cay,** which is filled with little cavelike catacombs, and **Fowl Cay National Reserve,** which contains wide tunnels and a variety of fish.

**Pelican Cays National Park** is a popular dive and snorkeling area south of Marsh Harbour. This shallow, 25-foot dive is filled with sea life; turtles are often sighted, as are spotted eagle rays and tarpon. The park is a 2,000-acre land and marine park protected and maintained by the Bahamas National Trust. Hook up your own boat to one of the moorings, or check with the local dive shops to see when trips to the park are scheduled. Snorkelers will want to visit Mermaid Beach, just off Pelican Shores Road in Marsh Harbour, where live reefs and green moray eels make for some of the Abacos' best snorkeling.

**Dive Abaco** (☎ 242/367–2787 or 800/247–5338 ⊕ www.diveabaco. com), at the Conch Inn in Marsh Harbour, offers scuba and snorkeling trips on their custom dive boats. Sites explored include reefs, tunnels, caverns, and wreck dives. Dive Abaco also maintains a boat and office at Abaco Beach Resort. **Rainbow Rentals** (☎ 242/367–4602) rents catamarans and snorkeling gear. **Sea Horse Boat Rentals** (☎ 242/367–2513) rents snorkeling gear.

TENNIS
**Abaco Beach Resort** (☎ 242/367–2158) opens its two lighted courts to visitors. A tennis pro is on hand for clinics and private lessons for adults and children, and there are regular round-robin tournaments for guests.

TOURS
**Abaco Island Tours** (☎ 242/367–2936 ⊕ www.abacoislandtours.com), inside Sapodilly's Restaurant, arranges tours of Marsh Harbour, Elbow Cay/Hope Town, Man-O-War Cay, Great Guana Cay, and Little Harbour. They can also help arrange diving, sailing, sea kayaking, fishing, and dolphin encounter tours through local guides.

WINDSURFING
Windsurfing equipment and sea kayaks are available free of charge to hotel and marina guests at the **Abaco Beach Resort** (☎ 242/367–2158).

## Shopping

At Marsh Harbour's traffic light, look for the turquoise-and-white stripe awnings of **Abaco Treasures** (☎ 242/367–3460), purveyors of fine china, crystal, perfumes, and gifts.

**Iggy Biggy** (✉ Queen's Hwy., Marsh Harbour ☎ 242/367–3596), inside a couple of bright-pink cottages, is your best bet for hats, sandals, tropical jewelry, sportswear, and souvenirs. If you are looking for gifts to take back home, you should be able to find something cool here.

Nassau straw hats and baskets, shell-encrusted coasters and candlesticks, and pillows and linens made in the Abacos are the best choices at **Island-Style Gifts** (✉ Royal Harbour Village ☎ 242/367–5861).

Sip an iced latte or a strong mug of joe while perusing the ceramics, quilts, pillows, carved wooden boats, and other locally produced artwork at **Java in Abaco** (✉ Royal Harbour Village ☎ 242/367–5523). There's also a book exchange where you can replenish your supply of paperbacks.

**John Bull** (✉ Queen's Hwy., Marsh Harbour ☎ 242/367–2473), on the water next to Mangoes, is a branch of a leading Nassau shop that sells Rolex and other brand-name watches, fine jewelry by designers such as David Yurman and Yvel, and makeup and perfume from Chanel, Christian Dior, Clinique, and Lancome. Fine leather goods, silk ties and scarves, and cool sunglasses are also on hand, along with a well-stocked humidor filled with Cuban cigars.

**Johnston Studios Art Gallery** (✉ Little Harbour ☎ 242/367–2720), 30 minutes south of Marsh Harbor, displays original bronzes by the Johnstons, as well as unique gold jewelry, prints, and gifts.

**Sand Dollar Shoppe** (✉ Royal Harbour Village ☎ 242/367–4405) sells resort wear, including a decent children's selection, and jewelry, featuring locally made Abaco Gold necklaces and earrings.

**Solomon's Mines** (✉ Queen Elizabeth Dr., Marsh Harbour ☎ 242/367–3191) sells upscale watches (think Tag Heuer and Patek Philippe), plus high-quality perfumes, cosmetics, and china, all duty-free. It's at the Abaco Beach Resort's entrance.

## Elbow Cay

★ ❻ In the charming village of **Hope Town**, most of the families of the 300-odd residents have lived here for at least several generations, in some cases as many as 10. Hope Town lies southeast of Marsh Harbour on Elbow Cay. A ferry from Marsh Harbour arrives several times a day.

You'll find few cars here, and although modern conveniences like high-speed Internet and satellite TV are becoming more common, they are a relatively new development. In fact, most residents remember well the day the island first got telephone service—back in 1988. Before that, everyone called each other the way many still do here and in the other Out Islands: by VHF, the party line for boaters. If you are boating, want to communicate well with the locals, or would like to make a dinner reservation on one of the cays, you should carry a VHF radio and have it tuned to Channel 16.

This laid-back community enthusiastically welcomes visitors. Upon arrival you'll first see a much-photographed Bahamas landmark, a 120-foot-tall, peppermint-striped lighthouse built in 1838. The light's construction was delayed for several years by acts of vandalism; then-residents feared it would end their profitable wrecking practice. Today, the **Hope Town lighthouse** is one of the Bahamas' last three hand-turned, kerosene-fueled beacons. Weekdays 10–4 the lighthouse keeper will welcome you at the top for a superb view of the sea and the nearby cays. There's no road between the lighthouse and the town proper. You can take your own boat here or use the ferry, but it probably won't be back for at least an hour.

For an interesting walking or bicycle tour of Hope Town, follow the two narrow lanes that circle the village and harbor. (Most of the village is closed to cars and golf carts.) The saltbox cottages—painted in brilliant blues, purples, pinks, and yellows—with their white picket fences, flowering gardens, and porches and sills decorated with conch shells, will remind you of a New England seaside community—Bahamian style. Some have fanciful names, like Summer Magic or Valentines, while others are charmingly practical. Your walk will take you past **Hope Town School,** the original 110-year-old, one-room schoolhouse, painted red and white. The hand-carved corners made by Loyalist shipwrights are still in evidence.

Stop by the **Cholera Cemetery,** a deceptively peaceful graveyard that contains the bodies of more than 100 victims of an outbreak of the deadly disease in the 1850s. The cemetery was closed after the outbreak, in hopes of further containing the epidemic.

You may want to stop at the **Wyannie Malone Historical Museum** (☎ 242/366–0293) on Queen's Highway, the main street. It contains Hope Town memorabilia and photographs. Admission is $3, but because the museum is staffed by volunteers, hours vary, and the museum closes completely in September and October. Many descendants of Mrs. Malone, who settled here with her children in 1875, still live on Elbow Cay.

Smack in the town's center stands an old, turquoise municipal building with offices clearly labeled "Commissioner," "Post Office," and "Visitor Information." Forget about the first two—they've long since relocated—but Hope Town's Visitor Information "office" is a cement room with a few well-papered bulletin boards on which everything from current happenings to restaurant menus is posted.

There are several churches in this tiny town. On Sunday morning, you'll hear sermons floating through open windows. Don't be surprised if you come upon an alfresco Catholic service in the dockside park. Residents joke that the priest has to stand in the hot sun while the congregation enjoys the shade of sprawling trees "so he won't talk so long."

### Where to Stay & Eat

¢–$$   ✕ **Harbour's Edge.** Hope Town's happening hangout, this bar and restaurant's deck is the best place to watch the goings-on in the busy harbor; you can tie you boat up right in front. Kick back and have an icy Kalik, or for extra punch, try a Kalik Gold—just make sure some else drives your golf cart or boat afterward. Live bands occasionally play on weekends, and this a great spot for an after-dinner drink. For lunch or dinner, try the tender conch burgers, grilled grouper, or lobster salad. Authentic Bahamian breakfasts are served on Sunday, and you can also rent bikes here for $8 a day. ☒ *Lower Rd., Hope Town* ☎ *242/366–0292 or 242/366–0087* ▭ *MC, V* ⊘ *Closed Tues.*

¢–$   ✕ **Cap'n Jack's.** There are a handful of booths and a small bar, but most of this casual eatery's seating is out on the pink-and-white-striped dock-patio. The menu is nothing fancy, but provides reliable grouper burgers, pork chops, and cracked conch. When it's in season, there's sometimes a lobster special. Cap'n Jack's serves three meals a day, offers a full bar, and has live music Wednesday and a DJ Friday nights mid-December through August. ☒ *Hope Town* ☎ *242/366–0247* ▭ *MC, V.*

¢–$   ✕ **On the Beach Bar and Grill.** Burgers, fries, conch, and fish are served up with a terrific Atlantic view at this open-air bar and grill perched high on the beach across the street from the small Turtle Hill resort. It's open only until sunset, and because all seating is open to the elements, a gullywasher of a storm closes the place down. ☒ *Queens Hwy., between Hope Town and White Sound, Hope Town* ☎ *242/366–0557* ⚐ *Reservations not accepted* ▭ *AE, MC, V* ⊘ *Closed Mon.*

$–$$$   ✕▤ **Hope Town Harbour Lodge.** You can have it all at this casually classy
Fodor's Choice   resort—spectacular views of the Atlantic Ocean and the beach, quality
★   amenities, and a location steps away from the town and harbor. Pleasant rooms are decorated island style, but treat yourself to one of the ocean-view or oceanfront cottages, with light pine paneling, terra-cotta tile floors, full kitchenettes, and French doors opening onto private decks. Lunch is poolside, with views of the ocean. At dinner in the Upper Terrace ($$–$$$), warm up with a key-lime martini rimmed with graham-cracker crumbs before tackling a steak or grilled wahoo with creamy butter and lime. ☒ *Upper Rd., Hope Town* ☎ *242/366–0095* ᐧ *242/366–0286* ⊕ *www.hopetownlodge.com* ☞ *12 rooms, 6 cabanas, 6 cottages, 1 private house* ⚭ *2 restaurants, some microwaves, some kitchenettes, pool, beach, dock, boating, 2 bars; no room phones, no room TVs* ⚐ *Reservations essential* ▭ *D, MC, V.*

$–$$$$   ▤ **Elbow Cay Properties.** Besides being the most cost-efficient way to stay on Elbow Cay, a private house or villa is also likely to be the most comfortable. This longstanding rental agency handles a variety of properties, from cozy two-bedroom, one-bath cottages to a six-bedroom, six-bath villa better described as a mansion. Many of the rental homes are on the water, with a dock or a sandy beach right out front. The owners are set on finding you a place to match your wishes and budget. They can also arrange boat rentals. There are no Sunday check-ins, as the agency is closed. ☒ *Western Harborfront, Hope Town* ☎᐀ *242/366–0569* ⊕ *www.elbowcayrentals.com* ☞ *50 units* ▭ *MC, V.*

★ $–$$$$   ▤ **Hope Town Hideaways.** Choose one of the comfy island homes scattered on 11 acres of gardens, with access to the harbor and the beach, or go more upscale with a West Indies–style Flamingo Villa, perfectly situated across from the lighthouse at the entrance to the harbor. The spacious two bedroom/two bath villas have large kitchens, satellite TV and Internet access, deluxe bedrooms with balconies, and wraparound decks with pools and barbecues. Owners Peggy and Chris Thompson also run a property-management company that rents more than 75 private cottages and houses. Most of these units sleep four or more, and some of the more upscale properties can accurately be described as mansions. Peggy and Chris can also arrange for everything from boat rentals to island excursions and fishing guides. ☒ *1 Purple Porpoise Pl., Hope Town* ☎ *242/366–0224* 🖷 *242/366–0434* ⊕ *www.hopetown.com* 📡 *75 units* ☲ *AE, D, MC, V.*

**$–$$$$** 🏨 **Sea Spray Resort and Marina.** Consider this resort if you're planning to catch any waves. The accommodations are just off Garbanzo Beach, which is popular with surfers. One-, two-, and three-bedroom villas have full kitchens, satellite TVs, air-conditioning, and large decks with outdoor grills. You can rent motorboats, bikes, and snorkeling gear. The on-site store sells everything from charcoal to surfboard wax. There's also a 60-slip full-service marina, a tiki bar, and a restaurant where you can enjoy the ocean view while feasting on steamed lobster or grilled, freshly caught grouper. ☒ *South end of White Sound* ☎ *242/366–0065* 🖷 *242/366–0383* ⊕ *www.seasprayresort.com* 📡 *7 villas* ⚒ *Restaurant, kitchenettes, pool, dock, snorkeling, boating, marina, fishing, bicycles, bar* ☲ *D, MC, V* ☾ *Closed Sept. and Oct.*

**$$–$$$** 🏨 **Turtle Hill Vacation Villas.** Bougainvillea- and hibiscus-lined walkways encircle the central swimming pool of this cluster of six villas, each with its own private patio. Inside, villas have central air-conditioning, full kitchens that open into the spacious dining–living room, light-wood paneling, tile floors, and rattan furnishings, as well as sleeper sofas. The lovely beach, the setting for the resort's bar and grill, is a two-minute walk away. Each villa comes with a golf cart for jaunts into town. Choose an upper villa for views of the ocean. ☒ *Off Queens Hwy. between Hope Town and White Sound, Hope Town* ☎ *508/540–2519 or 800/339–2124* 🖷 *242/366–0557* ⊕ *www.turtlehill.com* 📡 *4 2-bedroom villas, 2 3-bedroom villas* ⚒ *Fans, kitchenettes, microwaves, in-room VCRs, pool* ☲ *D, MC, V.*

**★ $–$$** 🏨 **Abaco Inn.** The motto here is "Barefoot elegance," making this beachfront resort the ideal place for a couples getaway. The cozy rooms—seven with ocean views and seven overlooking the harbor—have simple, comfortable furnishings and individual hammocks. Luxury villas have kitchenettes, small living areas, and sunrise and sunset water views. After your complimentary pickup in Hope Town, rent your own boat so you can zoom into town or to the smaller neighboring cays. Excellent reefs for surfing, snorkeling, and diving are nearby. The restaurant, which serves the freshest seafood on the island, is outstanding. The lounge has satellite TV and live music several nights a week. ☒ *2 mi south of Hope Town* ☎ *242/366–0133* 🖷 *242/366–0113* ⊕ *www.abacoinn.com* 📡 *14 rooms, 8 villas* ⚒ *Restaurant, pool, beach, boating, fishing, bicycles, bar, lounge, laundry facilities, airport shuttle; no room phones, no room TVs* ☲ *AE, D, MC, V.*

## Sports & the Outdoors

BOATING **Hope Town Hideaways** (☎ 242/366–0224) has 12 slips. **Island Marine** (☎ 242/366–0282) has 17- to 23-foot boats available for rent from $90 to $135 a day. **Sea Horse Boat Rentals** (☎ 242/367–2513) has Bimini-top boats ranging in length from 18 to 26 feet. They're located in Hope Town. **Sea Spray Resort and Marina** (☎ 242/366–0065) has a full-service marina with 60 slips.

FISHING Former Abaco bonefish champ **Justin Sands** (☎ 242/367–3526 or 242/359–6890 ⊕ www.thebahamian.com/justfish/) will guide you in the Marls or around Snake Cay, Little Harbour, or Cherokee Sound. Fly and spinfishing guides **Donny and Jimmy Lowe** (☎ 242/366–2275 ⊕ bonefishheaven@abacoinet.com) will take you to the waters surrounding Cherokee Sound, including the Bight of Old Robinson and Little Harbour. **Day's Catch** (☎ 242/366–0059) books charter fishing excursions on the nearby reefs with Will Key, who will even clean your fish afterward. Key is especially patient with children, who will enjoy learning about the fish as much as they'll enjoy landing one. **Seagull Charters** (☎ 242/366–0266) sets up guided deep-sea excursions with Captain Robert Lowe, who has more than 35 years' experience in local waters.

SCUBA DIVING & **Day's Catch** (☎ 242/366–0059) takes out small groups of snorkelers and SNORKELING divers in a 21-foot offshore boat. **Froggies Out Island Adventures** (☎ 242/366–0431) has snorkel and dive trips, scuba and resort courses, full-day adventure tours, island excursions, and dolphin encounters. You can also rent snorkeling and diving gear here.

WINDSURFING **Sea Spray Resort** (☎ 242/366–0065) attracts windsurfers to the choice waters just off Garbanzo Beach.

## Shopping

**Ebbtide** (☎ 242/366–0088) is on the upper path road in a renovated Loyalist home. Come here for such Bahamian gifts as batik clothes, original driftwood carvings and prints, and nautical jewelry. Browse through the extensive Bahamian book collection or pick up a magazine.

**Fantasy Boutique** (✉ Queen's Hwy. ☎ 242/366–0537) has a nice selection of souvenirs, beach wraps, T-shirts, arts and crafts, and Cuban cigars.

**Iggy Biggy** (✉ Queen's Hwy. ☎ 242/366–0354) is the only shop in Hope Town that carries the lovely Abaco ceramics handmade in Treasure Cay. They also sells wind chimes, sandals, resort wear, jewelry, and island music.

# Man-O-War Cay

❼ Less than 300 people live on skinny, 2.5-mi-long **Man-O-War Cay,** many of them descendants of early Loyalist settlers named Albury, who started the tradition of handcrafting boats more than two centuries ago. These residents remain proud of their heritage and continue to build their famous fiberglass boats today. This shipwrighting center of the Abacos lies south of Green Turtle and Great Guana cays, an easy 45-minute ride from Marsh Harbour by water taxi or aboard a small rented outboard dinghy. Man-O-War Cay also has a 28-slip marina, three churches, a one-room schoolhouse, several shops, two grocery stores, and restaurants that cater largely to visitors.

A mile north of the island, you can dive to the wreck of the USS *Adirondack,* which sank after hitting a reef in 1862. It lies among a host of cannons in 20 feet of water. The cay is also a marvelous place to walk or to take a rented golf cart for a spin—no cars are allowed on the island. Two main roads, Queen's Highway and Sea Road, are often shaded with arching sea grape trees interspersed with palms and pines. The island is secluded, but it has kept up-to-date with satellite television and full phone and Internet service. Still, the old-fashioned, family-oriented roots show in the local policy toward liquor: it isn't sold anywhere on the island. (But most folks won't mind if you bring your own.)

## Where to Stay & Eat

**$–$$** ✕ **Hibiscus Cafe.** This local favorite isn't fancy, but it turns out dependable Bahamian cooking. Lunchtime is casual, with burgers, grouper, and conch. Dinner, served Thursday through Saturday, is slightly more formal, with rack of lamb among the specialties. ⊠ *Waterfront* ☎ *242/365–6380* ▤ *No credit cards* ⊗ *Closed Sun.*

**$–$$** ✕ **The Pavilion.** Locals and tourists alike come here for Friday- and Saturday-night steak, chicken, ribs, or lamb dinners, served with the expected Bahamian sides of baked macaroni and cheese and peas 'n' rice. For lunch, chow down on grouper fingers, cracked conch, and coleslaw while you enjoy a view of the Man-O-War Marina. ⊠ *Waterfront* ☎ *242/365–6185 or 242/365–6008* ▤ *No credit cards* ⊗ *Closed Sun. Closed mid-Aug. and Sept.*

**$$** ▦ **Schooner's Landing.** Perched on a rocky promontory overlooking a long, isolated beach, this small, Mediterranean-style resort has four two-bedroom town-house condos with ocean views; two of these units include lofts for children or extra friends. Rooms are airy, with wicker furniture and ceramic tile floors, and include fully equipped kitchens, ceiling fans, TVs, and stereos with CD players. Gaze out to sea from the freshwater swimming pool's wraparound deck, or lounge in the gazebo, which has a barbecue and wet bar. There's no restaurant, but you can easily walk to almost every establishment, eating or otherwise, on the cay. The resort also has golf carts for rent, and the nearby grocery store delivers. ⊠ *Man-O-War Cay, Abaco* ☎ *242/365–6072 or 242/365–6143* 🖶 *242/365–6285* ⊕ *schoonerslanding.com* ⇗ *4 condominiums* ♿ *In-room VCRs, pool, beach, boating, fishing, laundry service* ▤ *AE, MC, V.*

## Sports & the Outdoors

BOATING **Man-O-War Marina** (☎ 242/365–6008) has 28 slips and rents 26-foot boats (and for landlubbers, golf carts. For people coming from Marsh Harbour or other cays, the Albury Ferry dock is adjacent.

SCUBA DIVING **Man-O-War Dive Shop** (⊠ Man-O-War Marina ☎ 242/365–6013) rents tanks and snorkeling equipment. Fowl Cay Undersea Park, located just north of Man-O-War Cay, is a good place for snorkeling.

### Shopping

★ **Albury's Sail Shop** (☎ 242/365–6014) is popular with boaters, who stock up on duffel bags, briefcases, jackets, hats, and purses, all made from duck, a colorful, sturdy canvas fabric traditionally used for sails.

**Island Treasures** (☎ 242/365–6072) has a wide selection of T-shirts, souvenirs, resort wear, candles, and ceramics.

**Joe's Studio** (☎ 242/365–6082) sells paintings by local artists, books, clothing, and other nautically oriented gifts, but the most interesting souvenirs are the half-models of sailing dinghies. These mahogany models, which are cut in half and mounted on boards, are meant to be displayed as wall hangings. Artist Joe Albury, one of the store's owners, also crafts full, 3-D boat models, which go for as much as $1,800.

## Great Guana Cay

❽ The essence of **Great Guana Cay** can be summed up by its unofficial motto,

Fodor'sChoice painted on a hand-lettered sign: IT'S BETTER IN THE BAHAMAS, BUT . . . IT'S

★ GOODER IN GUANA. This narrow island just off Great Abaco Island, accessible by ferry from Marsh Harbour or by private boat, is the kind of place people picture when they dream of running off to live on an exotic island, complete with alluring deserted beaches and grassy dunes. Only 100 full-time residents live on 7 mi-long Great Guana Cay, where you're more likely to run into a rooster than a car during your stroll around the tranquil village. Still, there are just enough luxuries here to make your stay comfortable, including a couple of small, laid-back resorts and a restaurant–bar with one of the best party scenes in the Abacos. The island also offers easy access to bonefishing flats you can explore on your own.

### Where to Stay & Eat

★ **$–$$$** ✕ **Nipper's Beach Bar & Grill.** With awesome ocean views and a snorkeling reef just 10 yards off its perfect beach, this cool bar and restaurant is a must-visit hangout. Linger over a lunch of burgers and sandwiches or a dinner of steak and lobster, then chill out in the solar-heated double pool, one for children and one with a swim-up bar for adults. The Sunday pig roasts are an all-day party, with mountains of food, live music, and dancing. Nurse a "Nipper Tripper"—a frozen concoction of five rums and two juices. If you down more than one or two of these, you'll be happy to take advantage of the Nippermobile, which provides free transport to and from the cay's public dock. ⊠ *Great Guana Cay* ☎ *242/365–5143* ⊕ *www.nippersbar.com* ▤ *AE, D, MC, V.*

**$–$$$$** ✕▥ **Dolphin Beach Resort.** You'll be tempted to stay forever at this up-

Fodor'sChoice scale haven. Spacious, uniquely designed rooms and larger cottages—

★ handcrafted of Abaco pine by Guana Cay shipwrights—are all painted in bright Junkanoo colors. Each island-style cottage is individually furnished and includes a private deck or terrace. Two cottages are set away from the resort, ideal for honeymooners. Outside, secluded showers are surrounded by bougainvillea and sea-grape trees. Boardwalk nature trails winding through the carefully tended 15-acre property lead to miles of secluded beach. The Blue Water Grill ($–$$$) is a special treat. For lunch, try the famous fried chicken, sandwich wraps, or quesadillas. At dinner, seafood curry, grilled tuna, and prime rib can be accompanied by a nice selection of wines. Dinner reservations are a must. ✉ *Great Guana Cay* ☎ *800/222–2646 or 242/365–5137* 📠 *242/365–5163* ⊕ *www.dolphinbeachresort.com* 🗨 *9 cottages, 4 rooms* ♿ *Restaurant, kitchenettes, pool, beach, dive shop, dock, snorkeling, windsurfing, boating, bicycles, bar, shops* ⊟ *AE, MC, V.*

$–$$$    ✕🏨 **Guana Seaside Village.** Close your eyes and picture an idyllic sea-
FodorśChoice   side resort with aqua-green water lapping at warm, white sand. Open
★   them and you're at this small bayside retreat set among tropical gardens and shaded by coconut palms. Eight airy island-style rooms are arranged around a lush courtyard and pool. An additional seven cottages, with porches and decks, are just steps from the beach. Each cottage has at least two bedrooms, two baths, and a full kitchen; some have washers and dryers. Guests can play with complimentary kayaks, snorkeling equipment, and paddleboats, or arrange fishing or diving trips. The specials at Hibiscus Restaurant and Bar ($–$$) include coconut shrimp, stuffed pork chops, lobster salad, and pastas of all kinds. The two-story restaurant is air-conditioned, but on breezy nights sit in the landscaped courtyard, a romantic option for dining alfresco. ✉ *Near Crossing Bay, Great Guana Cay* ☎ *877/681–3091 or 242/365–5106* 📠 *242/365–5146* ⊕ *www.guanaseaside.com* 🗨 *8 rooms, 7 cottages* ♿ *Restaurant, in-room VCRs, pool, beach, lounge; no phones in some rooms* ⊟ *D, MC, V* ☾ *Closed mid-Sept.–Oct.*

### Sports & the Outdoors

SCUBA DIVING   **Dive Guana** (☎ 242/365–5178), on the grounds of Dolphin Beach Resort, organizes scuba and snorkeling trips and island tours. The shop also rents boats, kayaks, and bicycles. Renting a boat, at least for a day, is the best way to get around and enjoy other nearby cays.

BOATING   **Orchid Bay Yacht Club and Marina** has 32 deep-water slips and full services for boaters at the entrance to the main settlement bay, across from the public docks. The club office rents luxury cottages and homes, and prime real estate is for sale. There's also a swimming pool and a restaurant overlooking the marina that serves delicious fresh seafood, steaks, and healthy salads.

## Treasure Cay

Running through large pine forests that are still home to wild horses and boars, the wide, paved Sherben A. Boothe Highway leads north from
❾   Marsh Harbour for 20 mi to **Treasure Cay**, which is technically not an
FodorśChoice   island but a large peninsula connected to Great Abaco by a narrow spit
★   of land. Here you'll find a small community of mostly winter residents, a 3,000-acre farm that grows winter vegetables and fruit for export, and a spectacular 3½-mi-long beach, often called the best in the Abacos.

While Treasure Cay is a large-scale real-estate development project, it's also a wonderful small community where expatriate residents share the laid-back, sun-and-sea atmosphere with long-time locals. The development's centerpiece is the Treasure Cay Hotel Resort & Marina, with its Dick Wilson–designed golf course and a 150-slip marina that has boat rentals, a dive shop, a swimming pool, and a restaurant and lively bar. Treasure Island's central location makes it a great base for exploring and enjoying the Abacos. Historic Elbow Cay, Man-O-War Cay, and Green Turtle Cay are all easily accessible by boat, and car rentals are available to travel north to Fox Town or south to Sandy Point.

Treasure Cay's commercial center consists of two rows of shops near the resort as well as a post office, laundromat, ice-cream parlor, a couple of well-stocked grocery stores, and the BaTelCo. You'll also find car-, scooter-, and bicycle-rental offices here.

## Where to Stay & Eat

**$–$$$** ✕ **Coconuts.** Tourists and locals flock to this popular spot, located at the intersection of Treasure Cay Road and the main highway. The well-appointed dining room's white tablecloths and classy dishware lend a bit of elegance to the island-casual atmosphere. A wide selection of American and Bahamian dishes includes fresh fish, broiled lobster, rack of lamb, pasta, and Bahamian chicken. The separate bar is a cool place to enjoy a cocktail or relax while waiting for a table. Reservations are a must, especially on the weekends. Free shuttle service is available from the parking lot in front of the Treasure Cay Marina. ⊠ *Queen's Hwy. at Treasure Cay Rd.* ☎ *242/365–8885* ▭ *MC, V.*

**$–$$** ✕ **Touch of Class.** Ten minutes north of Treasure Cay, this favorite dinner spot serves delicious traditional Bahamian dishes such as grilled freshly caught grouper, and minced local lobster stewed with tomatoes, onions, and spices. Reasonably priced appetizers, such as conch chowder and conch fritters, and a full bar make this a nice option for a night out. Free shuttle service is available from the parking lot in front of the Treasure Cay Marina. ⊠ *Queen's Hwy. at Treasure Cay Rd.* ☎ *242/365–8195* ▭ *MC, V.*

★ **¢–$** ✕ **Café La Florence.** Stop into this bakery-café in the Treasure Cay resort's main shopping strip for breakfast treats such as just-made muffins and the best cinnamon rolls in the universe. Or go for a light lunch of lobster quiche, conch chowder, or a spicy, Jamaican-style meat patty. Anglers can order fishing picnic lunches to go. You can also arrange for the chef to cater private dinners of lobster, steak, and the like in your rented condo. Florence's ice-cream parlor next door is your answer for treats à la mode. ⊠ *Treasure Cay* ☎ *242/365–8354* ▭ *No credit cards.*

**☾ $–$$$** ✕🏨 **Treasure Cay Hotel Resort & Marina.** Treasure Cay is best known for

**Fodor's**Choice
★

its 18-hole golf course, which *Golf Digest* frequently rates as the Bahamas' best, and its first-class 150-slip marina. The property has rooms and town house-style accommodations set along the marina's boardwalk. Room have mini-refrigerators, toaster ovens, and small dining counters; suites have vaulted ceilings, spacious living–dining areas, full modern kitchens, loft bedrooms, and balconies. The indoor–outdoor Spinnaker restaurant ($$–$$$) serves Bahamian and Continental cuisine. A more casual, kid-friendly option is Thursday night pizza at the Tipsy Seagull, the poolside bar and grill that is also a popular dance spot. The resort can arrange fishing, diving, and island excursions. ⊠ *On marina* ⌂ *2301 S. Federal Hwy., Fort Lauderdale, FL 33316* ☎ *242/365–8801 or 954/525–7711, 800/327–1584 reservations* ▤ *954/525–1699*

⊕ *www.treasurecay.com* ⤳ *54 rooms, 33 suites* ⚥ *Restaurant, dining room, kitchenettes, 18-hole golf course, 4 tennis courts, pool, beach, dive shop, dock, snorkeling, windsurfing, boating, marina, fishing, 2 bars, lounge, babysitting* ▤ *AE, D, MC, V* ⦿❙ *EP, FAP, MAP.*

★ **$$$–$$$$** 🏨 **Bahama Beach Club.** Ideal for families, these two- to five-bedroom condos are right off the famous Treasure Cay beach. Decor varies, but each unit has ceramic-tile floors and stylish rattan furniture with colorful accents, as well as a fully equipped kitchen and a large living room. Each unit has a patio or balcony overlooking the water and the grounds, which are landscaped with tropical palms. These are some of the nicest condos in the Abacos, and they are within a few minutes walk of the Treasure Cay Hotel Resort and Marina. ⌂ *Box AB 22275, Treasure Cay* ☎ *800/284–0382 or 242/365–8500* 🖷 *242/365–8501* ⊕ *www. bahamabeachclub.com* ⤳ *44 condos* ⚥ *Kitchens, pool, beach, laundry facilities* ▤ *AE, D, MC, V.*

**$$$** 🏨 **Treasure Houses.** Set around a courtyard of interconnected swimming pools, footbridges, and burbling waterfalls, these octagonal houses are perched on stilts for lovely beach views. Each two-bedroom guesthouse can sleep six and has airy, exposed-beam ceilings, lots of windows, and muted tropical-print textiles. Bedrooms open onto narrow private patios. Queen-size sleeper sofas, TVs with VCRs, and fully equipped kitchens are standard. Rent a golf cart or ride one of the gratis bicycles that accompany each unit. The Treasure Houses are 1 mi from the main resort and the Treasure Cay development's stores. ✉ *Treasure Cay beach* ☎ *242/365–8507 or 242/365–8777* 🖷 *242/365–8508* ⊕ *www. islandtreasurehouse.com* ⤳ *2 2-bedroom houses* ⚥ *BBQs, kitchenettes, pool, beach, snorkeling, bicycles, laundry facilities; no room phones* ▤ *MC, V.*

## Sports & the Outdoors

BICYCLING **Wendell's Bicycle Rentals** (☎ 242/365–8687) rents mountain bikes by the half-day, day, or week.

BOATING Located at the Treasure Cay Marina, **J. I. C. Boat Rentals** (☎ 242/365–8771) rents center-console boats for fishing and cruising the nearby cays; one-, three-, and seven-day rates are available. Try to reserve your boat at least two to three weeks in advance. Golf cart rentals are also available; book ahead for these as well. **Rich's Rentals** (☎ 242/365–8582) rents boats by the day, three-day block, or week. Daily rentals range from $130 to $160 for 21- to 26-foot Bimini-top fishing boats, perfect for island-hopping.

EVENTS A popular sportfishing destination, Treasure Cay hosts several fishing tournaments annually, including a leg of the **Bahamas Billfish Championship** in May. June brings the annual **Treasure Cay International Billfish Tournament.** Call **Treasure Cay Services** (☎ 954/525–7711 or 800/327–1584) for information about fishing and golf tournaments, regattas, and other special events.

FISHING Advanced reservations are a must to fish with **Justin Sands** (☎ 242/367–
★ 3526 or 242/359–6890 ⊕ www.thebahamian.com/justfish/), the Abaco's two-time bonefish champ.

★ Top professional bonefish guide **O'Donald Macintosh** (☎ 242/365–01263526) meets clients each day at Florence's Cafe in Treasure Cay for full or half days of guided bonefishing in the northern Marls or outside Coopers Town. In more than 20 years of guiding, O'D has built up a large, loyal base of repeat clients, so you'll need to book him well in advance—especially in the prime months of April, May, and June.

Arrange for local deep-sea fishing or bonefishing guides through **Treasure Cay Hotel Resort & Marina** (☎ 242/365–8250).

GOLF  A half mile from the **Treasure Cay Hotel Resort & Marina** (☎ 800/327–
★ 1584 or 954/525–7711 ⊕ www.golfbahamas.com) is the property's par-72, Dick Wilson–designed course, with carts available. There's no need to reserve tee times, and the course is usually delightfully uncrowded—ideal for a leisurely round. A driving range, putting green, and small pro shop are also on-site.

SCUBA DIVING &   No Name Cay, Whale Cay, and the Fowl Cay Preserve are popular ma-
SNORKELING  rine-life sites. The 1865 wreck of the steamship freighter **San Jacinto** also affords scenic diving and a chance to feed the resident green moray eel. **Treasure Divers** (☎ 242/365–8465 ⊕ www.treasure-divers.com), in the Treasure Cay Marina, rents equipment and takes divers and snorkelers out to a variety of sites.

TENNIS  **Treasure Cay Hotel Resort & Marina** (☎ 800/327–1584 or 242/365–8801) has six of the best courts in the Abacos, four of which are lighted for night play.

WINDSURFING  Windsurfers and a complete line of nonmotorized water craft are available for rent at the **Treasure Cay Hotel Resort & Marina** (☎ 242/365–8250).

## Shopping

Near Treasure Cay resort is **Abaco Ceramics** (☎ 242/365–8489 ⊙ Closed Sat. and Sun.), which offers its signature white clay pottery with blue fish designs.

# Green Turtle Cay

❿ A 10-minute ferry ride from a Treasure Cay dock will take you to **Green Turtle Cay.** The tiny island is steeped in Loyalist history; some residents can trace their heritage back to their ancestors' arrival from the U.S. colonies more than 200 years ago. The cay is surrounded by several deep bays, sounds, and a nearly continuous strip of fine beach.

**New Plymouth,** first settled in 1783, is Green Turtle's main community. Many of its approximately 550 residents earn a living by diving for conch or selling lobster and fish to the Abaco Seafood Company, but an increasing number depend on businesses catering to tourists and vacation-home owners. On some summer days during the height of Green Turtle's tourist season, the visitors on the island can outnumber the residents.

There are a few grocery and hardware stores, several gift shops, a post office, a bank, a handful of restaurants, and several offices—not to mention the homes that have been owned, in some cases, by the same families for generations. Narrow streets flanked by wild-growing flora (such as amaryllis, hibiscus, and poinciana) wind between rows of New England–style white-clapboard cottages with brightly colored shutters. During the Civil War, New Plymouth provided a safe haven for Confederate blockade runners. One Union ship, the USS *Adirondack,* was pursuing a gunrunner and wrecked on a reef in 1862 at nearby Man-O-War Cay. One of the ship's cannons now sits at the town harbor.

If your accommodations aren't in New Plymouth proper, you'll need transportation into town. Many hotels provide an occasional shuttle, and there's one taxi on the island, but most people travel via golf cart or boat. Your hotel can help to arrange a boat rental through one of several rental companies on the island. Don't worry, you won't miss having a car; even in the slowest golf cart, you can get from one end of the island to the other in 20 minutes or less.

New Plymouth's most frequently visited attraction is the **Albert Lowe Museum,** on the main thoroughfare, Parliament Street. The Bahamas' oldest historical museum, it's dedicated to a model-ship builder and direct descendant of the island's original European-American settlers. You can learn island history through local memorabilia from the 1700s, Lowe's model schooners, and old photographs, including one of the aftermath of the 1932 hurricane that nearly flattened New Plymouth. One of the galleries displays paintings of typical Out Island scenes by acclaimed artist Alton Lowe, Albert's son. Mrs. Ivy Roberts, the museum's director, enjoys showing visitors around and sharing stories of life in the Out Islands before the days of high-speed Internet and daily airline flights. ⊠ *Parliament St.* ☎ *242/365–4094* ⊠ *$5* ⊗ *Mon.–Sat. 9–11:45 and 1–4.*

Just a few blocks from the Albert Lowe Museum, on Victoria Street, is **Miss Emily's Blue Bee Bar** (☎ 242/365–4181), which stands next to the old gaol (jail), a tiny stone building thought to be more than 100 years old and, happily, no longer in use. Mrs. Emily Cooper, creator of the popular Goombay Smash drink, passed away in 1997, but her daughter Violet continues to serve up the famous rum, pineapple juice, and apricot brandy concoction. The actual recipe is top secret, and in spite of many imitators throughout the islands, you'll never taste a Goombay this good anywhere else. It's worth a special trip to try one. Mementos left by customers—business cards, expired credit cards, T-shirts, and autographed dollar bills—and Junkanoo masks cover the walls and ceiling.

The past is present in the **Memorial Sculpture Garden,** across the street from the New Plymouth Inn. (Note that it's laid out in the pattern of the British flag.) Immortalized in busts perched on pedestals are local residents who have made important contributions to the Bahamas. Plaques detail the accomplishments of British Loyalists, their descendants, and the descendants of those brought as slaves, such as Jeanne I. Thompson, a contemporary playwright and the country's second woman to practice law.

### Where to Stay & Eat

$–$$   ✕ **McIntosh Restaurant and Bakery.** At this simple, diner-style restaurant, lunch means excellent renditions of local favorites, such as fried grouper and cracked conch, and sandwiches made with thick slices of slightly sweet Bahamian bread. At dinner, large portions of pork chops, lobster, fish, and shrimp are served with rib-sticking sides like baked macaroni and cheese, peas 'n' rice, and coleslaw. Save room for a piece of pound cake or coconut cream pie, baked fresh daily and displayed in the glass case up front. Or, on a hot day, step next door to the attached Three Sisters' Ice Cream Shop for a scoop of homemade cookies 'n' cream or coconut ice cream. ⊠ *Parliament St.* ☎ *242/365–4625* ⊟ *D, MC, V.*

¢–$$    ✕ **Jolly Roger Bar and Bistro.** This casual eatery on the water in the Bluff House Marina offers tasty lunches and, in the evening, a less formal alternative to the reservation-only fine dining in the Clubhouse restaurant. Sitting under a canvas umbrella on the deck is the best way to enjoy the view of the sailboat-filled harbor, but you can also eat in the air-conditioned pub-style dining room. Menu choices range from standard Bahamian (conch fritters and burgers) to new American (roasted pork tenderloin with salsa, salads with goat cheese and roasted vegetables, and even, on occasion, sushi). Another fun option is to enjoy a rum drink from the bar while catching some rays at the pool. ⊠ *Between Abaco Sea and White Sound, at Bluff House Beach Hotel marina* ⌖ *Box AB 22886, Green Turtle Cay* ☎ *242/365–4247* ⊟ *AE, MC, V.*

$    ✕ **The Wrecking Tree.** The wooden deck at this casual restaurant was built around the wrecking tree, a place where 19th-century wrecking vessels brought their salvage. Today it's a cool place to linger over a cold Kalik and a hearty lunch of cracked conch, fish-and-chips, or zesty conch salad. Dinners may include turtle steak or grilled lobster—if you order by 5 PM. Otherwise, choose from dishes like fresh-caught grouper and fried chicken. They have great pastries too—take some back to your hotel or rental cottage. And ask for Phil Stubb's CD if you like island music. ⊠ *Bay St.* ☎ *242/365–4263* ⊟ *No credit cards* ⊙ *Closed Sun.*

$–$$$$    ✕▦ **Bluff House Beach Hotel.** From its perch on a rocky bluff overlook-
**Fodor'sChoice**    ing White Sound, this romantic hilltop hideaway provides sweeping views
★    of the sheltered harbor or the Sea of Abaco. Established in 1954 by wealthy Americans who loved to entertain, this elegant resort has grown and improved with age. Formal dinners are still served by reservation only in the dining room ($$$) adjoining the open-air, natural pine cocktail lounge and library. (It's only open during the main season, which starts in March.) The split-level suites have tropical-style wicker furniture, parquet-inlay floors, and double doors opening onto balconies with sensational ocean vistas. Even more spacious are the two-bedroom marine villas, with huge screened-in verandahs overlooking the marina. ⊠ *Between Abaco Sea and White Sound* ⌖ *Box AB 22886, Green Turtle Cay, Abaco* ☎ *242/365–4247 or 800/745–4911* 🖷 *242/365–4248* ⊕ *www.BluffHouse.com* ⇨ *4 rooms, 8 suites, 9 villas* ♨ *2 restaurants, refrigerators, tennis court, 2 pools, beach, dock, snorkeling, boating, marina, fishing, 2 bars, lounge, laundry service; no room phones, no room TVs* ⊟ *AE, D, MC, V* ⑩ *EP, MAP.*

★ $–$$$$    ✕▦ **Green Turtle Club.** Purchased by Ann Showell Mariner and Adam Lockhart Showell Sr. in 2004, the longstanding tradition of casual refinement continues at this well-known resort. The cheerful yellow cottages are scattered up a hillside amid lush trees and shrubs. Villa accommodations have decks overlooking the water and docks for rental boats; poolside rooms are more formal, furnished with mahogany Queen Anne–style furniture, gleaming hardwood floors, and Oriental rugs. Breakfasts and lunches are served on a screened, terra-cotta tile patio, but it's dinner under the harbor-view dining room's chandeliers—which transport you back to the 1920s—that makes the club shine. Choose from an ever-changing menu ($$–$$$) that might include fresh grilled lobster, sautéed lemon grouper, or rack of lamb, accompanied by the best selection of wines in the Abacos. ⊠ *North end of White Sound, Green Turtle Cay* ✉ *Box AB 22792, Green Turtle Cay* ☎ *242/365–4271 or 866/528–0539* 🖷 *242/365–4272* ⊕ *www.greenturtleclub.com* 🛏 *24 rooms, 2 suites, 8 villas* ⚭ *Restaurant, dining room, fans, refrigerators, some in-room VCRs, pool, beach, dock, snorkeling, boating, 40-slip marina, fishing, bar, laundry facilities; no room phones* ⊟ *AE, D, MC, V* ⦶ *EP, MAP.*

**$** ✕⊡ **New Plymouth Club & Inn.** This charming, two-story historic hostel with white balconies is in New Plymouth's center. Renovated in 2004 but originally built in 1830, the building had been a French mercantile exchange, a warehouse, and a private residence before it opened as a hotel in 1946. A patio pool is nestled in well-manicured tropical gardens, and the cozy rooms have canopy beds and terra-cotta tile baths. The rates are among the most affordable options on the cay and include breakfast. The dining room serves memorable Bahamian-style dinners of lobster, grouper, snapper, and chicken. Call for reservations and to see if they are open. ⊠ *Parliament St.* ☎ *242/365–4161* 🖷 *242/365–4138* 🛏 *9 rooms* ⚭ *Restaurant, fans, pool, bar, lounge* ⊟ *D, MC, V.*

**$–$$$$** ⊡ **Island Property Management.** A five-bedroom, oceanfront mansion with wraparound verandah, full-time staff, and a marble fireplace could be yours. Or rent a two-bedroom cottage in the heart of New Plymouth. This agency will find you a property to match your budget and needs, and can help arrange excursions and boat and golf cart rentals. Most homes have water views, and some have docks for your rental boat. ✉ *Box AB 22758, Green Turtle Cay, Abaco* ☎ *242/365–4047 or 561/202–8333* 🖷 *561/202–8478* ⊕ *www.go-abacos.com/ipm/* 🛏 *27 units* ⊟ *D.*

**$$** ⊡ **Coco Bay Cottages.** Sandwiched between one beach on the Atlantic and another calmer sandy stretch on the bay, these homey cottages all have views of the water. Each has attractive rattan furniture, a telephone, a modern kitchen, and linens. Snorkeling and diving are excellent around the reef that protects the Atlantic beach. The bay, where sunset views are fabulous, is prime territory for shell collecting and bonefishing. A separate building holds a library with games and books, satellite TV, and exercise equipment. ⊠ *Coco Bay, North of Green Turtle Club* ☎ *242/365–5464 or 800/752–0166* 🖷 *242/365–5465* ⊕ *www. cocobaycottages.com* 🛏 *4 cottages* ⚭ *Kitchenettes, gym, beach, dock, snorkeling, library* ⊟ *D, MC, V.*

**$$** ⊡ **Linton's Beach and Harbour Cottages.** These three classic Bahamian-style cottages are ideally placed between Long Bay and Black Sound. The two beachside cottages are on a rise overlooking Pelican Cay and the Atlantic. Each has two comfortable bedrooms, a screened-in porch, a combination living/dining room with built-in settees, a well-stocked library, and a fully equipped kitchen. The Harbour Cottage, with one air-conditioned bedroom, is on Black Sound, steps away from the dock. If you're renting a boat, you can tie it up right out front. Families, groups of friends, and couples looking for an escape will enjoy this location. ✉ *S. Loyalist Rd.* 🏠 *Box 64-3066 Vero Beach, FL 32964* ☎ *772/ 538–4680* 🌐 *www.lintoncottages.com* 🛏 *3 cottages* ⚲ *Fans, kitchenettes, boating, bicycles, library* ▤ *No credit cards.*

### Nightlife

At night, Green Turtle can be deader than dead or surprisingly lively. Bet on the latter if the local favorites, the **Gully Roosters,** are playing anywhere on the island. Known locally as just the Roosters, this reggae-calypso band is the most popular in the Abacos. Its mix of original tunes and covers can coax even the most reluctant reveler onto the dance floor. The band's home base is **Rooster's Rest** (☎ 242/365–4066), a pub and restaurant in a bright blue building at the entrance to New Plymouth. The band's schedule there is erratic; ask at your hotel or just drive by one of their haunts on a Friday or Saturday night to see what's happening. In addition to Rooster's Rest, try **Bluff House Beach Resort** (☎ 242/ 365–4247) and **Green Turtle Club** (☎ 242/365–4271), both of which also sell Rooster CDs, a good souvenir of your visit.

★ Other nighttime options include a visit to **Miss Emily's Blue Bee Bar** (☎ 242/ 365–4181), where you might find a singing, carousing crowd knocking back the world famous Goombay Smash. (Or not—many Goombay novices underestimate the drink's potency, and end up making it an early night.) Locals hang out at **Sundowner's** (☎ 242/365–4060), a waterside bar and grill where attractions include a pool table and, on weekend nights, a DJ spinning dance music on the deck under the stars.

### Sports & the Outdoors

BICYCLING  The flat roads of Green Turtle Cay are perfect for getting around by bicycle. **D&P Rentals** (☎ 242/365–4655) rents mountain bikes for $10 per day.

BOATING  It's highly recommended that you reserve your boat rental at the same time you book your hotel or cottage. If you're unable to rent a boat on Green Turtle Cay, try nearby Treasure Cay.

**Bluff House Beach Hotel** (☎ 242/365–4247) has a marina with 45 slips. **Green Turtle Club** (☎ 242/365–4271) has 40 slips and is home to Green Turtle Divers dive shop. **The Other Shore Club Marina and Cottages** (☎ 242/ 365–4226 or 242/365–4338 🌐 www.othershoreclub.com), tucked into quiet and protected Black Sound, is an ideal place to keep your small cay-hopping boat if you are staying in one of Green Turtle's many rental houses and cottages. The club has its own rental cottages and can arrange fishing, diving, and snorkeling trips.

**Donny's Boat Rentals** (☎ 242/365–4119) rents boats ranging from 14-foot Whalers to 23-foot Makos. **Paradise Boat Rentals** (☎ 242/365– 4359 🌐 www.abacoboatrentals.com) has custom-built Albury's Brothers 20-foot runabouts crafted on Man 'O War Cay. The Bimini tops are retractable, and boats include ice chests, anchors, paddles, first aid kits, life vests, compasses, VHF radios, rod holders, and large dry storage. **Reef Rentals** (☎ 242/365–4145) has fishing boats and pleasure crafts ranging from 19 to 21 feet.

EVENTS The **Bluff House Fishing Tournament** is held in May. In the beginning of July, the **Bahamas Cup** boat race, part of **Regatta Time in Abaco,** circumnavigates Green Turtle Cay. **All Abaco Regatta,** the work-boat race between Green Turtle and Treasure Cay, is held at the end of October. For information on special events, call the **Abaco Tourist Office** (☎ 242/367–3067). The **Out Island Promotion Board** (☎ 954/475–8315) has details on island tournaments and other seasonal events.

FISHING **Captain Rick Sawyer** (☎ 242/365–4261 ⊕ www.abacoflyfish.com) is one of Abaco's best guides, and the top recommendation on Green Turtle Cay. Rick's company, **Abaco Flyfish Connection and Charters,** offers bonefishing on 17-foot Maverick flats skiffs, and reef and offshore fishing aboard his 31-foot Tiara. Complete fishing packages are available, including accommodations at **Pineapple Bluff** (☎ 242/365–4045 ⊕ www.pineapplebluff.com). Book as far in advance as you can. **Ronnie Sawyer** (☎ 242/365–4070) works with Rick and on his own. Call **Joe Sawyer** (☎ 242/365–4173) for a morning of reef fishing in his 29-foot boat.

SCUBA DIVING & **Brendal's Dive Center** (☎ 242/365–4411 ⊕ www.brendal.com) leads
SNORKELING snorkeling and scuba trips, plus wild dolphin encounters, glass-bottom
★ boat cruises, and more. Personable owner Brendal Stevens has been featured on the Discovery Channel and CNN, and he knows the surrounding reefs so well that he's named some of the groupers, stingrays, and moray eels that you'll have a chance to hand-feed. Trips can include a seafood lunch, grilled on the beach, and complimentary rum punch. Kayak and canoe rentals are available.

Rent some snorkel gear or bring your own, and call **Lincoln Jones** (☎ 242/365–4223), known affectionately as "the Daniel Boone of the Bahamas," for an unforgettable snorkeling adventure. Lincoln will dive for conch and lobster (in season) or catch fish, then grill a sumptuous lunch on a deserted beach.

TENNIS **Bluff House Beach Hotel** (☎ 242/365–4247) has one hard-surface court; rackets and balls are provided.

## Shopping

**Golden Reef** (✉ Parliament St. ☎ 242/365–4511) sells jewelry, including Abaco Gold jewelry made in Marsh Harbour, plus resort wear, kids' clothing, swimwear, and gifts.

Colorful Abaco Ceramics, handmade in Treasure Cay, are the best bet at **Native Creations** (✉ Parliament St. ☎ 242/365–4206). The shop also sells beaded jewelry, picture frames, candles, postcards, and books.

Annexed to Plymouth Rock Liquors and Café, **Ocean Blue Gallery** (✉ Parliament St. ☎ 242/365–4234) is a small gallery with framed and unframed paintings, sculptures, and other works by more than 50 local artists. The adjoining liquor store sells Cuban cigars and more than 60 kinds of rum.

**Sid's Grocery** (☎ 242/365–4055) has the most complete line of groceries on the island, plus a gift section that includes books on local Bahamian subjects—great for souvenirs or for replenishing your stock of reading material.

**Vert's Model Ship Shop** (✉ Corner of Bay St. and Gully Alley ☎ 242/365–4170) has Vert Lowe's handcrafted two-mast schooners and sloops. Model prices range anywhere from $100 to $1,200. If Vert's shop door is locked—and it often is—knock at the white house with bright pink shutters next door. If you're still unsuccessful, inquire at the Green Turtle Club, where Vert has worked for more than 30 years.

## Spanish Cay

Only 3 mi long, this privately owned island was once the exclusive retreat of millionaires, and many visitors still arrive by yacht or by landing a private plane on the 5,000-foot airstrip. Although several private upscale homes dot the coast, a small resort also rents rooms and condos. A well-equipped marina, great fishing, and some fine beaches are among the attractions here.

### Where to Stay & Eat

$$ ×☐ **Spanish Cay Resort and Marina.** Take your pick here—either a beachfront room or a two-room hotel suite tucked away on a hill overlooking the marina and the Sea of Abaco. Decisions, decisions. Regardless of location, all rooms have tile floors, pastel draperies and bedspreads, private porches, king or double beds, and desks. Two- to four-bedroom condos and luxury villas are also available. The Pointe House ($$–$$$$) serves three meals daily; locally caught fish is your best bet for dinner. The 81-slip marina can handle yachts up to 250 feet, and boat rentals are available. ✑ *Cay Resorts Limited, 1110 N.E. 7th Ave., Dania, FL 33004* ☎ *242/365–0083* 🖷 *242/365–0453* ⊕ *www.spanishcay.com* ⇌ *18 rooms, 5 condos, 12 villas* ⟨ *Restaurant, microwaves, refrigerators, 4 tennis courts, pool, hot tub, 81-slip marina, bar; no room phones* ▤ *MC, V.*

# THE ABACOS ESSENTIALS

### BY AIR

There are two major public airports in the Abacos. Most flights land at the international airports in Marsh Harbour or Treasure Cay. Some private planes and charter carriers use the airstrip at Spanish Cay. There's also a small public airstrip in Sandy Cay.

Many carriers operate seasonal schedules to the Abacos. Some routes are flown daily from December through August, and three times a week from September through November. In addition, many airlines serving the Abacos are very small and change schedules frequently, even in season.

Air Sunshine flies from Fort Lauderdale to Marsh Harbour and Treasure Cay. American Eagle has a daily flight to Marsh Harbour from Miami. Bahamasair flies daily from Nassau to Marsh Harbour and Treasure Cay. Cherokee Air is the charter-plane service of choice for island hopping to or from the Abacos. Continental Connection flies into both Marsh Harbour and Treasure Cay from Miami and Fort Lauderdale. Island Express Airways has daily flights to Marsh Harbour and Treasure Cay from Fort Lauderdale. Twin Air has several flights per week to Treasure Cay from Fort Lauderdale, and flies to other parts of the Abacos by charter. Vintage Props and Jets flies into Marsh Harbour and Treasure Cay from four airports in Florida: Daytona Beach, Melbourne, Orlando, and New Smyrna Beach. Yellow Air Taxi has scheduled charters into Marsh Harbour and Treasure Cay from Fort Lauderdale and West Palm Beach.

**3**

▊ Airlines & Contacts **Air Sunshine** ☎ 954/434-8900 or 800/327-8900 ⊕ www. airsunshine.com. **American Eagle** ☎ 242/367-2231 or 800/433-7300 ⊕ www.aa.com. **Bahamasair** ☎ 242/367-2095 in Marsh Harbour, 242/365-8601 in Treasure Cay ⊕ www. bahamasair.com. **Cherokee Air** ☎ 242/367-2089 ⊕ www.cherokeeair.com. **Continental Connection** ☎ 242/367-3415 in Marsh Harbour, 242/365-8615 in Treasure Cay, 800/ 231-0856 ⊕ www.continental.com. **Island Express Airways** ☎ 954/359-0380 ⊕ http://oii. net/islandexpress/. **Twin Air** ☎ 954/359-8266 ⊕ www.flytwinair.com. **Vintage Props and Jets** ☎ 800/852-0275 ⊕ www.vpj.com. **Yellow Air Taxi** ☎ 888/935-5694 ⊕ www. flyyellowairtaxi.com.

## BY BOAT

Boats are a key method of transportation among the many islands of the Abacos. A good system of public ferries and boat rental agencies allows you to reach even the most remote cays. Assuming you have plenty of time and a sense of adventure, you can even arrive in the Abacos by mail boat.

BOAT RENTAL If you don't want to be bound by the somewhat limited schedule of the ferries, rent a small boat. Having your own boat also allows you the freedom to explore uninhabited cays, find your own favorite fishing and snorkeling spots, and picnic on secluded beaches. Most hotels and many rental cottages have docking facilities that allow you to keep your boat within easy reach. Boats can be rented on most islands with tourist facilities, but the best selections are at the main visitor destinations, including Marsh Harbour, Treasure Cay, Hope Town, and Green Turtle Cay.

In Marsh Harbour, Rich's Rentals has 21- and 26-foot Paramount powerboats. The boats at Rainbow Rentals in Marsh Harbour include custom-built 22-foot center-console powerboats. Sea Horse Boat Rentals has a large selection at its two offices in Marsh Harbour and Hope Town. In Treasure Cay, check out J. I. C. Boat Rentals, which rents boats on a daily, three-day, or weekly basis. In Green Turtle Cay, Donny's Boat Rentals and Reef Rentals both offer fishing boats that comfortably carry up to six passengers, and Paradise Boat Rentals has custom-built Albery 20-foot boats with retractable bimini tops.

▊ Boat Rental Information **Donny's Boat Rentals** ☎ 242/365-4119. **J. I. C. Boat Rentals** ☎ 242/365-8465. **Paradise Boat Rentals** ☎ 242/365-4359. **Rainbow Rentals** ☎ 242/367-4602. **Reef Rentals** ☎ 242/365-4145. **Rich's Rentals** ☎ 242/367-2742. **Sea Horse Boat Rentals** ☎ 242/367-2513.

FERRIES In contrast to the mail boats, the two major ferry services serving the Abacos are very punctual. Every day except Sunday and holidays, Albury's Ferry Service leaves Marsh Harbour for the 20-minute ride to

CLOSE UP

# Boating in the Abacos

**THE ABACOS PROVIDE SUPERB RECREATIONAL CRUISING GROUNDS.** If you tune your VHF radio to Chanel 16, you'll be able to communicate with just about everyone in the area.

In the northern portion of the archipelago, Grand Cay is a laid-back settlement of about 200 people and four times that many Bahamian potcakes (mixed breed dogs). Most yachters will find the anchorage off the community dock adequate, and the docks at Rosie's Place can take boats up to 80-feet, depending on traffic. Double anchors are advised to handle the harbor's tidal current.

Heading south from Grand Cay, you'll pass a clutch of tiny cays and islets, such as Double Breasted Cays, Roder Rocks, Barracuda Rocks, Miss Romer Cay, Little Sale Cay, and Great Sale Cay. Great Sale Harbour provides excellent shelter. Other small islands in the area are Carter Cay, Moraine Cay, Umbrella Cay, Guineaman Cay, Pensacola and Allen's cays (which are now virtually one island since a hurricane filled in the gap between them), and the Hawksbill Cays. Most offer varying degrees of lee anchorage. Fox Town, due south of Hawksbill Cay on Little Abaco's western tip, is the first refueling stop for powerboats traveling east from West End.

A narrow causeway joins Little Abaco to Great Abaco, where the largest community at the north end is Cooper's Town. Stock up here on provisions. You'll also find a coin laundry, a telephone station, a few restaurants, bakeries, and a resident doctor here. Just northeast of Cooper's Town is the private island 81-slip marina at Spanish Cay.

Cruising south, you'll pass Powell Cay, Nun Jack Cay, and Crab Cay on the way to Green Turtle Cay, which has excellent yachting facilities at White Sound to the north and Black Sound to the south. The Green Turtle Club dominates White Sound's northern end, whereas Bluff House, halfway up the sound, has docks on the inside and a dinghy dock below the club on the Sea of Abaco side.

South of New Plymouth on Great Abaco's mainland is the Treasure Cay Hotel Resort & Marina, with one of the area's longest and finest beaches. Complete facilities for boaters are available here; you can also stop over to play a round of golf.

Straight back out in the Sea of Abaco is Great Guana Cay and its famous 7-mi strip of pristine beaches. Just south is a New England–style charmer: Man-O-War Cay, a boatbuilding settlement with more deserted beaches and the 28-slip Man-O-War Marina.

Continuing south, the Bahamas' most photographed lighthouse sits atop Elbow Cay, signaling the harbor opening to Hope Town, an idyllic small resort community.

Back on Great Abaco, you'll find the Abacos's most populous settlement at Marsh Harbour, which has plenty of facilities for boaters. These include the modern 190-slip Boat Harbour Marina, a full-service operation on the island's east side. The other side of town has additional marinas, including the 80-slip Conch Inn Marina, Marsh Harbour Marina and its 68 slips, and a couple of smaller facilities.

Hope Town at 7:15, 9, 10:30, 12:15, 2, 4, and 5:45; ferries make the return trip at 8, 9:45, 11:30, 1:30, 3, 4, and 5. A same-day round-trip costs $15. One-way tickets cost $10. Albury's also provides service between Marsh Harbour and Man-O-War Cay or Guana Cay. Charter excursions can also be booked.

The Green Turtle Cay Ferry leaves the Treasure Cay airport dock at 8:30, 10:30, 11:30, 1:30, 2:30, 3:30, 4:30, and 5 (except Sunday) and returns from Green Turtle Cay at 8, 9, 11, 12:15, 1:30, 3, and 4:30. One-way fares are $8, and a same-day round-trip fare is $14. The ferry makes several stops in Green Turtle, including New Plymouth, the Green Turtle Club, and the Bluff House Beach Hotel.

**⚑ Ferry Information Albury's Ferry Service** ☎ 242/367-3147 or 242/365-6010 ⊕ www.oii.net/alburysferry. **Dockmaster's Office** ☎242/393-1064. **Green Turtle Cay Ferry** ☎242/365-4032.

MAIL BOATS  A mail boat is scheduled to depart every Tuesday from Potter's Cay, Nassau, for Marsh Harbour and Green Turtle Cay, returning to Nassau on Thursday. Another boat is supposed to depart Nassau each Friday for Sandy Point, at the southern tip of Great Abaco, and return to Nassau on Friday. However, the schedule is often affected by wind, rain, tides, mechanical problems, and other issues. Each one-way journey takes about six hours. For details, call the Dockmaster's Office at Potter's Cay.

### BY CAR

Cars are not necessary on most of the smaller cays in the Abacos; in fact, rental cars aren't even available in most locations. On Great Abaco, however, you'll need a car if you want to venture beyond Marsh Harbour or Treasure Cay. Rentals are expensive, at about $75 a day and up, and gasoline costs at least $3.50 per gallon. You might negotiate a better rate if you rent for a week or longer. In Marsh Harbour, you can rent automobiles from H & L Car Rentals, A & P Rentals, or Rental Wheels of Abaco. Just outside Treasure Cay Airport, Cornish Car Rentals has a large rental fleet.

**⚑ Local Agencies A & P Rentals** ☎ 242/367-2655. **Cornish Car Rentals** ☎ 242/365-8623. **H & L Car Rentals** ✉ Shell Gas Station ☎242/367-2854. **Rental Wheels of Abaco** ☎ 242/367-4643.

### BY GOLF CART

Golf carts are the vehicle of choice on the majority of the smaller cays, including Elbow Cay, Green Turtle Cay, Great Guana Cay, and Man-O-War Cay. Each can carry four adults comfortably, if slowly. The standard rates are $45 to $50 per day for a gas cart, or $240 per week. Electric-powered carts, which usually must be recharged nightly, are slightly cheaper. Big-wheel carts, which provide a smoother ride on the bumpy, pothole-filled roads common in the islands, cost a little more and are not available at all locations. Reservations are always recommended, but are essential in the busy travel months of April, May, June, and July.

In Hope Town, try Hope Town Cart Rentals, Island Cart Rentals, or T&N Cart Rentals. In Treasure Cay, you can rent carts from Cash's Resort Carts or Blue Marlin Rentals. On Green Turtle, Bay Street Rentals is on the grounds of the Bluff House Beach Hotel. D & P Rentals rents carts from an office at the Green Turtle Club. In New Plymouth, try Island Roadrunner or Seaside Carts. On Man-O-War, the Man-O-War Marina has golf carts.

🔲 **Bay Street Rentals** 📞 242/365-4070. **Blue Marlin Rentals** 📞 242/365-8687. **Cash's Resort Carts** 📞 242/365-8771. **D & P Rentals** 📞 242/365-4655. **Hope Town Cart Rentals** 📞 242/366-0064. **Island Cart Rentals** 📞 242/366-0448. **Island Roadrunner** 📞 242/365-4610. **Man-O-War Marina** 📞 242/365-6008. **Seaside Carts** 📞 242/477-5497. **T&N Cart Rentals** 📞 242/366-0069.

### BY TAXI

Only a few islands have taxi service—including Great Abaco, Green Turtle Cay, and Elbow Cay—but there are plenty of taxis in Treasure Cay and Marsh Harbour. Taxi services meet arriving planes at the airports and will take you to your hotel or to a ferry dock, where you can catch a water taxi to neighboring islands such as Green Turtle Cay, Great Guana, or Elbow Cay. Hotels will arrange for taxis to take you on short trips and back to the airport. Fares are generally $1.50 per mi. A 15% tip is customary.

## Contacts & Resources

### EMERGENCIES

The Marsh Harbour Clinic has a resident doctor and a nurse. There are also small government clinics staffed by nurses in Hope Town and New Plymouth, but hours are limited and change frequently. There are several private doctors in Marsh Harbour, and hotels will contact medical personnel upon request. Serious medical emergencies will require evacuation by plane to Nassau or Florida. It's a good idea to buy travel insurance that includes medical evacuation coverage.

🔲 **Marsh Harbour Clinic** 📞 242/367-2510. **Police or Fire Emergencies** 📞 919.

### TOUR OPTIONS

In Marsh Harbour, Abaco Island Tours books island tours, diving and sailing excursions, and customized trips. From Green Turtle, Brendal's Dive Center offers fully catered and captained sunset "booze cruises," and glass-bottom boat excursions where dolphin sightings are often a highlight. Froggies Out Island Adventures is the choice on Elbow Cay for sunset cruises and tours of the nearby cays.

🔲 **Abaco Island Tours** 📞 242/367-2936 ⊕ www.abacoislandtours.com. **Brendal's Dive Center** 📞 242/365-4411 or 800/780-9941 ⊕ www.brendal.com. **Froggies Out Island Adventures** 📞 242/366-0431 ⊕ www.froggiesabaco.com.

### VISITOR INFORMATION

Visit, call, or write Marsh Harbour's Abaco Tourist Office. It is open 9 AM to 5:30 PM, Monday through Friday.

🔲 Tourist Information **Abaco Tourist Office** ✉ Memorial Plaza, Queen Elizabeth Dr., Marsh Harbour ✆ Box AB 20663, Marsh Harbour, Abaco 📞 242/367-3067 📠 242/367-3068.

# Eleuthera &
# the Exumas

## 4

**WORD OF MOUTH**

"Eleuthera is spectacular, miles and miles of deserted beaches and not much more in the way of tourist amenities yet, so not much in the way of crowds. Go there now because it will not be that way in 5 years. There are some major developments going in and shortly it will be a lovely island with more touristy things to see and do."

—wantsomesun

"We love Exuma . . . There is very little to do here other than relax."

—AlwaysDreamin

Updated by
Chelle Koster
Walton

**ELEUTHERA AND THE EXUMAS ARE KNOWN FOR** their unspoiled and secluded sand beaches, turquoise water, and deep green forests populated
by sea grapes and coco plums. These islands are among the prettiest in
the Bahamas, with gentle hills, unspoiled "bush" (backwoods), and
gorgeous gardens. Hotels and inns are painted in the shades of a
Caribbean sunset and decorated with colorful hibiscus, bougainvillea,
and oleander. The laid-back, easy-going pace of the islands, not uncommon in the rest of the West Indies, guarantees a restful respite. The residents welcome visitors warmly; most will be happy to let you know
where to find the most secluded beaches or recommend the best restaurant for conch chowder. People here are serious about fishing, and can
show you the choice spots—while some of the other Out Islands attract
deep-sea fishermen seeking marlin and tarpon, the lure here is bonefish,
the elusive and feisty breed that prefers the shallow, sandy flats that punc-
tuate these islands.

Eleuthera was named in 1648 by a group from Britain fleeing religious
persecution; the name is taken from the Greek word for freedom. These
settlers, who called themselves the Eleutheran Adventurers, gave the
Bahamas its first written constitution. In the late 1800s, Eleuthera dominated the world's pineapple market, and these small, intensely sweet
fruits are still grown on small family farms dotting the island. On the
Exumas, you'll find wild cotton, left over from plantations established by Loyalists after the Revolutionary War. Breadfruit trees, which
a local preacher bought from Captain William Bligh in the late 18th
century, are in abundance as well. Today, the Exumas are known as
the Bahamas' onion capital, although many of the 3,600-odd residents
earn a living by fishing and farming. However, the tourism industry
has been the islands' top employer since the mammoth Four Seasons
Resort opened in 2003. Another yet-unidentified luxury resort is expected to follow suit in Williams Town, and the Old Island Beach Resort plans to set up shop in the historic buildings of the Old Island
Inn by 2007.

Your first impression of the people of the Exumas may be that almost
all of them have the surname Rolle. Dennis Rolle imported the first cotton seeds to these islands and his son, Lord John, had more than 300
slaves, to whom he bequeathed not only his name but also the 2,300
acres of land that were bestowed on him by the British government in
the late 18th century. Today Rolle's
descendants are still entitled to land
for building homes and farms.

## Exploring Eleuthera & the Exumas

Eleuthera is shaped like a praying
mantis, 110 mi long and just a few
miles wide. It lies 200 mi southeast of Florida and 60 mi east of
Nassau. One of the most picturesque parts of Eleuthera is Harbour Island, often compared with

> **DID YOU KNOW?**
>
> Folks are friendly in Eleuthera and
> the Exumas and will readily hail
> you on the street to chat. Under-
> stand that when a man greets a
> woman as "baby," it doesn't have
> a derogatory context; it's a term of
> endearment that women also use
> when addressing other women.

## GREAT ITINERARIES

*Numbers in the text correspond to numbers in the margins and on the Eleuthera and the Exumas maps.*

### IF YOU HAVE 3 DAYS

Fly into **North Eleuthera** and stay at a hotel along the famous 3-mi pink-sand beach on ▶ 🏠 **Harbour Island** ⑮, a taxi and boat ride from the airport. Leave your windows open so you can hear the free-roaming roosters wake you up in time to see the incredible pink and mauve sunrise. Take a morning walk on the beach, then veg out with a good book, interrupted only by lunch at an oceanside restaurant. Stroll through **Dunmore Town** in the afternoon, stopping at the craft stands and visiting the centuries-old churches. The next day, go scuba diving or snorkeling, or hire a guide and try to snag at least one of the elusive and feisty bonefish for which Eleuthera is famous. End the day with dinner in Dunmore Town. Take the ferry to **Spanish Wells** on your last day. Rent a golf cart and enjoy this prosperous lobster fishing island, with its neat, upscale homes and tiny alcove beaches. Be sure to try some fresh lobster before leaving.

### IF YOU HAVE 5 DAYS

Follow the suggested three-day itinerary, and on Day 4 take the ferry to "the mainland," what Harbour Island's residents call the main island of ▶ **Eleuthera** ① – ⑮. Drive south past **Glass Window** ⑫, where you can stand in one spot and see the Atlantic Ocean on one side and the Caribbean Sea on the other. Check out the cathedral-like cavern called **The Cave** ⑧ to prowl the stalagmites and hunt for bats and pirates' booty. In the afternoon, drive to **Hidden Beach** off James

**Point** for some private sunbathing or snorkeling. Continue south to 🏠 **Governor's Harbour** ⑥, the island's largest town, and grab dinner at one of the seaside restaurants overlooking the harbor. The next morning, drive to **Rock Sound** ① and then head either to **Ocean Hole** ②, a large inland saltwater lake, or to the challenging **Robert Trent Jones Jr. golf course** at **Cotton Bay Club** ③.

### IF YOU HAVE 7 DAYS

Add a hop to the Exumas to the three-day agenda above. The best way to fly between Eleuthera and the Exumas is through Fort Lauderdale on Continental Connection (unless you charter your own plane, which is exorbitantly expensive), which involves a three-hour layover with an evening arrival. You can also connect through Nassau on Bahamasair. After your flights, you'll be ready to relax in 🏠 **Exuma** ⑯ – ㉔ at the closest beach or bar to your hotel room. The next day, camp out on the beach, go golfing, or treat yourself to a massage. On Day 5, go diving at **Angel Fish Blue Hole** or snorkeling at **Stocking Island Mystery Cave,** a blue hole grotto filled with technicolor fish, accessible via a short ferry ride from **George Town** ⑯. Watch the sunset over dinner at an oceanside restaurant.

Finish the week at one of the beachfront hotels in 🏠 **George Town** ⑯, preferably including a Friday night so you can join in the festivities at **Palm Bay Beach Club,** where an outdoor barbecue and live band attract most of the island's inhabitants for a friendly evening of dancing.

Nantucket and reachable by a three-minute ferry ride from North Eleuthera. Harbour Island is famous worldwide for its 3-mi stretch of powdery pink-sand beach, usually included in lists of the most beautiful beaches on the planet. The Exumas begin less than 35 mi southeast of Nassau and stretch south for about 60 mi, flanked by the Great Bahama Bank and Exuma Sound. They are made up largely of some 365 fragmented little cays, mostly uninhabited. The two main islands, Great Exuma and Little Exuma, lie in the south, connected by a bridge; together they are about 50 mi long. The islands' capital, George Town, on Great Exuma, is the site of one of the Bahamas' most prestigious and popular sailing events, the Family Islands Regatta, in which locally built wooden work boats compete. In winter, George Town's Elizabeth Harbour is a haven for yachts. The surrounding waters are legendary for their desolate islands, coves, bays, and harbors.

> **DID YOU KNOW?**
>
> In Exuma, pea soup and dumplings (made with pigeon peas) is a specialty. Many local restaurants serve it as a weekly lunch special, usually on Wednesday.

Eleuthera and the Exumas are a quick flight from Miami or Nassau. You can also take a ferry from Nassau; the trip takes just a few scenic hours. It's easy to explore the islands by rented car, bicycle, or golf cart, although you'll need to rent a motorboat to reach some of the smaller and uninhabited islands.

## About the Restaurants

Although the ambience is usually casual, food is taken seriously here, especially island specialties like conch salad and fritters, the succulent Bahamian lobster most locals call crawfish, and barbecued pork or chicken. Fresh fish and seafood, usually pulled that morning from the waters just beyond the restaurant kitchen, is the highlight of most menus. If you've never had fresh conch, these two islands are the place to indulge, especially at one of the conch shacks favored by island residents. The conch is often so fresh that it may be sitting in a tank outside until you place your order. It is then diced, mixed with chopped red and green bell peppers and tomatoes, seasoned with each chef's own secret recipe of lemon, lime, and sour orange juices, and topped with a tangy dash of hot pepper sauce or minced chili pepper.

Most restaurants serve Bahamian food, with a few lamb dishes and steak thrown in. Italian, Continental, and Asian dishes may show up on the menu, too, offering alternatives for those who want a change in taste. Newer restaurants, particularly in Eleuthera, feature experimental and fusion cuisine, a trend that is becoming increasingly popular. Many dining establishments are closed two days a week, including Sunday, which is family day on these deeply religious and family-oriented islands.

## About the Hotels

Accommodations run the gamut from quaint, family-run guest houses in historic Colonial-era buildings to modern beachfront resorts. For information and reservations, you can call the Out-Island Promotion

## IF YOU LIKE

### CONCH SALAD

This Bahamian staple is akin to ceviche. Fresh-caught conch is removed from its shell, diced, and mixed with chopped onions and red or green bell peppers. The mix is drizzled with fresh lime and sour orange juices, and spiced with either homemade hot sauce or finely minced local hot peppers, or both. Often the best places to try conch salad are one-room shacks at the water's edge, such as the cluster of shacks called **Fish Fry** just north of George Town in Exuma, or at **Queen Conch** on Harbour Island, Eleuthera, where the salad is made right in front of you. In restaurants, conch salad can be an appetizer or a main course. Conch also is chopped and fried in fritters, stewed with potatoes as chowder, and fried up as cracked conch.

### PINK SANDS & SECLUDED HAVENS

Go to Eleuthera or the Exumas to sink your toes into soft sand and be lulled into a happy stupor by the sounds of gentle waves. The slightly curved 3-mi pink-sand beach on Harbour Island, Eleuthera, usually rates in the world's top 10 beaches, and deservedly so. Its sand is of such a fine consistency that it's almost as soft as talcum powder, and the gentle slope of the shore makes small waves break hundreds of yards offshore; you have to walk out quite a distance to get past your waist. On moonlit nights, the waves seem lit from underneath. On Exuma, head a few miles north or south from George Town, the island's main city, to find isolated spots of wide sand.

### SNORKELERS' PARADISE

The 176-square-mi Exuma Cays Land and Sea Park is a favorite of divers and snorkelers attracted by rare pillar coral and huge schools of multicolor fish, and sightseers who just want to enjoy the isolated and pristine ecosystem that flourishes here under the watchful eye of park rangers. They patrol in motorized boats to ensure that nobody damages the precious coral reefs, poaches fish, or bothers the dolphins and porpoises. Stretching some 22 mi between Compass Cay and Norman's Cay along the string of islands at the far northern end of the Exumas, this park is reachable only by seaplane or boat. That's part of its charm. The nearest "civilization" is an hour or more away in Staniel Cay, where there's a marina, restaurant, and tiny airport.

### A WARM BAHAMIAN WELCOME

Most of the people you'll meet on Exuma and Eleuthera have lived here for their entire lives, except maybe for a few years of college or work, or a brief visit to the United States. Their ties to their homeland and extended families tend to be strong and secure—perhaps this is why the local residents seem to be exceptionally friendly and have an uncanny openness about them. Everybody says "good morning" or "good afternoon" with a smile when they see you. Express the smallest interest in the history, food, or culture of the islands, and you'll probably be rewarded with an instant friendship, or at least a bit of interest and a brief conversation. Good manners are important here, and making guests feel welcome is at the top of the list.

## ELEUTHERA & THE EXUMAS' TOP 5

- **Dunmore Town.** Harbour Island's New England–style village begs to be explored on foot or by golf cart.

- **Surfer's Beach.** Gidget and Moondoggie would have loved the waves and the funky, junky beach shack here.

- **Stocking Island.** Gnarly waves, a beautiful beach, and ecofriendly eateries make this the ultimate getaway.

- **George Town.** Here's where it's all happening on Great Exuma; the best parties are late Friday afternoon.

- **Williams Town.** History runs deep in this quiet, old-island village—but rumor holds that it may be transformed into a resort town.

Board (☎ 800/688–4752). There's an undeniable appeal to staying at a place that treats you like family, and this type of establishment is not hard to come by in these parts. Most hotels have their own restaurants and offer several different meal plans. Many of the hotels are busy repainting and remodeling in response to the opening of the luxurious Four Seasons Resort Great Exuma at Emerald Bay in 2003, the largest and most upscale resort on the two islands. It has the only full-service spa on either island and the only golf course on Exuma. The development of the February Point resort estates community has also raised the stakes for lodging options in Exuma, and scuttlebutt claims that more luxury resort are on the way.

Note that most hotels add a government tax (6%–12%) and 10% gratuity to their rates.

| WHAT IT COSTS | | | | |
|---|---|---|---|---|
| **$$$$** | **$$$** | **$$** | **$** | **¢** |
| RESTAURANTS over $40 | $30–$40 | $20–$30 | $10–$20 | under $10 |
| HOTELS over $400 | $300–$400 | $200–$300 | $100–$200 | under $100 |

Restaurant prices are for a main course at dinner, excluding gratuity, typically 15%, which is often automatically added to the bill. Hotel prices are for two people in a standard double room in high season, excluding service charges and 6%–12% tax.

### Timing

All the Out Islands share similar weather, including a steamy late summer hurricane season and wintertime low temperatures that dip into the 60s. The high season for tourism is mid-December through April, when residents of cold weather climates head to the Caribbean to defrost and soak up some rays. For the cheapest hotel rates and some of the best deals on watersports packages, visit in early summer or fall to mid-December. For those who want to catch some action and don't mind crowds, the liveliest times to visit Eleuthera and the Exumas are around Christmas during the annual Junkanoo celebration of music and dance, and during the annual Family Islands Regatta in April, when the harbor of George Town, Exuma, is filled with hundreds of multimillion-dollar yachts.

# ELEUTHERA ISLAND

*Numbers in the margin correspond to points of interest on the Eleuthera map.*

## Rock Sound

**❶** One of Eleuthera's largest settlements, the village of **Rock Sound** has a small airport serving the island's southern part. **Front Street,** the main thoroughfare, runs along the seashore, where fishing boats are tied up. If you walk down the street, you'll eventually come to the pretty, white-washed **St. Luke's Anglican Church,** a contrast to the deep blue and green houses nearby, with their colorful gardens full of poinsettia, hibiscus, and marigolds. If you pass the church on a Sunday, you'll surely hear fervent hymn singing through the open windows. Rock Sound has the island's largest supermarket shopping center, where locals stock up on groceries and supplies.

**❷** **Ocean Hole,** a large inland saltwater lake a mile southeast of Rock Sound, is connected by tunnels to the sea. Steps have been cut into the coral on the shore so visitors can climb down to the lake's edge. Bring a piece of bread or some fries and watch the fish emerge for their hors d'oeuvres, swimming their way in from the sea. The hole had been estimated to be more than 100 fathoms (600 feet) deep, but, in fact, its depth was measured by a local diver at about 75 feet. He reports that there are a couple of cars at the bottom, too.

**❸** Ten miles south of Rock Sound, the old **Cotton Bay Club** hotel and its well-known, seaside Robert Trent Jones Jr. golf course are being resurrected by Starwood Hotels, which had plans to open a 73-room guesthouse and clubhouse by the end of 2006. Cotton Bay was once an exclusive club, the domain of Pan Am's founder, Juan Trippe, who would fly his friends to the island on a 727 Yankee Clipper for a weekend of golf.

**❹** The tiny settlement of **Bannerman Town** (population 40) is at the island's southern tip, which is punctuated by an old cliff-top lighthouse. From Eleuthera's north end (near Preacher's Cave), it's about a three-hour drive down the Queen's Highway. The beach here is gorgeous, and on a clear day you can see the Bahamas' highest point, Mt. Alvernia (elevation 206 feet), on distant Cat Island. The town lies about 30 mi from the **Cotton Bay Club,** past the quiet, little fishing villages of **Wemyss Bight** (named after Lord Gordon Wemyss, a 17th-century Scottish slave owner) and **John Millars** (population 15), barely touched over the years.

# Eleuthera

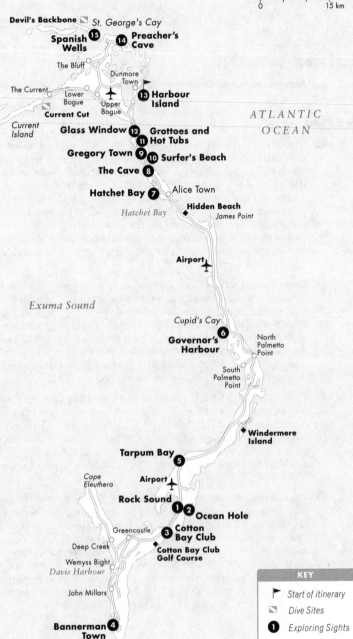

**Devil's Backbone** *St. George's Cay*

**Spanish Wells** ⑮  ⑭ **Preacher's Cave**

The Bluff

Dunmore Town

The Current

Lower Bogue

The Current

⑬ **Harbour Island**

**Current Cut**

Upper Bogue

*Current Island*

*ATLANTIC OCEAN*

**Glass Window** ⑫ **Grottoes and** ⑪ **Hot Tubs**

**Gregory Town** ⑨ ⑩ **Surfer's Beach**

**The Cave** ⑧

**Hatchet Bay** ⑦  Alice Town

*Hatchet Bay*  **Hidden Beach**

James Point

Airport

*Exuma Sound*

*Cupid's Cay*

⑥

**Governor's Harbour**

North Palmetto Point

South Palmetto Point

**Windermere Island**

**Tarpum Bay** ⑤

Airport

*Cape Eleuthera*

**Rock Sound**

① ② **Ocean Hole**

Greencastle

③ **Cotton Bay Club**

Deep Creek

**Cotton Bay Club Golf Course**

Wemyss Bight

*Davis Harbour*

John Millars

**Bannerman Town** ④

| KEY | |
|---|---|
| ▶ | *Start of itinerary* |
| ◪ | *Dive Sites* |
| ❶ | *Exploring Sights* |

0 ——— 10 miles
0 ——— 15 km

### Where to Eat

¢–$$  ✕ **Sammy's Place.** This spotless stop is owned by Sammy Culmer and managed mainly by his friendly daughter Margarita. It serves conch fritters, fried chicken and fish, and peas 'n' rice. ⊠ *Albury La.* ☎ *242/334–2121* ▭ *D.*

### Sports & the Outdoors

GOLF  **Robert Trent Jones Jr. Course** (⊠ Cotton Bay Club, Rock Sound ☎ 242/334–6101), an 18-hole, 7,068-yard, par-72 course, is Eleuthera's only course, and will be undergoing renovations as the Cotton Bay Club gets ready to reopen. You won't find a clubhouse or restaurant, and some fairways are poorly marked. The club has caddies, but no carts. Rates are $70 for 9 holes and $100 for 18 holes. Club rental is $15. Be sure to call ahead for reservations.

### Shopping

The **Almond Tree** (⊠ Queen's Hwy. ☎ 242/334–2385) is a blue house with white hibiscus–painted shutters. Inside, the quaint gift shop has a collection of handmade gifts, jewelry, and straw work.

## Tarpum Bay

❺ Waterfront **Tarpum Bay** is one of Eleuthera's loveliest settlements, with hilly roads flanked by weather-beaten homes with colored shutters, and goats roaming the streets.

### Where to Stay & Eat

¢  ▥ **Hilton's Haven.** Not to be confused with the well-known U.S. hotel chain, this Hilton is an unassuming 10-room motel across the road from a beach. A tidy and unpretentious place, it's run by a matronly local nurse named Mary Hilton. Rooms have private baths and patios, and Ms. Hilton serves good home cooking in her small restaurant. The hotel is a two-minute walk from the beach and about 8 mi from the Rock Sound Airport. Room rates are a bargain. ⊠ *Tarpum Bay* ☎ *242/334–4125* 🖨 *242/334–4231* ⬎ *10 rooms, 1 apartment* ⌂ *Dining room, cable TV, bar* ▭ *No credit cards* ⫚ *EP, MAP.*

### Shopping

You can stock up on groceries, souvenirs, and the like at **Tarpum Bay Shopping Centre** (☎ 242/334–4022).

EN ROUTE  About halfway between Rock Sound and Governor's Harbour, distinguished **Windermere Island** is the site of vacation homes of the rich and famous, including members of the British royal family. Don't plan on any drive-by ogling of these million-dollar homes, though; the security gate prevents sightseers from passing.

## Governor's Harbour

❻ **Governor's Harbour** is where the intrepid Eleuthera Adventurers landed. The drive between Governor's Harbour and Rock Sound takes about 35 minutes. Some of the island's wealthiest residents live in this pretty Victorian town looped around the harbor. If you're here when the mail boats M/V *Bahamas Daybreak III,* M/V *Captain Fox,* and M/V *Eleuthera Express* chug in, you'll witness the sight of residents unloading mattresses, lumber, mail, stacks of vegetables, and other household necessities. You might also see the same Eleutherans loading their own vegetables for export to Nassau. While they're here, they'll stop in at their mailboxes at the small post office in the town's pink government building.

If you're cooking during your stay, note that the Governor's Harbour waterfront is a great place to procure fresh fish and conch.

## Where to Stay & Eat

¢–$$   ✕ **Mate & Jenny's Restaurant & Bar.** A few miles south of Governor's Harbour, this neighborhood restaurant specializes in pizza. Try one topped with conch. Sandwiches, Bahamian specialties, and ice-cream sundaes are also served. The walls are painted with tropical sunset scenes and decorated with photos, and the jukebox and pool table add to the joint's local color. Pizza pie prices are $10, $15, and $24. ⊠ *S. Palmetto Point* ☎ 242/332–1504 ▭ *MC, V* ⊙ *Closed Tues.*

★ ¢–$   ✕ **Tippy's.** Despite its barefoot-casual atmosphere, the menu at this charming beachside restaurant-bar is sophisticated, with grouper Caesar, conch bruschetta, seared sushi-grade tuna and sushi, coconut crème brulée, plus pizza. This place may look like a beach-shack, but everything has been well-planned—they even imported an Italian chef to satisfy discriminating palates. Try to grab a table at the outdoor deck, which has a fantastic view of the beach. ⊠ *S. Palmetto Pt.* ☎ 242/332–3331 ▭ *No credit cards* ⊙ *Closed Wed.*

¢   ✕▥ **Buccaneer Club.** On a hillside overlooking the town and the harbor, this mid-19th-century farmhouse has been transformed into a family-run inn. Bougainvillea, hibiscus, and coconut palms flourish on the grounds. Guest rooms, with two double beds and full baths, are decorated with rattan furniture. The spacious third-floor room has a wonderful view of Governor's Harbour and the water. The beach is a leisurely five-minute stroll away, and the harbor, where you can also swim, is within shouting distance. Local artwork graces the walls at the Buccaneer Club, where you can sample such native specialties as grouper, conch, and crawfish (breakfast and lunch only). ⊕ *Box 86, Governor's Harbour* ☎ 242/332–2000 🖷 242/332–2888 ⊕ *www. eleutherainformer.com/buccanneGH.htm* 🗷 *5 rooms* ⌂ *Restaurant, pool, bar, shop* ▭ *D, MC, V.*

$–$$   ✕▥ **Cocodimama Charming Resort.** If decompressing in a hammock is your thing, you're in luck—you'll find one on the private patios of all 12 rooms at this sedate hotel, nestled on the Caribbean side of the island, 6 mi north of Governor's Harbour. Rooms are accented with teak furniture imported from Indonesia as well as Italian tiles, which reflect the taste of the married Italian expats who own and manage the property. Their influence also pervades the restaurant's Italian-Bahamian menu: buffalo mozzarella and other delicacies are flown in to complement the local fare. Snorkeling equipment and catamaran and kayak use are included in the rates. ⊕ *Box 122* ⊠ *Alabaster Bay, Governor's Harbour* ☎ 242/332–3150 🖷 242/332–3155 ⊕ *www.cocodimama.com* 🗷 *12 rooms* ⌂ *Restaurant, fans, shop, Internet* ▭ *MC, V* ⊙ *Closed Sept.–Nov.*

**$** ✕⊞ **Unique Village.** Just south of Governor's Harbour near North Palmetto Point, this resort has large, tile-floor rooms. The round restaurant, with its pagoda-style natural-wood ceiling, wraparound covered deck, and panoramic view of the beach, makes this village unique. Try the Caesar salad or any of the seafood specialties, especially the substantial lobster salad. The small bar has satellite TV, high captain's chairs, and views from second-story windows. The resort also organizes deep-sea fishing trips. ⬠ *Box EL 25187, Governor's Harbour* ☎ *242/332–1830* 🖷 *242/332–1838* ⊕ *www.bahamasvg.com/uniquevil.html* ⌻ *10 rooms, 4 villas* ⌂ *Restaurant, fans, some kitchens, cable TV, beach, snorkeling, fishing, bar* ⊟ *MC, V.*

**$$** ⊞ **Quality Cigatoo Inn.** Surrounded by a white picket fence, this resort sits high on a hill overlooking Governor's Harbour. It has crisp white buildings trimmed in vibrant hues with indoor and outdoor tropical gardens. Rooms have bright, sunny decors; modern furnishings; and private patios or balconies. The resort is a 15-minute walk from a pink-sand beach. The Cigatoo Room restaurant specializes in Bahamian and Chinese cuisine. The guest services department arranges bonefishing or deep-sea fishing trips, day trips to other islands, and car or bike rentals. Note that the resort is for guests 16 and up. ✉ *Queen's Hwy.* ☎ *242/332–3060* 🖷 *242/332–3061* ⌻ *22 rooms* ⌂ *Restaurant, cable TV, 2 tennis courts, pool, bar, Internet, meeting room; no kids under age 16* ⊟ *MC, V.*

**$** ⊞ **Duck Inn and Orchid Gardens.** Facing west into the sunset, overlooking beautiful Governor's Harbour, two colonial cottages and a home built in the 1850s nestle into a tropical hillside garden surrounded by a world-class orchid collection. John and Kay Duckworth bought the compound from a Canadian timber baron and restyled the houses. With one bedroom each, the cottages are perfect for couples, whereas the four-bedroom house can sleep eight. Each dwelling has a full kitchen (there are grocery stores just a block away) and a verandah. A full-time gardener tends to tropical fruit trees; guests are welcome to pick and eat—even the apples. ✉ *Queen's Hwy.* ☎ *242/332–2608* 🖷 *242/332–2160* ⊕ *www.theduckinn.com* ⌻ *2 cottages, 1 house* ⌂ *Fans, kitchenettes, cable TV, fishing* ⊟ *MC, V.*

**$** ⊞ **Laughing Bird Apartments.** English architect Dan Davies (designer of Windermere Island Club and Jacques Cousteau's villa) and his wife, Jean, own these four tidy apartments on an acre of land at the water's edge. Linens and crockery (including an English teapot and china cups) are furnished. You can stock your kitchen with produce from local stores or dine at any of the four restaurants within walking distance. This is a quiet, on-your-own kind of place, where relaxing and fishing are the name of the game. ⬠ *Box EL 25076, Governor's Harbour* ☎ *242/332–2012* 🖷 *242/332–2358* ⌻ *4 apartments* ⌂ *Kitchens, beach, fishing, shop, Internet* ⊟ *D, MC, V.*

## Sports & the Outdoors

SNORKELING If you have a four-wheel-drive vehicle, take the road east at the settlement of James Cistern to reach James Point, a beautiful beach with snorkeling and 3- to 10-foot waves for surfers. About 4 mi north of James Cistern on the Atlantic side, take the rough-hewn steps down to **Hidden Beach,** a sandy little hideaway sheltered by a rock-formation canopy, affording maximum privacy. It's also a great spot for novice snorkelers.

## Hatchet Bay & Environs

**❼ Hatchet Bay** has mid-Eleuthera's only marina. Be sure to notice the names of the town's side roads, which have such colorful designations as Lazy Road, Happy Hill Road, and Smile Lane. Just south of town, the Rainbow Inn and Restaurant is the hub of activity for this stretch of Eleuthera.

**❽** North of Hatchet Bay lies **The Cave,** a subterranean, bat-populated tunnel complete with stalagmites and stalactites. It was supposedly once used by pirates to hide their loot. An underground path leads for more than a mile to the sea, ending in a lofty, cathedral-like cavern. Within its depths, fish swim in total darkness. The adventurous may wish to explore this area with a flashlight (follow the length of guide string along the cavern's floor), but it's best to inquire first at one of the local stores or the Rainbow Inn for a guide. To find the cave, drive north from Hatchet Bay and watch for the vine-covered silo on Queen's Highway's north side. Take the left turn soon thereafter, marked by a white stripe down the center of Queen's Highway. En route to the Cave is Sweeting's Pond, the focus of all sorts of local myths. Some claim that there are Loch Ness–like creatures living in it. Others believe that a wrecked plane lies on the bottom.

### Where to Stay & Eat

**★ $** ✕🏠 **Rainbow Inn.** Immaculate, generously sized cabins—all with large private porches—dot the waterfront grounds. The restaurant is one of the island's best, with a classy but no-fuss atmosphere and exhibition windows that face gorgeous sunsets. Islanders drive great distances for a meal here, especially when the famed Dr. Seabreeze strums away and sings island tunes on rib night (Wednesday) and steak night (Friday). The Nautical Bar, hung with authentic ships' wheels salvaged from wrecks, drips with local color. Nurse Goombay Smashes as long as you like; cantankerous co-owner "Krabby" Ken won't be bashful about letting you know when it's time to leave. 🗐 *Box E-125053* ✉ *2½ mi south of Hatchet Bay, Governor's Harbour* 🕿🕿 *242/335–0294* 🕿 *800/688–0047* 🌐 *www.rainbowinn.com* 🛏 *4 apartments, 2 2-bedroom villas, 1 3-bedroom villa* ⚏ *Restaurant, BBQ, no room phones, kitchenettes, microwaves, tennis court, pool, fishing, bar* 🖭 *D, MC, V* ⦿ *EP, MAP* ⊘ *Closed Sept. 1–Nov. 15.*

## Gregory Town & Environs

**❾** The charming pastel homes of **Gregory Town** dot a hillside that slides down to the sea. The town's annual Pineapple Festival begins on the Thursday evening of the Bahamian Labor Day weekend, at the beginning of June. With live music, juicy ripe pineapple (served every possible way), and settlement-wide merriment continuing into the wee hours, this is Gregory Town's liveliest happening.

★ ⑩ Gregory Town's claim to fame lies about 2½ mi south of town, where **Surfer's Beach,** the site of a funky shack from the 1960s, still draws wave-catchers from December through May. If you don't have a jeep, you can walk the ¾ mi to this Atlantic-side beach—follow rough-and-bumpy Ocean Boulevard at Eleuthera Island Shores just south of town.

⑪ If you're too lulled by the ebb and flow of lapping waves and prefer your shores crashing with dramatic white sprays, perhaps a visit to Eleuthera's **Grottoes and Hot Tubs** will revive you. The sun warms these tidal pools—which the locals call "moon pools"—making them a markedly more temperate soak than the sometimes-chilly ocean. On most days, refreshing sprays and rivulets tumble into the tubs, but on some it can turn dangerous; if the waves are crashing over the top of the cove's centerpiece mesa, pick another day to stop here. If you're driving from Gregory Town, the entrance is approximately 5 mi north on the right (Atlantic) side of the Queen's Highway, across the road from two thin tree stumps. If you reach the one-lane Glass Window Bridge, you've gone too far.

⑫ At a narrow point of the island a few miles north of Gregory Town, the Glass Bridge, a slender concrete structure, links the two sea-battered bluffs that separate the Governor's Harbour and North Eleuthera districts. Sailors going south in the waters between New Providence and Eleuthera supposedly named this area the **Glass Window** because they could see through the narrow cavity to the Atlantic on the other side. Stop to watch the northeasterly deep-azure Atlantic swirl together under the bridge with the southwesterly turquoise Great Bahama Bank, producing a brilliant aquamarine froth. Artist Winslow Homer found the site stunning, too. He painted *Glass Window* in 1885. It's thought that the bridge was a natural span until the early 1900s, when rough currents finally washed it away.

## Where to Stay & Eat

¢–$  ╳ **Cush's Place.** Temporarily displaced to Nappy's (the cook's) home kitchen by Hurricane Frances in 2004, this is where locals come for a traditional Bahamian breakfast—chicken souse, sheep tongue souse, boil fish, and johnnycake. At lunchtime, Nappy cooks up fresh fish and local favorites such as barbecue pork with rice and beans. ⊠ *Queens Hwy., Gregory Town* ☎ *242/335–5301* ▭ *No credit cards.*

¢–$  ╳ **Elvina's Bar and Restaurant.** Shoot some pool and enjoy West Indian specialties such as curry chicken at this local favorite. Walls are covered with license plates and bumper stickers, and the surfboards hanging from the ceiling have been stowed there by surfer-regulars. Elvina's husband, known around these parts as "Chicken Ed," is from Louisiana, and the jambalaya here is the real thing. Be sure to call ahead, as Elvina and Ed don't open every night. There's karaoke on Tuesday and Friday nights, and Lenny Kravitz, who owns a home nearby, may show up. ⊠ *Queens Hwy., Governor's Harbour* ☎ *242/335–5032* ▭ *No credit cards.*

¢  ╳ **Thompson Bakery.** Located appropriately on Sugar Hill Street, Daisy Thompson bakes the island's best banana muffins, cinnamon rolls, pineapple bread, pizza, and pineapple, coconut, and lemon tarts in a tiny hilltop enclave. Her family reputedly developed the recipe for pineapple rum. ✉ *Sugar Hill St., Gregory Town* ☎ *242/335–5053* ⊘ *Closed weekends* 🖃 *No credit cards.*

🕒 **$**   ✕🖭 **The Cove Eleuthera.** Reopened with an updated look in 2005, 30
Fodor'sChoice   secluded acres set the tone for this relaxing seaside inn (formerly known
★   as Pineapple Cove). A rocky promontory separates two coves: one has
a small sandy beach with palapas, lounge chairs, and kayaks, the other
is rocky and ideal for snorkeling. The poolside patio is a good place for
breakfast or relaxing cocktails. Clustered rooms have ocean views, tile
floors, high slanted ceilings, 600-thread-count sheets, and white rattan
furnishings. MP3 players are available on request. Take in both the sunrise and the sunset from one of two suites in the Point House; it's built
on the promontory with a 180-degree view of the coves and the sea. The
spacious, window-lined dining room serves three meals a day, and the
resort's French chef blends classic Continental with Bahamian to produce delights such as lobster tail with lime and thyme beurre blanc, and
potato-crusted sea bass. A prix-fixe menu is available. ✉ *3 mi south of
Glass Window Bridge, 1½ mi north of Gregory Town* ⚘ *Box 1548,
Gregory Town* ☎ *242/335–5142 or 800/552–5960* 🖷 *242/335–5338*
⊕ *www.thecoveeleuthera.com* ⇔ *12 rooms, 8 1-bedroom suites, 2 2-
bedroom suites* ⚬ *Restaurant, 2 tennis courts, pool, dive shop, snorkeling, fishing, bicycles, bar, lounge, shop, Internet; no room phones,
no room TVs* 🖃 *D, MC, V.*

### Nightlife

The debonair **Dr. Seabreeze**—a friend of Lenny Kravitz, who lives
nearby—strums his acoustic guitar while singing island songs Wednesday and Friday night at the Rainbow Inn, Saturday at the Cove, and
Thursday night at Unique Village. On Tuesday and Friday you can
often find him playing at **Elvina's Bar and Restaurant.**

### Sports & the Outdoors

SURFING   In Gregory Town, stop by **Rebecca's** (☎ 242/335–5436), a general store
and crafts shop, where local surf guru "Ponytail Pete" stocks a few supplies and posts a chalkboard listing surf conditions and tidal reports.

### Shopping

**Island Made Shop** (✉ Queen's Hwy. ☎ 242/335–5369), run by Pam
and Greg Thompson, is a good place to shop for Bahamian arts and crafts,
including Androsia batik (made on Andros Island), driftwood paintings,
Abaco ceramics, and prints.

EN
ROUTE   Snorkelers and divers will want to spend some time at **Gaulding's Cay**
beach, 3 mi north of Gregory Town. Swim out to the tiny offshore island to witness a concentration of sea anemones so spectacular it daz-
zled even Jacques Cousteau's biologists (it's as if someone laid down a
carpet). Gaulding's Cay is also a nice 1,500-foot shelling stretch for beachcombers.

## Harbour Island

❸   **Harbour Island** has often been called the Nantucket of the Caribbean and
Fodor'sChoice   the prettiest of the Out Islands because of its 3 mi of powdery pink-sand
★   beach and its pastel-color clapboard houses with dormer windows, set

among white picket fences, narrow lanes, quaint shops, and tropical flowers. The residents have long called it Briland, their faster way of pronouncing "Harbour Island." The best way to get around is to rent a golf cart or bike; or hire a taxi, since climbing the island's hills can be quite strenuous in the midday heat. Within its 2 square mi are tucked some of the Bahamas' most attractive small hotels, each strikingly distinct. At several that are perched on a bluff above the shore, you can fall asleep with the windows open and listen to the waves lapping the beach. Harbour Island is reached via a five-minute ferry ride from the North Eleuthera dock. Fares are $5 per person in a boat of two or more, plus an extra dollar to be dropped off at the private docks of Romora Bay Club. The ferry also occasionally charges more for nighttime rides.

Old trees line the narrow streets of **Dunmore Town,** named after the 18th-century royal governor of the Bahamas, Lord Dunmore, who built a summer home here and laid out the town. The community was once second in the country to Nassau in terms of its prosperity. It's the only town on Harbour Island, and you can take in all its attractions during a 20-minute stroll. Stop first at the **Harbour Island Tourist Office** (☎ 242/333–2621), in the yellow building opposite the ferry dock. Get a map and ask about current events. Across the street is a row of strawwork stands, including Dorothea's, Pat's, and Sarah's, where you'll find straw bags, hats, accessories, T-shirts, and tourist bric-a-brac. Food stands sell conch, Kalik beer, and other local fare.

On Dunmore Street, you can visit the Bahamas' oldest Anglican church, **St. John's,** built in 1768, and the distinguished 1848 **Wesley Methodist Church.** Both hold services. On Bay Street, **Loyalist Cottage,** one of the original settlers' homes (circa 1797), has also survived. Many other old houses in the area, with gingerbread trim and picket fences, have such amusing names as "Beside the Point," "Up Yonder," and "The Royal Termite." Off the eastern, Atlantic shore lies a long coral reef, which protects the beach and has excellent snorkeling. You can see multicolor fish and a few old wrecks.

## Where to Stay & Eat

Note that most Harbour Island hotels and restaurants are closed from September through mid- to late October.

**$–$$$$** ✕ **Harbour Lounge.** Owners of the Bubble Room restaurant—a longtime Captiva Island, Florida, favorite—now own this pink building with green shutters across from the government dock. Arrive early if you want good seats on the front deck for watching the sunset over cocktails. The lunch and dinner fare might include smoked dolphinfish dip with garlic pita chips, grouper cake salad, cracked conch, and tequila shrimp. ⊠ *Bay St., Dunmore Town* ☎ *242/333–2031* ▤ *MC, V* ⊘ *Closed Mon.*

★ **$–$$$$** ✕ **Romora Bay Club.** The waterfront alfresco bar, Sunset on the Bay, is one of the best places to enjoy a cocktail, views of the Harbour Island sunset, and international cuisine. Arrive with plenty of time to secure your seat on the deck. Come nightfall, stroll through the gardens to the main hotel complex for fine post-dusk dining in an intimate dining room overlooking the infinity pool. Also make time for a drink in the jungle-hip Parrot Bar. ⊠ *South end of Dunmore St., Dunmore Town* ☎ *242/333–2325* ⌕ *Reservations essential* ▤ *AE, D, MC, V.*

★ **$–$$** ✕ **Sip Sip.** You can't miss this building—it's bright lime green with cobalt shutters—at the end of the block past the elementary school. Sit inside and enjoy the paintings by local artists and a little "sip sip" (Bahamian for gossip) with the locals, or dine on the shaded deck overlooking the beach. The menu is eclectic, with local fish dishes using Mediterranean and Asian ingredients. One of Harbour Island's most contemporary eateries, its specialties include hot and spicy conch chili, carrot cake with ginger-caramel frosting, and Sip Sip Rum Punch. Check out the blackboard for the daily specials. ⊠ *Court St., Dunmore Town* ☎ *242/333–3316* ▤ *MC, V* ☺ *Closed Tues.*

**¢–$** ✕ **Arthur's Bakery and Cafe.** *M\*A\*S\*H* screenwriter Robert Arthur and his Trinidadian wife, Anna, bake sensational bread every morning. Try the four-herb or jalapeño loaf. For lunch, order up a deli sandwich. Anna coordinates and caters weddings as well. ⊠ *Corner of Crown St. and Dunmore St., Dunmore Town* ☎ *242/333–2285* ▤ *No credit cards* ☺ *Closed Sun. No dinner.*

**¢–$** ✕ **Dunmore Deli.** Under a green-and-white striped awning shading a wooden deck, this exceptional deli serves alfresco breakfasts and hot-and-cold lunches—homemade soups, deli sandwiches, and green salads. It stocks a superb variety of international coffee, imported cheese, and other gourmet items you won't find anywhere else on the island. ⊠ *King St., Dunmore Town* ☎ *242/333–2644* ▤ *MC, V* ☺ *Closed Sun. No dinner.*

**¢** ✕ **Queen Conch.** A block and a half from the ferry dock on Bay Street,
Fodorś Choice Lavaughn and Richard Percentie's colorful snack stand overlooking
★ the harbor is renowned for its freshly caught conch salad ($7), which is diced in front of you, mixed with fresh vegetables, and served in deep bowls. Visitors from the world over place large orders to take home. ⊠ *Bay St., Dunmore Town* ☎ *No phone* ▤ *No credit cards* ☺ *Closed Sun.*

**$$$$** ✕⊡ **Dunmore Beach Club.** Classic Old Bahamian in style, the Dunmore
Fodorś Choice is proud of its guest-to-staff ratio (almost one-to-one) and the length of
★ service of its employees (10 years is not considered a long time here). Accommodations are private New England–style cottages with exquisite interiors, including gorgeous marble bathrooms with two-person whirlpool tubs, enormous stand-alone showers, and separate sink–vanity areas. In the cozy clubhouse you'll find a Villeroy & Boch–tile oceanview honor bar, comfy settees, a working fireplace, and a well-stocked library. This is the most formal place to stay or dine on the island. The restaurant serves a four-course international menu at 8 PM. The club's clientele consists predominantly of the yachting crowd. ⌂ *Box EL 27122, Harbour Island* ☎ *242/333–2200 or 877/891–3100* 🖷 *242/333– 2429* ⊕ *www.dunmorebeach.com* 🛏 *14 units in 8 cottages* ⌕ *Restaurant, some in-room hot tubs, refrigerators, tennis court, beach, bar, library, laundry service, Internet* ▤ *D, MC, V* ⑩ *FAP.*

★ **$$$$** ✕⊡ **Pink Sands.** Island Records founder Chris Blackwell transformed this old Harbour Island property—on the edge of the famous rosy-hue sands—into a luxury resort. Private, colorful one- or two-bedroom cottages, scattered across the lush, 25-acre property, include such frills as Aveda Spa-Bath toiletries, cordless phones, DVD players, and king-size beds with dual-controlled heaters. The main house has a hand-carved bar and imported Indian and Indonesian furniture and antiques. The richness extends to the library, which has a working fireplace and plump, comfy couches. Euro-Bahamian fare is served during lunch in the striking ocean-view Blue Bar, and in the evening there's a four-course "Chef Recommends" menu. ⌂ *Box 87, Harbour Island* ☎ *242/333–2030* 🖷 *242/333–2060* ⊕ *www.pinksandsresort.com* ✍ *25 1- and 2-bedroom cottages* ⌂ *2 restaurants, dining room, in-room safes, minibars, in-room data ports, some in-room hot tubs, in-room VCRs, 3 tennis courts, pool, gym, beach, snorkeling, billiards, 2 bars, library, shop, babysitting, laundry service, Internet* ▭ *AE, D, MC, V* ♨ *MAP* ⊗ *Closed 2 wks in mid-Oct.*

★ **$$$–$$$$** ✕🖾 **Rock House.** This complex of historic harborside buildings—including a 19th-century jail and a schoolhouse—has been lavishly renovated by the architectural design team that created Gianni Versace's Miami mansion. The owner's attention to detail is evident at every turn, from the constant tweaking of floral arrangements to the moonlight-like blue lights in the private cabanas ringing the heated pool (each room has its own cabana). Guest rooms each have a different name and accessory motif, and come with luxurious items like a picnic basket for beach forays and a custom-designed extra-padded mattress. Rock House has Harbour Island's only fully outfitted gym—one of the owners is a fitness nut. The restaurant serves gourmet fare in the front parlor and on the open porch. Try the seafood roll appetizer, a mix of lobster, crab, and tiger prawn in an Asian-style roll; don't miss the homemade ice cream for dessert. ✉ *Bay St., Harbour Island* ☎ *242/333–2053* 🖷 *242/333–3173* ⊕ *www.rockhousebahamas.com* ✍ *7 rooms, 3 suites* ⌂ *Restaurant, in-room safes, minibars, cable TV, in-room VCRs, bar, library, Internet room; no smoking* ▭ *AE, MC, V* ♨ *CP.*

♨ **$$–$$$** ✕🖾 **Coral Sands Hotel.** The resort sits on 9 hilly acres right above its namesake, the world-famous, 3-mi-long pink beach. The bright, individually decorated guest rooms have British Colonial–style furnishings. Upstairs rooms—reached by curving steps—have access to expansive rooftop terraces. Some rooms have child-size futons and adjoining bedrooms; all have small private balconies overlooking the ocean or lushly planted gardens through French doors. The restaurant offers an eclectic mix of Bahamian favorites and Italian classics, served on a balcony with open arches framing breathtaking views of the ocean. Lunch is served at a beach bar high above the rosy sand. ✉ *Chapel St., Harbour Island* ☎ *242/333–2350, 242/333–2320, or 800/468–2799* 🖷 *242/333–2368* ⊕ *www. coralsands.com* ✍ *32 rooms, 4 suites, 1 2-bedroom beach house* ⌂ *Restaurant, tennis court, pool, beach, snorkeling, boating, fishing, billiards, 2 bars, library, laundry service, Internet; no room TVs* ▭ *AE, D, MC, V* ♨ *EP, MAP.*

★ **$$** ✕🖾 **The Landing.** Built by uniting two early-19th-century homes, this lovely inn facing the harbor embodies an understated contemporary-rustic chicness. All seven plantation-style bedrooms have harbor views, pastel walls, hand-carved four-poster beds, and large, tiled bathrooms. The management, a former Miss Bahamas queen and her family, uses the original parlor with highly polished Abaco pine floors as an intimate restaurant, one of the island's finest. The menu is an elegantly prepared blend of Bahamian, European, and Asian cuisines. You can also dine on the porch overlooking the harbor, and in a lovely garden. The bar is fabulous, offering premium libations you can't find elsewhere on the island. A hearty breakfast is included in the rate. ⌧ *Bay St., Box 190* ☎ *242/333–2707 or 242/333–2740* 🖷 *242/333–2650* ⊕ *www.harbourislandlanding.com* 🗺 *7 rooms* ♿ *Restaurant, bar, library, Internet, business services; no room phones, no room TVs* ⊟ *D, MC, V* ⏐⏐ *BP* ☉ *Closed Sept. 10–Nov. 1.*

$ ✕⊞ **Tingum Village.** These rustic cottages have high pine ceilings, sea-color furnishings, netting above king-size beds, floor-to-ceiling corner windows, and two-person whirlpool tubs with garden views. In front of the hotel is Ma Ruby's Restaurant, purported home of Jimmy Buffett's original "Cheeseburger in Paradise," where you can sample Bahamian food on a breezy covered patio three times daily. Leave room for Ma Precentie's home-baked bread, coconut tarts, key lime pie, or pound cake. Tingum Village is on the town's south end and a short walk from Harbour Island's famous pink-sand beach. ⌧ *Next to Harbour Island Library, Harbour Island* 🖷🖷 *242/333–2161* 🗺 *12 rooms, 5 1-bedroom and 2 2-bedroom suites, 1 3-bedroom cottage* ♿ *Restaurant, bar* ⊟ *MC, V* ⏐⏐ *EP, MAP.*

★ $$$–$$$$ ⊞ **Runaway Hill Club.** What was once a private seaside mansion is now an enchanting inn perched on a bluff above Harbour Island's fabled beach. Most rooms face the sea; the rest overlook the gardens. All are individually decorated with wicker, original island artwork, lovely bed linens, and coordinating draperies. The newer hilltop villa has larger, more uniform rooms with colorful patchwork quilts and bookshelves with an array of titles. Stairs lead down to the freshwater pool near the beach. Be sure to make reservations early to check out the club's inventive menu, which focuses on fresh, local ingredients. A jacket is required at dinner in season. ⌖ *Box EL 27031, Dunmore Town* 🖷 *242/333–2150* 🖷 *242/333–2420* ⊕ *www.runawayhill.com* 🗺 *10 rooms* ♿ *Restaurant, fans, pool, beach, bar, lounge, airport shuttle; no kids* ⊟ *AE, D, MC, V* ⏐⏐ *EP, MAP.*

★ $$$ ⊞ **Romora Bay Club.** Clusters of cottages are scattered about the grounds at this eclectic and artsy resort on Harbour Island's bay side. Each guest room, suite, or villa is decorated with unique artwork and furnishings and has a private patio, cable TV, and CD player. Although the hotel is not on the famous pink beach, it's just a short golf-cart ride away. If you'd rather stay on the property, you won't be bored: watersports galore are yours for the taking; the library has hundreds of movies, CDs, and books for you to borrow; and the lovely pool deck has stunning bay views. ⌧ *South End of Dunmore St., Dunmore Town* 🖷 *242/333–2325* 🖷 *242/333–2500* ⊕ *www.romorabay.com* 🗺 *13 rooms, 6 suites* ♿ *2 restaurants, cable TV, in-room VCRs, tennis court, pool, gym, dock, waterskiing, fishing, billiards, 2 bars, library, Internet* ⊟ *AE, D, MC, V* ⏐⏐ *MAP.*

★ $  ⊞ **Bahama House Inn.** This upscale bed-and-breakfast was originally deeded in 1796 and built by Thomas W. Johnson, Briland's first justice of the peace. Set in a garden filled with bougainvillea, royal poincianas, and roses, this lovely five-bedroom house thrives thanks to the loving preservation work done by genial owner-hosts John and Joni Hersch. Each guest room has local artwork, four-poster beds with decorative netting, a comfy sofa, and gracious Queen Anne–style writing desks. Enjoy a continental breakfast each morning on the deck. ⊠ *Dunmore St.* ☎ *242/333–2201* 🖷 *242/333–2850* ⊕ *www.bahamahouseinn.com* ⇆ *7 rooms* ⌂ *Some kitchenettes, fans, library; no room TVs, no kids under age 12* ▤ *MC, V* ⏍ *CP* ⊗ *Closed Aug. and Sept.*

### Nightlife

Enjoy a brew on the wraparound patio of **Gusty's** (☎ 242/333–2165), on Harbour Island's northern point. This lively hot spot has sand floors, a few tables, and patrons shooting pool or watching sports on satellite TV. On weekends, holidays, and in high season, it's a very crowded and happening dance spot with a DJ.

Enter through the marine life–muraled hallway at **Seagrapes** (⊠ Colebrook and Gibson Sts. ☎ 242/333–2389) to a large nightclub with a raised stage that's home to the local Funk Gang band.

**Vic-Hum Club** (⊠ Barrack St. ☎ 242/333–2161) occasionally hosts live Bahamian bands in a room decorated with classic record album covers; otherwise, you'll find locals playing Ping-Pong and listening and dancing to loud recorded music, from calypso to American pop and R&B.

### Sports & the Outdoors

BICYCLING  Bicycles are a popular way to explore Harbour Island; rent one at **Michael's Cycles** (⊠ Harbour Island ☎ 242/333–2384).

BOATING &  There are abundant spots around the island to angle for bonefish and
FISHING  deep-sea fish. Charters cost about $150 for a half day. There's great bonefishing right off Dunmore Town at Girl Bay. The Harbour Island Tourist Office can help organize bone- and bottom-fishing excursions, as can all of the major hotels.

SCUBA DIVING &  **Current Cut,** the narrow passage between North Eleuthera and Current
SNORKELING  Island, is loaded with marine life and provides a roller-coaster ride on the currents. **Devil's Backbone,** in North Eleuthera, offers a tricky reef area with a nearly infinite number of dive sites and a large number of wrecks. **Fox Diving** (☎ 242/333–2323) rents scuba equipment and offers instruction, certification, dive packages, and daily dive trips. **Valentine's Dive Center** (☎ 242/333–2080 ⊕ www.valentinesdive.com) rents and sells equipment and provides all levels of instruction, certification, dive packages, and daily group and custom dives. **Pierre's Dive Shop** (☎ 242/335/3284) rents snorkel and scuba gear and arranges deep-sea fishing charters. It has locations at Spanish Wells and the Cove resort.

### Shopping

Most small businesses on Harbour Island close for a lunch break between 1 and 3, a practice unique in the Bahamas.

**Blue Rooster** (✉ Dunmore St. ☎ 242/333–2240) has a wonderful selection of Bahama Hand Prints clothing, bags, and elegant gift items from around the world. Closed Sunday.

**Briland's Androsia** (✉ Bay St. ☎ 242/333–2342) has a good selection of bathing suits, bags, and other items made from the bright batik fabric created on the island of Andros.

**Briland Brushstrokes** (✉ Bay St. ☎ 242/333–2085) is a gallery owned by Harvey Roberts, Briland's politician-artist. Many of Roberts' original acrylics and prints may be viewed and purchased in his office–art gallery. Artwork and sculptures by other local artists are also on display.

**Dilly Dally** (✉ Dunmore St. ☎ 242/333–3109) sells Bahamian-made jewelry, maps, decorations, and other fun souvenirs.

**John Bull** (✉ Bay St. ☎ 242/333–2950), a duty-free shop near the dock, sells watches, fine jewelry, perfume, cigars, and sunglasses. Closed Sunday.

**The Landing** (✉ Bay St. ☎ 242/333–2707) has an elegant and eclectic mix of beaded jewelry, sequined and embroidered caftans and shirts, and gift items. Closed Wednesday.

**Pink Sands Gift Shop** (✉ Pink Sands Resort ☎ 242/333–2030) is a good place for inexpensive jewelry, clothing, and trinkets.

**Princess Street Gallery** (✉ Princess St. ☎ 242/333–2788) features original oil and watercolor paintings, hand-loomed throws, painted linens, and wooden bowls by local artists. Closed Sunday.

**Sugar Mill** (✉ Bay St. ☎ 242/333–2173) sells prints by local artists, Bahamian coin jewelry, picture frames decorated with Eleutheran shells, and wooden puzzles from the nearby island of Spanish Wells. Closed Sunday.

## North Eleuthera

**⓮** At the island's tip, **Preacher's Cave** is where the Eleutheran Adventurers took refuge and held services when their ship hit a reef more than three centuries ago. Note the original stone altar inside the cave. The last 2 mi of the road to Preacher's Cave is rough, but passable if you go slowly. Across from the cave is a long succession of deserted pink-sand beaches.

## Spanish Wells

**⓯** Off Eleuthera's northern tip lies St. George's Cay, the site of **Spanish Wells.** The Spaniards used this as a safe harbor during the 17th century while they transferred their riches from the New World to the Old. Supposedly they dug wells from which they drew water during their frequent visits. Today, water comes from the mainland. Residents—the few surnames go back generations—live on the island's eastern end in clapboard houses that look as if they've been transported from a New England fishing village. Descendants of the Eleutheran Adventurers continue to sail these waters and bring back to shore fish and lobster (most of the Bahamas' langoustes are caught here), which are prepared and boxed for export in a factory at the dock. So lucrative is the trade in crawfish, the local term for Bahamian lobsters, that the 700 inhabitants may be the most prosperous Out Islanders in the Bahamas. Those who don't fish here grow tomatoes, onions, and pineapples. You can reach Spanish Wells by taking a five-minute ferry ride ($3) from the Gene's Bay dock at North Eleuthera.

Tourists have little to do here but hang out on the beach, dive, and dine on fresh seafood at **Jack's Out Back** (☎ 242/333–4219).

$ 🖼 **Abner's Rentals.** Abner Pinder's wife, Ruth, keeps these two attached two-bedroom houses as spotless as her own. A tiny, private sand beach overlooking Harbour Island is just steps from the patio. The house rental includes use of a golf cart so you can explore the island and pick up groceries at one of the local shops. There's a one-week minimum stay. ✉ *1st St., Spanish Wells* ☎ *242/333–4890* 🖨 *242/333–4895* 🛏 *2 houses* ♿ *Kitchens* 🟰 *MC, V.*

# ELEUTHERA ESSENTIALS

*To research prices, get advice from other travelers, and book travel arrangements, visit ⊕ www.fodors.com.*

## Transportation

### BY AIR

Eleuthera has three airports: North Eleuthera; Governor's Harbour, near the center of the island; and Rock Sound, in the southern part of the island. Head for the one closest to your hotel. Fly into Governor's Harbour if you're staying south of Gregory Town, and into North Eleuthera if you're staying in Gregory Town or to the north. Several North American carriers and national airlines fly to each of the airports.

Bahamasair has daily service from Nassau to all three airports. Cherokee Air makes scheduled flights from Marsh Harbour in the Abacos to North Eleuthera every Friday and Sunday. Lynx Air flies direct from Fort Lauderdale to Governor's Harbour four days each week. Southern Air flies charters three times daily from Nassau to North Eleuthera and Governor's Harbour. Continental Connection and United Airlines have daily flights to North Eleuthera from Miami and Fort Lauderdale. Continental also flies nonstop from Fort Lauderdale to Governor's Harbour. Twin Air flies from Fort Lauderdale four times a week to Governor's Harbour, Rock Sound, and North Eleuthera. Yellow Air Taxi flies on demand from Fort Lauderdale to North Eleuthera and Governor's Harbour.

🛈 Airlines & Contacts **Bahamasair** ☎ 800/222-4262. **Cherokee Air** ☎ 242/367-3450. **Continental Connection** ☎ 800/231-0856. **Lynx Air** ☎ 888/596-9247. **Southern Air** ☎ 242/323-6833, 242/335-1720 Governor's Harbour, 242/34-2035 North Eleuthera. **Twin Air** ☎ 954/359-8266. **United** ☎ 800/864-8331. **Yellow Air Taxi** ☎ 888/935-5694.

🛈 Airport Information **Governor's Harbour** ☎ 242/332-2321. **North Eleuthera** ☎ 242/335-1242. **Rock Sound** ☎ 242/334-2177.

## BY BOAT

The following mail boats leave from Nassau at Potter's Cay; for schedules, contact the Dockmaster's Office at Potter's Cay, Nassau.

M/V *Current Pride* sails to the Current, Lower Bogue, Upper Bogue, and Hatchet Bay on Thursday, returning Tuesday. M/V *Bahamas Daybreak III* leaves on Monday for South Eleuthera, stopping at Rock Sound, and returns on Tuesday. It then leaves Thursday from Nassau for the Bluff and Harbour Island, returning on Sunday. The *Eleuthera Express* sails for Governor's Harbour and Spanish Wells on Monday and Thursday, returning to Nassau on Tuesday and Sunday, respectively. The fare is $20 for all Eleutheran destinations.

Bahamas Ferries connects Nassau to Harbour Island, Governor's Harbour, and Spanish Wells daily. A round-trip fare costs $110; excursion rates (including a tour, lunch, and a trip to the beach) are somewhat higher. The trip from Bahamas Ferries terminal on Potter's Cay, Nassau to Harbour Island, with a stop on Spanish Wells, takes two hours. Ferries leave Nassau at 8 AM and return at 3:55 (2 on Sunday). Call to confirm departure times and rates; on busy days, an extra trip is sometimes added. Make reservations well in advance for trips around Columbus Day, the weekend of the annual North Eleuthera Regatta.

🛈 Boat & Ferry Information **Bahamas Ferries** ☎ 242/323-2166 🖷 242/322-8185 🌐 www.bahamasferries.com. **Dockmaster's Office** ☎ 242/393-1064.

## BY CAR

Visiting Eleuthera's main sights will require renting a car. North to south is about a three-hour drive. Governor's Harbour, which lies approximately at Eleuthera's midpoint, is a 40-minute drive from Glass Window in the north, and a 35-minute drive from Rock Sound in the south. You can also rent a bike or scooter to explore the island. On Harbour Island and Spanish Wells, you're better off renting a golf cart.

Arranging a car rental through your hotel will most likely be your least complicated option. You can usually have a vehicle delivered to you at the airport. Daily rentals run about $70. Request a four-wheel-drive if you plan to visit Preacher's Cave or Surfer's Beach. Gardiner's Automobile Rentals, Hilton's Car Rentals, and Stanton Cooper all rent cars from Governor's Harbour—call to discuss delivery of your automobile. In Rock Sound, Dingle Motor Service rents cars. Baretta's has cars and minivans.

🛈 Local Agencies **Baretta's** ✉ Harbour Island ☎ 242/333-2361. **Dingle Motor Service** ☎ 242/334-2031. **Gardiner's Automobile Rentals** ☎ 242/332-2665. **Hilton's Car Rentals** ☎ 242/335-6241. **Stanton Cooper** ☎ 242/359-7007 or 242/332-1620.

## BY GOLF CART

Even if you're a big walker, you'll want a golf cart if you spend more than a couple of days on Harbour Island; there are several golf-cart rental companies there. Cart rates start at $40 for a four-seater for three hours and go up according to size (a six-seater is the largest); definitely negotiate if you'll be renting for longer. You can rent a cart directly at the dock.

🚗 **Abner's Rentals** ☎ 242/333-4890. **Baretta's** ☎ 242/333-2361. **Dunmore Rentals** ☎ 242/333-2372. **Grant's** ☎ 242/333-2157. **Johnson's Rentals** ☎ 242/333-2376. **Ross's Garage** ☎ 242/333-2122. **R&J Golf Carts** ☎ 242/333-2116. **Sunshine Carts** ☎ 242/333-2509.

### BY TAXI

Taxis are available through your hotel. On Eleuthera, have your hotel call for a taxi about a half hour before you need it. On Harbour Island, taxis generally arrive a few minutes after being called. Taxis are almost always waiting at the North Eleuthera and Harbour Island water taxi docks.

Taxis also wait for incoming flights at all three airports. If you land at North Eleuthera and need to get to Harbour Island, off Eleuthera's north coast, take a taxi ($4 to $5 each) to the ferry dock (Three Island Dock) on Eleuthera, a water taxi ($4 to $5 each) to Harbour Island, and, on the other side, another taxi. Follow a similar procedure to get to Spanish Wells, also off Eleuthera's north shore, at Gene's Bay ($3 one-way). Taxi service from Governor's Harbour Airport to the Cove Eleuthera is $42 for two people, though the taxi fare from North Eleuthera to the Cove is only $27 for two people. The fare from Governor's Harbour to Rainbow Inn is $23.25.

🚕 Taxi Information **Governor's Harbour Taxi Stand** ☎ 242/332-2568.

## Contacts & Resources

### BANKS & EXCHANGING SERVICES

Banks on Eleuthera and its islands are open weekdays from 9:30 to 3, Friday until 5. First Caribbean International Bank has a branch in Governor's Harbour. Royal Bank of Canada runs Harbour Island's only bank, in addition to branches in Governor's Harbour and Spanish Wells. Scotia Bank has branches in North Eleuthera and Rock Sound.

🏦 **First Caribbean International Bank** ☎ 242/332-2300. **Royal Bank of Canada** ☎ 242/333-2250 Harbour Island, 242/332-2856 Governor's Harbour, 242/333-4131 Spanish Wells. **Scotia Bank** ☎ 242/335-1400, 242/335-1406, 242/334-2620 North Eleuthera, 242/335-1400, 242/335-1406, 242/334-2620 Rock Sound.

### EMERGENCIES

Governor's Harbour, Harbour Island, Rock Sound, and Spanish Wells each have their own police and medical emergency numbers.

🚑 **Medical Clinics** ☎ 242/332-2774 Governor's Harbour, 242/333-2227 Harbour Island, 242/334-2226 Rock Sound, 242/333-4064 Spanish Wells. **Police** ☎ 242/332-2111 Governor's Harbour, 242/333-2111 Harbour Island, 242/334-2244 Rock Sound, 242/335-5322 Gregory Town.

### SIGHTSEEING GUIDES

Arthur Nixon is probably the most knowledgeable authority on Eleuthera. His presentation will make you want to stand up and applaud. Tell him how much time you have and where you want to go, and he'll take you there, telling stories en route.

🧭 **Arthur Nixon** ☎ 242/332-1006, 242/332-2568, or 242/359-7879.

### VISITOR INFORMATION

Contact the Eleuthera Tourist Office in Governor's Harbour or the Harbour Island Tourist Office on Bay Street right off the dock for brochures and information about the islands. Both are open weekdays 9–5. Visit the Bahamas Ministry of Tourism Web site and the Out-Islands Promotion Board's site for additional information.

🗐 Tourist Information **Bahamas Ministry of Tourism** ☎ 242/302–2000 or 800/224–2627 🖷 242/302–2098 ⊕ www.bahamas.com. **Eleuthera Tourist Office** ⊠ Governor's Harbour ☎ 242/332–2142 🖷 242/332–2480. **Harbour Island Tourist Office** ⊠ Bay St. ☎ 242/333–2621 🖷 242/333–2622. **Out-Islands Promotion Board** ☎ 800/688–4752 ⊕ www.bahama-out-islands.com.

# THE EXUMAS

*Numbers in the margin correspond to points of interest on the Exumas map.*

## Little Exuma & Great Exuma

★ ⑯ The old village of **Williams Town** lies at Little Exuma Island's southern tip. Out here, you can see salt raking at certain times of the year, and wild cotton still grows along the way to the picturesque hilltop ruins of the **Hermitage,** a former plantation house. Ask for directions to Pelican's Bay, down an unmarked gravel road north of town. Besides finding a romantic, secluded beach, you can step across a line marking the Tropic of Cancer.

> **HERE'S WHERE**
>
> Ask anyone where to find the best conch fritters in the Exumas, and invariably you'll hear Santana's Grill, a little stand on the water in Williams Town.

★ At the juncture of Great and Little Exuma, a one-lane bridge crosses the short pass to **The Ferry,** Little Exuma's earliest settlement. The town holds the island's smallest church—St. Christopher's Anglican, built for one family's use—pretty gardens, and the home of the "Shark Lady," Gloria Patience, the now-deceased legendary shark hunter of Exuma. On the Great Exuma side, you can see the remains of the historic ferry landing. The bridge replaced the ferry in 1966 and is a great fishing spot.

⑰ **Rolle Town,** a typical Exuma village devoid of tourist trappings, sits atop a hill overlooking the sea, 5 mi south of George Town. Some of the buildings are 100 years old, and three tombs off the main road date back to the Loyalists.

**FRUGAL FUN**

To get to know Exuma islanders better, hook up with the **People-to-People Program** (242/336–2430, 242/336–2457). The group hosts a tea the first Friday of each month where visitors can learn about bush medicine and other aspects of local life. The location changes monthly; for more information, check with your hotel or at the airport.

# The Exumas

0 ⎯⎯⎯⎯ 20 miles
0 ⎯⎯⎯⎯ 30 km

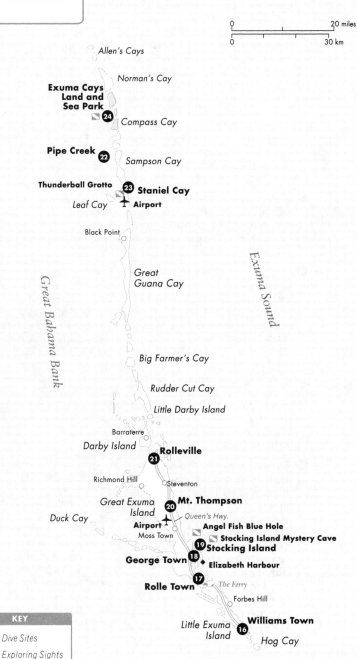

*Allen's Cays*

*Norman's Cay*

**Exuma Cays
Land and
Sea Park**

24 *Compass Cay*

**Pipe Creek** 22 *Sampson Cay*

**Thunderball Grotto** 23 **Staniel Cay**

*Leaf Cay* ✈ **Airport**

Black Point

*Great
Guana Cay*

*Exuma Sound*

*Great Bahama Bank*

*Big Farmer's Cay*

*Rudder Cut Cay*

*Little Darby Island*

Barraterre

*Darby Island* 21 **Rolleville**

Richmond Hill ○ Steventon

*Great Exuma
Island* 20 **Mt. Thompson**

*Duck Cay* *Queen's Hwy.*

✈ **Airport** **Angel Fish Blue Hole**

Moss Town **Stocking Island Mystery Cave**

19 **Stocking Island**

**George Town** 18 ◆ **Elizabeth Harbour**

17 **Rolle Town** *The Ferry*

Forbes Hill

*Little Exuma
Island* 16 **Williams Town**

*Hog Cay*

| KEY |
|-----|
| ◥ *Dive Sites* |
| **1** *Exploring Sights* |

**18** Although **George Town** is the island's hive of activity, it's still on the no-need-for-a-traffic-light scale. The most imposing structure here is in the town center—the white-pillared, sandy pink, colonial-style **Government Administration Building,** modeled on Nassau's Government House and containing the commissioner's office, police headquarters, courts, and a jail. Atop a hill across from the government building is the white-washed **St. Andrew's Anglican Church,** originally built around 1802 and renovated in 1991. Behind the church is the small, sea-fed Lake Victoria. A leisurely stroll around town will take you past a straw market and a few shops. You can buy fruit and vegetables and bargain with fishermen for some of the day's catch at the **Government Dock,** where the mail boat comes in. The wharf is close to **Regatta Point** (☎ 242/336–2206), an attractive guest house named after the annual Family Islands Regatta that curls around Kidd Cove, where the 18th-century pirate Captain Kidd supposedly tied up.

★ **Fish Fry** is the name given to a jumble of one-room beachside structures about 2 mi north of George Town, favored by locals for made-to-order fish and barbecue; there's even a sports bar with TVs in each corner. Some shacks are open weekends only, but most are open nightly until 11 PM or midnight.

★ **19** Slightly more than a mile off George Town's shore lies **Stocking Island.** The 5-mi-long island has only seven inhabitants, a gorgeous white beach rich in seashells and popular with surfers, and plenty of good snorkeling sites. Jacques Cousteau's team is said to have traveled some 1,700 feet into **Mystery Cave,** a blue-hole grotto 70 feet beneath the island. Club Peace & Plenty's ferry runs over to Stocking Island twice daily at 10 AM and 1 PM and charges $10 for nonguests. Near the Stocking Island pier, **Peace & Plenty Beach Club** provides changing rooms (with plumbing) and operates a lunch spot where Dora's hamburgers and famous conch burgers are the eats of choice. To enjoy the setting sun from Stocking Island, head for the **Chat & Chill,** a lively open-air restaurant and bar right on the point (but not reachable by foot from Peace & Plenty's club). Boaters hang out here, plus the restaurant picks up guests at Government Dock.

**20** From the top of **Mt. Thompson,** rising from the beach, there is a pleasing view of the **Three Sisters Rocks** jutting above the water just offshore. During your walks, you may glimpse peacocks on Great Exuma. Originally, a peacock and a peahen were brought to the island as pets by a man named Shorty Johnson, but when he left to work in Nassau, he abandoned the birds, who gradually proliferated into a colony. The birds used to roam the streets but development has forced

---

**DID YOU KNOW?**

Legend has it that Mt. Thompson's Three Sisters Rocks were formed when three sisters, all unwittingly in love with the same English sailor, waded out into deep water upon his departure, drowned, and turned into stone. If you look carefully next to each "sister," you'll see smaller boulders—the children the fickle sailor left with them.

them into the bush, so they are rarer sights these days. Mt. Thompson is about 12 mi north of George Town, past Moss Town.

㉑ The town of **Rolleville** (☎ 242/336–6038) sits on a hill above a harbor, 20 mi north of George Town. Its old slave quarters have been transformed into livable cottages. The town's most prominent citizen, Kermit Rolle, runs the **Hilltop Tavern,** a seafood restaurant and bar guarded by an ancient cannon.

## Where to Stay & Eat

**$–$$**  ✕ **Eddie's Edgewater.** The specialty at this popular spot is turtle steak, but the menu also offers fried chicken, lobster, T-bone steak, and cracked conch. Don't miss the rake 'n' scrape band on Monday; washtubs, saws, and screwdrivers serve as instruments. ⊠ *Charlotte St., George Town* ☎ *242/336–2050* ⊟ *D, MC, V* ⊙ *Closed Sun.*

★ **$**  ✕ **Sam's Place.** If you want to dine where the locals do, hit Sam's. Proprietor Sam Gray owns a complex of businesses in town, including the liquor store. Breakfast is especially favored and Exumians call ahead to see whether the day's menu includes stew fish, boil fish, or souse. Those who don't have time to sit down at the clean, modern café—which overlooks the bay—line up for takeout. Dinner selections are typical—lobster (called "crawfish" here), steak, lamb chops, and cracked conch. ⊠ *Queen's Hwy., George Town* ☎ *242/336–2579* ⊟ *MC, V.*

★ **¢–$**  ✕ **Chat & Chill.** Yacht folks, locals, and visitors alike rub shoulders at Kenneth Bowe's very hip and upscale—yet still casual—eatery on the point at Stocking Island. You may hear locals refer to it as KB's, for its owner. All of the incredible edibles are grilled over an open fire. Awesome conch burgers with secret spices and grilled fish with onions and potatoes are not to be missed. The Sunday pig roasts are fabulous. You can get here only by boat, but transportation is provided from the Government Dock. Since there's no phone, contact Chat & Chill via VHF 16. ⊠ *Stocking Island, George Town* ☎ *No phone* ⊟ *No credit cards.*

**¢–$**  ✕ **Iva Bowe's Central Highway Inn.** About 10 mi from George Town, close to the airport, this casual lunch and dinner spot has an island-wide reputation for having the best native food. Try one of the delectable shrimp dishes—coconut beer shrimp, spicy Cajun shrimp, or scampi, all for around $10. ⊠ *Queen's Hwy.* ☎ *242/345–7014* ⊟ *No credit cards* ⊙ *Closed weekends.*

**¢–$**  ✕ **Towne Café.** George Town's bakery serves breakfast (especially popular on Saturday)—consider trying the "stew" fish or chicken souse—and lunch—seafood sandwiches with three sides, or grilled fish. Towne Café is open until 5 PM. ⊠ *Marshall Complex, George Town* ☎ *242/336–2194* ⊟ *No credit cards* ⊙ *Closed Sun.*

**¢**  ✕ **Big D's Conch Shack.** For the freshest conch salad and the coldest beer, look for the splatter-painted seaside shack a stone's throw from the Four Seasons Emerald Bay resort. Daron Tucker does the fishing, wife Dianne heads the kitchen. ⊠ *Queen's Hwy., Steventon* ☎ *242/358–0059* ⊟ *No credit cards* ⊙ *Closed Mon.*

★ **¢**  ✕ **Jean's Dog House.** A bright-yellow former school bus is now a tiny, spotless kitchen on wheels. Noted for her 'dogs, divine lobster burger, and the "MacJean," a hearty breakfast sandwich with sausage or bacon and sometimes cheese on homemade Bahama bread, Jean cooks them all in her unique "dry-fry" method (no oil). The minibus is parked every weekday from 7 to around 3 at the bottom of schoolhouse hill (a well-known landmark). Jean has an effervescent personality and is a treasure trove of Exuma history. She's also a daughter of the famous "Shark Lady," who spent years going out regularly in her 13-foot Boston Whaler to catch sharks with a 150-foot-long hand line. ⊠ *Queen's Hwy., George Town* ☎ *No phone* ▭ *No credit cards* ⊘ *Closed weekends.*

🕙 **\$\$\$\$** ✕🖻 **Four Seasons Resort Great Exuma at Emerald Bay.** The luxurious Four FodorśChoice Seasons is the only full-service resort on Great Exuma Island. When it ★ opened in 2003, it changed the island's guesthouse demeanor, causing an upswing in the upscale. The 470 acres of pristine grounds lie adjacent to a mile-long strip of beach. There's an elaborate spa with two-person treatment rooms for couples, as well as watersports, tennis courts, the island's only golf course, and a children's area with its own pool; a casino opened in 2006. Guests stay in lemon yellow Colonial-style villas clustered on landscaped grounds. Rooms are decorated in rich, dark woods and rattan offset by pastel walls and sunny artwork. Each room has its own patio or balcony facing the bay. The emphasis is on service, with custom-stocked bars in each room and a 24-hour beach butler. The resort's three restaurants have Bahamian and continental dishes, heavy on the seafood. The signature restaurant, Il Cielo, looks out toward the sea through gaping windows and serves fine pastas, risottos, and seafood. The newest restaurant, Ting'm, sits outdoors at the edge of one of Exuma's most gorgeous beaches. ⌂ *Box EX 29005, Emerald Bay* ☎ *242/336–6800* 🖷 *242/336–6801* ⊕ *www.fourseasons.com* 🛏 *183 rooms, 43 suites* ♿ *2 restaurants, room service, in-room safes, in-room VCRs, in-room data ports, some kitchens, driving range, 18-hole golf course, pro shop, 3 pools, wading pool, snorkeling, windsurfing, boating, fishing, bar, casino, children's programs (ages 5–12), playground, laundry service, Internet, business services, car rental* ▭ *AE, D, MC, V.*

**\$\$\$\$** 🖻 **February Point Resort Estates.** At this writing, this gated residential community and resort had six vacation estates available for rent. There are plans to eventually offer more, and to transform the property's historic Army base housing into hotel rooms. The three-story, three-bedroom rental homes have magnificent harbor views of Flamingo Bay (though the flamingoes aren't as plentiful as they once were). Luxuriously decorated, the homes are serviced by maids every other day. Guests may use the community's fitness center, tennis courts, restaurants, and infinity pool. ⌂ *Box EX-29090, George Town* ☎ *242/336–2693 or 800/726–2988* 🖷 *242/336–2692* ⊕ *www.februarypoint.com* 🛏 *6 homes* ♿ *Restaurant, BBQs, in-room VCRs, cable TV, kitchens, 2 tennis courts, pool, gym, snorkeling, boating, marina, fishing, bar, laundry facilities, business services* ▭ *MC, V.*

★ **\$\$\$** ✕🖻 **Hotel Higgins Landing.** The only resort on undeveloped Stocking Island is this ecohotel, which is 100% solar powered—though everything still works when the weather's overcast. Wood cottages have screen windows with dark-green shutters and private, spacious decks with ocean views. Interiors have antiques, queen-size beds, tile floors, and folksy Americana decor. By day, the bar is an alfresco living room where you can play checkers or darts, or read books from the hotel's library. Colorful blossoms and tropical birds abound. Rates include full breakfasts and gourmet dinners, though be aware that the kitchen cannot accommodate *any* special dietary requests. No children under 16 during the winter season. ⌂ *Box EX 29146, Stocking Island, George Town* ☏ *866/289–0919 or 242/357–0008* ⊕ *www.higginslanding.com* ⇆ *5 cottages* ♨ *Restaurant, kitchens, gym, beach, dock, snorkeling, boating, fishing, bar, library, Internet; no smoking* ☐ *D, MC, V* ⑂ *MAP.*

★ $$ ✕⊞ **Peace & Plenty Bonefish Lodge.** The Out Islands' swankiest bonefishing lodge is on a peninsula 10 mi south of George Town. Dark wood and handsome hunter-green accents lend a gentleman's-club feel to the bar and dining room, where photos of anglers and their catches grace the walls; there's also a fly-tying station. The large rooms have white rattan furnishings, louvered wooden doors, and private balconies overlooking the water. Guests will find contemplative, restful spots on the large deck, upstairs verandah, or in a hammock on the sandy point that juts out beyond the lodge's fish pond. The dining room is open to outside guests for dinner four or five nights a week; lodge guests can opt for an all-inclusive plan or dine à la carte. The resort is closed from late June through October. ⌂ *Box EX 29173, George Town* ☏ *242/345–5555* 🖷 *242/345–5556* ⊕ *www.ppbonefishlodge.net* ⇆ *8 rooms* ♨ *Dining room, fans, cable TV, in-room VCRs, snorkeling, boating, fishing, bicycles, 2 bars, lobby lounge, library, Internet* ☐ *D, MC, V* ⑂ *BP, AI.*

★ ☾ $–$$ ✕⊞ **Palm Bay Beach Club.** Palm Bay, one of the George Town area's most modern accommodations, is all about light and color. The bungalows have brightly painted, gingerbread-trim exteriors (like turquoise with hibiscus pink) and cheerfully sunny interiors with one or two bedrooms. They're clustered on oleander-lined boardwalk paths along a pretty sand beach or across the street on a hillside. Each unit has a patio and a kitchenette or kitchen. Kayaks and paddle boats are available at no charge to guests. The huge circular poolside bar and patio area attracts what seems like everybody on the island for Saturday night parties with live music. The Canadian and English owners have plans to build another swimming pool and a spa in the hillside subdivision. The restaurant serves coconut shrimp, conch burgers, barbecue ribs, and a Bahamian special of the day. ⌂ *Box EX 9137, George Town* ☏ *888/396–0606 or 242/336–2787* 🖷 *242/336–2770* ⊕ *www.palmbaybeachclub.com* ⇆ *50 cottages* ♨ *Restaurant, cable TV, in-room-safes, in-room VCRs, some kitchens, some kitchenettes, pool, snorkeling, windsurfing, boating, waterskiing, fishing, bar, laundry service, business services* ☐ *AE, MC, V.*

★ $ ✕⊞ **Club Peace & Plenty.** The first of Exuma's hotels and granddaddy of the island's omnipresent Peace & Plenty empire, this pink, two-story hotel is in the heart of the action in George Town. Rooms have private balconies—most overlooking the pool with ocean views to the side, although some have full ocean vistas. It doesn't have a true on-property beach, but its Beach Club on Stocking Island is a 5-minute ferry shuttle away (free for guests); a land shuttle also transports guests to its sister property's beach. In high season the hotel is known for its Saturday-night parties on the pool patio, where Lermon "Doc" Rolle has been holding court at the bar since the '70s. The indoor bar, which was once a slave kitchen, attracts locals and a yachting crowd, especially during the Family Islands Regatta. At dinner, the hotel's restaurant goes the standard Out-Island route with huge portions of sweet and sour chicken and Danish baby back ribs, its two specialties; French rack of lamb; and porterhouse steak. Breakfast and dinner plans are available, with the flexibility of dining at the resort's sister property. ⌂ *Box EX 29055, George Town* ☎ *242/336–2551 or 800/525–2210* 🖷 *242/336–2093* ⊕ *www.peaceandplenty.com* 🛏 *32 rooms* ♻ *Restaurant, fans, refrigerators, cable TV, pool, beach, dive shop, dock, boating, fishing, 2 bars, Internet* ☰ *AE, MC, V* ⌘ *EP, MAP.*

**$** ✕🖼 **Coconut Cove Hotel.** The Paradise Suite at this intimate hotel has its own private terrace hot tub, a king-size bed, walk-in closet, and an immense bathroom with a black-marble Jacuzzi. Other rooms have queen-size beds, tile floors, and scenic views from private terraces. Bathrobes and fresh-daily floral arrangements add an elegant touch. The restaurant menu includes Angus beef, fresh pastas, and gourmet pizzas served outside on the deck or inside by the fireplace. ⌂ *Box EX 29299, George Town* ☎ *242/336–2659* 🖷 *242/336–2658* ⊕ *www.exumabahamas.com/coconutcove.html* 🛏 *12 rooms, 1 cottage* ♻ *Restaurant, fans, refrigerators, pool, dive shop, fishing, bar, laundry service* ☰ *AE, D, MC, V.*

⌘ **$** ✕🖼 **Peace & Plenty Beach Inn.** This 16-room resort on 300 feet of narrow beach is a mile west of its big brother, the Club Peace & Plenty; a shuttle runs between the two four times daily. The units have white-tile floors, simple tropical-print accents, and French doors opening onto private patios or balconies that overlook the pool and the ocean. The resort offers free scuba sessions in the pool. Once in the restaurant, marvel at the tiered, stained-pine cathedral ceiling and feast poolside on blackened mahimahi, New York–cut steak, or shrimp Parmesan. Specialties include lobster burgers and hand-rolled coconut shrimp. Reservations are required. ⌂ *Box EX 29055, George Town* ☎ *242/336–2250 or 800/525–2210* 🖷 *242/336–2253* ⊕ *www.peaceandplenty.com* 🛏 *16 rooms* ♻ *Restaurant, fans, refrigerators, cable TV, pool, beach, fishing, 2 bars* ☰ *AE, MC, V.*

**$$–$$$** 🖼 **Bahama Houseboats.** Brightly decorated floating accommodations offer all the comforts of home. There are five houseboats to choose from: three 35-foot boats with one bedroom and two 43-foot boats with two bedrooms. All have water slides that descend from the top deck. No special license or experience is required to rent the houseboats, and you'll be instructed on cruising parameters and safe operation before leaving the dock. The owners are always a radio call away to answer questions and provide peace of mind. Right out your "front door" you can fish, collect shells, snorkel, and cruise Elizabeth Harbour's multihued, incandescent waters. A three-day minimum stay is required. ⌂ *Box EX 29031, Government Dock, George Town* ☎ *242/336–2628* 🖷 *242/336–2645* ⊕ *www.bahamahouseboats.com* 🛏 *5 boats* ♻ *Kitchenettes* ☰ *MC, V.*

**$** 🖼 **Regatta Point.** Soft pink with hunter green shutters, this handsome two-story guest house overlooks Kidd Cove from its own petite island. Connected to George Town by a short causeway, the property is only a five-minute walk from town but far enough from the fray to have a secret hideaway's charm. Rooms have picturesque views of Elizabeth Harbour, large vaulted ceilings, and porches. Leave the louvered windows open to be lulled to sleep by the waves. The hotel has no restaurant, but units come with modern kitchens, and maid service is included. Dock usage and bicycles are available free to guests. ⊠ *Regatta Point across from George Town* ⌂ *Box EX 29006* ☎ *242/336–2206 or 888/ 720–0011* 🖷 *242/336–2046* ⊕ *www.regattapointbahamas.com* ⇨ *6 suites* ⌂ *Fans, kitchenettes, beach, dock, boating, fishing, bicycles, laundry service* ☰ *MC, V.*

## Nightlife

On Monday, head to **Eddie's Edgewater** (☎ 242/336–2050) for rousing rake 'n' scrape music. The front porch and the game room behind the restaurant are popular spots where locals hang out all week long, especially come Friday afternoon. **Two Turtles Inn** (☎ 242/336–2545) is the other hot spot on Friday, when everyone comes to town to celebrate the end of the work week. 2T, as it's known, puts on a barbecue with live music. A week is too long to wait, so the celebration is repeated on Tuesday nights. In season, the poolside bashes at **Club Peace & Plenty** (☎ 242/ 336–2551), with its resident band, George Wiley and the In-Crowd, keep Bahamians and vacationers on the dance floor Wednesday and Saturday nights. On Saturday, the live band and barbecue pack 'em in at **Palm Bay Beach Club.**

## Sports & the Outdoors

BICYCLING  **Starfish** (☎ 242/336–3033 ⊕ www.kayakbahamas.com) rents bicycles with helmets and maps starting at $15 per half-day, $100 per week. In George Town's Scotia Bank building, **Thompson's Rentals** (☎ 242/336–2442) has bicycles.

BOATING  Because of its wealth of safe harbors and regatta events, the Exumas is a favorite spot for yachtsmen. Renting a boat allows you to explore the cays near George Town and beyond, and a number of area hotels allow guests to tie up rental boats at their docks. For those who want to take a water jaunt through Stocking Island's hurricane holes, sailboats are ideal.

**Minns Water Sports** (☎ 242/336–3483 ⊕ www.mwsboats.com) rents Boston Whalers ranging from 15- to 22-feet. You can reserve a full-day (8 to 5) rental; half-day (four hour) rentals are available on a first-come, first-served basis. Rates start at $65 for a half-day.

★ **Starfish** (☎ 242/336–3033 ⊕ www.kayakbahamas.com) rents Hobie Cat and Sea Pearl sailboats with gear starting at $50 for a half-day.

To sail the Exumas without the hassle of owning or captaining, book a day charter on the *Emerald Lady* (☎ 242/357–0441). Snacks and meals are provided, plus there's extra fun to be had sliding into the water and snorkeling.

EVENTS  The **Annual New Year's Day Cruising Regatta** is held at the Staniel Cay Yacht Club, with international yachts taking part in a series of races. At the beginning of March, the **Cruiser's Regatta** hosts visiting boats for a week of races, cookouts, and partying in George Town. The **Family Is-**

**lands Regatta** is the Bahamas most important yachting event of the year. It takes place in April. Starting the race in Elizabeth Harbour in George Town, island-made wooden sailboats compete for trophies. Onshore, the town is a three-day riot of Junkanoo parades, Goombay music, arts-and-crafts fairs, and continuous merriment. The **Music & Heritage Festival** is held each March in Regatta Park.

FISHING Exuma is a fishing haven, a great place to hunt the elusive bonefish (in season year-round and highly prized among fly fishermen). Most hotels can arrange for local guides, and a list is available from the **Exuma Tourist Office** (☎ 242/336–2430). **Cooper's Charter Service** (☎ 242/336–2711) will take you out for a day of deep-sea fishing, $300 per half day, $500 per full day. **Fish Rowe Charters** (☎ 242/357–0870 ⊕ www.fishrowecharters.com) has a 40-foot Hatteras that holds up to four fishermen. Deep water charters run $800 for a half-day, $1,600 for a full day. **Trevor B Fishing Guide** (☎ 242/336–2674) is a highly recommended for bonefishing. **Cely Smith** (☎ 242/345–2341) is both a bonefishing and fly-fishing guide. Fisherman and boat owner **Gus Thompson** (☎ 242/345–5214) will help you hook big game as well as feisty bonefish.

GOLF Golf legend Greg Norman designed the 18-hole, par-72 championship course, featuring six oceanside holes, at **Four Seasons Resort Great Exuma at Emerald Bay** (☎ 242/336–6800), the island's only golf course. There are preferred tee times for hotel guests, who pay $145, including golf cart; the fee for nonguests is $175.

KAYAKING **Starfish** (☎ 242/336–3033 ⊕ www.kayakbahamas.com) has guided ★ half-day kayak trips to Crab Cay and Moriah Cay National Park in sturdy flat-bottom ocean-going kayaks. Adults pay $55; children pay $44 for three- to four-hour excursions. Kayak lessons are free with rentals, which start at $30 for a half day in a single. Deliveries are available on rentals of three days or longer.

SCUBA DIVING **Angel Fish Blue Hole,** minutes from George Town, is a popular dive site filled with angel fish, spotted rays, snapper, and the occasional reef shark. **Dive Exuma** (☎ 242/336–2893 ⊕ www.dive-exuma.com) offers dive instruction, certification courses, and scuba trips. One-tank dives are $75; blue hole and night dives are $100. **Stocking Island Mystery Cave** is full of mesmerizing schools of colorful fish but is for experienced divers only.

SNORKELING **Starfish** (☎ 242/336–3033 ⊕ www.kayakbahamas.com) rents snorkel equipment by the half-day, day, or week.

TENNIS Four Har-Tru tennis courts, which are lighted for night play, are available to nonguests at **Four Seasons Resort Great Exuma at Emerald Bay** (☎ 242/336–6800), depending on availability, for $25 per hour. Nonguests can use the two Laycold cushion-surfaced courts at **February Point** (☎ 242/336–2693 or 877/839–4253) for $30 a day; use of the adjacent fitness center is an additional $15.

## Shopping

In the Exumas, George Town is the place to shop, but expect mostly local goods and crafts. **Exuma Markets** (✉ Across from Scotia Bank, George

Town ☎ 242/336–2033) was the island's largest grocery until Emerald Island opened in 2005 at Emerald Bay, near the Four Seasons. Yachties tie up at the skiff docks in the rear, on Lake Victoria. FedEx, emergency e-mail, and faxes for visitors are accepted here as well.

**Exuma Master Tailor Shop** (⊠ Across street from Exuma Markets, George Town ☎ 242/554–2050), with one- to two-day service at very reasonable prices, will duplicate a favorite designer dress or suit while you are out sunning. Bring your own material, buttons, and zippers.

**Peace & Plenty Boutique** (⊠ Opposite Club Peace & Plenty ☎ 242/336–2551) has a good selection of Androsia fabrics, plus gifts, resort logo items, and the town's best selection of women's fashions, from casual to dressy.

**Sandpiper Arts & Crafts** (⊠ Queen's Hwy. ☎ 242/336–2084) has upscale souvenirs, from high-quality cards and books to batik clothing and art.

## Cays of the Exumas

A band of cays—with names like Rudder Cut, Big Farmer's, Great Guana, and Leaf—stretches north from Great Exuma.

**㉒** Boaters will want to explore the waterways known as **Pipe Creek** (☎ 242/355–2034), a winding passage through the tiny islands between Staniel and Compass cays. There are great spots for shelling, snorkeling, diving, and bonefishing. The **Samson Cay Yacht Club,** at the creek's halfway point, is a good place for lunch or dinner.

**㉓** **Staniel Cay** is a favorite destination of yachters and makes the perfect home base for visiting the Exuma Cays Land and Sea Park. The island has an airstrip, two hotels, and one paved road. Virtually everything is within walking distance. Oddly enough, as you stroll past brightly painted houses and sandy shores, you are as likely to see a satellite dish as a woman pulling a bucket of water from a roadside well. At one of three grocery stores, boat owners can replenish their supplies. The friendly village also has a small red-roof church, a post office, and a straw vendor.

Fodor'sChoice ★

Just across the water from the Staniel Cay Yacht Club is one of the Bahamas' most unforgettable attractions: **Thunderball Grotto,** a beautiful marine cave that snorkelers (at low tide) and experienced scuba divers can explore. In the central cavern, shimmering shafts of sunlight pour through holes in the soaring ceiling and illuminate the glass-clear water. You'll see right away why this cave was chosen as an exotic setting for such movies as 007's *Thunderball* and *Never Say Never Again,* and the mermaid tale *Splash.*

**㉔** Above Staniel Cay, near the Exumas' northern end, lies the 176-square-mi **Exuma Cays Land and Sea Park,** which spans 22 mi between Conch Cut and Wax Cay Cut. You must charter a small boat or seaplane to reach the park, which has more than 20 mi of petite cays. Hawksbill Cay and Warderick Wells (both with remains of 18th-century Loyalist settlements) have marked hiking trails, as does Hall's Pond. At Shroud

# Islands of the Stars

**THE BAHAMAS HAS SERVED AS** a source of inspiration for countless artists, writers, and directors. Just about any day of the year, there's a film crew somewhere in the islands shooting scenes for a movie, music video, or television commercial.

The Bahamian movie legacy dates back to the era of silent films, including the now-legendary original black-and-white version of Jules Verne's *20,000 Leagues Under the Sea,* which was filmed here in 1907. Since the birth of color film, the draw has only increased—directors are lured by the possibility of using the islands' characteristic white sands and luminous turquoise waters as a backdrop. Among the more famous movies shot in the Bahamas are *Jaws,* the cult favorite whose killer shark has terrified viewers for two decades; *Flipper,* the family classic about a boy and a porpoise; *Splash,* whose main character is a mermaid who becomes human; and *Cocoon,* about a group of elderly friends who discover an extraterrestrial secret to immortality. Most recently, parts of the two sequels to *Pirates of the Caribbean* were shot on location in the Exumas.

Another memorable film, *Thunderball,* gave Great Exuma Island the distinction of being the only island in the Caribbean where not one, but two James Bond movies were filmed. *Thunderball* and *Never Say Never Again* were both shot on location in Staniel Cay, one of the northernmost islands of the Exumas chain.

You can swim and snorkel in **Thunderball Cave,** site of the pivotal chase scene in the 1965 Sean Connery film. The ceiling of this huge, dome-shape cave is about 30 feet above the water, which is filled with yellowtails, parrots, blue chromes, and yellow and black striped sergeant majors. Swimming into the cave is the easy part—the tide draws you in—but paddling back out can be strenuous, especially because if you stop moving, the tide will pull you back.

Well before Connery gave the cave its name, Ian Fleming, the creator of 007, set his book *Dr. No* on Great Inagua. **Ernest Hemingway** wrote about the Bahamas as well. He visited Bimini regularly in the 1930s, dubbing it the "Sportsfishing Capital of the World." His hangout was the Compleat Angler, a bar that housed a small Hemingway museum until it burned down in January 2006. Among the items the museum displayed were Hemingway's drawings for *The Old Man and the Sea*—rumor has it that the protagonist looks suspiciously like one of the Angler's former bartenders.

The Bahamas not only seem to spark the imaginations of artists, but have also become a playground for the rich and famous in recent years. The stars of Cocoon, the late **Hume Cronyn** and **Jessica Tandy,** were regular visitors to Goat Cay, a private island just offshore from George Town, Exuma. Many world-famous celebrities and athletes hide out at **Musha Cay,** an exclusive retreat in the northern part of the Exumas, where a week's stay can set you back five figures. Although the cay won't name its guests, the all-knowing taxi drivers at the George Town airport mention **Oprah Winfrey** and **Michael Jordan** as a few of the esteemed visitors.

Cay, jump into "Camp Driftwood," where the strong current creates a natural whirlpool that whips you around a rocky outcropping to a powdery beach. Part of the Bahamas National Trust, the park appeals to divers, who appreciate the vast underworld of limestone, reefs, drop-offs, blue holes of freshwater springs, caves, and a multitude of exotic marine life, including one of the Bahamas' most impressive stands of rare pillar coral. Strict laws prohibit fishing and removing coral, plants, or even shells as souvenirs. A list of park rules is available at the head-quarters on Warderick Wells.

North of the park is **Norman's Cay,** an island with 10 mi of rarely trod white beaches, which attracts an occasional yachter. It was once the pri-vate domain of Colombian drug smuggler Carlos Lehder. It's now owned by the Bahamian government. **Allen's Cays** are at the Exumas' northernmost tip and are home to the rare Bahamian iguana.

## Where to Stay & Eat

$  ✕⌂ **Staniel Cay Yacht Club.** The club once drew such luminaries as Mal-colm Forbes and Robert Mitchum. It's now a low-key getaway for yachties and escapists. The cottages, perched on stilts along a rocky bank, have broad ocean vistas and dramatic sunsets, which you can treasure from a chaise longue on your spacious private balcony. Take a tour of the cay in one of the club's golf carts. Meal plans for breakfast and din-ner cost an extra $35 per person per day. All-inclusive packages are also available. ⊠ *Staniel Cay* ⌖ *2233 S. Andrews Ave., Fort Lauderdale, FL 33316* ☎ *242/355–2024 or 954/467–8920* ⎙ *242/355–2044* ⊕ *www. stanielcay.com* ⇌ *5 1-bedroom cottages, 3 2-bedroom cottages, 1 3-bedroom cottage* ⚖ *Restaurant, fans, refrigerators, boating, fishing, bar, piano, Internet, business services, airstrip; no room phones, no room TVs* ▤ *AE, MC, V* ⎜◯⎜ *EP, MAP, AI.*

¢–$  ✕⌂ **Happy People Marina.** You may find this casual hotel a bit isolated if you're not interested in yachting. The property is close to Staniel Cay, but it's a long way from the George Town social scene. A local band, however, plays at the Royal Entertainer Lounge, and a small restaurant serves meals. The simple motel-style rooms are on the beach. ⊠ *Staniel Cay* ☎ *242/355–2008* ⇌ *8 rooms, 1 2-bedroom apartment* ⚖ *Restau-rant, dining room, beach, dock, bar* ▤ *No credit cards.*

## Nightlife

**Club Thunderball** (⊠ East of Thunderball Grotto ☎ 242/355–2012) is a sports bar–dance club built on a bluff overlooking the water. Run by a local pilot, it serves lunch every day and has Friday evening barbe-cues. **Royal Entertainer Lounge** (⊠ Happy People Marina ☎ 242/355–2008) has live Bahamian bands performing on special occasions.

## Sports & the Outdoors

BICYCLING  Contact **Chamberlain Rentals** (☎ 242/355–2020) if you want to pedal around Staniel Cay.

BOATING &  **Staniel Cay Yacht Club** (☎ 242/355–2024) rents 13-foot Whalers and
FISHING  arranges for fishing guides.

**Exuma Cays Land and Sea Park** and **Thunderball Grotto** are excellent snorkeling and dive sites. **Staniel Cay Yacht Club** (☎ 242/355–2024) rents masks and fins for snorkeling, and Staniel fills tanks from its compressor. Call ahead or plan to bring your own scuba gear.

## Exumas Essentials

### BY AIR

You can fly from Fort Lauderdale, St. Petersburg, Sarasota, or Miami to the Exuma International Airport, the Exumas' official airport and official port of entry. Located 9 mi from George Town, the airport is in the process of rebuilding due to a fire in 2005 (though it is still open). You can also fly into Staniel Cay, near the top of the chain, which has a 3,000-foot airstrip that accepts charter flights and private planes—but you must clear customs at the Andros, Nassau, or Exuma airport first.

Air Sunshine flies on demand from Fort Lauderdale to George Town. American Eagle has daily service from Miami; call for summer scheduling. Bahamasair has daily flights from Nassau to George Town. Continental Connection/Gulfstream flies twice daily between Fort Lauderdale and George Town. US Airways flies direct from Charlotte, NC, to George Town every Saturday. Watermakers Air offers charters from Fort Lauderdale Executive Airport to Staniel Cay Yacht Club. Lynx Air International flies from Fort Lauderdale to George Town on Thursday, Friday, and Saturday.

🛪 Airlines & Contacts **Air Sunshine** ☎ 954/435-8900 or 800/327-8900. **American Eagle** ☎ 800/433-7300. **Bahamasair** ☎ 800/222-4262. **Continental/Gulfstream** ☎ 800/231-0856. **Lynx Air International** ☎ 888/596-9247. **US Airways** ☎ 800/428-4322. **Watermakers Air** ☎ 954/467-8920.

### BY BOAT

M/V *Grand Master* travels from Nassau to George Town on Tuesday and returns to Nassau on Friday. Travel time is 12 hours, and fares range from $35 to $40 depending on your destination. M/V *Ettienne & Cephas* leaves Nassau on Tuesday for Staniel Cay, Big Farmer's Cay, Black Point, and Barraterre, returning to Nassau on Saturday. The full trip takes 21 hours. Call for fares to specific destinations. For further information, contact the Dockmaster's Office at Potter's Cay, Nassau.

Bahama Ferries' air-conditioned *Seawind* and *Sealink* carry passengers and vehicles from Nassau to George Town Monday and Wednesday, returning to Nassau Tuesday and Thursday.

To reach Stocking Island from George Town, the Club Peace & Plenty Ferry leaves from the hotel's dock twice daily at 10 and 1. The ferry departs from the Stocking Island dock at 10:30 and 1:30. The fare is $10 round-trip for non–Peace & Plenty guests.

You can stay in George Town proper and enjoy touring Great Exuma by car, but if you want a closer look at any of the hundreds of deserted Exuma cays nearby, you'll appreciate the greater freedom of a boat. If you want to go to Staniel Cay, through Pipe Creek, or to the Exuma

Cays Land and Sea Park, water passage via the Exuma Sound or Great Bahama Bank is the only route.

🗐 Boat & Ferry Information **Bahamas Ferries** ☎ 242/323-2166. **Club Peace & Plenty Ferry** ☎ 242/336-2551. **Dockmaster's Office** ☎ 242/393-1064.

### BY BUS
Exuma Bus Service travels daily for the main purpose of delivering staff to the Four Seasons Resort and back home in the afternoon. Rates range between $3 and $5 per person, depending upon pick-up/drop-off location.

### BY CAR
Thompson's Rentals rents cars. Exuma Transport is a car-rental establishment in George Town. Hotels can also arrange car rentals.

🗐 Local Agencies **Airport Rent a Car** ☎ 242/345-0090. **Exuma Transport** ☎ 242/336-2101. **Raquel's Car Rental** ☎ 242/358-5011. **Thompson's Rentals** ☎ 242/336-2442. **Uptown Car Rentals** ☎ 242/336-2822.

### BY GOLF CART
Staniel Cay Yacht Club rents golf carts for exploring Staniel Cay.

🗐 Staniel Cay Yacht Club ☎ 242/355-2024.

### BY SCOOTER
In George Town, Prestige Scooter Rental rents motor scooters for $60 a day.

🗐 Prestige Scooter Rental ☎ 242/357-0066.

### BY TAXI
Taxis wait at the airport for incoming flights. The cost of a ride from the airport to George Town is about $25 for two people.

Your George Town hotel will arrange for a taxi if you wish to go exploring or need to return to the airport. Kermit Rolle or Luther Rolle Taxi Service will take you where you need to go. Or try Exuma Transit Services.

🗐 Exuma Transit Services ☎ 242/345-0232 ⊕ www.exumatransitservices.com. **Kermit Rolle** ☎ 242/345-6038. **Luther Rolle Taxi Service** ☎ 242/345-5003.

## Contacts & Resources

### BANKS & EXCHANGING SERVICES
The Scotia Bank in George Town is open weekdays 9–3 and Saturday 9–1. Since the Four Seasons came to town, two new banks have opened, Royal Bank of Canada and Bank of the Bahamas.

### EMERGENCIES
🗐 In George Town: **Police** ☎ 242/336-2666 or 911. **Health Clinic** ☎ 242/336-2088. In Staniel Cay: **Police** ☎ 242/355-2042.

### TOURS OPTIONS
From George Town, Captain Cole arranges overnight trips up to the Exuma Cays Land and Sea Park. Exuma Glass Bottom Boat keeps you

dry as you explore local reefs and blue holes. Luther Rolle will take you on an informative tour of Little and Great Exuma, or contact Christine's Island Tours, which does bush medicine tours, or Exuma Transit Services, whose island tours include lunch at a native restaurant or dinner with rake 'n' scrape music.

🚩 **Captain Cole** ☎ 242/345-0074. **Christine's Island Tours** ☎ 242/358-4016. **Exuma Transit Services** ☎ 242/334-0232. **Exuma Glass Bottom Boat** ☎ 242/357-0570. **Luther Rolle** ☎ 242/345-5003.

## VISITOR INFORMATION

The Exuma Tourist Office is in George Town, across the street from the Exuma Markets, one block from the Government Administration Building. Visit the Bahamas Ministry of Tourism Web site and the Out-Islands Promotion Board's site for additional information.

🚩 Tourist Information **Exuma Tourist Office** ☎ 242/336-2430 🖶 242/336-2431 ⊕ www.bahamas.com. **Out-Islands Promotion Board** ☎ 800/688-4752 ⊕ www.bahama-out-islands.com.

# The Other Out Islands

**WORD OF MOUTH**

"What you will find in the Out Islands is peace and quiet, and a lively bar or two (depending on the night). You'll find spectacular beaches with nary a soul in sight, a handful of like-minded travelers, and charming—but oftentimes bare bones—accommodations. The luxury comes from the quiet and the closeness to nature, not from marble baths and spa pedicures."

–Callaloo

Updated by
Stephen F.
Vletas

**THE QUIET, SIMPLER WAY OF LIFE** of the Bahama Out Islands, sometimes referred to as the Family Islands, is startlingly different from Nassau's and Freeport's fast-paced glitz and glitter. Outside New Providence and Grand Bahama, on the dozen or so islands that are equipped to handle tourists, you'll leave the sophisticated resorts, nightclubs, casinos, and shopping malls behind. If you love the outdoors, however, you'll be in fine shape: virtually all the Out Islands have good to excellent fishing, boating, and diving, and you'll often have endless stretches of beach all to yourself.

For the most part, you won't find hotels that provide the costly creature comforts that are taken for granted in Nassau and Freeport, with the exception of Kamalame Cay on Andros, and Club Med–Columbus Isle on San Salvador. Out Islands accommodations are generally modest lodges, rustic cottages, and small inns—many without telephones and TV (inquire when making reservations if these are important to you). Making a phone call, or receiving one, will sometimes require a trip to the local BaTelCo (Bahamas Telecommunications Corporation) telephone station.

Along with the utter lack of stress of an Out Islands holiday, you'll find largely unspoiled environments. Roughing it in Inagua, for example, is a small price to pay for the glorious spectacle of 60,000 pink flamingos taking off into the sky. And a day of sightseeing can mean little more than a stroll down narrow, sand-strewn streets in a fishing village, past small, pastel homes where orange, pink, and bright-red bougainvillea spill over the walls. Meals, even those served in hotels, almost always incorporate local specialties, from conch and fresh-caught fish to chicken with peas 'n' rice. Island taverns are tiny and usually noisy with chatter. You can make friends with locals over a beer and a game of pool or darts much more quickly than you would in the average stateside cocktail lounge. Nightlife may involve listening to a piano player or a small village rake 'n' scrape combo in a clubhouse bar, or joining the crowds at a local disco playing everything from R&B to calypso.

The Out Islands were once mostly the purview of private plane and yacht owners. The tourist who discovered a hideaway on Andros, Eleuthera, or in the Exumas would cherish it and return year after year to find the same faces as before. But the islands are now becoming more and more popular, largely because of increased airline activity. Most islands are served from Nassau or Florida daily. Others may only have a couple of incoming and outgoing flights a week. If you want to partake of simple island life without feeling completely cut off, choose a slightly busier spot that is closer to the mainland United States, such as Bimini. If you go farther away from the mainland, to a place like Cat Island or San Salvador, you'll feel much more like you're getting away from it all.

## Exploring the Out Islands

The Out Islands span a sweeping area of shallow seas and deep ocean—from the Biminis, just off southern Florida, to Great Inagua, northeast

# GREAT ITINERARIES

*Numbers in the text correspond to numbers in the margins and on the Andros, the Biminis, Cat Island, Long Island, and San Salvador maps.*

### IF YOU HAVE 3 DAYS

If you've decided to sample the natural treasures of the Out Islands, the ▶ 🔳 **South Bight** of **Andros** is a clear-cut choice. Fly to **Congo Town airport,** then take your first day to relax on the beach; or jump right in with a kayaking tour of the nearby cays and **Lisbon Creek.** On your second day, sign up for a guided snorkeling exploration of the area's vivid blues holes and the black-coral barrier reef swarming with sea life. In the afternoon go on a nature hike in a pine forest in search of wild orchids and exotic birds. Enjoy sunset cocktails on the beach. For your last day, set out on a boating adventure to the secluded **West Side** for fishing, exploring, and picnicking. Here, the aquamarine water melds with the sky in a dreamy purple haze that creates a dazzling portrait of tranquility.

If you're a bonefishing enthusiast, spend your three days in 🔳 **Cargill Creek.** Fish for the elusive gray ghost with top professional guides in the **North and Middle Bights** and along the white-sand beaches of **Big Wood Cay.** The lodges in the area can also arrange diving and snorkeling excursions, and island sightseeing tours.

### IF YOU HAVE 5 DAYS

Follow the suggested three-day itinerary, then transfer to 🔳 **Fresh Creek** ❸. On the way you can stop at the **Androsia Batik Works Factory** in 🔳 **Andros Town** ❷, and shop for colorful island-made

fabrics and other gifts at the **Androsia Outlet Store.** After settling in, get your adrenaline flowing with an "over the wall" dive in the **Tongue of the Ocean.** If you're not certified, you can take the **Small Hope Bay Lodge** resort course, and begin diving around the nearby reef in the afternoon. Or lounge on the beach, swim, and snorkel over shallow-water coral heads. Sip sunset cocktails and relax in the evening. Your last day can be filled with other watersports and activities—windsurfing, snorkeling, fishing, or exploring from Fresh Creek to **Captain Bill's Blue Hole,** where you can enjoy a leisurely picnic and a cooling swim. If you're looking for some serious exercise, make this trip on a bicycle, about 6 mi one-way from **Fresh Creek.**

Dedicated anglers don't need to move anywhere else. A continued stay at 🔳 **Cargill Creek** will mean fishing more of the countless flats throughout the Bights. Venture to the **West Side,** where you can pursue tarpon and permit along with bonefish.

### IF YOU HAVE 7 DAYS

Add on to the five-day itinerary above by flying to 🔳 **Bimini** for your last two days. Charter a deep-sea fishing boat or dive over the famous ▶ **Atlantis** lost city site. On your final day, hop the ferry to South Bimini to wander the white-sand beaches, snorkel and swim, shop in the **Native Straw and Craft Market,** or visit the **Bimini Museum.**

5

of Cuba. The northern islands of the Biminis, the Berries, and Andros are quick and easy to reach from Florida via scheduled and chartered flight service. Dominated by the Great Bahama Bank, these islands are tailor-made for sportfishing, diving, snorkeling, swimming, and boating. Bimini receives more boaters than any other island and is a weekend party spot. Great Harbour, the largest of the Berry Islands, is sedate, self-contained, and oriented toward family beach and watersport vacationing. Andros is vast, an ultimate retreat for bonefishing and diving. The northern islands are mostly flat, lush with mangroves, rimmed with white-sand beaches, and laced with miles of creeks and lakes. People walk between settlements, or ride bikes or golf carts. Exploring is best done by boat, not car, though taxis are available to cover longer distances.

The southern islands are more remote, exposed to the open Atlantic, and ruggedly dramatic. They're usually reached by air from Nassau. Good roads on Cat and Long Islands allow for convenient exploration by car. Here you'll find miles of pink-sand beaches, bonefish flats, and aquamarine bays waiting. Settlements are spread out, and services, including gas stations, are not always available. The weather is a few degrees warmer and more consistent south of the Tropic of Cancer, which slices through the center of Long Island. Club Med on San Salvador, designed for pampered relaxation, is the essence of quiet luxury. Crooked and Acklins Islands, with populations of about 400 people each, are outposts for the self-sufficient adventurer. The same is true for Great Inagua, where the best way to explore is with a local guide.

## About the Restaurants

Dining is a casual "get together" experience, and rarely involves anything fancy. Restaurants, lodges, and inns serve traditional Bahamian fare—fresh seafood, grilled chicken, johnnycakes, and barbecued pork with all the fixings (potato salad, coleslaw, peas 'n' rice, and baked macaroni and cheese). Most islands have restaurants that are open during normal mealtime hours, but there are exceptions. Call ahead whenever possible, especially on Crooked, Acklins, and Great Inagua islands. Beachside restaurants are often small, with simple wooden tables and casual dress. Sunset cocktails are one of the pleasures of daily life. Thatched conch stands and colorful roadside bars are a treat—and a cool way to mingle with local residents. During regatta season, life on the Out Islands gets merrily crazy, and pig roasts with live music are not-to-be-missed events.

## About the Hotels

Accommodations to suit most tastes can be found, from a handful of luxury properties on private cays and remote beaches to simple fishing lodges and funky hotels with swinging nightlife. You need to have a good idea of what you want—the overall experience, service, amenities, activities—then do your homework before making a reservation. Many resorts and lodges don't have air-conditioning, or only have it in certain rooms. If this is important to you, be sure to ask at the time of your booking. A number of lodges cater specifically to anglers and divers and are not well suited to overall vacationing.

# IF YOU LIKE

### OUT ISLANDS CUISINE

Out Islands restaurants are often family-run and focus on home-style dishes. They typically serve a combination of Bahamian, Continental, and American fare. Instead of the menu, it's the ingredients and individual flare of the chef that set one place apart from the next. While fried food, especially seafood, is a staple, more chefs are experimenting with alternate cooking methods, especially baking and grilling. If you see grilled or blackened hog snapper on a menu, give it a try, as this is one of the most popular island dishes. Lobster chunks marinated in wine and sautéed is another specialty.

To get a sense of what the locals eat at home, try ordering any fish prepared "Bahamian style," meaning baked and smothered in tomatoes and spices. For a true taste of Out Islands food, don't go home without sampling conch salad with lemon and hot peppers. If you're on the hunt for the freshest conch salad, look for one of the out-of-the-way stands where the commercial fishermen clean their catch. Another worthy culinary challenge is the quest for the best key lime pie, a local dessert favorite.

### YOUR OWN PRIVATE PARADISE

Aside from the large resorts, most hotels on the Out Islands are small and owner-operated, which ensures a personal touch. Some accommodations use an honor-bar system—mix your own and sign for it—so you really feel at home. These are the places that people return to year after year to visit the locals who have become their friends.

Although such hotels may not be any cheaper than the big, plush resorts, many visitors feel that it's hard to put a price on the total escape that the more low-key accommodations have to offer. What would you pay for a powdery pink beach that stretches for miles with no footprints but your own? Or water so clear that snorkeling makes you feel like you're flying?

### THE AGE-OLD SPORT OF FISHING

Fishing is believed to have been an integral part of Bahamian culture for as long as people have inhabited the islands. The majority of settlements in the Out Islands were established for subsistence fishing and sponging. Commercial fishing, focused on lobster, grouper, and snapper, is what drives the economies of many of these communities today. Sportfishing began with an emphasis on offshore angling—trolling an assortment of lures, rigged baits, and teasers on conventional tackle rods and reels to entice deepwater gamefish into striking distance—for marlin, tuna, wahoo, and dolphin. Bonefishing—stalking bonefish on foot or in a poled boat across clear shallow-water flats, and then sight-casting your bait, jig, lure, or fly to specific fish that you spot—entered the mix in the 1920s and 1930s. Now, big-game blue water fishing and fly-fishing the flats are ingrained in the local fabric. Fishing guides are often second- or third-generation professionals with a contagious enthusiasm for their sport and an encyclopedic knowledge of the best spots.

5

## OUT ISLANDS' TOP 5

- **Charter a boat.** Explore the necklace of islands that comprise the Biminis and the Berrys. Start in Bimini, and end up in Chub Cay. It's quite possible that you may not choose to come back . . .

- **Dive and Bonefish on Andros Island.** Go with the diving experts at Small Hope Bay and drop "over-the-wall." Then cruise the West Side flats with top professional guides in pursuit of the elusive "gray ghost."

- **Explore Long Island.** Possibly the most alluring of all the Out Islands, Long Island is an absolute jewel. Base yourself at Stella Maris Resort, rent a car,

and head out. Don't forget your snorkeling gear, fishing rods, and a cooler of goodies.

- **Go deep-sea fishing at Pittstown Point Landing.** This is wild blue-water fishing the way it used to be: marlin, tuna, dorado, wahoo, and more, with no other boats in sight. Eat, drink, fish, sleep . . . eat, drink, fish, sleep . . . you get the idea. The bonefishing isn't bad either.

- **Hide on Cat Island.** If you're looking for romance, hole up with that special person at Fernandez Bay Village. There's sun, sea, and sand—what more do you need?

Comfortable motel-style accommodations are most common, and these lodges usually have a restaurant and bar. Places located on the water are better cooled by ocean breezes, which are a huge help in keeping down the bugs—mosquitoes, sand flies, and doctor flies. Family-owned and operated properties tend to be exceptionally warm and friendly, though you can generally expect a welcoming reception wherever you go. Off-season rates usually begin in May, with some of the best discounted package deals available in October, November, and early December. Club Med–Columbus Isle offers early-bird booking bonuses and runs pricing promotions year-round.

| WHAT IT COSTS | | | | |
|---|---|---|---|---|
| | $$$$ | $$$ | $$ | $ | ¢ |
| RESTAURANTS | over $40 | $30–$40 | $20–$30 | $10–$20 | under $10 |
| HOTELS | over $400 | $300–$400 | $200–$300 | $100–$200 | under $100 |

Restaurant prices are for a main course at dinner, excluding gratuity, typically 15%, which is often automatically added to the bill. Hotel prices are for two people in a standard double room in high season, excluding service charges and 6%–12% tax.

### Timing

The peak tourist season is mid-December through April for visitors in the sun-sea-and-sand vacation mode. From the beginning of May, and on through the fall, room rates tend to drop by as much as a third. May,

June, July, October, and November are good months for diving, snorkeling, boating, and beach activities at discount prices. Hurricane season technically runs from June through November, though June, July and November are less of a concern. August and September (the most likely months for hurricanes) can be hot and steamy, and many resorts and restaurants are closed.

Off-season discount rates often won't include lodges focused on fishing, as April through June are prime months for flats and offshore anglers. This is also the perfect time to combine fishing with diving, snorkeling, and beach exploring. October and November are excellent fishing months as well, and the winter period of December through March is good when the weather cooperates. Winter cold fronts—a relative term, with temperatures only dropping into the high-60s to low-70s—move down from Florida and can bring wind and clouds for several days, which makes swimming, sunning, and fishing less appealing. To play the weather odds, your best bet is to go to the southern islands (Long Island, San Salvador, Crooked, Acklins, and Great Inagua) December through March. Cold fronts often stall out before reaching these southern islands, and daily temperatures average about five degrees warmer than on the northern islands.

You'll rarely have to worry about crowds in the Out Islands. However, sailing regattas on Andros, Long, and Cat Islands and fishing tournaments in the Biminis and Berries are popular events that bring out the partying spirit in locals and visitors alike.

## ANDROS

The Bahamas' largest island (100 mi long and 40 mi wide) and one of the least explored, Andros's land mass is carved up by myriad channels, creeks, lakes, and mangrove-covered cays. The North, Middle, and South Bights cut through the width of the island, creating boating access to both coasts. Andros is best-known for its bonefishing and diving, and is also a glorious ecotourism spot with snorkeling, blue hole exploration, sea kayaking, and nature hikes. More than a dozen small lodges on the eastern shore cater to sun and sea revelers.

The Spaniards who came here in the 16th century called it *La Isla del Espíritu Santo*—the Island of the Holy Spirit—and it has retained its eerie mystique to this day. In fact, the descendants of a group of Seminole Indians and runaway slaves who left the Florida Everglades in the mid-19th century settled in Andros and remained hidden until a few decades ago. They continue to live as a tribal society. Their village, near the island's northern tip, is called Red Bay, and they make a living by

### DID YOU KNOW?

In the Bahamas, mail is still delivered by mailboats, as it has been for centuries. Mailboats leave Nassau's Potter's Cay carrying mail, cars, produce, and passengers on trips to more than 30 Bahamian islands. The voyages range from the 4-hour cruise to Andros to the overnight trip to Inagua in the south.

weaving straw goods. The Seminoles are credited with originating the myth of the island's legendary (and elusive) chickcharnies—red-eyed, bearded, green-feathered creatures with three fingers and three toes that hang upside down by their tails from pine trees. These mythical characters supposedly wait deep in the forests to wish good luck to the friendly passerby and vent their mischief on the hostile trespasser.

Andros's undeveloped West Side adjoins the Great Bahama Bank, a vast shallow-water haven for lobster and gamefish, including tarpon. Shifting shoals and sandbars, and flats that go dry during low tides, create hazards for boaters. Immense bays, tiny sloughs, and mangrove swamps snake in and out of the chalk-color shoreline. The island's lush green interior is covered with wild orchids and dense pine and mahogany forests. The forests provide nesting grounds for parrots, partridges, quail, white-crowned pigeons, and whistling ducks, and hunters come to Andros from September through March in search of game.

The island's roughly 8,000 residents live in about a dozen settlements on the eastern shore, from Morgan's Bluff in the north to Mars Bay in the south. Farming and commercial fishing are the mainstays of the economy, and the island is the country's largest source of fresh water.

The Andros Barrier Reef—the world's third-largest reef—is within a mile of the east shore and runs for 140 mi. It has an enchanting variety of marine life and is easily accessible to divers. Sheltered waters within the reef average 6–15 feet, but on the other side of the reef ("over the wall") lie the depths (more than 6,000 feet) of the Tongue of the Ocean, where the U.S. and British navies test submarines and underwater weapons. Operating under the acronym AUTEC (Atlantic Underwater Test and Evaluation Center), their base is near Andros Town.

*Numbers in the margin correspond to points of interest on the Andros map.*

## Nicholl's Town

❶ **Nicholl's Town**, at Andros's northeastern corner, is the island's largest village, with a population of about 600. This friendly community has stores for supplies and groceries, a few hotels, a public medical clinic, a telephone station, and small restaurants. A few miles north of Nicholl's Town is a crescent beach and a headland known as **Morgan's Bluff**, named after the 17th-century pirate Henry Morgan, who allegedly dropped off some of his stolen loot in the area. Morgan's Bluff is the site of the All Andros Crabfest in June, an annual party with a craft fair, sailboat races, live music, and plenty of Bahamian food and drink.

Several miles south of Nicholl's Town, **Conch Sound** is a wide protected bay with long strands of white sand and tranquil waters. Swimmers and bonefishers can wade on their own on the easily accessible flats.

### Where to Stay & Eat

¢–$  ✕▥ **Conch Sound Resort Inn.** The inn has six simple and spacious motel-style rooms with carpeting, mahogany furniture, handmade quilts, soft-cushioned chairs, and satellite TV. There are also four two-bedroom suites

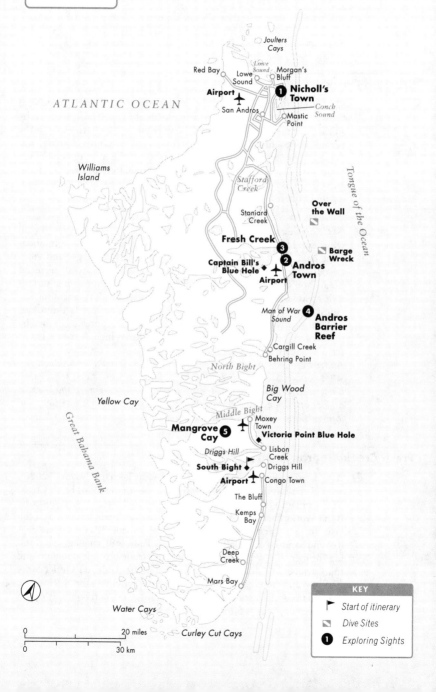

# Andros

*Joulters Cays*

Red Bay

*Lowe Sound*

Lowe Sound

Morgan's Bluff

**Airport**

San Andros

**1 Nicholl's Town**

*Conch Sound*

Mastic Point

ATLANTIC OCEAN

*Williams Island*

*Stafford Creek*

Staniard Creek

*Tongue of the Ocean*

**Over the Wall**

**Fresh Creek**

**3**

**2 Andros Town**

**Captain Bill's Blue Hole**

**Airport**

**Barge Wreck**

*Man of War Sound*

**4 Andros Barrier Reef**

Cargill Creek

Behring Point

*North Bight*

*Big Wood Cay*

*Yellow Cay*

*Middle Bight*

**Mangrove Cay 5**

Moxey Town

**Victoria Point Blue Hole**

*Driggs Hill*

Lisbon Creek

**South Bight**

Driggs Hill

**Airport**

Congo Town

*Great Bahama Bank*

The Bluff

Kemps Bay

Deep Creek

Mars Bay

*Water Cays*

0    20 miles

0    30 km

*Curley Cut Cays*

| KEY | |
|---|---|
| ⚑ | *Start of itinerary* |
| ◣ | *Dive Sites* |
| **❶** | *Exploring Sights* |

with kitchenettes. If you'd prefer not to cook, go to the restaurant for basic Bahamian fare. The inn is on the road between Nicholl's Town and Conch Sound. The beach is a 10-minute walk away, but the hotel will provide transportation. Bonefishing and diving can be arranged. ⚐ *Box 23029, Conch Sound Hwy.* ☎ *242/329–2060* 🖷 *242/329– 2338* ➔ *6 rooms, 4 suites* ⚒ *Restaurant, kitchenettes, pool, bar; no room phones* ▤ *No credit cards.*

## Staniard Creek

Sand banks that turn gold at low tide lie off the northern tip of **Staniard Creek,** a small island settlement 9 mi north of Fresh Creek, accessed by a bridge off the main highway. Coconut palms and casuarinas shade the oceanside beaches, and offshore breezes are pleasantly cooling. **Kamalame Cove** and its nearby private cay are at the northern end of the settlement. Three creeks snake into the mainland, forming extensive mangrove-lined back bays and flats. The surrounding areas are good for wading and bonefishing.

### Where to Stay & Eat

★ **$$$$** ✕▥ **Kamalame Cay.** This 96-acre resort sits on a private cay laced with white-sand beaches and coconut palms. Gleaming, airy accommodations have plush furnishings, linens, and towels. Cottages and villas are on the beach, with sitting areas, soaking tubs, and private terraces. Meals and cocktails are served in the verandah-wrapped plantation-style great house, which is adorned with oversize furniture and antiques. Guests feast on fresh fruits, prime beef, homemade breads and soups, and innovative seafood dishes. You can fish, dive, snorkel, lounge by the pool, or head to the deluxe spa facility. Rates include meals, taxes, service charges, and airport transfers. ⚐ *Kamalame Cay, Staniard Creek, Andros* ☎ *242/368–6281* 🖷 *242/368–6279* ⊕ *www.kamalame.com* ➔ *4 rooms, 5 cottages, 2 villas* ⚒ *2 dining rooms, fans, some minibars, refrigerators, Wi-Fi, tennis court, pool, massage, spa, beach, dive shop, dock, snorkeling, boating, marina, fishing, bicycles, bar, lounge, library, laundry service; no room phones, no room TVs* ▤ *MC, V* ⦿ *AI.*

## Fresh Creek–Andros Town

❷ Batik fabric called Androsia is made in **Andros Town** (☎ 242/368–2080), a small community in central Andros on the south side of Fresh Creek. This brilliantly colored fabric is designed and dyed at the **Androsia Batik Works Factory,** a 3-mi drive from Andros Town airport. You can visit the factory and see how the material is made. It's open weekdays 8–4 and Saturday 9–5. Batik fabric is turned into wall hangings and clothing for men and women, which are sold throughout the Bahamas and the Caribbean. Adjacent to the factory is the **Androsia Outlet Store** (⊕ www.androsia.com), where you can buy original fabrics, clothing, Bahamian carvings and straw baskets, maps, CDs, and books. It's open 9–5 every day except Sunday.

On the north side of Fresh Creek (and about 30 mi south of Nicholl's
**3** Town on the east coast) is the small hamlet of **Fresh Creek**. A few restaurants, including **Hank's Place**, line the waterfront, along with several
boat docks and a small hotel with a convenience store. (Hank put his
business up for sale in November 2005, but plans to continue operations indefinitely.) A few blocks in from the creek are a couple of markets, shops, and offices. The creek itself cuts over 16 mi into the island,
creating tranquil bonefishing flats and welcoming mangrove-lined bays
that can be explored by boaters and sea kayakers.

Andros lures fishing enthusiasts to its fabulous bonefishing flats, and
**4** divers can't get enough of the sprawling **Andros Barrier Reef**, just off Fresh
Creek–Andros Town. Snorkelers can explore such reefs as the Three Sisters, where visibility is clear 15 feet to the sandy floor and jungles of
elkhorn coral snake up to the surface. Divers can delve into the 60-foot-
deep coral caves of the Petrified Forest, beyond which the wall slopes
down to depths of 6,000 feet. Anglers can charter boats to fish offshore
or over the reef, and bonefishers can wade the flats on their own in Fresh
Creek.

## Where to Stay & Eat

★ ¢–$$  ✕ **Hank's Place Restaurant and Bar.** On the north side of Fresh Creek, a
block or so east of the bridge, this restaurant and bar is shaded by co-
conut palms and graced with clear views of the water. Bahamian spe-
cialties—panfried grouper, baked hog snapper, and fresh conch
salad—make it a favorite hangout for locals and visitors. Fresh lob-
ster, prepared to your liking, is available in season (August–March).
Hank's signature cocktail, aptly named "Hanky Panky," is a dynamite
frozen rum and fruit juice concoction. This business has been for sale
since November 2005, but Hank plans to continue operations until he
finds a buyer. ⊠ *Fresh Creek, Andros* ☎ *242/368–2447* ⊕ *hanks-
place.com* ⌦ *Reservations not accepted* ☐ *MC, V* ☾ *Closing hrs are
erratic, call ahead.*

$  ✕🖼 **Andros Lighthouse Yacht Club and Marina.** This is the best place on
Andros to park your boat and hang out. You're sure to meet an ever-
changing parade of people in the cocktail lounge and restaurant ($–$$),
which serves a Bahamian buffet lunch on Sunday. The spacious rooms
and villas are comfortable, but in need of renovation. Boat rentals and
fishing guides can be arranged. It's a five-minute walk across the bridge
to Hank's Place Restaurant and Bar and the convenience stores of the
main settlement area. ⊠ *Andros Town, Andros* ☎ *242/368–2305*
🖨 *242/368–2300* ⊕ *www.androslighthouse.com* ⤳ *12 rooms, 8 villas* ⌂ *Restaurant, fans, refrigerators, pool, beach, dock, snorkeling,
boating, marina, fishing, bicycles, bar, lounge* ☐ *AE, D, MC, V.*

★ ☼ $–$$  ✕🖼 **Small Hope Bay Lodge.** This casual, palm-shaded oceanfront prop-
erty has a devoted following of divers, snorkelers, eco-adventurers, anglers, and families. Rooms with Androsia batik prints and straw work
are in beachside cottages made of coral rock and Andros pine. The homey
main lodge—with a dining room, bar-lounge, game room, and reading
area—is the center of activity. Tasty Bahamian meals include lavish

seafood buffets and pig roasts. For an additional charge you can select bonefishing and specialty diving packages, such as guided explorations of blue holes, diving instruction and certification, and "over-the-wall" dives. Rates include meals, taxes, service charges, and airport transfers. ⊠ *Small Hope Bay, Fresh Creek* ✆ *Box 21667, Fort Lauderdale, FL 33335* ☎ *242/368–2014 or 800/223–6961* 🖷 *242/368–2015* ⊕ *www. smallhope.com* ➷ *20 cottages* ♿ *Dining room, fans, hot tub, massage, beach, dive shop, dock, snorkeling, windsurfing, boating, fishing, bicycles, 2 bars, lounge, library, recreation room, babysitting, laundry service, Internet room; no a/c, no room phones, no room TVs* ▭ *AE, D, MC, V* ⊗ *AI.*

### Sports & the Outdoors

BICYCLING  In Andros Town, bicycles are available at **Andros Lighthouse Yacht Club and Marina** (☎ 242/368–2305). Cruise around Fresh Creek after renting a bike from **Small Hope Bay Lodge** (☎ 242/368–2014).

BOATING &  **Small Hope Bay Lodge** (☎ 242/368–2014 or 800/223–6961) has bone-,
FISHING  deep-sea, fly-, reef, and seasonal tarpon fishing, as well as a "west side overnight"—a two-night camping, bone- and tarpon-fishing trip to the island's uninhabited western end. Rates run $250–$300 for a half day and $375–$500 for a full day (full-day trips include all gear and lunch).

## Cargill Creek

Fishing—bonefishing in particular—is this tranquil area's principal appeal, with wadable flats winding along the shoreline all the way to Behring Point. Cargill Creek is approximately 20 mi south of Andros Town (30 minutes by taxi). Taxi fare is about $40 one-way for two passengers. Bonefishing packages run $350 to $450 per person per day at the half dozen lodges in the area.

### Where to Stay & Eat

$$–$$$$  ✕▥ **Andros Island Bonefishing Club.** If you're a hard-core bonefisher, this is the lodge for you. Guests have access to 100 square mi of lightly fished flats. Owner Captain Rupert Leadon is a gregarious, attention-grabbing presence with many a story of the elusive bonefish. Captain Leadon purchased the adjacent Creekside Lodge in spring 2003 and joined it with AIBC. Rooms are comfortable, with two queen-size beds, mini-refrigerators, and ceiling fans. The dining room–lounges have satellite TV and fly-tying tables. Meals are hearty, with Bahamian fare such as seafood and peas 'n' rice served up family style. Rates include room, meals, and airport transfers. ⊠ *Cargill Creek, Andros* ☎ *242/368–5167* 🖷 *242/368–5397* ⊕ *www.androsbonefishing.com* ➷ *30 rooms* ♿ *2 dining rooms, fans, refrigerators, pool, dive shop, dock, snorkeling, boating, fishing, billiards, 2 bars, lounge, recreation room, laundry service; no room phones, no room TVs* ▭ *AE, D, MC, V* ⊗ *AI.*

### Sports & the Outdoors

FISHING  Some of the best private bonefishing guides in the Bahamas work out of Cargill Creek and Behring Point. **Andy Smith** (☎ 242/368–4261 or 242/368–4044) is highly recommended for guiding anglers through the

CLOSE UP

## Undersea Adventures in Andros

**ANDROS PROBABLY HAS** the largest number of dive sites in the country. With the third-longest barrier reef in the world (behind those of Australia and Belize), the island offers about 100 mi of drop-off diving into the Tongue of the Ocean.

Uncounted numbers of **blue holes** are forming in the area. In some places, these constitute vast submarine networks that can extend more than 200 feet down into the coral (Fresh Creek, 40–100 feet; North Andros, 40–200-plus feet; South Bight, 40–200 feet). Blue holes are named for their inky-blue aura when viewed from above and for the light-blue filtered sunlight that is visible from many feet below. Some of the holes have vast cathedral-like interior chambers with stalactites and stalagmites, offshoot tunnels, and seemingly endless corridors. Others have distinct thermoclines (temperature changes) between layers of water or are subject to tidal flow.

The dramatic Fresh Creek site provides an insight into the complex Andros cave system. There isn't much coral growth, but there are plenty of midnight parrot fish, big southern stingrays, and some blacktip sharks. Similar blue holes are found all along the barrier reef, including several at Mastic Point in the north and the ones explored and filmed off South Bight.

Undersea adventurers also have the opportunity to investigate wrecks such as the *Potomac,* a steel-hulled freighter that sank in 1952 and lies in 40 feet of water off Nicholl's Town. And off the waters of Fresh Creek, at 70 feet, lies the 56-foot-long World War II LCM (landing craft mechanized) known only as the **Barge Wreck,** which was sunk in 1963 to create an artificial reef. Now encrusted with coral, it has become home to a school of groupers and a blizzard of tiny silverfish. There is a fish-cleaning station where miniature cleaning shrimp and yellow gobies clean grouper and rockfish by swimming into their mouths and out their gills, picking up food particles. It's an excellent subject matter for close-up photography.

The split-level **Over the Wall** dive at Fresh Creek takes novices to the 80-foot ledge and experienced divers to a pre–Ice Age beach at 185 feet. The wall is covered with black coral and all kinds of tube sponges. **Small Hope Bay Lodge** is the most respected dive resort on Andros. It's a friendly, informal place where the only thing taken seriously is diving. There's a fully equipped dive center with a wide variety of specialty dives, including customized family-dive trips with a private dive boat and dive master. If you're not certified, check out the lodge's morning "resort course" and be ready to explore the depths by afternoon.

Bights and on the West Side. Charlie Neymour is also a highly regarded bonefishing guide. Contact **Nottages Cottages** (☎ 866/963-7870 or 242/368–4293) to hire him. Call **Tranquility Hill Fishing Lodge** (☎☎ 242/368–4132) at Behring Point to book Barry Neymour, Frankie Neymour, Deon Neymour, Ivan Neymour, Dwain Neymour, Ray Mackey, and Ricardo Mackey, all recommended guides. Rooms and all-inclusive fishing packages are available at Tranquility Hill.

## Mangrove Cay

❺ Remote **Mangrove Cay** is sandwiched between two sea-green bights, separating it from north and south Andros and creating an island of black coral shorelines, gleaming deserted beaches, and dense pine forests. **Moxey Town,** known locally as Little Harbour, rests on the northeast corner in a coconut grove. Pink piles of conch shells and mounds of porous sponges dot the small harbor of this commercial fishing and sponging community. Anglers come on a mission, in search of giant bonefish on flats called "the promised land" and "land of the giants." A five-minute boat ride takes fly-fishers to Gibson Cay to wade hard sand flats sprinkled with starfish. The bar at **Moxey's Guest House and Bonefish Lodge** (☎ 242/362–2080), across the road from the harbor, is the place for an après fishing Kalik, or a piece of Pearl Moxey's legendary johnnycake. The **Victoria Point Blue Hole** is good for snorkeling and diving, and there are a number of pristine spots sure to please naturalists looking for birds or wild orchids. The cay's main road runs south from Moxey Town, past the airport, then along coconut-tree shaded beaches to the settlement of Lisbon Creek. From here, a free government ferry (☎ 242/369–0331) makes trips twice daily (usually at 8 and 4) across the South Bight to Driggs Hill, South Andros.

### Where to Stay & Eat

**$–$$** ✕⬚ **Mangrove Cay Inn.** Set in a coconut grove with wild orchid and hibiscus gardens, the inn caters to those who want to get away from it all. The rooms are decorated in peach and green with light Andros pine walls. Enjoy your favorite fresh seafood dish or a cold Kalik while relaxing in the restaurant ($–$$) and bar. Rent a bicycle to explore the cay, roam miles of nearby beach, or hire a fishing guide. A three-bedroom cottage with full kitchen, overlooking a saltwater lake filled with baby tarpon and snappers, is also available for rent. Rates include taxes and gratuity. ⬚ *General Post Office, Mangrove Cay, Andros* ☎ *242/369–0069* 🖨 *242/369–0014* ⊕ *www.mangrovecayinn.net* 🛏 *12 rooms, 2 cottages* ⚐ *Restaurant, fans, fishing, bicycles, bar; no room phones, no room TVs* ⊟ *No credit cards.*

**★ $** ✕⬚ **Seascape Inn.** Five individual cottages with private decks overlook the glass-clear ocean. Owners Mickey and Joan McGowan have decorated each one with handcrafted wooden furniture and original art. The elevated restaurant ($–$$) and bar is *the* place to relax, swap stories, and enjoy cocktails with the locals. Grilled steaks, coconut grouper, and chicken in white wine sauce are dinner highlights. The hearty breakfasts (included in the rate) are also delicious. Joan bakes killer banana bread and an assortment of yummy muffins. Mickey leads the diving program and can arrange for a fishing guide. ⊠ *Mangrove Cay, Andros* ☎ *242/369–0342* ⊕ *www.seascapeinn.com* 🛏 *4 1-bedroom cottages, 1 cottage suite* ⚐ *Restaurant, fans, beach, dive shop, snorkeling, boating, fishing, bicycles, bar, library, Internet room; no a/c, no room phones, no room TVs* ⊟ *AE, MC, V* ⦿⦿ *BP.*

## Sports & the Outdoors

DIVING & SNORKELING
The dive shop at **Seascape Inn** (☎ 242/369–0342) has snorkeling and diving excursions, and rents dive equipment and kayaks. A minimum of four people is required per group. You need to call a day in advance.

BICYCLING
Rent a bicycle from **Seascape Inn** (☎ 242/369–0342) and pedal around the island.

# South Andros–Driggs Hill

**Driggs Hill**, on South Andros, is a small settlement of pastel houses, a tiny church, a grocery store, the government dock, and the Emerald Palms Resort of South Andros (formerly the Ritz Beach Resort). A mile south is the Congo Town airport. Eight miles farther south, the Bluff settlement sprawls atop a hill overlooking miles of golden beaches, lush cays, and the Tongue of the Ocean. Here skeletons of Arawak natives were found huddled together. A local resident attests that another skeleton was found—this one of a 4-foot-tall, one-eyed owl, which may have given rise to the legend of the mythical, elflike chickcharnie.

5

## Where to Stay & Eat

$–$$$$
✕⊡ **Emerald Palms Resort of South Andros.** This upscale property has 22 one- and two-bedroom cottages with individual gardens and private decks surrounded by palm trees. The cottages have marble floors, mahogany furniture, and king-size beds. The spacious clubhouse rooms run along the blue-tile pool and out to the glimmering beach. Ask for one of the beachfront rooms or cottages. A cabana bar overlooks the gin-clear sea. Hearty Bahamian breakfasts, light zesty lunches, and theme-night four-course dinners are served in the poolside restaurant ($$–$$$). Grilled seafood and whole lobsters are specialties. ⌂ *Box 800, Driggs Hill, Andros* ☎ *242/369–2713* 🖶 *242/369–2711* ⊕ *www.emerald-palms.com* ☞ *20 rooms, 22 suites* ⌖ *Restaurant, in-room hot tubs, kitchenettes, refrigerators, pool, outdoor hot tub, beach, snorkeling, windsurfing, boating, fishing, bicycles, bar, lounge, laundry service, Internet room, car rental; no room phones* ▭ *AE, D, DC, MC, V.*

$$
Fodor's Choice
★
✕⊡ **Tiamo Resorts.** You arrive at this low-key yet sophisticated South Bight ecoresort via private ferry. A cold drink awaits in the lodge—a stress-free gathering place with wood-beam ceilings that naturally combines bar, lounge, library, and dining room. Individual bungalows with wraparound porches are strung out along the powdery beach, shaded by coconut palms. Commodious bedrooms with soft linens are positioned to receive the cooling ocean breeze. Leisurely meals include seafood delights, homemade breads, and luscious desserts. To explore the wilds of sea and land, guided snorkeling, sea kayaking, nature hike, and fishing excursions can be arranged at your whim. ⌂ *General Delivery, Driggs Hill, South Andros Island* ☎ *954/242–8171 or 242/357–2489* 🖶 *305/768–7707* ⊕ *www.tiamoresorts.com* ☞ *11 bungalows* ⌖ *Dining room, fans, beach, dive shop, dock, snorkeling, boating, fishing, bar, lounge, library, laundry service; no a/c, no room phones, no room TVs* ▭ *AE, D, DC, MC, V* ⎰⎱ *AI.*

## Sports & the Outdoors

FISHING **Emerald Palms Resort of South Andros** (☎ 242/369–2711) can arrange boat rentals and schedule guides for bonefishing, reef fishing, or deep-sea fishing.

# ANDROS ESSENTIALS

## Transportation

### BY AIR

There are four airports on Andros. The San Andros airport is in North Andros; the Andros Town airport is in Central Andros; and the South Andros airport is in Congo Town. There's also an airport on Mangrove Cay. Check with your hotel for the closest airport. Several small airlines and charter companies have flights from Nassau. Daily charter service is also available from Fort Lauderdale and Freeport.

Bahamasair does not offer consistent service to Andros. Western Air has two flights per day from Nassau to each of the four Andros airports; it offers the best and cheapest service to Andros. Lynx Air International flies from Fort Lauderdale to Congo Town three days a week. Major Air has charter service from Freeport to all four airports, and regular service Friday and Sunday. Small Hope Bay Lodge offers flights from Fort Lauderdale to Andros Town for a minimum of two passengers and can arrange charter flights for island hopping.

🛪 Airlines & Contacts **Bahamasair** ☎ 242/339-4415 or 800/222-4262. **Lynx Air International** ☎888/596-9247. **Major Air** ☎242/352-5778. **Small Hope Bay Lodge** ☎242/368-2014 or 800/223-6961. **Western Air** ☎ 242/377-2222 Nassau, 242/329-4000 San Andros, 242/368-2759 Andros Town, 242/369-0003 Mangrove Cay, 242/369-2222 Congo Town.

🛪 Airport Information **Andros Town** ☎242/368-2030. **Congo Town** ☎242/369-2640. **Mangrove Cay** ☎ 242/369-0083. **San Andros** ☎ 242/329-4224.

### BY BOAT

A free government ferry makes the half-hour trip between Mangrove Cay and South Andros twice daily. It departs South Andros at 8 AM and 4 PM and departs Mangrove Cay at 8:30 AM and 4:30 PM, but schedules are subject to change. Call the Commissioner's Office for more information.

From Potter's Cay Dock in Nassau, the M/V *Lisa J III* sails to Morgan's Bluff and Nicholl's Town in the north of the island every Wednesday, returning to Nassau the following Tuesday. The trip takes six hours and costs $30. The M/V *Lady D* leaves Nassau on Tuesday for Fresh Creek (with stops at Stafford Creek, Blanket Sound, and Behring Point) and returns to Nassau on Sunday. The trip takes 5½ hours, and the fare is $35. The M/V *Mangrove Cay Express* leaves Nassau on Thursday evening for Driggs Hill, Mangrove Cay, and Cargill Creek and returns on Tuesday afternoon. The trip takes 5½ hours and costs $30. The M/V *Captain Moxey* leaves Nassau on Monday and calls at Kemp's Bay, Long Bay Cays, and the Bluff on South Andros. It returns to Nassau on Wednesday. The trip takes 7½ hours; the fare is $35. Schedules are subject to change due to weather conditions or occasional dry-docking. For more information, contact the Dockmaster's Office at Potter's Cay.

**⁊ Boat & Ferry Information Commissioner's Office** ☎ 242/369-0331. **Dockmaster's Office** ☎ 242/393-1064.

### BY CAR
The main roads are generally in good shape, but watch out for potholes and remember to drive on the left. Cab drivers will charge $80–$120 for a half-day tour of the island. Even a short taxi ride is usually $10. Many visitors opt to get around by bicycle. If you need a rental car, your best bet is to have your hotel make arrangements. It's smart to book a week in advance during high season, as the number of vehicles is limited.

### BY TAXI
Taxis meet incoming planes at the airports, but they can also be arranged ahead of time through hotels. Rates are around $1.50 a mile, though most fares are set from one location to another. You should always agree on a fare before your ride begins.

## Contacts & Resources

### BANKS & EXCHANGE SERVICES
The Canadian Imperial Bank of Commerce in San Andros is open Wednesday 10:30–2:30. There are also banks in Fresh Creek and on Mangrove Cay that are open two to three days a week, usually Monday and Wednesday, and sometimes Friday.

**⁊ Bank Information Canadian Imperial Bank of Commerce** ☎ 242/329-2382.

### EMERGENCIES
Telephone service is available only through the front desk at Andros hotels, so emergencies should be reported to the management. A doctor lives in San Andros. Medical clinics are in Mastic Point, Nicholl's Town, and Lowe Sound; each has a resident nurse. A health center at Fresh Creek has both a doctor and a nurse. A clinic at Mangrove Cay has a nurse.

**⁊ Police** ☎ 919 North Andros, 242/368-2626 Fresh Creek/Central Andros, 242/369-4733 Kemp's Bay/South Andros. **Medical Clinics** ☎ 242/329-2055 Nicholl's Town/North Andros, 242/368-2038 Fresh Creek, 242/369-0089 Mangrove Cay, 242/369-4849 Kemp's Bay/South Andros.

# THE BERRY ISLANDS

The Berry Islands consist of more than two dozen small islands and almost a hundred tiny cays stretching in a sliver moon-like curve north of Andros and New Providence Island. Although a few of the islands are privately owned, most of them are uninhabited—except by rare birds using the territory as their nesting grounds or by visiting yachters dropping anchor in secluded havens. The Berry Islands start in the north at

Great Stirrup Cay, where a lighthouse guides passing ships, and they end in the south at Chub Cay, only 35 mi north of Nassau.

Most of the islands' 700 residents live on Great Harbour Cay, which is 10 mi long and 1½ mi wide. Its main settlement, Bullock's Harbour, has a few small restaurants and a grocery store. The Great Harbour Cay resort, a few miles away from Bullock's Harbour, was developed in the early 1970s. It's geared toward fishing enthusiasts. Both Chub and Great Harbour cays are close to the Tongue of the Ocean, where big game fish roam. Remote flats south of Great Harbour, from Anderson Cay to Money Cay, are excellent bonefish habitats, as are the flats around Chub Cay. Deeper water flats hold permit and tarpon.

The Berry Islands appear just north of Andros Island on the Bahamas map at the front of the book.

# Chub Cay

## Where to Stay & Eat

$–$$$$ ✕ Chub Cay Marina & Resort. This is one of the best sportfishing locations anywhere, with the Tongue of the Ocean at its doorstep and the Great Bahama Bank bending around to the Joulters Cays. The luxury resort planed to reopen in spring 2006 with a new two-story manor-style clubhouse with a restaurant, bar, pool, meeting rooms, reception area, offices, and a living room gathering area. The marina is being expanded to 205 slips with floating concrete docks, and the 5,000 foot airstrip is being repaved. The resort will offer 57 new townhouse–villas for sale, with daily rentals through the club. Upon reopening, six villas are expected to be ready, and six more should be available each month after that. ⊠ *Chub Cay Resort & Marina, Chub Cay, Berry Islands* ☎ *242/325–1490 or 877/234–2482* ☒ *954/761–8925* ⊕ *www. chubcay.com* ⇝ *57 villas* ⚭ *Restaurant, dining room, grocery, refrigerators, tennis court, pool, beach, dock, snorkeling, boating, marina, waterskiing, fishing, bicycles, 2 bars, laundry facilities; no room phones* ▭ *AE, MC, V.*

## Sports & the Outdoors

BOATING The clarity of Bahamian waters is particularly evident when you cross the Great Bahama Bank from the Bimini area, then cruise along the Berry Islands on the way to Nassau. The water's depth is seldom more than 20 feet here. Grass patches and an occasional coral head or flat coral patch dot the light sand bottom. Starfish abound, and you can often catch a glimpse of a gliding stingray or eagle ray. You might spot the odd turtle, and if you care to jump over the boat's side with a mask, you might also pick up a conch or two in the grass. Especially good snorkeling and bonefishing, and peaceful anchorages, can be found on the lee shores of the Hoffmans and Little Harbour Cays. When it's open, **Flo's Conch Bar,** at the southern end of Little Harbour Cay, serves fresh conch prepared every way you can imagine.

## Great Harbour Cay

### Where to Stay & Eat

**$–$$$$** ✕⊡ **Tropical Diversions Bahamas.** This resort, also called Great Harbour Cay and Resort, rents privately owned homes, beach villas, and marina town houses with docks on a daily or weekly basis. The furnishings and layouts differ, but all have sundecks, daily maid service, and coffeemakers. Most units have full kitchens. The management meets you at the airport and can help you find fishing guides. Have a light lunch at the Beach Club ($–$$) or sit down for a full meal at the Wharf Restaurant ($–$$) in the marina. A more expensive fish-and-seafood buffet is served a couple of nights each week at the **Tamboo Club** (☎ 242/367–8203), ($–$$$). Please be aware that some rentals and services are not always available. When you make a reservation, be sure to ask specific questions about the characteristics of the unit you are renting. ⌂ *3512 N. Ocean Dr., Hollywood, FL 33019* ☎ *242/367–8838 or 954/921–9084* 🖷 *242/367–8115 or 954/921–9089* 🛏 *13 beach villas and homes, 4 town houses* ⚒ *3 restaurants, beach, dock, snorkeling, boating, fishing; no room phones* ▤ *AE, MC, V.*

### Sports & the Outdoors

BOATING In the upper Berry Islands, the full-service **Great Harbour Cay Marina** (☎ 242/367–8005) has 70 slips that can handle boats up to 150 feet. Accessible through an 80-foot-wide channel from the bank side, the marina has one of the Bahamas' most pristine beaches running along its east side. **Happy People's** (☎ 242/367–8117) has boats available for exploring the island. They also rent bikes and jeeps.

FISHING The man to see about bonefishing is **Percy Darville** (☎ 242/367–8005), who knows the flats of the Berrys better than anyone. He can arrange for guides, or point you in the right direction to fish on your own. You should call him as far in advance as possible to book a guide or rent a boat. He can also be reached through the Great Harbour Cay Marina.

# THE BERRY ISLANDS ESSENTIALS

## Transportation

### BY AIR

Air Charter Bahamas flies to Great Harbour Cay and Chub Cay from South Florida. Private flights are chartered to fit your schedule, although the company, with advance notice and flexibility on your part, can attempt to group you with other passengers to provide you with a better fare. A number of other air charter companies fly to Great Harbour and Chub Cay from Nassau.

🖪 Airlines & Contacts **Air Charter Bahamas** ☎ 305/885-6665 or 866/359-4752 ⊕ www.aircharterbahamas.com.

### BY BOAT

*Captain Gurth Dean* leaves Potter's Cay, Nassau, Friday evening for Bullock Harbour, with stops in Sandy Point and Moore's Island, Abaco.

The trip takes about seven hours and costs $40 one-way. Return is Sunday morning. For schedules and specific destinations, call the Dockmaster's Office at Potter's Cay.

*Bimini Mack* leaves Potter's Cay, Nassau, Thursday afternoon for Chub Cay, with stops in Bimini and Cat Cay, which is just south of Bimini. The trip takes about 12 hours and costs $45 one-way. Return is Monday morning. For schedules and specific destinations, call the Dockmaster's Office at Potter's Cay.

🚢 Boat & Ferry Information **Dockmaster's Office** ☎ 242/393-1064.

## Contacts & Resources

### EMERGENCIES
Immediately contact the police or a doctor in case of an emergency.
🚢 **Great Harbour Cay Medical Clinic** ☎ 242/367-8400. **Police** ✉ Bullock's Harbour, Great Harbour Cay ☎ 242/367-8344.

# THE BIMINIS

The Biminis have long been known as the Bahamas' big-game-fishing capital. The nearest of the Bahamian islands to the U.S. mainland, they consist of a handful of islands and cays just 50 mi east of Miami, across the Gulf Stream that sweeps the area's western shores. Most visitors spend their time on North Bimini. Throughout the year, more than a dozen billfish tournaments draw anglers to the Gulf Stream and the Great Bahama Bank from the United States, Canada, Britain, and the rest of Europe. Marinas such as Weech's Bimini Dock, the Bimini Big Game Marina, and Blue Water Marina—all on skinny North Bimini's eastern side—provide more than 150 slips for oceangoing craft, many of them belonging to weekend visitors who make the short trip from Florida ports. South Bimini now has a 35-slip marina complete with a customs and immigration center at the Bimini Sands resort complex. North Bimini's western side, along Queen's Highway, is one long stretch of beautiful beach.

Most of the hotels, restaurants, churches, and stores in the Biminis are along North Bimini's King's and Queen's highways, which run parallel to each other. Everything on North Bimini, where most of the islands' 1,600 inhabitants reside, is so close that you do not need a car to get around. Sparsely populated South Bimini, separated from its big brother by a narrow ocean passage, is where Juan Ponce de León allegedly looked for the Fountain of Youth in 1513. Tourists have easy access to the Fountain of Youth site by way of a very good road, close to South Bimini's little airstrip.

Ernest Hemingway did battle with his share of game fish around North Bimini, which he visited for the first time in 1935 from his home in Key West. He made frequent visits, and wrote much of *To Have and Have Not* and *Islands in the Stream* here. He is remembered in the area as a picaresque hero, not only for his graphic descriptions of fishing exploits,

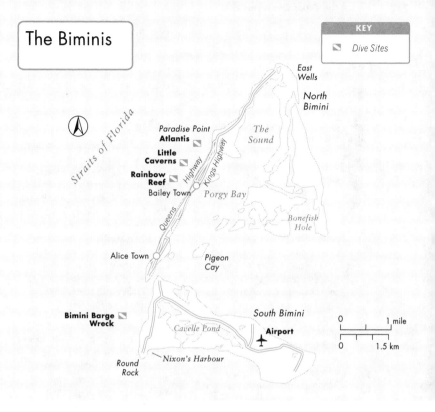

**KEY**

◤ Dive Sites

East
Wells

North
Bimini

*Straits of Florida*

Paradise Point
**Atlantis** ◤

**Little
Caverns** ◤

*The
Sound*

Highway

Kings Highway

**Rainbow
Reef** ◤

Bailey Town   *Porgy Bay*

Queens Highway

*Bonefish
Hole*

Alice Town

Pigeon
Cay

**Bimini Barge
Wreck** ◤

South Bimini

*Cavelle Pond*   **Airport** ✈

Round
Rock   Nixon's Harbour

0          1 mile

0        1.5 km

but for his drinking and brawling, including a fistfight he had with his brother Leicester on the Bimini dock.

Other notables lured to the island have included Howard Hughes and Richard Nixon. The American with the strongest ties to the Biminis was entrepreneur Michael Lerner. He discovered Bimini years before Hemingway and is the man credited with teaching him how to catch giant tuna. Lerner was a great friend to the Biminis and established, among other things, the Lerner Marine Research Laboratory, which conducted research on dolphins and sharks from 1947 to 1974.

The Biminis also have a notorious history as a jumping-off place for illicit dealings; first during the Civil War, when it was a refuge for profiteers bringing in war supplies from Europe, and then during Prohibition, when it was a haven for rumrunners. Today things are pretty quiet—rumrunners have been replaced by anglers and Floridians. Spring break brings hordes of students who cruise over from Fort Lauderdale for wild nights. Unlike the rest of the Out Islands, Bimini experiences its busy season in the summer, owing to the invasion of vacationing boaters from Florida.

# Running for Rum

**FOLLOWING BRITAIN'S DEFEAT** in the American Revolutionary War, Southern loyalists brought their slaves to the Bahamas. They grew cotton under the Crown's protection, maintaining the "cotton connection" through the Civil War, when Bahamians got rich running Confederate cotton to English mills and sending military equipment to Southern rebels.

A century later, Bahamians grew wealthy once again, this time smuggling a precious liquid from Britain—liquor. After the Civil War, temperance took hold in America, and soon made its way across the water. Although many Bahamians "took the pledge" not to drink, their government did not follow the U.S. path to **Prohibition.** With alcohol legal and certain islands less than 60 mi from American shores, the Bahamas once again became an important trans-shipping point for contraband.

British and Scottish whiskey, rum, and gin distillers began transporting large quantities of liquor to the Bahamas. Their ships were too large to dock at Nassau harbor, so they anchored offshore, out of view of the American Consul and revenue agents. The goods were off-loaded onto smaller vessels and stored in a network of warehouses on shore, which became known as **"rum row."** Some supplies were taken to the Out Islands for further transport. U.S. ships, often sailing under another flag to avoid detection, smuggled the bootleg booze to thirsty Americans, carrying the cargo through international waters, and ending up at drop-off points from Florida to New Jersey. But first, smugglers had to avoid U.S. Coast Guard ships that were prowling close to the Bahamas—this may have been the origin of the term **"rum-running."**

After Prohibition was repealed, the Bahamas lapsed into economic stagnation, but the United States maintained its interest in the islands due to their proximity. During **World War II,** the U.S. military set up camp, establishing an air and sea station in the Bahamas. Though the station is no longer in use, the islands still house military communications facilities, plus drug enforcement agents that guard against today's generation of smugglers.

In 1962 **Bacardi & Company,** the world's largest rum producer, opened a distillery in Nassau. Although there's also a Bahamian brewery, which produces the ever-popular **Kalik** beer, rum is the alcoholic beverage of choice in the Bahamas. The basic cocktail formula is simple: one or more types of rum plus fruit juice. You can order these drinks at every bar. This trio is the most popular:

**Bahama Mama**—light rum, coconut rum, Nassau Royale (vanilla-flavored rum), orange and pineapple juices.

**Rum Punch**—dark rum, orange and pineapple juices, grenadine, a dash of bitters.

**Goombay Smash**—light rum, coconut rum, pineapple juice, a dash of Galiano.

## Alice Town

Bimini's main community, Alice Town, is at North Bimini's southern end. It's neat and tidy, and painted in happy Caribbean pastels. In a prominent location stand the ruins of the **Bimini Bay Rod and Gun Club**, a resort and casino built in the early 1920s and destroyed by a hurricane in 1926. A short walk away is the **Bimini Native Straw and Craft Market**, which bustles on weekends and during fishing tournaments. **Chalks-Ocean** seaplanes splash down in the harbor a block south of town, lumber ashore, and park adjacent to the pink customs and immigration office building. Taxis, passenger vans, and a bus meet all arriving flights, though they're not necessary unless you have a lot of luggage.

The back door of the small, noisy **End of the World Bar** is always open to the harbor. This place—with a sandy floor and visitors' graffiti, business cards, and other surprises on every surface—is a good spot to meet local folks over a beer and a backgammon board. In the late '60s, the bar became a hangout of the late New York congressman Adam Clayton Powell, who retreated to North Bimini while Congress investigated his alleged misdemeanors. A marble plaque in his honor is displayed in the bar. The bar is 100 yards from the Bimini Bay Rod and Gun Club ruins. ⊠ *King's Hwy.* 📷 *No phone* ☾ *Daily 9 AM–3 AM.*

### Where to Stay & Eat

**$–$$** ✕ **Red Lion Pub.** Venture through twin doors emblazoned with the red Tudor lions for fresh seafood and Bahamian dishes in this no-smoking restaurant (uncommon in the Bahamas). There's a view out the back sliding-glass doors onto a small bay between the marinas. ⊠ *King's Hwy.* 📷 *242/347–3259* ▬ *No credit cards.*

**¢–$$** ✕ **Opal's Restaurant.** This diminutive, 12-seat dining room delivers huge helpings of ribs and seafood and is noted for its green turtle steaks. It's on the hill across from the Bimini Big Game Resort & Marina. ⊠ *Sherman La.* 📷 *242/347–3082* ▬ *No credit cards* ☾ *Closed Sun.*

**¢–$** ✕ **Big Game Sports Bar.** Part of the Bimini Big Game Resort & Marina, this is a popular anglers' hangout. The menu has pub fare like burgers and sandwiches along with fritters, chowder, and conch pizza. The bar overlooks the marina. ⊠ *King's Hwy.* 📷 *242/347–3391* ▬ *AE, MC, V.*

**¢–$** ✕ **Big John's.** For a hearty breakfast or lunch, this cheerful dining room with bright tablecloths and friendly staff is a favorite. Boiled fish and peas 'n' rice are specialties. ⊠ *King's Hwy., across from Gateway Gallery* 📷 *242/347–3117* ▬ *No credit cards* ☾ *No dinner.*

★ **$$–$$$** ✕🏠 **Bimini Sands Resort & Marina.** Overlooking the Straits of Florida, this luxury property rents one- or two-bedroom condominiums. The bright, high-ceiling houses have balconies and patios with views of the tropical surroundings, the marina, or the beach. The Petite Conch ($–$$) serves three meals a day, blending Bahamian staples with American favorites. There's a 150-slip marina and a convenient customs office, so guests with boats can tie up and clear their paperwork without venturing to North Bimini customs. An all-night water taxi shuttles you to North Bimini to shop, dine, and party. ⊠ *Bimini Sands, South Bimini* 📷 *242/347–3500* 📠 *242/347–3407* ⊕ *www.biminisands.com*

🛏 21 1- or 2-bedroom condominiums ⚭ 2 restaurants, kitchenettes, tennis court, pool, beach, marina, fishing, volleyball, bar, Internet room, laundry facilities ▤ AE, MC, V.

★ $–$$$ ✕▦ **Bimini Big Game Resort & Marina.** This resort is a favorite among the fishing and yachting crowd who take advantage of the full-service 74-slip marina. Anglers might prefer the spacious cottages, each with a built-in wet bar, refrigerator, and outdoor grill. First-floor rooms have views of the lush gardens or pool, while second-floor rooms have superb bayfront views. The beach is only a five-minute walk away. The Clubhouse Restaurant ($–$$$) presents the island's most upscale dining, with cuisine ranging from grilled tuna with pineapple to T-bone steaks. If you plan to stay during one of the major fishing tournaments, reserve well in advance. ✉ *King's Hwy., at pink wall, Box 699* ☎ *242/347–3391 or 800/737–1007* 🖷 *242/347–3392* ⊕ *www.biminibiggame.com* 🛏 *35 rooms, 12 cottages, 4 penthouses* ⚭ *2 restaurants, tennis court, pool, boating, marina, fishing, 3 bars, shops, babysitting, laundry service; no room phones* ▤ *AE, D, MC, V.*

¢–$$$ ▦ **Sea Crest Hotel and Marina.** Tucked between the beach and the marina, this three-story hotel has comfortable, simply furnished rooms with tile floors, refrigerators, cable TV, balconies, and one of the island's friendliest owner-management teams. Pick a room or suite on the third floor; they have lofty, open-beam ceilings and lovely sea- or marina views. The marina is across the street (King's Highway). Diving, snorkeling, and fishing charters can be arranged. There's a 5% surcharge for credit cards. ✉ *King's Hwy., Box 654* ☎ *242/347–3071* 🖷 *242/347–3495* ⊕ *www.seacrestbimini.com* 🛏 *23 rooms, 1 2-bedroom suite, 1 3-bedroom suite* ⚭ *Refrigerators, cable TV, marina; no room phones* ▤ *D, MC, V.*

$–$$ ✕▦ **Bimini Sands Beach Club.** Adjacent to Bimini's southern tip, the Beach Club is the sister property to the Bimini Sands Condos. Ocean- and marina-view rooms have light-color interiors and thoughtful touches, like good lighting, flowers, and throw rugs on gleaming terrazzo tile floors. The beach club offers a reception-lounge area with large couches placed in front of a working fireplace, a billiard room, a tiny bar that overlooks the sparkling pool, and a restaurant ($–$$) with tasty Bahamian cuisine and unparalleled views of the surrounding waters. ✉ *Bimini Sands Beach Club, South Bimini* ☎ *242/357–3500* 🖷 *242/347–3407* ⊕ *www.biminisands.com* 🛏 *38 rooms, 2 suites* ⚭ *Restaurant, pool, beach, marina, billiards, volleyball, bar, Internet* ▤ *AE, MC, V.*

¢–$$ ✕▦ **Bimini Blue Water Resort.** You can still rent Marlin Cottage, the place where Hemingway wrote parts of *Islands in the Steam,* and knock back daiquiris in the wood-paneled bar. Rooms in the main building are well-worn but comfortable. Additional rooms and suites, which have large windows and private patios, have a circa-1960 South Florida theme. The Anchorage restaurant ($–$$), overlooking the ocean, serves excellent fresh seafood and has satellite TV. The 32-slip marina and dockside pool are across the road on the lee side of the island. ✉ *King's Hwy., Box 601* ☎ *242/347–3166* 🖷 *242/347–3293* ⊕ *bluewaterresort@boipb.com* 🛏 *9 rooms, 4 suites, 1 3-bedroom cottage* ⚭ *Restaurant, pool, beach, marina, fishing, bar* ▤ *MC, V.*

## Sports & the Outdoors

BICYCLING  **Bimini Undersea** (☎ 242/347–3089) rents bikes for $7 per hour or $20 per day.

BOATING & FISHING  **Bimini Big Game Resort & Marina** (☎ 242/347–3391 or 800/737–1007 ⊕ www.biminibiggame.com), a 74-slip marina, charges $800–$900 for a day ($475–$500 for a half day) of deep-sea fishing. **Blue Water Marina** (☎ 242/347–3166), with 32 modern slips, charges from $750 a day, and from $450 a half day, with captain, mate, and gear included. **Bimini Sands Marina** (☎ 242/347–3500), on South Bimini, is a top-notch 35-slip marina capable of accommodating vessels up to 100 feet. Convenient customs clearance for guests is at the marina. Rent a 15-foot Whaler for $140 per day or a Wave Runner for $50 per half hour. Rental fishing gear (flats and blue water) is also available. **Weech's Bimini Dock** (☎ 242/347–3028), with 15 slips, has four Boston Whalers, which it rents for $135 a day or $75 a half day.

The following are highly recommended bonefish guides: **Bonefish Ansil** (☎ 242/347–2178 or 242/347–3098); **Bonefish Ebbie** (☎ 242/347–2053 or 242/359–8273); **Bonefish Ray** (☎ 242/347–2269); and **Bonefish Tommy** (☎ 242/347–3234).

EVENTS  The Biminis host a series of fishing tournaments and boating events throughout the year, including the **Mid-Winter Wahoo Tournament** (February), the **Annual Bacardi Rum Billfish Tournament** (March), the **Bimini Break and Blue Marlin Tournament** (April), the **Bimini Festival of Champions** (May), the **Annual Bimini Native Tournament** (August), the **Bimini Family Fishing Tournament** (August), the **Small BOAT—Bimini Open Angling Tournament** (September), and the **Wahoo Championship Tournament** (November). The island also hosts an annual **Bimini Regatta,** which takes place in the spring. For information on dates, tournament regulations, and recommended guides, call the **Bahamas Tourist Office** (☎ 800/327–7678) in Florida and ask for the sportfishing section.

SCUBA DIVING  The Biminis offer excellent diving opportunities, particularly for watching marine life. The **Bimini Barge Wreck** (a World War II landing craft) rests in 100 feet of water. **Little Caverns** is a medium-depth dive with scattered coral heads, small tunnels, and swim-throughs. **Rainbow Reef** is a shallow dive popular for fish gazing. And, of course, there's **Atlantis,** thought to be the famous "lost city." Dive packages are available through most Bimini hotels.

**Bimini Undersea** (☎ 242/347–3089 or 800/348–4644 ⊕ www.biminiundersea.com), headquartered at Bimini Big Game Resort & Marina, lets you snorkel near a delightful pod of Atlantic spotted dolphins for $119 per person. You can also rent or buy snorkel and diving gear. One-, two-, and three-tank dives cost $49, $89, and $119 per person, respectively.

The **Scuba Bimini Dive Center** (☎ 242/347–4444 or 954/524–6090 ⊕ www.scubabimini.com), at the rustic South Bimini Yacht Club, is a Neal Watson Undersea affiliate offering specialty wreck dives and a sensational blacktip- and reef shark–feeding one-tank dive experience for $75. (The dive masters feed them while you watch.) Call for package rates.

## Shopping

Upstairs in the Burns House Building, the **Gateway Gallery** (✉ King's Hwy. ☎ 242/347–3131) sells top-quality Bahamian arts and crafts, original artwork by Biminites, hand-sculpted figures depicting daily Bahamian life, and Bahamian music.

**Pritchard's Grocery** (✉ Queen's Hwy., next to Baptist church ☎ No phone) is known as the home of the sweet Bimini native bread. Consider placing an order to take home.

**Bimini Native Straw and Craft Market** (✉ Next door to Bahamas Customs Bldg.) has about 20 vendors, including Nathalie's Native Bread stand.

## Elsewhere on North Bimini

Toward King's Highway's north end, you'll see bars, grocery shops, clothing stores, the pink medical center, and a group of colorful fruit stalls. The island's northwestern part bears the ruins of an unrealized luxury development—Bimini Bay—that was to include a marina, private homes, and a hotel. The original developers ran out of money and abandoned the project.

The **Bimini Museum**, sheltered in the restored (1920) two-story original post office and jail—a three-minute walk from the seaplane ramp—showcases varied artifacts, including Adam Clayton Powell's domino set, Prohibition photos, rum kegs, Martin Luther King Jr.'s immigration card from 1964, and a fishing log and rare fishing films of Papa Hemingway. The exhibit includes film shot on the island as early as 1922. ✉ *King's Hwy.* ☎ *242/347–3038* 🖅 *$2* ☉ *Mon.–Sat. 9–9, Sun. noon–9.*

**Atlantis,** a curious rock formation under about 20 feet of water, 500 yards offshore at Bimini Bay, is shaped like a backward letter J, some 600 feet long at the longest end. It's the shorter 300-foot extension that piques the interest of scientists and visitors. The precision patchwork of large, curved-edge stones form a perfect rectangle measuring about 30 feet across. A few of the stones are 16 feet square. It's purported to be the "lost city" whose discovery was predicted by Edgar Cayce (1877–1945), a psychic with an interest in prehistoric civilizations. Archaeologists estimate the formation to be between 5,000 and 10,000 years old. Carvings in the rock appear to some scientists to resemble a network of highways. Skeptics have pooh-poohed the theory, conjecturing that they are merely turtle pens built considerably more recently.

Most of the island's residents live in **Bailey Town** in small, pastel-color concrete houses. Bailey Town lies on King's Highway, north of the Bimini Big Game Resort & Marina Hotel. Check out Kim's Fruit Stand for a good selection of fresh fruit.

**OFF THE BEATEN PATH**

**HEALING HOLE** – Locals recommend a trip here for curing what ails you—gout and rheumatism are among the supposedly treatable afflictions. Ask your hotel to arrange a trip out to this natural clearing in North Bimini's mangrove flats. You can take a leap of faith into the water and, if nothing else, enjoy a refreshing dip.

# THE BIMINIS ESSENTIALS

### BY AIR

The two U.S. gateways to the Biminis are Fort Lauderdale and Miami. If you've just arrived at Miami International Airport, the taxi ride (about $15) to the Watson Island terminal for Chalks-Ocean Airway, across from the Port of Miami, will take about the same time it takes to get to North Bimini. You can also fly to Bimini from Nassau.

Island Air offers charter flights from Fort Lauderdale's Jet Center to South Bimini aboard a seven-passenger Islander. Chalks-Ocean Airway has several 25-minute flights daily into Alice Town, North Bimini, from Miami's terminal at Watson Island on the MacArthur Causeway, and from Fort Lauderdale International Airport (40 minutes). North Bimini is also served from Chalks-Ocean Airway base in Nassau–Paradise Island. Chalks-Ocean Airway uses 17-passenger turbo Mallard amphibians, with takeoffs and landings on water. Baggage allowance is 30 pounds per passenger. Western Air flies to Bimini from Nassau's domestic air terminal.

**Airlines & Contacts** **Chalks-Ocean Airway** ☎ 800/424–2557, 242/347–3024, or 305/373–1120 ⊕ www.flychalks.com. **Island Air** ☎ 954/359–9942 or 800/444–9904. **Western Air** ☎ 242/347–4100 or 242/377–2222 ⊕ www.westernairbahamas.com.

### BY BOAT

M/V *Bimini Mack* sails from Potter's Cay, Nassau, to Bimini, Cat Cay, and Chub Cay on Thursday afternoon. The return is Monday morning. The trip takes 12 hours and costs $45 one-way. For information, call the Dockmaster's Office at Potter's Cay.

Boaters often travel from Florida to Bimini, mostly from West Palm Beach, Fort Lauderdale, and Miami. Crossing the Gulf Stream, however, should only be done by skippers who can plot a course using charts for that purpose. There are a half dozen or so routes that are most commonly used to cross the Stream from Florida to the Bahamas, with the route from Fort Lauderdale to Bimini being the most popular for sailboats and power craft. The distance is 48 nautical mi. The time to make the crossing depends on the type of craft and the boat's speed. Sailors often like to make an evening departure, and arrive in the morning. Speed boaters sometimes zip over to Bimini for lunch or dinner and then return home. It's important for boaters to consult official government charts for obstructions, sands banks, and other impediments, and to be familiar with harbor entrances and procedures. If using proper safety, the crossing is a delight, and the fishing to and from can be sensational.

**Boat & Ferry Information** **Dockmaster's Office** ☎ 242/393–1064.

### BY BUS
Taxi 1 & 2, operated by Sam Brown, has minibuses available for a tour of the island. Arrangements can be made through your hotel.

### BY CAR
Visitors do not need a car on North Bimini and usually walk wherever they go; there are no car-rental agencies.

### BY GOLF CART
Rental golf carts are available at the Sea Crest Hotel Marina and Bimini Blue Water Marina from Capt. Pat's for $60 a day or $20 for the first hour and $10 for each additional hour.

🚩 **Capt. Pat's** ☎ 242/347-3477.

### BY TAXI
If you don't have heavy luggage, you might decide to walk to your hotel from the seaplane terminal in Alice Town, North Bimini's main settlement. Sam Brown's Taxi 1 & 2 meets planes and takes incoming passengers to Alice Town in 12-passenger vans. The cost is $3. A $5 taxi-and-ferry ride takes visitors from the South Bimini airport to Alice Town.

## Contacts & Resources

### BANKS & EXCHANGE SERVICES
The Royal Bank of Canada is open Monday, Wednesday, and Friday from 9:30 to 3. Cash advances are given on MasterCard and Visa only.

🚩 Bank Information **Royal Bank of Canada** ☎ 242/347-3030.

### EMERGENCIES
To reach the police and fire department in an emergency, **call** ☎ 919. North Bimini Medical Clinic has a resident doctor and a nurse.

🚩 **North Bimini Medical Clinic** ☎ 242/347-2210.

### VISITOR INFORMATION
The Biminis Tourist Office is open weekdays from 9 to 5:30 and also has a booth at the straw market. The building it occupies was the site of the Lerner Marine Laboratory.

🚩 Tourist Information **Biminis Tourist Office** ✉ Government Bldg., Alice Town ☎ 242/347-3529 🖷 242/347-3530.

# CAT ISLAND

Cat Island is 130 mi southeast of Nassau and is a close neighbor of San Salvador, the reputed landing place of Christopher Columbus. Many Cat Islanders maintain, however, that Columbus landed here instead and that Cat Island was once known as San Salvador. Sir Sidney Poitier is a famous local; he left as a youth before becoming a famed movie actor and director. His daughter Ann lives here and spearheads the annual Rake 'N' Scrape Festival held in June.

The island was named after a frequent notorious visitor, Arthur Catt, a piratical contemporary of Edward "Blackbeard" Teach. Slender Cat Island is about 50 mi long and boot shaped, with high cliffs and dense forest. The Cat, as it's often called, is filled with living history, including semiruined, vine-covered mansions and crumbling remnants of slave villages that are perfect for exploring.

Good roads, including Queen's Highway, stretch from Orange Creek in the north to Port Howe and Hawk's Nest in the south. You'll rarely see another car, but watch out for local kids using the highway as a basketball court. The Cat's shores are ringed with mile upon mile of exquisite beaches edged with casuarina trees. Most of these beaches are on the "north shore," or windward side of the island, and can be reached via rough and rugged dirt and rock roads cut through the heavy vegetation.

Some of the original inhabitants' descendants, who migrated long ago to the United States, are slowly returning here. Large new homes have started to appear throughout the island, whose population is about 2,000. Residents fish, farm, and live a peaceful day-to-day existence guided by the philosophy, "What nature and the Lord will provide." The biggest event of the year is the Annual Cat Island Regatta in August.

*Numbers in the margin correspond to points of interest on the Cat Island map.*

## Arthur's Town & Bennett's Harbour

**6** The claim to fame of **Arthur's Town** is that it was the boyhood home of actor Sidney Poitier, who wrote about growing up here in his autobiography. His parents and relatives were farmers. The village has a BaTelCo station, a few stores, and Pat Rolle's **Cookie House Bakery** (☎ 242/354–2027)—a lunch or dinner spot and an island institution. When you drive south from Arthur's Town, which is nearly at the island's northernmost tip, you'll wind along a road that passes through small villages and past bays where fishing boats are tied up.

One of the island's oldest settlements of small, weather-beaten houses, **7** **Bennett's Harbour** is some 15 mi south of Arthur's Town. Fresh baked breads and fruit are available at makeshift stands at the government dock. There is good bonefishing in the creek.

### Where to Stay

$–$$$ ▦ **Pigeon Cay Beach Club.** Set in a wide bay a mile off the main road—just south of Alligator Point—the club has seven deluxe cottages perched steps away from a 3-mi stretch of sugary white beach. The native stone and stucco cottages have wood and tile floors, colorful island furniture, complete kitchenware, and ceiling fans. You can cook yourself, or the club will provide a cook. Either way, they will stock your cottage before your arrival (just send your grocery list). Snorkel, kayak, canoe, sail a Hobie cat, fish, swim, or just lay on the beach. The beach bar serves breakfast every morning. ⊠ *Pigeon Cay, Cat Island* ☎☎ *242/354–5084* ⊕ *www.pigeoncay-bahamas.com* ➾ *7 cottages* △ *Picnic area,*

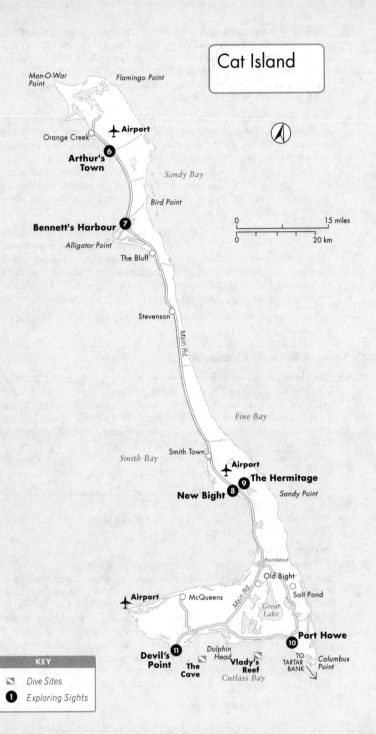

Cat Island

Man-O-War Point

Flamingo Point

Orange Creek

✈ Airport

Arthur's Town ⑥

Sandy Bay

Bird Point

Bennett's Harbour ⑦

Alligator Point

The Bluff

Stevenson

Main Rd.

Fine Bay

Smith Town

Smith Bay

✈ Airport

⑧ ⑨ The Hermitage

New Bight

Sandy Point

Roundabout

Old Bight

✈ Airport

McQueens

Salt Pond

Great Lake

Main Rd.

Port Howe ⑩

Devil's Point ⑪

The Cave

Dolphin Head

Vlady's Reef

Cutlass Bay

TO TARTAR BANK

Columbus Point

0          15 miles
0          20 km

KEY

◥ Dive Sites

① Exploring Sights

*kitchens, refrigerators, beach, snorkeling, fishing, bicycles, bar; no a/c, no room phones, no room TVs ☐ AE, MC, V.*

## New Bight

❽ The settlement of **New Bight,** where you'll find a small grocery store, a bakery, and the Bridge Inn, is near the New Bight (also called "The Bight") airport, south of Fernandez Bay Village. The Village, which is actually a resort on a bay, is where most Cat Island visitors stay.

Between the airport and the town is the small blue **First and Last Chance Bar,** run by Iva Thompson. This is a good place to have a beer with the locals, play dominoes, and check out Miss Iva's straw work, which is some of the Bahamas' best.

New Bight is the home of the **Twin Palms** (☎ 242/342–3108), a bar perched right on the ocean, where on Saturday night you may be fortunate enough to hear the famous Blind Blake play guitar and rake 'n' scrape.

❾ At the top of 206-foot Mt. Alvernia, **The Hermitage** is the final resting place of Father Jerome. Above the tomb's entrance, carved in stone, is the epitaph BLESSED ARE THE DEAD WHO DIE IN THE LORD, and inside, past the wooden gate that hangs on its hinges, his body lies interred. He died in 1956 at the age of 80 and was supposedly buried with his arms outstretched, in a pose resembling that of the crucified Christ.

Father Jerome, born John Hawes, traveled the world and eventually settled in the Bahamas. An Anglican who converted to Roman Catholicism, he built two churches, St. Paul's and St. Peter's, in Clarence Town, Long Island, as well as the St. Augustine Monastery in Nassau. He retired to Cat Island to live out his last dozen years as a hermit, and his final, supreme act of religious dedication was to carve the steps up to the top of Mt. Alvernia. Along the way, he also carved the 12 Stations of the Cross. At the summit, he built a child-size abbey with a small chapel, a conical bell tower, and living quarters comprising three closet-size rooms.

The pilgrimage to the Hermitage begins next to the commissioner's office at New Bight, at a dirt path that leads to the foot of Mt. Alvernia. Try not to miss the slightly laborious experience of climbing to the top. The Hermitage provides a perfect, inspired place to pause for quiet contemplation. It also has glorious views of the ocean on both sides of the island. A caretaker clears the weeds around the tomb—which islanders regard as a shrine—and lights a candle in Father Jerome's memory.

### Where to Stay & Eat

★ **$–$$** ✕▦ **Fernandez Bay Village.** This is one of the best kick-back retreats in the islands. Brick-and-stone villas and cottages are spread along a dazzling, horseshoe-shape white-sand beach shaded by casuarina pines and hibiscus. Villas have kitchens, terraces facing the sea, private gardens, and accommodations for four to six people. Cottages are for two people, and have private patios and garden baths. Canoes, Sunfish sailboats, and kayaks are free to use. Boats and guides can be hired for fishing or snorkeling expeditions. Delicious native dishes are served in the lodge dining room (¢–$$) and on the beachside patio. ☒ *1 mi west of New Bight airport* ① *7744 Peters Rd., Suite 310, Plantation, FL 33324* ☎ *242/342–3043 or 800/940–1905* ⊕ *954/474–4864* ⊕ *www.fernandezbayvillage.com* ⇆ *6 villas, 9 cottages* ⌂ *Dining room, grocery, kitchenettes, beach, snorkeling, boating, waterskiing, fishing, bicycles, bar, laundry service; no room phones, no room TVs* ☰ *AE, MC, V.*

¢ ✕▦ **Bridge Inn.** Use this friendly, family-run motel and apartment property as a base for exploring the island on your own—including the nearby beach. The wood-panel rooms have high ceilings, private baths, and cable TV. The snappy apartments have 2 bedrooms, 1.5 baths, cable TV, and full kitchens. The dining room (¢–$$) serves tasty local fare for breakfast. They can pack you a picnic lunch, and there's fresh seafood for dinner, along with live entertainment most Friday and Saturday nights. Rooms with air-conditioning cost extra. Complimentary shuttle service is available from the New Bight airport. ☒ *New Bight* ☎ *242/342–3013* ⊕ *242/342–3041* ✉ *newbightservicestation@yahoo.com* ⇆ *12 rooms, 6 2-bedroom apartments* ⌂ *Dining room, beach, snorkeling, boating, bicycles, billiards, bar, babysitting; no a/c in some rooms* ☰ *MC, V.*

## Port Howe

❿ At the conch shell–lined traffic roundabout, head east out toward **Port Howe,** believed by many to be Cat Island's oldest settlement. Nearby lie the ruins of the **Deveaux Mansion,** a stark two-story, whitewashed building overrun with vegetation. Once it was a grand house on a cotton plantation owned by Captain Andrew Deveaux of the British Navy, who was given thousands of acres of Cat Island property as a reward for his daring raid that recaptured Nassau from the Spaniards in 1783. Just beyond the mansion ruin is the entrance road to the Greenwood Beach Resort, which sits on an 8-mi stretch of umblemished velvet-sand beach.

### Where to Stay & Eat

★ ¢–$ ✕▦ **Greenwood Beach Resort.** Set on an 8-mi stretch of a pink shell-strewn sand, this remote resort is about 45 minutes from the New Bight airport. The large clubhouse, with its purple-and-white walls and vivid tropical paintings, is the center of activity. You can relax at the attractive bar or on the stone verandah, which has open vistas of the violet-blue Atlantic; or catch some rays at the pool or beach. Rooms are bright and cheerfully decorated with colorful fish stencils. Dinner (¢–$$) is served family-style. Picnic lunches are prepared for day excursions. The resort is an ideal location for divers and for anglers to fish on their own for bonefish. ☒ *Port Howe* ☎ *242/342–3053* ⊕ *242/342–3053* ⊕ *www. greenwoodbeachresort.com* ⇆ *20 rooms* ⌂ *Dining room, fans, pool, hot tub, beach, dive shop, snorkeling, boating, fishing, bicycles, billiards, bar, laundry service, Internet room, car rental; no a/c in some rooms, no room phones, no room TVs* ☰ *AE, MC, V.*

### Sports & the Outdoors

DIVING & **Cat Island Dive Centre** (⊠ Greenwood Beach Resort, Port Howe ☎ 242/
SNORKELING 342–3053) is the island's premier dive facility, with a 30-foot dive boat
and great snorkeling right off the beach. Beginners can take the $80 crash
course, and seasoned divers can plunge deep with spectacular wall-div-
ing just offshore. Take a half-day guided snorkeling trip, or rent snorkeling gear and head off on your own. Boat rentals are available for reef
fishing and island exploring.

FISHING Bonefishing guides for fishing the numerous nearby creeks can be
arranged through **Cat Island Dive Centre** (⊠ Greenwood Beach Resort,
Port Howe ☎ 242/342–3053).

## Devil's Point

⓫ The small village of **Devil's Point,** with its pastel-color, thatch-roof houses,
lies about 10 mi west of Columbus Point. Beachcombers will find great
shelling on the pristine beach. You'll also come across the ruins of the
**Richman Hill–Newfield plantation.**

### Where to Stay

$–$$$$ ✕⊡ **Hawk's Nest Resort & Marina.** At Cat Island's southwestern tip, this
waterfront resort, just yards from a long sandy beach, has its own run-
way and a 28-slip marina. The patios of the guest rooms, the dining room,
and the lounge overlook the expansive Exuma Sound. With cheerful peach
walls and bright bedspreads, rooms have either one king-size or two queen-
size beds with baths that have both tubs and showers. A hearty break-
fast is included in the daily rate. Fresh grilled wahoo, mahimahi, and
roasted rack of lamb are dinner specialties ($–$$). The marina can
arrange fishing and diving adventures. ⊠ *Devil's Point, Cat Island*
☎ *242/342–7050* 🖷 *242/342–7051* ⊕ *www.hawks-nest.com* 🛏 *10
rooms, 1 2-bedroom house* ⚭ *Restaurant, in-room VCRs, pool, beach,
dive shop, snorkeling, boating, marina, fishing, bicycles, 2 bars, lounge;
no room phones, no room TVs* ⊟ *MC, V* ⦿ *BP.*

### Sports & the Outdoors

SCUBA DIVING Contact your hotel, the Cat Island Dive Centre, or Dive Cat Island for
more information on any of these sites, or to arrange a dive.

**Tartar Bank** is an offshore site known for its abundant sea life, including sharks, triggerfish, turtles, eagle rays, and barracuda. **The Cave** has
a big channel with several exits to deeper ocean. Reef sharks, barracudas, and other tropical fish are frequently seen here. **Vlady's Reef,** also
known as "The Chimney," is near the Guana Cays. Coral heads have
created numerous canyons, chimneys, and swim-throughs. You're likely
to catch a glimpse of large stingrays.

**Dive Cat Island** (☎ 242/342–7050) at Hawk's Nest Marina, conducts daily
guided diving adventures, rents diving and snorkeling gear, and has equipment and sundries for sale. The running time to dive sites off the southern tip of the island is 15 to 30 minutes in the shop's 27-foot Panga,
outfitted with VHF and GPS.

5

FISHING Charter a boat from **Hawk's Nest Marina** (☎ 242/342–7050) and experience dynamite offshore fishing. Look for wahoo, yellowfin tuna, dolphin, and white and blue marlin along the Exuma Sound drop-offs, Devil's Point, Tartar Bank, and Columbus Point. March through July is prime time.

# CAT ISLAND ESSENTIALS

## Transportation

### BY AIR

Cat Island Air flies daily to New Bight from Nassau and is the best and cheapest service to the southern part of the island. Southern Air flies from Nassau to Arthur's Town and is the best service for the northern portion of the island. Bahamasair flies from Nassau to Arthur's Town or New Bight twice weekly. Lynx Air and Gulfstream (Continental's commuter) fly into New Bight from Fort Lauderdale.

If you are going to Greenwood Beach Resort or Hawk's Nest Resort, fly into New Bight. Fernandez Bay Village, Greenwood Beach Resort, and Hawk's Nest Resort & Marina offer charter flights from Nassau. Check with your destination for the most convenient airport.

🛈 Airlines & Contacts **Bahamasair** ☎ 800/222-4262. **Cat Island Air** ☎ 242/377-3318. **Fernandez Bay Village** ☎ 800/940-1905. **Greenwood Beach Resort** ☎ 242/342-3053. **Gulfstream/Continental** ☎ 800/523-3273. **Hawk's Nest Resort & Marina** ☎ 800/688-4752. **Lynx Air** ☎ 954/772-9808 or 888/596-9247. **Southern Air** ☎ 242/377-2014.

### BY BOAT

The *Lady Rosalind* leaves Potter's Cay, Nassau, every Thursday for Bennett's Harbour and Orange Creek, returning on Saturday. The trip takes 14 hours and costs $40 one-way. *Sea Hauler* leaves Potter's Cay on Tuesday for Smith Bay, and Old and New Bight, returning on Monday. The trip is 12 hours, and the fare is $40 one-way. For information, call the Dockmaster's Office at Potter's Cay.

🛈 Boat & Ferry Information **Dockmaster's Office** ☎ 242/393-1064.

### BY CAR

The New Bight Service Station rents cars and can pick you up from New Bight airport. You can rent a car from Candy's Market, which also picks up from the airport. Greenwood Beach Resort arranges car rentals for guests. Rates depend on the number of days you're renting, but $75 per day is average.

🛈 **Candy's Market** ☎ 242/342-3011. **New Bight Service Station** ☎ 242/342-3014.

### BY TAXI

TRANSFERS Fernandez Bay Village meets guests at New Bight airport, and the transfer is complimentary. If you miss your ride or no taxis are available, just ask around the parking lot for a lift. Anyone going in your direction (there's only one road) will be happy to drop you off.

## Contacts & Resources

### EMERGENCIES

Cat Island has three medical clinics—at Smith Town, Old Bight, and Arthur's Town. There are few telephones on the island, but your hotel's front desk will be able to contact the nearest clinic in case of an emergency.

# CROOKED & ACKLINS ISLANDS

Historians of the Bahamas tell us that as Columbus sailed down the lee of Crooked Island and its southern neighbor, Acklins Island (the two are separated by a short water passage), he was riveted by the aroma of native herbs wafting out to his ship. Soon after, Crooked Island, which lies 225 mi southeast of Nassau, became known as one of the "Fragrant Islands." The first known settlers didn't arrive until the late 18th century, when Loyalists brought their slaves from the United States and established cotton plantations. It was a doomed venture because of the island's poor soil, and those who stayed made a living of sorts by farming and fishing. A salt and sponge industry flourished for a while on Fortune Island, now called Long Cay. The cay, across the cut of French Well off the southwestern corner of Crooked Island, is the proposed home of a large new marina and resort development near the mostly abandoned settlement of Albert Town. The cay is also home to a flock of over 500 flamingos.

Today, Crooked and Acklins islands inhabitants, about 400 people on each island, continue to survive by farming and fishing. The islands are best known for splendid diving and bone, tarpon, and offshore fishing—and not much else. They're about as remote as populated islands in the Bahamas get. A number of residents rely on generators for electricity. Phone service, where available, often goes out for days at a time.

Although the plantations have long since crumbled, two relics of that era are preserved by the Bahamas National Trust on Crooked Island's northern part, which overlooks the Crooked Island Passage separating the cay from Long Island. Spanish guns have been discovered at one ruin, **Marine Farm,** which may have been used as a fortification. An old structure, **Hope Great House,** has orchards and gardens that are still tended by the Bahamas National Trust.

Crooked Island is 30 mi long and surrounded by 45 mi of barrier reefs that are ideal for diving. They slope from 4 feet to 50 feet, then plunge to 3,600 feet in the Crooked Island Passage, once one of the most important sea roads for ships following the southerly route from the West Indies to the Old World. The one-room airport is in **Colonel Hill,** across the main road from a wide bay and white-sand bonefish flat. If you drive up to the settlement, you get an uninterrupted view of the region all the way to the narrow passage at Lovely Bay between Crooked Island and Acklins Island. There are two houses. The sparkling white **Bird Rock Light-**

**house** (built in 1872) in the north once guarded the Crooked Island Passage. The rotating flash from its 115-foot tower still welcomes pilots and sailors to the Pittstown Point Landings resort, currently the islands' best lodging facility.

The **Castle Island** lighthouse (built in 1867), at Acklins Island's southern tip, formerly served as a beacon for pirates who used to retreat there after attacking ships.

Crooked and Acklins islands appear southeast of Long Island on the Bahamas map at the front of this guide.

### Where to Stay & Eat

$–$$$$  ✕⌂ **Pittstown Point Landings.** Purchased by new owners in September 2005, this is one of the best fishing destinations in the Bahamas. Shaded by coconut palms, this remote property on Crooked Island's northwestern tip has miles of open beach at its doorstep and unobstructed views of the emerald water surrounding Bird Rock Lighthouse. Rooms are motel-style units with double beds. Ask for an ocean view and air-conditioning. The main lodge—which has a restaurant, bar, and library—once housed the Bahamas' first post office. Fresh grilled wahoo and hog snapper are sure winners on the dinner menu (¢–$$). Captain Robbie Gibson leads snorkeling, diving, reef, and offshore fishing adventures. All-inclusive bonefishing packages are available with top guides. ⌂ *9274 S.E. Hawk's Nest Ct., Hobe Sound, FL 33455* ☎ *242/344–2507 or 561/ 282–6800* ⊕ *www.pittstownpoint.com* ⇆ *12 rooms* ⚵ *Restaurant, Wi-Fi, beach, snorkeling, fishing, bicycles, shuffleboard, volleyball, bar, lounge, library, shop, airstrip; no a/c in some rooms, no room phones, no room TVs* ▭ *AE, MC, V.*

¢–$  ⌂ **Casuarina Villas.** Four modern cottages sit on a ½-mi stretch of white-sand beach between Landrail Point and Pittstown Point Landings. Each has a full kitchen, satellite TV, and western facing decks. A local market, gas station, and restaurant are 2 mi away in Landrail Point, or you can eat at Pittstown Point. A rental car and fishing guide can be arranged. Diving excursions are led by owner Ellis Moss. ✉ *Landrail Point, Crooked Island* ☎ *242/344–2197, 242/344–2036, or 242/636–4056* ⇆ *4 cottages* ⚵ *Kitchens, beach, snorkeling, fishing, laundry facilities; no room phones* ▭ *No credit cards.*

### Sports & the Outdoors

SCUBA DIVING **The Wall** starts at around 45 feet deep and goes down thousands more. It's about 50 yards off Crooked Island's coast and follows the shoreline for many miles. For more information, contact the Pittstown Point Landings hotel.

FISHING Crooked Island has a number of highly regarded bonefishing guides with quality boats and fly-fishing tackle. Most can be booked through Pittstown Point Landings, but the guides also take direct bookings. Be aware that telephone service to and from Crooked and Acklins islands is not always operational.

**Michael Carroll** (☎ 242/636–7020), **Clinton Scavalla** (☎ 242/422–3596 or 242/344–2197), **Elton "Bonefish Shakey" McKinney** (☎ 242/344–2507),

**Jeff Moss** (☎ 242/457–0621), **Randy McKinney** (☎ 242/422–3276), and **Derrick Ingraham** (☎ 242/556–8769) are all knowledgeable professional guides.

**Captain Robbie Gibson** (☎ 242/344–2507) can be contacted through Pittstown Point Landings. He is the most experienced reef and offshore fishing captain on Crooked Island, where astounding fishing in virgin waters is the rule. Many wahoo weighing more than 100 pounds are landed each season with his assistance. Robbie's personal best wahoo is a whopping 180 pounds. He's also a skilled guide for anglers pursuing tuna, marlin, sharks, barracuda, jacks, snapper, and grouper.

# CROOKED & ACKLINS ISLANDS ESSENTIALS

## Transportation

### BY AIR
Bahamasair flies from Nassau to Crooked and Acklins Islands twice a week. Airports are in Colonel Hill on Crooked Island and at Spring Point on Acklins Island. Pittstown Point Landings can pick up its guests flying into Colonel Hill by prior arrangement. The private airstrip at Pittstown Point Landings is complimentary for hotel guests. Nonguests pay landing and parking fees. This airstrip is most convenient for private and charter flights if you're staying in the area of Pittstown and Landrail Point.

🗗 Airlines & Contacts **Bahamasair** ☎ 800/222-4262.

### BY BOAT
M/V *United Star* sails from Potter's Cay in Nassau to Acklins Island, Crooked Island, and Long Cay once a week on a varying schedule. Call the Dockmaster's Office in Potter's Cay for schedule information. The fare is $70 one-way, and the trip takes 18 hours. Ferry service between Cove Landing, Crooked Island, and Lovely Bay, Acklins Island, usually operates twice daily on varying schedules between 9 and 4.

🗗 Boat & Ferry Information **Dockmaster's Office** ☎ 242/393-1064.

### BY CAR
Cars are hard to come by. You should reserve a car prior to your arrival with your hotel, but even with a reservation, be prepared for the possibility of not having one. Gas is also not always available on the island, as it's delivered by mail boats, which are sometimes delayed. Fortunately, it's easy to get a ride to most places with locals.

## Contacts & Resources

### EMERGENCIES
The police and commissioner are on Crooked Island. The two government medical clinics on Acklins Island are at Spring Point and Chesters Bay. Crooked Island's clinic is at Landrail Point. The resident doctor and nurse for the area live in Spring Point. Nurses are also available at

Colonel Hill on Crooked Island, and Masons Bay on Acklins. You can contact these medical professionals through your hotel.

**Commissioner** ☎ 242/344-2197. **Police** ☎ 242/344-2599.

# INAGUA

Great Inagua, the Bahamas' third-largest island, is 25 mi wide and 45 mi long. The terrain is mostly flat and covered with scrub. An unusual climate of little rainfall and continual trade winds created rich salt ponds, which have brought prosperity to the island over the years. The Morton Salt Company harvests a million tons of salt annually at its Matthew Town factory. About a quarter of the Inaguan population earns its living by working for the company. Inagua is best known for the huge flocks of shy pink flamingos that reside in the island's vast national park and on the property belonging to the salt company. In addition to the famous flamingos, the island is home to one of the largest populations of the rare Bahamian parrot, as well as herons, egrets, owls, cormorants, and more than a hundred other species of birds.

Although the birds have moved in wholeheartedly, the island remains virtually undiscovered by outsiders. Avid bird-watchers make up the majority of the tourists who undertake the long trip to this most southerly of the Out Islands, about 300 mi southeast of Nassau and 50 mi off the coast of Cuba. Lack of exposure means that people are still friendly and curious about each new face in town. You won't feel like just another tourist. And since crowds and traffic are nonexistent, there's nothing to bother you but the rather persistent mosquito population (be sure to bring strong insect repellent). On the other hand, tourist facilities are very few and far between. There's no official visitor information office on the island. The only inhabited settlement on Inagua is Matthew Town, a small, dusty grid of workers' homes and essential services. The "hotels" are functional at best, and are often difficult to contact.

If you're a beach lover, Inagua is not for you. Although there are a couple of small swimming areas near Matthew Town and a few longer stretches farther north, no perfect combination of hotel and beach has been built here. However, the virgin reefs off the island have caused a stir among intrepid divers who bring in their own equipment. The buzz is that Inagua could become a hot dive destination. Adventurous self-sufficient bonefishers have also discovered untouched flats with large bones on the northwest and southwest shorelines.

Great Inagua Island appears in the southeast corner of the Bahamas map at the front of this guide.

## Matthew Town

About 1,000 people live on Inagua, whose capital, Matthew Town, is on the west coast. The "town" is about a block long. The large, pink, run-down government building (with the commissioner's office, post office, and customs office) is the dominant structure, along with a power plant and several Morton Salt Company machine shops. There's a grocery and liquor store, a bank, a clinic with a resident doctor, a small cinema, several guesthouses, a few restaurants and bars that keep irregular hours, and the small Kiwanis park that has a bench for sunset-gazing. Huge, no longer functional satellite dishes are prominently displayed in the yards of many houses, attesting to the money that flowed through the island in the heady drug-smuggling days of the 1980s. With smuggling on the rise again, the Royal Bahamas Defense Force (in cooperation with the United States DEA) has established a Southern Satellite Base here as part of a revised drug interdiction program.

The **Erickson Museum and Library** is a welcome part of the community, particularly the surprisingly well-stocked, well-equipped library. The Morton company built the complex in the former home of the Erickson family, who came to Inagua in 1934 to run the salt giant. The museum displays the island's history, to which the company is inextricably tied. ⊠ *Gregory St., on northern edge of town across from police station* ☎ *242/ 339–1863* 🖅 *Free* ⊙ *Weekdays 9–1 and 3–6, Sat. 9–1.*

The desire to marvel at the salt process lures few visitors to Inagua, but the **Morton Salt Company** (☎ 242/339–1300) is omnipresent on the island: it has more than 2,000 acres of crystallizing ponds and more than 34,000 acres of reservoirs. More than a million tons of salt are produced every year for such industrial uses as salting icy streets. (More is produced when the Northeastern United States has a bad winter.) Even if you decide not to tour the facility, you can see the mountains of salt glistening in the sun from the plane. In an unusual case of industry assisting its environment, the crystallizers provide a feeding ground for the flamingos. As the water evaporates, the concentration of brine shrimp in the ponds increases, and the flamingos feed on these animals. Tours are available.

### Where to Stay & Eat

¢–$ ✕ **Cozy Corner.** Cheerful and loud, this lunch spot—locals just call it Cozy's—is the best on the island. It has a pool table and a large seating area with a bar. Stop in for a chat with locals over a Kalik and a Bahamian conch burger. Cozy's also serves excellent island-style dinners on request—steamed crawfish, grilled snapper, baked chicken and fries, homemade slaw, macaroni and cheese, and fresh johnnycake. If they're not open when you stop by, they may still fix you food and a drink if you ask. ⊠ *Matthew Town* ☎ *242/339–1440* 🖃 *D.*

$ ▦ **Sunset Apartments.** A good bet for accommodations on Inagua, these apartments sit right along the water on Matthew Town's southern side. The cement units all have modern Caribbean-style terra-cotta tile floors, rattan furniture, small terraces, a picnic area, and a gas grill. About a five-minute walk away is a small, secluded beach called the Swimming Hole. Ezzard Cartwright, the owner, is the only fly-fishing guide on the island. He offers all-inclusive bonefishing packages. ⌂ *C/o Ezzard Cartwright, Matthew Town, Great Inagua* ☎ *242/339–1362* 🛏 *2 apartments* ⚙ *Fans, kitchenettes, cable TV, boating; no room phones* 🖃 *No credit cards.*

¢ 🏠 **The Main House.** The Morton Salt Company operates this small, affordable guesthouse. On the second of two floors, air-conditioned rooms share a sitting area with couches and a telephone. Rooms are spotless and spacious with dark-wood furnishings, Masonite-panel walls, and floral-print drapes and spreads. The green-and-white hotel is right in Matthew Town, behind the grocery store and directly across the street from the island's noisy power plant. ⊠ *Matthew Town, Great Inagua* 🕾 *242/339–1266 or 242/339–1267* 🛏 *5 rooms* 🕭 *Refrigerators, cable TV; no room phones* 🖃 *No credit cards.*

¢ 🏠 **Walkine's Guest House.** On the main drag and in the mix of the residential community, this cinder block duplex has five motel-style air-conditioned rooms with cable TV. All rooms are bright and comfortable, with two twin beds. Three rooms have private baths, and two share a bath. The owner, Eleanor Walkine, lives in the duplex next door, and will prepare meals on request. ⊠ *Matthew Town, Great Inagua* 🕾 *242/339–1612* 🛏 *5 rooms* 🕭 *Fans, cable TV; no room phones* 🖃 *No credit cards.*

### Sports & the Outdoors

BICYCLING The **Pour More Bar** (🕾 242/339–1232) rents bikes for exploring the island.

## Elsewhere on the Island

Although you'll spot them in salt ponds throughout the island, birds and other wildlife also reside in the **Inagua National Park,** managed by **The Bahamas National Trust** (BNT), which spreads over 287 square mi and occupies most of the island's western half. Nature lovers, ornithologists, and photographers are drawn to the area and to Lake Windsor (a 12-mi-long brackish body of water in the island's center) to view the spectacle of more than 60,000 flamingos feeding, mating, or flying (although you will rarely see all those birds together in the same place). When planning your trip, keep in mind that November through June is the best time to see the birds, and the breeding season is March through May. Flamingos live on Inagua year-round, but the greatest concentrations come at these times. If you visit right after hatching, the scrambling flocks of fuzzy, gray baby flamingos—they can't fly until they're older—are quite entertaining. On the northwest side of the Park is the **Union Creek Reserve,** where BNT is working with the Caribbean Conservation Corporation on marine turtle research. To tour any part of the park or reserve, you must be accompanied by a BNT warden. Contact the **Bahamas National Trust's Nassau office** (🕾 242/393–1317 🖷 242/393–4978 ⊕ www.thebahamasnationaltrust.org/) to make reservations for your visit. BNT will send a visitor reservation form that you must fill out and return with your flight information, length of stay, and number of people in your party. You must also pay for your tour before arrival on Inagua.

From **Southwest Point,** a mile or so south of the capital, you can see Cuba's coast—slightly more than 50 mi west—on a clear day from atop the lighthouse (built in 1870 in response to a huge number of shipwrecks on offshore reefs). This is one of the last four hand-operated kerosene light-houses in the Bahamas. Be sure to sign the guest book after your climb.

# INAGUA ESSENTIALS

## Transportation

### BY AIR

Bahamasair has flights on Monday, Wednesday, and Friday from Nassau to the Matthew Town Airport.

🔃 Airlines & Contacts **Bahamasair** ☎ 242/339-4415 or 800/222-4262.

### BY BOAT

M/V *Trans Cargo II* makes weekly trips from Nassau to Matthew Town, also stopping at Abraham's Bay, Mayaguana. The cost is $70 one-way, and the trip takes approximately 24 hours. For information on specific schedules contact the Dockmaster's Office at Potter's Cay, Nassau.

🔃 Boat & Ferry Information **Dockmaster's Office** ☎ 242/393-1064.

### BY CAR

Inagua Trading Ltd. has several cars for rent by the day. They're often difficult to contact by phone. BNT Warden Henry Nixon can also arrange for vehicle rentals.

🔃 Local Agency **Inagua Trading Ltd.** ☎ 242/339-1330. **Warden Henry Nixon** ☎ 242/339-1616.

### BY TAXI

Taxis sometimes meet incoming flights, though taxi service is not always reliable. It's best to make prior arrangements with your hotel.

🔃 Airport Information **Matthew Town Airport** ☎ 242/339-1254.

## Contacts & Resources

### BANKS & EXCHANGING SERVICES

The Bank of the Bahamas in Matthew Town is open Monday through Thursday 9:30–2 and Friday 9:30–5:30.

🔃 **Bank of the Bahamas** ☎ 242/339-1815.

### EMERGENCIES

There's no general emergency number in Inagua—call the police or hospital directly in case of an emergency.

🔃 **Hospital** ☎ 242/339-1249. **Police** ☎ 242/339-1263.

### TOUR OPTIONS

Warden Henry Nixon leads most tours into Inagua National Park and to Union Creek Reserve. Mr. Nixon is also a certified birding tour guide. He can arrange for rental vehicles and generally point you in the right direction for all activities on Inagua.

🔃 **Warden Henry Nixon** ☎ 242/339-1616.

# LONG ISLAND

Never more than 4 mi wide but close to 80 mi long, Long Island truly lives up to its name. The Queen's Highway traverses its length, through the Tropic of Cancer and some 35 settlements and farming towns. The island is known for its astonishing contrasts in geography, with chalk-white limestone cliffs, forested hillsides, mangrove swamps, and stark flatlands where salt is produced. Exposed to the open Atlantic, the east coast consists of black iridescent reefs, protected coves, long strands of shelling beaches, and craggy bluffs that drop precipitously into the deep blue sea. The tranquil west coast is composed of powdery-white beaches, wide-open sandy flats, and calm turquoise bays.

Long Island was one of Columbus's early stopping-off places. In 1790 American Loyalists from the Carolinas brought their slaves to the island, where they built plantations and planted more than 4,000 acres of cotton. The rich soil made crop growing more successful here than on any other Out Island, but with the abolition of slavery, the plantations failed. Agriculture, however, remains a thriving part of the local economy, and pothole farming is the favored method of growing corn, peas, squash, pineapples, bananas, and other fruits.

The island has blossomed into an Out Island jewel, with the population growing to more than 5,500 residents in 2004 and tourism on the rise. Resort, diving, and snorkeling services have been enhanced in recent years, and vast, unexplored bonefish flats are drawing anglers who enjoy remote fishing. Sailing enthusiasts will find Joe's Sound—sandwiched between Cape Santa Maria beach and Glenton Sound—to be a protected haven that rivals any in the Bahamas. A sheltered deep-water marina with fuel and other services in Clarence Town has created more convenient boating access to the southern islands.

*Numbers in the margin correspond to points of interest on the Long Island map.*

## Cape Santa Maria & Stella Maris

★ **⑫** Columbus originally named the island's northern tip **Cape Santa Maria** in honor of one of his ships. He called the entire island Fernandina, out of respect for his Spanish sponsor. Cape Santa Maria is known for its irresistibly dazzling beaches, which are considered among the best in the country.

Take a side trip on the unpaved road out to **Columbus Cove**, 1½ mi north of the Cape Santa Maria resort. The monument and plaque that commemorate Columbus's landing are here, as well as tremendous views of the protected harbor he sailed into. Divers can explore the wreck of a ship, the M/V *Comberbach,* which lies just off the headland. The Stella Maris Resort sunk the leaky 103-foot freighter in 1985 to create an artificial reef and an excellent dive site nearly 100 feet under. The road to the cove is too rough for most vehicles, but it happens to be a fine walk.

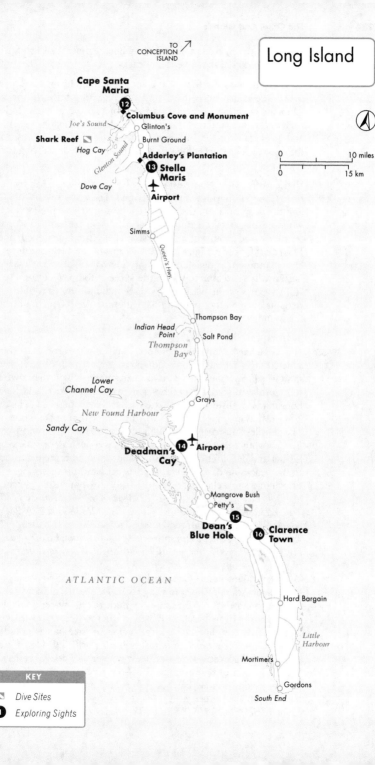

TO
CONCEPTION
ISLAND

Long Island

**Cape Santa
Maria**

⑫

**Columbus Cove and Monument**

*Joe's Sound*

○ Glinton's

**Shark Reef** ◣

○ Burnt Ground

*Hog Cay*

*Glenton Sound*

◆ **Adderley's Plantation**

⑬ **Stella
Maris**

*Dove Cay*

✈
**Airport**

○ Simms

*Queen's Hwy.*

○ Thompson Bay

*Indian Head
Point*

○ Salt Pond

*Thompson
Bay*

*Lower
Channel Cay*

*New Found Harbour*

○ Grays

*Sandy Cay*

✈
⑭ **Airport**

**Deadman's
Cay**

○ Mangrove Bush

○ Petty's ◣

⑮

**Dean's
Blue Hole**

⑯ **Clarence
Town**

*ATLANTIC OCEAN*

○ Hard Bargain

*Little
Harbour*

○ Mortimers

○ Gordons

*South End*

0 ———————— 10 miles
0 ———————— 15 km

**KEY**

◣  *Dive Sites*

①  *Exploring Sights*

An easier way to reach the cove is by boat. Anglers can fish for bone-fish and tarpon at the lower tidal stages.

**⑬ Stella Maris,** meaning Star of the Sea, lies about 12 mi south of Cape Santa Maria. It's home to the all-encompassing Stella Maris Resort Club, along with an airport. In a world of its own, the resort has a marina, yacht club, and tiny shopping complex with a bank, a post office, and a general store. If you're interested in aquatic adventures, contact the resort, which runs numerous daily outings, including diving and fishing trips.

**Shark Reef,** about 4 mi west of Hog Cay, is easily reached by boaters from Cape Santa Maria and Joe's Sound. The water is startlingly clear, and the drop-off from the white-sand bottom to deep blue is a visual wonder. You can take a guided diving excursion and watch a scuba master safely feed groups of a dozen sharks at a time. Just north of Stella Maris, off Queen's Highway, are the ruins of the 19th-century **Adderley's Plantation.** Long Island was another Bahamian island where fleeing Loyalists attempted, with little success, to grow cotton. You can still see parts of the plantation's three buildings up to roof level. The remains of two other plantations, **Dunmore's** and **Gray's,** are also on the island.

### Where to Stay & Eat

★ **$$–$$$**  ✕🏨 **Cape Santa Maria Beach Resort.** This cushy resort has 10 colonial-style cottages spread along a gorgeous, 4-mi stretch of velvety white-sand beach. Spacious one- or two-bedroom units have their own large, fully furnished screened porches steps away from the turquoise water. Four new 1,800-square-foot luxury villas were completed in December 2005. Another four are scheduled for completion in December 2006. The marble-floor reception building contains a small gym and TV room. In the brightly colored dining room ($–$$), you can feast on superb broiled lobster and delicious conch salads. Magenta sunsets are the trademark of the beachside bar. The watersports activities office arranges Hobie cat sailing, snorkeling, and deep-sea, reef, or bonefishing excursions. ⌂ *Oak Bay Marine Group, 1327 Beach Dr., Victoria, BC V8S 2N4* ☎ *242/338–5273 or 800/663–7090* 🖷 *242/338–6013 or 250/598–3366* ⊕ *www.capesantamaria.com* ⇝ *20 1- to 2-bedroom villas* △ *Restaurant, gym, beach, snorkeling, windsurfing, boating, waterskiing, fishing, bicycles, bar, shops, babysitting, laundry facilities; no room phones, no room TVs* ▭ *AE, MC, V.*

★ **$**  ✕🏨 **Stella Maris Resort Club.** Sitting atop a hilly east-coast ridge overlooking the Atlantic, this sprawling resort's range of daily activities make it a Bahamian classic. You can swim in three freshwater pools, lounge on a series of private beaches, or explore sandy coves with excellent snorkeling. Dive, fish, hike, or take advantage of free morning and afternoon activity programs. The resort has colorful hillside rooms and cottages, and oceanfront houses, a few with private pools. Fresh seafood is the highlight of the restaurant's ($–$$) rotating menus. The weekly cave party on Monday has buffet barbecue, music, and dancing set in a cavern on the property. ⌂ *1100 Lee Wagener Blvd., No. 310, Fort Lauderdale, FL 33315* ☎ *242/338–2051 or 800/426–0466* 🖷 *242/*

*338–2052* ⊕ *www.stellamarisresort.com* ↩ *20 rooms, 12 1-bedroom cottages, 7 2-bedroom cottages, 4 beach houses* ♿ *Restaurant, grocery, some kitchenettes, refrigerators, 3 pools, dive shop, snorkeling, boating, marina, waterskiing, fishing, bicycles, billiards, Ping-Pong, bar, recreation room, shop, complimentary weddings, laundry service; no room phones, no room TVs* ▤ *AE, D, MC, V.*

## Simms & South

Simms is one of Long Island's oldest settlements, 8 mi south of Stella Maris past little pastel-color houses. Some of these homes display emblems to ward off evil spirits, an indication of the presence of Obeah, the voodoolike culture found on many of the Bahamian islands. There are a few quirky roadside eats to be had on this stretch of Queen's Highway. On the road's east side, look for a small conch-salad stand that's intermittently open and prepares the snack right before your eyes. Immediately south of Simms, you may see rising smoke and tables out in the front yard of **Jeraldine's Jerk Pit** (☎ No phone). The barbecued chicken and pork are delectable.

The annual Long Island Regatta, featuring Bahamian-made boats, is held in **Salt Pond** every June. The regatta is the island's biggest event, attracting contestants from all over the islands. Three days of partying and pig roasts are sparked at night by lively local bands. Salt Pond is 10 mi south of Simms.

⑭ The town of **Deadman's Cay** is the island's largest settlement. Here you'll find a few shops, churches, and schools. Just east of Deadman's Cay, **Cartwright's Cave** has stalactites and stalagmites and eventually leads to the sea. The cave has apparently never been completely explored, although Arawak drawings were found on one wall. For guided cave tours, contact **Leonard Cartwright** (☎ 242/337–0235). There are several other caves, supposedly pirate-haunted, around Simms, Millers, and Salt Pond; a local should be able to point you in the right direction.

Between Deadman's Cay and Clarence Town, just past the settlement of Petty's, watch for the pink-and-white pillars that line the turnoff for ⑮ **Dean's Blue Hole.** At 660 feet, it's thought to be the world's second deepest blue hole. Curious divers will want to contact the **dive shop at Stella Maris** (☎ 242/338–2050).

⑯ **Clarence Town** has Long Island's most celebrated landmarks, **St. Paul's Church** (Anglican) and **St. Peter's Church** (Catholic). They were both built by Father Jerome, a priest who is buried in a tomb in the Hermitage atop Cat Island's Mt. Alvernia. As an Anglican named John Hawes, he constructed St. Paul's. Later, after converting to Catholicism, he built St. Peter's. The architecture of the two churches is similar to that of the missions established by the Spaniards in California in the late 18th century. Clarence Town is simply gorgeous, fringed by white-sand beaches, and fronted by a stunning oval-shape bay of clear aqua-blue water dotted with coral heads, sand bars, and small green cays. The harbor is also home to the local government headquarters and dock.

### Where to Stay & Eat

¢–$  ✕ **Earlie's Tavern.** The Knowles family runs this dining room, bar, and pool room. Try the delicious lobster, grouper, or cracked conch. Burgers, sandwiches, and boxed fishing lunches are made to order. This is a lively night spot some weekends, and the place rocks on occasional special events, including the Long Island Regatta. ⊠ *Queen's Hwy., Mangrove Bush* ☎ *242/337–1628* ▭ *No credit cards.*

¢–$  ✕ **Kooters.** Grab a seat on the deck at this casual spot for a lovely view of Mangrove Bush Point and watch bonefish and tarpon cruise the adjacent shallow flat. Enjoy a conch burger, club sandwich with homemade fries, or a cold Kalik. Daily specials range from ribs to seafood. Save room for one of the many flavors of ice cream. ⊠ *Queen's Hwy., Mangrove Bush* ☎ *242/337–0340* ▭ *No credit cards* ☉ *Closed Sun.*

¢–$  ✕ **Max's Conch Grill and Bar.** If you sit all day on a stool at this pink-, green-, and yellow-stripe roadside gazebo, nursing beers and nibbling on conch, you'll become a veritable expert on Long Island and the life of its residents. Such is the draw of this laid-back watering hole, open 9 to 9 daily—sometimes later when the bar is hopping. Have a chat with Max while sampling his conch salad ($3.50 or $6), conch dumplings (6 for $1), or daily specials like baked ham and steamed pork. ⊠ *Deadman's Cay* ☎ *242/337–0056* ▭ *MC, V.*

★ $  ✕▦ **Chez Pierre Bahamas.** Six elevated cottages with generous bedrooms, bath, and airy screened porches line this remote Millers Bay beach location, halfway between Stella Maris and Deadman's Cay. Owners Pierre and Anne deliver exceptional personalized service, however, guests here should be self-sufficient and adventurous. Chef Pierre whips up fresh innovative dishes with homegrown ingredients and daily caught seafood in the relaxing oceanfront restaurant (¢–$$). Explore nearby cays in sea kayaks, wade the adjacent flats for bonefish, or schedule a diving adventure through the Stella Maris marina. Fishing guides, car rentals, and airport transfers can be arranged. ✑ *Box S-30811, Simms, Long Island* ☎ *418/694–4046, 242/338–8809, or 242/357–1374* ⊕ *www. chezpierrebahamas.com* ➫ *6 cottages* ⚭ *Restaurant, fans, beach, snorkeling, fishing, bicycles, bar, lounge, babysitting, Internet; no a/c, no room phones, no room TVs* ▭ *AE, MC, V* ⋈ *MAP.*

¢  ✕▦ **The Forest.** Just south of Clarence Town on the west side of the highway, this popular laid-back restaurant (¢–$$) serves spicy wings, potato skins, cracked conch, barbecued chicken, and grouper fingers in a large open room furnished with simple tables and chairs. Enjoy a drink at the bar—which is made of seashells embedded in glossy resin—and a game of pool. Every other weekend there's live music and dancing. Six spacious motel rooms are in a concrete building behind the bar. Each room has white-tile floors and bright wood furnishings, including two double beds, satellite TV, and a private bath. ⊠ *Queen's Hwy., Miley's* ☎ *242/337–3287* 🖷 *242/337–3288* ⊕ *pattydean@batelnet.bs* ➫ *6 rooms* ⚭ *Restaurant, cable TV, bar; no room phones* ▭ *No credit cards.*

$  ▦ **Lochabar Beach Lodge.** Mellow and remote, the brightly painted two-story lodge consists of two thoughtfully constructed 600-square-foot guest studios downstairs that overlook a pristine beach and dramatic blue hole.

There are dinette islands with stools, although you can also eat alfresco on your deck. The larger upstairs suite includes a full kitchen and private bedroom. At low tide, you can stroll the cove's entire beach and round the point into Clarence Town. You'll need to rent a car to stay here. Bonefishing guides and car rentals can be arranged by the management. ⊠ *1 mi south of Clarence Town* ⌂ *Box CT-30330, Long Island, Bahamas* ☎ *242/337–0400 or 242/337–3123* ☒ *242/337–6556* ⊕ *www.lochabar-beach-lodge.com* ⇆ *2 studios, 1 suite* ☖ *Fans, kitchenettes, snorkeling, fishing; no a/c in some rooms* ▭ *No credit cards.*

### Nightlife

Just south of Clarence Town, **The Forest** (⊠ Queen's Hwy., Miley's ☎ 242/337–3287) has dancing and partying to live bands playing rock, Calypso, and reggae music every other weekend.

### Shopping

**Bonafide Tackle Shop and Cafe** (⊠ Queen's Hwy., Stella Maris ☎ 242/338–2025) sells fly-fishing tackle and accessories, clothing, souvenirs, and snacks. You can book a fishing trip here, and arrange for fishing gear rental. Internet access is available.

**Wild Tamarind** (⊠ About ½ mi east of Queen's Hwy., Petty's ☎ 242/337–0262) is Denis Knight's ceramics studio. Stop in for a lovely bowl, vase, or sculpture, but call first in case he's out fishing.

### Sports & the Outdoors

SCUBA DIVING For more information about these sites or to arrange a dive, contact the Stella Maris Resort Club.

**Dean's Blue Hole** is lauded by locals as one of the world's deepest ocean holes. It's surrounded by a powder-beach cove. **Conception Island Wall** is an excellent wall dive, with hard and soft coral, plus interesting sponge formations. **Shark Reef** is the site of the Bahamas' first shark dive. The Stella Maris Resort has been running trips there for more than 25 years.

FISHING **Bonafide Bonefishing** (☎ 242/338–2025) is run by guide James "Docky"
★ Smith and his wife, Jill. Highly regarded as one of the best guides in the Bahamas, Docky conducts full- and half-day guided trips in his state-of-the-art 16-foot Hewes flats skiffs, and also runs reef fishing trips. The operation is based out of Bonafide Tackle Shop and Cafe at Stella Maris, which rents conventional and fly-fishing gear, prepares snacks and box lunches, and sells a range of tackle, clothing, and flies.

The 15-slip **Flying Fish Marina** (⊠ Lighthouse Point Road, Clarence Town ☎ 242/337–3430) in the northern corner of Clarence Town Harbour can take boats up to 130 feet. Bathrooms, showers, and laundry facilities are available to marina guests only. Bonefishing, reef, and offshore guides can be arranged by the management with advance notice.

**Silver Strike Fishing** (☎ 242/337–1555 or 242/337–0329 ⊠ Box 30646, Deadman's Cay) is operated by guide Cecil Knowles and his wife, Judy Knowles. You can book guides by the day, or a complete bonefishing package with accommodations at Lochabar Beach Lodge.

# LONG ISLAND ESSENTIALS

## Transportation

### BY AIR

Bahamasair flies most days from Nassau to Stella Maris and Deadman's Cay. Flights from Fort Lauderdale are available during the winter season. Stella Maris has charter flights from Exuma and Nassau to Stella Maris. If you're a pilot, the island is a great base for exploring other islands. Stella Maris rents well-maintained planes—a four-seat Piper Seneca and a six-seat Piper Navajo—for about $90 an hour. Island Wings, an air charter company owned by Captain Marty Fox, has charter flight service to and from any Bahamian island with a legal airstrip, and to and from Stella Maris or Deadman's Cay.

If you're a guest at Cape Santa Maria or Stella Maris, fly into the Stella Maris airport. Use the Deadman's Cay airport if you're staying in Clarence Town.

 Airlines & Contacts **Bahamasair** ☎ 242/339-4415 or 800/222-4262. **Island Wings** ☎ 242/338-2022 or 242/357-1021. **Stella Maris** ☎ 800/426-0466, 954/359-8236, or 242/338-2051 ⊕ www.stellamarisresortairservice.com.

### BY BOAT

M/V *Mia Dean* makes a 12-hour weekly trip from Nassau to Clarence Town, on the island's south end. The boat leaves Nassau on Tuesday and returns on Thursday; the fare is $45 one-way. The M/V *Sherice M* leaves Nassau on Tuesday with stops in Salt Pond, Deadman's Cay, and Seymour's. The return trip is on Friday. Travel time is 15 hours; the fare is $45 one way. For more information, contact the Dockmaster's Office at Potter's Cay, Nassau.

 Boat & Ferry Information **Dockmaster's Office** ☎ 242/393-1064.

### BY CAR

Taylor's Rentals rents high-quality cars for the most reasonable rates on the island. Hotels and lodges will also arrange for guests' automobile rentals.

 Local Agency **Taylor's Rentals** ☎ 242/338-7001.

### BY TAXI

Taxis meet incoming flights at both airports. From the Stella Maris airport, the fare to Stella Maris Resort is $4; to Cape Santa Maria, it's $40. Check with your hotel to see which airport you should use—landing at the wrong airport could mean a $120 cab ride—in which case, renting a car will save you money. Guests staying at Chez Pierre pay $25 one-way for the taxi from Stella Maris, and $35 one-way for the taxi from Deadman's Cay.

## Contacts & Resources

### BANKS & EXCHANGING SERVICES

At Stella Maris Resort Club, the Bank of Nova Scotia is open Tuesday and Thursday 9:30–2 and Friday 9:30–5. Farther south, the Deadman's

Cay branch is open Monday–Thursday 9–1 and Friday 9–5. Royal Bank of Canada has a branch on Deadman's Cay; hours are Monday–Thursday 9–1 and Friday 9–5.

🏦 **Bank of Nova Scotia** ☎ 242/338-2057 Stella Maris, 242/338-2002 Deadman's Cay. **Royal Bank of Canada** ☎ 242/337-1044.

**EMERGENCIES**

Clarence Town, Deadman's Cay, and Simms each have their own police departments.

🏦 **Police** ☎ 242/337-0999 Clarence Town, 242/337-0444 Deadman's Cay, 242/338-8555 Simms.

# SAN SALVADOR

On October 12, 1492, Christopher Columbus disrupted the lives of the peaceful Lucayan Indians by landing on the island of Guanahani, which he named San Salvador. Apparently he knelt on the beach and claimed the land for Spain. (Skeptics of this story point to a study published in a 1986 *National Geographic* article in which Samana Cay, 60 mi southeast, is identified as the exact point of the weary explorer's landing.) Three monuments on the island commemorate Columbus's arrival, and the 500th anniversary of the event was officially celebrated here.

A 17th-century pirate named George Watling, who frequently sought shelter on the island, changed San Salvador's name to Watling's Island. The Bahamian government switched the name back to San Salvador in 1926.

The island is 12 mi long—roughly the length of Manhattan—and about 5 mi wide along the lake-filled portion of its interior. The Queen's Highway forms an oval that skirts the coastline. Most visitors come for the peaceful isolation and the diving; there are about 950 residents and over 50 dive sites. There's also world-renowned offshore fishing and good bonefishing.

*Numbers in the margin correspond to points of interest on the San Salvador map.*

## Fernandez Bay to Riding Rock Point

In 1492 the inspiring sight that greeted Christopher Columbus by moonlight at 2 AM was a terrain of gleaming beaches and far-reaching forest. The peripatetic traveler and his crews—"men from Heaven," the locals called them—steered the *Niña, Pinta,* and *Santa María* warily among ❶ the coral reefs and anchored, so it's recorded, in **Fernandez Bay.** A cross erected in 1956 by Columbus scholar Ruth C. Durlacher Wolper Malvin stands at his approximate landing spot. Ms. Malvin's **New World Museum** (☎ No phone), near North Victoria Hill on the east coast, contains artifacts from the era of the Lucayans. Admission to the museum is free; it's open by appointment only (your hotel can make arrangements). An underwater monument marks the place where the *Santa María* an-

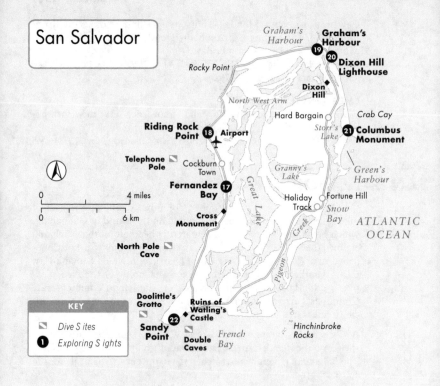

## San Salvador

chored. Nearby, another monument commemorates the Olympic flame's passage on its journey from Greece to Mexico City in 1968.

Fernandez Bay is just south of what is now the main community of **Cockburn Town,** mid-island on the western shore. Queen's Highway encircles the island from Cockburn Town, where the weekly mail boat docks. This small village's narrow streets contain two churches, a commissioner's office, a police station, a courthouse, a library, a clinic, a drugstore, and a telephone station.

**⑱** Columbus first spotted and made a record of **Riding Rock Point.** The area now serves as the home for the Riding Rock Inn, a popular resort for divers. Just north of the point is the island's other resort, the Club Med–Columbus Isle, at the foot of a gorgeous 2-mi-long beach. Riding Rock Point is about a mile north of Cockburn Town.

### Where to Stay & Eat

★ **$$$–$$$$** ✕🍴 **Club Med–Columbus Isle.** The 80-acre oceanfront village is one of Club Med's most luxurious resorts, with state-of-the-art dive facilities, including three custom-made 45-foot catamarans and a decompression chamber. All rooms have patios or balconies and handcrafted furniture. Guided bike tours introduce vacationers to island life beyond the resort.

This resort caters primarily to upscale couples, and the atmosphere is more low-key than at most. It's one of the most recommended by Club Med fanatics. With advance notice, nonguests can partake of the sumptuous lunches and dinners ($$$–$$$$). All-inclusive packages including air are available. ⊠ *3 mi north of Riding Rock Point* ⌂ *40 W. 57th St., New York, NY 10019* ☎ *888/932–2582 or 242/331–2000* 🖷 *242/ 331–2458* ⊕ *www.clubmed.com* ⤳ *288 rooms* ♨ *3 restaurants, refrigerators, Wi-Fi, 9 tennis courts, pool, gym, hair salon, massage, beach, dive shop, bicycles, lounge, nightclub, theater, laundry service, Internet room, car rental* ⊟ *AE, D, MC, V* ⏍ *AI.*

$ ✕▥ **Riding Rock Resort and Marina.** A diver's dream, this motel-style resort offers three dives per day to pristine offshore reefs and a drop-off wall teeming with life. It's also the only place to stay on San Salvador if you want to manage your own activities. The inn's three buildings house rooms facing either the ocean or the freshwater pool. All rooms have washed-oak furniture and a sitting area with a table and chairs; oceanside rooms have refrigerators and queen-size beds. The restaurant (¢–$$) serves grilled wahoo and tuna right off the boat as well as hearty pancake breakfasts. There's good bonefishing you can do on your own. ⊠ *Riding Rock Point* ⌂ *1170 Lee Wagener Blvd., Suite 103, Fort Lauderdale, FL 33315* ☎ *954/359–8353 or 800/272–1492* 🖷 *954/ 359–8254* ⊕ *www.ridingrock.com* ⤳ *42 rooms, 2 villas* ♨ *Restaurant, some refrigerators, cable TV, tennis court, pool, dive shop, fishing, bicycles, bar, Internet room, car rental* ⊟ *D, MC, V.*

### Sports & the Outdoors

BICYCLING **Riding Rock Inn** (☎ 800/272–1492 or 954/359–8353) rents bicycles for $8 a day.

SCUBA DIVING **Club Med** (☎ 242/331–2000) has dive boats and a decompression chamber. There's also tennis, sailing, and windsurfing, among other sports.

**Riding Rock Inn** (☎ 800/272–1492) is affiliated with Guanahani Dive Ltd., which uses mostly buoyed sites to avoid damaging the marine environment by dropping anchor. It also offers resort and certification courses, and a modern underwater photographic facility. It rents all kinds of camera gear and does slide shows of divers' work. Riding Rock also rents bicycles and snorkeling gear and will arrange fishing trips ($400 for a half day and $600 for a full day). The waters hold tuna, blue marlin, dorado, and, in the winter, wahoo.

## Around San Salvador

⓳ Columbus describes **Graham's Harbour** in his diaries as large enough "to hold all the ships of Christendom." A complex of buildings near the harbor houses the **Bahamian Field Station,** a biological and geological research institution that attracts scientists and students from all over the world.

⓴ A couple of miles south of Graham's Harbour stands **Dixon Hill Lighthouse.** Built around 1856, it's still hand-operated. The lighthouse keeper must wind the apparatus that projects the light, which beams out to sea every 15 seconds to a maximum distance of 19 mi, depending on visibility. A climb to the top of the 160-foot landmark offers a fabulous view of the island, which includes a series of inland lakes. The keeper is present 24 hours a day. Knock on his door, and he'll take you up to the top and explain the machinery. Drop $1 in the box when you sign the guest book on the way out.

**㉑** No road leads to the **Columbus Monument** on Crab Cay; you have to make your way along a bushy path. This initial tribute to the explorer was erected by the *Chicago Herald* newspaper in 1892, far from the presumed site of Columbus's landing. A series of little villages—Polly Hill, Hard Bargain, Fortune Hill, Holiday Track—winds south of here for several miles along Storr's Lake. You can still see the ruins of several plantations, and the deserted white-sand beaches on this eastern shore are some of the most spectacular in the islands. A little farther along is Pigeon Creek, which is a prime spot for bonefishing.

**㉒** **Sandy Point** anchors the island's southwestern end, overlooking French Bay. Here, on a hill, you'll find the **ruins of Watling's Castle,** named after the 17th-century pirate. The ruins are more likely the remains of a Loyalist plantation house than a castle from buccaneering days. A 5- to 10-minute walk from Queen's Highway will take you to see what's left of the ruins, which are now engulfed in vegetation.

### Sports & the Outdoors

SCUBA DIVING   For more information about these and other sites, contact the Riding Rock Inn or visit ⊕ www.ridingrock.com

**Doolittle's Grotto** is a popular site featuring a sandy slope down to 140 feet. There are lots of tunnels and crevices for exploring, and usually a large school of horse-eye jacks to keep you company. **Double Caves**, as the name implies, has two parallel caves leading out to a wall at 115 feet. There's typically quite a lot of fish activity along the top of the wall. **North Pole Cave** has a wall that drops sharply from 40 feet to more than 150 feet. Coral growth is extensive, and you might see a hammerhead or two. **Telephone Pole** is a stimulating wall dive where you can watch stingrays, grouper, snapper, and turtles in action.

# SAN SALVADOR ESSENTIALS

## Transportation

### BY AIR

Air Sunshine flies from Fort Lauderdale into Cockburn Town. Riding Rock Inn has charter flights every Saturday from Fort Lauderdale. American Eagle flies from Miami on the weekends. Bahamasair flies into Cockburn Town from Nassau and also offers direct service from Miami three days a week.

🛈 Airlines & Contacts **Air Sunshine** ☎ 954/434–8900 or 800/327–8900. **American Eagle** ☎ 800/433–7300 ⊕ www.aa.com. **Bahamasair** ☎ 242/339–4415 or 800/222–4262. **Riding Rock Inn** ☎ 800/272–1492 or 954/359–8353.

### BY BOAT

M/V *Lady Francis,* out of Nassau, leaves Tuesday for San Salvador and Rum Cay. The trip takes 12 hours, and the fare is $40 one-way. The return trip is on Sunday. For information on specific schedules and fares, contact the Dockmaster's Office at Potter's Cay, Nassau.

🚢 Boat & Ferry Information **Dockmaster's Office** ☎ 242/393-1064.

### BY CAR

Riding Rock Inn rents cars for $85 a day.

🚗 **Riding Rock Inn** ☎ 800/272-1492 or 954/359-8353.

### BY TAXI

Taxis meet arriving planes at Cockburn Town Airport. Club Med meets all guests at the airport (your account is charged $10 for the three-minute transfer). Riding Rock provides complimentary transportation for guests.

## Contacts & Resources

### EMERGENCIES

🏥 **Medical Clinic** ☎ 207. **Police** ☎ 218.

# OUT ISLANDS ESSENTIALS

*To research prices, get advice from other travelers, and book travel arrangements, visit* ⊕ *www.fodors.com.*

## Contacts & Resources

### EMERGENCIES

There are health centers and clinics scattered throughout the islands, but in the event of emergency, illness, or accident requiring fast transportation to the United States, AAPI Air Ambulance Services provides aeromedical services out of Fort Lauderdale Executive Airport. Its three jet aircraft are equipped with sophisticated medical equipment and a trained staff of nurses and flight medics.

🚑 **AAPI Air Ambulance Services** ☎ 954/491-0555 or 800/752-4195.

### TOURS OPTIONS

Florida Yacht Charters, at the high-tech Boat Harbour Marina in Marsh Harbour, offers an endless supply of boats (trawlers, sailboats, and catamarans with inflatable dinghies) and amenities, such as air-conditioning, refrigeration, and GPS. Licensed captains, instruction, and provisioning are also available. For captained yacht charters, contact the Moorings in Marsh Harbour. This is the Bahamas' division of one of the largest yacht-charter agencies in the world, which provides many services needed for yachties, from provisions to professional captains. Swift Yacht Charters also has yacht charters. If you're looking for a guided kayak tour, call Ibis Tours.

🚤 Tour-Operator Recommendations In the Bahamas: **The Moorings** 📮 Box AB-20469, Marsh Harbour, Abaco ☎ 242/367-4000 or 800/535-7289 ⊕ www.go-abacos.com/ conchinn/moorings. In the U.S.: **Changes in L'Attitudes** 📮 3080 East Bay Dr., Largo,

FL 33771 ☎ 727/573-3536 or 800/330-8272 ⊕ www.changes.com. **Florida Yacht Charters** ☎ 305/532-8600 or 800/537-0050 ⊕ www.floridayacht.com. **Future Vacations** ⌂ 110 E. Broward Blvd., Box 1525, Fort Lauderdale, FL 33301 ☎ 954/522-1440 or 800/456-2323 🖶 954/357-4687. **Ibis Tours** ⌂ Box 208, Pelham, NY 10803 ☎ 800/525-9411 ⊕ www.ibistours.com. **Swift Yacht Charters** ⌂ 209 S. Main St., Sherborn, MA 01770 ☎ 800/866-8340 or 508/647-1554 ⊕ www.swiftyachts.com. In Canada: **Americanada** ⌂ 139 Sauve O, Montréal, Québec H3L LY4 ☎ 514/384-6431 or 800/361-8242. **Holiday House** ⌂ 110 Richmond St. E, Suite 304, Toronto, Ontario M5C 1P1 ☎ 416/364-2433.

## VISITOR INFORMATION

The Bahama Out Islands Promotion Board has a fantastic staff that provides information about lodging, travel, and activities in the islands and can book reservations at many of the hotels. On request, the board will send color brochures about island resorts.

The Bahamas Ministry of Tourism's Bahamas Tourist Office can assist with travel plans and information.

The best overall Web sites for information on all the islands are the Ministry of Tourism and the Out Island Promotion Board's Web sites. Also try ⊕ www.bahamasvg.com and ⊕ www.bahamasnet.com. The best site for planning a fishing vacation is ⊕ www.bahamasflyfishingguide.com. 🛈 Tourist Information **Bahama Out Islands Promotion Board** ⌂ 19495 Biscayne Blvd., Suite 809, Aventura, FL 33180 ☎ 305/931-6612 or 800/688-4752 🖶 305/931-6867 ⊕ www.bahama-out-islands.com. **Bahamas Tourist Office** ⌂ Box N-3701, Market Plaza, Bay St., Nassau ☎ 242/322-7500 🖶 242/328-0945 ⊕ www.bahamas.com.

# Turks & Caicos Islands

**WORD OF MOUTH**

"We actually did less than we intended. We blamed it on the high beach gravity around there. Once you got on the beach relaxing, it was so hard to get up the gumption to do anything. We're really looking forward to returning."

—Ken_in_Mass

# WELCOME TO THE TURKS & CAICOS ISLANDS

TO BAHAMAS

Caicos Passage

Three Mary's Cays

Parrot Cay

Fort George Cay

Football Fields

Pine Cay

Little Water Cay

Northwest Point

Providenciales

Grace Bay

Cheshire Hall **2**

Caicos Conch Farm **1**

Sapodilla Hill **3**

Southwest Bluff

Juba Point

West Caicos

Southwest Reef

see Providenciales map on pages 252-253
**1** - **22**

Molasses Reef

Spanish Point

Highas Cay

Juniper Hole

Platic Poin

North Caicos

North Caicos **4**

Middle Caico

Middl Caico **5**

Ocean Hole

Vine Point

Toll Cra Point

C    A    I    C    O    S         I    S    L

The largest but least developed of the islands is Middle Caicos. It's 48 square mi (124 square km) but has only 300 residents and an extensive system of limestone caves.

CAICOS BANK

Little Ambergris C

SEAL CA

White Cay

0 _____ 14 miles
0 _____ 21 km

**KEY**

| | |
|---|---|
| Dive Sites |
| **1** Exploring Sights |
| **1** Hotels & Restaurants |

Only 8 of these 40 islands between the Bahamas and Haiti are inhabited. Divers and snorkelers can explore one of the world's longest coral reefs. Land-based pursuits don't get much more taxing than teeing off at Provo's Provo Golf Club, or sunset-watching from the seaside terrace of a laid-back resort.

## GEOGRAPHICAL INFO

Though Providenciales is a major offshore banking center, sea creatures far outnumber humans in this archipelago of 40 islands, where the total population is a mere 25,000. From developed Provo to sleepy Grand Turk to sleepier South Caicos, the islands offer miles of undeveloped beaches, crystal-clear water, and laidback luxury resorts.

Little Grand Turk is the capital of the Turks & Caicos, but it's known more for excellent beach diving and whale-watching than for anything else.

ATLANTIC OCEAN

Paulover Point
Long Bay
Joe Grant Cay
Drum Point
East Caicos
Southern Bush
Big Cameron Cay
Middle Creek Cay
Sail Rock Island
Horse Cay
South Caicos
6 South Caicos
High Point
Long Cay
Hill Cays
Fish Cays
Big Ambergris Cay
MBERGRIS CAYS
Bush Cay
ot Cay

Columbus Passage

Black Forest
The Library
TURKS ISLANDS
Cotton Cay
Salt Cay 9
38 - 43
South Point
Salt Cay

see Grand Turk map on page 273
7 - 8  28 - 37

Grand Turk Island
Grand Turk
Gibb's Cay
Long Cay
East Cay
Toney Rock

Big Sand Cay

Mouchoir Passage

## TOP 4 REASONS TO VISIT THE TURKS & CAICOS ISLANDS

1. Even on well-developed Provo, there are still miles of deserted beaches without any footprints or beach umbrellas in sight.

2. The third-largest coral reef system in the world is among the world's top dive sites.

3. Island-hopping beyond the beaten path will give you a feel of the past in the present.

4. Destination spas, penthouse suites, and exclusive villas and resorts make celebrity spotting a popular sport.

# TURKS & CAICOS PLANNER

## Getting to the Turks & Caicos

Several major airlines fly nonstop to Providenciales from the U.S., London, and Toronto; there are also connecting flights through Montego Bay and San Juan. Club Med has nonstop charter service from the northeast during the high season. If you are going to one of the smaller islands, you'll usually need to make a connection in Provo.

All international flights arrive at Providenciales International Airport (PLS). There are smaller airports on Grand Turk (GDT), North Caicos NCS), Middle Caicos (MDS), South Caicos (XSC), and Salt Cay (SLX). All have paved runways in good condition. Providenciales International Airport has modern, secure arrival and check-in services.

**Hassle Factor:** Low to Medium-High

## Activities

The vast majority of people come to the Turks & Caicos to relax and enjoy the clear, turquoise water and luxurious **hotels**. The smaller islands provide a more relaxed environment and are substantially less developed. Provo has excellent **beaches**, particularly the long, soft beach along Grace Bay, where most of the island's hotel development has taken place. Some of the smaller, more isolated islands in the chain have even better beaches. Reefs are plentiful and are often close to shore, making **snorkeling** excellent. The reef and wall **diving** are among the best in the Caribbean. The same reefs that draw colorful tropical fish draw big-game fish, so deep-sea **fishing** is also very good. If you are a **golfer**, Provo has one of the Caribbean's finest courses.

## On the Ground

You can find taxis at the airports, and most resorts provide pickup service as well. A trip between Provo's airport and most major hotels runs about $15. On Grand Turk a trip from the new airport to Cockburn Town is about $8; it's $8 to $15 to hotels outside town on Grand Turk. Transfers can cost more on the smaller islands, where gas is much more expensive.

## Renting a Car

If you are staying on Provo, you may find it useful to have a car since the island is so large and the resorts so far-flung, if only for a few days of exploring or to get away from your hotel for dinner. A bus service, the Gecko Shuttle, was introduced in 2005, and many people may find that sufficient for their needs. On Grand Turk, you can rent a car, but you probably won't need to.

Car- and jeep-rental rates average $35 to $80 per day on Provo, plus a $15 surcharge per rental as a government tax. Reserve well ahead of time during the peak winter season. Most agencies offer free mileage and airport pickup service. Several agencies—both locally owned and larger chains—operate on Provo, but Ed Ricos Car Rental is the only player on Grand Turk.

## Where to Stay

Providenciales in particular is a fairly upscale destination, and there are few moderately-priced options, but gorgeous beaches and decent restaurants make it the major draw for tourists. Since virtually all the island's development is on Grace Bay, only the budget-minded are likely to stay elsewhere, though some villas are scattered around the island. You'll find a few upscale properties on the outer islands—including the famous Parrot Cay—but the majority of places are smaller inns. What you give up in luxury, however, you gain back tenfold in island charm. Many of the smaller islands are fairly isolated, and that's arguably what makes them so attractive in the first place, making your trip more of a redeeming journey than a hassle.

### TYPES OF LODGINGS

**Resorts:** Most of the resorts on Provo are upscale; many are condo-style, so at least you will have a well-furnished kitchen for breakfast and a few quick lunches. There are two all-inclusive resorts on Provo. A handful of other luxury resorts are on the smaller islands.

**Small Inns:** Aside from the exclusive, luxury resorts, most of the places on the outlying islands are smaller, modest inns with relatively few amenities. Some are devoted to diving.

**Villas & Condos:** Villas and condos are plentiful, particularly on Provo and usually represent a good value for families. However, you need to plan a few months in advance to get one of the better choices, less if you want to stay in a more developed condo complex.

## When to Go

High season in Turks and Caicos runs roughly from January through March, with the usual extra-high rates during the Christmas and New Year's holiday period. Several hotels on Provo offer shoulder-season rates in April and May. During the off-season, rates are reduced substantially, as much as 40%.

There aren't really any major festivals or events to draw travelers. The main draw in the islands is consistently good weather (except for the occasional tropical storm).

6

## Hotel & Restaurant Costs

Assume that hotels operate on the European Plan (**EP**—with no meals) unless we specify that they use either the Continental Plan (**CP**—with a Continental breakfast), Breakfast Plan (**BP**—with full breakfast), or the Modified American Plan (**MAP**—with breakfast and dinner). Other hotels may offer the Full American Plan (**FAP**—including all meals but no drinks) or may be All-Inclusive (**AI**—with all meals, drinks, and most activities).

WHAT IT COSTS in Dollars

|  | $$$$ | $$$ | $$ | $ | ¢ |
|---|---|---|---|---|---|
| **Restaurants** | over $30 | $20–$30 | $12–$20 | $8–$12 | under $8 |
| **Hotels\*** | over $350 | $250–$350 | $150–$250 | $80–$150 | under $80 |
| **Hotels\*\*** | over $450 | $350–$450 | $250–$350 | $125–$250 | under $125 |

\*EP, BP, CP    \*\*AI, FAP, MAP
Restaurant prices are for a main course excluding 10% tax and tip. Hotel prices are for two people in a  double room in high season, excluding 10% tax, 10%–15% service charge, and meal plans (except at all-inclusives).

Updated by
Jackie Mulligan

**LINDSAY—OR, AS HE LIKES TO BE KNOWN, "ZEUS"—**has a rusty saw balanced precariously against his upper thigh. His eyes are understandably focused on it. He strums an old screwdriver against its teeth, bending the saw in perfect rhythm and harmony with the drummers and guitar player of his Turks Island ripsaw band. This performance, a common sight for the friendly local crowd, leaves a lasting impression on me. I file the picture beside the indelible images of the turquoise blue patchwork of water and white-sand beaches and decide to stay right here. Right here in these tiny islands, where everybody knows your name and everyone has a story to tell.

A much-disputed legend has it that Columbus first discovered these islands in 1492. Despite being on the map for longer than most other island groups, the Turks and Caicos Islands (pronounced *kay*-kos) still remain part of the less-discovered Caribbean. More than 40 islands—only 8 inhabited—make up this self-governing British overseas territory that lies just 575 mi (862 km) southeast of Miami on the third-largest coral reef system in the world.

While ivory-white, soft sandy beaches and breathtaking turquoise waters are shared among all the islands, the landscapes are a series of contrasts; from the dry, arid bush and scrub on the flat, coral islands of Grand Turk, Salt Cay, South Caicos, and Providenciales to the greener, foliage-rich undulating landscapes of Middle Caicos, North Caicos, Parrot Cay, and Pine Cay.

The political and historical capital island of the country is Grand Turk, but most of the tourism development, which consists primarily of boutique hotels and condo resorts, has occurred in Providenciales, thanks to the 12-mi (18-km) stretch of ivory sand that is Grace Bay. Once home to a population of around 500 people plus a few donkey carts, Provo has become a hub of activity, resorts, spas, restaurants, and water sports with a population of around 18,000. It's the temporary home for the majority of visitors who come to the Turks and Caicos.

Despite the fact that most visitors land and stay in Provo, the Turks & Caicos National Museum—predictably a stickler for tradition—is in Grand Turk. The museum tells the history of the islands that have all, at one time or another, been claimed by the French, Spanish, and British as well as many pirates, long before the predominately North American visitors discovered its shores.

Marks of the country's colonial past can be found in the wooden and stone, Bermudian-style clapboard houses—often wrapped in deep-red bougainvillea—that line the streets on the quiet islands of Grand Turk, Salt Cay, and South Caicos. Donkeys roam free in and around the salt ponds, which are a legacy from a time when residents of these island communities worked hard as both slaves and then laborers to rake salt (then known as "white gold") bound for the United States and Canada. In Salt Cay the remains of wooden windmills are now home to large Osprey nests. In Grand Turk and South Caicos, the crystal-edge tidal ponds are regularly visited by flocks of rose pink flamingos hungry for the shrimp to be found in the shallow, briny waters.

Sea Island Cotton, believed to be the highest quality, was produced on the Loyalist plantations in the Caicos Islands from the 1700s. The native cotton plants can still be seen dotted among the stone remains of former plantation houses in the more fertile soils of Middle Caicos and North Caicos. Here communities in tiny settlements have retained age-old skills using fanner grasses, silver palms, and sisal to create exceptional straw baskets, bags, mats, and hats.

In all, only 25,000 people live in the Turks and Caicos Islands; more than half are Belongers, the term for the native population, mainly descended from African and Bermudian slaves who settled here beginning in the 1600s. The majority of residents work in tourism, fishing, and off-shore finance, as the country is a haven for the overtaxed. Indeed for residents and visitors, life in "TCI" is anything but taxing. But while most visitors come to do nothing—a specialty in the islands—this does not mean there's nothing to do.

# THE CAICOS

## Providenciales

6

Passengers typically become oddly silent when their plane starts its descent, mesmerized by the shallow, crystal clear turquoise waters of Chalk Sound National Park. This island, nicknamed Provo, was once called Blue Hills after the name of its first settlement. Just south of the airport and downtown area, Blue Hills still remains the closest thing you can get to a more typical Caicos Island settlement on this, the most developed of the island chain. Most of the modern resorts, exquisite spas, water-sports operators, shops, business plazas, restaurants, bars, cafés, and the championship golf course are on or close by the 12-mi stretch of Grace Bay beach. In spite of the ever increasing number of taller and grander condominium resorts—either completed or under construction—it's still possible to find deserted stretches on this priceless, ivory white shoreline. For guaranteed seclusion, hire a car and go explore the southern shores and western tip of the island, or set sail for a private island getaway on one of the many deserted cays nearby.

While you may be kept quite content enjoying the beachscape and top-notch amenities of Provo itself, it's also a great starting point for island-hopping tours by sea or by air as well as fishing and diving trips. Resurfaced roads and a regular bus service—the Gecko Shuttle—should help you get around and make the most of the main tourism and sightseeing spots.

### Where to Stay

For approximate costs, *see* the dining and lodging price chart on the Turks & Caicos Planner, at the beginning of this chapter.

VILLA RENTALS  A popular option on Provo is renting a self-catering villa or private home. For the best villa selection, plan to make your reservations three to six months in advance.

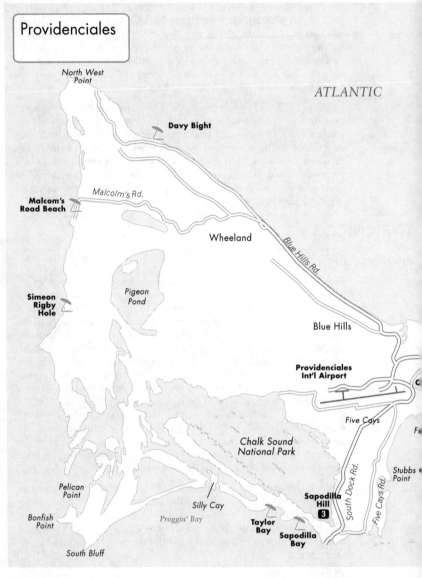

# Providenciales

*North West Point*

*ATLANTIC*

**Davy Bight**

*Malcolm's Rd.*

**Malcom's Road Beach**

Wheeland

*Blue Hills Rd.*

**Simeon Rigby Hole**

*Pigeon Pond*

Blue Hills

**Providenciales Int'l Airport**

Five Cays

*Chalk Sound National Park*

*South Dock Rd.*

*Five Cays Rd.*

Stubbs Point

**Pelican Point**

Silly Cay

**Sapodilla Hill**
**3**

**Bonfish Point**

*Proggin' Bay*

**Taylor Bay**

**Sapodilla Bay**

*South Bluff*

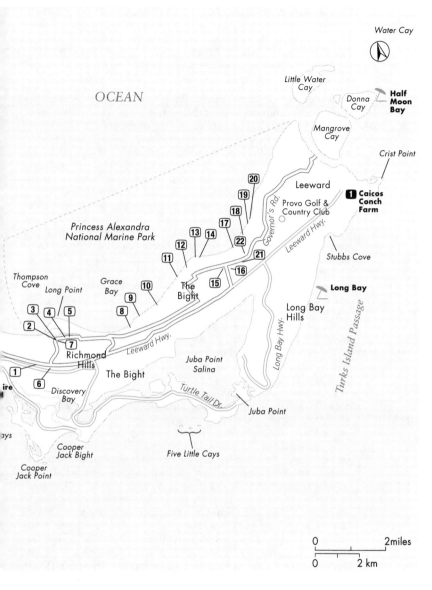

**Elliot Holdings & Management Company** (🖂 Box 235 ☎ 649/946–5355 ⊕ www.elliotholdings.com) offers a wide selection of modest to magnificent villas in the Leeward, Grace Bay, and Turtle Cove areas of Providenciales. **T. C. Safari** (🖂 Box 64 ☎ 649/941–5043 ⊕ www.tcsafari. tc) has exclusive oceanfront properties in the beautiful and tranquil Sapodilla Bay–Chalk Sound neighborhood on Provo's southwest shores.

HOTELS & RESORTS

★ ☾ $$$$ 🏨 **Beaches Turks & Caicos Resort & Spa.** The largest resort in the Turks and Caicos Islands can satisfy families as eager to spend time apart as together. Younger children and teenagers will appreciate a children's park, complete with video-game center, water slides, a swim-up soda bar, and even a teen disco. Parents may prefer the extensive spa, pretty beach, and complimentary scuba diving. Rooms, suites, and cottage villas are decorated in standard tropical themes, but the resort's major draw is found outside the rooms, where there are numerous activities and a choice of dining options, from a 1950s-style diner to a Japanese restaurant. This is one of the company's top resorts, with a generally helpful staff and excellent amenities. Butler service is included for the presidential and penthouse suites. ⊠ *Lower Bight Rd., Grace Bay* ☎ *649/946–8000 or 800/726–3257* 🖷 *649/946–8001* ⊕ *www.beaches.com* ⤶ *359 rooms, 103 suites ♤ 9 restaurants, in-room safes, cable TV with movies, miniature golf, 4 tennis courts, 5 pools, health club, hair salon, 3 hot tubs, spa, beach, dive shop, snorkeling, windsurfing, boating, parasailing, fishing, bicycles, 12 bars, nightclub, recreation room, theater, video game room, shops, babysitting, children's programs (ages newborn–12), concierge, meeting rooms, car rental* ▤ *AE, MC, V* ⭗ *All-inclusive.*

★ ☾ $$$$ 🏨 **Grace Bay Club & Villas at Grace Bay Club.** This small and stylish resort retains a loyal following because of its helpful, attentive staff and aura of unpretentious elegance. The architecture is reminiscent of Florence, with terra-cotta rooftops and a shaded courtyard, complete with fountain. Suites, all with sweeping sea views, have earthy tiles, luxurious white Egyptian cotton–covered beds, and Elemis toiletries. The ground-floor suites, fronted by large arched patios and lush azaleas, have a palatial feel and turquoise water views. New, ultraluxurious villas offer families a Grace Bay experience with large pool, a bar and grill, and an impressive range of children's activities, bouncy castle in Kids Town as well as kayaking trips and all sorts of "edutainment" to keep even teenagers well occupied. There are also cookies, of course. Anacaona remains one of the island's best restaurants; cocktails and tapas are offered in the Lounge, a Provo hot spot that gently cascades down to the beach. 🖂 *Box 128, Grace Bay* ☎ *649/946–5050 or 800/946–5757* 🖷 *649/946– 5758* ⊕ *www.gracebayclub.com* ⤶ *21 suites ♤ Restaurant, room service, in-room safes, kitchens, cable TV with movies, in-room VCRs, in-room broadband, Wi-Fi, golf privileges, 2 tennis courts, 2 pools, hot tub, spa, beach, snorkeling, windsurfing, boating, parasailing, bicycles, bar, shop, babysitting, laundry facilities, laundry service, concierge, Internet room, business services, meeting rooms* ▤ *AE, D, MC, V* ⭗ *CP.*

$$$$ 🏨 **Le Vele Resort.** The Armani family (not those Armanis, but with a similar savoir faire) have created a well-run, family-friendly condominium resort, though prices are steep given the lack of many resort-style amenities. Design, inside and out, is sleek and modern, with interiors that fuse

**CLOSE UP**

# From Salt Glows to Thalassotherapy

A TURKS ISLAND SALT GLOW, where the island's sea salt is mixed with gentle oils to exfoliate, smooth, and moisturize the skin, is just one of the treatments you can enjoy in one of the island spas. Being pampered spa-style has become as much a part of a Turks and Caicos vacation as sunning on the beach. Marine-based ingredients fit well with the Grace Bay backdrop at the Thalasso Spa at **Point Grace,** where massages take place in two simple, bleached-white cottages standing on the dune line, which means you have a spectacular view of the sea-blue hues if you manage to keep your eyes open. The spa at **The Reef Residences at Grace Bay** offers similarly sweeping vistas at its two-story treatment center specializing in Ayurveda treatments. In this spa, guests are treated head to toe and through dietary recommendations and

menu items to suit their body types. But the widest choice of Asian-inspired treatments (and the most unforgettable scenery) can be found at the 6,000-square-foot Como Shambhala Spa at the **Parrot Cay Resort,** which has outdoor whirlpools and a central beechwood lounge overlooking the shallow turquoise waters and mangroves. Provo also has a noteworthy day spa that's not in one of the Grace Bay resorts. Manager Terri Tapper of **Spa Tropique** (⊠ Ports of Call, Grace Bay Rd. ☎ 649/941–5720 ⊕ www.spatropique.com) blends Swedish, therapeutic, and reflexology massage techniques using oils made from natural plants and products produced locally and within the Caribbean region. The Turks Island Salt Glow has become one of her most popular treatments.

**6**

natural fibers with contemporary furnishings, cutting-edge appliances, and plenty of space. If you're a fan of top-notch Italian modern design, book eastside Suite 102. The glass-fronted show-room-style reception over-looks the infinity pool. Though the resort lacks any dining options, the staff will transport you to the restaurant of your choice. Local islander and manager Beverly Williams is helpful and informative. ⌂ *Box 240, Grace Bay* ☎ *649/941–8800* 🖷 *649/941–8001* ⊕ *www.levele.tc* ⇥ *18 suites* ⚒ *In-room safes, in-room hot tubs, kitchens, cable TV, in-room VCRs, in-room data ports, Wi-Fi, pool, gym, beach, snorkeling, boating, laundry facilities, concierge, Internet room* ═ *AE, D, MC, V* ⵔ *EP.*

**$$$$** 🏨 **Point Grace.** Provo's answer to Parrot Cay has attracted such celebrities as Donatella Versace. Asian-influenced rooftop domes blend with Romanesque stone pillars and wide stairways in this plush resort, which offers spacious beachfront suites and romantic cottages surrounding the centerpiece: a turquoise infinity pool with perfect views of the beach. Antique furnishings, four-poster beds, and art reproductions give a classic style to the rooms. The second-story cottage suites are especially romantic. Bleached-wood cottages, on the sand dune, house a thalassotherapy spa presided over by elegant French spa manager Edmonde Sidibé. Other highlights include the restaurants, particularly the beautiful Grace's Cottage. Honeymooners can arrange a transfer in an authentic London taxi. ⌂ *Box 700, Grace Bay* ☎ *888/924–7223 or*

*649/946–5096* 🖨 *970/513–0657 or 649/946–5097* ⊕ *www.pointgrace. com* 🖭 *23 suites, 9 cottage suites, 2 villas* & *2 restaurants, room service, in-room fax, in-room safes, some in-room hot tubs, kitchens, kitchenettes, microwaves, cable TV with movies, in-room VCRs, pool, spa, beach, snorkeling, windsurfing, boating, parasailing, fishing, bicycles, 2 bars, library, babysitting, laundry service, concierge, Internet room, business services, car rental, no-smoking rooms* ☰ *AE, D, MC, V* ⊘ *Closed Sept.* ⦶⊙⦶ *CP.*

**$$$$** 🏨 **Turks & Caicos Club.** On the quieter, western end of Grace Bay, this intimate all-suite hotel is one of a handful with a gated entrance. The buildings are in a colonial style with lovely gingerbread trim. Though the resort aims for an aura of exclusivity, the staff is warm and friendly. Safari-theme suites, complete with raised four-poster beds and spacious balconies, are a definite plus to this quiet retreat, which gets less bustle than either Grace Bay Club or Point Grace, its main competitors. ⊠ *West Grace Bay Beach, Box 687, West Grace Bay* ☎ *888/482–2582 or 649/ 946–5800* 🖨 *649/946–5858* ⊕ *www.turksandcaicosclub.com* 🖭 *21 suites* & *Restaurant, room service, fans, in-room safes, kitchens, cable TV, in-room VCRs, in-room data ports, Wi-Fi, pool, gym, beach, snorkeling, windsurfing, kayaks, bicycles, bar, laundry facilities* ☰ *AE, MC, V* ⊘ *Closed Sept.* ⦶⊙⦶ *CP.*

**$$$–$$$$** 🏨 **Club Med Turkoise.** Guests still fly in from the United States, Europe, and Canada to enjoy the scuba diving, windsurfing, and waterskiing on the turquoise waters at the doorsteps of the area's first major resort. Rooms in the village are basic and set in small, colorful bungalows (ask for a renovated room to avoid disappointment). In contrast to the otherwise tranquil Grace Bay resorts, this energetic property has a vibrant party atmosphere, nightly entertainment, and even a flying trapeze, catering primarily to fun-loving singles and couples. ⊠ *Grace Bay* ☎ *649/946– 5500 or 888/932–2582* 🖨 *649/946–5497* ⊕ *www.clubmed.com* 🖭 *293 rooms* & *2 restaurants, cable TV with movies, 8 tennis courts, pool, health club, hot tub, massage, beach, dive shop, snorkeling, windsurfing, boating, fishing, bicycles, billiards, soccer, volleyball, 3 bars, dance club, theater, shops, laundry service; no kids* ☰ *AE, D, MC, V* ⦶⊙⦶ *All-inclusive.*

★ **$$$–$$$$** 🏨 **The Reef Residences on Grace Bay.** André Niederhauser has brought his own Caribbean flair to this intimate beachfront hotel, which was refurbished and expanded in 2006. The staff is friendly, and Niederhauser is especially attentive. Turtle sightings, thanks to a location opposite one of the island's most popular snorkeling spots, are just one of the highlights. All but the cheapest rooms have sweeping views of the much less-developed western end of Grace Bay; the suites in particular are breathtaking. The resort's location, the exquisite two-story Ayurveda Spa, and romantic on-beach dining experience at the Tide Affair make this a romantic and gastronomic delight. ⊠ *Penn's Rd., Box 281, The Bight* ☎ *649/941–3713 or 800/950–2862* 🖨 *649/941–5171* ⊕ *www. cunadevida.com* 🖭 *54 suites* & *2 restaurants, room service, in-room safes, kitchens, cable TV with movies, in-room VCRs, in-room data ports, Wi-Fi 3 pools, hair salon, spa, beach, dive shop, snorkeling, boating, fishing, boccie, 2 bars, laundry facilities, concierge, Internet room, car rental* ☰ *AE, MC, V* ⦶⊙⦶ *CP.*

★ ▣ **Ocean Club Resorts.** Enormous locally painted pictures of hibiscus make
☾ **$$–$$$$** a striking first impression as you enter the reception area at one of the
island's most well-established condominium resorts. Regular shuttles run
along the ½-mi (1-km) stretch of Grace Bay Beach between two artfully
landscaped properties, Ocean Club and Ocean Club West. Both resorts
claim some of Provo's best amenities. Ocean Club has the advantage of
a quieter location away from most of the development and is just a short
walk from Provo Golf & Country Club. Ocean Club West has a larger
pool with a swim-up bar. Management and service are superb, as are
the special value packages offered throughout most of the year. Plenty
of beach and pool toys make Ocean Club a good family option. ▱ *Box
240, Grace Bay* ☎ *649/946–5880 or 800/457–8787* ▤ *649/946–5845*
⊕ *www.oceanclubresorts.com* ➥ *174 suites, 86 at Ocean Club, 88 at
Ocean Club West* ৬ *2 restaurants, in-room safes, some kitchens, some
kitchenettes, cable TV with games and movies, in-room VCRs, in-room
data ports, Wi-Fi, golf privileges, tennis court, 2 pools, gym, spa, beach,
dive shop, snorkeling, boating, 2 bars, shops, laundry facilities, concierge,
Internet room, meeting room, car rental* ▤ *AE, D, MC, V* ⊙ *EP.*

★ **$$–$$$$** ▣ **Royal West Indies Resort.** With a contemporary take on colonial architecture and the outdoors feel of a botanical garden, this unpreten-
tious resort has plenty of garden-view and beachfront studios and suites
for moderate self-catering budgets. Room 135 on the western corner has
the most dramatic ocean views. Right on Grace Bay Beach, the property has a small restaurant and bar for poolside cocktails and dining.
Ask at the reception desk for help and advice on where to go explore.
Special packages and free-night offers are available during the low season. ▱ *Box 482, Grace Bay* ☎ *649/946–5004 or 800/332–4203* ▤ *649/
946–5008* ⊕ *www.royalwestindies.com* ➥ *99 suites* ৬ *Restaurant,
fans, in-room safes, kitchenettes, cable TV with movies, in-room VCRs,
in-room data ports, in-room broadband, 2 pools, hot tub, massage, beach,
snorkeling, boating, bicycles, bar, babysitting, laundry facilities, laundry service, concierge, car rental, no-smoking rooms* ▤ *AE, MC, V* ⊙ *EP.*

☾ **$$–$$$$** ▣ **The Sands at Grace Bay.** Spacious gardens and two pools are surrounded
by six rather impersonal three-story buildings at this otherwise well-ap-
pointed resort. Guests can expect friendly and helpful staff and excel-
lent amenities, including a spa, good-size fitness room, and a beachside
cabana restaurant called Hemingway's. Sparkling ocean views from
huge screened patios and floor-to-ceiling windows are best in the ocean-
front suites in blocks 3 and 4, which are also closest to the beach,
restaurant, and pool. There are good discount packages in the off-sea-
son. ▱ *Box 681, Grace Bay* ☎ *649/941–5199 or 877/777–2637* ▤ *649/
946–5198* ⊕ *www.thesandsresort.com* ➥ *118 suites* ৬ *Restaurant,
in-room safes, some kitchens, some kitchenettes, cable TV with movies,
in-room data ports, tennis court, 2 pools, gym, hot tub, spa, beach, snor-
keling, boating, bicycles, bar, shops, babysitting, laundry facilities, laun-
dry service, concierge, Internet room, car rental, some pets allowed,
no-smoking rooms* ▤ *AE, MC, V* ⊙ *EP.*

**$$** ▣ **Comfort Suites.** This franchise hotel provides satisfactory accommodations for budget travelers thanks to good service, brightly colored and
neat rooms, and a convenient location near restaurants and bars, a dive

6

shop, a day spa, and an Internet café at Ports of Call. Rooms, though basic, are comfortable and are set around an attractively landscaped pool, which makes up for the fact that the property is across the street from the beach. A basic Continental breakfast buffet is included in the price. The bar manager, a North Caicos native named Watson, is more than happy to share his insights about the local culture. The bar attracts government officials on business trips, so it is a useful base for those seeking insights into island living. ⓓ *Box 590, Governor's Rd., Grace Bay* 🕾 *649/946–8888 or 888/678–3483* 🖷 *649/946–5444* ⊕ *www. comfortsuitestci.com* ⟋ *100 suites* ⚲ *Fans, in-room safes, refrigerators, cable TV with movies, in-room data ports, pool, bar, shops, travel services* ⊟ *AE, D, MC, V* ⦿ *CP.*

**$–$$** ▦ **Caribbean Paradise Inn.** Not far from Grace Bay Beach—but tucked away inland about a 10-minute walk from the beach—this two-story B&B has terra-cotta walls and cobalt blue trimmings. If you get to know manager Jean-Luc Bohic, you can sometimes persuade him to prepare a barbecue. Indeed, the Parisian's passion for cooking means that as well as a delicious Continental breakfast, you might be able to join him for lunch and dinner, too. Rooms are smaller than the usual Provo fare and are simply decorated with balconies overlooking the palm-fringed pool. ⓓ *Box 673, Governor's Rd., Grace Bay* 🕾 *649/946–5020* 🖷 *649/946–5020* ⊕ *www. paradise.tc* ⟋ *16 rooms* ⚲ *Fans, in-room safes, some kitchenettes, cable TV, pool, bar, Internet room, no-smoking rooms* ⊟ *AE, MC, V* ⦿ *CP.*

**$–$$** ▦ **Sibonné.** Dwarfed by most of the nearby resorts, the smallest hotel on Grace Bay beach has snug (by Provo's spacious standards) but pleasant rooms with Bermuda-style balconies and a completely circular but tiny pool. Of course, the pool is hardly used because the property is right on the beach. Rooms on the second floor have airy, vaulted ceilings; downstairs rooms have views of and access to the attractively planted courtyard garden, replete with palms, yellow elder, and exotic birdlife. The popular beachfront Bay Bistro serves breakfast, lunch, and dinner. Book early to get one of the two simple value rooms or the beachfront apartment, complete with four-poster bed, which is four steps from the beach; all three are usually reserved months in advance. ⓓ *Box 144, Grace Bay* 🕾 *649/946–5547 or 800/528–1905* 🖷 *649/946–5770* ⊕ *www. sibonne.com* ⟋ *29 rooms, 1 apartment* ⚲ *Restaurant, in-room safes, cable TV, in-room data ports, pool, beach, snorkeling, boating, bicycles, bar, laundry service* ⊟ *AE, MC, V* ⦿ *CP.*

**$** ▦ **Miramar Resort.** This ridge-top property, on one of the few hills in Provo, overlooks Turtle Cove Marina and provides a different point of view from the beachfront accommodations. Pretty but basic marina-facing and poolside rooms and cottages—which seem to be precariously balanced on the hillside—are a great value. The Magnolia Wine Bar & Restaurant has one of the best sunset views on the island. Free transfers to Grace Bay are available to guests, or it's a 15- to 20-minute walk to the closest beach. ⊠ *Turtle Cove Marina, Box 131, Turtle Cove* 🕾 *649/946–4240* 🖷 *649/946–4704* ⊕ *www.miramarresort.tc* ⟋ *19 rooms, 4 suites* ⚲ *Restaurant, refrigerators, cable TV, in-room data ports, tennis court, pool, marina, fishing, bar* ⊟ *AE, MC, V* ⦿ *EP.*

**$** ▦ **Turtle Cove Inn.** This pleasant two-story inn offers affordable and comfortable lodging in Turtle Cove Marina. All rooms have either a private balcony or patio overlooking the lush tropical gardens and pool or the marina. Besides the dockside Aqua Bar & Terrace, there's also a souvenir shop and liquor store. The inn is ideally situated for divers looking to roll from their beds into the ocean. ⊠ *Turtle Cove Marina, Box 131, Turtle Cove* ☎ 649/946–4203 or 800/887–0477 ☐ 649/946–4141 ⊕ *www. turtlecoveinn.com* ➦ *28 rooms, 2 suites* ⚴ *Restaurant, in-room safes, refrigerators, cable TV with movies, pool, marina, fishing, bicycles, bar, shops, car rental, no-smoking rooms* ☐ *AE, D, MC, V* ⦿| *EP.*

## Where to Eat

There are more than 50 restaurants on Provo, from casual to elegant, with cuisine from Asian to Tex-Mex (and everything in between). You can spot the islands' own Caribbean influence no matter where you go, exhibited in fresh seafood specials, colorful presentations, and a tangy dose of spice.

For approximate costs, *see* the dining and lodging price chart on the Turks & Caicos Planner, at the beginning of this chapter.

CARIBBEAN ✕ **Simba.** Fish-bowl-size glassware is all part of the charm at this larger-
$$–$$$ than-life, safari-theme poolside restaurant at the quieter end of Grace Bay. For the price, presentation of the Caribbean-inspired dishes with fruity twists like the grouper with curry and mango sauce is above expectations. ⊠ *Turks & Caicos Club, West Grace Bay* ☎ 649/946–5888 ⚴ *Reservations essential* ☐ *D, MC, V* ⊘ *No dinner Wed.*

DELI ✕ **Angela's Top o' the Cove New York Style Delicatessen.** Order deli sand-
¢–$ wiches, salads, and enticingly rich desserts and freshly baked pastries at this island institution on Leeward Highway, just south of Turtle Cove. From the deli case you can buy the fixings for a picnic; the shelves are stocked with an eclectic selection of fancy foodstuffs, as well as beer and wine. It's open at 6:30 AM for a busy trade in coffees, cappuccinos, and frappaccinos. ⊠ *Leeward Hwy., Turtle Cove* ☎☎ 649/946–4694 ☐ *No credit cards* ⊘ *No dinner.*

ECLECTIC ✕ **Coyaba Restaurant.** Hidden behind the former Coral Gardens, this posh
★ $$$$ eatery serves nostalgic favorites with tempting twists in conversation-piece crockery and in a palm-fringed setting. Chef Paul Newman uses his culinary expertise for the daily-changing main courses, which include exquisitely presented dishes such as crispy whole yellow snapper fried in Thai spices. To minimize any possible pretension, he keeps the resident expat crowd happy with traditional favorites like lemon meringue pie, albeit with his own tropical twist. The service is seamless. ⊠ *Coral Gardens Resort, Penn's Rd., The Bight* ☎ 649/946–5186 ⚴ *Reservations essential* ☐ *AE, MC, V* ⊘ *Closed Tues. No lunch.*

$$$$ ✕ **Grace's Cottage.** At one of the prettiest dining settings on Provo, tables are artfully set under wrought-iron cottage-style gazebos and around the wraparound verandah, which skirts the gingerbread-covered main building. In addition to such tangy and exciting entrées as the panfried red snapper served with roasted pepper sauce or the melt-in-your-mouth grilled beef tenderloin served with truffle-scented mashed potatoes, the soufflés are well worth the 15-minute wait and the top-tier price tag.

⊠ *Point Grace, Grace Bay* ☎ *649/946–5096* ⌂ *Reservations essential* ⊟ *D, MC, V* ☯ *No lunch.*

★ **$$$–$$$$** ✕ **Anacaona.** At the Grace Bay Club, this palapa-shaded restaurant has become a favorite of the country's chief minister. In spite of this, the restaurant continues to offer a memorable dining experience minus the tie, the air-conditioning, and the attitude. Start with a bottle of fine wine; then enjoy the light and healthy Mediterranean-influenced cuisine. The kitchen utilizes the island's bountiful seafood and fresh produce. Oil lamps on the tables, gently revolving ceiling fans, and the murmur of the trade winds add to the Eden-like environment. The entrancing ocean view and the careful service make it an ideal choice when you want to be pampered. ⊠ *Grace Bay Club, Grace Bay* ☎ *649/946–5050* ⌂ *Reservations essential* ⊟ *AE, D, MC, V* ☞ *No kids under 12.*

🕐 **$$–$$$$** ✕ **Gecko Grille.** You can eat indoors surrounded by giant, painted banana-leaf murals of camouflaged geckoes or out on the garden patio, where the trees are interwoven with tiny twinkling lights. Creative "Floribbean" fare combines native specialties with exotic fruits and zesty island spices and includes Black Angus steaks grilled to perfection. Pecan-encrusted grouper is a long-time menu favorite. ⊠ *Ocean Club, Grace Bay* ☎ *649/946–5885* ⊟ *AE, D, MC, V* ☯ *Closed Mon. and Tues.*

**$$$** ✕ **Caicos Café.** There's a pervasive air of celebration on the tree-shaded terrace of this popular eatery. Choose from grilled seafood, steak, lamb, or chicken served hot off the outdoor barbecue. Owner-chef Pierrik Marziou adds a French accent to his appetizers, salads, and homemade desserts, along with an outstanding collection of fine French wines. ⊠ *Grace Bay* ☎ *649/946–5278* ⊟ *AE, D, MC, V* ☯ *No lunch.*

★ **$$$** ✕ **Magnolia Wine Bar & Restaurant.** Restaurateurs since the early 1990s, hands-on owners Gianni and Tracey Caporuscio make success seem simple. Expect well-prepared, uncomplicated choices that range from European to Asian to Caribbean. The atmosphere is romantic, the presentations attractive, and the service careful. It's easy to see why the Caporuscios have a loyal following. The adjoining wine bar includes a hand-picked list of specialty wines, which can be ordered by the glass. ⊠ *Miramar Resort, Turtle Cove* ☎ *649/941–5108* ⊟ *AE, D, MC, V* ☯ *Closed Mon. No lunch.*

**$–$$** ✕ **Barefoot Café.** This lively indoor-outdoor café is always bustling, drawing residents and tourists with hearty, affordable fare that includes farm-raised conch. Fresh-roasted gourmet coffee, homemade muffins and pastries, and breakfast sandwiches start the day. Huge burgers, grinders, and savory pizzas are popular lunchtime options, along with fresh fruit smoothies and ice cream. Dinner fare always includes fresh island seafood—the barefoot seafood platter is a must for fish fanatics. Look for value-priced evening specials, such as the popular $15 Caribbean Tuesday dinner. Centrally located on the lower level of Ports of Call shopping plaza, it's also a great place to people-watch. ⊠ *Ports of Call, Governor's Rd., Grace Bay* ☎ *649/946–5282* ⊟ *AE, MC, V.*

ITALIAN ✕ **Baci Ristorante.** Aromas redolent of the Mediterranean waft from the **$$–$$$** open kitchen as you enter this intimate eatery east of Turtle Cove. Outdoor seating is on a romantic canal-front patio. The menu offers a small but varied selection of Italian dishes. Veal is prominent on the menu, but main courses also include pasta, chicken, fish, and brick-oven pizzas. House wines are personally selected by the owners and complement the tasteful wine list. Try the tiramisu for dessert with a flavored coffee drink. ⊠ *Harbour Town, Turtle Cove* ☎ *649/941–3044* ▤ *AE, MC, V.*

SEAFOOD ✕ **Aqua Bar & Terrace.** This popular restaurant on the grounds of the Turtle Cove Inn has an inviting waterfront dining deck. Specializing in locally caught seafood and farm-raised conch, the menu includes longtime favorites like wahoo sushi, pecan-encrusted conch fillets, and grilled fish served with flavorful sauces. A selection of more casual entrées, including salads and burgers, appeals to the budget-conscious. There are plenty of child-friendly menu options. ⊠ *Turtle Cove Inn, Turtle Cove Marina, Turtle Cove* ☎ *649/946–4763* ▤ *AE, MC, V.*

$–$$ ✕ **Banana Boat.** Buoys and other sea relics deck the walls of this lively restaurant-bar on the wharf. Grilled grouper, lobster salad sandwiches, conch fritters, and conch salad are among the options. Tropical drinks include the rum-filled Banana Breeze—a house specialty. ⊠ *Turtle Cove Marina, Turtle Cove* ☎ *649/941–5706* ▤ *AE, D, MC, V.*

TEX-MEX ✕ **Hey Jose's Caribbean Cantina.** Frequented by locals, this restaurant south of Turtle Cove claims to serve the island's best margaritas. Customers also return for the tasty Tex-Mex treats: tacos, tostadas, nachos, burritos, fajitas, and special-recipe hot chicken wings. Thick, hearty pizzas are another favorite—especially the Kitchen Sink, with a little bit of everything thrown in. ⊠ *Leeward Hwy., Central Square* ☎ *649/946–4812* ▤ *D, MC, V* ⊘ *Closed Sun.*

## Beaches

The best of the many secluded beaches and pristine sands around Provo can be found at **Sapodilla Bay** (⊠ North of South Dock, at end of South Dock Rd.), a peaceful ¼-mi (½-km) cove protected by Sapodilla Hill, where calm waves lap against the soft sand, and yachts and small boats move with the gentle tide. **Half Moon Bay** (⊠ 15 minutes from Leeward Marina, between Pine Cay and Water Cay, accessible only by boat) is a natural ribbon of sand linking two uninhabited cays; it's only inches above the sparkling turquoise waters and only a short boat ride away from Provo. **Grace Bay** (⊠ Grace Bay, on north shore), a 12-mi (18-km) sweeping stretch of ivory-white, powder-soft sand on Provo's north coast is simply breathtaking and home to migrating starfish as well as shallow snorkeling trails. The majority of Provo's beachfront resorts are along this shore.

## Sports & the Outdoors

BICYCLING Provo has a few steep grades to conquer, but they're short. Unfortunately, traffic on Leeward Highway makes pedaling here a less than relaxing experience, so it's best to stick to the main Grace Bay and Lower Bight roads. Most hotels have bikes available. **Provo Fun Cycles** (⊠ Ports of Call, Providenciales ☎ 649/946–5868 ⊕ www.provo.net/provofuncycles) rents double-seater scooters and bicycles (as well as jeeps, vans, cars, and SUVs). Rates are $16 per day for bicycles and $32 to $44 per day for scooters. You can rent mountain bikes at **Scooter Bob's** (⊠ Turtle Cove Marina, Turtle Cove ☎ 649/946–4684) for $15 a day.

**BOATING &** Provo's calm, reef-protected seas combine with constant easterly trade
**SAILING** winds for excellent sailing conditions. Several multihull vessels offer charters with snorkeling stops, food and beverage service, and sunset vistas. Prices range from $39 for group trips to $600 or more for private
charters. **Sail Provo** (☎ 649/946–4783 ⊕ www.sailprovo.com) runs 52-
foot and 48-foot catamarans on scheduled half-day, full-day, sunset, and
kid-friendly glow-worm cruises, where underwater creatures light up the
sea's surface for several days after each full moon. The *Atabeyra*, run
by **Sun Charters** (☎ 649/941–5363 ⊕ www.suncharters.tc), is a retired
rum runner and the choice of residents for special events.

For sightseeing below the waves, try the semisubmarine operated by **Caicos
Tours** (✉ Turtle Cove Marina, Turtle Cove ☎ 649/231–0006 ⊕ www.
caicostours.com). You can stay dry within the small, lower observatory
as it glides along on a one-hour tour of the reef, with large viewing windows on either side. The trip costs $39.

**DIVING &** The island's many shallow reefs offer excellent and exciting snorkel-
**SNORKELING** ing relatively close to shore. Try **Smith's Reef,** over Bridge Road east of
**Fodor's**Choice Turtle Cove.
★

Scuba diving in the crystalline waters surrounding the islands ranks among
the best in the Caribbean. The reef and wall drop-offs thrive with bright,
unbroken coral formations and lavish numbers of fish and marine life.
Mimicking the idyllic climate, waters are warm all year, averaging 76°F
to 78°F in winter and 82°F to 84°F in summer. With minimal rainfall
and soil runoff, visibility is usually good and frequently superb, ranging from 60 feet to more than 150 feet. An extensive system of marine
national parks and boat moorings, combined with an eco-conscious mind-
set among dive operators, contributes to an uncommonly pristine underwater environment.

Dive operators in Provo regularly visit sites at **Grace Bay** and **Pine Cay**
for spur-and-groove coral formations and bustling reef diving. They make
the longer journey to the dramatic walls at **North West Point** and **West
Caicos** depending on weather conditions. Instruction from the major
diving agencies is available for all levels and certifications, even tech-
nical diving. An average one-tank dive costs $45; a two-tank dive, $90.
There are also two live-aboard dive boats available for charter working out of Provo.

**Provo Turtle Divers** (✉ Turtle Cove Marina, Turtle Cove ☎ 649/946–4232
or 800/833–1341 ⊕ www.provoturtledivers.com), which also operates
satellite locations at the Ocean Club and Ocean Club West, has been
on Provo since the 1970s. The staff is friendly, knowledgeable, and unpretentious. With a certified marine biologist on staff, **Big Blue Unlimited** (✉ Leeward Marina, Leeward ☎ 649/946–5034 ⊕ www.bigblue.
tc) specializes in eco-friendly diving adventures, including special trips
for kids involving kayaking through the mangroves or walking along
nature trails. It also offers Nitrox and Trimix. **Caicos Adventures** (✉ La
Petite Pl., Grace Bay ☎☎ 649/941–3346 ⊕ www.tcidiving.com), run
by friendly Frenchman Fifi Kuntz, offers daily trips to West Caicos, French
Cay, and Molasses Reef. **Dive Provo** (✉ Ports of Call, Grace Bay ☎ 649/

## Diving the Turks & Caicos Islands

CLOSE UP

**SCUBA DIVING WAS THE** original water sport to draw visitors to the Turks and Caicos Islands in the 1970s. Aficionados are still drawn by the abundant marine life, including humpback whales in winter, sparkling clean waters, warm and calm seas, and the coral walls and reefs around the islands. Diving in the Turks and Caicos—especially off Grand Turk, South Caicos, and Salt Cay—is still considered among the best in the world.

Off Providenciales, dive sites are along the north shore's barrier reef. Most sites can be reached in anywhere from 10 minutes to 1½ hours. Dive sites feature spur-and-groove coral formations atop a coral-covered slope. Popular stops like **Aquarium, Pinnacles,** and **Grouper Hole** have large schools of fish,

turtles, nurse sharks, and gray reef sharks. From the south side dive boats go to **French Cay, West Caicos, South West Reef,** and **Northwest Point.** Known for typically calm conditions and clear water, the West Caicos Marine National Park is a favorite stop. The area has dramatic walls and marine life, including sharks, eagle rays, and octopus, with large stands of pillar coral and huge barrel sponges.

Off Grand Turk, the 7,000-foot coral wall **drop-off** is actually within swimming distance of the beach. Buoyed sites along the wall have swim-through tunnels, cascading sand chutes, imposing coral pinnacles, dizzying vertical drops, and undercuts where the wall goes beyond the vertical and fades beneath the reef.

---

946–5040 or 800/234–7768 ⊕ www.diveprovo.com) is a PADI five-star operation that runs daily one- and two-tank dives to popular Grace Bay sites. The **Turks and Caicos Aggressor II** (☎ 800/348–2628 ⊕ www.turksandcaicosaggressor.com), a live-aboard dive boat, plies the islands' pristine sites with weekly charters from Turtle Cove Marina.

FISHING   The island's fertile waters are great for angling—anything from bottom- and reef-fishing (most likely to produce plenty of bites and a large catch) to bonefishing and deep-sea fishing (among the finest in the Caribbean). Each July the Caicos Classic Catch & Release Tournament attracts anglers from across the islands and the United States who compete to catch the biggest Atlantic blue marlin, tuna, or wahoo. For any fishing activity, you are required to purchase a $15 visitor's fishing license; operators generally furnish all equipment, drinks, and snacks. Prices range from $100 to $375, depending on the length of trip and size of boat. For deep-sea fishing trips in search of marlin, sailfish, wahoo, tuna, barracuda, and shark, look up **Gwendolyn Fishing Charters** (⊠ Turtle Cove Marina, Turtle Cove ☎ 649/946–5321 ⊕ www.fishingtci.com). You can rent a boat with a captain for a half- or full-day of bottom- or bone-fishing through **J&B Tours** (⊠ Leeward Marina, Leeward ☎ 649/946–5047 ⊕ www.jbtours.com). Capt. Arthur Dean at **Silver Deep** (⊠ Leeward Marina, Leeward ☎ 649/946–5612 ⊕ www.silverdeep.com) is said to be among the Caribbean's finest bonefishing guides.

GOLF
Fodor'sChoice
★

The par-72, 18-hole championship course at **Provo Golf & Country Club** (⊠ Governor's Rd., Grace Bay ☎ 649/946–5991) is a combination of lush greens and fairways, rugged limestone outcroppings, and freshwater lakes and is ranked among the Caribbean's top courses. Fees are $130 for 18 holes with shared cart. Premium golf clubs are available.

HORSEBACK
RIDING

Provo's long beaches and secluded lanes are ideal for trail rides on horseback. **Provo Ponies** (☎ 649/946–5252 ⊕ www.provo.net/provoponies) offers morning and afternoon rides for all levels of experience. A 45-minute ride costs $45; an 80-minute ride is $65.

PARASAILING

A 15-minute parasailing flight over Grace Bay is available for $70 (single) or $120 (tandem) from **Captain Marvin's Watersports** (☎ 649/231–0643 ⊕ www.captainmarvinsparasail.com), who will pick you up at your hotel for your flight. The views as you soar over the bite-shape Grace Bay area, with spectacular views of the barrier reef, are truly unforgettable.

TENNIS

You can rent equipment at **Provo Golf & Country Club** (⊠ Grace Bay ☎ 649/946–5991 ⊕ www.provogolf.com) and play on the two lighted courts, which are among the island's best courts.

WINDSURFING

Windsurfers find the calm, turquoise water of Grace Bay ideal. **Windsurfing Provo** (⊠ Ocean Club, Grace Bay ☎ 649/946–5649 ⊠ Ocean Club West, Grace Bay ☎ 649/231–1687 ⊕ www.windsurfingprovo.tc) rents kayaks, motorboats, Windsurfers, and Hobie Cats and offers windsurfing instruction.

## Shopping

There are several main shopping areas in Provo: Market Place and Central Square are on Leeward Highway about ½ mi to 1 mi (1 to 1½ km) east of downtown; Grace Bay has the new Saltmills complex and La Petite Place retail plaza as well as the original Ports of Call shopping village. Two newly constructed markets on the beach near the Ocean Club and the Beaches Resort allow for barefooted shopping. Hand-woven straw baskets and hats, polished conch-shell crafts, paintings, wood carvings, model sailboats, handmade dolls, and metalwork are crafts native to the islands and nearby Haiti. The natural surroundings have inspired local and international artists to paint, sculpt, print, craft, and photograph; most of their creations are on sale in Providenciales.

★ **Anna's Art Gallery & Studio** (⊠ The Saltmills, Grace Bay ☎ 449/231–3293) sells original artworks, silk-screen paintings, sculptures, and handmade sea-glass jewelry. **ArtProvo** (⊠ Ocean Club Plaza, Grace Bay ☎ 649/941–4545) is the island's largest gallery of designer wall art; also shown are native crafts, jewelry, hand-blown glass, candles, and other gift items.

★ **Bamboo Gallery** (⊠ Leeward Hwy., The Market Place ☎☎ 649/946–4748) sells Caribbean art, from vivid Haitian paintings to wood carvings and local metal sculptures, with the added benefit that artists are usually on-hand to describe their works. **Caicos Wear Boutique** (⊠ La Petite Pl., Grace Bay Rd., Grace Bay ☎ 649/941–3346) is filled with casual resort wear, including Caribbean-print shirts, swimsuits from Brazil, sandals, beach jewelry, and gifts. **Greensleeves** (⊠ Central Sq., Leeward

Hwy., Turtle Cove 🖼 649/946–4147) offers paintings and pottery by local artists, baskets, jewelry, and sisal mats and bags. **Marilyn's Craft** (✉ Ports of Call, Grace Bay 🕾 No phone) sells handmade dolls, rag rugs, and wood carvings, plus tropical clothing and knickknacks. **Royal Jewels** (✉ Providenciales International Airport 🕾 649/941–4513 ✉ Arch Plaza 🕾 649/946–4699 ✉ Beaches Turks & Caicos Resort & Spa, Grace Bay 🕾 649/946–8285 ✉ Club Med Turkoise, Grace Bay 🕾 649/946–5602) sells gold and other jewelry, designer watches, perfumes, fine leather goods and cameras—all duty-free—at several outlets. Termed "the best little water-sports shop in Provo," **Seatopia** (✉ Ports of Call, Grace Bay 🕾 649/941–3355) sells reasonably priced scuba and snorkeling equipment, swimwear, beachwear, sandals, hats, and related water gear and swim toys. The **Tourist Shoppe** (✉ Central Sq., Leeward Hwy., Turtle Cove 🕾 649/946–4627) has a large selection of souvenirs, including CDs, cards and postcards, beach toys, and sunglasses. If you need to supplement your beach-reading stock or are looking for island-specific materials, ★ ☾ visit the **Unicorn Bookstore** (✉ In front of Graceway IGA Mall, Leeward Hwy., Grace Bay 🕾 649/941–5458) for a wide assortment of books and magazines, lots of information and guides about the Turks and Caicos Islands and the Caribbean, and a large children's section with crafts, games, and art supplies.

For a large selection of duty-free liquor, visit **Discount Liquors** (✉ Leeward Hwy., east of Suzie Turn Rd. 🕾 649/946–4536). Including a large fresh-produce section, bakery, gourmet deli, and extensive meat counter, **Graceway IGA Supermarket** (✉ Leeward Hwy., Grace Bay 🕾 649/941–5000), Provo's largest, is likely to have what you're looking for. Be prepared for sticker shock, as prices are much higher than you would expect at home. Besides having a licensed pharmacist on duty, **Lockland Trading Co.** (✉ Neptune Plaza, Grace Bay 🕾 649/946–8242)Stay sells flavored coffees, snacks, ice cream, and a selection of souvenirs.

## Nightlife

Residents and tourists alike flock to the **BET Soundstage & Gaming Lounge** (✉ Leeward Hwy., Grace Bay 🕾 649/941–4318) for video lottery games, live music, and other entertainment, a casino, and a late-night disco almost every night. **Bonnie's** (✉ Lower Bight Rd., Grace Bay 🕾 649/941–8452) is a favorite local spot for sports events, movie nights, and endless happy hour specials. On Friday nights you can find a local band and lively crowd at **Calico Jack's Restaurant & Bar** (✉ Ports of Call, Grace Bay 🕾 649/946–5129). A popular gathering spot for locals to shoot pool, play darts, slam dominoes, and catch up on gossip is **Club Sodax Sports Bar** (✉ Leeward Hwy., Grace Bay 🕾 649/941–4540). You won't go hungry with snacks such as conch and fish fingers, jerk pork, and typical native dishes.

## Exploring Providenciales

*Numbers in the margin correspond to points of interest on the Turks & Caicos Islands map.*

☾ ❶ **Caicos Conch Farm.** On the northeast tip of Provo, this is a major mariculture operation where mollusks are farmed commercially (more than

3 million conch are here). Guided tours are available; call to confirm times. The small gift shop sells conch-related souvenirs, and the world's only pet conchs, Sally and Jerry, seem more than happy to come out of their shells. ⊠ *Leeward-Going-Through, Leeward* ☎ *649/946–5330* ⊠ *$6* ⊙ *Mon.–Sat. 9–4.*

**❷ Cheshire Hall.** Standing eerily just west of downtown Provo are the remains of a circa-1700 cotton plantation owned by Loyalist Thomas Stubbs. A trail weaves through the ruins, where interpretive signs tell the story of the island's doomed cotton industry. A variety of local plants are also identified. To visit, you must arrange for a tour through the Turks & Caicos National Trust. The lack of context can be disappointing for history buffs; a visit to North Caicos Wades Green Plantation or the Turks & Caicos National Museum could well prove a better fit. ⊠ *Near downtown Providenciales* ☎ *649/941–5710 for National Trust* ⊕ *www.turksandcaicos.tc/nationaltrust* ⊠ *$5* ⊙ *Daily by appointment.*

**❸ Sapodilla Hill.** On this cliff overlooking the secluded Sapodilla Bay, you can discover rocks carved with the names of shipwrecked sailors and dignitaries from TCI maritime and colonial past. The less adventurous can see molds of the carvings at Provo's International Airport. ⊠ *Off South Dock Rd., west of South Dock.*

## Little Water Cay

★ ☾ This small, uninhabited cay is a protected area under the Turks & Caicos National Trust. On these 150 acres are two trails, small lakes, red mangroves, and an abundance of native plants. Boardwalks protect the ground, and interpretive signs explain the habitat. The cay is home to about 2,000 rare, endangered rock iguanas. Experts say the iguanas are shy, but these creatures actually seem rather curious. They waddle right up to you, as if posing for a picture. Several water-sports operators from Provo and North Caicos include a stop on the island as a part of their snorkel or sailing excursions. There's a $5 fee for a permit to visit the cay, and the proceeds go toward conservation in the islands.

## Parrot Cay

Once said to be a hideout for pirate Calico Jack Rackham and his lady cohorts Mary Reid and Anne Bonny, the 1,000-acre cay, between Fort George Cay and North Caicos, is now the site of an ultraexclusive hideaway resort.

For approximate costs, *see* the dining and lodging price chart on the Turks & Caicos Planner, at the beginning of this chapter.

★ **$$$$** 🏨 **Parrot Cay Resort.** This private paradise—a favorite for celebrities and aspiring ones—comes with all the trimmings you'd expect for the substantial price. Elaborate oceanfront villas border the island, and their wooden, Far Eastern feel contrasts with the rather bland hillside terracotta and stucco building that houses the spacious suites. Suite and villa interiors are a minimalist and sumptuous mix of cool-white interiors, Indonesian furnishings, and four-poster beds. The villas are the ultimate indulgence, with heated lap-edge pools, hot tubs, and butler service. The resort's main pool is surrounded by a round, thatched bar and the Asian-inspired Lotus restaurant. The giant Como Shambhala Spa takes destination spas to a whole new level with Indonesian and Balinese therapists. If you have traveled far, Shambhala's own jetlag tea will put the zing back in your ying. If you wish to splash out in Parrot style without remortgaging your home, look out for special three- to five-night packages in the off-season. ⊠ *Parrot Cay* ✆ *Box 164, Providenciales* ☎ *649/946–7788* 🖶 *649/946–7789* ⬚ *www.parrotcay.como.bz* ⬚ *42 rooms, 4 suites, 14 villas* ⚹ *2 restaurants, room service, in-room safes, some kitchens, some kitchenettes, minibars, cable TV with movies, in-room VCRs, in-room data ports, Wi-Fi, 2 tennis courts, pool, health club, hot tub, Japanese baths, sauna, spa, Turkish bath, beach, snorkeling, windsurfing, boating, waterskiing, fishing, 2 bars, library, babysitting, laundry service, Internet room, airport shuttle* ▭ *AE, MC, V* ⦿ *BP.*

## Pine Cay

Pine Cay's 2½-mi-long (4-km-long) beach is among the most beautiful in the archipelago. The 800-acre private island is home to a secluded resort and around 37 private residences.

For approximate costs, *see* the dining and lodging price chart on the Turks & Caicos Planner, at the beginning of this chapter.

**$$$$**   🔲 **Meridian Club.** You might feel unplugged when you step onto Pine
Fodor'sChoice   Cay, since there are no televisions, telephones, or traffic to be found on
★   the tiny private island. The charm of this resort, which was built in the 1970s, is that it never changes, and unlike Parrot Cay, it prides itself on simplicity rather than celebrity. The simple beachfront cottages, most of the staff, and what is perhaps the world's smallest airport (in truth, a gazebo) have all stayed pretty much the same for years. The 2½-mi (4-km)stretch of beach is deserted, and instead of roads you can find nature trails and sun-dappled paths that crisscross the island, which can be explored by bike or on foot. Rates are fully inclusive and even include the flight from Provo. Cuisine is excellent, with fresh seafood and delicious cakes and tarts served at lunch, dinner, and afternoon tea. Far from being an ivory tower experience, the club enables you to become a part of a small community. Guests are mostly overstressed executives, mature couples, and honeymooners; a large percentage of guests are repeats. Families are welcomed in June. ⊠ *Pine Cay* ☎ *866/746–3229 or 770/500–1134* 🖶 *649/941–7010, 203/602–2265 in the U.S.* ⊕ *www.meridianclub.com* ⬚ *12 rooms, 7 cottages* ⚹ *Restaurant, fans, tennis court, pool, beach, snorkeling, windsurfing, boating, fishing, bicycles, hiking, bar, library, laundry service, Internet room, airstrip; no a/c, no room phones, no room TVs, no kids under 12* ▭ *No credit cards* ⦿ *AI* ⊗ *Closed Aug.–Oct.*

## North Caicos

❹   Thanks to abundant rainfall, this 41-square-mi (106-square-km) island is the lushest of the Turks and Caicos. Bird lovers can see a large flock

## Coming Attractions

**THE BUZZ ABOUT TURKS AND CAICOS** has increased steadily over the last five years, a fact that hasn't been lost on the ears of developers. Grace Bay, a 12-mi (19-km) stretch of ivory sand on Providenciales, is still a favored location for new properties. At the time of writing, several new resorts had almost been completed on Grace Bay, including the breathtaking **Somerset**, a luxurious retreat owned by the Sheikh of Qatar, and **Seven Stars,** a seven-story condominium resort that will be taking the destination to new heights, quite literally. Given the volume of construction, it is worth asking your hotel about nearby construction projects to avoid the noise, dust, and obstructed views that can sometimes result. Investors are looking beyond this golden north-shore strip. An

**Aman** resort is planned for Provo's North West Point, for example.

West Caicos, the most westerly cay—closest to one of the best dive sites around Turks and Caicos—will be home to **Molasses Reef,** a resort owned by Ritz-Carlton. On North Caicos, the handful of small guesthouses will be joined by **St. Charles,** a five-story condominium resort on Horse Stable Beach, and the three-story **Royal Reef Resort at Sandy Point.** Even South Caicos, the islands' sleepy fishing capital, has three new hotels under construction; the **South Caicos Lodge** and the **Old Commissioner's House** are under renovation at this writing. All of this adds up to more choice for vacationers wanting to explore and be pampered in the very near future.

---

of flamingos here, anglers can find shallow creeks full of bonefish, and history buffs can visit the ruins of a Loyalist plantation. Although there's no traffic, almost all the roads are paved, so bicycling is an excellent way to sightsee. The island is predicted to become one of the next tourism hot spots, and foundations have been laid for condo resorts on Horse Stable beach and Sandy Point. Even though it's a quiet place, you can find some small eateries around the airport and in Whitby, giving you a chance to try local and seafood specialties, sometimes served with homegrown okra or corn.

### Where to Stay

For approximate costs, *see* the dining and lodging price chart on the Turks & Caicos Planner, at the beginning of this chapter.

**$$** 🏨 **Pelican Beach Hotel.** North Caicos islanders Susan and Clifford Gardiner built this small palmetto-fringed hotel in the 1980s on the quiet, mostly deserted Whitby Beach. The couple's friendliness and insights into island life, not to mention Susan's home-baked bread and island dishes (Cliff's favorite is her cracked conch and island lobster), are the best features. Over the years upkeep of the property has been somewhat inconsistent, but rooms are nevertheless comfortable. Best, the line of cottage-style rooms 1 through 6 is exactly 5 steps from the windswept beach. ✉ *Whitby* 🕾 *649/946–7112* 🖷 *649/946–7139* ⊕ *www. pelicanbeach.tc* 🛏 *14 rooms, 2 suites* ⌂ *Restaurant, beach, snorkeling,* *fishing, bar; no room phones, no room TVs* ⊟ *MC, V* ⊘ *Closed Aug. 15–Sept. 15* ⦿ *MAP.*

**$–$$** 🏨 **Ocean Beach Hotel & Condominiums.** On Whitby Beach, this horseshoe-shape two-story, solar-paneled resort offers ocean views, comfortable and neatly furnished apartments, and a freshwater pool at quite reasonable rates. The Silver Palm restaurant is a welcome addition to the on-site amenities, which also include a dive and water-sports operation called Beach Cruiser. Unit 5 has the best views over the beach—especially for honeymooners, who automatically receive a 10% discount. You pay extra for air-conditioning, however. ✉ *Whitby* ☎ *649/946–7113, 800/710–5204, 905/690–3817 in Canada* 📠 *649/946–7386* ⊕ *www.turksandcaicos.tc/oceanbeach* 🛏 *10 suites* ⚘ *Restaurant, fans, some kitchenettes, pool, beach, dive shop, snorkeling, boating, fishing, bicycles, bar, car rental; no room TVs* ⊟ *AE, D, MC, V* ⊘ *Closed June 15–Oct. 15* ⦿ *EP.*

### Beaches

The beaches of North Caicos are superb for shallow snorkeling and sunset strolls, and the waters offshore have excellent scuba diving. Horse Stable Beach is the main beach for annual events and beach parties. Whitby Beach usually has a gentle tide, and its thin strip of sand is bordered by palmetto plants and taller trees.

### Exploring North Caicos

**Flamingo Pond.** This is a regular nesting place for the beautiful pink birds. They tend to wander out in the middle of the pond, so bring binoculars.

**Kew.** This settlement has a small post office, a school, a church, and ruins of old plantations—all set among lush tropical trees bearing limes, papayas, and custard apples. Visiting Kew will give you a better understanding of the daily life of many islanders.

🔄 **Wades Green.** Visitors can view well-preserved ruins of the greathouse, overseer's house, and surrounding walls of one of the most successful plantations of the Loyalist era. A lookout tower provides views for miles. Contact the National Trust for tour details. ✉ *Kew* ☎ *649/941–5710 for National Trust* 🎫 *$5* ⊘ *Daily, by appointment only.*

## Middle Caicos

**❺** At 48 square mi (124 square km) and with fewer than 300 residents, this is the largest and least developed of the inhabited islands in the Turks and Caicos chain. A limestone ridge runs to about 125 feet above sea level, creating dramatic cliffs on the north shore and a cave system farther inland. Middle Caicos has rambling trails along the coast; the **Crossing Place Trail**, maintained by the National Trust, follows the path used by the early settlers to go between the islands. Inland are quiet settlements with friendly residents.

### Where to Stay

For approximate costs, *see* the dining and lodging price chart on the Turks & Caicos Planner, at the beginning of this chapter.

**$$** 🏠 **Blue Horizon Resort.** At this resort, undulating cliffs skirt one of the most dramatic beaches in the Turks and Caicos. Blue-tin roofs mark the small self-contained open-plan cottages. Screened-in porches and careful positioning ensure that all of the cottages have unobstructed views along the cliffs and out to sea. Owners Mike and Nikki Witt can purchase your groceries before you get there, as resources and amenities on the island are minimal. But the lack of amenities and development is actually what makes this spot so special. Tropical Cottage has large, attractive murals; Dragon View cottage has spectacular views of Dragon Cay and is closest to the Crossing Place trail that winds along the clifftops. ⊠ *Mudjin Harbor, Conch Bar* ☎ *649/946–6141* 🖷 *649/946–6139* ⊕ *www.bhresort.com* 🛏 *5 cottages, 2 villas* ⚬ *Fans, some kitchens, some kitchenettes, cable TV with movies, beach, snorkeling, fishing, bicycles, hiking, laundry service; no a/c in some rooms, no phones in some rooms, no TV in some rooms* 🖃 *AE, MC, V* 🍽 *EP.*

### Exploring Middle Caicos

🖐 **Conch Bar Caves.** These limestone caves have eerie underground lakes and milky-white stalactites and stalagmites. Archaeologists have discovered Lucayan Indian artifacts in the caves and the surrounding area. The caves are inhabited by some harmless bats. If you visit, don't worry—they don't bother visitors. It's best to get a guide. If you tour the caves, be sure to wear sturdy shoes, not sandals.

CAVE TOURS  Taxi driver and fisherman **Cardinal Arthur** (☎ 649/946–6107) can give you a good cave tour. Local cave specialist and taxi driver **Ernest Forbes** (☎ 649/946–6140) is also happy to oblige with a cave tour and may even arrange a fixed-fee lunch at his house afterward if you ask nicely.

## South Caicos

**6** This 8½-square-mi (21-square-km) island was once an important salt producer; today it's the heart of the fishing industry. Nature prevails, with long, white beaches, jagged bluffs, quiet backwater bays, and salt flats. Diving and snorkeling on the pristine wall and reefs are a treat enjoyed by only a few.

### Beaches

The beaches at **Belle Sound** on South Caicos will take your breath away, with lagoonlike waters. On the opposite side of the ridge from Belle Sound, **Long Bay** is an endless stretch of beach, but it can be susceptible to rough surf; however, on calmer days this stretch makes you feel you're on a deserted island. Due south of South Caicos is **Big Ambergris Cay,** an uninhabited cay about 14 mi (23 km) beyond the Fish Cays, with a magnificent beach at Long Bay. To the north of South Caicos, uninhabited **East Caicos** has a beautiful 17-mi (27-km) beach on its north coast. The island was once a cattle range and the site of a major sisal-growing industry. Both places are accessible only by boat.

### Exploring South Caicos

At the northern end of the island are fine white-sand beaches; the south coast is great for scuba diving along the drop-off; and there's excellent

## All in the Family

BELONGERS, from the taxi driver meeting you to the chef feeding you, are often connected. "Oh, him?" you will hear. "He my cousin!" As development has been mercifully slow, such family connections, as well as crafts, bush medicine, ripsaw music, storytelling, and even recipes, have remained constant. But where do such traditions come from? Recently, researchers came closer to finding out. Many Belongers had claimed that their great-great-grandparents had told them their forebears had come directly from Africa. For decades their stories were ignored. Indeed, most experts believed that Belongers were descendants of mostly second-generation Bermudian and Caribbean slaves.

In 2005, museum researchers continued their search for a lost slave ship called *Trouvadore*. The ship, which wrecked off East Caicos in 1841, carried a cargo of 193 Africans, captured to be sold into slavery, almost all of whom miraculously survived the wreck. As slavery had

been abolished in this British territory at the time, all the Africans were found and freed in the Turks and Caicos Islands. Since there were only a few thousand inhabitants in the islands at the time, these first-generation African survivors were a measurable minority (about 7% of the population then). Researchers have concluded that all the existing Belongers may be linked by blood or marriage to this one incident.

During one expedition, divers found a wrecked ship of the right time period. If these remains are *Trouvadore*, the Belongers may finally have a physical link to their past, to go with their more intangible cultural traditions. So while you're in the islands, look closely at the intricately woven baskets, listen carefully to the African rhythms in the ripsaw music, and savor the stories you hear. They may very well be the legacy of *Trouvadore* speaking to you from the past. For more information, check out ⊕ www.slaveshiptrouvadore.com.

6

snorkeling off the windward (east) coast, where large stands of elkhorn and staghorn coral shelter several varieties of small tropical fish. Spiny lobster and queen conch are found in the shallow Caicos Bank to the west and are harvested for export by local processing plants. The bone-fishing here is some of the best in the West Indies. **Beyond the Blue** (⊠ Cockburn Harbour ☎ 649/231–1703 ⊕ www.beyondtheblue.com) offers bonefishing charters on a specialized airboat, which can operate in less than a foot of water. Lodging packages are available

**Boiling Hole.** Abandoned salinas make up the center of this island—the largest, across from the downtown ballpark, receives its water directly from an underground source connected to the ocean through this boiling hole.

**Cockburn Harbour.** The best natural harbor in the Caicos chain hosts the South Caicos Regatta, held each year in May.

# THE TURKS

## Grand Turk

Just 7 mi (11 km) long and a little over 1 mi (2½ km) wide, this island, the capital and seat of the Turks and Caicos government, has been a longtime favorite destination for divers eager to explore the 7,000-foot-deep pristine coral walls that drop down only 300 yards out to sea. On shore, the tiny, quiet island is home to white-sand beaches, the National Museum, and a small population of wild horses and donkeys, which leisurely meander past the white-walled courtyards, pretty churches, and bougainvillea-covered colonial inns on their daily commute into town. A new cruise-ship dock that opened at the southern end of the island in 2006 is set to bring around 300,000 visitors per year. In spite of the dramatic changes this could make to this peaceful tourist spot, the dock is likely to be self-contained and is about 3 mi (5 km) from the tranquil, small hotels of Cockburn Town, Pillory Beach, and the Ridge and far from most of the western-shore dive sites. However, some development will alter and in some cases open up a few new historic sites, including Grans Turk's Old Prison, Gun Hill, and the Lighthouse.

### Where to Stay

Accommodations include original Bermudian inns, more modern but small beachfront hotels, and very basic to well-equipped self-catering suites and apartments. Almost all hotels offer dive packages, which are an excellent value.

**$$** **The Arches of Grand Turk.** Upstairs and downstairs, east- and west-facing balconies from these four ridgetop town houses ensure nicely framed views of both sunrise and sunset. Canadian husband-and-wife team Wally and Cecile Wennick left Florida in the 1990s after more than a decade in the hospitality industry to create this hillside home away from home, less than a five-minute walk from the deserted east beach. The well-equipped town houses are peppered with Cecille's handicrafts, including painted glass bottles, embroidery, and wall hangings that combine to give the airy houses a homespun feel. Weekly housekeeping is included in the rate, but daily maid service costs extra. ⊠ *Lighthouse Rd., Box 226* 🏠 *649/946–2941* ⊕ *www.grandturkarches.com* 🛏 *4 town houses* ⚲ *BBQs, fans, kitchens, cable TV with movies, pool, bicycles, laundry service* ☰ *D, MC, V* ⦿ *EP.*

**$$** **Bohio Dive Resort & Spa.** Formerly the Pillory Beach Resort, this resort sits on an otherwise deserted stretch of beach. It's a dream come true for British couple Kelly Shanahan and Nick Gillings, who have created their own retreat on Grand Turk after years of visiting the tiny island. The resort's restaurant is the best on the island. You can relax with yoga sessions or party with the locals at the Sunday sail and kayak races or Thursday night's "pit party" with roasted meats and music. ⊠ *Pillory Beach* 🏠 *649/946–2135* 🖨 *649/946–2135* ⊕ *www.bohioresort.com* 🛏 *12 rooms, 4 suites* ⚲ *Restaurant, some kitchenettes, cable TV, pool, spa, beach, dive shop, snorkeling, 2 bars, Internet room* ☰ *AE, MC, V* ⦿ *EP.*

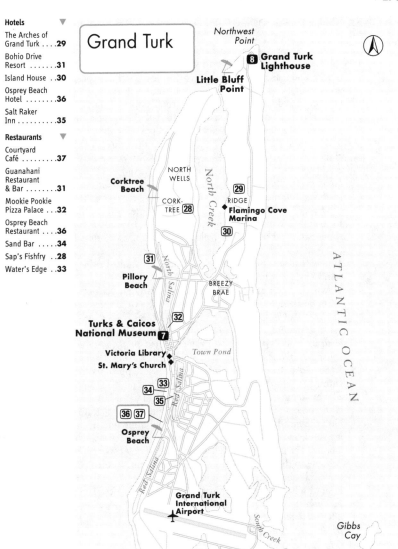

# Grand Turk

*Northwest Point*

**8** **Grand Turk Lighthouse**

**Little Bluff Point**

NORTH WELLS

**Corktree Beach**

*North Creek*

CORK-TREE **28**

**29** RIDGE

◆ **Flamingo Cove Marina**

**30**

**31** *North Salina*

**Pillory Beach**

BREEZY BRAE

ATLANTIC OCEAN

**32**

**Turks & Caicos National Museum** **7**

**Victoria Library** ◆
**St. Mary's Church** ◆

*Town Pond*

**34** **33**
**35**

*Red Salina*

**36** **37**

**Osprey Beach**

*Red Salina*

**Grand Turk International Airport** ✈

*South Creek*

*Gibbs Cay*

*Hawks Pond*

WATERLOO

*Round Cay*

**Governor's Beach**

◆ **Former U.S. A.F.B.**

◆ **Hawks Nest Plantation**

*Hawks Nest Salina*

**Cruise Ship Port** 🚢

**White Sands Beach**

**Columbus' Landfall** ◆

0       1/2 mi
0       1/2 km

☾ **$$** ▦ **Island House.** Owner Colin Brooker gives his guests a personal introduction to the capital island, thanks to his family's long history here. His years of business travel experience have gone into the comfortable, peaceful suites that overlook North Creek. Balcony barbecues, shaded hammocks, and flatscreen TVs are served against a backdrop of splendid island and ocean views. Suites 3 and 7 command the best sunset views. Graduated terraces descend the hillside to a small pool surrounded by pink-and-white climbing bougainvillea, creating the feel of a Mediterranean hideaway. An array of inflatable toys keeps kids happy. The deserted east beach is a 12-minute walk away. If you stay more than three nights, a car is included in the rental price. ⊠ *Lighthouse Rd., Box 36* ☎ *649/946–1519* 🖷 *649/946–2646* ⊕ *www.islandhouse-tci.com* ➴ *8 suites* ♻ *BBQs, kitchenettes, cable TV with movies, pool, dock, fishing, bicycles, laundry facilities, Internet room, some pets allowed* ⊟ *AE, D, MC, V* ⦿ *EP.*

**$–$$** ▦ **Osprey Beach Hotel.** Grand Turk veteran hotelier Jenny Smith has transformed this two-story oceanfront hotel with her artistic touches. Palms, frangipani, and deep green azaleas frame it like a painting. Inside, evocative island watercolors, painted by her longtime friend, Nashville artist Tupper Saussay, thread through the property. Vaulted ceilings and Indonesian four-poster beds are the highlight of upstairs suites 51, 52, and 53. Downstairs you can enjoy beach access through your own garden. On the opposite side of Duke Street, 13 new suites were slated to open in 2006. ⊠*Duke St., Cockburn Town* ☎*649/946–2666* 🖷*649/946–2817* ⊕*www.ospreybeachhotel.com* ➴ *11 rooms, 16 suites* ♻ *Restaurant, some kitchenettes, cable TV with movies, golf privileges, pool, beach, snorkeling, bar, some pets allowed* ⊟ *AE, MC, V* ⦿ *EP* ☞ *3-night minimum.*

**$** ▦ **Salt Raker Inn.** A large anchor on the sun-dappled pathway marks the entrance to this 19th-century house, which is now an unpretentious inn. The building was built by a shipwright and has a large, breezy balcony with commanding views over the sea, but its best feature is hidden behind the facade: a secret garden of tall tamarind and neme trees, climbing vines, hanging plants, potted hibiscus, climbing bougainvillea, and even a pond. The greenery, as well as providing a quiet spot for natural shade, is home to the inn's Secret Garden Restaurant. Rooms A2, B2, and C2 are nicely shaded havens but have no sea views. Upstairs, Rooms G and H share a balcony with unobstructed views of the ocean and Duke Street. ⊠ *Duke St., Box 1, Cockburn Town* ☎ *649/946–2260* 🖷 *649/946–2263* ⊕ *www.hotelsaltraker.com* ➴ *10 rooms, 3 suites* ♻ *Restaurant, refrigerators, cable TV, in-room data ports, bar* ⊟ *D, MC, V* ⦿ *EP.*

## Where to Eat

Conch in every shape and form, fresh grouper, and lobster (in season) are the favorite dishes at the laid-back restaurants that line Duke Street in Grand Turk and Balfour Town in Salt Cay. Away from these more touristy areas, smaller and less-expensive eateries serve chicken and ribs, curried goat, peas and rice, and other native island specialties. Prices are more expensive than in the United States, as most of the produce has to be imported.

AMERICAN ✕ **Water's Edge.** Seamus, the British owner of this lively, well-established bar and restaurant, is locally known as Shameless, owing to the
☾ **$$–$$$**

potent concoctions he creates and pours. Arrive early to secure a table on the deck for spectacular views of the sunset and the legendary green flash. The eclectic menu includes seafood and chicken quesadillas, conch salads, and burgers. There's live music on weekends and special internationally themed evenings once a week, so check the board for details. Service can be slow, so order before you're too hungry. ⊠ *Duke St., Cockburn Town* ☎ *649/946–1680* ▤ *MC, V.*

**$–$$** ✕ **Sand Bar.** Run by two Canadian sisters, this popular beachside bar is a good value, though the menu is limited to fish-and-chips, quesadillas, and similarly basic bar fare. The tented wooden terrace jutting out on to the beach provides shade during the day, making it an ideal lunch spot. The service is friendly, and the local crowd often spills into the street. ⊠ *Duke St., Cockburn Town* ▤ *MC, V.*

**¢–$** ✕ **Courtyard Café.** A great spot for people-watching, this spot offers omelets, wraps, and giant subs, as well as cakes for those with sweeter tastes. Daily specials range from lasagna and quiche to island-style beef patties. ⊠ *Duke St., Cockburn Town* ☎ *649/946–1453* ▤ *AE, MC, V.*

CARIBBEAN ✕ **Osprey Beach Restaurant.** At the top of Duke Street, this has become
★ **$$–$$$** the place to be on Sunday and Wednesday nights, when a sizzling barbecue of ribs, chicken, and lobster combines with live "rake-and-scrape" music from a local group called High Tide to draw an appreciative crowd. Arrive before 8 PM to secure beachside tables and an unrestricted view of the band. The rest of the week, enjoy more elegant and eclectic fare accompanied by an increasingly impressive wine list. ⊠ *Duke St., Cockburn Town* ☎ *649/946–2666* ▤ *MC, V.*

**¢–$** ✕ **Mookie Pookie Pizza Palace.** Local husband-and-wife team "Mookie" and "Pookie" have created a wonderful backstreet parlor that has gained well-deserved popularity over the years as much more than a pizza place. At lunchtime, the tiny eatery is packed with locals ordering specials like steamed beef, curried chicken, and curried goat. You can also get burgers and omelets, but stick to the specials if you want fast service, and dine in if you want to get a true taste of island living. By night, the place becomes Grand Turk's one and only pizza take-out and delivery service, so if you're renting a villa or condo, put this spot on speed dial. ⊠ *Hospital Rd.* ☎ *649/946–1538* ▤ *No credit cards* ☼ *Closed Sun.*

ECLECTIC ✕ **Guanahani Restaurant & Bar.** Off the town's main drag, this restau-
★ **$$–$$$** rant sits on a stunning but quiet stretch of beach. The food goes beyond the usual Grand Turk fare, thanks to the talents of Canadian-born chef Zev Beck, who takes care of the evening meals. His pecan-encrusted mahimahi and crispy sushi rolls are to die for. For lunch, Middle Caicos native Miss Leotha makes juicy jerk chicken to keep the crowd happy. The menu changes daily. ⊠ *Bohio Dive Resort & Spa, Pillory Beach* ☎ *649/946–2135* ▤ *MC, V.*

SEAFOOD ✕ **Sap's Fishfry.** Down a lesser-known road that runs to the west of North
**$–$$$** Creek lies an even lesser-known restaurant. If you survive the potholed road trip, you will undoubtedly feel you deserve a taste of the freshly caught grouper, conch, and lobster specialties served at this small hideaway on the water. This is a favorite (if slightly scandalous) spot, where

local married men like to bring their "sweethearts." The prices and food are certainly good enough to make it the best choice for a cheap date. ⊠ *North Creek* ☎ *649/242–1723* ▤ *No credit cards* ⊗ *No lunch.*

## Beaches

Grand Turk is spoiled for choices when it comes to beach options: Sunset strolls along miles of deserted beaches, picnics in secluded coves, beachcombing on the coralline sands, snorkeling around shallow coral heads close to shore, and admiring the impossibly turquoise-blue waters. **Governor's Beach**, a secluded crescent of powder-soft sand and shallow, calm turquoise waters that fronts the official British Governor's residence, called Waterloo, is framed by tall casuarina trees that provide plenty of natural shade. For more of a beachcombing experience, **Little Bluff Point Beach**, just west of the Grand Turk Lighthouse, is a low, limestone cliff-edged, shell-covered beach that looks out onto shallow waters, mangroves, and often flamingos, especially in spring and summer.

★

## Sports & the Outdoors

CYCLING  The island's mostly flat terrain isn't very taxing, and most roads have hard surfaces. Take water with you: there are few places to stop for refreshment. Most hotels have bicycles available, but you can also rent them for $10 to $15 a day from **Oasis Divers** (⊠ Duke St., Cockburn Town ☎☎ 649/946–1128 ⊕ www.oasisdivers.com).

DIVING &  In these waters you can find undersea cathedrals, coral gardens, and count-
SNORKELING  less tunnels, but note that you must carry and present a valid certificate card before you'll be allowed to dive. As its name suggests, the **Black Forest** offers staggering black-coral formations as well as the occasional black-tip shark. In the **Library** you can study fish galore, including large numbers of yellowtail snapper. At the Columbus Passage separating South Caicos from Grand Turk, each side of a 22-mi-wide (35-km-wide) channel drops more than 7,000 feet. From January through March, thousands of Atlantic humpback whales swim through en route to their winter breeding grounds.

★

Dive outfitters can all be found in Cockburn Town. Two-tank boat dives generally cost $60 to $75. **Blue Water Divers** (⊠ Duke St., Cockburn Town ☎☎ 649/946–2432 ⊕ www.grandturkscuba.com) has been in operation on Grand Turk since 1983 and is the only PADI Gold Palm five-star dive center on the island. Owner Mitch will doubtless put some of your underwater adventures to music in the evenings when he plays at the Osprey Beach Hotel or Salt Raker Inn. **Oasis Divers** (⊠ Duke St., Cockburn Town ☎☎ 649/946–1128 ⊕ www.oasisdivers.com) specializes in complete gear handling and pampering treatment. It also supplies Nitrox and rebreathers. Besides daily dive trips to the Wall, **Sea Eye Diving** (⊠ Duke St., Cockburn Town ☎☎ 649/946–1407 ⊕ www.seaeyediving.com) offers encounters with friendly stingrays on a popular snorkeling trip to nearby Gibbs Cay.

## Nightlife

On weekends and holidays the younger crowd heads over to the **Nookie Hill Club** (⊠ Nookie Hill ☎ No phone) for late-night drinking and dancing. Every Wednesday and Sunday, there's lively "rake-and-scrape" music at the **Osprey Beach Hotel** (⊠ Duke St., Cockburn Town ☎ 649/946–2666). On Friday, "rake-and-scrape" bands play at the **Salt Raker Inn** (⊠ Duke St., Cockburn Town ☎ 649/946–2260). A fun crowd gathers most nights and for live music each Saturday at the **Water's Edge** (⊠ Duke St., Cockburn Town ☎ 649/946–1680).

## Exploring Grand Turk

Pristine beaches with vistas of turquoise waters, small local settlements, historic ruins, and native flora and fauna are among the sights on Grand Turk. Fewer than 5,000 people live on this 7½-square-mi (19-square-km) island, and it's hard to get lost, as there aren't many roads.

**Cockburn Town.** The buildings in the colony's capital and seat of government reflect a 19th-century Bermudian style. Narrow streets are lined with low stone walls and old street lamps, which are now powered by electricity. The once-vital salinas have been restored, and covered benches along the sluices offer shady spots for observing wading birds, including flamingos that frequent the shallows. Be sure to pick up a copy of the Tourist Board's Heritage Walk guide to discover Grand Turk's rich architecture.

**7** In one of the oldest stone buildings on the islands, the **Turks & Caicos National Museum** houses the Molasses Reef wreck, the earliest shipwreck—dating to the early 1500s—discovered in the Americas. The natural-history exhibits include artifacts left by Taíno, African, North American, Bermudian, French, and Latin American settlers. The museum has a 3-D coral reef exhibit, a walk-in Lucayan cave with wooden artifacts, and a gallery dedicated to Grand Turk's little-known involvement in the Space Race. An interactive children's gallery keeps knee-high visitors even more "edutained." ⊠ Duke St., Cockburn Town ☎ 649/946–2160 ⊕ www.tcmuseum.org ☞ $5 ⊙ Mon., Tues., Thurs., and Fri. 9–4, Wed. 9–5, Sat. 9–1.

**8** **Grand Turk Lighthouse.** More than 150 years old, the lighthouse, built in the United Kingdom and transported piece by piece to the island, used to protect ships in danger of wrecking on the northern reefs. Use this panoramic landmark as a starting point for a breezy clifftop walk by following the donkey trails to the deserted eastern beach. ⊠ Lighthouse Rd., North Ridge.

# Salt Cay

**9** Fewer than 100 people live on this 2½-square-mi (6-square-km) dot of land, maintaining an unassuming lifestyle against a backdrop of quaint stucco cottages, stone ruins, and weathered wooden windmills standing sentry in the abandoned salinas. The beautifully preserved island is bordered by picturesque beaches, where weathered green and blue sea glass and pretty shells often wash ashore. Beneath the waves, 10 dive sites are minutes from shore.

## Where to Stay

For approximate costs, *see* the dining and lodging price chart on the Turks & Caicos Planner, at the beginning of this chapter.

**$$$$** ⊞ **Windmills Plantation.** Arched balconies frame the perfect north-shore
Fodor'sChoice beach views in this outstanding small luxury hotel, which is presided
★ over by former Meridian Club managers Jim and Sharon Shafer. Wooden
decking winds through an eclectic plantation-inspired arrangement of
colorful buildings that hide a delightful mix of atmospheric, romantic
hideaways complete with dark wooden beams, four-poster beds, and original art. Jim, clearly a frustrated pirate, serves possibly the country's best
piña coladas from his cozy bar. Sharon, a natural and gracious hostess,
oversees her own boutique, a quiet library, and—most important—
scrumptious meals with desserts like blueberry crème brûlée and out-
standingly decadent breakfast pancakes that are to die for. Rates include
full board. ⊠ *North Beach Rd.* ☎ *649/946–6962 or 203/602–2265*
🖶 *649/946–6930* ⊕ *www.windmillsplantation.com* 🛏 *4 rooms, 4
suites* ⚲ *Restaurant, pool, beach, snorkeling, fishing, hiking, horseback riding, bar, library; no a/c, no room phones, no room TVs, no kids,
no smoking* ⊟ *AE, MC, V* ⏶⏷ *FAP.*

**$–$$** ⊞ **Pirate's Hideaway & Blackbeard's Quarters.** Owner Candy Herwin—
true to her self-proclaimed pirate status—has smuggled artistic treasures across the ocean and even created her own masterpieces to deck
out this lair. Quirkily decorated rooms show her original style and sense
of humor. The African and Crow's Nest suites have private baths; Blackbeard's Quarters is a four-bedroom house with rooms that can be rented
separately but share a living room and kitchen (one room has an en-
suite bath; the others share a single bath). On a good day, Candy will
cook, but only if you entertain her and other guests—whether by
reading a sonnet or singing a song. If you love eclectic and artistically
inspiring surroundings and want to meet a true pirate queen, this
could well be your perfect hideaway. ⊠ *Victoria St., South District*
☎ *649/946–6909* 🖶 *649/946–6909* ⊕ *www.saltcay.tc* 🛏 *2 rooms,
1 4-bedroom house* ⚲ *Some kitchens, beach, snorkeling, fishing, bicycles; no a/c in some rooms, no room phones, no room TVs* ⊟ *MC,
V* ⏶⏷ *EP.*

**$–$$** ⊞ **Sunset Reef.** A blue whale on the rooftop denotes this Victoria Street
property, which has two very basic villas with excellent ocean views and
a whale-watching balcony ideal for communal dining. You must pay extra
to use the air-conditioning. ⊠ *Victoria St., Balfour Town* ☎ *649/941–
7753* 🖶 *649/941–7753* ⊕ *www.sunsetreef.com* 🛏 *1 1-bedroom villa,
1 2-bedroom villa* ⚲ *Fans, in-room fax, in-room safe, kitchens, in-
room VCRs, beach, snorkeling, fishing, laundry facilities, some pets allowed; no room phones* ⊟ *MC, V* ⏶⏷ *EP.*

**$–$$** ⊞ **Tradewinds Guest Suites.** Yards away from Dean's Dock, a grove of
whispering casuarina trees surrounds these five single-story, basic
apartments, which offer a moderate-budget option on Salt Cay with the
possibility of all-inclusive and dive packages. Screened porches, hammocks overlooking the comings and goings of the small dock, and the
friendly staff are the best features. You must pay extra to use the air-
conditioning. ⊠ *Victoria St., Balfour Town* ☎ *649/946–6906* 🖶 *649/
946–6940* ⊕ *www.tradewinds.tc* 🛏 *5 suites* ⚲ *Some kitchens, some
kitchenettes, beach, snorkeling, fishing, bicycles; no room phones, no
room TVs* ⊟ *MC, V* ⏶⏷ *EP.*

## Where to Eat

**$–$$** ✕ **Island Thyme Bistro.** Owner Porter Williams serves potent alcoholic creations like "The Wolf" and other creatures, as well as fairly sophisticated local and international cuisine. Look for steamed, freshly caught snapper served in a pepper wine sauce with peas and rice or spicy-hot chicken curry served with a tangy range of chutneys. The airy, trellis-covered spot overlooks the Salinas. ⊠ *North District* ☎ *649/946–6977* ▭ *MC, V* ☉ *Closed Wed.*

**$–$$** ✕ **Pat's Place.** Born and bred on the island, Pat Simmons can give you a lesson in the medicinal qualities of her garden plants and periwinkle flowers as well as excellent native cuisine for a down-home price in her typical Salt Cay home. Try conch fritters for lunch and her steamed grouper with okra rice for dinner. Be sure to call ahead, as she cooks only when there's someone to cook for. ⊠ *South District* ☎ *649/946–6919* ⌂ *Reservations essential* ▭ *No credit cards.*

## Beaches

★ The north coast of **Salt Cay** has superb beaches, with tiny, pretty shells and weathered sea glass. Accessible by boat with the on-island tour operators, **Big Sand Cay,** 7 mi (11 km) south of Salt Cay, is tiny and totally uninhabited, but it's also known for its long, unspoiled stretches of open sand.

## Sports & the Outdoors

DIVING & SNORKELING   Scuba divers can explore the wreck of the *Endymion,* a 140-foot wooden-hull British warship that sank in 1790. It's off the southern point of Salt Cay. **Salt Cay Divers** (⊠ Balfour Town ☎ 649/946–6906 ⊕ www.saltcaydivers.tc) conducts daily trips and rents all the necessary equipment. It costs around $80 for a two-tank dive.

WHALE-WATCHING   During the winter months (January through April), Salt Cay is a center for whale-watching, when some 2,500 humpback whales pass close to ☉ shore. Whale-watching trips can most easily be organized through your inn or guesthouse.

## Exploring Salt Cay

Salt sheds and salinas are silent reminders of the days when the island was a leading producer of salt. Now the salt ponds attract abundant birdlife. Island tours are often conducted by motorized golf cart. From January through April, humpback whales pass by on the way to their winter breeding grounds.

**Balfour Town.** What little development there is on Salt Cay is found here. It's home to several small hotels and a few cozy stores, as well as the main dock and the Green Flash Gazebo, where locals hang out with tourists to watch the sunset and sink a beer.

The grand stone **White House,** which once belonged to a wealthy salt merchant, is testimony to the heyday of Salt Cay's eponymous industry. Still privately owned by the descendants of the original family, it's sometimes opened up for tours. It's worth asking your guesthouse or hotel owner—or any local passer-by—if Salt Cay Islander "Uncle Lionel" is on-island, as he may give you a personal tour to see the still-intact, original furnishings, books, and medicine cabinet that date back to the early 1800s. ⊠ *Victoria St.*

# TURKS & CAICOS ESSENTIALS

*To research prices, get advice from other travelers, and book travel arrangements, visit www.fodors.com.*

## Transportation

### BY AIR

The main gateways into the regions are Providenciales International Airport and Grand Turk International Airport. For private planes, Provo Air Center is a full service FBO (Fixed Base Operator) offering refueling, maintenance, and short-term storage, as well as on-site customs and immigration clearance, a lounge, and concierge services.

Although carriers and schedules can vary according to season, you can find nonstop and connecting flights to Providenciales from several U.S. cities on American, Delta, and USAirways; Air Jamaica provides connecting service on Air Jamaica Express through Montego Bay. During the high season, there are weekly charters from a number of North American cities (Club Med, for example, organizes its own weekly charter from the New York City area). Air Canada flies nonstop from Toronto. British Airways flies from the United Kingdom. There are also flights from the Bahamas and parts of the Caribbean on Bahamasair, Air Turks & Caicos, and Sky King; these airlines also fly to some of the smaller islands in the chain from Provo.

🛪 Airline Contacts **Air Canada** ☎ 888/247-2262. **Air Jamaica Express** ☎ 800/523-5585 ⊕ www.airjamaica.com. **Air Turks & Caicos** ☎ 649/946-4181 or 649/941-5481 ⊕ www.airturksandcaicos.com. **American Airlines** ☎ 649/946-4948 or 800/433-7300. **Bahamasair** ☎ 649/946-4999 or 800/222-4262 ⊕ www.bahamasair.com. **British Airways** ☎ 649/941-3352 or 800/247-9297. **Delta** ☎ 800/241-4141. **SkyKing** ☎ 649/941-5464 ⊕ www.skyking.tc. **US Airways** ☎ 800/622-1015.

🛪 Airport Contacts **Grand Turk International Airport** ☎ 649/946-2233. **Providenciales International Airport** ☎ 649/941-5670. **Provo Air Center** ☎ 649/946-4181 ⊕ www.provoaircenter.com.

### BY BOAT & FERRY

Surprisingly, there's no scheduled boat or ferry service between Provo and the other Turks and Caicos Islands. Instead, islanders tend to catch rides leaving from the marina at Leeward-Going-Through. There's a thrice-weekly ferry from Salt Cay to Grand Turk.

### BY CAR

Major reconstruction of Leeward Highway on Providenciales has been completed, and most of the road is now a four-lane divided highway complete with roundabouts. However, the paved two-lane roads through the settlements on Providenciales can be quite rough, although signage is improving. The less-traveled roads in Grand Turk and the family islands are, in general, smooth and paved. Gasoline is expensive, much more so than in the United States.

Driving here is on the left side of the road, British style; when pulling out into traffic, remember to look to your right. Give way to anyone entering a roundabout, as roundabouts are still a relatively new concept in the Turks and Caicos; stop even if you are on what appears to be the primary road. The maximum speed is 40 mph, 20 mph through settlements, and limits, as well as the use of seat belts, are enforced.

Avis and Budget have offices on the islands. You might also try local agencies such as Provo Rent-a-Car, Rent a Buggy, and Tropical Auto Rentals.

🚗 **Avis** ☎ 649/946-4705 ⊕ www.Avistci.com. **Budget** ☎ 649/946-4079 ⊕ www. provo.net/budget. **Provo Rent-a-Car** ☎ 649/946-4404 ⊕ www.provo.net/rentacar. **Rent a Buggy** ☎ 649/946-4158 ⊕ www.rentabuggy.tc. **Tropical Auto Rentals** ☎ 649/ 946-5300 ⊕ www.provo.net/tropicalauto.

### BY TAXI

Cabs (actually large vans) in Providenciales are now metered, and rates are regulated by the government at $2 per person per mile traveled. In Provo call the Provo Taxi & Bus Group for more information. In the family islands, cabs may not be metered, so it's usually best to try to negotiate a cost for your trip when you book your taxi. Many resorts and car-rental agencies offer complimentary airport transfers. Ask ahead of time.

🚖 **Provo Taxi & Bus Group** ☎ 649/946-5481.

## Contacts & Resources

### BANKS & EXCHANGE SERVICES

Prices quoted in this chapter are in U.S. dollars, which is the official currency in the islands. Major credit cards and traveler's checks are accepted at many establishments. The islands' few ATMs are primarily at the banks.

Scotiabank and FirstCaribbean have offices on Provo, with branches on Grand Turk. Many larger hotels can take care of your money requests. Bring small denominations to the less-populated islands.

### BUSINESS HOURS

Banks are open Monday through Thursday from 9 to 3, Friday 9 to 5. Post offices are open weekdays from 8 to 4. Shops are generally open weekdays from 8 or 8:30 to 5.

### ELECTRICITY

Electricity is fairly stable throughout the islands, and the current is suitable for all U.S. appliances (120/240 volts, 60 Hz).

### EMERGENCIES

🚨 Emergency Services **Ambulance & Fire** ☎ 999 or 911. **Police** ☎ 649/946-2499 in Grand Turk, 649/946-7116 in North Caicos, 649/946-4259 in Provo, 649/946-3299 in South Caicos.

🏥 Hospitals **Associated Medical Practices** ✉ Leeward Hwy., Glass Shack, Providenciales ☎ 649/946-4242. **Grand Turk Hospital** ✉ Hospital Rd., Grand Turk ☎ 649/946-2040.

💊 Pharmacies **Grand Turk Hospital** ✉ Grand Turk Hospital, Grand Turk ☎ 649/946-2040. **Grace Bay Medical Center** ✉ Neptune Plaza, Grace Bay, Providenciales ☎ 649/ 941-5252.

◪ Scuba Diving Emergencies **Associated Medical Practices** ✉ Leeward Hwy., Glass Shack, Providenciales ☎ 649/946-4242.

## HOLIDAYS

Public holidays are New Year's Day, Commonwealth Day (2nd Mon. in Mar.), Good Friday, Easter Monday, National Heroes Day (last Mon. in May), Queen's Birthday (3rd Mon. in June), Emancipation Day (1st Mon. in Aug.), National Youth Day (last Mon. in Sept.), Columbus Day (2nd Mon. in Oct.), International Human Rights Day (last Mon. in Oct.), Christmas Day, and Boxing Day (Dec. 26).

## INTERNET, MAIL & SHIPPING

The post office is in downtown Provo at the corner of Airport Road. Collectors will be interested in the wide selection of stamps sold by the Philatelic Bureau. It costs 50¢ to send a postcard to the United States, 60¢ to Canada and the United Kingdom, and $1.25 to Australia and New Zealand; letters, per ½ ounce, cost 60¢ to the United States, 80¢ to Canada and the United Kingdom, and $1.40 to Australia and New Zealand. When writing to the Turks and Caicos Islands, be sure to include the specific island and "Turks and Caicos Islands, BWI" (British West Indies). Delivery service is provided by FedEx, with offices in Provo and Grand Turk.

◪ **FedEx** ☎ 649/946-4682 on Provo. **Philatelic Bureau** ☎ 649/946-1534.

## MEDIA

The *Turks and Caicos Free Press* and the *Turks and Caicos Weekly News* are English-language newspapers that appeal to those interested in gaining some insight into the local culture. Magazines include the wonderful *Times of the Islands,* the upscale *S3,* and *Baller.* WIV provides local television programming, usually channel 4. Radio Turks and Caicos broadcasts laid-back discussions and sounds from the islands on 97.3FM

## PASSPORT REQUIREMENTS

U.S. and Canadian citizens need some proof of citizenship, such as a birth certificate (original or certified copy), plus a photo ID or a current passport. All other travelers, including those from the United Kingdom, Australia, and New Zealand, require a current passport. Everyone must have an ongoing or return ticket. A valid passport will be a requirement to all U.S. citizens traveling to the Turks and Caicos beginning January 1, 2007.

## SAFETY

Although crime is not a major concern in the Turks and Caicos Islands, petty theft does occur here, and you're advised to leave your valuables in the hotel safe-deposit box and lock doors in cars and rooms when unattended.

## TAXES & SERVICE CHARGES

The departure tax is $35 and is usually built into the cost of your tickets. If not, it's payable only in cash or traveler's checks. Restaurants and hotels add a 10% government tax. Hotels also add 10% to 15% for service.

## TELEPHONES

The area code for the Turks and Caicos is 649. Just dial 1 plus the 10-digit number, including area code, from the United States. To make local calls, dial the seven-digit number. To make calls from the Turks and Caicos, dial 0, then 1, the area code, and the number.

All telephone service is provided by Cable & Wireless. Many U.S.–based cell phones work on the islands; use your own or rent one from Cable & Wireless. Internet access is available via hotel-room phone connections or Internet kiosks on Provo and Grand Turk. You can also connect to the World Wide Web from any telephone line by dialing C-O-N-N-E-C-T to call Cable & Wireless and using the user name *easy* and the password *access*. Calls from the islands are expensive, and many hotels add steep surcharges for long-distance. Talk fast.

🔗 **Cable & Wireless** ☎ 649/946–2200, 800/744–7777 for long distance, 649/266–6328 for Internet access, 811 for mobile service ⊕ www.tcimall.tc.

## TIPPING

At restaurants, tip 15% if service isn't included in the bill. Taxi drivers also expect a token tip, about 10% of your fare.

## TOUR OPTIONS

Whether by taxi, boat, or plane, you should try to venture beyond your resort's grounds and beach. The natural environment is one of the main attractions of the Turks and Caicos, yet few people explore beyond the natural wonder of the beach. Big Blue Unlimited has taken ecotouring to a whole new level with educational ecotours, including three-hour kayak trips and more land-based guided journeys around the family islands. The Coastal Ecology & Wildlife tour is a kayak adventure through red mangroves to bird habitats, rock iguana hideaways, and natural fish nurseries. The North Caicos Mountain Bike Eco Tour gets you on a bike exploring the island, the plantation ruins, the inland lakes, and a flamingo pond with a stop-off at Susan Butterfield's home for lunch. Package costs range from $85 to $225 per person. J&B Tours offers sea and land tours, including trips to Middle Caicos, the largest of the islands, for a visit to the caves, or to North Caicos to see flamingos and plantation ruins. Nell's Taxi offers taxi tours of the islands, priced between $25 and $30 for the first hour and $25 for each additional hour.

Special day excursions are available from local airline Air Turks & Caicos. Trips include whale-watching in Salt Cay, and if you venture to Middle Caicos and North Caicos, in addition to flights, you get a map, water, a lunch voucher, and a mountain bike to explore for the day. Trips start from $99, which includes round-trip air tickets. Day trips to Grand Turk are available with SkyKing. For around $155, you get a round-trip flight to the capital island, a short tour, admission to the Turks & Caicos National Museum, a stop off for lunch, and time to explore on your own.

🔗 **Air Turks & Caicos** ☎ 649/946–5481 or 649/946–4181 ⊕ www.airturksandcaicos.com. **Big Blue Unlimited** ✉ Leeward Marina, Leeward ☎ 649/946–5034 ⊕ www.bigblue.tc. **J&B Tours** ☎ 649/946–5047 ⊕ www.jbtours.com. **Nell's Taxi** ☎ 649/231–0051. **SkyKing** ☎ 649/941–5464 ⊕ www.skyking.tc.

## VISITOR INFORMATION

The tourist offices on Grand Turk and Providenciales are open daily from 9 to 5.

🗐 Before You Leave **Turks & Caicos Islands Tourist Board** ✉ 2715 E. Oakland Park Blvd., No. 101, Fort Lauderdale, FL 33316 ☎ 954/568-6588 or 800/241-0824 ⊕ www.turksandcaicostourism.com.

🗐 In Turks & Caicos Islands **Turks & Caicos Islands Tourist Board** ✉ Front St., Cockburn Town, Grand Turk ☎ 649/946-2321 ✉ Stubbs Diamond Plaza, The Bight, Providenciales ☎ 649/946-4970 ⊕ www.turksandcaicostourism.com.

## WEDDINGS

Beautiful oceanfront backdrops, endless starlight nights, and a bevy of romantic accommodations make the islands an ideal wedding destination. The residency requirement is only 24 hours, after which you can apply for a marriage license to the registrar in Grand Turk; the ceremony can take place at any time after the application has been granted, generally within two to three days. You must present a passport, original birth certificate, and proof of current marital status, as well as a letter stating both parties' occupations, ages, addresses, and fathers' full names. No blood tests are required, and the license fee is $50. The ceremony is conducted by a local minister, justice of the peace, or the registrar. The marriage certificate is filed in the islands, although copies can be sent to your home. There are a number of wedding coordinators on-island, and many resorts offer special wedding packages, which include handling all the details.

🗐 **Nila Destinations Wedding Planning** ☎ 649/941-4375 ⊕ www.nilavacations.com.

# UNDERSTANDING
# THE BAHAMAS

# BAHAMAS AT A GLANCE

## Fast Facts

**Type of government:** Constitutional parliamentary democracy
**Capital:** Nassau
**Administrative divisions:** 21 districts: Acklins and Crooked Islands, Bimini, Cat Island, Exuma, Freeport, Fresh Creek, Governor's Harbour, Green Turtle Cay, Harbour Island, High Rock, Inagua, Kemps Bay, Long Island, Marsh Harbour, Mayaguana, New Providence, Nichollstown and Berry Islands, Ragged Island, Rock Sound, Sandy Point, San Salvador and Rum Cay
**Independence:** July 10, 1973 (from the United Kingdom)
**Legal system:** Based on English common law; Privy Council Supreme Court, Court of Appeal, magistrates courts
**Legislature:** Bicameral parliament: upper house: 16-member appointed Senate; lower house: 40-member elected House of Assembly
**Population:** 303,770
**Birth Rate:** 17.57 births per 1,000 population

**Infant Mortality:** 24.68 deaths per 1,000 live births; female: 18.96; male: 30.29
**Language:** English, Creole (among Haitian immigrants), and strong Bahamian dialect
**Ethnic groups:** Bahamians are mainly of African descent—85% black, 12% white, and 3% Asian and Hispanic
**Life expectancy:** Male, 62.24; female, 69.03
**Literacy:** Total population: 95.6%; male: 94.7%; female, 96.5%
**Religion:** Dominant religion: Christianity; largest three denominations: Baptist, 35.4%; Anglican, 15.1%; and Roman Catholic, 13.5%; Other denominations and religions represented: Assembly of God, Ba'hai faith, Brethren, Christian and Missionary Alliance, Christian Science, Church of God of Prophecy, Greek Orthodox, Jehovah's Witnesses, Jewish, Latter-day Saints (Mormon), Lutheran, Methodist, Presbyterian, and Seventh Day Adventist

## Geography

**Location:** The archipelago of the islands of the Bahamas is in the Atlantic Ocean, extending more than 650 miles from the eastern coast of Florida to the southeastern tip of Cuba. Of the some 700 islands and almost 2,500 small islets of cays, approximately 30 are inhabited.
**Coastline:** 2,201 mi
**Area:** Total: 5,382 square mi; land, 3,888 square mi; water, 1,494 square mi; about the size of the state of Connecticut in the U.S.
**Climate:** Tropical marine; moderated by warm waters of the Gulf Stream
**Terrain:** Long, flat coral formations with some low, rounded hills

**Islands:** New Providence Island, home to the capital Nassau; Grand Bahama Island; and other inhabited islands officially called the Family Islands but commonly known as the Out Islands, including The Abacos, Andros, Cat Island, The Biminis, The Berries, Eleuthera, The Exumas, and Long Island
**Natural resources:** Salt, aragonite, timber, arable land
**Natural hazards:** Hurricanes and other tropical storms that cause extensive flooding and wind damage

## Economy

**Inflation:** 1.4%
**Unemployment:** 10.2%
**GDP per capita:** $20, 200
**GDP:** $6.1 billion (2005)
**Agriculture:** Citrus, vegetables, and poultry
**Industry:** Tourism, banking, cement, salt, rum, oil transshipment, aragonite, pharmaceuticals, and spiral-welded steel pipe
**Work force:** Tourism, 50%; other services, 40%; industry, 5%; agriculture, 5%
**Currency:** Bahamian dollar (U.S. dollar widely accepted)
**Exchange rate:** One Bahamian dollar per U.S. dollar

**Debt (external):** $342.6 million (2004)
**Economic aid:** $5 million (2004)
**Major export products:** animal products, rum, mineral products and salt, chemicals, fruit and vegetables
**Export partners:** U.S., 40.5%; Poland, 13.4%; Spain, 12.3%; Germany, 5.9%; France, 4.3%
**Imports:** Machinery and transport equipment, manufactures, chemicals, mineral fuels, food and live animals
**Import partners:** U.S., 22.4%; South Korea, 18.9%; Brazil, 9.2%; Japan, 7.9%; Italy 7.8%; Venezuela, 6.6%

## Environment

**Environmental issues:** Coral reef decay, solid waste disposal

## Did You Know?

• The Bahamas is a stable, developing nation; its economy is predominantly dependent on tourism and offshore banking.

• Tourism and tourism-driven construction and manufacturing account for 60% of the GDP and employ about half of the labor force.

• Arawak Indians inhabited the islands when Christopher Columbus first landed in the New World on San Salvador in 1492.

• British settlement of the islands began in 1647; they became a colony in 1783.

• Since attaining independence from the U.K. in 1973, the Bahamas has prospered through tourism, international banking, and investment management.

• Because of its geography, the country is a major transshipment point for illegal drugs, particularly shipments to the U.S., and its territory is used for smuggling illegal migrants into the U.S.

# IN THE WAKE OF COLUMBUS: A SHORT HISTORY OF THE BAHAMAS

**YOU MIGHT CALL CHRISTOPHER COLUMBUS** the first tourist to hit the Bahamas, although he was actually trying to find a route to the East Indies with his *Niña*, *Pinta*, and *Santa María*. Columbus is popularly believed to have made his first landfall in the New World on October 12, 1492, at San Salvador, in the southern part of the Bahamas. Researchers of the National Geographic Society, however, have come up with the theory that he may first have set foot ashore Samana Cay, some 60 mi southeast of San Salvador. The Bahamians have taken this new theory under consideration, if not too seriously; tradition dies hard in the islands, and they are hardly likely to tear down the New World landfall monument on San Salvador.

The people who met Columbus on his landing day were Arawak Indians, said to have fled from the Caribbean to the Bahamas to escape the depredations of the murderous Caribs around the turn of the 9th century. The Arawaks were a shy, gentle people who offered Columbus and his men their hospitality. He was impressed with their kindness and more than slightly intrigued by the gold ornaments they wore. But the voracious Spaniards who followed in Columbus's footsteps a few years later repaid the Indians' kindness by forcing them to work in the conquistadors' gold and silver mines in Cuba and Haiti; the Bahamas' indigenous peoples were virtually wiped out in the next 30 years, despite the fact that the Spaniards never settled their land.

In 1513 another well-known seafarer stumbled upon the westernmost Bahamian islands. Juan Ponce de León had been a passenger on Columbus's second voyage, in 1493. He conquered Puerto Rico in 1508 and then began searching thirstily for the Fountain of Youth. He thought he had found it on South Bimini, but he changed his mind and moved on to visit the site of St. Augustine, on the northeast coast of Florida.

In 1629 King Charles I claimed the Bahamas for England, though his edict was not implemented until the arrival of English pilgrims in 1648. Having fled the religious repression and political dissension then rocking their country, they settled on the Bahamian island they christened Eleuthera, the Greek word for freedom. Other English immigrants followed, and in 1656 another group of pilgrims, from Bermuda, took over a Bahamian island to the west and named it New Providence because of their links with Providence, Rhode Island. By the last part of the 17th century, some 1,100 settlers were trying to eke out a living, supplemented by the cargoes they salvaged from Spanish galleons that ran aground on the reefs. Many settlers were inclined to give nature a hand by enticing these ships onto the reefs with lights.

Inevitably, the British settlers were joined by a more nefarious subset of humanity, pirates and buccaneers like Edward Teach (better known as Blackbeard, he was said to have had 14 wives), Henry Morgan, and Calico Jack Rackham. Rackham numbered among his crew two violent, cutlass-wielding female members, Anne Bonney and Mary Read, who are said to have disconcerted enemies by swinging aboard their vessels topless. Bonney and Read escaped hanging in Jamaica by feigning pregnancy.

For some 40 years until 1718, pirates in the Bahamas constantly raided the Spanish galleons that carried booty home from the New World. During this period, the Spanish government, furious at the raids, sent ships and troops to destroy the New Providence city of Charles Town, which was later rebuilt and renamed Nassau, in

1695, in honor of King William III, formerly William of Orange-Nassau.

In 1718 King George I appointed Captain Woodes Rogers the first royal governor of the Bahamas, with orders to clean up the place. Why the king chose Rogers for this particular job is unclear—his thinking may well have been that it takes a pirate to know one, for Woodes Rogers had been a privateer. But he did take control of Nassau, hanging eight pirates from trees on the site of what was to become the British Colonial Hotel. Today, a statue of the former governor stands at the hotel entrance, and the street that runs along the waterfront is named after him. Rogers also inspired the saying *Expulsis piratis, restitua commercia* (Piracy expelled, commerce restored), which remained the country's motto until Prime Minister Lynden O. Pindling replaced it with the more appropriate and optimistic Forward, Upward, Onward Together, on the occasion of independence from Britain in 1973.

Although the Bahamas enjoyed a certain measure of tranquillity, thanks to Rogers and the governors who followed him, the British colonies in America at the same time were seething with a desire for independence. The peace of the islanders' lives was to be shattered during the Revolutionary War by a raid in 1778 on Nassau by the American navy, which purloined the city's arms and ammunition without even firing a shot. Next, in 1782, the Spanish came to occupy the Bahamas until the following year. Under the Treaty of Versailles of 1783, Spain took possession of Florida, and the Bahamas reverted to British rule.

\* \* \*

**THE BAHAMAS WERE ONCE AGAIN OVERRUN,** between 1784 and 1789, this time by merchants from New England and plantation owners from Virginia and the Carolinas who had been loyal to the British and were fleeing the wrath of the American revolutionaries. Seeking asylum under the British flag, the Southerners brought their families and slaves with them. Many set up new plantations in the islands, but frustrated by the islands' arid soil, they soon opted for greener pastures in the Caribbean. The slaves they left behind were set free in 1834, but many retained the names of their former masters. That is why you'll find many a Johnson, Saunders, and Thompson in the towns and villages throughout the Bahamas.

The land may have been less than fertile, but New Providence Island's almost perfect climate, marred only by the potential for hurricanes during the fall, attracted other interest. Tourism was foreseen as far back as 1861, when the legislature approved the building of the first hotel, the Royal Victoria. Though it was to reign as the grande dame of the island's hotels for more than a century, its early days saw it involved in an entirely different profit-making venture. During the U.S. Civil War, the Northern forces blockaded the main Southern ports, and the leaders of the Confederacy turned to Nassau, the closest neutral port to the south. The Royal Victoria became the headquarters of the blockade-running industry, which reaped huge profits for the British colonial government from the duties it imposed on arms supplies. (In October 1990, the Royal Victoria Hotel burned down.)

A similar bonanza, also at the expense of the United States, was to come in the 1920s, after Prohibition was signed into U.S. law in 1919. Booze brought into the Bahamas from Europe was funneled into a thirsty United States by rumrunners operating out of Nassau, Bimini, and West End, the community on Grand Bahama Island east of Palm Beach. Racing against, and often exchanging gunfire with, Coast Guard patrol boats, the rumrunners dropped off their supplies in Miami, the Florida Keys, and other Florida destinations, making their contribution to the era known as the Roaring '20s.

Even then, tourists were beginning to trickle into the Bahamas, many in opulent yachts belonging to the likes of Whitney, Vanderbilt, and Astor. In 1929 a new airline, Pan American, started to make daily flights from Miami to Nassau. The Royal Victoria, shedding its shady past, and two new hotels, the Colonial (now the British Colonial Hilton Nassau) and the Fort Montagu Beach, were all in full operation. Nassau even had instant communication with the outside world: A few miles northwest of the Colonial, a subterranean telegraph cable had been laid linking New Providence with Jupiter, Florida. It took no flash of inspiration to name the area Cable Beach.

One of the most colorful and enigmatic characters of the era, Sir Harry Oakes, came to Nassau in the 1930s from Canada. He built the Bahamas Country Club and the Cable Beach Golf Course; he also built Nassau's first airport in the late '30s to lure the well-heeled and to make commuting easier for the wealthy residents. Oakes Field can still be seen on the ride from Nassau International Airport to Cable Beach.

Oakes was to die in an atmosphere of eerie and mysterious intrigue. Only his good friend, the late Sir Harold Christie, a powerful real-estate tycoon, was in the house at the time that Oakes' body was found, battered and burned. This was a period when all of the news that was fit to print was coming out of the war theaters in Europe and the Far East, but the Miami newspapers and wire services had a field day with the society murder.

Although a gruff, unlikable character, Oakes had no known enemies, but there was speculation that mob hit men from Miami had come over and taken care of him because of his unyielding opposition to the introduction of gambling casinos to the Bahamas. Finally, two detectives brought from Miami pinned the murder on Oakes' son-in-law, Count Alfred de Marigny, for whom the Canadian was known to have a strong dislike. De Marigny was tried and acquitted in an overcrowded Nassau court. Much of the detectives' research and testimony was later discredited. For many years afterward, however, the mysterious and still unsolved crime was a sore point with New Providence residents.

During World War II, New Providence also played host to a noble, if unlikely, couple. In 1936 the Duke of Windsor had forsaken the British throne in favor of "the woman I love," an American divorcée named Wallis Warfield Simpson, and the couple temporarily found a carefree life in Paris and the French Riviera. When the Nazis overran France, they fled to neutral Portugal. Secret papers revealed after the war suggest that the Germans had plans to use the duke and duchess, by kidnapping if necessary, as pawns in the German war against Britain. This would have taken the form of declaring them king and queen in exile, and seating them on the throne when Hitler's assumed victory was accomplished.

Word of the plot might have reached the ears of Britain's wartime prime minister, Winston Churchill, who encouraged King George VI, the duke's younger brother and his successor, to send the couple as far away as possible out of harm's way. In 1939 the duke had briefly returned to England, offering his services to his brother in the war effort. He was given a position of perhaps less import than he had expected, for he and Wallis suddenly found themselves in the Bahamas, with the duke as governor and commander in chief.

\* \* \*

## CHANGES IN THE BAHAMAS' POLITICAL CLIMATE

had to wait for the war's end. For more than 300 years, the country had been ruled by whites; members of the United Bahamian Party (UBP) were known as the Bay Street Boys, after Nassau's main business thoroughfare, because they controlled the islands' commerce. But the voice of the overwhelmingly black majority was making itself heard. In 1953 a London-educated black barrister named Lynden O. Pindling joined the opposition Progressive Liberal Party (PLP); in 1956 he was elected to Parliament.

Pindling continued to stir the growing resentment most Bahamians now had for the Bay Street Boys, and his parliamentary behavior became more and more defiant. In 1965, during one parliamentary session, he picked up the speaker's mace and threw it out the window. Because this mace has to be present and in sight at all sessions, deliberations had to be suspended; meanwhile, Pindling continued his harangue to an enthusiastic throng in the street below. Two years later, Bahamian voters threw the UBP out, and Pindling led the PLP into power.

Pindling's magnetism kept him in power through independence from Britain in 1973 (though loyalty to the mother country led the Bahamians to choose to remain within the Commonwealth of Nations, recognize Queen Elizabeth II as their sovereign, and retain a governor-general appointed by the queen). For his services to his nation, the prime minister was knighted by the queen in 1983. His deputy prime minister Clement Maynard received the same accolade in 1989.

In August 1992 there came the biggest political upset since Pindling took power in 1967. His Progressive Liberal Party was defeated in a general election by the Free National Movement party, headed by lawyer Hubert Alexander Ingraham. The 45-year-old former chairman of the PLP and Cabinet member under Pindling had been expelled from the party by Pindling in 1986 because of his outspoken comments on alleged corruption inside the government. Ingraham's continued emphasis on this issue during the 1992 campaign did much to lead to Pindling's defeat and Ingraham's taking over as prime minister. Ingraham was reelected for another five-year term in 1996. In May 2002, the PLP again took the reigns with the election of the Right Honourable Perry G. Christie.

Residents, for the most part, are proud of their country and are actively involved in bettering their own lot—the last complete census showed about 27% of the population was attending school at one level or another. And in the spirit of their national motto—Forward, Upward, Onward Together—they graciously welcome the ever-increasing numbers of outsiders who have discovered their little piece of paradise.

— Ian Glass

# CASHING IN: A CASINO GAMBLING PRIMER

For a short-form handbook on the rules, the plays, the odds, and the strategies for the most popular casino games—or to decide on the kind of action that's for you and suits your style—read on. You must be 18 to gamble; Bahamians and permanent residents are not permitted to indulge.

## The Good Bets

The first part of any viable casino strategy is to risk the most money on wagers that present the lowest edge for the house. Blackjack, craps, video poker, and baccarat are the most advantageous to the bettor in this regard. The two types of bets at baccarat have a house advantage of a little more than 1%. The basic line bets at craps, if backed up with full odds, can be as low as ½%. Blackjack and video poker, at times, can not only put you even with the house (a true 50–50 proposition), but actually give you a slight long-term advantage.

How can a casino possibly provide you with a 50–50 or even a positive expectation at some of its games? First, because a vast number of suckers make the bad bets (those with a house advantage of 5%–35%, such as roulette, keno, and slots) day in and day out. Second, because the casino knows that very few people are aware of the opportunities to beat the odds. Third, because it takes skill—requiring study and practice—to be in a position to exploit these opportunities the casino presents. However, a mere hour or two spent learning strategies for the beatable games will put you light years ahead of the vast majority of visitors who give the gambling industry an average 12% to 15% profit margin.

## Baccarat

The most "glamorous" game in the casino, baccarat (pronounced *bah*-kuh-rah) is a version of *chemin de fer,* popular in European gambling halls, and is a favorite with high rollers, because thousands of dollars are often staked on one hand. The Italian word *baccara* means "zero"; this refers to the point value of 10s and picture cards. The game is run by four pit personnel. Two dealers sit side by side in the middle of the table; they handle the winning and losing bets and keep track of each player's "commission" (explained below). The "caller" stands in the middle of the other side of the table and dictates the action. The ladderman supervises the game and acts as final judge if any disputes arise.

**How to Play.** Baccarat is played with eight decks of cards dealt from a large "shoe" (or cardholder). Each player is offered a turn at handling the shoe and dealing the cards. Two two-card hands are dealt, the "player" and the "bank" hands. The player who deals the cards is called the banker, though the house, of course, banks both hands. The players bet on which hand, player or banker, will come closest to adding up to 9 (a "natural"). The cards are totaled as follows: ace through 9 retain face value, while 10s and picture cards are worth zero. If you have a hand adding up to more than 10, the number 10 is subtracted from the total. For example, if one hand contains a 10 and a 4, the hand adds up to 4. If the other holds an ace and 6, it adds up to 7. If a hand has a 7 and 9, it adds up to 6.

Depending on the two hands, the caller either declares a winner and loser (if either hand actually adds up to 8 or 9), or calls for another card for the player hand (if it totals 1, 2, 3, 4, 5, or 10). The bank hand then either stands pat or draws a card, determined by a complex series of rules depending on what the player's total is and dictated by the caller. When one or the other hand is declared a winner, the dealers go into action to pay off the winning wagers, collect the losing wagers, and add up the commission (usually 5%) that the house collects on the bank hand. Both bets have a house advantage of slightly more than 1%.

The player-dealer (or banker) continues to hold the shoe as long as the bank hand wins. As soon as the player hand wins, the shoe moves counterclockwise around the table. Players are not required to deal; they can refuse the shoe and pass it to the next player. Because the caller dictates the action, the player responsibilities are minimal. It's not necessary to know any of the card-drawing rules, even if you're the banker.

**Baccarat Strategy.** Making a bet at baccarat is very simple. All you have to do is place your money in either the bank, player, or tie box on the layout, which appears directly in front of where you sit at the table. If you're betting that the bank hand will win, you put your chips in the bank box; bets for the player hand go in the player box. (Only real suckers bet on the tie.) Most players bet on the bank hand when they deal, since they "represent" the bank, and to do otherwise would seem as if they were betting "against" themselves. This isn't really true, but it seems that way. In the end, playing baccarat is a simple matter of guessing whether the player or banker hand will come closest to 9, and deciding how much to bet on the outcome.

## Blackjack

**How to Play.** Basically, here's how it works: You play blackjack against a dealer, and whichever of you comes closest to a card total of 21 is the winner. Number cards are worth their face value, picture cards are worth 10, and aces are worth either 1 or 11. (Hands with aces in them are known as "soft" hands. Always count the ace first as an 11; if you also have a 10, your total will be 21, not 11.) If the dealer has a 17 and you have a 16, you lose. If you have an 18 against a dealer's 17, you win (even money). If both you and the dealer have a 17, it's a tie (or "push") and no money changes hands. If you go over a total of 21 (or "bust"), you lose immedi-

ately, even if the dealer also busts later in the hand. If your first two cards add up to 21 (a "natural"), you're paid 3 to 2. However, if the dealer also has a natural, it's a push. A natural beats a total of 21 achieved with more than two cards.

You're dealt two cards, either face down or face up, depending on the custom of the particular casino. The dealer also gives herself two cards, one face down and one face up (except in double-exposure blackjack, where both the dealer's cards are visible). Depending on your first two cards and the dealer's up card, you can **stand**, or refuse to take another card. You can **hit**, or take as many cards as you need until you stand or bust. You can **double down**, or double your bet and take one card. You can **split** a like pair; if you're dealt two 8s, for example, you can double your bet and play the 8s as if they're two hands. You can **buy insurance** if the dealer is showing an ace. Here you're wagering half your initial bet that the dealer *does* have a natural; if so, you lose your initial bet, but are paid 2 to 1 on the insurance (which means the whole thing is a push). You can **surrender** half your initial bet if you're holding a bad hand (known as a "stiff") such as a 15 or 16 against a high-up card like a 9 or 10.

**Blackjack Strategy.** Playing blackjack is not only knowing the rules—it's also knowing *how* to play. Many people devote a great deal of time to learning complicated statistical schemes. However, if you don't have the time, energy, or inclination to get that seriously involved, the following basic strategies, which cover more than half the situations you'll face, should allow you to play the game with a modicum of skill and a paucity of humiliation:

- When your hand is a stiff (a total of 12, 13, 14, 15, or 16) and the dealer shows a 2, 3, 4, 5, or 6, always stand.

- When your hand is a stiff and the dealer shows a 7, 8, 9, 10, or ace, always hit.

- When you hold 17, 18, 19, or 20, always stand.

- When you hold a 10 or 11 and the dealer shows a 2, 3, 4, 5, 6, 7, 8, or 9, always double down.

- When you hold a pair of aces or a pair of 8s, always split.

- Never buy insurance.

## Craps

Craps is a dice game played at a large rectangular table with rounded corners. Up to 12 players can crowd around the table, all standing. The layout is mounted at the bottom of a surrounding "rail," which prevents the dice from being thrown off the table and provides an opposite wall against which to bounce the dice. It can require up to four pit personnel to run an action-packed, fast-paced game of craps. Two dealers handle the bets made on either side of the layout. A "stickman" wields the long wooden "stick," curved at one end, which is used to move the dice around the table; the stickman also calls the number that's rolled and books the proposition bets made in the middle of the layout. The "boxman" sits between the two dealers and oversees the game; he settles any disputes about rules, payoffs, mistakes, and so on.

**How to Play.** To play, just stand at the table wherever you can find an open space. You can start betting casino chips immediately, but you have to wait your turn to be the shooter. The dice move around the table in a clockwise fashion: The person to your right shoots before you, the one to the left after (the stickman will give you the dice at the appropriate time). It's important, when you're the "shooter," to roll the dice hard enough so they bounce off the end wall of the table; this ensures a random bounce and shows that you're not trying to control the dice with a "soft roll."

**Craps Strategy.** Playing craps is fairly straightforward; it's the betting that's complicated. The basic concepts are as follows: If, the first time the shooter rolls the dice, he or she turns up a 7 or 11, that's called a "natural"—an automatic win. If a 2, 3, or 12 comes up on the first throw (called the "come-out roll"), that's termed "craps"—an automatic lose. Each of the numbers 4, 5, 6, 8, 9, or 10 on a first roll is known as a "point": The shooter keeps rolling the dice until the point comes up again. If a 7 turns up before the point does, that's another loser. When either the point or a losing 7 is rolled, this is known as a "decision," which happens on average every 3.3 rolls.

But "winning" and "losing" rolls of the dice are entirely relative in this game, because there are two ways you can bet at craps: "for" the shooter or "against" the shooter. Betting for means that the shooter will "make his point" (win). Betting against means that the shooter will "seven out" (lose). (Either way, you're actually betting against the house, which books all wagers.) If you're betting "for" on the come-out, you'd place your chips on the layout's "pass line." If a 7 or 11 is rolled, you win even money. If a 2, 3, or 12 (craps) is rolled, you lose your bet. If you're betting "against" on the come-out, you place your chips in the "don't pass bar." A 7 or 11 loses, a 2, 3, or 12 wins. A shooter can bet for or against himself or herself, as well as for or against the other players.

There are also roughly two dozen wagers you can make on any single specific roll of the dice. Craps strategy books can give you the details on Come/Don't Come, Odds, Place, Buy, Big Six, Field, and Proposition bets.

## Roulette

Roulette is a casino game that utilizes a perfectly balanced wheel with 38 numbers (0, 00, and 1 through 36), a small white ball, a large layout with 11 different betting options, and special "wheel chips." The layout organizes 11 different bets into six "inside bets" (the single numbers, or those closest to the dealer) and five "outside bets" (the grouped bets, or those closest to the players).

The dealer spins the wheel clockwise and the ball counterclockwise. When the ball slows, the dealer announces, "No more bets." The ball drops from the "back track" to the "bottom track," caroming off built-in brass barriers and bouncing in and out of the different cups in the wheel before settling into the cup of the winning number. Then the dealer places a marker on the number and scoops all the losing chips into her corner. Depending on how crowded the game is, the casino can count on roughly 50 spins of the wheel per hour.

**How to Play.** To buy in, place your cash on the layout near the wheel. Inform the dealer of the denomination of the individual unit you intend to play (usually 25¢ or $1, but it can go up as high as $500). Know the table limits (displayed on a sign in the dealer area)—don't ask for a 25¢ denomination if the minimum is $1. The dealer gives you a stack of wheel chips of a different color from those of all the other players, and places a chip marker atop one of your wheel chips on the rim of the wheel to identify its denomination. Note that you must cash in your wheel chips at the roulette table before you leave the game. Only the dealer can verify how much they're worth.

**Roulette Strategy.** With **inside bets,** you can lay any number of chips (depending on the table limits) on a single number, 1 through 36 or 0 or 00. If the number hits, your payoff is 35 to 1, for a return of $36. You could, conceivably, place a $1 chip on all 38 numbers, but the return of $36 would leave you $2 short, which divides out to 5.26%, the house advantage. If you place a chip on the line between two numbers and one of those numbers hits, you're paid 17 to 1 for a return of $18 (again, $2 short of the true odds). Betting on three numbers returns 11 to 1, four numbers returns 8 to 1, five numbers pays 6 to 1 (this is the worst

bet at roulette, with a 7.89% disadvantage), and six numbers pays 5 to 1.

To place an **outside bet,** lay a chip on one of three "columns" at the lower end of the layout next to numbers 34, 35, and 36; this pays 2 to 1. A bet placed in the first 12, second 12, or third 12 boxes also pays 2 to 1. A bet on red or black, odd or even, and 1 through 18 or 19 through 36 pays off at even money, 1 to 1. If you think you can bet on red *and* black, or odd *and* even, in order to play roulette and drink for free all night, think again. The green 0 or 00, which fall outside these two basic categories, will come up on average once every 19 spins of the wheel.

## Slot Machines

Around the turn of the 20th century, Charlie Fey built the first mechanical slot in his San Francisco basement. Slot-machine technology has exploded in the past 20 years, and now there are hundreds of different models, which accept everything from pennies to specially minted $500 tokens. The major advance in the game, however, is the progressive jackpot. Banks of slots within a particular casino are connected by computer, and the jackpot total is displayed on a digital meter above the machines. Generally, the total increases by 5% of the wager. If you're playing a dollar machine, each time you pull the handle (or press the spin button), a nickel is added to the jackpot.

**How to Play.** To play, insert your penny, nickel, quarter, silver dollar, or dollar token into the slot at the far right edge of the machine. Pull the handle or press the spin button, then wait for the reels to spin and stop one by one, and for the machine to determine whether you're a winner (occasionally) or a loser (the rest of the time). It's pretty simple—but because there are so many different types of machines nowadays, be sure you know exactly how the one you're playing operates.

**Slot-Machine Strategy.** The house advantage on slots varies widely from machine to machine, between 3% and 25%. Casinos that advertise a 97% payback are telling you that at least one of their slot machines has a house advantage of 3%. Which one? There's really no way of knowing. Generally, $1 machines pay back at a higher percentage than quarter or nickel machines. On the other hand, machines with smaller jackpots pay back more money more frequently, meaning that you'll be playing with more of your winnings.

One of the all-time great myths about slot machines is that they're "due" for a jackpot. Slots, like roulette, craps, keno, and Big Six, are subject to the Law of Independent Trials, which means the odds are permanently and unalterably fixed. If the odds of lining up three sevens on a 25¢ slot machine have been set by the casino at 1 in 10,000, then those odds remain 1 in 10,000 whether the three 7s have been hit three times in a row or not hit for 90,000 plays. Don't waste a lot of time playing a machine that you suspect is "ready," and don't think if someone hits a jackpot on a particular machine only minutes after you've finished playing on it that it was "yours."

## Video Poker

Like blackjack, video poker is a game of strategy and skill, and at select times on select machines, the player actually holds the advantage, however slight, over the house. Unlike slot machines, you can determine the exact edge of video poker machines. Like slots, however, video poker machines are often tied into a progressive meter; when the jackpot total reaches high enough, you can beat the casino at its own game. The variety of video poker machines is already large, and it's growing steadily larger. All of the different machines are played in similar fashion, but the strategies are different. This section deals only with straight-draw video poker.

**How to Play.** The schedule for the payback on winning hands is posted on the machine, usually above the screen. It lists the returns for a high pair (generally jacks or better), two pair, three of a kind, a flush, full house, straight flush, four of a kind, and royal flush, depending on the number of coins played—usually 1, 2, 3, 4, or 5. Look for machines that pay with a single coin played: one coin for "jacks or better" (meaning a pair of jacks, queens, kings, or aces; any other pair is a stiff), two coins for two pairs, three for three of a kind, six for a flush, nine for a full house, 50 for a straight flush, 100 for four of a kind, and 250 for a royal flush. This is known as a 9/6 machine—one that gives a nine-coin payback for the full house and a six-coin payback for the flush with one coin played. Other machines are known as 8/5 (8 for the full house, 5 for the flush), 7/5, and 6/5.

You want a 9/6 machine because it gives you the best odds: The return from a standard 9/6 straight-draw machine is 99.5%; you give up only a half percent to the house. An 8/5 machine returns 97.3%. On 6/5 machines, the figure drops to 95.1%, slightly less than roulette. Machines with varying paybacks are scattered throughout the casinos. In some you'll see an 8/5 machine right next to a 9/6, and someone will be blithely playing the 8/5 machine!

As with slot machines, it's always optimum to play the maximum number of coins to qualify for the jackpot. You insert five coins into the slot and press the "deal" button. Five cards appear on the screen—say, 5, J, Q, 5, 9. To hold the pair of 5s, you press the hold buttons under the first and fourth cards. The word "hold" appears underneath the two 5s. You then press the "draw" button (often the same button as "deal") and three new cards appear on the screen—say, 10, J, 5. You have three 5s; with five coins bet, the machine will give you 15 credits. Now you can press the "max bet" button: five units will be removed from your number of credits, and five new cards will appear on the screen. You repeat the hold and draw process; if you hit a winning hand, the proper payback will be added to your credits. Those who want coins rather than credit can hit the "cash out" button at any time. Some machines don't have credit counters and automatically dispense coins for a winning hand.

**Video-Poker Strategy.** Like blackjack, video poker has a basic strategy that's been formulated by the computer simulation of hundreds of millions of hands. The most effective way to learn it is with a video poker computer program that deals the cards on your screen, then tutors you in how to play each hand properly. If you don't want to devote that much time to the study of video poker, memorizing these six rules will help you make the right decision for more than half the hands you'll be dealt:

- If you're dealt a completely "stiff" hand (no like cards and no picture cards), draw five new cards.

- If you're dealt a hand with no like cards but with one jack, queen, king, or ace, always hold on to the picture card; if you're dealt two different picture cards, hold both. But if you're dealt three different picture cards, only hold two (the two of the same suit, if that's an option).

- If you're dealt a pair, always hold it, no matter what the face value.

- Never hold a picture card with a pair of 2s through 10s.

- Never draw two cards to try for a straight or a flush.

- Never draw one card to try for an inside straight.

# SMART TRAVEL TIPS

*There are planners and there are those who, excuse the pun, fly by the seat of their pants. We happily place ourselves among the planners. Our writers and editors try to anticipate all the issues you may face before and during any journey, and then they do their research. This section is the product of their efforts. Use it to get excited about your trip to the Bahamas, to inform your travel planning, or to guide you on the road should the seat of your pants start to feel threadbare.*

## ADDRESSES

"Whimsical" might best describe Bahamas addresses. Streets change name for no apparent reason, and many buildings have no numbers. In more remote locations, such as the Out Islands, street addresses often aren't used. To find your destination, you might have to ask a local. Postal codes aren't used throughout the Bahamas.

## AIR TRAVEL

Most international flights to the Bahamas—to Nassau, Freeport, and the Out Islands alike—connect through airports in Florida, New York, Charlotte, Atlanta, Newark, or Philadelphia, depending on the airline. Most domestic flights make a quick stop in Miami or Fort Lauderdale. If you're flying to the Out Islands, you may have to make a connection in both Florida and Nassau—and you still may have to take a ferry or a water taxi to your final destination, as many of the smaller islands do not have airports.

A direct flight from New York City to Nassau takes approximately three hours. The flight from Charlotte to Nassau is two hours, and the flight from Miami to Nassau takes about an hour. It's about a 35-minute flight from Fort Lauderdale to Freeport, and traveling from Miami or Fort Lauderdale to Marsh Harbour takes about an hour. Most flights between the islands of the Bahamas take less than 90 minutes—most of them far less. You'll most likely spend more time on the ground waiting than in the air.

## CARRIERS

Air service to the Bahamas and the Turks
and Caicos varies seasonally, with the
biggest choice of flights usually available
in the Christmas-to-Easter window. Things
can change substantially from year to year.
Carriers come and go, especially in the
Out Islands, which are served mostly by
smaller commuter airlines and charters.
Schedules change frequently. The smallest
cays may have scheduled service only a
few days a week, or may rely mostly on
charters. In the Out Islands, ask your hotel
for flight recommendations, as they are
likely to have the most up-to-date information on carriers and schedules; some
can even help you book air travel.

**▶ To & From the Bahamas ▶ Major Airlines
from the U.S. & Canada Air Canada** ☎ 888/247-
2262 ⊕ www.aircanada.com. **AirTran** ☎ 800/247-
8726 ⊕ www.airtran.com. **American Eagle** ☎ 800/
433-7300 ⊕ www.aa.com. **Continental Airlines**
☎ 800/523-3273 for U.S. and Mexico reservations,
800/231-0856 for international reservations
⊕ www.continental.com. **Delta** ☎ 800/221-1212 or
800/241-4141 ⊕ www.delta.com. **JetBlue** ☎ 800/
538-2583 ⊕ www.jetblue.com. **Northwest Airlines**
☎ 800/225-2525 for U.S. reservations, 800/447-
4747 for international destinations ⊕ www.nwa.
com. **Spirit Airways** ☎ 800/772-7117 ⊕ www.
spiritair.com. **US Airways** ☎ 800/428-4322
⊕ www.usair.com.

**▶ Smaller Airlines Air Sunshine** ☎ 800/327-
8900 or 954/434-8900 ⊕ www.airsunshine.com.
**Bahamasair** ☎ 800/222-4262 ⊕ www.
bahamasair.com. **Chalks Ocean Airways** ☎ 800/
424-2557 ⊕ www.flychalks.com. **Cherokee Air**
☎ 242/367-3450 ⊕ www.cherokeeair.com. **Comair**
☎ 800/221-1212 ⊕ www.comair.com. **Gulfstream
International Airways** ☎ 800/231-0856 ⊕ www.
gulfstreamair.com. **Island Express** ☎ 954/359-
0380 ⊕ www.oii.net/islandexpress. **Lynx Air International** ☎ 888/596-9247 ⊕ www.lynxair.com.
**Twin Air** ☎ 954/359-8266 ⊕ www.flytwinair.com.
**Vintage Props and Jets** ☎ 800/852-0275 ⊕ www.
vpj.com. **Yellow Air Taxi** ☎ 888/935-5694
⊕ www.flyyellowairtaxi.com.

**▶ Within the Bahamas Air Charter Bahamas**
☎ 866/359-4752 ⊕ www.aircharterbahamas.com.
**Bahamasair** ☎ 242/377-5505 ⊕ www.bahamasair.
com. **LeAir** ☎ 242/377-2356 ⊕ www.leaircharters.
com. **Take Flight Air Charters** ☎ 242/362-1877
⊕ www.takeflightcharters.com.

**▶ Within the Turks & Caicos Air Turks and Caicos**
☎ 649/941-5481 ⊕ www.airturksandcaicos.com.
**Global Airways** ☎ 649/941-3222 ⊕ www.
globalairways.tc. **Sky King** ☎ 649/941-3136
⊕ www.skyking.tc.

## CHECK-IN & BOARDING

**Double-check your flight times,** especially
if you made your reservations far in advance. Airlines change their schedules, and
alerts may not reach you. Always **bring a
government-issued photo ID to the airport**
(even when it's not required, a passport is
best), and **arrive when you need to and
not before.** Check-in usually at least an
hour before domestic flights and two to
three hours for international flights. But
many airlines have more stringent advance
check-in requirements at some busy airports. The TSA estimates the waiting time
for security at most major airports and
publishes the information on its Web site.
Not that if you aren't at the gate at least
10 minutes before your flight is scheduled
to take off (sometimes earlier), you won't
be allowed to board.

**Don't stand in a line if you don't have to.**
Buy an e-ticket, check in at an electronic
kiosk, or—even better—check in on your
airline's Web site before you leave home. If
you don't need to check luggage, you
could bypass all but the security lines.
These days, most domestic airline tickets
are electronic; international tickets may be
either electronic or paper.

You usually pay a surcharge (up to $50) to
get a paper ticket, and its sole advantage is
that it may be easier to endorse over to another airline if your flight is canceled and
the airline with which you booked can't
accommodate you on another flight. With
an e-ticket, the only thing you receive is an
e-mailed receipt citing your itinerary and
reservation and ticket numbers. Be sure to
carry this with you as you'll need it to get
past security. If you lose your receipt,
though, you can simply print out another
copy or ask the airline to do it for you at
check-in.

Particularly during busy travel seasons and
around holiday periods, if a flight is over-
sold, the gate agent will usually ask for
volunteers and will offer some sort of

compensation if you're willing to take a different flight. (This is a common occurrence in Miami.) **Know your rights.** If you are bumped from a flight *involuntarily,* the airline must give you some kind of compensation if an alternate flight can't be found within one hour. If your flight is delayed because of something within the airline's control (so bad weather doesn't count), then the airline has a responsibility to get you to your destination on the same day, even if they have to book you on another airline and in an upgraded class if necessary. Read your airline's Contract of Carriage; it's usually buried somewhere on the airline's Web site.

**Be prepared** to quickly adjust your plans by programming a few numbers into your cell: your airline, an airport hotel or two, your destination hotel, your car service, and/or your travel agent. Bring snacks, water, and sufficient diversions, and you'll be covered if you get stuck in the airport, on the tarmac, or even in the air during turbulence.

## CUTTING COSTS

It's always good to **comparison shop.** Web sites (aka consolidators) and travel agents can have different arrangements with the airlines and offer different prices for exactly the same flight and day. Certain Web sites have tracking features that will e-mail you immediately when good deals are posted. Other people prefer to stick with one or two frequent-flier programs, racking up free trips and accumulating perks that can make trips easier. On some airlines, perks include a special reservations number, early boarding, access to upgrades, and more roomy economy-class seating.

**Check early and often.** Start looking for cheap fares up to a year in advance, and keep looking until you see something you can live with; you never know when a good deal may pop up. That said, **jump on the good deals.** Waiting even a few minutes might mean paying more. For most people, saving money is more important than flexibility, so the more affordable nonrefundable tickets work. Just remember that you'll pay dearly (often as much as $100) if you must change your travel

plans. Check on prices for departures at different times of the day and to and from alternate airports, and look for departures on Tuesday, Wednesday, and Thursday, typically the cheapest days to travel. Remember to **weigh your options,** though. A cheaper flight might have a long layover rather than being nonstop, or landing at a secondary airport might substantially increase your ground transportation costs.

Note that many airline Web sites—and most ads—show prices *without* taxes and surcharges. Don't buy until you know the full price. Government taxes add up quickly. Also **watch those ticketing fees.** Surcharges are usually added when you buy your ticket anywhere but on an airline's own Web site. (By the way, that includes on the phone—even if you call the airline directly—and for paper tickets regardless of how you book).

**Look into air passes.** Many airlines, singly or in collaboration, offer discount air passes that allow foreigners to travel economically in a particular country or region. These visitor passes usually must be reserved and purchased before you leave home. Information about passes often can be found on most airlines' international Web pages, which tend to be aimed at travelers from outside the carrier's home country. Also, try typing the name of the pass into a search engine, or search for "pass" within the carrier's Web site.

When you fly as a courier, you trade your checked-luggage space for a ticket deeply subsidized by a courier service. There are restrictions on when you can book and how long you can stay. Some courier companies list with membership organizations, such as the Air Courier Association and the International Association of Air Travel Couriers; these require you to become a member before you can book a flight.

🛪 Online Consolidators **AirlineConsolidator.com** ⊕ www.airlineconsolidator.com; for international tickets. **Best Fares** ⊕ www.bestfares.com; $59.90 annual membership. **Cheap Tickets** ⊕ www.cheaptickets.com. **Expedia** ⊕ www.expedia.com. **Hotwire** ⊕ www.hotwire.com; Hotwire is a discounter. **lastminute.com** ⊕ www.lastminute.com; specializes in last-minute travel; the main site is for the UK, but it has a link to a U.S. site. **Luxury Link** ⊕ www.luxurylink.com; has auctions (surprisingly good deals) as well as offers at the high-end side of travel. **Orbitz** ⊕ www.orbitz.com. **Onetravel.com** ⊕ www.onetravel.com. **Priceline.com** ⊕ www.priceline.com; Priceline is a discounter that also allows bidding. **Travel.com** ⊕ www.travel.com; allows you to compare its rates with those of other booking engines. **Travelocity** ⊕ www.travelocity.com; charges a booking fee for airline tickets but promises good problem resolution.

▣ Courier Resources **Air Courier Association/ Cheaptrips.com** ☏ 800/461-8856 ⊕ www.aircourier.org or www.cheaptrips.com; $39 annual membership. **Courier Travel** ☏ 303/570-7586 ⊕ www.couriertravel.org; $40 one-time membership fee. **International Association of Air Travel Couriers** ☏ 308/632-3273 ⊕ www.courier.org; $45 annual membership.

### ENJOYING THE FLIGHT

**Get the seat you want.** Avoid those on the aisle directly across from the lavatories. Most frequent fliers say those are even worse than the seats that don't recline (e.g., those in the back row and those in front of a bulkhead). For more legroom, you can request emergency-aisle seats, but only do so if you're capable of moving the 35- to 60-pound airplane exit door—a Federal Aviation Administration requirement of passengers in these seats. Seats behind a bulkhead also offer more legroom, but they don't have under-seat storage. Often, you can pick a seat when you buy your ticket on an airline's Web site. But it's not always a guarantee, particularly if the airline changes the plane after you book your ticket; check back before you leave. SeatGuru.com has more information about specific seat configurations, which vary by aircraft.

Fewer airlines are providing free food for passengers in economy class. **Don't go hungry.** If you're scheduled to fly during meal times, verify if your airline offers anything to eat; even when it does, be prepared to pay. If you have dietary concerns, request special meals. These can be vegetarian, low-cholesterol, or kosher, for example. It's a good idea to pack some healthful snacks and a small (plastic) bottle of water in your carry-on bag.

**Ask the airline about its children's menus, activities, and fares.** On some lines infants and toddlers fly for free if they sit on a parent's lap, and older children fly for half price in their own seats. Also inquire about policies involving car seats; having one may limit where you can sit. While you're at it, ask about seatbelt extenders for car seats. And note that you can't count on a flight attendant to automatically produce an extender; you may have to inquire about it again when you board.

### HOW TO COMPLAIN

If your baggage goes astray or your flight goes awry, complain right away. Most carriers require that you **file a claim immediately.** The Aviation Consumer Protection Division of the Department of Transportation publishes *Fly-Rights,* which discusses airlines and consumer issues and is available online. You can also find articles and information on mytravelrights.com, the Web site of the nonprofit Consumer Travel Rights Center.

▣ Airline Complaints **Office of Aviation Enforcement and Proceedings** (Aviation Consumer Protection Division) ☏ 202/366-2220 ⊕ airconsumer.ost.dot.gov. **Federal Aviation Administration Consumer Hotline** ☏ 866/835-5322 ⊕ www.faa.gov.

### AIRPORTS

The major gateways to the Bahamas include Freeport International Airport (FPO), on Grand Bahama Island, and Nassau International Airport (NAS), on New Providence Island. There are also some direct flights from Florida to Out Islands airports such as Marsh Harbour (MHH) and Treasure Cay (TCB) in the Abacos. For more airports, ⇨ Essentials *in* individual chapters.

▣ Airport Information **Freeport International Airport** ☏ 242/352-6020. **Nassau International Airport** ☏ 242/377-7281. **Airline and Airport Links.com** ⊕ www.airlineandairportlinks.com has links to many of the world's airlines and airports.

▣ Airline Security Issues **Transportation Security Agency** ⊕ www.tsa.gov/public has answers for almost every question that might come up.

### BIKE TRAVEL

Biking in the Bahamas is fairly easy due to the flat island terrain. Some hotels offer bikes as amenities to their guests, or rent them out. So do general stores. In the Out Islands and Turks and Caicos, bikes are often the most logical way to get around on land and match the laid-back pace of life. For the location of bike rental outlets, ⇨ Biking *in* individual chapters.

### BIKES IN FLIGHT

Most airlines accommodate bikes as luggage, provided they are dismantled and boxed; check with individual airlines about packing requirements. Some airlines sell bike boxes, which are often free at bike shops, for about $20 (bike bags can be considerably more expensive). International travelers often can substitute a bike for a piece of checked luggage at no charge; otherwise, the cost is about $100. Most U.S. and Canadian airlines charge $40–$80 each way.

### BOAT & FERRY TRAVEL

If you're of an adventurous frame of mind, and have time to spare, you can revert to the mode of transportation that islanders used before the advent of air travel: ferries and the traditional mail-boats, which regularly leave Nassau from Potter's Cay, under the Paradise Island bridge. Although fast, modern, air-conditioned boats now make some of the trips, some of the more remote destinations are still served by slow, old-fashioned craft with few amenities. Especially if you choose the mailboat route, you may even find yourself sharing company with goats or chickens, and making your way on deck through piles of lumber and crates of cargo; on these lumbering mailboats, expect to spend 5 to 12 or more hours slowly making your way between island outposts. **Don't plan to arrive or depart punctually**; the flexible schedules can be thrown off by bad weather. Remember, too, that they operate on Bahamian time, which is a casual, unpredictable measure. The larger ferries now can be booked ahead of time, and even online, but mail-boats cannot generally be booked in advance, and services are limited. In Nassau, check details with the dockmaster's office at Potter's Cay. You can purchase tickets from the dockmaster or from the captain or mate just before departure.

From Florida, the Discovery Cruise Line travels to Grand Bahama Island daily with its 1,100-passenger Discovery Sun, complete with swimming pool, casino, live entertainment, disco, and buffets. Passengers can either make it just a day trip, arriving in the Bahamas in the morning and departing that afternoon, or stay on the island for a few days. Round-trip fares start at about $120.

Within the Bahamas, Bahamas Fast Ferry has the most, and most comfortable, options for island-hopping, with air-conditioned boats that offer food and beverages served by cabin attendants. As with most things in the Bahamas, schedules do change rather frequently; if you're planning to ferry back to an island to catch a flight, check and double-check the departure times, and build in extra time in case the weather's bad or the boat inexplicably doesn't make the trip you'd planned on. Ferries serve most of the major tourist destinations from Nassau, including Spanish Wells, Governor's Harbour, Harbour Island, Abaco, Exuma, and Andros. The high-speed ferry that runs between Nassau and Spanish Wells, Governor's Harbour, and Harbour Island costs $110 one-way, and takes about two hours each way.

Local ferries in the Out Islands transport islanders and visitors from the main island to smaller cays. Usually, these ferries make several round-trips daily, and keep a more punctual schedule than the longer-haul ferry. The Out Island ferry captains keep in close touch with the airports, so, for instance, if your flight is delayed, the last ferry of the day might wait around a while for stragglers. (Or, it might not. Check with your hotel or rental villa to see what types of alternate transportation they can arrange in case you miss the day's last ferry.) From the ferry docks, if you've missed the boat, so to speak, you can sometimes catch a ride to outlying cays with locals, but if you do, always offer to chip in for gas, which is expensive in the Bahamas.

If you're setting sail yourself, note that cruising boats must clear customs at the nearest port of entry before beginning any diving or fishing. The fee is $150 for boats 35 feet and under and $300 for boats 36 feet and longer, which includes fishing permits and departure tax for up to four persons. Each additional person above the age of four will be charged the $15 departure tax. Stays of longer than 12 months must be arranged with Bahamas customs and immigration officials.

### FARES & SCHEDULES

🚣 Boat & Ferry Information **Bahamas Fast Ferry** ☎ 242/323-2166 🖨 242/322-8185 🌐 www.bahamasferries.com. **Discovery Cruise Line** ☎ 888/213-8253 🌐 www.discoverycruise.com. **Potter's Cay dockmaster** ☎ 242/393-1064.

## BUSINESS HOURS

### BANKS & OFFICES

Banks are generally open Monday–Thursday 9 or 9:30 to 3 or 4 and Friday 9 to 5. However, on the Out Islands, banks may keep shorter hours—on the smallest cays, they may be open only a day or two each week. ATMs are common on the larger and more heavily populated islands, but don't count on finding one when you need it on some of the more remote cays. (Most ATMs, by the way, dispense Bahamian dollars.) Most Bahamian offices observe bank hours.

### MUSEUMS & SIGHTS

Hours for attractions vary. Most open between 9 and 10 and close around 5.

### PHARMACIES

Though most drugstores typically abide by normal store hours, some stay open 24 hours.

### SHOPS

Shops in downtown Nassau are open Monday–Saturday 9 to 5. Grand Bahama's International Bazaar and Port Lucaya Marketplace are open 10 to 6. Most stores, with the exception of straw markets and malls, close on Sunday. **Shop in the morning,** when streets are less crowded. Remember that when you're shopping in Nassau, Freeport, and Port Lucaya, you may be competing with the hordes of passengers that pour off cruise ships daily.

## BUS TRAVEL

Buses on New Providence Island and Grand Bahama are called jitneys, and are actually vans. Route numbers are clearly marked, and there's usually service from early morning until dusk. Exact change (usually $1 around town; more for long-distance travel) is required, and although there are established stops, you can sometimes hail a jitney. Let the driver know where you would like to get off. There's no bus service on most of the Out Islands.

## CAMERAS & PHOTOGRAPHY

Frothy waves in a turquoise sea and palm-lined crescents of beach are relatively easy to capture on film if you **don't let the brightness of the sun on sand and water fool your light meter.** You'll need to compensate or else work early or late in the day when the light isn't as brilliant and contrast isn't such a problem. Try to **capture expansive views** of waterfront, beach, or village scenes; consider shooting down onto the shore from a clearing on a hillside or from a rock on the beach. Or **zoom in on something colorful,** such as a delicate tropical flower or a craftsman at work. Always **ask permission to take pictures of locals or their property** and **offer a gratuity.** The *Kodak Guide to Shooting Great Travel Pictures* (available at bookstores everywhere) is loaded with tips.

📷 Photo Help **Kodak Information Center** 🌐 www.kodak.com.

### EQUIPMENT PRECAUTIONS

**Don't pack film or equipment in checked luggage,** where it's much more susceptible to damage. X-ray machines used to view checked luggage are extremely powerful and therefore are likely to ruin your film. Try to ask for hand inspection of film, which becomes clouded after repeated exposure to airport X-ray machines, and keep videotapes and computer disks away from metal detectors. Always keep film, tape, and computer disks out of the sun. Carry an extra supply of batteries, and be prepared to turn on your camera, camcorder, or laptop to prove to airport security personnel that the device is real.

## FILM & DEVELOPING

If you're using a digital camera, bring plenty of memory with you. Although digital accessories are available in the larger cities and resort areas, the selection is limited, and what you find is likely to cost quite a bit more than it would back home. Similarly, film is expensive in the Bahamas, so it's best to bring it with you. Popular brands of film are available in Nassau and Freeport, with a more limited selection in the Out Islands. Likewise, you'll find film-developing stores (some with one-hour service) in shopping centers in Nassau and Freeport, but developing will likely be pricier and more difficult to find in the Out Islands.

## CAR RENTAL

To rent a car, you must be 21 years of age or older in both the Bahamas and the Turks and Caicos, the latter of which charges a flat tax of $10 on all rentals.

Request car seats and extras such as GPS when you book, and make sure that a confirmed reservation guarantees you a car. Agencies sometimes overbook, particularly for busy weekends and holiday periods. Rates are sometimes—but not always—better if you book in advance or reserve through a rental agency's Web site. There are other reasons to book ahead, though: for popular destinations, during busy times of the year, or to ensure that you get a certain type of car (vans, SUVs, exotic sports cars).

Your driver's license may not be recognized outside your home country. You may not be able to rent a car without an International driving permit (IDP), which can be used only in conjunction with a valid driver's license and which translates your license into 10 languages. Check the AAA Web site for more info as well as for IDPs ($10) themselves.

▣ Major Agencies **Alamo** ☎ 800/522-9696 ⊕ www.alamo.com. **Avis** ☎ 800/331-1084 ⊕ www. avis.com. **Budget** ☎ 800/472-3325 ⊕ www.budget. com. **Hertz** ☎ 800/654-3001 ⊕ www.hertz.com. **National Car Rental** ☎ 800/227-7368 ⊕ www. nationalcar.com.

▣ Automobile Associations U.S.: **American Automobile Association (AAA)** ☎ 315/797-5000 ⊕ www.aaa.com; most contact with the organization is through state and regional members. **National Automobile Club** ☎ 650/294-7000 ⊕ www. thenac.com; membership is open to California residents only.

## CUTTING COSTS

**Really weigh your options.** Find out if a credit card you carry or organization or frequent-renter program to which you belong has a discount program. And check that such discounts really are the best deal. You can often do better with special weekend or weekly rates offered by a rental agency. (And even if you only want to rent for five or six days, ask if you can get the weekly rate; it may very well be cheaper than the daily rate for that period of time.)

Price local car-rental companies as well as the majors. Also investigate wholesalers, which don't own fleets but rent in bulk from those that do and often offer better rates (note you must usually pay for such rentals before leaving home). Consider adding a car rental onto your air–hotel vacation package; the cost will often be cheaper than if you had rented the car separately on your own.

When traveling abroad, **look for guaranteed exchange rates,** which protect you against a falling dollar. With your rate locked in, you won't pay more, even if the price goes up in the local currency. (Note to self: not the best thing if the dollar is surging rather than plunging.)

**Beware of hidden charges.** Those great rental rates may not be so great when you add in taxes, surcharges, cancellation penalties, taxes, drop-off charges (if you're planning to pick up the car in one city and leave it in another), and surcharges (for being under or over a certain age, for additional drivers, or for driving over state or country borders or out of a specific radius from your point of rental).

Note that airport rental offices often add supplementary surcharges that you may avoid by renting from an agency with an office just off airport property. Don't buy the tank of gas that's in the car when you rent it unless you plan to do a lot of driving. Avoid hefty refueling fees by filling the tank at a station well away from the rental agency (those nearby are often more expensive) just before you turn in the car.

## INSURANCE

Everyone who rents a car wonders about whether the insurance that the rental companies offer is worth the expense. No one—not even us—has a simple answer. This is particularly true abroad, where laws are different than at home.

If you own a car, your personal auto insurance may cover a rental to some degree, though not all policies protect you abroad; always read your policy's fine print. If you don't have auto insurance, then seriously consider buying the collision- or loss-damage waiver (CDW or LDW) from the car-rental company, which eliminates your liability for damage to the car. Some credit cards offer CDW coverage, but it's usually supplemental to your own insurance and rarely covers SUVs, minivans, luxury models, and the like. If your coverage is secondary, you may still be liable for loss-of-use costs from the car-rental company. But no credit-card insurance is valid unless you use that card for *all* transactions, from reserving to paying the final bill. All companies exclude car rental in some countries, so be sure to find out about the destination to which you're traveling.

Some countries require you to purchase CDW coverage or require car-rental companies to include it in quoted rates. Ask your rental company about issues like these in your destination. In most cases, it's cheaper to add a supplemental CDW plan to your comprehensive travel insurance policy ( ⇨ Trip Insurance *under* Things to Consider *in* Getting Started, *above*) than to purchase it from a rental company. That said, you don't want to pay for a supplement if you're required to buy insurance from the rental company.

Note that you can decline the insurance from the rental company and purchase it through a third-party provider such as Travel Guard (www.travelguard.com)—$9 per day for $35,000 of coverage. That's sometimes just under half the price of the CDW offered by some car-rental companies. Also, Diners Club offers primary CDW coverage on all rentals reserved and paid for with the card. This means that Diners Club's company—not your own car insurance—pays in case of an accident. It *doesn't* mean your car-insurance company won't raise your rates once it discovers you had an accident.

## CAR TRAVEL

### EMERGENCY SERVICES

In case of road emergency, **stay in your vehicle with emergency flashers engaged and wait for help,** especially after dark. If someone stops to help, relay information through a small opening in the window. If it's daylight and help does not arrive, walk to the nearest phone and call for help. In the Bahamas, motorists readily stop to help drivers in distress.

### ROAD CONDITIONS

In and around Nassau, roads are good, although a bit crowded in peak season. From 7 to 10 AM and 3 to 6 PM, downtown Nassau and most major arteries are congested with cars and pedestrians. When cruise ships are in, pedestrian traffic further stifles the flow. On Grand Bahama Island and the Out Islands, conditions vary from the perfectly paved and manicured boulevards in Freeport to narrow and winding countryside roads that are filled with potholes. **Make sure you have a spare tire in good condition and necessary tools.**

### ROAD MAPS

Bahamas Trailblazer Maps and AT&T Road Maps, which are fairly dependable (some small streets and roads are not included), are distributed for free throughout the islands.

### RULES OF THE ROAD

Remember, like the British, islanders **drive on the left side of the road,** which can be confusing because most cars are American with the steering wheel on the left. It is illegal, however, to make a left-hand turn on a red light. Many streets in downtown Nassau are one-way. Roundabouts pose further confusion to Americans. Remember to keep left and yield to oncoming traffic as you enter the roundabout and at GIVE WAY signs.

## CHILDREN IN THE BAHAMAS

Small visitors will generally receive a very warm welcome from Bahamians, especially in the smaller settlements, where children will receive special attention and, sometimes, little treats at restaurants and cafés. Be sure to plan ahead and **involve your youngsters** as you outline your trip. Take them to the library and **find children's books about life in the islands** to prepare them for the new culture they will be experiencing. Check out *The Bahamas* from the Enchantment of the World Book Series, by Martin and Stephen Hintz (recommended for ages 8 to 12), to get your kids up to speed. When packing, include things to keep them busy en route. On sight-seeing days, try to schedule activities of special interest to your children. Besides beaches, the Bahamas offers a variety of kid-friendly parks, museums, natural attractions, and opportunities to learn how to make local crafts. Many large resorts supervise children's programs. The Out Islands are less accommodating, but even the most remote areas, with their rich culture and family-centric lifestyles, are intriguing to children. **Make your visit a learning experience for the children** whenever possible.

If you're renting a car, don't forget to arrange for a car seat when you reserve.

## FLYING TO THE BAHAMAS

If your children are two or older, ask about children's airfares. As a general rule, infants under two not occupying a seat fly at greatly reduced fares or even for free. But if you want to guarantee a seat for an infant, you have to pay full fare. Consider flying during off-peak days and times; most airlines will grant an infant a seat without a ticket if there are available seats. When booking, confirm carry-on allowances if you're traveling with infants. In general, for babies charged 10% to 50% of the adult fare you're allowed one carry-on bag and a collapsible stroller; if the flight is full, the stroller may have to

be checked or you may be limited to less carry-on baggage.

Experts agree that it's a good idea to use safety seats aloft for children weighing less than 40 pounds. Airlines set their own policies: if you use a safety seat, U.S. carriers usually require that the child be ticketed, even if he or she is young enough to ride free, because the seats must be strapped into regular seats. And even if you pay the full adult fare for the seat, it may be worth it, especially on longer trips. Do **check your airline's policy about using safety seats during takeoff and landing.** Safety seats are not allowed everywhere in the plane, so get your seat assignments as early as possible.

When reserving, request children's meals or a freestanding bassinet (not available at all airlines) if you need them. But note that bulkhead seats, where you must sit to use the bassinet, may lack an overhead bin or storage space on the floor.

If you plan on taking your child to the Bahamas alone (without the other parent being present on the same flight), be prepared to show additional documentation. This may include a notarized statement from the other parent giving permission to take the child into the country. If the parent and the child do not share the same last name, it may even be necessary to show a marriage license or divorce decree to prove the relationship. Check with your airline well in advance of the trip to avoid surprises at the airport.

## FOOD

Nassau and Freeport have all the fast-food chains children love. Try to **introduce them to local cuisine,** which is entirely palatable to children. Peas 'n' rice, macaroni and cheese, and chicken are common specialties. Adventurous little ones will think it's fun eating local specialties such as conch fritters, grouper "burgers"—essentially fried-fish sandwiches—and johnnycake.

## LODGING

Most hotels in the Bahamas allow children under a certain age to stay in their parents' room at no extra charge, but others charge for them as extra adults; be sure to find out the cutoff age for children's discounts. Breezes, Sandals, some small inns, and some exclusive rental villas discourage or don't permit children. Be sure to ask. Other large resorts are designed around families. Resorts with fine kids' facilities and programs include Atlantis in Paradise Island, Radisson Cable Beach Resort, Nassau Marriott Resort, Our Lucaya in Grand Bahama Island, Small Hope Bay in Andros, and Beaches in Providenciales.

## PRECAUTIONS

Babies' and children's skin is highly susceptible to the strength of the tropical sun. Child-grade sun protection is available in Nassau, Freeport, and other large towns. If you're staying on an Out Island, **bring your own child-grade sun protection.** It's also best to bring along your own child-friendly insect repellent, which can be hard to find on some islands. Some small children object less to insect repellent in the form of creams and towelettes than to the traditional aerosol versions.

It's also a good idea to check with locals before you head for a swim at a deserted beach—currents can sometimes be too rough for kids, and for many adults.

## SIGHTS & ATTRACTIONS

Places that are especially appealing to children are indicated by a rubber-duckie icon (☝) in the margin.

## SUPPLIES & EQUIPMENT

Disposable diapers, baby formula, and other necessities are widely available throughout the Bahamas, though at a higher price than you would pay at home. **Take your own disposable diapers** so you will have the extra space for souvenirs on the trip home. For older children, you can find toys and games at stores throughout the islands, again at up to double what they would cost in the States. Straw markets sell inexpensive maracas and folk dolls. Think twice before lugging a heavy stroller along; if you're spending much of your time at the beach, it will be useless. Instead, a lightweight, basic umbrella stroller, or a baby carrier in the form of a sling or a backpack, may be more convenient.

## COMPUTERS ON THE ROAD

If you're carrying a laptop into the Bahamas, you must **fill out a Declaration of Value form** upon arrival, noting make, model, and serial number. **Bring an extra battery.** They're not always readily available in out-of-the-city locations. Bahamian electrical current is compatible with U.S. computers. If you're traveling from abroad, **pack a standard adaptor.** Wireless Internet service is becoming more available throughout the islands, but there are still pockets where service is impossible or difficult to get, and it's likely to be slower than you may be accustomed to. If Internet service is an important consideration to you, ask your hotel representative about service before traveling.

## CONSUMER PROTECTION

Whether you're shopping for gifts or purchasing travel services, **pay with a major credit card** whenever possible, so you can cancel payment or get reimbursed if there's a problem (and you can provide documentation). If you're doing business with a particular company for the first time, contact your local Better Business Bureau and the attorney general's offices in your state and (for U.S. businesses) the company's home state as well. Have any complaints been filed? Finally, if you're buying a package or tour, always consider travel insurance that includes default coverage (⇨ Insurance on page 313).

⇨ Insurance on page 313

🛈 BBBs **Council of Better Business Bureaus** ☎ 703/276-0100 ⊕ www.bbb.org.

## CRUISE TRAVEL

A cruise can be one of the most pleasurable ways to see the islands. A multi-island excursion allows for plenty of land-time because of the short travel times between destinations. Be sure to shop around before booking.

🛈 Cruise Lines **Carnival Cruise Line** ☎ 305/599-2600 or 800/227-6482 ⊕ www.carnival.com. **Celebrity Cruises** ☎ 305/539-6000 or 800/437-3111 ⊕ www.celebrity.com. **Costa Cruises** ☎ 954/266-5600 or 800/462-6782 ⊕ www.costacruise.com. **Crystal Cruises** ☎ 310/785-9300 or 800/446-6620 ⊕ www.crystalcruises.com. **Discovery Cruise Line**

☎ 800/866-8687 ⊕ www.discoverycruise.com.
**Disney Cruise Line** ☎ 407/566-3500 or 800/951–
3532 ⊕ www.disneycruise.com. **Holland America
Line** ☎ 206/281-3535 or 877/932-4259 ⊕ www.
hollandamerica.com. **Norwegian Cruise Line**
☎ 305/436-4000 or 800/327-7030 ⊕ www.ncl.
com. **Oceania Cruises** ☎ 305/514-2300 or 800/531-
5658 ⊕ www.oceaniacruises.com. **Princess Cruises**
☎ 661/753-0000 or 800/774-6237 ⊕ www.
princess.com. **Regent Seven Seas Cruises** ☎ 954/
776-6123 or 800/477-7500 ⊕ www.rssc.com. **Royal
Caribbean International** ☎ 305/539-6000 or 800/
327-6700 ⊕ www.royalcaribbean.com. **Silversea
Cruises** ☎ 954/522-4477 or 800/722-9955 ⊕ www.
silversea.com. **Windjammer Barefoot Cruises**
☎ 305/672-6453 or 800/327-2601 ⊕ www.
windjammer.com.

## CUSTOMS & DUTIES

You're always allowed to bring goods of a certain value back home without having to pay any duty or import tax. There's also a limit on the amount of tobacco and liquor you can bring back duty-free, and some countries have separate limits for perfumes; for exact figures, check with your customs department. The values of so-called "duty-free" goods are included in these amounts. When you shop abroad, save all your receipts as customs inspectors may ask to see them as well as the items you purchased. If the total value of your goods is more than the duty-free limit, then you'll have to pay a tax (most often a flat percentage) on the value of everything beyond that limit.

### INFORMATION IN THE BAHAMAS & TURKS & CAICOS

Customs allows you to bring in 1 liter of wine or liquor and five cartons of cigarettes in addition to personal effects, purchases up to $100, and all the money you wish. Certain types of personal belongings may get a raised eyebrow—an extensive collection of CDs or DVDs, for instance—if they suspect you may be planning to try to sell them while in the country. However, real hassles at immigration are rare, since officials realize tourists are the lifeblood of the economy. But **don't even think of smuggling** in marijuana or any kind of narcotic. Justice is swift and severe in the Bahamas.

You would be well advised to **leave pets at home,** unless you're considering a prolonged stay in the islands. An import permit is required from the Ministry of Agriculture and Fisheries for all animals brought into the Bahamas. The animal must be more than six months old. You'll also need a veterinary health certificate issued by a licensed vet. The permit is good for one year from the date of issue, costs $15, and the process must be completed immediately before departure.

🛈 **Ministry of Agriculture and Fisheries** ⊠ Box N3028, Nassau ☎ 242/325-7502.

### U.S. INFORMATION

U.S. residents who have been out of the country for at least 48 hours may bring home $800 worth of foreign goods duty-free, as long as they have not used the $800 allowance or any part of it in the past 30 days. If you're returning from a U.S. insular possession, such as the U.S. Virgin Islands (USVI), the duty-free allowance is $1,600. If your travel included the USVI and another country—say, the Dominican Republic—the $1,600 allowance still applies, but at least $800 worth of goods has to be from the USVI.

U.S. residents 21 and older may bring back 2 liters of alcohol duty-free, as long as one of the liters was produced in a Caribbean Basin Initiative (CBI) country. In addition, regardless of your age, you are allowed 200 cigarettes and 100 non-Cuban cigars. Antiques, which U.S. Customs and Border Protection defines as objects more than 100 years old, enter duty-free, as do original works of art done entirely by hand, including paintings, drawings, and sculptures. This doesn't apply to folk art or handicrafts, which are in general dutiable. You may also send packages home duty-free, with a limit of one parcel per addressee per day (except alcohol or tobacco products or perfume worth more than $5). You can mail up to $200 worth of goods for personal use; label the package PERSONAL USE and attach a list of its contents and their retail value. If the package contains your used personal belongings, mark it PERSONAL GOODS RETURNED to avoid paying duties. You may send up to $100 worth of goods as a gift; mark the package UNSOLICITED GIFT. Mailed items do not affect your duty-free allowance on your return.

◪ **U.S. Customs and Border Protection** ✉ For inquiries and equipment registration, 1300 Pennsylvania Ave. NW, Washington, DC 20229 ⊕ www.cbp. gov ☎ 877/287-8667 or 202/354-1000 ✉ For complaints, Customer Satisfaction Unit, 1300 Pennsylvania Ave. NW, Room 5.2C, Washington, DC 20229.

## DISABILITIES & ACCESSIBILITY

In general, the Bahamas offer good options for those with limited mobility: the terrain throughout the islands is relatively flat; many hotels have been built or renovated with features that can accommodate wheelchairs or walkers; and downtown Nassau took into account wheelchair accessibility when it underwent redevelopment in 1995. The Bahamas Association for the Physically Disabled has a bus for hire that can pick up people with disabilities from the airport or provide other transportation. Reservations must be made well in advance.

◪ Local Resources **Bahamas Association for the Physically Disabled** ☎ 242/322-2393.

## LODGING

Most major hotels throughout the Bahamas have special facilities for people with disabilities, in the way of elevators, ramps, and easy access to rooms and public areas. However, some properties may have only a few rooms designed to accommodate wheelchairs, for instance, and in the Out Islands, what locals consider accessible may not be up to the standards to which travelers are accustomed.

If you have mobility problems, ask for the lowest floor on which accessible services are offered. If you have a hearing impairment, check whether the hotel has devices to alert you visually to the ring of the telephone, a knock at the door, and a fire/emergency alarm. Some hotels provide these devices without charge. Discuss your needs with hotel personnel if this equipment isn't available, so that a staff member can personally alert you in the event of an emergency.

If you're bringing a guide dog, get authorization ahead of time and write down the name of the person with whom you spoke.

### RESERVATIONS

When discussing accessibility with an operator or reservations agent, ask hard questions. Are there any stairs, inside *or* out? Are there grab bars next to the toilet *and* in the shower/tub? How wide is the doorway to the room? To the bathroom? For the most extensive facilities meeting the latest legal specifications, opt for newer accommodations. If you reserve through a toll-free number, consider also calling the hotel's local number to confirm the information from the central reservations office. Get confirmation in writing when you can.

### SIGHTS & ATTRACTIONS

The beaches of the Bahamas and the Turks and Caicos are generally accessible. In Grand Bahama Island, the two largest shopping malls—International Bazaar and Port Lucaya—have some second-story restaurants not accessible by wheelchair. The Dolphin Experience can make special arrangements for travelers with disabilities. In Nassau, Ardastra Gardens is accessible in most areas, Government House has limited access, and Parliament Square is fully accessible.

### TRANSPORTATION

The U.S. Department of Transportation Aviation Consumer Protection Division's online publication *New Horizons: Information for the Air Traveler with a Disability* offers advice for travellers with a disability, and outlines basic rights. Visit DisabilityInfo.gov for general information.

◪ Information and Complaints **Aviation Consumer Protection Division** (⇨ Air Travel for airline-related problems; ⊕ airconsumer.ost.dot.gov/publications/horizons.htm for airline travel advice and rights). **Departmental Office of Civil Rights** ☎ 202/366-4648, 202/366-8538 TTY ⊕ www.dotcr. ost.dot.gov. **Disability Rights Section** ☎ ADA information line 202/514-0301, 800/514-0301, 202/514-0383 TTY, 800/514-0383 TTY ⊕ www.ada.gov. **U.S. Department of Transportation Hotline** ☎ for disability-related air-travel problems, 800/778-4838 or 800/455-9880 TTY.

## TRAVEL AGENCIES

In the United States, the Americans with Disabilities Act requires that travel firms serve the needs of all travelers. Some agencies specialize in working with people with disabilities.

**Travelers with Mobility Problems** **Access Adventures/B. Roberts Travel** ⊠ 206 Chestnut Ridge Rd., Scottsville, NY 14624 ☎ 585/889-9096 ⊕ www.brobertstravel.com ✎ dltravel@prodigy. net, run by a former physical-rehabilitation counselor. **CareVacations** ⊠ No. 5, 5110-50 Ave., Leduc, Alberta, Canada T9E 6V4 ☎ 780/986-6404 or 877/ 478-7827 🖶 780/986-8332 ⊕ www.carevacations. com, for group tours and cruise vacations. **Flying Wheels Travel** ⊠ 143 W. Bridge St., Box 382, Owatonna, MN 55060 ☎ 507/451-5005 🖶 507/451-1685 ⊕ www.flyingwheelstravel.com.

**Travelers with Developmental Disabilities** **Sprout** ⊠ 893 Amsterdam Ave., New York, NY 10025 ☎ 212/222-9575 or 888/222-9575 🖶 212/222-9768 ⊕ www.gosprout.org.

## EATING OUT

The restaurants we list are the cream of the crop in each price category. You'll find all types, from cosmopolitan to the most casual restaurants, serving all types of cuisine.

Price categories are as follows:

| CATEGORY | COST* |
|----------|-------|
| $$$$ | over $40 |
| $$$ | $30-$40 |
| $$ | $20-$30 |
| $ | $10-$20 |
| ¢ | under $10 |

*Per person for a main course at dinner

For information on food-related health issues ⇨ Health *below.*

Was the service stellar or not up to snuff? Did the food give you shivers of delight or leave you cold? Did the prices and portions make you happy or sad? Rate restaurants and write your own reviews in Travel Ratings or start a discussion about your favorite places in Travel Talk on www.fodors.com. Your comments might even appear in our books. Yes, you, too, can be a correspondent!

## RESERVATIONS & DRESS

Regardless of where you are, it's a good idea to make a reservation if you can. In some places (Hong Kong, for example), it's expected. We only mention specifically when reservations are essential (there's no other way you'll ever get a table) or when they are not accepted. For popular restaurants, book as far ahead as you can (often 30 days), and reconfirm as soon as you arrive. (Large parties should always call ahead to check the reservations policy.) We mention dress only when men are required to wear a jacket or a jacket and tie. Otherwise you can assume that dining out is a casual affair.

## ECOTOURISM

There are 25 National Parks in the Bahamas, all of which are managed by the Bahamas National Trust. Included in those areas is the Andros Barrier Reef, the third largest living coral reef in the world, and the 287-square-mi Inagua National Park, home to world's largest flock (about 50,000) of brilliant pink West Indian flamingos. Environmental consciousness has been heightened in the Bahamas, and 10 new national parks were created in 2002 (doubling the size of the system). More than 700,000 acres have been safeguarded, and officials hope to add more. Efforts to protect sea turtles and replenish populations of conch and lobster (crawfish) are among the conservation projects that have been undertaken in recent years.

Tour operators have begun focusing on kayaking, hiking, birding, and mountain biking—as well as on the islands' traditional sports of fishing, diving, and boating—and local guides have become more in tune with their environment. The Bahamas offers a full array of adventures in places untainted by civilization; designated wildlife preserves lie right outside Freeport. In the Out Islands, especially Abaco, Andros, and Great Inagua, you'll find rare and endangered animals, pristine "bush," and vital reefs. Near Providenciales (Turks and Caicos), the Little Water Cay Nature Trail takes you into the habitat of the rare West Indian rock iguana. You can do your part to keep the Bahamas beautiful—don't purchase products made from endangered species, use care when diving to avoid damage to reefs, don't leave any of your belongings or trash behind (or, in outdoor parlance, pack out what you pack in), and properly dispose of anything you can't remove. Also, be sure your ecotour really is, in fact, eco-friendly, and not just a regular tour wrapped up in a pretty marketing campaign.

▸ Ecotourism Resources **The Bahamas National Trust** ✆ Box N-4105, Nassau ☎ 242/393-1317 ⊕ www.thebahamasnationaltrust.org.

## ELECTRICITY

Electricity is 120 volts/60 cycles AC, which is compatible with all U.S. appliances.

## EMERGENCIES

The emergency telephone number in the Bahamas is **911.**

When you're on the road, it's a good idea to get in touch with your country's consulate or embassy officials to let them know you're in the area. This is especially true if you plan to get way off the beaten path (or lost), or think that you might be in harm's way where you're traveling. They are also key in replacing lost passports, or with assistance in emergencies.

▸ Embassy Contacts **United States** ✉ Mosmar Bldg., Queen St., Nassau ☎ 242/322-1181.

## ETIQUETTE & BEHAVIOR

Bahamians greet people with a proper British "good morning," "good afternoon," or "good evening." When approaching an islander to ask directions or information, **preface your request with such a greeting,** and ask "how are you?" **Smile, and don't rush into a conversation,** even if you're running late.

Humor is a wonderful way to relate to the islanders, but don't force it. Don't try to talk their dialect unless you are adept at it. This takes long exposure to the culture, and though most Bahamians are too polite to show it, you'll either offend them or amuse them if you make a bad attempt at local lingo. Church is central in the lives of the Bahamians. They dress up in their fanciest finery; it's a sight to behold on Saturday evening and Sunday morning. To show respect, dress accordingly if you plan to attend religious ceremonies. No

doubt you'll be outdone, but do dress up regardless.

## BUSINESS ETIQUETTE

Business in the Bahamas is conducted very much like it is in the United States. Handshakes, business card swapping, and other protocols are the same. Meetings are usually held in office conference rooms, and occasionally at a local restaurant for lunch, in which case either the person who invites pays, or all pay their own tab. Islanders wear suits and typical business attire for work and meetings, so **don't be tempted to wear resort dress** in an office atmosphere.

## GAY & LESBIAN TRAVEL

▸ Gay- & Lesbian-Friendly Travel Agencies **Different Roads Travel** ☎ 760/325-6964 or 800/429-8747 (Ext. 14) ✍ lgernert@tzell.com. **Skylink Travel and Tour/Flying Dutchmen Travel** ☎ 707/546-9888 or 800/225-5759; serving lesbian travelers.

## HEALTH

The major health risk in the Bahamas is traveler's diarrhea. This is most often caused by ingesting fruits, shellfish, and drinks to which your body is unaccustomed. **Go easy at first on new foods such as mangoes, conch, and rum punch.** There are rare cases of contaminated fruit, vegetables, or drinking water. If you're susceptible to digestive problems, **avoid ice, uncooked food, and unpasteurized milk and milk products,** and **drink bottled water,** or water that has been boiled for several minutes, even when brushing your teeth. Mild digestive treatments might include Imodium (known generically as loperamide) or Pepto-Bismol, both of which can be purchased over the counter. Travelers prone to travel-related stomach disorders who are comfortable with alternative medicine might pick up some *po chai* tablets from a doctor of Oriental medicine or Asian pharmacy—it's a great stomach cure-all. Drink plenty of purified water or tea; chamomile is a good folk remedy. In severe cases, rehydrate yourself with a salt-sugar solution (½ teaspoon salt and 4 tablespoons sugar per quart of water).

Consult a doctor—preferably your own physician, and prior to your trip—before ingesting any medication that's new to you. Pack familiar digestive remedies with your belongings, **but also have them on you** if you're out traveling for the day.

No-see-ums (sand fleas) and mosquitoes can be bothersome. Some travelers have allergies to sand-flea bites, and the itching can be extremely annoying. To prevent the bites, **use a recommended bug repellent.** To ease the itching, **rub alcohol on the bites.** Some Out Island hotels provide sprays or repellents such as mosquito coils or citronella candles, but it's a good idea to bring your own.

Hospitals and other health care facilities are readily available in Nassau, Freeport, and Grand Turk. In the Out Islands, facilities range from clinics to private practitioners. For more serious emergencies, an airlift can be arranged from any location. The most serious accidents and illnesses may require treatment in the U.S., most likely in a hospital in Florida; less severe emergency cases will be sent to Nassau or Freeport. The costs of a medical evacuation, especially to the U.S., can quickly run into the thousands of dollars, and your personal health insurance may not cover such costs. If you're planning on pursuing inherently risky activities, such as scuba diving, or if you have an existing medical condition, check your existing policy. You may want to consider buying a medical insurance policy that lasts the duration of your trip.

🛂 Major Local Hospitals **Princess Margaret Hospital** ✉ Shirley St., Box N-3730, Nassau ☎ 242/352-2861. **Rand Memorial Hospital** ✉ East Atlantic Dr., Box 40071, Freeport ☎ 242/352-6735.

## DIVERS' ALERT
**Do not fly within 24 hours of scuba diving.**

Always know where your nearest decompression chamber is *before* you embark on a dive expedition, and how you would get there in an emergency.

🛂 Decompression Chamber **Bahamas Hyperbaric Centre** ✉ Box CB-10981, Nassau ☎ 242/362-5765.

## OVER-THE-COUNTER REMEDIES
Pharmacies carry most of the same pain relief products you find in the United States, but often at a higher price, so **pack any over-the-counter medications you regularly use.** They also sell a product called 2-2-2, which is equal parts aspirin, caffeine, and codeine. It's an effective pain killer but can cause upset stomach.

## SHOTS & MEDICATIONS
A vaccination against yellow fever is required if you're arriving from Angola, Benin, Bolivia, Brazil, Burkina Faso, Colombia, Cameroon, Democratic Republic of Congo, Ecuador, French Guiana, Gabon, Gambia, Ghana, Guinea, Liberia, Nigeria, Sierra Leone, Peru, and Sudan. Travelers must be vaccinated 10 days prior to entering the Bahamas and must have a valid certificate of vaccination against yellow fever. Otherwise, no special shots are required before visiting the Bahamas.

## SUNBATHING
Basking in the sun is one of the great pleasures of a Bahamian vacation, but because the sun is closer to Earth the farther south you go, it will burn your skin more quickly, so take precautions against sunburn and sunstroke. On a sunny day, even people who are not normally bothered by strong sun should **cover up with a long-sleeve shirt, a hat, and pants or a beach wrap** while on a boat or midday at the beach. **Carry UVA/UVB sunblock** (with a sun protection factor, or SPF, of at least 15) for your face and other sensitive areas. If you're engaging in water sports, be sure the sunscreen is waterproof. Wear sunglasses because eyes are particularly vulnerable to direct sun and reflected rays. Be sure to **drink enough liquids—water or fruit juice preferably—** and avoid coffee, tea, and alcohol. Above all, limit your sun time for the first few days until you become accustomed to the rays. Do not be fooled by an overcast day. Quite often you will get the worst sunburns when you least expect them. The safest hours for sunbathing are 4–6 PM, but even then it's wise to limit initial exposure.

🛂 Health Warnings **National Centers for Disease Control & Prevention** (CDC) ☎ 877/394-8747 international travelers' health line ⊕ www.cdc.gov/travel. **World Health Organization** (WHO) ⊕ www.who.int.

## HOLIDAYS

The grandest holiday of all is Junkanoo, a carnival that embraces the Christmas season. **Don't expect to conduct any business during the week of festivities.** During other legal holidays, most offices close, and some may extend the holiday by keeping earlier (or no) hours the day before or after. In the Bahamas, official holidays include New Year's Day, Good Friday, Easter, Whit Monday (last Mon. in May), Labour Day (1st Mon. in June), Independence Day (July 10), Emancipation Day (1st Mon. in Aug.), Discovery Day (Oct. 12), Christmas Day, and Boxing Day (Dec. 26). In Turks and Caicos, islanders also celebrate Commonwealth Day (Mar.), Easter Monday, National Heroes Day (May), the Queen's Birthday (June), National Youth Day (Sept.), and International Human Rights Day (Oct.). They celebrate Emancipation Day (Aug. 1) but do not celebrate Whit Monday, Labour Day, or Independence Day.

## INSURANCE

What kind of coverage do you honestly need? Do you even need trip insurance at all? Take a deep breath and read on.

We believe that comprehensive trip insurance is especially valuable if you're booking a very expensive or complicated trip (particularly to an isolated region) or if you're booking far in advance. Who knows what could happen six months down the road? But whether you get insurance has more to do with how comfortable you are assuming all that risk yourself.

Comprehensive travel policies typically cover trip-cancellation and interruption, letting you cancel or cut your trip short because of a personal emergency, illness, or, in some cases, acts of terrorism in your destination. Such policies also cover evacuation and medical care. Some also cover you for trip delays because of bad weather or mechanical problems as well as for lost or delayed baggage. Another type of coverage to look for is financial default—that is, when your trip is disrupted because a tour operator, airline, or cruise line goes out of business. Generally you must buy this when you book your trip or shortly

thereafter, and it's only available to you if your operator isn't on a list of excluded companies.

If you're going abroad, consider buying medical-only coverage at the very least. Neither Medicare nor some private insurers cover medical expenses anywhere outside of the United States besides Mexico and Canada (including time aboard a cruise ship, even if it leaves from a U.S. port). Medical-only policies typically reimburse you for medical care (excluding that related to preexisting conditions) and hospitalization abroad and provide for evacuation. You still have to pay the bills and await reimbursement from the insurer, though.

Expect comprehensive travel insurance policies to cost about 4% to 7% of the total price of your trip (it's more like 12% if you're over age 70). A medical-only policy may or may not be cheaper than a comprehensive policy. Always read the fine print of your policy to make sure that you're covered for the risks that are of the most concern to you. Compare several policies to make sure you're getting the best price and range of coverage available.

Just as an aside: you know you can save a bundle on trips to warm-weather destinations by traveling in rainy season. But there's also a chance that a severe storm will disrupt your plans. The solution? Look for hotels and resorts that offer storm-hurricane guarantees. Although they rarely allow refunds, most guarantees do let you re-book later if a storm strikes.

⚑ Insurance Comparison Sites **Insure My Trip. com** ⊕ www.insuremytrip.com. **Square Mouth.com** ⊕ www.quotetravelinsurance.com.

⚑ Comprehensive Travel Insurers **Access America** ☎ 866/807-3982 ⊕ www.accessamerica.com. **CSA Travel Protection** ☎ 800/873-9855 ⊕ www. csatravelprotection.com. **HTH Worldwide** ☎ 610/254-8700 or 888/243-2358 ⊕ www.hthworldwide. com. **Travelex Insurance** ☎ 888/457-4602 ⊕ www.travelex-insurance.com. **Travel Guard International** ☎ 715/345-0505 or 800/826-4919 ⊕ www.travelguard.com. **Travel Insured International** ☎ 800/243-3174 ⊕ www.travelinsured.com.

⚑ Medical-Only Insurers **Wallach & Company** ☎ 800/237-6615 or 504/687-3166 ⊕ www.wallach.

com. **International Medical Group** ☏ 800/628-4664 ⊕ www.imglobal.com. **International SOS** ☏ 215/942-8000 or 713/521-7611 ⊕ www.internationalsos.com.

## LANGUAGE

Islanders speak English with a lilt influenced by their British and/or African ancestry. When locals talk among themselves in local dialect, it's virtually impossible for the unaccustomed to understand them. They take all sorts of shortcuts and pepper the language with words all their own. When islanders speak to visitors, they will use standard English.

## LODGING

The lodgings we list are the cream of the crop in each price category. We always list the facilities that are available—but we don't specify whether they cost extra: when pricing accommodations, always ask what's included. Properties marked ✕🖼 are lodging establishments whose restaurants warrant a special trip.

Most hotels and other lodgings require you to give your credit card details before they will confirm your reservation. If you don't feel comfortable e-mailing this information, ask if you can fax it (some places even prefer faxes). However you book, get confirmation in writing and have a copy of it handy when you check in. If you book through an online travel agent, discounter, or wholesaler, you might even want to confirm your reservation with the hotel before leaving home—just to be sure everything was processed correctly.

Be sure you understand the hotel's cancellation policy. Some places allow you to cancel without any kind of penalty—even if you prepaid to secure a discounted rate—if you cancel at least 24 hours in advance. Others require you to cancel a week in advance or penalize you for the cost of one night. Small inns and B&Bs are most likely to require you to cancel far in advance. Most hotels allow children under a certain age to stay in their parents' room at no extra charge, but others charge for them as extra adults; find out the cutoff age for discounts.

Assume that hotels operate on the European Plan (**EP**, no meals) unless we specify that they use the Breakfast Plan (**BP**, with full breakfast), Continental Plan (**CP**, continental breakfast), Full American Plan (**FAP**, all meals), Modified American Plan (**MAP**, breakfast and dinner) or are **all-inclusive** (all meals and most activities).

| CATEGORY | COST* |
|---|---|
| **$$$$** | over $400 |
| **$$$** | $300–$400 |
| **$$** | $200–$300 |
| **$** | $100–$200 |
| **¢** | under $100 |

*All prices are for a standard double room in high season, excluding 6%–12% tax and 10%–15% service charge. Note that the government hotel tax doesn't apply to guesthouses with fewer than four rooms.

Did the resort look as good in real life as it did in the photos? Did you sleep like a baby, or were the walls paper thin? Did you get your money's worth? Rate hotels and write your own reviews in Travel Ratings or start a discussion about your favorite places in Travel Talk on www.fodors.com. Your comments might even appear in our books. Yes, you, too, can be a correspondent!

### APARTMENT & VILLA OR HOUSE RENTALS

If you want a home base that's roomy enough for a family and comes with cooking facilities, consider a furnished rental. These can save you money, especially if you're traveling with a group. Home-exchange directories sometimes list rentals as well as exchanges.

🚩 **At Home Abroad** ☏ 212/421-9165 ⊕ www.athomeabroadinc.com. **Bahamas Home Rentals** ✉ 2722 Riverview Dr., Melbourne, FL 32901 ☏ 888/881-2867 or 321/725-9790 ⊕ www.bahamasweb.com. **Bahamas Vacation Homes** ✉ Box EL 27528, Spanish Wells, Bahamas ☏ 242/333-4080 ⊕ www.bahamasvacationhomes.com. **Barclay International Group** ☏ 516/364-0064 or 800/845-6636 ⊕ www.barclayweb.com. **Hope Town Hideaways** ✉ 1 Purple Porpoise Pl., Hope Town, Elbow Cay, Abacos ☏ 242/366-0224 🖷 242/366-0434 ✍ www.hopetown.com. **Vacation Home Rentals Worldwide** ☏ 201/767-9393 or 800/633-3284

⊕ www.vhrww.com. **Villanet** ☎ 206/417-3444 or 800/964-1891 ⊕ www.rentavilla.com. **Villas & Apartments Abroad** ☎ 212/213-6435 or 800/433-3020 ⊕ www.vaanyc.com. **Villas of Distinction** ☎ 707/778-1800 or 800/289-0900 ⊕ www.villasofdistinction.com. **Villas International** ☎ 415/499-9490 or 800/221-2260 ⊕ www.villasintl.com. **Wimco** ☎ 800/449-1553 ⊕ www.wimco.com.

## HOME EXCHANGES

With a direct home exchange, you stay in someone else's home while they stay in yours. Some outfits also deal with vacation homes, so you're not actually staying in someone's full-time residence, just their vacant weekend place.

⌘ Exchange Clubs **HomeLink International** ☎ 800/638-3841 ⊕ www.homelink.org; $80 yearly for Web-only membership; $125 with Web access and two directories. **Home Exchange.com** ☎ 800/877-8723 ⊕ www.homeexchange.com; $59.95 for a 1-year online listing. **Intervac U.S.** ☎ 800/756-4663 ⊕ www.intervacus.com; $78.88 for Web-only membership; $126 includes Web access and a catalog.

## HOSTELS

Hostels offer bare-bones lodging at low, low prices—often in shared dorm rooms with shared baths—to people of all ages, though the primary market is young travelers, especially students. Most hostels serve breakfast; dinner and/or shared cooking facilities may also be available. In some hostels, you aren't allowed to be in your room during the day, and there may be a curfew at night. Nevertheless, hostels provide a sense of community, with public rooms where travelers often gather to share stories. Many hostels are affiliated with Hostelling International (HI), an umbrella group of hostel associations with some 4,500 member properties in more than 70 countries. Other hostels are completely independent and may be nothing more than a really cheap hotel.

Membership in any HI association, open to travelers of all ages, allows you to stay in HI-affiliated hostels at member rates. One-year membership is about $28 for adults; hostels charge about $10–$30 per night. Members have priority if the hostel is full; they're also eligible for discounts

around the world, even on rail and bus travel in some countries.

The Bahamas, like most of the Caribbean, has very few hostels; some that advertise as such are really just budget hotels or inns, perhaps with some shared bathroom facilities or dorm-like rooms that sleep several guests.

⌘ **Hostelling International–USA** ☎ 301/495-1240 ⊕ www.hiusa.org.

## HOTELS

**Weigh all your options (we can't say this enough).** Join "frequent guest" programs. You may get preferential treatment in room choice and/or upgrades in your favorite chains. Check general travel sites and hotel Web sites as not all chains are represented on all travel sites. Always research or inquire about special packages and corporate rates. If you prefer to book by phone, note you can sometimes get a better price if you call the hotel's local toll-free number (if one is available) rather than the central reservations number.

Note that many properties charge peak-season rates for your entire stay even if your travel dates straddle peak and off-peak seasons. High-end chains catering to businesspeople are often busy only on weekdays and often drop rates dramatically on weekends to fill up rooms. **Ask when rates go down.**

**Watch out for hidden costs,** including resort fees, energy surcharges, and "convenience" fees for such things as unlimited local phone service you won't use and a free newspaper—possibly written in a language you can't read. Always verify whether local hotel taxes are or are not included in the rates you are quoted, so that you'll know the real price of your stay. In some places, taxes can add 20% or more to your bill. **Look for price guarantees,** which protect you against a falling dollar. With your rate locked in, you won't pay more, even if the price goes up in the local currency.

Smaller lodges and resorts offer easier access to local life and are attractive to travelers who want a cultural experience or a sequestered getaway focused on fishing, diving, and other watery pastimes. Many small, family-run hotels throughout the Bahamas, including the occasional B&B, offer low-key, warm accommodations. All hotels listed have private bath unless otherwise noted. But remember: the Bahamas is not particularly known as a budget traveler's destination. Hotel prices reflect the cost of shipping supplies to the islands, which is common in the region, plus the existence of a labor force that is relatively well-paid and well-educated compared to some of the other Caribbean islands. Finding a decent room for less than $100 a night, especially in high season, is becoming more and more difficult, if not impossible, on some islands.

🛈 Discount Hotel Rooms **Accommodations Express** ☎ 800/444-7666 or 800/277-1064. **Hotels. com** ☎ 800/219-4606 or 800/364-0291 ⊕ www. hotels.com. **Quikbook** ☎ 800/789-9887 ⊕ www. quikbook.com. **Turbotrip.com** ☎ 800/473-7829 ⊕ w3.turbotrip.com.

## MAIL & SHIPPING

Regardless of whether the term "snail mail" was coined in the Bahamas, you're likely to arrive home long before your postcards do—it's not unheard of for letters to take two to four weeks to reach their destinations. No postal (zip) codes are used in the Bahamas—all mail is collected from local area P.O. boxes.

First-class mail to the United States is 65¢ per half-ounce. Airmail postcards to the United States require a 50¢ stamp in the Bahamas; the stamps must be Bahamian. In Turks and Caicos, prices are comparable. Postcard stamps good for foreign destinations are usually sold at shops selling postcards, so you don't have to make a special trip.

Mailing time to the United States from the Bahamas is 4 to 15 days—but this is only an estimate. Don't be surprised if it takes longer. From the United States, a postcard sent to the Bahamas costs 75¢ and an airmail letter is 84¢.

### SHIPPING PACKAGES

FedEx delivers to Nassau, Freeport, Abaco, Andros, Eleuthera, Long Island, Providenciales, and Grand Turk; UPS has

service to numerous Bahamas locales. However, even premium mail services do not necessarily provide the door-to-door service you might be accustomed to, especially in farther-flung locales—you might have to go pick up your mail at an office. True overnight service is often not available, but second- or third-day delivery is usually reliable.

🛈 Major Services **FedEx** ☎ Freeport: 242/352-3402 or 242/352-3403, Nassau: 242/322-5656 or 242/322-5657, Abaco: 242/367-2817, Andros: 242/368-2540, Eleuthera: 242/332-2720 or 242/335-1600, Long Island: 242/337-6786, Grand Turk: 649/946-2542, Providenciales: 649/946-4682, U.S. international customer service: 800/247-4747 ⊕ www. fedex.com. **UPS** ☎ Abaco, Marsh Harbour: 242/367-2333, Freeport: 242/352-6253, Nassau: 242/393-3795, Providenciales: 649/941-5006 ⊕ www.ups. com.

## MEDIA

### NEWSPAPERS & MAGAZINES

You'll get all the Bahamian news and a good idea of what's going on internationally in the *Tribune, Bahama Journal,* and *Nassau Guardian* on New Providence and in the *Freeport News* on Grand Bahama. The twice-weekly tabloid, *The Punch,* enjoys the highest circulation of locally produced papers and also delivers the most "sip-sip"—Bahamian slang for gossip. These local newspapers are available in most of the Out Islands one day after publication. If you want up-to-date news on what's happening around the world, you can also get the *Miami Herald,* the *Wall Street Journal, USA Today,* and the *New York Times* daily at newsstands in the larger resort areas.

### TELEVISION

Cable and satellite TV are widely available throughout the Bahamas, and at the very least, hotels that offer TV usually give guests a choice of the major networks, CNN, and ESPN. Luxury hotels often have a much bigger selection. The local TV station is ZNS, but it has a limited number of locally produced programs and offers up a schedule that consists largely of old movies, soap operas, and sports programming.

## MONEY MATTERS

Generally, prices in the Bahamas reflect the exchange rate: they are about the same as in the United States. A hotel can cost anywhere from $75 a night (for cottages and apartments in downtown Nassau and in the Out Islands) to $200 and up (at the ritzier resorts on Paradise Island, Harbour Island, Freeport, and Lucaya), depending on the season. Add at least $35 per person per day for meals. Four-day, three-night and eight-day, seven-night package stays offered by most hotels can cut costs considerably. In the Out Islands, you'll notice that meals and simple goods can be expensive; prices are high due to the remoteness of the islands and the costs of importing.

Banks rarely have every foreign currency on hand, and it may take as long as a week to order. If you're planning to exchange funds before leaving home, don't wait until the last minute.

Prices throughout this guide are given for adults. Substantially reduced fees are almost always available for children, students, and senior citizens. For information on taxes, ⇨ Taxes on page 324.

### ATMS

Your own bank will probably charge a fee for using ATMs abroad; the foreign bank you use may also charge a fee. Nevertheless, you'll usually get a better rate of exchange via an ATM than you will at a currency-exchange office or even when changing money in a bank. And extracting funds as you need them is a safer option than carrying around a large amount of cash. Note that PIN numbers with more than four digits are not recognized at ATMs in many countries.

There are ATMs at banks, malls, resorts, and shops throughout the major islands. However, in more remote locations, be sure to take a bit more cash than you think you might need; there are few or no ATMs on some small cays, and on weekends or holidays, those that exist may run out of cash.

🔳 **ATM Locations MasterCard/Cirrus** ☎ 800/424-7787 ⊕ www.mastercard.com provides locations in the Bahamas and worldwide. **Visa/Plus** ☎ 800/843-7587 ⊕ www.visa.com has information for locations in the United States and international destinations.

### CREDIT CARDS

Throughout this guide, the following abbreviations are used: **AE**, American Express; **D**, Discover; **DC**, Diners Club; **MC**, MasterCard; and **V**, Visa.

It's a good idea to inform your credit card company before you travel, especially if you're going abroad and don't travel internationally very often. Otherwise, the credit-card company might put a hold on your card owing to unusual activity—not a good thing halfway through your trip. Record all your credit card numbers—as well as the phone numbers to call if your cards are lost or stolen—in a safe place so you're prepared should something go wrong. Both MasterCard and Visa have general numbers you can call (collect if you're abroad) if your card is lost, but you're better off calling the number of your issuing bank since MasterCard and Visa usually just transfer you to your bank; your bank's number is usually printed on your card.

If you plan to use your credit card for cash advances, you'll need to apply for a PIN at least two weeks before your trip. Although it's usually cheaper (and safer) to use a credit card abroad for large purchases (so you can cancel payments or be reimbursed if there's a problem) note that some credit card companies *and* the banks that issue them add substantial percentages to all foreign transactions, whether they're done in a foreign currency or not. Check on these fees before leaving home so that there won't be any surprises when you get the bill.

Before you charge something, ask the merchant whether he or she plans to do a dynamic currency conversion (DCC). In such a transaction the credit-card *processor* (shop, restaurant, or hotel, not Visa or MasterCard) converts the currency and charges you in dollars. In most cases you'll pay the merchant a 3% fee for this service in addition to any credit-card company and issuing-bank foreign-transaction surcharges.

DCC programs are becoming increasingly widespread. Merchants who participate in them are supposed to ask whether you want to be charged in dollars or the local currency, but they don't always do so. And even if they do offer you a choice, they may well avoid mentioning the additional surcharges. The good news is that you *do* have a choice. And if this practice really gets your goat, you can avoid it entirely thanks to American Express; with its cards, DCC simply isn't an option.

Some smaller hotels in the islands do not accept credit cards.

⚑ Reporting Lost Cards **American Express** ☎ 800/992-3404 in U.S., 336/393-1111 collect from abroad ⊕ www.americanexpress.com. **Diners Club** ☎ 800/234-6377 in U.S., 303/799-1504 collect from abroad ⊕ www.dinersclub.com. **Discover** ☎ 800/347-2683 in U.S., 801/902-3100 collect from abroad ⊕ www.discovercard.com. **MasterCard** ☎ 800/622-7747 in U.S., 636/722-7111 collect from abroad ⊕ www.mastercard.com. **Visa** ☎ 800/847-2911 in U.S., 410/581-9994 collect from abroad ⊕ www.visa.com.

## CURRENCY & EXCHANGE

The U.S. dollar is on par with the Bahamian dollar and is accepted all over the Bahamas. Bahamian money runs in bills of $1, $5, $10, $20, $50, and $100. The U.S. dollar is the currency of the Turks and Caicos.

In the Bahamas, only U.S. cash will be exchanged freely in hotels, stores, or restaurants, and since the U.S. currency is accepted throughout, there really is no need to change to Bahamian. Also, you won't incur any transaction fees for currency exchange, or worry about getting stuck with unspent Bahamian dollars. **Carry small bills when bargaining at straw markets.**

Even if a currency exchange booth has a sign promising no commission, rest assured that there's some kind of huge, hidden fee. (Oh . . . that's right. The sign didn't say no *fee*.). And, in terms of rates, you're almost always better off getting foreign currency through an ATM or exchanging money at a bank.

⚑ Currency Conversion **Google** ⊕ www.google.com does currency conversion. Just type in the

amount you want to convert and an explanation of how you want it converted (e.g., "14 Swiss francs in dollars"), and then voila. **Oanda.com** ⊕ www.oanda.com also allows you to print out a handy table with the current day's conversion rates. **XE.com** ⊕ www.xe.com is a good currency conversion Web site.

## TRAVELER'S CHECKS & CARDS

Some consider this the currency of the cave man, and it's true that fewer establishments accept traveler's checks these days. Nevertheless, they're a cheap and secure way to carry extra money, particularly on trips to urban areas. Both Citibank (under the Visa brand) and American Express issue traveler's checks in the United States, but Amex is better known and more widely accepted; you can also avoid hefty surcharges by cashing Amex checks at Amex offices. Whatever you do, keep track of all the serial numbers in case the checks are lost or stolen.

American Express now offers a stored-value card called a Travelers Cheque Card, which you can use wherever American Express credit cards are accepted, including ATMs. The card can carry a minimum of $300 and a maximum of $2,700, and it's a very safe way to carry your funds. Although you can get replacement funds in 24 hours if your card is lost or stolen, it doesn't really strike us as a very good deal. In addition to a high initial cost ($14.95 to set up the card, plus $5 each time you "reload"), you still have to pay a 2% fee for each purchase in a foreign currency (similar to that of any credit card). Further, each time you use the card in an ATM you pay a transaction fee of $2.50 on top of the 2% transaction fee for the conversion— add it all up and it can be considerably more than you would pay for simply using your own ATM card. Regular traveler's checks are just as secure and cost less.

⚑ **American Express** ☎ 888/412-6945 in U.S., 801/945-9450 collect outside of U.S. to add value or speak to customer service ⊕ www.americanexpress.com.

## PACKING

Why do some people travel with a convoy of suitcases the size of large-screen TVs and yet never have a thing to wear? How do others pack a toaster-oven-size duffel with a week's worth of outfits *and* supplies for every possible contingency? We realize that packing is a matter of style—a very personal thing—but there's much to be said for traveling light. The tips in this section will help you win the battle of the bulging bag.

**Make a list.** In a recent Fodor's survey, 29% of respondents said they make lists (and often pack) at least a week before a trip. Lists can be used at least twice—once to pack and once to repack at the end of your trip. You'll also have a record of the contents of your suitcase, just in case it disappears in transit.

**Think it through.** What's the weather like? Is this a business trip or a cruise or resort vacation? Going abroad? In some places and/or sights, traditions of dress may be more or less conservative than you're used to. As your itinerary comes together, jot activities down and note possible outfits next to each (don't forget those shoes and accessories).

**Edit your wardrobe.** Plan to wear everything twice (better yet, thrice) and to do laundry along the way. Stick to one basic look—urban chic, sporty casual, etc. Build around one or two neutrals and an accent (e.g., black, white, and olive green). Women can freshen looks by changing scarves or jewelry. For a week's trip, you can look smashing with three bottoms, four or five tops, a sweater, and a jacket you can wear alone or over the sweater.

**Be practical.** Put comfortable shoes at the top of your list. (Did we need to tell you this?) Pack items that are lightweight, wrinkle resistant, compact, and washable. (Or this?) Try a simple wrinkling test: intentionally fold a piece of fabric between your fingers for a couple minutes. If it refuses to crease, it will probably come out of your suitcase looking fresh. That said if you stack and then roll your clothes when packing, they'll wrinkle less.

**Check weight and size limitations.** In the United States you may be charged extra for checked bags weighing more than 50 pounds. Abroad some airlines don't allow

you to check bags weighing more than 60 to 70 pounds, or they charge outrageous fees for every pound your luggage is over. Carry-on size limitations can be stringent, too.

**Be prepared to lug it yourself.** If there's one thing that can turn a pack rat into a minimalist, it's a vacation spent lugging heavy bags over long distances. Unless you're on a guided tour or a cruise, select luggage that you can readily carry. Porters, like good butlers, are hard to find these days.

**Lock it up.** Several companies sell locks (about $10) approved by the Transportation Safety Administration that can be unlocked by all U.S. security personnel should they decide to search your bags. Alternatively, you can use simple plastic cable ties, which are sold at hardware stores in bundles.

**Tag it.** Always put tags on your luggage with some kind of contact information; use your business address if you don't want people to know your home address. Put the same information (and a copy of your itinerary) inside your luggage, too.

**Don't check valuables.** On U.S. flights, airlines are only liable for about $2,800 per person for bags. On international flights, the liability limit is around $635 per bag. But just try collecting from the airline for items like computers, cameras, and jewelry. It isn't going to happen; they aren't covered. And though comprehensive travel policies may cover luggage, the liability limit is often a pittance. Your homeowners' policy may cover you sufficiently when you travel—or not. You're really better off stashing baubles and gizmos in your carry-on—right near those prescription meds.

**Report problems immediately.** If your bags—or things in them—are damaged or go astray, file a written claim with your airline *before you leave the airport*. If the airline is at fault, it may give you money for essentials until your luggage arrives. Most lost bags are found within 48 hours, so alert the airline to your whereabouts for two or three days. If your bag was opened for security reasons in the United States and something is missing, file a claim with the TSA.

🛈 Complaints **U.S. Transportation Security Administration Contact Center** ☎ 866/289-9673 🌐 www.tsa.gov.

## WHAT YOU'LL NEED IN THE BAHAMAS

The reason you're going to the Bahamas is to get away from all of that suit-shirt-and-tie turmoil, so your wardrobe should reflect the informality of the experience. Aside from your bathing suit, which will be your favorite uniform, take lightweight clothing (short-sleeve shirts, T-shirts, cotton slacks, lightweight jackets for evening wear for men; light dresses, shorts, and T-shirts for women). If you're going during the high season, between mid-December and April, toss in a sweater for the occasional cool evening. Cover up in public places for downtown shopping expeditions, and save that skimpy bathing suit for the beach at your hotel.

Some of the more sophisticated hotels require jackets for men and dresses for women at dinner. The Bahamas' casinos do not have dress codes.

## PASSPORTS & VISAS

Starting December 31, 2006, all visitors to the Bahamas will need to present a passport to enter the country. This is due to the Western Hemisphere Travel Initiative, which has toughened entry requirements for countries throughout the Americas and the Caribbean. Until that date, U.S. citizens can gain entry to the Bahamas with just a photo ID and proof of citizenship (Starting December 31, 2006, U.S. citizens will also need a valid passport to re-enter the United States from the Bahamas—or any other country they are returning from via air or sea travel).

Residents of the United States can stay in the Bahamas for up to eight months. You also must show proof of a return or onward ticket; if you show up at the airport counter with a one-way ticket, be prepared to shell out for a return flight on the spot or be denied boarding.

For specific entry questions, contact the Bahamas Immigration Department or the nearest consulate.

🛈 **Bahamas Department of Immigration** ✉ Hawkins Hill, Box N-831, Nassau ☎ 242/322-7530.

## PASSPORTS

We're always surprised at how few Americans have passports—only 25% at this writing. This number is expected to grow in coming years, when it becomes impossible to re-enter the United States from trips to neighboring Canada or Mexico without one. Remember this: A passport verifies both your identity and nationality—a great reason to have one.

U.S. passports are valid for 10 years. You must apply in person if you're getting a passport for the first time; if your previous passport was lost, stolen or damaged; or if your previous passport has expired and was issued more than 15 years ago or when you were under 16. All children under 18 must appear in person to apply for or renew a passport. Both parents must accompany any child under 14 (or send a notarized statement with their permission) and provide proof of their relationship to the child.

There are 13 regional passport offices, as well as 7,000 passport acceptance facilities in post offices, public libraries, and other governmental offices. If you're renewing a passport, you can do so by mail. Forms are available at passport acceptance facilities and online.

The cost to apply for a new passport is $97 for adults, $82 for children under 16; renewals are $67. Allow six weeks to process the paperwork for either a new or renewed passport. For an expediting fee of $60, you can reduce the time to about two weeks. If your trip is less than two weeks away, you can get a passport even more rapidly by going to a passport office with the necessary documentation. Private expediters can get things done in as little as 48 hours but charge hefty fees for their services.

Before your trip, make two copies of your passport's data page (one for someone at home and another for you to carry separately). Or scan the page and e-mail it to someone at home and/or yourself.

🔲 U.S. Passport Information **U.S. Department of State** ☎ 877/487-2778 ⊕ http://travel.state.gov/passport

## VISAS

Visas are essentially formal permissions to travel to a country. They allow countries to keep track of you and other visitors and to generate revenue (from visa fees). You *always* need a visa to enter a foreign country; however, many countries routinely issue tourist visas on arrival, particularly to U.S. citizens. When your passport is stamped or scanned in the immigration line, you're actually being issued a visa. Sometimes you have to stand in a separate line and pay a small fee to get your stamp before going through immigration, but you can still do this at the airport on arrival. Getting a visa isn't always that easy. Some countries require you to arrange for one in advance of your trip. There's usually—but not always—a fee involved, and said fee may be nominal ($10 or less) or substantial ($100 or more).

If you must apply for a visa in advance, you can usually do it in person or by mail. When you apply by mail, you send your passport to a designated consulate, where your passport will be examined and the visa issued. Expediters—usually the same ones who handle expedited passport applications—can do all the work to obtain your visa for you; however, there's always an additional cost (often more than $50 per visa).

Most visas limit you to a single trip—basically during the actual dates of your planned vacation. Other visas allow you to visit as many times as you wish for a specific period of time. Remember that requirements change, sometimes at the drop of a hat, and the burden is on you to make sure that you have the appropriate visas. Otherwise, you'll be turned away at the airport or, worse, deported after you arrive in the country. No company or travel insurer gives refunds if your travel plans are disrupted because you didn't have the correct visa.

🔲 U.S. Passport & Visa Expediters **A. Briggs Passport & Visa Expeditors** ☎ 800/806-0581 or 202/464-3000 ⊕ www.abriggs.com. **American Passport Express** ☎ 800/455-5166 or 603/559-9888 ⊕ www.americanpassport.com. **Passport Express** ☎ 800/362-8196 or 401/272-4612 ⊕ www.passportexpress.com. **Travel Document Systems** ☎ 800/874-5100 or 202/638-3800 ⊕ www.traveldocs.com. **Travel the World Visas** ☎ 866/886-8472 or 301/495-7700 ⊕ www.world-visa.com.

## PHONES

The good news is that you can now make a direct-dial telephone call from virtually any point on earth. The bad news? You can't always do so cheaply. Calling from a hotel is almost always the most expensive option; hotels usually add huge surcharges to all calls, particularly international ones. In some countries, you can phone from call centers or even the post office. Calling cards usually keep costs to a minimum, but only if you purchase them locally. And then there are mobile phones ⇨ *below*, which are sometimes more prevalent—particularly in the developing world—than land lines; as expensive as mobile phone calls can be, they are still usually a much cheaper option than calling from your hotel.

BaTelCo (Bahamas Telecommunications Corporation) is the phone company in the Bahamas. Most public phones require BaTelCo phone cards (available at outlets throughout the islands) and also use AT&T calling cards. Check on the surcharge from your calling card provider prior to making calls, and always ask at your hotel desk about what charges will apply when you make card calls from your room. There's usually a charge for making toll-free calls to the United States.

When you're calling the Bahamas, the country code is 242. The country code for the Turks and Caicos is 649. You can dial either number from the United States as you would make an interstate call. The country code is 1 for the United States.

### CALLING WITHIN THE BAHAMAS

Within the Bahamas, to make a local call from your hotel room, dial 9, then the number. If your party doesn't answer before the fifth ring, hang up or you'll be charged for the call. Some 800 and 888 numbers—particularly airline and credit card numbers—can be called from the Bahamas. Others can be reached by substituting an 880 prefix and paying for the call.

Dial 916 for directory information and 0 for operator assistance.

## CALLING OUTSIDE THE BAHAMAS

AT&T, MCI, and Sprint access codes make calling long-distance relatively convenient, but you may find the local access number blocked in many hotel rooms. First ask the hotel operator to connect you. If the hotel operator balks, ask for an international operator, or dial the international operator yourself. One way to improve your odds of getting connected to your long-distance carrier is to travel with more than one company's calling card (a hotel may block Sprint, for example, but not MCI). If all else fails, call from a pay phone.

🛈 Access Codes Access codes are as numerous as the number of calling plans offered by the major phone carriers. Be sure to write your access number, phone, and PIN numbers in more than one location before you leave home.

## CALLING CARDS

To place a call from a public phone using your own calling card, dial 0 for the operator, who will then place the call using your card number.

Pay phones accept BaTelCo phone cards and AT&T calling cards.

🛈 **BaTelCo** ☎ 242/302–7000.

## MOBILE PHONES

If you have a multiband phone (some countries use different frequencies than what's used in the United States) and your service provider uses the world-standard GSM network (as do T-Mobile, Cingular, and Verizon), you can probably use your phone abroad. Roaming fees can be steep, though: 99¢ a minute is considered reasonable. And overseas you normally pay the toll charges for incoming calls. It's almost always cheaper to send a text message than to make a call since text

messages have a low set fee (often less than 5¢).

If you just want to make local calls, consider buying a new SIM card (note that your provider may have to unlock your phone for you to use a different SIM card) and a prepaid service plan in the destination. You'll then have a local number and can make local calls at local rates. If your trip is extensive you could also simply buy a new cell phone in your destination as the initial cost will be offset over time.

If you travel internationally frequently, save one of your old mobile phones or buy a cheap one on the Internet; ask your cell phone company to unlock it for you, and take it with you as a travel phone, buying a new SIM card with pay-as-you-go service in each destination.

BaTelCo has roaming agreements with several U.S. cellular service providers, but the charges can add up fast; check with your provider before traveling to find out the per-minute charge. If you use a cell phone, it may be difficult or impossible to get a signal on some remote Out Islands, and even in the bigger population centers, service can be spotty.

🛈 **Cellular Abroad** ☎ 800/287–5072 ⊕ www.cellularabroad.com rents and sells GMS phones and sells SIM cards that work in many countries. **Mobal** ☎ 888/888–9162 ⊕ www.mobalrental.com rents mobiles and sells GSM phones (starting at $49) that will operate in 140 countries. Per-call rates vary throughout the world. **Planet Fone** ☎ 888/988–4777 ⊕ www.planetfone.com rents cell phones, but the per-minute rates are expensive.

## RESTROOMS

Most attractions, restaurants, and shopping areas have reasonably clean, and sometimes attended, public restrooms. Beaches away from the resorts often have no facilities. **Headquarter your beach escape near a bar or restaurant** for restroom access.

The Bathroom Diaries is a Web site that's flush with unsanitized info on restrooms the world over—each one located, reviewed, and rated.

🛈 Find a Loo **The Bathroom Diaries** ⊕ www.thebathroomdiaries.com

## SAFETY

Distribute your cash, credit cards, IDs, and other valuables between a deep front pocket, an inside jacket or vest pocket, and a hidden money pouch. Don't reach for the money pouch once you're in public.

Crime against tourists is rare, and, unlike some of the Caribbean countries, the Bahamas has little panhandling. But take the precautions you would in any foreign country: be aware of your wallet or handbag at all times, and keep your jewelry in the hotel safe. **Be especially wary in remote areas, always lock your rental vehicle, and don't keep any valuables in the car, even in the locked trunk.**

### GOVERNMENT ADVISORIES

Consider registering online with the state department ( ⊕ https://travelregistration. state.gov/ibrs/), so the government will know to look for you should a crisis occur in the country you're visiting.

If you travel frequently also look into the Registered Traveler program of the Transportation Security Administration (TSA; ⊕ www.tsa.gov). The program, which is still being tested in five U.S. airports, is designed to cut down on gridlock at security checkpoints by allowing prescreened travelers to pass quickly through kiosks that scan an iris and/or a fingerprint. How sci-fi is that?

🛂 **U.S. Department of State** ⊕ www.travel.state. gov.

### WOMEN IN THE BAHAMAS & TURKS & CAICOS

If you carry a purse, choose one with a zipper and a thick strap that you can drape across your body; adjust the length so that the purse sits in front of you at or above hip level. (Don't wear a money belt or a waist pack.) Store only enough money in the purse to cover casual spending. Distribute the rest of your cash and any valuables between deep front pockets, inside jacket or vest pockets, and a concealed money pouch.

Women traveling alone should not go out walking unescorted at night in Nassau or in remote areas. Crime is low, but there's

no need to take unnecessary risks. In most other cases, women are safe and treated with respect. To avoid unwanted attention, **dress conservatively and cover up swimsuits off the beach.**

### SENIOR-CITIZEN TRAVEL

To qualify for age-related discounts, mention your senior-citizen status up front when booking hotel reservations (not when checking out) and before you're seated in restaurants (not when paying the bill). Be sure to have identification on hand. When renting a car, ask about promotional car-rental discounts, which can be cheaper than senior-citizen rates.

🎓 **Educational Programs** Elderhostel ✉ 11 Ave. de Lafayette, Boston, MA 02111–1746 ☎ 877/426–8056, 978/323–4141 international callers, 877/426–2167 TTY ⎙ 877/426–2166 ⊕ www.elderhostel.org.

### SHOPPING

There's enough of a savings over U.S. prices (30%–50%, in many cases) to make duty-free shopping profitable on New Providence and Grand Bahama. On all the islands, be sure to visit the straw markets, where you can bargain for low-price hats, baskets, place mats, T-shirts, and other items. But be aware that most of the straw goods you find in a straw market are actually imported from Taiwan or other places. Remember also that duty-free means that the shop doesn't have to pay taxes, not that you don't: if your purchases exceed your exemption—in most cases, $800 per person for U.S. residents—you'll be liable for duty when you go through customs at home.

### SMART SOUVENIRS

For authentic souvenirs, check out the art and crafts galleries you will find throughout the Bahamas. Most are concentrated in Nassau. Bahamian artists hold their own in the burgeoning marketplace for Caribbean art.

Trademark products include Junkanoo-inspired art, wood sculpture, painted straw masks, handmade batik, model ships, and hand-plaited straw work. Jackson Burnside is one master of Junkanoo art. His Doongalik Studios in Nassau sells his work and that of other artists.

Long Island is known for its hand-plaiting, which has survived the onslaught of cheap imported goods. The island of Andros is home to the Androsia Batik factory, which produces island-style batik cloth and clothing that is available throughout the islands.

On the island of Green Turtle Cay, the Lowe brothers are famous. Albert Lowe is the official Bahamian artist, whose masterpieces dwell in the four- and five-figure price range. Vertram Lowe assembles realistic models of sailing ships, which start around $700.

In Providenciales in the Turks and Caicos, Bamboo Gallery carries fine local, Haitian, and other Caribbean sculpture and paintings. You can contribute to the well-being of the islands' environment by taking home handmade crafts that don't include such natural items as coral, feathers, and rare shells.

**WATCH OUT**

U.S. Customs does not allow any product made from black coral or tortoise shell into the country. **Smoke your Cuban cigars in the Bahamas.** They're illegal in the United States, and the fine is stiff.

**STUDENTS IN THE BAHAMAS**

**TRAVEL AGENCIES**

Students of marine ecology and biology flock to the Bahamas like West Indian flamingos. If you're a student visitor, there are resources to help save money—**look into deals available through student-oriented travel agencies.** To qualify you'll need a bona fide student ID card. Members of international student groups are also eligible.

🖪 **I.D.s & Services STA Travel** ☎ 212/627-3111, 800/781-4040 24-hr service center ⊕ www.sta.com. **Travel Cuts** ☎ 800/592-2887 in the U.S. ⊕ www.travelcuts.com.

**TAXES**

There's no sales tax in the Bahamas. However, there's a $15 per-person departure tax (travelers under age four aren't charged this fee). The departure tax from Turks and Caicos is $35 for persons older than age two. Tax on your hotel room is 6%–12%, depending on the island visited;

in some resorts, a small service charge of up to 5% may be added to cover housekeeping and bellman service. U.S. visitors can take home $800 worth of duty-free goods. The next $1,000 is taxed at 10% (⇨ Customs and Duties, *above*).

**TAXIS**

There are taxis waiting at every airport, in Nassau along Bay Street, and outside all of the main hotels and cruise ship docks. Beware of "hackers"—drivers who don't display their license (and may not have one). You can negotiate a fare, but you must do so before you enter the taxi. On Grand Bahama and New Providence, taxi rates are usually zoned, but they may also be metered; again, check before getting in. Some sample fares around Nassau: airport to Cable Beach, $15; airport to Paradise Beach, $27; airport to downtown, $22. Sample fares around Grand Bahama: airport to Lucaya, $19; harbor to Port Lucaya Marketplace, $24. These prices are for two passengers; each additional passenger costs another $3. In the Out Islands, rates are negotiated, but drivers usually don't want to budge by more than a few dollars on their prices (and you might find that renting a car is more economical). Upon arriving, you're likely to find that Bahamian taxi drivers are more loquacious than their U.S. counterparts, so by the time you've reached your hotel, you'll be already familiar with points of interest. A 15% tip is suggested.

**TIME**

The Bahamas and the Turks and Caicos lie within the Eastern Standard Time (EST) Zone, which means that it's 7 AM in the Bahamas (or New York) when it's noon in London and 10 PM in Sydney. In summer, the islands switch to Eastern Daylight Time (EDT).

**TIPPING**

The usual tip for service from a taxi driver or waiter is 15% and $1–$2 a bag for porters. Many hotels and restaurants automatically add a 15% gratuity to your bill.

**TOURS & PACKAGES**

**GUIDED TOURS**

Guided tours are a good option when you don't want to do it all yourself. You travel along with a group (sometimes large, sometimes small), stay in prebooked hotels, eat with your fellow travelers (sometimes included in the price of your tour, sometimes not), and follow a schedule. But not all guided tours are a "If This is Tuesday, It Must Be Belgium" kind of experience. A knowledgeable guide can take you places that you might never discover on your own, and you may be pushed to see more than you would have otherwise. Tours aren't for everyone, but they can be just the thing for trips to places where making travel arrangements is difficult or time-consuming (particularly when you don't speak the language). Whenever you book a guided tour, find out what's included and what isn't. A "land-only" tour includes all your travel (by bus, in most cases) in the destination, but not necessarily your flights to or even within it. Also, in most cases, prices in tour brochures don't include fees and taxes. And remember that you'll be expected to tip your guide (in cash) at the end of the tour.

### VACATION PACKAGES

Packages *are not* guided tours. Packages combine airfare, accommodations, and perhaps a rental car or other extras (theater tickets, guided excursions, boat trips, reserved entry to popular museums, transit passes), but they let you do your own thing. During busy periods, packages may be your only option because flights and rooms may be otherwise sold out. Packages will definitely save you time. They can also save you money, particularly in peak seasons, but—and this is a really big "but"—you should price each part of the package separately to be sure. And be aware that prices advertised on Web sites and in newspapers rarely include service charges or taxes, which can up your costs by hundreds of dollars.

Note that local tourism boards can provide information about lesser-known and small-niche operators that sell packages to just a few destinations. And don't always assume that you can get the best deal by booking everything yourself. Some packages and cruises are sold only through travel agents.

Each year consumers are stranded or lose their money when packagers—even large ones with excellent reputations—go out of business. How can you protect yourself? First, always pay with a credit card; if you have a problem, your credit-card company may help you resolve it. Second, buy trip insurance that covers default. Third, choose a company that belongs to the U.S. Tour Operators Association, whose members must set aside funds ($1 million) to cover defaults. Finally choose a company that also participates in the Tour Operator Program of the American Society of Travel Agents (ASTA), which will act as mediator in any disputes. You can also check on the tour operator's reputation among travelers by posting an inquiry on one of the Fodors.com forums.

**Organizations American Society of Travel Agents** (ASTA) ☎ 703/739-2782, 800/965-2782 24-hr hotline ⊕ www.astanet.com. **United States Tour Operators Association** (USTOA) ☎ 212/599-6599 ⊕ www.ustoa.com.

### TRAVEL AGENCIES

If you use an agent—brick-and-mortar or virtual—you'll pay a fee for the service. And know that the service you get from some online agents isn't comprehensive. For example Expedia or Travelocity don't search for prices on budget airlines like JetBlue, Southwest, or small foreign carriers. That said, some agents (online or not) *do* have access to fares that are difficult to find otherwise, and the savings can more than make up for any surcharge.

A knowledgeable brick-and-mortar travel agent can be a godsend if you're booking a cruise, a package trip that's not available to you directly, an air pass, or a complicated itinerary including several overseas flights. What's more, travel agents that specialize in a destination may have exclusive access to certain deals and insider information on things such as charter flights. Agents who specialize in types of travelers (senior citizens, gays and lesbians, naturists) or types of trips (cruises, luxury travel, safaris) can also be invaluable.

A top-notch agent planning your trip to Russia will make sure you get the correct visa application and complete it on time;

the person booking your cruise may get you a cabin upgrade or arrange to have bottle of champagne chilling in your cabin when you embark. And complain about the surcharges all you like, but when things don't work out the way you'd hoped, it's nice to have an agent to put things right.

🔏 Agent Resources **American Society of Travel Agents** ☎ 703/739-2782 ⊕ www.travelsense.org. 🔏 Online Agents **Expedia** ⊕ www.expedia.com. **Onetravel.com** ⊕ www.onetravel.com. **Orbitz** ⊕ www.orbitz.com. **Priceline.com** ⊕ www.priceline.com. **Travelocity** ⊕ www.travelocity.com.

## VISITOR INFORMATION

🔏 Tourist Information **Bahamas Ministry of Tourism** ☎ 800/224-2627 or 242/322-7500 ⊕ www.bahamas.com ✉ Box N-3701, Nassau 🖷 242/302-2098 ✉ 150 E. 52nd St., 28th fl., north, New York, NY 10022 ☎ 800/823-3136 or 212/758-2777 🖷 212/753-6531 ✉ 3450 Wilshire Blvd., Suite 1204, Los Angeles, CA 90010 ☎ 213/385-0033 🖷 213/383-3966. **Bahamas Out Islands Promotion Board** ✉ 1200 S. Pine Island Rd., Suite 700, Plantation, FL 33324 ☎ 954/475-8315 🖷 954/236-8354 ⊕ www.myoutislands.com. **Caribbean Tourism Organization** ✉ 80 Broad St., 32nd fl., New York, NY 10014 ☎ 212/635-9530 🖷 212/635-9511 ⊕ www.doitcaribbean.com. **Grand Bahama Island Tourism Board** ✉ Box F-40650, Freeport ☎ 800/448-3386 ⊕ www.grand-bahama.com. **Nassau/Paradise Island Promotion Board** ✉ 1200 S. Pine Island Rd., Suite 700, Plantation, FL 33324 ☎ 888/627-7281 or 800/327-9019 ⊕ www.nassauparadiseisland.com.

**Turks and Caicos Islands Tourist Board** ✉ 60 East 42nd St., Suite 2817, New York, NY 10165 ☎ 800/241-0824 ⊕ www.turksandcaicostourism.com.

## WEB SITES

We're really proud of our Web site: Fodors.com is a great place to begin any journey. Scan Travel Wire for suggested itineraries, travel deals, restaurant and hotel openings, and other up-to-the-minute info. Check out Booking to research prices and book plane tickets, hotel rooms, rental cars, and vacation packages. Head to Talk for on-the-ground pointers from travelers who frequent our message boards. You can also link to loads of other travel-related resources.

After your trip, be sure to rate the places you visited and share your experiences and travel tips with us and other Fodorites in Travel Ratings and Talk on www.fodors.com.

🔏 Weather **Accuweather.com** ⊕ www.accuweather.com is an independent weather-forecasting service with especially good coverage of hurricanes. **Weather.com** ⊕ www.weather.com is the Web site for the Weather Channel.

🔏 Other Resources **CIA World Factbook** ⊕ www.odci.gov/cia/publications/factbook/index.html has profiles of every country in the world. It's a good source if you need some quick facts and figures.

# INDEX